The New York Public Library
Science Desk Reference

The New York Public Library

Science
Desk
Reference

Patricia Barnes-Svarney

Editorial Director

A STONESONG PRESS BOOK

MACMILLAN • USA

MACMILLAN
A Simon & Schuster Macmillan Company
1633 Broadway
New York, NY 10019

Library of Congress Cataloging-in-Publication Data

Barnes-Svarney, Patricia L.
The New York Public Library science desk reference / by Patricia Barnes-Svarney.
    p.   cm.
    "A Stonesong Press book."
    Includes bibliographical references and index.
    ISBN 0-02-860403-2
    1. Science—Miscellanea. 2. Science—Handbooks, manuals, etc. 3. New York Public Library.
    I. Title. II. Title: Science desk reference.
Q173.B25 1995
500—dc20   94-40445
                                      CIP

The New York Public Library Project Sponsors

A Note from the Editors

Every attempt has been made to ensure that this publication is as accurate as possible and as comprehensive as space would allow. We are grateful to the many researchers, librarians, teachers, reference editors, and friends who contributed facts, figures, time, energy, ideas, and opinions. Our choice of what to include was aided by their advice and their voices of experience. The contents, however, remain subjective to some extent, because we could not possibly cover everything that one might look for in basic information. If errors or omissions are discovered, we would appreciate hearing from you, the user, as we prepare future editions. Please address suggestions and comments to The Stonesong Press in care of Macmillan General Reference, 1633 Broadway, New York, NY 10019.

We hope you find our work useful.

Contents

Italicized entries denote illustrations and tables.

Introduction   xix

1.   Scientific Measurements   1

Why Is Measurement Important to Science?   2
Early Measurements   2
Scientific Notation   3
    Powers of 10   3
    Large Number Names   4
    SIDEBAR: Measuring Percents and Parts   4
Fundamentals of Science   4
U.S. Conventional System   5
    Dry and Liquid Weights   5
    Measures   5
    Miscellaneous   6
The SI System   6
    SIDEBAR: Going Metric?   7
    Liquid and Dry Weights   7
    Measures   7
Common U.S. Conventional and SI Equivalents   8
    Distance and Length   8
    Area and Volume   8
    Mass, Weight, and Capacity   9
    Power and Efficiency   9
Miscellaneous Measurements   9
    Common Measurements and Equivalents   9
    Circular and Arc Measurement   9
    Nautical Distances   9
    Conversions for U.S. Conventional and SI Systems   10
Dimensions and Coordinates   15
    Rectangular Coordinates   15
    Two- and Three-dimensional Coordinate Systems   15
    Polar Coordinates   15

Spherical Coordinates   16
Scale of the Universe   16
    A Relative Scale of the Universe   16
    SIDEBAR: How Does It Measure?   17
Special Scientific Measurements   17
    Sound Units   17
    Electrical Units   18
    Density and Volume   18
    Altitude and Azimuth   19
    *Altitude and Azimuth in a Horizontal Coordinate
        System   19*
Measuring Speeds   20
    Converting Common Speeds   20
    Comparing Speeds   20
Scientific Scales   20
    Common Ruler   20
        Ruler with Inches and Millimeters   21
    Engineer's Scale   21
        Engineer's Scale   21
    Metric Scale   21
        Metric Scale   21
    Micrometers   22
        Micrometer   22
    Electrical Multimeters   22
        Two Types of Analogue Multimeters   22
        SIDEBAR: Measuring Interference   23
Logarithms   23
Temperature   23
    Temperature Conversions   23
    Temperature Ranges in the Universe   24
    Temperature Conversion Table   25
Astronomical Distances   27
    Some Astronomical Measurements   27
Mathemathics and Measurement   28
    Evolution of Numbers   28
    SIDEBAR: Same Sum—Every Time   28
    Naming Numbers   29

SIDEBAR: Finding Prime Numbers   30
Decimal and Percent Equivalents of Common Fractions   30
Decimal Equivalents of Common Fractions of an Inch   30
Power and Exponents   31
Geometric Shapes   32
Common Geometric Shapes   32
Circular Measurements   33
Names for Polygons   33
Common Formulas for Geometric Shapes   33
Conic Sections   34
Ratios of Common Angles   35
SIDEBAR: A Chiral Universe?   35
Major Mathematicians   35
Significant Discoveries in Measurement and Mathematics   39
Common Terms in Measurement and Mathematics   40
Additional Sources of Information   44

Amino Acids   56
Symbols in Chemistry   56
Common Chemical Symbols   56
Chemical Elements   57
Symbols for Chemical Charges   57
Chemical Formulas and Structures   58
Symbols in Astronomy and Physics   58
Astronomical Symbols   58
Physics Symbols   59
Symbols in Earth Science   59
Geological Symbols for Maps   59
Paleontology Symbols—Fossils   60
Symbols Used for Rock Types   60
Symbols Used on Topographic Maps   61
Symbols in Meteorology   62
Symbols for Storms, Wind, and Fronts   62
Symbols for Precipitation   62
Cloud Symbols   63
Symbols Used for Weather Station Data   63
Symbols in Environmental Science   64
SIDEBAR: Changing Signs   64
Symbols in Electrical Engineering   65
Electrical Engineering Symbols   65
Additional Sources of Information   66

2.   Scientific Symbols and Signs   45

What Are Symbols and Signs?   46
Symbols, Signs, and Graphics   46
Early Symbols and Signs   46
SIDEBAR: The Astrological Signs   47
Astrological Signs and Symbols   47
The Greek Alphabet   48
Upper- and Lower-Case Greek Letters   48
Greek Letters Used in Science   48
Selected Roman Letters Used in Science   49
Numbers and Symbols   51
Symbols for Number Prefixes   51
Symbols and Signs in Mathematics   51
Set Theory Symbols   53
Symbols in Biology   54
Plant Symbols   54
Animal Symbols   54
Symbols in Biomedical Science   55
Biomedical Symbols   55
Deoxyribonucleic Acid (DNA) and Ribonucleic Acid (RNA)   55

3.   Time   67

Why Is Time Important to Science?   68
SIDEBAR: Is Time Travel Possible?   68
Measured Time   68
SIDEBAR: Biological Clocks   68
Common Divisions of Time   69
Years, Months, and Days   69
The Year   69
The Months   70
Sidereal and Synodic Months   70
Names of the Months   71
SIDEBAR: The Sun and the Sundial   71
The Days   71
Sidereal and Solar Days   72
Names of the Days   72
SIDEBAR: Early Scientific Clock Watching   73
Standard and 24-Hour Time Systems   73
What Is a Second?   74

Other Times   74
  Seasonal Times   74
  Equinox   75
  Solstice   75
      *The Sun Through the Northern Hemisphere's
        Seasons   75*
  Tidal Time   76
      Average High and Low Tides   76
  SIDEBAR: Earth-Moon Future Time   76
  Ephemeris Time   77
  Atomic Time   77
  SIDEBAR: Keeping Track of Today's Time   77
  Geologic Time   78
  SIDEBAR: How Tree Rings Keep Time   78
Moon and Sun Times   78
  Calendars   78
      Three Calendars   78
      Hebrew   79
      Muslim (Islam)   79
      Julian   79
      Gregorian   79
      The World Calendar   80
      Worldsday Calendar   80
      SIDEBAR: Taking a Leap   80
Time Around the World   81
  Latitude and Longitude   81
      Reading Latitude and Longitude   81
  Standard Time   82
  Coordinated Universal Time   82
  Universal Time (Greenwich Mean Time) and the
    Prime Meridian   82
  International Date Line   82
  U.S. Time Zones   83
  International Time Zones   84
Worldwide Time Variations   85
  Daylight Savings Time (United States)   85
  Differences in International Time   85
Additional Sources of Information   85

4. *Biology*   87

What Is Biology?   88
Biology and Life   88
  What Is Life?   88

  SIDEBAR: New Life Under the Sea   88
  Building Blocks of Life   89
  Theories of the Origin of Life   89
  SIDEBAR: The Space and Life Connection   90
  Self-replicating Mechanisms   90
Evolution   91
  What Is Evolution?   91
  SIDEBAR: Wiping Out Organisms   92
  Possible Early Evolution   92
  Possible Evolution of Living Organisms   93
  SIDEBAR: Is Evolution Going on Today?   93
Heredity   93
Classifying Organisms   94
  An Example: Human Beings   95
  Number of Species   95
  SIDEBAR: Dividing Organisms   95
  Groups of Organisms   96
**Example of a Five-Kingdom Classification of
  Living Organisms   97**
Kingdom Descriptions   98
  Kingdom: Monera   98
      Parts of a Bacterium   99
      SIDEBAR: Bacteria and Us   99
  Kingdom: Protista   100
  Kingdom: Fungi   100
  Kingdom: Archaebacteria   100
Distinguishing Plants from Animals   101
  Composition of Organisms   101
  Human Elements   101
  SIDEBAR: Glowing in the Dark:
        Bioluminescence 102
  Cells   102
  Cell Comparisons   102
  A Typical Animal Cell   103
  A Typical Plant Cell   103
The Plant Kingdom   104
  What Is Botany?   104
  What Are Plants?   104
      Parts of a Flowering Plant   106
      Parts of a Flower   106
      Cross-section of a Leaf   107
      SIDEBAR: Meat-eating Plants
  Plant Reproduction   109
  SIDEBAR: Of Trees and Seeds   110
  Plant Photosynthesis   110
  Botanical Names of Plants   110
  SIDEBAR: Plants and Pollution   114
  Poisonous Cultivated and Wild Plants   115

Common Herbs   117
Germination Tables for Flowers and Vegetables   119
The Animal Kingdom   120
What Is Zoology?   120
Animal Reproduction   120
Invertebrates   120
SIDEBAR: The Real Killer Bees   121
The Vertebrates   122
SIDEBAR: Animal Patterns   124
Orders of Mammals   124
Subclasses of Mammals   126
Mammal Gestation Periods   127
SIDEBAR: Animal Navigation   129
Poisonous Animals   129
Animal Lists   130
SIDEBAR: Fastest of All   131
SIDEBAR: Amber and the Pits   131
Extinct Animals   132
Endangered Animals   134
SIDEBAR: The New Zoos   135
Major Biologists   136
Significant Scientific Discoveries in Biology   141
Common Terms in Biology   144
Additional Sources of Information   150

5. The Human Body and Biomedical Science   151

Human Blood   152
What Is Blood?   152
Composition of Blood   152
Blood Types   153
SIDEBAR: Donating Blood   154
Common Blood Disorders   155
Disease Carriers in the Blood   155
SIDEBAR: Keeping It Cold   156
Nonblood Components and Needs of the Human Body   156
Proteins   156
Carbohydrates   156
Minerals   157
Vitamins   157
List of Vitamins   158

Fats   159
SIDEBAR: The Problem with Lipoproteins   159
The Food Pyramid—A Guide to Daily Food Choices   160
Human Cells   160
Cell Comparisons   160
SIDEBAR: Theories on Aging   161
Systems of the Human Body   161
The Hormonal System   161
Important Hormones   162
The Circulatory System   163
The Circulatory System   164
The Heart   164
The Urinary Tract   165
SIDEBAR: What Does Your Blood Pressure Mean?   165
The Digestive System   165
The Digestive System   166
The Muscle System   166
The Muscle System   167
The Nervous System   167
The Brain   168
The Nervous System   169
The Ear   170
The Eye   170
Olfactory System   170
Areas of Taste on the Tongue   171
The Reproductive System   171
The Male Reproductive System   171
The Female Reproductive System   172
Menstruation and Menopause   172
The Respiratory System   173
The Respiratory System   173
The Skeletal System   174
The Skeletal System   175
The Immune System   174
The Lymphatic System   176
The Skin   177
SIDEBAR: What Is Skin Cancer?   177
Genetics   178
Classical Genetics   178
Modern Genetics and Chromosomes   179
What Is DNA?   180
DNA   181
The Genetic Code in DNA   182
SIDEBAR: Genetic Fingerprints   182
What Is RNA?   182
Genetic Engineering   183
Types of Health Care Providers   184

SIDEBAR: How Do Wounds Heal? 186
Common Medical Problems 187
Communicable Diseases 187
Hereditary or Genetic Diseases 190
Chronic Diseases 192
Other Medical Problems 193
SIDEBAR: Your Type of Allergy 194
Animal- and Insect-Borne Diseases 200
SIDEBAR: Epidemics of the Past 201
Biomedical Laboratory Technology 201
Invasive Techniques 201
Noninvasive Techniques 202
SIDEBAR: Frozen Organ Assets 203
Other Methods for Maintaining Health 204
Life Expectancy by Race, Sex, and Age 205
Deaths and Death Rates, by Selected Causes 206
Dental Technology 209
The Teeth 209
The Human Mind and Psychology 209
Psychoses and Major Mood Disorders 209
Neuroses 210
SIDEBAR: Phobic Neuroses 211
Other Mental Disorders 212
Major Biomedical and Biological Scientists 212
**Significant Scientific Discoveries in Biomedical
Science 217**
Common Terms in Biomedical Science 219
Additional Sources of Information 223

6. Chemistry 225

What Is Chemistry? 226
Early Chemical Studies 226
Branches of Chemistry 227
**Classifying Matter: Elements, Compounds, and
Mixtures 227**
Elements and Compounds 228
*Elements, Compounds, and Mixture
Relationships 227*
Mixtures: Solutions and Suspensions 228
Kinds of Solutions 228
*Solubility Curves for Selected Solutes in Water
229*

Some Common Solutes 229
SIDEBAR: Why Does Antifreeze Work in Your
Automobile? 229
Collodial Dispersions 230
Atomic Structure 230
What Are Protons, Neutrons, and Electrons? 230
The Three Major Subatomic Particles 230
Atoms, Ions, and Molecules 231
Atomic Nomenclature 231
Oxygen Atom 231
Names and Charges of Common Ions 232
SIDEBAR: How Is Your Water Softened? 232
Atomic Models 233
Electron Models 233
Electron Configuration of the Elements 234
Measuring Molecules 235
Matter as a Solid, Liquid, or Gas 235
Solids 235
Liquids 235
Gases 235
Plasma 236
SIDEBAR: Glass: A Supercooled Liquid 236
Physical Properties of Matter 236
*Freezing and Boiling Points of Common
Substances 236*
Densities of Common Substances 236
SIDEBAR: Unusual Properties of Water 237
The Periodic Table of the Elements 238
What Is the Periodic Table of the Elements? 238
History of the Periodic Table 238
Mendeleev's Periodic Table 239
Divisions of the Periodic Table 239
Periods of the Table 239
The Periodic Table of Elements 240
Groups of Elements
Metals 240
Nonmetals 241
Properties of Metals and Nonmetals 241
Activity of Some Elements 241
Semimetals 242
SIDEBAR: Semiconductor Technology 242
Noble Gases 242
Groups of Elements of the Periodic Table 243
SIDEBAR: How Do You Name a New Element?
243
Chemical Formulas and Equations 244
Stoichiometry 244

Formulas   244
Equations   244
Chemical Kinetics   245
Chemical Kinetics and the Gas Laws   245
Vapor Pressure of Water   245
Chemical Bonding and Reactions   246
Bonding   246
Ionic and Covalent Bonds   246
Types of Chemical Reactions   247
Catalysts   248
Terms and Common Chemical Substances   248
Organic Chemistry   249
Hydrocarbons   249
Structural Formula of Benzene   250
Functional Groups   250
Polymers   251
SIDEBAR: Discovering Buckyballs   251
Acids and Bases   251
What Is an Acid?   251
What Is a Base?   251
Common Acids and Bases   252
Measures of pH Values   252
Neutralization   253
Chemical Indicators   253
Electrochemistry of Batteries   253
Basic Batteries   254
SIDEBAR: Better with Batteries   254
Radiochemistry   255
What Is Radioactivity?   255
Isotopes   255
Types of Radioactive Particles   255
Decay of Radioactive Uranium   256
Half-life of Some Radioactive Nuclei   256
SIDEBAR: Preserving Food   257
Radioactive Dating   257
Carbon Dating   257
Chemical Laws and Rules   257
Major Chemists   259
Significant Scientific Discoveries in Chemistry   263
Common Terms in Chemistry   266
Additional Sources of Information   270

7.   Physics   271

What Is Physics?   272
Branches of Physics   272
Mass and Gravitation   272
Motion   273
Speed and Velocity   273
Acceleration   273
Force   274
Torque   274
Momentum   274
Inertia   274
Centripetal and Centrifugal Forces   274
Angular Momentum   275
Newton's Laws of Motion   275
Work and Energy   276
Work   276
Power   276
Kinetic and Potential Energies   276
Conservation of Energy   277
Newton's Universal Law of Gravitation   277
SIDEBAR: Black Holes and Gravity Waves   278
Orbits   278
SIDEBAR: Into Orbit   178
Einstein and Relativity   279
SIDEBAR: Can It Be Warp Speed?   279
Einstein's Theories   279
The Energy Equivalent of Mass   280
General Relativity   280
Basic Forces in Nature   281
Grand Unified Theories   281
SIDEBAR: Finding GUT   282
Heat and Temperature   282
Common Temperature Scales   282
Absolute Zero   283
Thermodynamics   283
Entropy   284
SIDEBAR: Getting to Know Superconductivity   284
Waves   284
Parts of a Wave   284
Diagram of a Wave   285
Wave Properties   286
Transverse and Longitudinal Wave Motions   286

Wave Relationships 286
Electromagnetic Waves 286
    The Electromagnetic Spectrum 287
Interference 287
SIDEBAR: On the Radio 287
What Is Light? 287
    Dispersion of Color: White Light Through a Prism 288
    SIDEBAR: Lighten Up! 288
Refection and Refraction 288
    Reflection and Refraction of Light 289
    SIDEBAR: Diamonds and Fiber Optics 289
Sound Waves 290
Speed of Sound 290
The Doppler Effect 290
Electricity 291
Electrostatics 291
Electric Current 292
    Turning on a Light 292
Ohm's Law—Formulas 293
Kilowatts Used by Common Appliances 293
Magnetism 293
    Magnetic Lines of Force 294
Electromagnetism 294
Maxwell's Equations 294
Particles of the Universe 295
Physics of the Atom 295
Models of Atoms 295
Isotopes 296
Radioactivity 296
SIDEBAR: Antiparticles in the Universe 297
Subatomic Particles 297
SIDEBAR: Neutrino Detectors 298
Nuclear Physics 299
Fission—Nuclear Power and Chain Reactions 299
SIDEBAR: How Big Is the Atom? 299
Splitting the Atom 299
SIDEBAR: Nuclear Reactions in the Backyard 300
Fusion—Thermonuclear Reactions 300
Quantum Physics 300
Quanta 300
Quantum Mechanics 300
    SIDEBAR: How Lasers Work 301
The Uncertainty Principle 301
Exclusion Principle 302
Major Physicists 302
Significant Scientific Discoveries in Physics 307

Common Terms in Physics 309
Additional Sources of Information 312

8. Astronomy 313

What Is Astronomy? 314
The Universe 314
The First Moments of the Universe 314
SIDEBAR: Evidence for the Big Bang 314
Cosmology and the Universe 315
Age of the Universe 315
SIDEBAR: Astronomical Theories and Discoveries 316
The Solar System 317
Birth of Our Solar System 317
Distribution of Mass in the Solar System 318
The Sun 318
    Layers and Features of the Sun 320
The Planets and Satellites 320
    Planetary Statistics 321
    Planetary Distances 321
    Size Comparisons of the Planets 322
    Planets from Earth 322
    Satellites of Our Solar System 323
    SIDEBAR: Kepler's Laws of Planetary Motion 324
Comets 324
    SIDEBAR: Farthest Out? 325
    Short-Period Comet Returns 325
Asteroids 326
    Sampling of Asteroids 326
Impacts on the Earth 327
    SIDEBAR: An Impact Today 328
    Terrestrial Impact Craters 328
Meteors 328
    Major Meteor Showers 329
    SIDEBAR: Samples from Space? 329
Between the Planets 330
The Earth's Moon 330
    SIDEBAR: Origin of the Moon? 331
    The Moon Around the Earth 331
    Faces of the Moon 332
    Phases of the Moon 333

Eclipses of the Sun and Moon   334
    Lunar and Solar Eclipses   334
    *Chart of Lunar and Solar Eclipses
    (1995–2010)   335*
Constellations   336
    *The Constellations (Northern and Southern
        Hemispheres)   336*
The Stars   337
    Star Classification   337
    Lives of the Stars   337
        Hertzsprung-Russell Diagram   337
    Types of Stars   338
        Brightest Stars   339
        Closest Stars   339
        SIDEBAR: The Closest Star System   340
Galaxies   340
    What Is a Galaxy?   340
        Shapes of Galaxies   341
        SIDEBAR: Members of the Local Group   341
Other Astronomical Objects   342
    SIDEBAR: Cataloging Space   342
Common Telescopes   342
    Reflecting and Refracting Telescopes   343
    SIDEBAR: Using CCDs   344
    World's Largest Telescopes   344
    Radio Astronomy   346
    SIDEBAR: The Other Telescopes   347
The Space Age   347
    Space Firsts   347
    Human Missions to the Moon   348
    Special Spacecraft   349
        SIDEBAR: The First Space Shuttle   350
        Unmanned Spacecraft to the Planets   351
        SIDEBAR: Where Are They Now?   353
        SIDEBAR: The Search for Others   354
Major Astronomers and Space Scientists   354
Significant Scientific Discoveries in Astronomy   360
Common Terms in Astronomy   362
Additional Sources of Information   365

9. *Earth Science*   367

The Earth   368
    The Early Earth   368

Earth in Space   368
    Rotation   368
    SIDEBAR: Why Slow Down?   369
    Revolution   369
    Earth's Seasons   370
        Earth Around the Sun   370
    Precession of the Equinoxes   370
        Earth's Precession   371
    SIDEBAR: The Earth's Magnetic Field   371
    Earth's Movement Through the Galaxy   371
Lists of the Earth   372
    Earth Facts and Figures   372
    Largest Lakes   373
    Principle Waterfalls   374
    Principle Rivers   374
    Principle Mountain Peaks   375
    Highest and Lowest Continental Points   375
    Principle Deserts   375
    SIDEBAR: Natural Wonders   376
Geology   376
    What Is Geology?   376
    Layers of the Earth   377
        Earth's Layers   378
        SIDEBAR: Deepest in the Earth   378
        Composition of the Earth's Crust   378
    Plate Tectonics   379
        Crustal Plates Around the World   380
        SIDEBAR: Switching North and South   380
        The Earth Through Time   381
    Rocks and Minerals   382
        SIDEBAR: False Diamonds   382
        Common Crystal Shapes   383
        SIDEBAR: Curious Crystals   384
        Mineral Hardness Scale   384
        Rock Cycle   385
        *Common Igneous, Sedimentary, and Metamor-
          phic Rocks   386*
    What Is Soil?   386
        Typical Soil Profiles   387
        Soil Taxonomy   387
    Geologic Time Scale   387
        Geologic Time Scale   388
        SIDEBAR: Ice in the Earth's Past and Today   389
Earthquakes and Volcanoes   389
    Earthquakes   389
        SIDEBAR: The Threat of Tsunamis   389
        Modified Mercalli Scale   390

Richter Scale   390

Comparison of Richter Magnitude and Energy Released   391

SIDEBAR: *Famous Earthquakes   391*

Major Earthquake and Volcanic Zones   392

Volcanoes   393

Recent Active Volcanoes   393

SIDEBAR: Aftermath of a Modern Volcano   394

Marine Science   395

The Earth's Oceans and Seas   395

SIDEBAR: Why Do We Need the Oceans?   395

Ocean Facts and Figures   395

SIDEBAR: Hot Vents and Ocean Life   396

Composition of Sea Water   396

Ocean Shoreline   397

Ocean Surface Currents   398

Ocean Zones   399

Ocean Features   399

SIDEBAR: Are There Other Oceans?   400

Ocean Tides   400

How Neap and Spring Tides Are Produced   401

Past Life   401

Paleontology   401

SIDEBAR: Extinctions of the Past   401

SIDEBAR: Keeping Up With the Dinosaurs   402

How Fossils Are Preserved   403

Physical Anthropology   404

One Possible Lineage to Homo sapiens   405

Comparing the Skull   406

SIDEBAR: Evidence of Ancient Humans   407

Major Earth Scientists   407

Significant Scientific Discoveries in Earth Science   411

Common Terms in Earth Science   412

Additional Sources of Information   417

10.   Meteorology   419

What Is Meteorology?   420

The Earth's Atmosphere   420

Atmospheric Layers   420

Divisions of the Earth's Atmosphere   421

SIDEBAR: Colorful Skies   422

Composition of Dry Air at Sea Level   423

The Earth's Winds   423

Planetary Winds   423

The Earth's General Circulation   424

Secondary Winds   424

Regional Winds   425

SIDEBAR: Wind Shear and Microbursts   426

Beaufort Wind Scale: Land and Sea   426

SIDEBAR: Wind Chill Chart   427

The Earth's Weather   428

Air Masses   428

Major Air Masses in the United States   428

SIDEBAR: Old Weather Ways   428

The Jet Streams   429

Air Temperature   429

Weather Fronts   430

Average Monthly High Temperatures, Precipitation, and Snowfall for Selected U.S. Cities   431

World's Highest and Lowest Temperatures   433

Humidity and Relative Humidity   433

Apparent Temperature Chart   434

Barometric (Air) Pressure   434

Weather Predictions Using the Barometer   435

Clouds

Common Clouds   437

Cloud Altitudes   438

Hydrometeors and Precipitation   438

Liquid Precipitation   438

High and Low Precipitation Records   439

Highest Normal Annual Precipitation in the United States   440

SIDEBAR: How Hail Forms   440

Definitions of Major Storms   441

Comparisons of Storms   441

Rainstorms   441

SIDEBAR: Rainbows and Halos   441

Snowstorms   442

Temperature and Ice Crystal Shapes   443

U.S. Greatest Annual Snowfalls   444

Thunderstorms   444

Hurricanes   445

Forming Tropical Storms Around the World   446

Major Hurricanes Since 1950   446

SIDEBAR: How are Hurricanes Named?   447

Saffir-Simpson Hurricane Damage Potential Scale   448

Tornadoes   448

Fujita and Pearson Wind Damage Scale   449

When and Where? Tornadoes in the United States 449

Weather Forecasting 450
SIDEBAR: Weather From Space 450
Storm Watches and Warnings 450
SIDEBAR: Radar Watches the Weather 450

Major Meteorologists 451
Significant Scientific Discoveries in Meteorology 453
Common Terms in Meteorology 454
Additional Sources of Information 456

11. Environmental Science 457

What Is Environmental Science? 458
What Is Ecology? 458
Natural Cycles of the Earth 458
The Water Cycle 458
The Carbon Cycle 458
The Nitrogen Cycle 458
The Oxygen Cycle 458
Global Water Cycle 459
Organic Carbon Cycle 459
The Nitrogen Cycle 460
The Oxygen Cycle 460
The Earth's Climate Zones 461
Earth's Climate Zone Classification 461
The Earth's Environments 461
SIDEBAR: What Do They Eat? 462
Terrestrial Ecology 463
Altitudinal and Latitudinal Life Zones (Eastern North America) 464
World's Tundra and Taiga 465
World's Rainforests 466
World's Grasslands and Savannas 467
World's Deserts 468
Mountain Belts 468
Freshwater Ecology 469
Marine Ecology 469
Environmental Pollution 469
Air Pollution 470
World's Primary Air Pollutants 470
Known and Suspected Effects of Common Air Pollutants on Human Health 470
United States Air-Quality Index Values 471

Water Pollution 472
SIDEBAR: A Shrinking Sea 473
The Earth's Water 473
Percent of Water Used in the United States 473
How Is Water Used? 474
Common Water Pollutants 474
Known or Suspected Effects of Common Water Pollutants on Human Health 474
SIDEBAR: The "Other" Pollutions 475
Current Environmental Concerns 476
Wetland Loss 476
Acid Rain 476
Waste Disposal 477
SIDEBAR: The Problems with Landfills 477
Landfill Loads 477
SIDEBAR: Digging Garbage 478
SIDEBAR: Not in My Backyard 478
Radon 479
Indoor Air Levels for Radon 479
Lead Contamination 479
SIDEBAR: The Debate Over EMFs 480
Soil Erosion 480
Global Environmental Concerns 480
The Earth's Natural Warming Cycle 480
The Earth as a Greenhouse 480
Major Greenhouse Gases and Sources 481
Is There Global Warming? 481
Deforestation 481
SIDEBAR: Reading the Ice 482
The Disappearing Ozone? 482
SIDEBAR: What Is Ozone? 483
SIDEBAR: El Niño and the World Climate 484
Urbanization and Overpopulation 484
Recycling 484
What Is Recycling? 484
What Our Garbage Contains 485
What Is Recycling Worth? 485
Our Energy Sources 486
Energy Sources 486
SIDEBAR: Gasoline Alternatives 487
Preserving Nature 487
SIDEBAR: Holding on to the Last Wilderness 488
Major Environmentalists 489
Significant Scientific Discoveries in Environmental Science 490
Common Terms in Environmental Science 491
Additional Sources of Information 494

12.   Computer Science   495

What Is Computer Science?   496
SIDEBAR: Binary Computing   496
Early Computing   497
Early Abacus   497
SIDEBAR: When a Computer Catches a Virus   497
Personal Computers   498
A Typical Computer Keyboard   499
Computer Necessities   499
SIDEBAR: Computer Talk   501
Adding On   501
SIDEBAR: More and More From Your PC   502
The Personal Computer   502
Printers   502
Memory   503
Other Personal Computers   504
More Powerful Computing   504
Programs and the Personal Computer   504
SIDEBAR: Getting With the Program   505
High Performance Computers   505
Mainframe   505
Supercomputers   505
SIDEBAR: Finding Fractals   506
Massive Parallel Processing   506
Computer Languages   506
SIDEBAR: Creating Chaos   506
High-Level Programming Languages   507
SIDEBAR: Sticking Together   508
Programming Codes   508
Partial List of ASCII Codes   509
Computer Uses in Science and Technology   510
Artificial Intelligence   510
CAD/CAM Animation   511
Desktop Publishing and Multimedia   511
SIDEBAR: The Virtual World   511
Computer Information and Retrieval Services   511
SIDEBAR: Making Computers Work   512
Major Computer Scientists   513
Significant Discoveries in Computer Science   514
Common Terms in Computer Science   516
Additional Sources of Information   522

13.   Engineering and Technical Science   523

What Are Engineering and Technical Science?   524
Tallest Buildings   524
Types of Engineering   524
SIDEBAR: Six Basic Machines   527
Highlights of Technology   528
SIDEBAR: Getting Small   531
Significant Discoveries and Inventions   531
Common Terms in Technical Science and Engineering   546
Additional Sources of Information   548

14.   Useful Science Resources   549

Museums, Planetariums, and Observatories   550
Zoos and Aquariums   580
National Parks Listing   592
National Wildlife Refuges   598
Notable Caves and Caverns   614
Deepest Caves Measured   614
Longest Caves Measured   614
Most Visited United States Caves   614
Useful Science Information   614
Nobel Prize Awards (1901–1994)   614
Scientific Organizations   630
Government Agencies   632
Popular Science Publications   633
Additional Sources of Information: General Science Books   637

Index   639

Introduction

"Men, in fact, desire from science nothing else but the benefits; not the arguments, but the definitions. Accordingly, our intention in this book is to shorten long-winded discourses and synthesize the various ideas. Our intention, also, however, is not to neglect the advice of the ancients."
    —IBN BOTLAN, "THE PHYSICIAN," FROM THE PREFACE TO THE TACUINUM SANITATIS, 15TH CENTURY A.D.

Science, at its very heart, is never constant. The study of any science entails looking at things, measuring and defining them, analyzing their properties, or figuring out how they work. Along with the observing and measuring are the ever-changing new technologies to accomplish these goals. Add all of these factors together, and it is easy to see why science is constantly changing and growing.

And as any lover of science will tell you, it's precisely this dynamism that keeps science exciting.

But there are also the basics—basics that the reader requires to form an understanding and definition of the intricacies within a science field. With this book, we attempt to offer to readers a chance to understand the basics of most of the commonly studied sciences. The first section of each chapter tells why a particular scientific field is important. Essential information—in the form of descriptions, charts, and illustrations—follows. Finally, each science chapter is capped with brief biographies of famous people in the field, highlights of the science through history, terminology, and additional sources of information.

Choosing the information for this book was not an easy task: An entire book covering all the minute details of all the sciences would encompass volumes. While we try to cover the most commonly sought information in each field, we had to make subjective decisions about what would be too detailed or technical for our audience. What we offer you is condensed treatment of science facts and figures, with interesting science tidbits in the sidebars that answer many science queries, without—to quote from Ibn Botlan—being long-winded.

Even as this book was being completed, there were changes and additions to the text to keep it current with the ever-changing science world. For the first time in history, we witnessed the fragments of a space object striking another world (Jupiter); and we saw DNA become a major contender in the field of forensic science. Because of the rapid changes in science, we chose to offer you as many solid facts and figures as possible. And, in keeping with the dynamics of science, we also added several of the more popular debates in all the sciences, mentioning many sides of each chosen scientific story.

We would like to thank the New York Public Library for their support during the writing of this book. We are also indebted to three editors for their comments and insights: Gerry Helferich, who helped sharpen our focus while always keeping the reader in mind; Bryan Bunch, whose vast knowledge of the sciences and friendly spirit (not to mention the sharing of his wonderful knowledge from his own books) improved the book immensely; and John Michel, who inherited the work, added to it, and saw the book through design and production.

—Patricia Barnes-Svarney

Chapter 1

Scientific Measurements

Why Is Measurement Important to Science? 2

Early Measurements 2

Scientific Notation 3

Fundamentals of Science 4

U.S. Conventional System 5

The SI System 6

Common U.S. Conventional and
SI Equivalents 8

Miscellaneous Measurements 9

Dimensions and Coordinates 15

Scale of the Universe 16

Special Scientific Measurements 17

Measuring Speeds 20

Scientific Scales 20

Logarithms 23

Temperature 23

Astronomical Distances 27

Mathematics and Measurement 28

Geometric Shapes 32

Major Mathematicians 35

Significant Discoveries in Measurement and
Mathematics 39

Common Terms in Measurement and
Mathematics 40

Additional Sources of Information 44

1

WHY IS MEASUREMENT IMPORTANT TO SCIENCE?

One of the most important developments in the history of science was the scientific method, the procedure scientists use to acquire knowledge in any field of science. Measurement of phenomena is essential to the scientific method—including measuring the initial phenomena and/or measuring the phenomena after an experiment—because it helps to quantify the experiment's results. The general format of the scientific method is as follows:

1. *The observation of the phenomena and the recording of facts.* The phenomena are what occurs in the environment; the facts are descriptions of what is observed.
2. *The formulation of physical laws from the generalization of the phenomena.* Physical laws are the way nature usually behaves based on what has been observed in the past.
3. *The development of a theory that is used to predict new phenomena.* The theory is a general statement that explains the facts. A theory can lead to a new conclusion or the discovery of a phenomenon. Developments of a theory often result in a change in paradigm—that is, looking at or thinking about a scientific problem in a totally different way.

EARLY MEASUREMENTS

The earliest measurements were based on familiar objects and lengths. A *foot* was originally the length of a man's foot from the heel to the end of the big toe. The foot was divided into 12 increments by the Romans. But by the seventeenth century, there was disagreement between countries concerning a foot's division. For example, the Dutch divided the foot into 11 inches.

England's Henry I (ruled 1100–1135) fixed the *yard* as the distance from the tip of his nose to the tip of his outstretched thumb. England's Edward I (ruled 1272–1307) determined that 1 yard would be equal to 3 feet (0.91 meter). The *acre*, from the Latin word *ager* ("field") was once the amount of land a yoke of oxen could plow in a day. The modern definition of an acre was also determined by Edward I—an area 40 by 4 rods, or 43,560 square feet (4,047 square meters), where a rod is equal to 16.5 feet (5.03 meters).

The *mile* was devised by the Romans and represented 1,000 paces (*mille* is Latin for "one thousand"). Each pace was 5 feet (1.52 meters) long, so a mile was 5,000 feet (1,524 meters). Today, 1 *mile* is equal to 5,280 feet (1,609.34 meters).

The *nautical mile* used by ships and airplanes was established much later. Each nautical mile represents $1/60$ of a degree of longitude along the equator, or 6,082.66 feet (1,853.99 meters). Because the Earth is not a perfect sphere, the nautical mile differs by a few decimals in different parts of the world. The United States uses the *international nautical mile*, or 6,076.1033 feet (1,851.9962 meters). In Britain, the *admiralty mile* is equal to 6,080 feet (1,853.18 meters).

The first accurate measurements of the Earth's circumference and diameter were made by the Hellenic librarian and astronomer Eratosthenes, who lived some 2,200 years ago. He knew that the Sun's light at noon reached the bottom of a deep well at Syene; he then measured the angle of the Sun's shadow at Alexandria at the same time to determine the angular measure between Syene and Alexandria. He determined that the Earth's circumference was 250,000 stadia, which was later revised to 252,000 stadia—or about 25,054 miles (40,320 kilometers). The actual circumference of the Earth is 24,857 miles (40,009 kilometers) around the poles, and

24,900 miles (40,079 kilometers) around the equator. From these data, Eratosthenes calculated the diameter of the Earth as 7,850 miles (12,631 kilometers)—close to today's mean value of 7,918 miles (12,740 kilometers). Eratosthenes is known as the father of geodesy, or the science of Earth measurement.

SCIENTIFIC NOTATION

Scientific notation is a way of writing numbers that makes it easier to work with the very large and small numbers often found in scientific measurements.

When a number is written in scientific notation, the number is written as the base number (or mantissa) times ten raised to a power (or exponent), expressed as *mantissa* $\times 10^{power}$. The exponent determines how many decimal places are in the actual number.

A negative exponent means that the numerical result after the multiplication will move the decimal point to the left, with as many decimal point movements to the left as in the exponent. For example, 6.723×10^{-3} translates to 0.006723, while 0.006723×10^{-3} translates to 0.000006723. A positive exponent means to move the decimal point that number of places to the right, adding zeros as needed. For example, 6.723×10^5 translates to 672,300, while 6.72300×10^3 translates to 6723.00.

There are a few rules to follow in using scientific notation:

- Any number written without an exponent has the number 1 for its exponent. For example, $10 = 10^1$.
- Any number (except 0 or 0^0) with an exponent of 0 is equal to 1. For example, $10^0 = 1$.
- A power indicates how many times the number is multiplied by 10. For example, $10^4 = 10 \times 10 \times 10 \times 10$.
- If the decimal point is moved to the left to create the scientific notation, the power of 10 will be positive. For example, $246 = 2.46 \times 10^2$.
- If the decimal point is moved to the right to create the scientific notion, the power of 10 will be negative. For example, $0.04 = 4 \times 10^{-2}$.

Powers of 10

Place Value	Place Name	Power of 10
1,000,000.	millions	10^6
100,000.	hundred thousands	10^5
10,000.	ten thousands	10^4
1,000.	thousands	10^3
100.	hundreds	10^2
10.	tens	10^1
1.	ones, or units	10^0
.	decimal point	
.1	tenths	10^{-1}
.01	hundredths	10^{-2}
.001	thousandths	10^{-3}
.0001	ten thousandths	10^{-4}
.00001	hundred thousandths	10^{-5}
.000001	millionths	10^{-6}

Large Number Names

Number of Zeros	United States Name	British, German, French Name
6	million	million
9	billion	milliard
12	trillion	billion
15	quadrillion	1,000 billion
18	quintillion	trillion
21	sextillion	1,000 trillion
24	septillion	quadrillion
27	octillion	1,000 quadrillion
30	nonillion	quintillion
33	decillion	1,000 quintillion

MEASURING PERCENTS AND PARTS

Substances in solution, such as salt in ocean water, are measured in percents, or as "parts per" a certain concentration. For example, if 5 grams of table salt were dissolved in 95 grams of water, there would be 100 grams of the solution, thus a 5 percent (%) salt solution by mass.

Another way of expressing the percent of substances in solution is by "parts per" readings. A 5% salt solution by mass would be recorded as 5 parts per hundred of salt, or 5 pph salt. This same solution would read 50 parts per thousand (ppt) or 50,000 parts per million (ppm).

Why use the higher numbers such as parts per thousand or million? For solutions having smaller quantities of solute, such as dissolved gases in water, these units are more convenient, since they allow us to use whole numbers. For example, most fish cannot live in water with a dissolved oxygen level of less than 4 ppm (0.004 grams per 1,000 grams of solution). To understand the amounts involved in a 4 ppm solution, visualize 1 million stacked pennies (the stack would be a mile high)—with the four top pennies representing the dissolved oxygen in solution.

FUNDAMENTALS OF SCIENCE

Most phenomena in nature include more than one fundamental property and are measured using combinations of standard units. Standard units are measured values that are fixed and reproducible. Other measurements are compared with the standards to determine their accuracy or their deviation from the standard readings.

- To measure locations and sizes, scientists use the fundamental property of *length*, or the measurement of space in any direction.
- The fundamental property of *time* is described as a continuous, forward flow of an event or series of events.
- *Mass* is a fundamental property defined as the measurement of an object's quantity of matter.
- *Electric charge* is a fundamental property of matter that can be either positive or negative; when mass with an electric charge moves, it produces an electric current.

U.S. CONVENTIONAL SYSTEM

The United States is one of the few places using a measuring system inherited (but now modified) from the British Imperial system of measurement. It also is called the U.S. Conventional System or the gravitational system of measurement.

U.S. Conventional System—Dry and Liquid Weights
Fluid Volume

1 teaspoon = $1/3$ tablespoon = $1/6$ fluid ounce
1 tablespoon = 3 teaspoons = $1/2$ fluid ounce
1 fluid ounce = 2 tablespoons = 6 teaspoons
1 gill = $1/2$ cup = 4 fluid ounces
1 cup = 16 tablespoons = 8 fluid ounces
1 pint = 2 cups = 16 fluid ounces = 33.6 cubic inches
1 quart = 2 pints = 4 cups = 32 fluid ounces
1 gallon = 4 quarts = 8 pints = 16 cups = 128 fluid ounces = 0.1337 cubic feet = 231 cubic inches
   = 8.34 pounds of water
1 bushel = 8 gallons = 32 quarts
1 barrel = 31.5 U.S. gallons (a petroleum barrel = 42 U.S. gallons)

Weights

1 dram = 27 $^{11}/_{32}$ grains
1 ounce = 16 drams
1 pound = 16 ounces
1 short hundredweight = 100 pounds
1 short ton = 20 hundredweight = 2,000 pounds
1 quintal (long hundredweight) = 220.26 pounds avoirdupois = 100,000 grams
1 long ton = 2,240 pounds = 20 long hundredweights

U.S. Conventional System—Measures
Linear Measurement

1 foot = 12 inches
1 yard = 3 feet = 36 inches
1 mile = 1 statute mile = 1,760 yards = 5,280 feet = 8 furlongs
1 nautical mile = 1.15 statute miles = 6,076 feet
1 rod = 16.5 feet
1 furlong = 40 rods = 660 feet

Cubic Measurement (or Volume)

1 cubic foot = 1,728 cubic inches
1 standard gallon = 231 cubic inches
1 cubic yard = 27 cubic feet (46,656 cubic inches)

Square Measurement (or Area)

1 square foot = 144 square inches
1 square yard = 9 square feet = 1,296 square inches
1 square rods = 30.25 square yards = 272.25 square feet
1 road = 40 square rods
1 acre = 4 roads = 4,840 square yards = 43,560 square feet = 160 square rods
1 square mile = 1 section = 640 acres

Power and Efficiency

1 slug = mass to which 1 poundal (a unit of force) equals an acceleration of 1 foot per second
   = about 32.17 pounds
1 foot-pound = work when a force of 1 poundal moves something 1 foot
1 horsepower = 550 foot-pounds per second

U.S. Conventional System—Miscellaneous

1 cubic foot of water = 62.425 pounds (weight)
1 cubic feet per second = 448.83 gallons per minute (water flow)
1 pound per square inch = 27.7 inches of water (pressure)
1 pound per square inch = 2.31 feet of water (pressure)
1 pound per square inch = 2.036 inches of mercury (pressure)
1 kilowatt-hour = 2.655×10^6 foot-pounds (energy)
1 mile per hour = 88.028 feet per minute (velocity)
1 mile per hour = 1.467 feet per second (velocity)

THE SI SYSTEM

The metric system was devised by scientists appointed by the French National Assembly during the French Revolution. The system was developed mainly as a standard to replace the numerous measurement systems in use throughout the country, but the system also stood for defiance against the previous government's standard measurement system.

Unlike the U.S. Conventional System, the metric system was not based on measurements of human anatomy. The first measurement, the *meter*, was based on the circumference of the Earth measured on a line through Paris and the north and south poles. The line was divided by 40,000,000, and each division was called a meter (from the Greek word *metron*, "measure"). The standards of length were defined by multiplying or dividing the meter by various factors of 10. Later, the meter was further defined as the length equal to 1,650,763.73 times the wavelength of orange light emitted when a gas consisting of a pure isotope of krypton (mass number 86) is excited in an electrical discharge. In 1983, the wavelength definition was replaced by the distance light travels in a vacuum in $^1/_{299,792,458}$ second.

Other metric measurements also have certain set standards. For example, the *gram* was originally set as the mass of 1 cubic centimeter of water under standard conditions. The modern kilogram (1,000 grams) is equal to the mass of an international kilogram stored at Sèvres, France; a prototype is also located at the United States Bureau of Standards.

The metric system has been incorporated into the International System of Units (shortened to SI, from the French *Système International d'Unités*), which is now the standard measurement system for most fields of science. Within the SI system, the units are multiplied by factors of 10 when converting from one unit to another.

There are seven base units of the SI system: the *meter* (m, a measure of length), the *kilogram* (kg, a measure of weight), the *second* (s, a measure of time), the *ampere* (A, a measure of electric current), the *Kelvin* (K, a measure of temperature), the *mole* (mol, a measure of the amount of a substance), and the *candela* (cd, a measure of luminous intensity), and two supplementary units, the *radian* (plane angles) and *steradian* (solid angles).

GOING METRIC?

The United States and Burma are the only countries that do not use the metric system for their principal units of measurement. Resistance to the metric system dates to the U.S.'s infancy, when Thomas Jefferson was unable to persuade Congress to adopt the French decimal system. The metric system was again introduced to the United States in 1866, just after the Civil War, but it was ignored. In 1975, then-President Gerald Ford signed a bill that would establish the U.S. Metric Board and gradually convert the United States to the metric system. The attempt failed because of the entrenchment of the popular U.S. Conventional System and the voluntary nature of the changeover. By 1982, the board had been abolished.

There is still a call for the United States to "go metric"—but a great deal of resistance remains. In the Trade Act of 1988, government agencies were supposed to adopt the SI system; by 1992, most agencies had switched to the metric system. A 1988 law also called for the conversion of highway signs to metric by 1992; the deadline passed and by 1994, there was still resistance—not only to spending money for the change but, again, to the conversion itself. U.S. professionals and students in most scientific fields must learn the SI system—but for everyday life, they must still know the U.S. Conventional System, which is still solidly in place.

SI System—Liquid and Dry Weights
Liquid (Capacity or Fluid Volume)

1 liter (L) = 1,000 milliliters (mL) = 0.001 cubic meter = 1,000 cubic centimeters
1,000 liters = 1 kiloliter (kL)
1 centiliter (cL) = 10 milliliters
1 deciliter (dL) = 10 centiliters = 100 milliliters
1 hectoliter = 10 dekaliters (daL) = 100 liters

Mass

1 gram = 10 decigrams = 100 centigrams = 1,000 milligrams
1,000 grams = 1 kilogram
1,000 kilograms = 1 metric ton

SI System—Measures
Linear Measurement

1 angstrom (Å) = 0.0001 micrometer = 0.0000001 millimeter
1 micrometer = 0.001 millimeter
    (a micrometer is also known as a micron)
10 millimeters = 1 centimeter
10 centimeters = 1 decimeter
1 meter = 10 decimeters = 100 centimeters = 1,000 millimeters

10 meters = 1 dekameter
100 meters = 1 hectometer
10 hectometers = 1 kilometer = 1,000 meters

Cubic Measurement (or Volume)

1,000 cubic millimeters = 1 cubic centimeter
1 cubic decimeter = 1,000 cubic centimeters
1 cubic meter = 1,000 cubic decimeters
1,000 cubic meters = 1 cubic dekameter

Square Measurement (or Area)

100 square millimeters = 1 square centimeter
1 square meter = 100 square decimeters = 10,000 square centimeters
100 square meters = 1 are
10,000 square meters = 1 hectare = 100 ares
100 hectares = 1 square kilometer = 1,000,000 square meters

COMMON U.S. CONVENTIONAL AND SI EQUIVALENTS

Distance and Length

1 foot = 0.3048 meters
1 inch = 2.54 centimeters
0.04 inch = 1 millimeter
0.3937 inch = 1 centimeter
3.28084 feet = 1 meter = 1.093613 yards
1 yard = 0.9144 meter
0.62137 mile = 1 kilometer
1 mile = 1.609344 kilometers
1 rod = 5.092 meters
1 furlong = 201.168 meters

Area and Volume

1 square inch = 6.4516 square centimeters
1 square centimeter = 0.1550003 square inch
1 square foot = 0.09290304 square meter
1 square meter = 10.76 square feet = 1.196 square yards
1 square yard = 0.83612736 square meter
1 cubic inch = 16.387064 cubic centimeters
1 cubic centimeter = 0.06102374 cubic inch
1 cubic foot = 0.028316847 cubic meter
1 cubic meter = 35.31467 cubic feet = 1.307951 cubic yards = 61,023.74 cubic inches
1 acre = 4,046.8564 square meters = 0.40468564 hectare
1 hectare = 107,639.1 feet = 2.4710538 acres = 0.003861006 square mile
1 are = 119.6 square yards

Mass, Weight, and Capacity

0.035 ounce (avoirdupois) = 1 gram
1 ounce = 28.3495 grams
1 dry quart = 1.101 liters
1 liquid quart = 0.9463529 liter
1 gallon = 0.0038 cubic meter = 3.78541 liters
1 bushel = 35.23907 liters
1 avoirdupois pound = 453.59237 grams
1 gram = 0.03527 ounces
1 kilogram = 0.0685 slug = 2.2046 avoirdupois pounds = 35.2736 ounces
1 liter = 1.0567 liquid quarts = 33.814 fluid ounces = 0.908 dry quart = 4.2268 cups = 2.113 pints
1 metric ton = 1.1023 short tons = 2,205 pounds

Power and Efficiency

1 joule = 9.480×10^{-4} British thermal units (Btu) = 2.777×10^{-7} kilowatt-hour
1 horsepower = 0.746 kilowatt
1 kilowatt = 1.3 horsepower
1 kilometer per liter = 2.3521458 miles per gallon

MISCELLANEOUS MEASUREMENTS

Common Measurements and Equivalents

1 angstrom = 10^{-10} meter
1 radian = 57.2958 degrees
1 atmosphere = 14.696 pounds per square inch (pressure) = 29.921 inches of mercury
1 pound per square inch = 6.804×10^{-2} atmosphere

Circular and Arc Measurement

60 seconds = 1 minute
60 minutes = 1 degree
30 degrees = 1 sign
60 degrees = 1 sextant
90 degrees = 1 quadrant
4 quadrants = 360 degrees = 1 circle
1 minute = 60 seconds of arc = 60 seconds
1 degree = 60 minutes of arc = 60 minutes

Nautical Distances

1 fathom = 6 feet
1 cable = 120 fathoms = 720 feet
1 international nautical mile = 8.44 cables = 6,076.1033 feet = 1,851.9962 meters

Conversions for U.S. Conventional and SI Systems

Multiply	By	To Obtain
Acres	43560	Square feet
Acres	4047	Square meters
Acres	0.0016	Square miles
Acres	4840	Square yards
Acre feet	43560	Cubic feet
Acre feet	1233.48	Cubic meters
Angstroms	10^{-2}	Centimeters
Atmospheres	76.0	Centimeters—mercury
Atmospheres	29.92	Inches—mercury
Atmospheres	14.70	Pounds/square inch
Atmospheres	1.058	Tons/square foot
Barrels—oil	42	Gallons—oil
Board feet	144	Cubic inches
British thermal units	777.6	Foot-pounds
British thermal units	3.927×10^{-4}	Horsepower-hours
British thermal units	2.928×10^{-4}	Kilowatt-hours
Btu/minute	12.96	Foot-pounds/second
Btu/minute	0.0236	Horsepower
Btu/minute	17.57	Watts
Centares (Centiares)	1	Square meters
Centigrams	0.01	Grams
Centimeters	0.3937	Inches
Centimeters	0.01	Meters
Centimeters	10	Millimeters
Centimeters—mercury	0.0132	Atmospheres
Centimeters—mercury	0.4460	Feet—water (4°C)
Centimeters—mercury	136.0	Kilograms/square meter
Centimeters—mercury	27.85	Pounds/square foot
Centimeters—mercury	0.1934	Pounds/square inch
Centimeters/second	0.0328	Feet/second
Centimeters/second	0.036	Kilometers/hour
Centimeters/second	0.6	Meters/minute
Centimeters/second	0.0224	Miles/hour
Centimeters/second	0.0004	Miles/minute
Cubic centimeters	3.531×10^{-5}	Cubic feet
Cubic centimeters	0.0610	Cubic inches
Cubic centimeters	1×10^{-6}	Cubic meters
Cubic centimeters	1.3079×10^{-6}	Cubic yards
Cubic centimeters	2.642×10^{-4}	Gallons
Cubic centimeters	0.0010	Liters
Cubic centimeters	0.0021	Pints (liquid)
Cubic centimeters	0.0011	Quarts (liquid)
Cubic feet	1728	Cubic inches
Cubic feet	0.0283	Cubic meters
Cubic feet	7.4805	Gallons
Cubic feet	28.32	Liters
Cubic feet	59.84	Pints (liquid)
Cubic feet	29.92	Quarts (liquid)
Cubic feet/minute	0.1247	Gallons/second
Cubic feet/minute	0.4719	Liters/second
Cubic feet/second	448.831	Gallons/minute
Cubic inches	16.39	Cubic centimeters
Cubic inches	0.0005787	Cubic feet

Multiply	By	To Obtain
Cubic inches	1.6387×10^{-3}	Cubic meters
Cubic inches	2.1433×10^{-5}	Cubic yards
Cubic inches	0.004329	Gallons
Cubic inches	0.0164	Liters
Cubic inches	0.0346	Pints (liquid)
Cubic inches	0.0173	Quarts (liquid)
Cubic meters	1×10^{6}	Cubic centimeters
Cubic meters	35.31	Cubic feet
Cubic meters	61023	Cubic inches
Cubic meters	1.308	Cubic yards
Cubic meters	264.2	Gallons
Cubic meters	1000	Liters
Cubic meters	2113	Pints (liquid)
Cubic meters	1057	Quarts (liquid)
Cubic yards	27	Cubic feet
Cubic yards	46.656	Cubic inches
Cubic yards	0.7645	Cubic meters
Cubic yards	202.0	Gallons
Cubic yards	764.5	Liters
Cubic yards	1616	Pints (liquid)
Cubic yards	807.9	Quarts (liquid)
Cubic yards/minute	0.45	Cubic feet/second
Cubic yards/minute	3.367	Gallons/second
Cubic yards/minute	12.74	Liter/second
Degrees (angle)	60	Minutes
Degrees (angle)	0.0174	Radians
Degrees (angle)	3600	Seconds
Degree/second	0.1667	Revolutions/minute
Degree/second	0.0028	Revolutions/second
Drams	27.34	Grains
Drams	0.0625	Ounces
Drams	1.7718	Grams
Fathoms	6	Feet
Feet	30.48	Centimeters
Feet	12	Inches
Feet	0.3048	Meters
Feet	0.3333	Yards
Feet—water (4°C)	0.8826	Inches—mercury
Feet—water	62.43	Pounds/square foot
Feet/minute	0.5080	Centimeters/second
Feet/minute	0.0183	Kilometers/hour
Feet/minute	0.3048	Meters/minute
Feet/minute	0.0114	Miles/hour
Feet/second	30.48	Centimeters/second
Feet/second	1.097	Kilometers/hour
Feet/second	18.29	Meters/minute
Feet/second	0.6818	Miles/hour
Feet/second	0.0114	Miles/minute
Foot-pounds	0.0013	British thermal units
Foot-pounds	5.0505×10^{-7}	Horsepower-hours
Foot-pounds	3.766×10^{-7}	Kilowatt-hours
Foot-pounds/minute	0.0167	Foot-pounds/second
Foot-pounds/minute	3.030×10^{-3}	Horsepower
Foot-pounds/minute	2.2597×10^{-3}	Kilowatts

Conversions for U.S. Conventional and SI Systems (cont'd)

Multiply	By	To Obtain
Gallons	3785	Cubic centimeters
Gallons	0.1337	Cubic feet
Gallons	231	Cubic inches
Gallons	0.0038	Cubic meters
Gallons	3.785	Liters
Gallons	8	Pints (liquid)
Gallons	4	Quarts (liquid)
Gallons, imperial	1.2009	U.S. gallons
Gallons, U.S.	0.8327	Imperial gallons
Gallons—water	8.34	Pounds—water
Grams	980.7	Dynes
Grams	15.43	Grains
Grams	0.0353	Ounces
Grams	0.0322	Ounces (troy)
Grams	0.0022	Pounds
Grams/cubic centimeter	0.0361	Pounds/cubic inch
Hectares	2.471	Acres
Horsepower	42.44	Btu/minute
Horsepower	33000	Foot-pounds/minute
Horsepower	550	Foot-pounds/second
Horsepower	1.014	Horsepower (metric)
Horsepower	0.7457	Kilowatts
Horsepower-hours	0.7457	Kilowatt-hours
Inches	2.540	Centimeters
Inches—mercury	0.033	Atmospheres
Inches—mercury	345.3	Kilograms/square meter
Inches—mercury	70.73	Pounds/square foot
Inches—water	0.0735	Inches—mercury
Kilograms	980665	Dynes
Kilograms	2.205	Pounds
Kilometers	3281	Feet
Kilometers	1000	Meters
Kilometers	0.6214	Miles
Kilometers	1094	Yards
Kilometers	1.0570×10^{-11}	Light-year
Kilometers/hour	54.68	Feet/minute
Kilometers/hour	0.5396	Knots
Kilowatts	56.82	Btu/minute
Kilowatts	44253.7	Foot-pounds/minute
Kilowatts	737.6	Foot-pounds/second
Kilowatts	1.341	Horsepower
Kilowatt-hours	3410	British thermal units
Kilowatt-hours	2.655×10^{6}	Foot-pounds
Kilowatt-hours	1.341	Horsepower-hours
Light-years	9.4605×10^{12}	Kilometers
Light-years	0.3066	Parsecs
Liters	0.0353	Cubic feet
Liters	61.02	Cubic inches
Liters	0.0010	Cubic meters
Liters	0.2642	Gallons
Liters	2.113	Pints (liquid)
Liters	1.057	Quarts (liquid)
Meters	10^{-10}	Angstroms

Multiply	By	To Obtain
Meters	3.281	Feet
Meters	39.37	Inches
Meters	0.001	Kilometers
Meters	1.094	Yards
Meters/minute	3.281	Feet/minute
Meters/minute	0.06	Kilometers/hour
Meters/minute	0.0373	Miles/hour
Meters/second	196.8	Feet/minute
Meters/second	3.281	Feet/second
Meters/second	3.6	Kilometers/hour
Meters/second	0.03728	Miles/minute
Microns	1×10^6	Meters
Microns	10^4	Angstroms
Miles	5280	Feet
Miles	1.609	Kilometers
Miles	1760	Yards
Miles/hour	44.70	Centimeters/second
Miles/hour	88	Feet/minute
Miles/hour	1.467	Feet/second
Miles/hour	1.609	Kilometers/hour
Miles/hour	0.8690	Knots
Miles/hour	26.82	Meters/minute
Miles/minute	2682	Centimeters/second
Miles/minute	88	Feet/second
Miles/minute	1.609	Kilometers/minute
Miles/minute	60	Miles/hour
Milligrams	0.001	Grams
Milliliters	0.001	Liters
Millimeters	0.1	Centimeters
Millimeters	0.0394	Inches
Ounces	16	Drams
Ounces	437.5	Grains
Ounces	0.0625	Pounds
Ounces	0.9115	Ounces (troy)
Ounces	2.8349×10^{-5}	Tons (metric)
Ounces (troy)	1.0971	Ounces (avoirdupois)
Ounces (fluid)	1.805	Cubic inches
Ounces (fluid)	0.0296	Liters
Parsecs	3.086×10^{13}	Kilometers
Parsecs	3.2617	Light-years
Pounds	16	Ounces
Pounds	256	Drams
Pounds	7000	Grains
Pounds	0.0005	Tons (short)
Pounds	1.2153	Pounds (troy)
Pounds/cubic inch	1728	Pounds/cubic foot
Pounds/square foot	1488	Kilograms/meter
Pounds/inch	178.6	Grams/centimeter
Pounds/square foot	4.882	Kilograms/square meter
Pounds/square inch	0.0680	Atmospheres
Pounds/square inch	2.036	Inches—mercury
Quadrants (angle)	1.571	Radians
Quarts (liquid)	57.75	Cubic inches
Quintal, metric	220.46	Pounds

Conversions for U.S. Conventional and SI Systems (cont'd)

Multiply	By	To Obtain
Radians	57.30	Degrees
Radians	3438	Minutes
Radians	0.637	Quadrants
Radians/second	9.549	Revolutions/minute
Revolutions/second	360	Degrees/second
Revolutions/second	6.283	Radians/second
Revolutions/second	60	Revolutions/minute
Seconds (angle)	4.8481×10^{-6}	Radians
Square centimeters	0.0011	Square feet
Square centimeters	0.1550	Square inches
Square centimeters	0.0001	Square meters
Square centimeters	100	Square millimeters
Square feet	2.2957×10^{-5}	Acres
Square feet	929.0	Square centimeters
Square feet	144	Square inches
Square feet	0.0929	Square meters
Square feet	3.5870×10^{-8}	Square miles
Square feet	0.1111	Square yards
Square inches	6.452	Square centimeters
Square inches	0.0069	Square feet
Square kilometers	247.1	Acres
Square kilometers	1.0764×10^{7}	Square feet
Square kilometers	1×10^{6}	Square meters
Square kilometers	0.3861	Square miles
Square kilometers	1.1960×10^{6}	Square yards
Square meters	10.76	Square feet
Square meters	1.1960	Square yards
Square miles	640	Acres
Square miles	2.590	Square kilometers
Square miles	3.0976×10^{6}	Square yards
Square millimeters	0.01	Square centimeters
Square millimeters	0.0016	Square inches
Square yards	9	Square feet
Square yards	0.8361	Square meters
Square yards	3.2283×10^{-7}	Square miles
Tons (metric)	1000	Kilograms
Tons (metric)	2205	Pounds
Tons (short)	2000	Pounds
Tons (short)	0.89286	Tons (long)
Tons (short)	0.9072	Tons (metric)
Watts	0.0586	Btu (mean)/minute
Watts	0.7377	Foot-pounds/second
Watts	0.0013	Horsepower
Watts	0.001	Kilowatts
Watts	10^{7}	Ergs/second
Watt-hours	3.4144	British thermal units
Watt-hours	2655	Foot-pounds
Watt-hours	0.00134	Horsepower-hours
Watt-hours	0.001	Kilowatt-hours
Yards	91.44	Centimeters
Yards	3	Feet
Yards	36	Inches

Multiply	By	To Obtain
Yards	0.9144	Meters
Years	3.156×10^7	Seconds

DIMENSIONS AND COORDINATES

Rectangular Coordinates

A *rectangular coordinate system* is a standard way to draw a two- or three-dimensional graph. It uses x and y coordinates to determine two-dimensional positions along the x (horizontal) and y (vertical) axes; the z coordinate is added to describe a three-dimensional coordinate system. The x, y, and z coordinates are all perpendicular to each other, and pass through the origin of the graph.

Two- and Three-dimensional Coordinate Systems

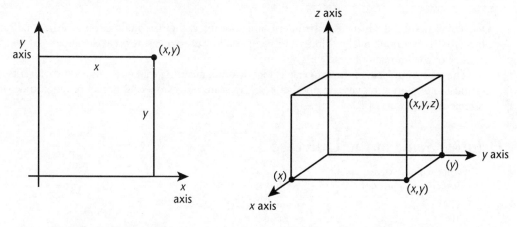

Two-Dimensional Coordinates   Three-Dimensional Coordinates

Polar Coordinates

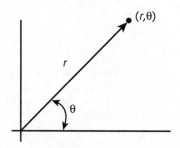

Spherical Coordinates

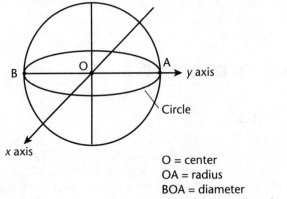

O = center
OA = radius
BOA = diameter
The circle cuts the sphere in half.

SCALE OF THE UNIVERSE

Due to technological advances, instruments are now able to help us analyze some of the smallest objects, such as atomic nuclei. Modern telescopes allow us to measure great distances—close to the edge of the known universe.

The following scale of the universe is logarithmic, meaning that each division represents a 10-fold increase in size over the one before. The scale ranges over 40 orders of magnitude or increments of powers of 10.

A Relative Scale of the Universe

Approximate Measurement (order of magnitude)	Object
10^{-14}	atomic nuclei
10^{-10}	atoms
10^{-9}–10^{-7}	molecules and viruses
10^{-7}–10^{-6}	visible light waves
10^{-4}	single-celled protozoa (0.1 millimeter across)
10^{-3}–10^{-2}	limit of visibility of the unaided eye
1–10	human beings to elephants (the largest land creature)
10^{4}–10^{5}	largest cities
10^{5}	largest asteroid
10^{6}	Moon
10^{7}–10^{8}	Earth
10^{9}–10^{10}	Sun
10^{11}–10^{12}	Earth's orbit
10^{13}	solar system
10^{17}	nebulae where stars are born
10^{20}–10^{21}	galaxies
10^{24}	local group of galaxies
10^{26}–10^{27}	observable universe

HOW DOES IT MEASURE?

How do you visualize sizes, distances, or other standard measurements? Some objects are too small or too large to comprehend, and some distances are too far to judge. The only way to understand some measurements is to compare them with something more familiar:
- An angstrom can be visualized as the change in level of a 164 by 66-foot (50 by 20-meter) swimming pool caused by the landing of a fly on the water's surface.
- The planet Jupiter has 318 times the mass of the Earth; Jupiter's Great Red Spot is about three times the size of the Earth.
- In Europe, tidal ranges along the coast vary from the Baltic Sea, which has virtually no tide, to the Bristol Channel, which has spring tide variations of more than 33 feet (10 meters)— or about as high as the average three-story building.

SPECIAL SCIENTIFIC MEASUREMENTS

Sound Units

A *sound* is a vibration that travels in waves through almost any medium, including air and water (sound cannot travel in a vacuum). Sound is measured by its pitch, loudness, and speed (for more information on sound and sound waves, see Chapter 7, "Physics").

Pitch

Pitch is the highness or lowness of a sound. It is measured by the frequency of its waves in hertz, or the number of waves (or cycles) per second. Fast, vibrating, and high-frequency waves cause a *high pitch*, whereas low frequency waves produce a *low pitch*.

Pitches too high to be heard by humans (with frequencies above 15,000 hertz) are called *ultrasonic*. Ultrasonic devices are widely used in medical diagnosis and in industry. Pitches too low to be heard by humans (with frequencies below 50 hertz) are called *infrasonic*. Though we cannot hear infrasound vibrations, we can often feel them, because parts of the body resonate in this range.

Pitch Ranges

Subject	Approximate Frequency Range of Hearing (in Hertz)
Humans	50–15,000
Dolphins	150–150,000
Bats	1,000–120,000
Dogs	15–50,000
Cats	60–65,000

Decibels

Decibels are the units used to measure relative loudness. The smallest amount of change that can be detected by the human ear is 1 decibel. The decibel scale is not linear; it is exponential. For example, a 20-decibel sound is 10 times louder than a 10-decibel sound; a 30-decibel sound is 100 times louder than a 10-decibel sound.

Decibel Scale

Sound Intensity Factor	Level of Sound (in decibels)	Common Sources
1,000,000,000,000,000,000	180	rocket engine
1,000,000,000,000,000	150	jet taking off
1,000,000,000,000	120	thunderclap
100,000,000,000	110	auto horn at 3 feet (1 meter); riveter
10,000,000,000	100	inside a subway
1,000,000,000	90	lawn mower; food blender
100,000,000	80	garbage disposal; hair dryer; alarm clock
10,000,000	70	vacuum cleaner; freeway traffic
1,000,000	60	ordinary conversation; air-conditioning at 20 feet (6 meters) away
100,000	50	light traffic noise
10,000	40	quiet office; living room (average)
1,000	30	library; soft whisper
10	10	rustling leaves
1	0	threshold of hearing

Speed of Sound

The *speed of sound* is usually measured at about 1,088 feet (331.4 meters) per second at 32°F (0°C) in dry air at sea level. The exact figure of the speed of sound varies because environmental conditions such as air pressure, humidity, and air purity can change the speed.

When an aircraft travels faster than the speed of sound, a "sonic boom" (or "supersonic boom") is heard as the craft passes over the observer. This is caused by a sharp air pressure rise in front and back of the craft. A double sonic boom occurs when a space shuttle enters the atmosphere. It is also caused by the air pressure rises at the front and back of the craft, but the rapid decent of the shuttle allows both shock waves to be heard (jets move too slowly for us to distinguish between the two booms).

Electrical Units

There are numerous units used to measure electricity, all based on a specific experimental standard. Electrical units include the following common divisions in the SI system (for more information on electricity, see Chapter 7, "Physics").

ampere (amp)   A unit of the rate of electric current

coulomb   A unit quantity of electrical charge

ohm   A unit of electrical resistance

volt   A unit of electromotive force; the difference in electrical potential required to move a current of 1 ampere through a resistance of 1 ohm

Density and Volume

Density is the measure of a substance's mass per unit volume, thus the density times the volume is equal to the object's mass (for more information on atoms and substances, see Chapter 6, "Chemistry").

For example, gold has a density of 19.28 grams per cubic centimeter and an atomic weight of 196.967. If you have a cube of gold, 0.5 centimeter per side, the following equations will determine the mass of the cube, the number of atoms in the cube, and the volume and mass of one atom of gold.

mass of the cube   Density times volume is equal to the mass of the cube: $19.28 \times 0.5^3 = 2.41$ grams

number of atoms   The mass of the cube divided by the atomic weight times Avogadro's number gives the number of atoms in the cube:
$$\frac{2.41 \text{ grams}}{196.967} \times \left(6.02217 \times 10^{23}\right) = 7.3685 \times 10^{21} \text{ atoms}$$

volume of an atom   The volume of an atom is the volume of the cube divided by the number of atoms in the cube: $\dfrac{0.5^3}{7.3685 \times 10^{21}} = 1.6964 \times 10^{-23}$ cubic centimeter

mass of an atom   The mass of an atom is the mass of the cube divided by the number of atoms in the cube: $\dfrac{2.41}{7.3685 \times 10^{21}} = 3.2707 \times 10^{-22}$ gram

Altitude and Azimuth

The most obvious measurements of a coordinate system are based on the observer's horizon and zenith (the point directly overhead). Lines called vertical circles intersect the horizon at right angles. The altitude equals the degrees measured at a point on that circle. The azimuth is the number of degrees along the horizon to the vertical circle from a reference point on the horizon.

Altitude and Azimuth in a Horizontal Coordinate System

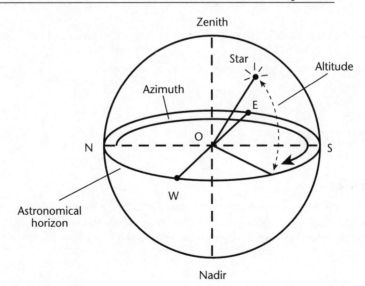

MEASURING SPEEDS

Measuring the speed of an object is important to many scientific fields. Some speeds are constant in the known universe, such as the speed of light.

Converting Common Speeds

To convert one unit of speed to another, multiply the unit of measurement in the left column by the number in the column of the desired measurement. For example, 1 mile per hour is equal to 44.7 centimeters per second.

Unit of measurement	miles/hour	centimeters/second	feet/second	knots
miles/hour	—	44.7	1.47	0.868
centimeters/second	0.0224	—	0.0328	0.0194
feet/second	0.682	30.5	—	0.592
knots	1.15	51.5	1.69	—

Comparing Speeds

Speed of light (in a vacuum, as in space)	186,000 miles per second; 2.9979×10^8 meters per second (more accurately 186,291 miles—299,792,458 meters—per second)
Speed of sound (0°C in dry air at surface)	1,088 feet per second; 331.4 meters per second (Mach 1)
Speed of jet stream (fastest measured)	597 feet per second; 182 meters per second
Speed of Earth's rotation at equator	1,532 feet per second; 467 meters per second
Speed of Moon around Earth (average)	0.634 miles per second; 1.02 kilometers per second
Speed of Earth around Sun (average)	18.52 miles per second ; 29.8 kilometers per second
Speed of Sun around galactic center	136.7 miles per second; 220 kilometers per second

SCIENTIFIC SCALES

Common Ruler

The common ruler represents a scale based on the U.S. Conventional System. Units are the foot, inch, and fractions of an inch. Some rulers also include the metric divisions of centimeters and millimeters, usually along the opposite side from the Conventional System measurements displayed.

Ruler with Inches and Millimeters

Engineer's Scale

The civil engineer's scale, or decimal scale, is divided into 10 minor divisions to 1 major division. This three-sided ruler has a triangular-shaped cross section. The scales can be used to represent most units of measure, including inches, feet, yards, and miles. Fractions of units are read in decimals; for example, the measure 2 feet 6 inches is read as 2.5 feet.

To read the upper scale in the following diagram, 1 inch equals 1 unit (e.g., 1 inch = 1 foot). For the lower scale, 1 inch equals 2 units (e.g., 1 inch = 2 feet). Other engineer's scales differ.

Engineer's Scale

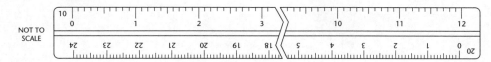

Metric Scale

The metric scale is used to make accurate drawings of machinery or structures in metric units. The scale represents ratios and can be used for various reductions and enlargements. For example, a 1:1 ratio represents a full-size drawing; a 1:2 reduction scale means, for example, that 1 millimeter on the drawing equals 2 millimeters on the object being drawn (or the drawing is half the size of the object), and so on. There are more than 20 typical ratios, including 1:1, 1:2, 1:20, and 1:100.

Metric Scale

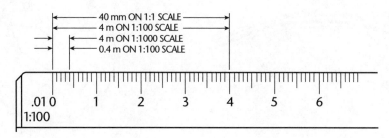

Micrometers

Micrometers are used to make extremely accurate linear measurements, usually no larger than a few inches. Standard inch micrometers measure to thousands of an inch (0.001 inch); vernier micrometers measure to ten thousandths of an inch (0.0001 inch). Standard metric micrometers measure to hundredths of a millimeter (0.01 millimeter); vernier metric micrometers measure to two thousandths of a millimeter (0.002 millimeter). To measure an object, the spindle is opened and the object is held in place at the opening. The thimble is turned to touch the object along the dimension that is to be read, and the measurement is read on the sleeve.

Micrometer

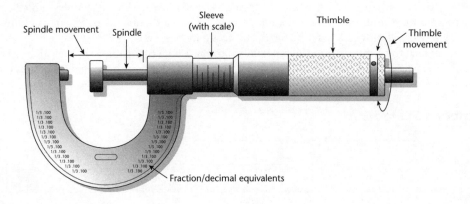

Electrical Multimeters

Electrical multimeters, either as analogue or digital meters, are used to measure electrical units, including voltage, resistance, and current. The units on a multimeter include direct current volts (DCV), alternating current volts (ACV), ohms (Ω), and direct current milliamps (DCmA).

Two Types of Analogue Multimeters

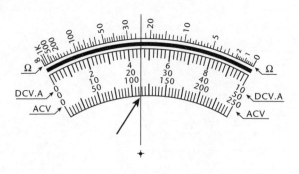
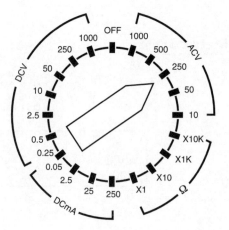

MEASURING INTERFERENCE

An interferometer separates waves—from acoustical to radio waves—into two or more parts by reflection, then eventually reunites the parts after they take different optical paths. The different paths produce interference—the high part of the wave is shifted in one of the otherwise identical waves. Even an extremely small shift can be observed, because some parts of the wave will be reinforced while others will be reduced.

Such precise measurements of wavelengths can be used to determine small distances and thickness. For example, acoustic interferometers are used for measuring velocity and absorption of sonic or ultrasonic waves in a gas or liquid. The combination of two or more radio telescopes used in radio astronomy act as interferometers; the separation of the two telescopes is called the *interferometer baseline*. A laser interferometer can measure lengths up to 200 inches (508 centimeters) to accuracies of better than 20 millionths of an inch (0.000000127 centimeters), such as the minute movement of a fault at the Earth's surface.

LOGARITHMS

There are several varieties of logarithm used extensively in mathematics and some areas of science. *Common logarithms* (in older sources called *Briggsian logarithms*) are logarithms with a base of 10. Today, logarithms with bases of any number are used about as often as common logarithms, and they are written with the number as the base. For example, $\log_2 8 = 3$ is a true statement about a logarithm to the base 2. It is true because $2^3 = 8$. The logarithms used most often are *natural logarithms* that have a base of e (which is about 2.7). Natural logarithms are usually abbreviated ln. The statement $\ln e^x = x$ is the normal way to write the logarithm; in long hand, it is written as $\log_e e^x = x$.

Common rules of logarithms include the following:

$\log (ab) = \log a + \log b$
$\log (^a/_b) = \log a - \log b$
$\log (^1/_a) = -\log a$
$\log a^b = b \log a$

TEMPERATURE

The temperature scale most commonly used in science is the Celsius scale. For very high or very low temperatures (those near absolute zero, the theoretical boundary where all molecules stop moving), the Kelvin (absolute) scale is used (for more information on temperature, see Chapter 7, "Physics").

Temperature Conversions

Name of Measurement	Conversion
Degrees Rankine (°R) (obsolete; thermodynamic temperature)	$R = {}^9/_5 K$

Temperature Ranges in the Universe

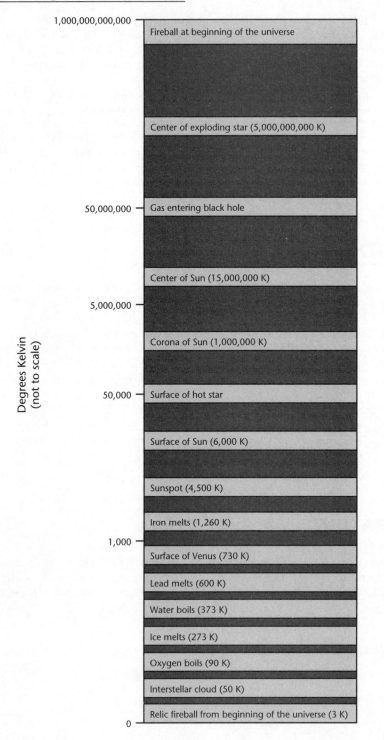

Degrees Kelvin (not to scale)

- 1,000,000,000,000 — Fireball at beginning of the universe
- Center of exploding star (5,000,000,000 K)
- 50,000,000 — Gas entering black hole
- Center of Sun (15,000,000 K)
- 5,000,000 —
- Corona of Sun (1,000,000 K)
- 50,000 — Surface of hot star
- Surface of Sun (6,000 K)
- Sunspot (4,500 K)
- Iron melts (1,260 K)
- 1,000 — Surface of Venus (730 K)
- Lead melts (600 K)
- Water boils (373 K)
- Ice melts (273 K)
- Oxygen boils (90 K)
- Interstellar cloud (50 K)
- Relic fireball from beginning of the universe (3 K)
- 0 —

Name of Measurement	Conversion
Degrees Reaumur (°R) (obsolete; thermodynamic temperature)	$R = \frac{4}{9}(F - 32)$; $R = \frac{4}{5}C$
Degrees Celsius (°C)	$C = \frac{5}{9}(F - 32)$; $C = \frac{5}{4}R$
Degrees Fahrenheit (°F)	$F = (\frac{9}{5}C) + 32$; $F = (K - 273)\frac{9}{5} + 32$
Degrees Kelvin (°K) (Absolute zero (0°K) = –459.69°F or –273.16°C)	$K = C + 273.16$

The following is a table of conversions from 0° to 212°. To convert from either Celsius or Fahrenheit, find the number in middle column and read left to convert to Celsius and right to convert to Fahrenheit.

Temperature Conversion Table

°C	°F or °C	°F	°C	°F or °C	°F
–17.8	0	32.0	3.9	39	102.2
–17.2	1	33.8	4.4	40	104.0
–16.7	2	35.6	5.0	41	105.8
–16.1	3	37.4	5.6	42	107.6
–15.6	4	39.2	6.1	43	109.4
–15.0	5	41.0	6.7	44	111.2
–14.4	6	42.8	7.2	45	113.0
–13.9	7	44.6	7.8	46	114.8
–13.3	8	46.6	8.3	47	116.6
–12.8	9	48.2	8.9	48	118.4
–12.2	10	50.0	9.4	49	120.2
–11.7	11	51.8	10.0	50	122.0
–11.1	12	53.6	10.6	51	123.8
–10.6	13	55.4	11.1	52	125.6
–10.0	14	57.2	11.7	53	127.4
–9.4	15	59.0	12.2	54	129.2
–8.9	16	60.8	12.8	55	131.0
–8.3	17	62.6	13.3	56	132.8
–7.8	18	64.4	13.9	57	134.6
–7.2	19	66.2	14.4	58	136.4
–6.7	20	68.0	15.0	59	138.2
–6.1	21	69.8	15.6	60	140.0
–5.6	22	71.6	16.1	61	141.8
–5.0	23	73.4	16.7	62	143.6
–4.4	24	75.2	17.2	63	145.4
–3.9	25	77.0	17.8	64	147.2
–3.3	26	78.8	18.3	65	149.0
–2.8	27	80.6	18.9	66	150.8
–2.2	28	82.4	19.4	67	152.6
–1.7	29	84.2	20.0	68	154.4
–1.1	30	86.0	20.6	69	156.2
–0.6	31	87.8	21.1	70	158.0
0.0	32	89.6	21.7	71	159.8
0.6	33	91.4	22.2	72	161.6
1.1	34	93.2	22.8	73	163.4
1.7	35	95.0	23.3	74	165.2
2.2	36	96.8	23.9	75	167.0
2.8	37	98.6	24.4	76	168.8
3.3	38	100.4	25.0	77	170.6

Temperature Conversion Table (cont'd)

°C	°F or °C	°F		°C	°F or °C	°F
25.6	78	172.4		54.4	130	266.0
26.1	79	174.2		55.0	131	267.8
26.7	80	176.0		55.6	132	269.6
27.2	81	177.8		56.1	133	271.4
27.8	82	179.6		56.7	134	273.2
28.3	83	181.4		57.2	135	275.0
28.9	84	183.2		57.8	136	276.8
29.4	85	185.0		58.3	137	278.6
30.0	86	186.8		58.9	138	280.4
30.6	87	188.6		59.4	139	282.2
31.1	88	190.4		60.0	140	284.0
31.7	89	192.2		60.6	141	285.8
32.2	90	194.0		61.1	142	287.6
32.8	91	195.8		61.7	143	289.4
33.3	92	197.6		62.2	144	291.2
33.9	93	199.4		62.8	145	293.0
34.4	94	201.2		63.3	146	294.8
35.0	95	203.0		63.9	147	296.6
35.6	96	204.8		64.4	148	298.4
36.1	97	206.6		65.0	149	300.2
36.7	98	208.4		65.6	150	302.0
37.2	99	210.2		66.1	151	303.8
37.8	100	212.0		66.7	152	305.6
38.3	101	213.8		67.2	153	307.4
38.9	102	215.6		67.8	154	309.2
39.4	103	217.4		68.3	155	311.0
40.0	104	219.2		68.9	156	312.8
40.6	105	221.0		69.4	157	314.6
41.1	106	222.8		70.0	158	316.4
41.7	107	224.6		70.6	159	318.2
42.2	108	226.4		71.1	160	320.0
42.8	109	228.2		71.7	161	321.8
43.3	110	230.0		72.2	162	323.6
43.9	111	231.8		72.8	163	325.4
44.4	112	233.6		73.3	164	327.2
45.0	113	235.4		73.9	165	329.0
45.6	114	237.2		74.4	166	330.8
46.1	115	239.0		75.0	167	332.6
46.7	116	240.8		75.6	168	334.4
47.2	117	242.6		76.1	169	336.2
47.8	118	244.4		76.7	170	338.0
48.3	119	246.2		77.2	171	339.8
48.9	120	248.0		77.8	172	341.6
49.4	121	249.8		78.3	173	343.4
50.0	122	251.6		78.9	174	345.2
50.6	123	253.4		79.4	175	347.0
51.1	124	255.2		80.0	176	348.8
51.7	125	257.0		80.6	177	350.6
52.2	126	258.8		81.1	178	352.4
52.8	127	260.6		81.7	179	354.2
53.3	128	262.4		82.2	180	356.0
53.9	129	264.2		82.8	181	357.8

°C	°F or °C	°F		°C	°F or °C	°F
83.3	182	359.6		92.2	198	388.4
83.9	183	361.4		92.8	199	390.2
84.4	184	363.2		93.3	200	392.0
85.0	185	365.0		93.9	201	393.8
85.6	186	366.8		94.4	202	395.6
86.1	187	368.6		95.0	203	397.4
86.7	188	370.4		95.6	204	399.2
87.2	189	372.2		96.1	205	401.0
87.8	190	374.0		96.7	206	402.8
88.3	191	375.8		97.2	207	404.6
88.9	192	377.6		97.8	208	406.4
89.4	193	379.4		98.3	209	408.2
90.0	194	381.2		98.9	210	410.0
90.6	195	383.0		99.4	211	411.8
91.1	196	384.8		100.0	212	413.6
91.7	197	386.6				

ASTRONOMICAL DISTANCES

Distances in space are so immense that astronomers have developed special measurements. The standard units are astronomical units, light-years, and parsecs.

An *astronomical unit* (AU) is the mean distance from the Sun to the Earth, or 92,960,117 miles (149,573,881 kilometers); for simplicity, an AU is usually rounded off to 93,000,000 miles (149,637,000 kilometers).

A *light-year* is the distance light (and other types of electromagnetic radiation) travels in 1 year in a vacuum. At an average speed of 186,291 miles (299,792 kilometers) per second, this equals approximately 5.88 trillion miles (9.4607 trillion kilometers), or 63,246 astronomical units

The light-year also is divided into light-minutes and light-seconds. For example, the Moon is 1.3 light-seconds from the Earth; the Sun is 8.3 light-minutes away from the Earth. Though a light-year is a measurement of distance and not time, it does imply time. For example, the light from a star that is 10 light-years from the Earth takes 10 years to reach the Earth. Therefore, an observer on Earth is seeing the star as it appeared 10 years ago.

Some Astronomical Measurements

Location	Distance from the Sun (Approximate)
Earth	1 AU; 93 million miles (149,637,000 kilometers)
Pluto	29 AU; 2.7 billion miles (4.344 billion kilometers)
Alpha Centauri	270,000 AU; 4.3 light-years; 25 trillion miles (40 trillion kilometers)
Rigel (star in Orion)	57 million AU; 900 light-years; 5.25 quadrillion miles (8.45 quadrillion kilometers)
M13 (globular cluster in Hercules)	1.7 billion AU; 26,700 light-years; 160 quadrillion miles (257.4 quadrillion kilometers)

Location	Distance from the Sun (Approximate)
Center of Milky Way galaxy	2 billion AU; 32,000 light-years; 190 quadrillion miles (305.7 quadrillion kilometers)
Nearest observed galaxies	4.8 billion AU; 75,000 light-years; 450 quadrillion miles (724 quadrillion kilometers)
Andromeda galaxy	140 billion AU; 2.2 million light-years; 1.3×10^{19} miles (2.09×10^{19} kilometers)
Nearest quasar	63 trillion AU; 1 billion light-years; 6×10^{21} miles; (9.7×10^{21} kilometers)

MATHEMATICS AND MEASUREMENT

Mathematics is the deductive study of quantities, magnitudes, and shapes with the use of numbers and symbols. Applied mathematics investigates physical phenomena, whereas pure mathematics explores mathematical structures or theoretical design. Every branch of science and engineering depends on mathematics; many measurements in science also depend on mathematics.

Evolution of Numbers

SAME SUM—EVERY TIME

There is a way to get the same sum—in this case 1,089—every time you add certain numbers together. (1) Take any three-digit number in which the first digit is larger than the last digit. (2) Reverse the number and subtract the smaller number from the larger one. (3) Reverse the result and add this number to the result. (4) The answer is 1,089 every time.

For example, use the number 725. The reverse of the number is 527. Subtract 527 from 725 to get 198. The reverse of the result is 891. Add this number to 198—and the answer is 1,089. If the result from step 2 is a two-digit number, such as 99, simply put a 0 in front of the 99 before reversing it (the reverse of 099 is 990). The answer will still be the same.

Naming Numbers

There are certain characteristics of numbers that allow them to be classified.

An **abstract number** is a number with no associated units.

Complex numbers were first devised as solutions to quadratic equations such as $x^2 + 2x + 2 = 0$. They are numbers of the form $a + bi$, where a and b are real and i is $\sqrt{-1}$.

The first **imaginary numbers** were created by determining the square root of –1. Today, imaginary numbers are the square roots of negative numbers.

Irrational numbers are numbers that are not the quotient of two integers. Mathematicians do not know if the first irrational number was the result of applying the Pythagorean theorem to a right triangle with legs of length 1 ($\sqrt{2^3}$) or the golden ratio from the use of the golden triangle ($1 + (\sqrt{5}/2)$).

Literal numbers are letters used to represent a number. They are usually found in algebraic formulas.

A **mixed number** is one that contains both a whole number and a fraction.

A **natural number,** often referred to as a counting number, is any whole number that is not equal to zero.

Along a number line, the numbers to the left of zero are **negative numbers.** They are written with a minus sign (–) before them.

A **perfect number** is equal to the sum of its proper divisors. For example, 6 is a perfect number because its proper divisors (1,2, and 3) total 6. Other perfect numbers are 28 and 496. No odd perfect number has ever been found; but that does not mean that one does not exist. By 1603, only seven perfect numbers were known—the sixth is 8,859,869,056, and the seventh is 137,438,691,328.

Along a number line, the numbers to the right of zero are **positive numbers.** They are written with either a blank space or a plus sign (+) before them.

A **prime number** is a positive whole number (greater than 1) that cannot be divided by any other positive number other than itself or 1. Certain rules concerning prime numbers have been discovered: 2 is the only even prime number; no prime number other than 5 can end in 5; the products of two prime numbers can never be a perfect square; if a prime number other than 2 or 3 is increased or decreased by 1, one of the results is always divisible by 6; and after the unit primes of 2, 3 , 5, and 7, all other prime numbers must end in 1, 3, 7, or 9.

A **rational number** can be expressed as the quotient of two integers when the denominator is not zero.

Any irrational or rational number that does not contain an even root of a negative number is a **real number.**

A **signed number** has either a positive or negative position relative to zero, usually in reference to a number line.

A **transcendental number** is a number that cannot be expressed as a solution of an algebraic equation. For example, pi (π) is a transcendental number.

A **whole number** represents zero or any positive number, with no fractional parts.

FINDING PRIME NUMBERS

Euclid, a Greek mathematician who lived during the third century B.C., proved that no one will ever find the "largest" prime number. Today, millions of prime numbers are known to exist—and mathematicians and computer scientists are still adding more.

To date, one of the largest primes is $(391,581 \times 2^{216,193})-1$—a prime with 65,087 digits. An even larger prime number was found in 1992, by a French team of researchers using a CRAY supercomputer in England. The number is $2^{756,839} - 1 \ldots$, and on, with a total of 227,832 digits—a prime number long enough to fill thirty-two pages of computer paper!

The larger prime numbers are called Mersenne primes, named after Father Marin Mersenne (died 1648), who found several prime numbers. The Mersenne primes (only about thirty-two are known to exist) take the form of $2^m - 1$, where m is a prime. In fact, calculations from Mersenne primes are often used in the search for perfect numbers.

Decimal and Percent Equivalents of Common Fractions

Fraction	Decimal	Percent	Fraction	Decimal	Percent
$^1/_{32}$	0.03125	3.125	$^{17}/_{32}$	0.53125	53.125
$^1/_{16}$	0.0625	6.25	$^9/_{16}$	0.5625	56.25
$^3/_{32}$	0.09375	9.375	$^{19}/_{32}$	0.59375	59.375
$^1/_{10}$	0.1	10	$^3/_5$	0.6	60
$^1/_8$	0.125	12.5	$^5/_8$	0.625	62.5
$^5/_{32}$	0.15625	15.625	$^{21}/_{32}$	0.65625	65.625
$^3/_{16}$	0.1875	18.75	$^2/_3$	0.6666+	66.666+
$^1/_5$	0.2	20	$^{11}/_{16}$	0.6875	68.75
$^7/_{32}$	0.21875	21.875	$^7/_{10}$	0.7	70
$^1/_4$	0.25	25	$^{23}/_{32}$	0.71875	71.87
$^9/_{32}$	0.28125	28.125	$^3/_4$	0.75	75
$^3/_{10}$	0.3	30	$^{25}/_{32}$	0.78125	78.125
$^5/_{16}$	0.3125	31.25	$^4/_5$	0.8	80
$^1/_3$	0.3333+	33.333+	$^{13}/_{16}$	0.8125	81.25
$^{11}/_{32}$	0.34375	34.375	$^{27}/_{32}$	0.84375	84.375
$^3/_8$	0.375	37.5	$^7/_8$	0.875	87.5
$^2/_5$	0.4	40	$^9/_{10}$	0.9	90
$^{13}/_{32}$	0.40625	40.625	$^{29}/_{32}$	0.90625	90.625
$^7/_{16}$	0.4375	43.75	$^{15}/_{16}$	0.9375	93.75
$^{15}/_{32}$	0.46875	46.875	$^{31}/_{32}$	0.96875	96.875
$^1/_2$	0.5	50			

Decimal Equivalents of Common Fractions of an Inch

Fractional Inch	Decimal Inch	Millimeter	Fractional Inch	Decimal Inch	Millimeter
$^1/_{64}$	0.015625	0.397	$^5/_{32}$	0.15625	3.969
$^1/_{32}$	0.03125	0.794	$^{11}/_{64}$	0.171875	4.366
$^3/_{64}$	0.046875	1.191	$^3/_{16}$	0.1875	4.762
$^1/_{16}$	0.0625	1.588	$^{13}/_{64}$	0.203125	5.159
$^5/_{64}$	0.078125	1.984	$^7/_{32}$	0.21875	5.556
$^3/_{32}$	0.09375	2.381	$^{15}/_{64}$	0.234375	5.953
$^7/_{64}$	0.109375	2.778	$^1/_4$	0.25	6.350
$^1/_8$	0.125	3.175	$^{17}/_{64}$	0.265625	6.747
$^9/_{64}$	0.140625	3.572	$^9/_{32}$	0.28125	7.144

Fractional Inch	Decimal Inch	Millimeter	Fractional Inch	Decimal Inch	Millimeter
$^{19}/_{64}$	0.296875	7.541	$^{21}/_{32}$	0.65625	16.669
$^{5}/_{16}$	0.3125	7.938	$^{43}/_{64}$	0.671875	17.066
$^{21}/_{64}$	0.328125	8.334	$^{11}/_{16}$	0.6875	17.462
$^{11}/_{32}$	0.34375	8.731	$^{45}/_{64}$	0.703125	17.859
$^{23}/_{64}$	0.359375	9.128	$^{23}/_{32}$	0.71875	18.256
$^{3}/_{8}$	0.375	9.525	$^{47}/_{64}$	0.734375	18.653
$^{25}/_{64}$	0.390625	9.922	$^{3}/_{4}$	0.75	19.05
$^{13}/_{32}$	0.40625	10.319	$^{49}/_{64}$	0.765625	19.447
$^{27}/_{64}$	0.421875	10.716	$^{25}/_{32}$	0.78125	19.844
$^{7}/_{16}$	0.4375	11.112	$^{51}/_{64}$	0.796875	20.241
$^{29}/_{64}$	0.453125	11.509	$^{13}/_{16}$	0.8125	20.638
$^{15}/_{32}$	0.46875	11.906	$^{53}/_{64}$	0.828125	21.034
$^{31}/_{64}$	0.484375	12.303	$^{27}/_{32}$	0.84375	21.431
$^{1}/_{2}$	0.5	12.700	$^{55}/_{64}$	0.859375	21.828
$^{33}/_{64}$	0.515625	13.097	$^{7}/_{8}$	0.875	22.225
$^{17}/_{32}$	0.53125	13.494	$^{57}/_{64}$	0.890625	22.622
$^{35}/_{64}$	0.546875	13.891	$^{29}/_{32}$	0.90625	23.019
$^{9}/_{16}$	0.5625	14.288	$^{59}/_{64}$	0.921875	23.416
$^{37}/_{64}$	0.578125	14.684	$^{15}/_{16}$	0.9375	23.812
$^{19}/_{32}$	0.59375	15.081	$^{61}/_{64}$	0.953125	24.209
$^{39}/_{64}$	0.609375	15.478	$^{31}/_{32}$	0.96875	24.606
$^{5}/_{8}$	0.625	15.875	$^{63}/_{64}$	0.984375	25.003
$^{41}/_{64}$	0.640625	16.272	1	1.0	25.400

Power and Exponents

A power is the product of the multiplication of a number by itself. When numbers are extremely large or small, it is convenient to express them as powers of 10.

Number	Exponential Form
1	1×10^0
10	1×10^1
100	1×10^2
1,000	1×10^3
10,000	1×10^4
100,000	1×10^5
1,000,000	1×10^6
0.1	1×10^{-1}
0.01	1×10^{-2}
0.001	1×10^{-3}
0.0001	1×10^{-4}
0.00001	1×10^{-5}
0.000001	1×10^{-6}

Exponents are superscripts that indicate how many times a number is multiplied by itself.
The laws of exponents are rules used to simplify expressions that use exponents.
- A number raised to the 1 power is the number itself: $10^1 = 10$
- A number raised to the 0 power is 1: $10^0 = 1$ (except for 0^0)
- A number without an exponent has an exponent of 1: $10 = 10^1$

- For positive powers: $1 \times 10^4 = 1 \times 10 \times 10 \times 10 \times 10 = 10{,}000$
- For negative powers: $1 \times 10^{-4} = 1 \div 10 \div 10 \div 10 \div 10 = 0.0001$
- To multiply powers: $(1 \times 10^4) \times (3 \times 10^5) = 1 \times 3 \times 10^{4+5} = 3 \times 10^9 = 300{,}000{,}000$
- To divide powers: $10^3/10 = 10^{3-1} = 10^2 = 100$
- To multiply like exponents: $10^2 \times 2^2 = (10 \times 2)^2 = 400$

GEOMETRIC SHAPES

There are numerous geometric shapes used in mathematics. The most common are listed below.

circle   A continuous line or the plane bounded by such a line, in which every point of the line is equidistant from the central point lying on the plane. A circle is commonly described by its radius—a straight line extending from the center of the circle to any point on the perimeter— and its diameter—a straight line extending from a point on the perimeter, through the center, to a point on the perimeter on the other side of the circle (it is also expressed as twice the radius).

square   A four-sided figure that has four lines at 90° angles. The opposite sides are parallel to each other and all sides are of equal length.

triangle   A three-sided figure that can take several shapes. In general, it has three inside angles, which add up to 180°. Triangles are divided into three basic types: obtuse, right, and acute; triangles named by the characteristics of their sides are equilateral, isosceles, and scalene.

polygon   A geometric figure that is bound by many straight lines (see also "Names for Polygons," later this chapter).

rectangle   A four-sided figure that has four lines at 90° angles. The opposite sides are parallel to each other and are equal in length, but are not equal in length to the lines that run perpendicular to them.

cube   A solid that has six square sides, with each at right angles to each adjacent side.

cylinder   A solid that has two equal-sided circular bases and a third side that joins the bases.

sphere   A solid that is bounded by a curved surface. Any point measured from the outside of the sphere to the center of the sphere is equal in distance.

rectangular prism   A solid that has four sides, with each junction at 90° angles. The opposite sides are equal in length and parallel to each other, but they are not equal in length to the sides that run perpendicular to them.

Common Geometric Shapes

Two-dimensional

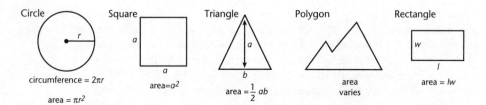

Circle   circumference = $2\pi r$ area = πr^2

Square   area=a^2

Triangle   area =$\frac{1}{2} ab$

Polygon   area varies

Rectangle   area = lw

Three-dimensional

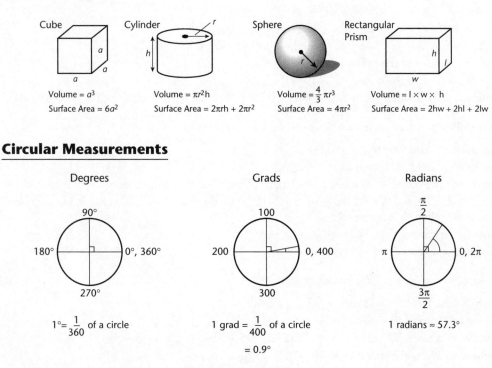

Cube

$Volume = a^3$
$Surface\ Area = 6a^2$

Cylinder

$Volume = \pi r^2 h$
$Surface\ Area = 2\pi rh + 2\pi r^2$

Sphere

$Volume = \frac{4}{3}\pi r^3$
$Surface\ Area = 4\pi r^2$

Rectangular Prism

$Volume = l \times w \times h$
$Surface\ Area = 2hw + 2hl + 2lw$

Circular Measurements

Degrees

$1° = \frac{1}{360}$ of a circle

Grads

$1\ grad = \frac{1}{400}$ of a circle

$= 0.9°$

Radians

$1\ radians \approx 57.3°$

The three common sets of mathematical units used to indicate angular measure are degrees, radians, and grads.

Names for Polygons

Number of Sides	Name
3	Triangle
4	Square
5	Pentagon
6	Hexagon
7	Heptagon
8	Octagon
9	Nonagon (or ennagon)
10	Decagon
11	Undecagon
12	Dodecagon

Common Formulas for Geometric Shapes

The following formulas are for determining area:

square   length × width, or length of one side (x) squared (or x^2)

rectangle   length × width

triangle $^1/_2$ × base × perpendicular height

cube square of the length of one side × 6
pentagon (5 sides) square of the length of one side × 1.720
hexagon (6 sides) square of the length of one side × 2.598
octagon (8 sides) square of the length of one side × 4.828
sphere square of the radius × 3.1416 (pi) × 4
circle square of the radius × 3.1416 (pi)
ellipse long diameter × short diameter × 0.7854, or short radius × long radius × 3.1416 (pi)

The following formulas are for determining the perimeter:

square 4 × the length of one side
rectangle 2 × (the length of one long side + the length of one short side)
triangle the length of one side × the length of one side × the length of one side
circle 2 × the radius × 3.1416 (pi), or 3.1416 (pi) × the diameter (The perimeter of a circle is generally called the circumference.)
regular pentagon 5 × the length of one side
regular hexagon 6 × the length of one side

The following formulas are for determining volume:

cube cube (x^3) of the length (x) of one side
pyramid area of the base × height × $^1/_3$
cylinder square of the radius (r^2) of the base × 3.1416 (pi) × height
sphere cube of the radius (r^3) × 3.1416 (pi) × $^4/_3$
cone square of the radius (r^2) of the base × 3.1416 (pi) × height × $^1/_3$
rectangular solid length × width × height

Conic Sections

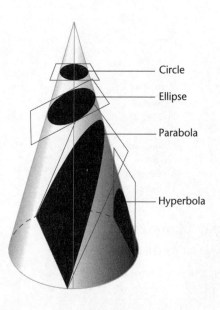

Circle

Ellipse

Parabola

Hyperbola

A conic section is a curve formed by the intersection of a plane with various parts of a cone.

Ratios of Common Angles

	0°	30°	45°	60°	90°	120°	135°	150°	180°
Sine	0	$\frac{1}{2}$	$\frac{1}{\sqrt{2}}$	$\frac{\sqrt{3}}{2}$	1	$\frac{\sqrt{3}}{2}$	$\frac{1}{\sqrt{2}}$	$\frac{1}{2}$	0
		Increasing and positive				**Decreasing and positive**			
Cosine	1	$\frac{\sqrt{3}}{2}$	$\frac{1}{\sqrt{2}}$	$\frac{1}{2}$	0	$-\frac{1}{2}$	$-\frac{1}{\sqrt{2}}$	$-\frac{\sqrt{3}}{2}$	1
		Decreasing and positive				**Decreasing and negative**			
Tangent	0	$\frac{1}{\sqrt{3}}$	1	$\sqrt{3}$	∞	$-\sqrt{3}$	-1	$-\frac{1}{\sqrt{3}}$	0
		Increasing and positive				**Decreasing and positive**			

A CHIRAL UNIVERSE?

Does anyone really know why certain systems in nature follow left- or right-handedness—or what scientists call chirality? Not really, but there are plenty of chiral and achiral objects to study. For example, chiral objects, such as screws, cannot be superimposed on their mirror image; whereas achiral objects, such as spheres, can be superimposed on their mirror image. And while the universe is filled with objects large and small that show handedness, apparently nature seems to favor the right, just as most humans are right-handed.

But this may all be conjecture. It's true that seashells, plants, and bacteria are right-handed. Yet the building blocks of life, amino acids, are mainly left-handed. Maybe the answer will come if scientists and mathematicians discover the chirality of the four forces that govern the universe—gravity, electromagnetic, strong nuclear, and weak interactive.

MAJOR MATHEMATICIANS

Archimedes (c. 287–212 B.C.)   Greek mathematician who is considered to be the greatest mathematician and engineer of ancient times. He discovered the lever and the principle of buoyancy, and he came close to inventing calculus.

Banach, Stefan (1892–1945)   Russian mathematician who founded modern functional analysis. He also developed the theory of topological vector spaces.

Barrow, Isaac (1630–1677)   British mathematician who was one of the teachers of Isaac Newton. He later developed several ideas on calculus, including that integration and differentiation are inverse operations.

Bernoulli, Daniel (1700–1782)   Netherlands-born Swiss mathematician who also studied extensively in medicine, biology, astronomy, and physics. He is known for his work on the math and physics behind fluid flow.

Brahmagupta (c. 598–c. 665)   Indian mathematician and astronomer, who wrote works on measuring, trigonometry, and algebra. He was also one of the first to incorporate negative numbers in his work (see also Chapter 8, "Astronomy").

Cantor, Georg (Ferdinand Ludwig Philipp) (1845–1918)   German mathematician who founded set theory, which became an entirely new subject in the mathematics of the infinite.

Cauchy, Augustin Louis, Baron (1789–1857)   French mathematician who was considered one of the greatest of modern mathematicians; his work concentrated on analysis, the theory of numbers, and the theory of substitution groups.

Chu Shih-Chieh (Han-ch'ing) (fl. c.1280–1303)   One of the greatest Chinese mathematicians of all time. His major contribution was to the theory of equations.

Conon of Samos (fl. 245 B.C.)   Greek mathematician and astronomer who worked on conic sections (named after him). He also developed a calendar to forecast the rising and setting of stars. He was a long-time friend of Archimedes.

Diophantus of Alexandria (fl. 250)   Greek mathematician, who was famous for his work in algebra, though most of his writings have been lost.

Euclid (c. 330–c. 260 B.C.)   Greek, one of the most famous of all mathematicians, who developed a major treatise on geometry, *Elements*, that set forth the ideas that are still used in Euclidean geometry.

Euler, Leonhard (1707–1783)   Swiss mathematician and physicist who was one of the founders of pure mathematics. He contributed to all fields of math (calculus, geometry, mechanics, and number theory) and demonstrated applications of mathematics for the technical and public affairs fields.

Fermat, Pierre de (1601–1665)   French mathematician who helped lay the foundation for analytical geometry. He was also the founder of the modern theory of numbers.

Fibonacci, Leonardo (Leonardo of Pisa) (c. 1170–c. 1250)   Italian mathematician who introduced Hindu-Arabic numerals to Europe (though they were already known to a few). He is also known for the Fibonacci series, numbers in which each term is the sum of the two preceding terms (1, 1, 2, 3, 5, 8, 13, 21 . . .).

Fontana, Niccoló (see *Tartaglia*)

Fourier, Jean Baptiste Joseph, Baron (1768–1830)   French mathematician whose work influenced mathematical physics. The Fourier series (involving the heat of solid bodies), Fourier number (a dimensionless number used in flow problems), and Fourier transform (an integral transform) are named after him.

Frege, Friedrich Ludwig Gottlob (1848–1925)   German philosopher and mathematician; the founder of modern mathematical logic.

Gauss, Karl Friedrich (1777–1855)   German mathematician who worked on electricity and magnetism, and planetary orbits. He is considered one of the greatest mathematicians of all time.

Gödel, Kurt (1906–1978)   Austrian-born American mathematician who developed the Gödel proof.

Grassmann, Hermann Günther (1809–1877)   German mathematician who was one of the first to develop the general calculus of vectors.

Green, George (1793–1841)   British mathematician who was one of the first to attempt to formulate a mathematical theory of electricity and magnetism.

Hamilton, Sir William Rowan (1805–1865)   Irish mathematician and astronomer who introduced some of the landmark theories in the development of algebra. He also discovered the phenomenon of conical refraction.

Hardy, Godfrey Harold (1877–1947)   British mathematician who developed numerous solutions in the prime number theory.

Hariot (Harriot), Thomas (1560–1621)   British mathematician, astronomer, and physicist who founded the English school of algebra.

Hero of Alexandria (fl. first century A.D.)   Greek mathematician and inventor who was best known for his formulation for the area of a triangle. He was also the inventor of the first known steam-powered engine.

Hypatia (c. 370– 415)   Egyptian mathematician and philosopher who was the first notable women in mathematics.

Lamb, Sir Horace (1849–1934)   British mathematician and geophysicist who was one of the major contributors to mathematical physics, including the study of airflow over airplane surfaces.

Lambert, Johann Heinrich (1728–1777)   German mathematician, physicist, astronomer, and philosopher who proved that π is an irrational number.

Legendre, Adrien-Marie (1752–1833)   French mathematician who described polynomial solutions for differential equations, did extensive work on the elliptic and its functions, and published the most-used basic geometry text of his time.

Leibniz, Gottfried Wilhelm (1646–1716)   German mathematician, philosopher, historian, and physicist who—besides devising a calculating machine and introducing the concept of binary numbers used in computing—is credited with discovering the series for $\pi/4$ (though he was not the first), or Leibniz's theorem. He also corresponded on mathematical ideas with Isaac Newton and was the first to discover how to differentiate any integral or fractional power of x (some of the first attempts at differential and integral calculus).

Lindemann, Carl Louis Ferdinand von (1875–1939)   German mathematician who proved that π is a transcendental number.

Liouville, Joseph (1809–1882)   French mathematician who excelled in mathematical analysis, theory of numbers, and differential geometry. He also discovered transcendental numbers.

Minkowski, Hermann (1864–1909)   Russian-born German mathematician who developed the geometrical theory of numbers and used geometrical methods to solve problems in number theory, math, physics, and the theory of relativity.

Möbius, August Ferdinand (1790–1868)   German mathematician who discovered the figure that has only one side and one edge, called the Möbius strip. He also made major contributions to analytical geometry and topology.

Müller, Johann (1436–?)   German mathematician who was one of the first to give a major summary of trigonometry.

Napier (Neper), John (1550–1617)   British mathematician who invented the logarithm as a mathematical device to aid in calculations, including tables and rules for their use.

Omar Khayyám (1048–?)   Persian mathematician and astronomer who solved cubics, or a general cubic equation of the third degree. (Tartaglia is also often given credit: Omar's solution was geometric; Tartaglia's was algebraic.) His work was a step toward the unification of algebra and geometry.

Oresme, Nicolas (c. 1325–1382)   French mathematician who devised a "latitude of forms," the precursor of analytic geometry, calculus, and the idea of a forth dimension. He also introduced rational and irrational powers.

Oughtred, William (1574–1660)   British mathematician who invented the earliest form of the slide rule.

Pacioli, Luca (c. 1445–?)   Italian mathematician who wrote the first algebra book. It was the most influential math book of its time.

Pappus of Alexandria (fl. 320 A.D.)   Greek mathematician who wrote a compendium of eight books covering mathematical knowledge of his time.

Pascal, Blaise (1623–1662)   French mathematician, physicist, and religious philosopher who founded the modern theory of probabilities.

Penrose, Roger (1931–)   British mathematician and theoretical physicist who developed Penrose tiling.

Pythagoras (c. 580 B.C.–c. 500 B.C.)   Greek mathematician and philosopher, though none of his work survives, he is credited with developing the theory of functions, significance of numbers, and the Pythagorean theorem for right triangles.

Ramanujan, Srinivasa Aaiyangar (1887–1920)   Indian mathematician who, among other mathematical determinations, developed the theory of numbers.

Riemann, Georg Friedrich Bernhard (1826–1866)   German mathematician whose work had a great influence on geometry and analysis. His work on the geometry of space greatly influenced modern theoretical physics.

Russell, Bertrand Arthur William, Earl (1872–1970)   British philosopher and mathematician who had great influence in mathematical logic. He was an influential writer and was considered one of the brightest intellectuals of the twentieth century.

Stirling, James (1692–1770)   British mathematician who advanced the theory of infinite series and infinitesimal calculus.

Tartaglia (Niccoló Fontana) (1500–1557)   Italian mathematician, topographer, and military scientist who, among other mathematical feats, solved the general cubic. (Omar is also often given credit: Omar's solution was geometric; Tartaglia's was algebraic.)

Taylor, Brook (1685–1731)   British mathematician who solved the problem of center oscillation (waves). His work also advanced the field of calculus.

Vernier, Pierre (c. 1580–1637)   French mathematician who developed the vernier caliper, an instrument to make accurate linear measurements.

Whittaker, Sir Edmund Taylor (1873–1956)   British mathematician and physicist who contributed to special functions, a branch of mathematics of interest to mathematical physicists.

SIGNIFICANT DISCOVERIES IN MEASUREMENT AND MATHEMATICS

B.C.	~28,000	Counting began in Europe
	~10,000	A system of counting using baked clay tokens began to develop in the Near East
	~3,000	Egyptians developed a systematic numbering system (predating writing)
	~2,000	Olmecs (from what is now Mexico) had a complex numeration system
		Arithmetic was in use in Egypt
	~1,900	Mesopotamians discovered what is now called the Pythagorean theorem
		First multiplication tables appeared in Mesopotamia
	~1350	First decimal numbers used in China
	876	First symbol for 0 (zero) used in India, though it is not known when it became a number (it was mainly used as a place holder)
	~600	First mathematical proofs by Thales of Miletus
	~540	Great progression in mathematics, as several cultures further developed arithmetic and geometry principles
	~450	Greeks developed a method of writing numbers based on letters of the alphabet
	~300	Euclid's *Elements* summarized three centuries of Greek mathematical knowledge; the book would be the basic mathematical text for the next 2,000 years
	~180	The 360° circle introduced to Greek mathematics by Hypsicles
	100	Chinese mathematicians first used negative numbers
	1	First decimal fraction used in China
A.D.	190	First powers of ten used in China
	~500	First abacus used in Europe, though boards based on the same system were used by ancient Greeks and Romans a thousand years earlier
	1464	First major summary of trigonometry given by Johann Müller, but it would not be published until 1533
	1489	First printed document published by Johann Widmann that used the plus (+) and minus (−) signs, though they were translated as surplus and deficit
	1492	Pedro Nunes developed the first instrument to measure angles
	1514	First use of plus (+) and minus (−) as signs in algebraic expressions, by Vander Hoecke
	1572	First application shown of complex numbers to solve equations, by Rafael Bombelli
	1591	First publication used vowels for variables and consonants for constants in an equation, by Franciscus Vieta
	1593	First description of modern abacus appears in China
	1614	John Napier explained the use of logarithms (though in 1620, Swiss mathematician Joost Bürgi reported the independent discovery of logarithms)
	1629	Pierre de Fermat developed ideas that led to analytic geometry (by 1636, but not published until 1670)
	1631	The symbols for greater than (>) and less than (<) are introduced by Thomas Harriot
	1637	René Descartes published work that includes information on analytic geometry, (though Fermat had already developed the idea but not published)
	1659	The sign for division (÷) is introduced by Johann Rahn
	1666	Isaac Newton introduced his first works on calculus
	1692	Wilhelm Leibniz introduced the terms coordinate, abscissa, and ordinate
	1733	The normal distribution curve is discovered by Abraham de Moivre
	1736	Euler published a textbook on mechanics based on differential equations
	1794	Adrien-Marie Legendre published the basic geometry textbook, used extensively in France and the United States for most of the nineteenth century
	1796	Karl Gauss proved the law of quadratic reciprocity

1799   First printed account of descriptive geometry—geometry in three dimensions—by Gaspard Monge

1806   Legendre published the method of least squares, a technique to find the best approximation to observed data (it had been discovered 10 years earlier by Gauss, but not published)

1829   Nikolai Lobachevski was first to publish on non-Euclidean geometry (though others had known about it, including Gauss in 1816)

1851   Joseph Liouville discovered that transcendental numbers exist

1858   Florence Nightingale published a paper that included numerous statistical diagrams and charts—several that she invented

1895   Topology founded as a branch of mathematics by Henri Poincaré

1906   Functional calculus developed

1919   Felix Hausdorff first to propose the use of fractals to describe small-scale structure of mathematical shapes

1955   A cross between abstract algebra and algebraic topology was developed, called homological algebra, by Henri Cartan and Samuel Eilenberg

1971   First time a number with 40 digits was factored

1975   Benoil Mandelbrot developed a theory of fractals

1977   The "bootstrap" method for statistics was developed, or determining a more accurate statistical analysis that depends on high-speed computers

1985   Another prime number was found by Hugh Williams and Harvey Dunbar, by putting 1,031 ones in a row

1988   A method to generate purely random numbers was found by Silvio Micali
        First time a number with 100 digits was factored

1990   First time a number with 155 digits was factored

COMMON TERMS IN MEASUREMENT AND MATHEMATICS

abscissa   The horizontal coordinate on a plane. It is measured from the y (vertical) axis.

absolute value   The magnitude of a number. It is the number with the sign (+ or −) removed and is symbolized using two vertical straight lines ($|4|$).

accuracy   How close a measurement comes to the actual (or true) value. The true value is the value currently accepted by, for example, a certain field of science.

approximate   Not precise; a measurement that is close enough to the true number to be useful.

arc   A portion of the circumference of a circle that is represented as a curved line.

area   The measurement of a two-dimensional surface.

axiom   Any of the assumptions on which a mathematical theory is based.

average   The sum of several quantities divided by the number of quantities.

avoirdupois   Units used to measure the mass of any substance (except precious gems and metals, and drugs). It includes the pound, short and long tons, ounce, and dram.

balance   An instrument for measuring the mass of an object. With a conventional balance, the object is placed in a pan while a known weight is placed in a pan opposite a fulcrum. If the pans are level, the materials in the two pans are of equal weight.

circumference   A line or boundary that forms the perimeter of a circle; also the circle that circumscribes a rounded body.

coefficient   A number or letter before a variable in an algebraic expression that is used as a multiplier.

common denominator   A denominator (the bottom number in a fraction) that is common to all the fractions within an equation.

constant   A constant is a quality of a measurement that never changes in magnitude. For example, gravitational forces on Earth or any other planet is constant and does not change.

conversion   The change from one measurement system to another by use of a common value, such as the conversion of feet to meters.

coordinate   A set of numbers in any coordinate system that locates the position of the point; in the rectangular coordinate system, a coordinate is represented by x,y values.

cube root   The factor of a number that, when it is cubed, gives that number.

curve   A line that is continuously bent, as in the arc of a circle.

decimal system   The system of notation for real numbers that uses place values and base 10. The numbers to the right of the decimal point represent a fractional part of a whole number.

degree   A unit of angular measurement. For example, a circle is divided into 360 degrees.

denominator   The bottom number in a fraction.

dependent variable   A variable whose value depends on the value of another variable.

diameter   A straight line that passes from side to side through the center of a sphere or circle; the end points of a diameter are points on the circumference of the circle.

digit   In the decimal system, the numbers 0 through 9.

dimension   Either the length and/or width of a flat surface or the length, width, and/or height of a solid. For example, solids have three dimensions and a flat surface has two dimensions.

E-notation   Another term for scientific (or exponential) notation.

equation   Generally, an algebraic statement in which two equal algebraic expressions are written on either side of an equals sign. It is also commonly used to define any mathematical statement.

equilibrium   The state of balance between opposing forces or effects. When forces balance each other, they are said to be in equilibrium.

error (or experimental error)   One-half the precision used in making the measurement, usually given as a range around a reported measurement using a ± amount. For example, a measurement of 72 inches to the nearest inch has an error of 0.5 inch, reported often as 72 ± 0.5 inches.

factorial   The product of a series of consecutive positive integers from 1 to a given number. It is expressed with the symbol !. For example, $4! = 4 \times 3 \times 2 \times 1 = 24$.

factoring   To break down a number into factors; for example, to find all the numbers that divide into it with no remainders. It is the reverse of finding a product.

fraction   A portion of a whole amount; the term usually applies only to ratios of integers (for example, $^1/_2$, $^6/_1$, or $^{30}/_{32}$).

gauge   An instrument used to determine dimensions, amounts, or force.

Gödel's proof   This proof states that within any rigidly logical mathematical system, there are certain questions that cannot be proved or disproved on the basis of axioms within the system. Therefore, it is uncertain that the basic axioms of arithmetic will not give rise to contradictions.

graph   A diagram that represents the relationship and variations between two or more factors (or functions), mainly by means of a series of connected points, bars, curves, or lines.

hypotenuse   The longest side of a right triangle. It is opposite the right angle of the triangle.

improper fraction   A fraction whose numerator is the same as or larger than the denominator.

independent variable   The variable that determines the value of the dependent variable. For example, in the equation $y = f(x)$, x is the independent variable.

infinite   Having no boundaries, limits, or end.

initial   The term applied to the measurement that is the first to be considered.

instantaneous   Actions that happen in an instant, with no discernible time passing between the cause and the effect.

integer   Any whole number: positive and negative numbers and zero.

lowest common denominator   The integer or polynomial that is the lowest and is exactly divisible by each denominator in a group of fractions.

magnitude   The size of a measurement. For example, 2 miles and 3.22 kilometers equal the same distance, and thus have the same magnitude, but represent different measurements. Also, the absolute value of a number (see also *absolute value*).

mass   The measured amount of a material. All materials possess mass, and that mass never changes no matter where it resides in the universe. Two separate masses are compared by weight or the force of gravity acting on them (for more information on mass, see also Chapter 7, "Physics").

measurement   The result of measuring or the act of measuring; or a comparison of the physical quantity that is measured with a standard unit.

numerator   The top number in a fraction; the number indicates what part of the denominator is used.

numerical coefficient   Generally, a number that is placed before a letter in an algebraic equation. For example, 2 is the numerical coefficient in the expression $2x$.

ordered pair   The x and y coordinates that define a point on a graph or number line.

ordinate   The vertical coordinate on a plane. It is measured from the x (horizontal) axis.

origin   The point on a number line or graph that represents the ordered pair $(0,0)$. It is where the x and y axes meet.

parallel   Lines or planes that are equidistant from each other and are nonintersecting. Any perpendicular distance between parallel lines or planes is the same at any location.

percent   A quantity based on parts of 100. For example, 20 percent is equivalent to $^{20}/_{100}$.

percentage difference   The ratio, expressed as a percent, of the absolute difference between the experimental values and an average of the experimental values.

percentage error   The ratio, expressed as a percent, of the absolute difference between the experimental and the accepted value, divided by the accepted value.

perpendicular   At right angles to a line or plane.

precision   The size of the unit actually used to make a measurement; a person's height measured as to the nearest inch (e.g., 73 inches) is more precise than if it were measured to the nearest foot (6 feet).

product   The result of a multiplication problem.

proper fraction   A fraction in which the numerator is smaller than the denominator.

proportion   An equality of two ratios.

quadrant   One of the four quarters into which the plane of a rectangular coordinate system is divided.

quantification   The act of quantifying or giving a numerical value to a measurement.

quantify   To determine the quantity of a measurement.

quotient   The result of a division problem.

radical sign   The symbol for a root of a number ($\sqrt{}$).

radius   The distance between the center of a circle and any point on the circle's circumference.

rate   The relationship between two measurements of different units. For example, change in distance with respect to time (miles per hour).

ratio   The relationship between two numbers or measurements, usually with the same units.

reciprocal   The inverse of a number; the reciprocal is formed by inverting the numerator and denominator of a fraction.

rounding   To give a close approximation of a number by dropping the least significant numbers. For example, a number can be rounded up or down to the nearest whole number; 56.8 can be rounded up to 57, and 56.3 can be rounded down to 56.

scalar   A quantity that has magnitude but no direction, such as mass and density.

scale   A set of marks on a measuring instrument, usually with numbers in increments from low to high values.

significant   Use of the digits in a measurement that reflects the actual measurement. For example, a lot frontage measured to the nearest foot as 172 feet has three significant figures; the same lot measured to the nearest yard as 54 yards has two significant figures, and a measurement to the nearest tenth of a foot as 172.3 feet has four significant digits.

solid   A solid is an object with three dimensions: length, width, and height.

spring balance   An instrument used to measure weight. The object is placed on a hook attached to a spring and the weight is read on a scale.

standard   A measured unit that is used as the basis for measuring other things. For example, a foot and meter are standards of length.

troy weight   A system of weights used to measure precious metals.

uniform   Speed, velocity, or acceleration that does not change with time. It also refers to an object that is of the same color or appearance throughout.

unit   A standard measurement; for example, the standard unit of inches is used to measure length in the U.S. Conventional System.

variable   A symbol, such as a letter or number, used to represent two or more numbers. In algebra, variables are often represented by letters in an equation. Or a quantity that can change or be changed; for example, the variable speed may change over time.

vernier   The part of a measuring instrument that moves along the main scale.

volume   The amount of space an object occupies or the capacity of an object. It is often expressed as cubic, as in cubic inches or cubic centimeters.

ADDITIONAL SOURCES OF INFORMATION

Asimov, I. *Asimov on Numbers*. Pocket Books, 1978.

Asimov, I. *The Measure of the Universe*. Harper & Row, 1983.

Blocksma, M. *Reading the Numbers: A Survival Guide to the Measurements, Numbers, and Sizes Encountered in Everyday Life*. Viking, 1989.

Carman, Robert A. *Quick Arithmetic*. Wiley, 1984.

Field, Michael, and Golubitsky, Martin. *Symmetry in Chaos: A Search for Pattern in Mathematics, Art, and Nature*. Oxford Univ. Press, 1992.

Julius, Edward H. *Rapid Math Tricks and Tips*. Wiley, 1992.

Pappas, T. *The Joy of Mathematics*. Wide World, 1986.

Pappas, T. *More Joy of Mathematics*. Wide World, 1991.

Chapter 2

Scientific Symbols and Signs

What Are Symbols and Signs?   46

The Greek Alphabet   48

Selected Roman Letters Used in Science   49

Numbers and Symbols   51

Symbols and Signs in Mathematics   51

Symbols in Biology   54

Symbols in Biomedical Science   55

Symbols in Chemistry   56

Symbols in Astronomy and Physics   58

Symbols in Earth Science   59

Symbols in Meteorology   62

Symbols in Environmental Science   64

Symbols in Electrical Engineering   65

Additional Sources of Information   66

WHAT ARE SYMBOLS AND SIGNS?

Symbols, Signs, and Graphics

A symbol, from the Greek word *symbolon* ("a mark"), is an object or drawing chosen by a group of people to represent or stand for something else, especially an abstract idea or quality or a physical object or process. For example, the symbol for recycling is represented by an arrow that forms a triangle ♻. In science, a symbol—such as a character, mark, or sign—represents a concept, object, or phenomenon. For example, the symbol Ca in chemistry represent the element calcium; the symbol ☉ stands for the Sun in astronomy. In mathematics, symbols are used extensively to represent values, operations, relationships, and so on.

An *ideogram* is a special type of symbol that represents an idea or concept. The concept of rain and the physical phenomenon of rain falling from the sky are symbolized by an inverted triangle with a period on top of the triangle (see "Precipitation Symbols," later in this chapter).

A *sign* is an inscription conveying information of some kind. For example, the + (plus) and – (minus) in mathematics are signs.

A *graphic symbol*, or graph, is a sign that is drawn, written, engraved, or painted in a special way. In engineering (especially mechanical engineering), graphics are incorporated into drawings, engravings, and computer drawings as lines and curves that conform to mathematical rules. Graphics in computer science represents artwork that can be drawn and manipulated on the computer screen (for more information on computer graphics, see Chapter 12, "Computer Science").

When a graphic symbol depicts a person or an object, it is called an *icon*; a *noniconic* sign is a picture that does not represent the actual person or object but is a created visual interpretation of an object or process that can be interpreted by most people, such as a symbol of a rock slide that indicates a falling rock zone.

Early Symbols and Signs

Four basic elements found in most symbols and signs can be traced back to some 10,000 to 20,000 years ago. These symbols include the straight line, circle segment (half circle), spiral, and dot. From about 8,000 to 4,000 B.C. it appears that few new written symbols were developed. Then around 4,000 B.C., the Egyptians invented the symbol of a sunwheel (or Earth symbol); the Mesopotamians developed the cuneiform script, and the Chinese and Egyptians developed forms of hieroglyphics (from the Greek word for "sacred writings" or "carvings").

These early symbols eventually lead to an alphabet (from the first two Greek letters: alpha and beta)—phonetic symbols that were eventually combined to form words. About 2,000 to 1,700 B.C., the north Semitic culture at the eastern end of the Mediterranean was probably first to make this breakthrough. The north Semitic alphabet also spread into East Asia as the Aramaic alphabet, which eventually developed into Asian alphabets, such as used to write Hindi. It also evolved into the Arabic, Hebrew, and Phoenician alphabets. The Phoenician alphabet led to the Greek alphabet, which led to the Roman alphabet (now used in all modern western European languages, including English) and Cyrillic alphabet (now used in eastern Europe and Russia).

From the sixteenth through the nineteenth centuries, new symbols and words were developed to represent scientific processes and objects. By the twentieth century, old symbols and science terms were modified, and others were created to fit new technologies. For example, the fields of atomic energy and meteorology invented new symbols and words as these disciplines developed.

THE ASTROLOGICAL SIGNS

Astronomy has its roots in astrology, one of the oldest "sciences" (astronomy and astrology were once thought of as the same science). Astrology is the relationship said to exist between the changing positions of the planets, Sun, and stars and the characteristics, occurrence of events, and personal development that exist in a person's life. Modern astronomy is considered a science; modern astrology is relegated to the study of human affairs.

Astrologers use between 40 and 50 signs to determine future events that will influence a person's life. The principal signs, or patterns, are contained in the astrological chart (usually the natal chart, or horoscope). The 12 sectors represent the zodiac's 12 signs, beginning and ending in the spring with the sign Aries (the sign Libra represents the autumnal equinox). From there, the signs are Taurus, Gemini, Cancer, Leo, Virgo, Libra, Scorpius, Sagittarius, Capricornus, Aquarius, and Pisces.

Astrological Signs and Symbols

TAURUS (The Bull)
April 20 to May 20

GEMINI (The Twins)
May 21 to June 21

CANCER (The Crab)
June 22 to July 22

LEO (The Lion)
July 23 to Aug. 22

VIRGO (The Virgin)
Aug. 23 to Sept. 22

LIBRA (The Balance)
Sept. 23 to Oct. 23

SCORPIUS (The Scorpion)
Oct. 24 to Nov. 21

SAGITTARIUS (The Archer)
Nov. 22 to Dec. 21

CAPRICORNUS (The Goat)
Dec. 22 to Jan. 19

AQUARIUS (The Water Bearer)
Jan. 20 to Feb. 18

PISCES (The Fishes)
Feb. 19 to March 20

ARIES (The Ram)
March 21 to April 19

THE GREEK ALPHABET

Upper- and Lower-Case Greek Letters

Upper- /Lower-Case Letter	Name	Upper- /Lower-Case Letter	Name
A, α	Alpha	N, ν	Nu
B, β	Beta	Ξ, ξ	Xi
Γ, γ	Gamma	O, o	Omicron
Δ, δ	Delta	Π, π	Pi
E, ε	Epsilon	P, ρ	Rho
Z, ζ	Zeta	Σ, σ, ς	Sigma
H, η	Eta	T, τ	Tau
Θ, θ	Theta	Y, υ	Upsilon
I, ι	Iota	Φ, φ	Phi
K, κ	Kappa	X, χ	Chi
Λ, λ	Lambda	Ψ, ψ	Psi
M, μ	Mu	Ω, ω	Omega

Greek Letters Used in Science

Greek letters are used to symbolize several objects and phenomena in science. Common uses are listed below (the list is not all-inclusive). Note that for some letters, both the upper- and the lower-case letter are used.

alpha (α)   alpha-particle, alpha-rhythm (brain waves), right ascension, absorptance, the principal or brightest star in a constellation

beta (β)   beta-particle, beta-ray, beta-wave (brain waves), pressure coefficient

gamma (γ)   photon, electrical conductivity, a unit of magnetic field intensity, gamma-ray, surface tension

delta (Δ)   double bond in an organic compound ($\Delta-$)

delta (δ)   declination, thickness

epsilon (ε)   obliquity of ecliptic

eta (η)   efficiency, eta-particle, viscosity

zeta (ζ)   zeta-potential (or electrokinetic potential)

theta (Θ)   characteristic temperature

theta (θ)   a polar coordinate, sidereal time

kappa (κ)   compressibility, conductivity

lambda (Λ)   permeance, lambda-particle

lambda (λ)   wavelength, decay constant, thermal conductivity

mu (μ)   micron, muon, magnetic moment of particle, permeability, proper motion, friction coefficient

nu (ν)   neutrino, frequency, kinematic viscosity

xi (Ξ) xi-particle

xi (ξ) extent of reaction

pi (Π) osmotic pressure

pi (π) ratio of circumference of a circle to its diameter (a mathematical constant), solar parallax, pion (pi-meson)

rho (ρ) density, specific resistance, reflectance, mass concentration

sigma (Σ) sum of

sigma (σ) electrical conductivity, surface tension, cross section

tau (τ) time constant, shear stress, tauon

phi (Φ) potential energy, magnetic flux

phi (ϕ) luminous flux, fluidity, electric potential, a polar coordinate

chi (χ) electrical susceptibility, magnetic susceptibility

psi (Ψ) wave function, electric flux

omega (Ω) ohm, omega-particle ($\Omega-$)

omega (ψ) angular velocity, angular frequency

SELECTED ROMAN LETTERS USED IN SCIENCE

Note: Certain items on the list can be represented with both upper- and lower-case letters. For example, *pressure* can be "P" or "p." Certain letters are also often italicized, although they are not noted here. For example, acceleration is often denoted as "*a*."

A a blood antigen, angstrom (Å), absolute temperature, acid, first van der Waals constant

a anode, a number prefix (atto-), acre, acceleration, ampere, area, semimajor axis, arc

B base, a blood antigen, magnetic field

b base

C Coulomb, a computer language, degrees Celsius, constant

c a number prefix (centi-), heat capacity, per mole, speed of light in vacuum, calorie, curie, cathode, constant

D diameter

d diameter, day, a number prefix (deci-), relative density, degree, angular distance, declination

E a number prefix (exa-), energy, electrical field, a polar coordinate (east), electromotive force

e charge of electron, orbital eccentricity, base of natural logarithms

F degrees Fahrenheit, farad, Faraday constant

f a number prefix (femto-), frequency, electron state (*f*-number), force

G a number prefix (giga-), universal gravitational constant, conductance, specific gravity

g gram, acceleration due to gravity

H   strength or intensity of magnetic field, Hubble constant, horizontal component of the Earth's magnetism

h   a number prefix (hecto-), Planck's constant, height, hour, hardness

I   electric current strength, intensity of luminosity, acoustic intensity, inertia

i   angle of incidence, electric current strength, vapor pressure constant

J   joule, current density, radiant intensity

j   current density

K   degrees Kelvin, kilobyte, equilibrium constant

k   a number prefix (kilo-), Boltzmann constant, kilobit, carat, cathode, cumulus clouds, thermal conductivity, knot

L   liter, luminosity, inductance, kinetic potential

l   length, latent heat per unit mass

M   a number prefix (mega-), megabyte, molecular weight, absolute magnitude, momentum, Mach

m   a number prefix (milli-), meter, molecular weight, mass, apparent magnitude, miles, minute, month, arithmetic mean, meridian

N   newton, a polar coordinate (north), Avogadro constant

n   a number prefix (nano-), neutron, index of refraction

O   a blood antigen

o   ohm

P   a number prefix (peta-), pressure, orbital period, probability ratio

p   a number prefix (pico-), pressure, proton, parallax, para- (*p*-), fluid density, probability ratio

Q   stored charge (*Qs*)

q   quart, dynamic pressure, electric charge

R   resistance, roentgen, radius, universal gas constant, retrograde

r   radius, roentgen, retrograde, distance in parsecs, angle of reflection, relative humidity

S   entropy, a polar coordinate (south)

s   second, speed

T   a number prefix (tera-), time (*T* for half-life), temperature

t   ton, time, temperature, meridian angle

U   potential energy, total internal energy

u   density of radiant energy, unified atomic mass

V   volt, volume

v   volume, velocity, vector

W   watt, work, a polar coordinate (west)

w   weight, width, work

X   reactance, magnification

x   a Cartesian coordinate (horizontal axis, or abscissa), magnification

Y   a number prefix (yotta-)

y   a number prefix (yacto-), a Cartesian coordinate (vertical axis, or ordinate), year

Z   a number prefix (zetta-), atomic number, impedance, azimuth, zenith

z   a number prefix (zepto-), a Cartesian coordinate

NUMBERS AND SYMBOLS

Symbols for Number Prefixes

Symbol	Prefix	Power of 10	Symbol	Prefix	Power of 10
a	atto	10^{-18}	M	mega	10^6
c	centi	10^{-2}	n	nano	10^{-9}
d	deci	10^{-1}	p	pico	10^{-12}
da	deka	10	P	peta	10^{15}
E	exa	10^{18}	T	tera	10^{12}
f	femto	10^{-15}	y	yocto	10^{-20}
G	giga	10^9	Y	yotta	10^{24}
h	hecto	10^2	z	zepto	10^{-21}
k	kilo	10^3	Z	zetta	10^{21}
m	milli	10^{-3}	μ	micro	10^{-6}

SYMBOLS AND SIGNS IN MATHEMATICS

+	plus (sign of addition), positive sign
−	minus (sign of subtraction), negative sign
±	plus or minus
∓	minus or plus
×, •	multiplication signs
$a \times b, a \cdot b, ab$	a times b
÷	sign of division
$a/b, \dfrac{a}{b}, ab^{-1}$	a divided by b
:	ratio of, is to
::	proportional to
≙	corresponds to
%	percent
<	less than
>	greater than
≦, ≤	less than or equal to
≧, ≥	greater than or equal to
≪	much less than
≫	much greater than
≯	not greater than
≮	not less than
≡, ≡	identical with
x^n	x raised to the power of n

∞	infinity
$\sqrt{a}, \sqrt{a}$	square root of a
$\sqrt[3]{a}$	cube root of a
$\sqrt[n]{a}$	nth root of a
$\parallel$	parallel to
$\perp$	perpendicular to
$(\ ), \{\}, [\ ]$	parentheses, braces, brackets
$1.\overline{672}$	repeating decimal (for example)
$\circ$	degrees
$'$	minutes, minutes of arc, prime
$''$	seconds, seconds of arc, double prime
$\angle, \measuredangle$	angle
$\llcorner$	right angle
$n!$	factorial
Δx	increment of x
$\int$	integral
$\int_b^a$	integral between the limits of a and b
$\dot{x}$	first derivative of x with respect to time
$\ddot{x}$	second derivative of x with respect to time
$[\ ]$	greatest integer function
Σ	summation of
$\cong$	congruent to
$=$	equal to
$\neq$	not equal to
$\sim$	similar to
$\doteq$	approaches
$\approx$	approximately equals
$f(x)$	function of x
(x, y)	rectangular coordinates of point in a plane
$\bar{a}, <a>$	mean value of a
$P_{(x)}$	polynomial
$\begin{pmatrix} a \\ b \end{pmatrix}$	binomial coefficient
$\therefore$	therefore
π	pi
y^{-1}	inverse of y
$\bigcirc$	ellipse

△	triangle
▭	rectangle
▱	rhombus
▢	square, cube
○	circle
$\overset{n}{\Sigma}$	summation of n term, one for each positive
Π	product
$\lvert b \rvert$	absolute value of b, magnitude of b
$\mathbf{A} \times \mathbf{B}$	vector product
$\mathbf{A} \cdot \mathbf{B}$	scalar product
∇^2	vector differential operator
∂	partial differential
dx	total differential of x
$\sim$	horizontal integral
$\oint$	contour integral
$\log x$	logarithm of x ($\log$ of x)
e^x	exponential function
$\partial y / \partial x$	partial derivative of y with respect to x
$\overline{AB}$	length of line from A to B
$\bar{e}$	base of nature system of logarithms, $2{,}718 \ldots$
$\varnothing$	diameter
$x \wedge y$	conjunction of x and y
$\forall x$	for all x
$x \rightarrow y$	if x, then y
$x \leftrightarrow y$	x equivalent to y

Set Theory Symbols

$\{\}$	notation of a set
$\{2\}$	a set in which 2 is the only element
$\{2,3,4\}$	a set in which 2, 3, and 4 are the only elements
$\cup$	the universal set
$\wedge, \varnothing$	empty set, null set
$A \cup B$	union of A and B
$A \subseteq B$	set inclusion
$A \subset B$	any set inclusion, but usually proper set
$A \cap B$	intersection of A and B
$\in$	is an element of
$b \in B$	b is an element of set B
A'	complement of A
$X = \{x \mid x \text{ is a real number}\}$	the set of all real numbers

SYMBOLS IN BIOLOGY

Plant Symbols

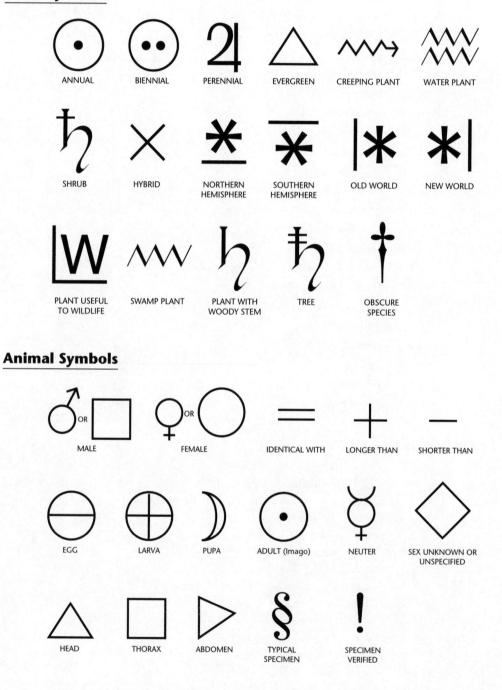

| ANNUAL | BIENNIAL | PERENNIAL | EVERGREEN | CREEPING PLANT | WATER PLANT |

| SHRUB | HYBRID | NORTHERN HEMISPHERE | SOUTHERN HEMISPHERE | OLD WORLD | NEW WORLD |

| PLANT USEFUL TO WILDLIFE | SWAMP PLANT | PLANT WITH WOODY STEM | TREE | OBSCURE SPECIES |

Animal Symbols

| MALE | FEMALE | IDENTICAL WITH | LONGER THAN | SHORTER THAN |

| EGG | LARVA | PUPA | ADULT (Imago) | NEUTER | SEX UNKNOWN OR UNSPECIFIED |

| HEAD | THORAX | ABDOMEN | TYPICAL SPECIMEN | SPECIMEN VERIFIED |

SYMBOLS IN BIOMEDICAL SCIENCE

Biomedical Symbols

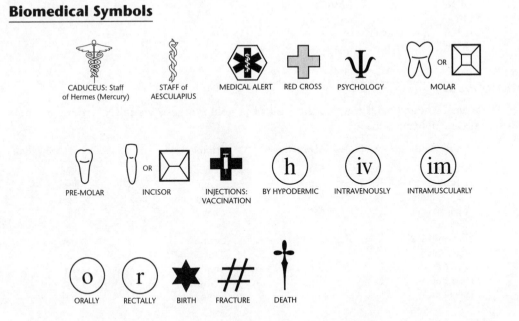

Deoxyribonucleic Acid (DNA) and Ribonucleic Acid (RNA)

Deoxyribonucleic acid (DNA) is a two-stranded, linear polymer made up of repeating units called bases; ribonucleic acid (RNA) has only one strand and the sugar is ribose, not dioxyribose (for more information on DNA and RNA, see Chapter 5, "The Human Body and Biomedical Science").

When replicating, two strands of the parent DNA molecule separate. The replicated daughter strands pair with certain bases. The bases are linked to each other, but because of their structures, they can link only in a specific way: A links with T, and G links with C.

The symbols for the DNA bases are as follows.

A   Adenine
T   Thymine
G   Guanine
C   Cytosine

Biologists use symbols for particular types of DNA as follows:

cDNA   complementary DNA
ctDNA   DNA within chloroplast
dsDNA   double-stranded DNA
mtDNA   DNA found in mitochondrial structures
rDNA   DNA found in ribosomal structures
ssDNA   single-stranded DNA

The bases in RNA are the same as in DNA, but the thymine is replaced by a base called uracil (U) that links to the adenine. The following symbols are used for the various types of RNA:

mRNA	messenger RNA
nRNA	nuclear RNA
sRNA	soluble RNA
tRNA	transfer RNA

Amino Acids

There are 20 amino acids that are the basis of protein synthesis via mRNA. Here are their symbols and abbreviations.

Amino Acid	Symbol	Abbreviation	Amino Acid	Symbol	Abbreviation
Alanine	A	Ala	Leucine	L	Leu
Arginine	R	Arg	Lysine	K	Lys
Asparagine	N	Asn	Methionine	M	Met
Aspartic acid	D	Asp	Phenylalanine	F	Phe
Cysteine	C	Cys	Proline	P	Pro
Glutamic acid	E	Glu	Serine	S	Ser
Glutamine	Q	Gln	Threonine	T	Thr
Glycine	G	Gly	Tryptophan	W	Trp
Histidine	H	His	Tyrosine	Y	Tyr
Isoleucine	I	Ile	Valine	V	Val

SYMBOLS IN CHEMISTRY

Common Chemical Symbols

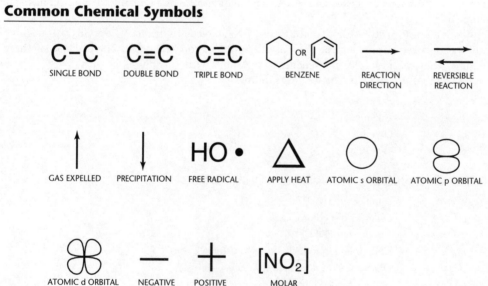

Chemical Elements

Ac	Actinium	Ge	Germanium	Pr	Praseodymium
Ag	Silver	H	Hydrogen	Pt	Platinum
Al	Aluminum	He	Helium	Pu	Plutonium
Am	Americium	Hf	Hafnium	Ra	Radium
Ar	Argon	Hg	Mercury	Rb	Rubidium
As	Arsenic	Ho	Holmium	Re	Rhenium
At	Astatine	I	Iodine	Rh	Rhodium
Au	Gold	In	Indium	Rn	Radon
B	Boron	Ir	Iridium	Ru	Ruthenium
Ba	Barium	K	Potassium	S	Sulfur
Be	Beryllium	Kr	Krypton	Sb	Antimony
Bi	Bismuth	La	Lanthanum	Sc	Scandium
Bk	Berkelium	Li	Lithium	Se	Selenium
Br	Bromine	Lu	Lutetium	Si	Silicon
C	Carbon	Lr	Lawrencium	Sm	Samarium
Ca	Calcium	Md	Mendelevium	Sn	Tin
Cd	Cadmium	Mg	Magnesium	Sr	Strontium
Ce	Cerium	Mn	Manganese	Ta	Tantalum
Cf	Californium	Mo	Molybdenum	Tb	Terbium
Cl	Chlorine	N	Nitrogen	Tc	Technetium
Cm	Curium	Na	Sodium	Te	Tellurium
Co	Cobalt	Nb	Niobium	Th	Thorium
Cr	Chromium	Nd	Neodymium	Ti	Titanium
Cs	Cesium	Ne	Neon	Tl	Thallium
Cu	Copper	Ni	Nickel	Tm	Thulium
Dy	Dysprosium	No	Nobelium	U	Uranium
Er	Erbium	Np	Neptunium	V	Vanadium
Es	Einsteinium	O	Oxygen	W	Tungsten
Eu	Europium	Os	Osmium	Xe	Xenon
F	Fluorine	P	Phosphorus	Y	Yttrium
Fe	Iron	Pa	Protactinium	Yb	Ytterbium
Fm	Fermium	Pb	Lead	Zn	Zinc
Fr	Francium	Pd	Palladium	Zr	Zirconium
Ga	Gallium	Pm	Promethium		
Gd	Gadolinium	Po	Polonium		

Symbols for Chemical Charges

$-, --, ---$; or $^{-1}, ^{-2}, ^{-3}$, etc.	denotes a single, double, and triple negative charge, respectively
$+, ++, +++$; or $^{+1}, ^{+2}, ^{+3}$, etc.	denotes a single, double, and triple positive charge, respectively
', '', ''', etc.	denotes a single, double, and triple charge, or valence, respectively

Chemical Formulas and Structures

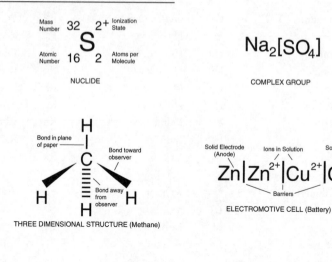

Mass Number 32 S^{2+} Ionization State

Atomic Number 16   2   Atoms per Molecule

NUCLIDE

$Na_2[SO_4]$

COMPLEX GROUP

Bond in plane of paper

Bond toward observer

Bond away from observer

THREE DIMENSIONAL STRUCTURE (Methane)

Solid Electrode (Anode)   Ions in Solution   Solid Electrode (Cathode)

$Zn \mid Zn^{2+} \mid Cu^{2+} \mid Cu$

Barriers

ELECTROMOTIVE CELL (Battery)

Fe^{II}

INDICATION of DIVALENCY

NO^*

ELECTRONIC EXCITED STATE

SYMBOLS IN ASTRONOMY AND PHYSICS

Astronomical Symbols

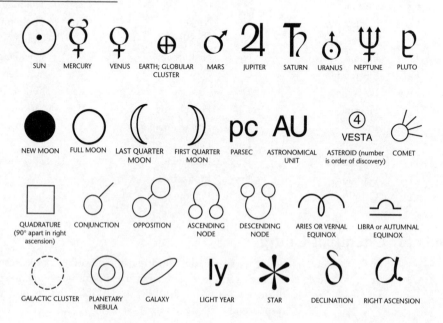

| SUN | MERCURY | VENUS | EARTH; GLOBULAR CLUSTER | MARS | JUPITER | SATURN | URANUS | NEPTUNE | PLUTO |

| NEW MOON | FULL MOON | LAST QUARTER MOON | FIRST QUARTER MOON | PARSEC | ASTRONOMICAL UNIT | ASTEROID (number is order of discovery) | COMET |

VESTA

pc   AU

| QUADRATURE (90° apart in right ascension) | CONJUNCTION | OPPOSITION | ASCENDING NODE | DESCENDING NODE | ARIES OR VERNAL EQUINOX | LIBRA or AUTUMNAL EQUINOX |

| GALACTIC CLUSTER | PLANETARY NEBULA | GALAXY | LIGHT YEAR | STAR | DECLINATION | RIGHT ASCENSION |

ly

Physics Symbols

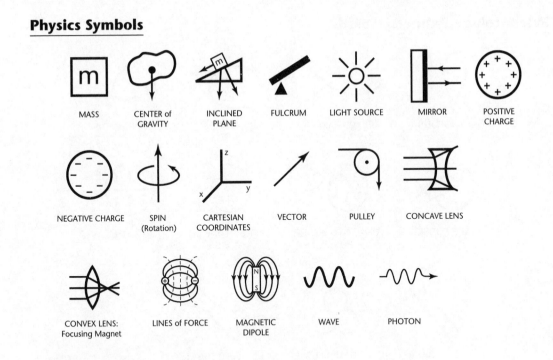

MASS   CENTER of GRAVITY   INCLINED PLANE   FULCRUM   LIGHT SOURCE   MIRROR   POSITIVE CHARGE

NEGATIVE CHARGE   SPIN (Rotation)   CARTESIAN COORDINATES   VECTOR   PULLEY   CONCAVE LENS

CONVEX LENS: Focusing Magnet   LINES of FORCE   MAGNETIC DIPOLE   WAVE   PHOTON

SYMBOLS IN EARTH SCIENCE

Geological Symbols for Maps

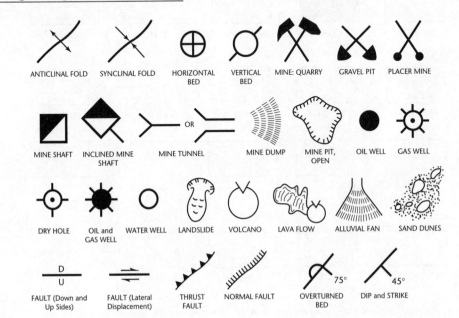

ANTICLINAL FOLD   SYNCLINAL FOLD   HORIZONTAL BED   VERTICAL BED   MINE: QUARRY   GRAVEL PIT   PLACER MINE

MINE SHAFT   INCLINED MINE SHAFT   MINE TUNNEL   OR   MINE DUMP   MINE PIT, OPEN   OIL WELL   GAS WELL

DRY HOLE   OIL and GAS WELL   WATER WELL   LANDSLIDE   VOLCANO   LAVA FLOW   ALLUVIAL FAN   SAND DUNES

FAULT (Down and Up Sides)   FAULT (Lateral Displacement)   THRUST FAULT   NORMAL FAULT   OVERTURNED BED   75°   DIP and STRIKE   45°

Paleontology Symbols—Fossils

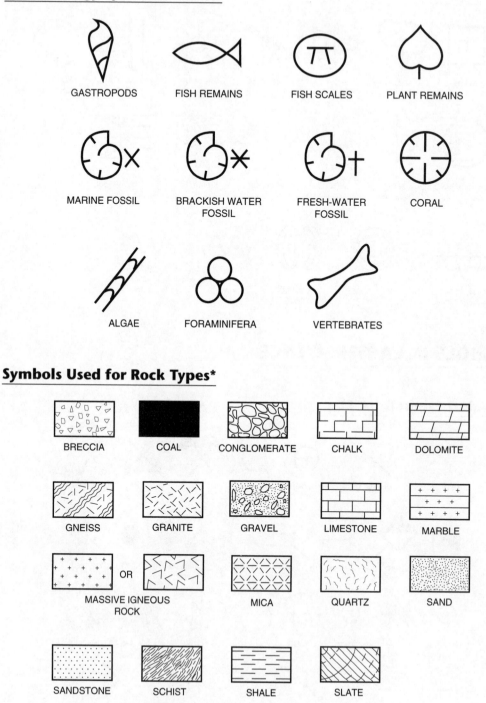

GASTROPODS   FISH REMAINS   FISH SCALES   PLANT REMAINS

MARINE FOSSIL   BRACKISH WATER FOSSIL   FRESH-WATER FOSSIL   CORAL

ALGAE   FORAMINIFERA   VERTEBRATES

Symbols Used for Rock Types*

BRECCIA   COAL   CONGLOMERATE   CHALK   DOLOMITE

GNEISS   GRANITE   GRAVEL   LIMESTONE   MARBLE

OR   MASSIVE IGNEOUS ROCK   MICA   QUARTZ   SAND

SANDSTONE   SCHIST   SHALE   SLATE

All markings are black unless otherwise noted. Variations may be found on older maps.

Symbols Used on Topographic Maps*

Primary highway, hard surface	
Secondary highway, hard surface	
Light-duty road, hard or improved surface	
Unimproved road	
Trail	
Railroad: single track	
Railroad: multiple track	
Bridge	
Drawbridge	
Tunnel	
Footbridge	
Overpass–Underpass	
Power transmission line with located tower	
Landmark line (labeled as to type)	_TELEPHONE_

Dam with lock	
Canal with lock	
Large dam	
Small dam: masonry – earth	
Buildings (dwelling, place of employment, etc.)	
School – Church – Cemeteries	Cem
Buildings (barn, warehouse, etc.)	
Tanks; oil, water, etc. (labeled only if water)	Water Tank
Wells other than water (labeled as to type)	o Oil . . o Gas
U.S. mineral or location monument – Prospect	▲ X
Quarry – Gravel pit	X X
Mine shaft – Tunnel or cave entrance	◼ . . . . . Y
Campsite – Picnic area	
Located or landmark object – Windmill	o
Exposed wreck	
Rock or coral reef	
Foreshore flat	
Rock: bare or awash	* ☀

Horizontal control station	△
Vertical control station	BM ×672 ×671
Road fork – Section corner with elevation	429 +58
Checked spot elevation	X5970
Unchecked spot elevation	X5970

Boundary: national	
State	
county, parish, municipio	
civil township, precinct, town, barrio	
incorporated city, village, town, hamlet	
reservation, national or state	
small park, cemetery, airport, etc.	
land grant	
Township or range line, U.S. land survey	
Section line, not U.S. land survey	
Township line, not U.S. land survey	
Section line, not U.S. land survey	
Fence line or field line	
Section corner: found – indicated	+ . . . . . . +
Boundary monument: land grant – other	⊡ . . . . . ⊡

Index contour		Intermediate contour	
Supplementary cont.		Depression contours	
Cut – Fill		Levee	
Mine dump		Large wash	
Dune area		Tailings pond	
Sand area		Distorted surface	
Tailings		Gravel beach	

Glacier		Intermittent streams	
Perennial streams		Aqueduct tunnel	
Water well–Spring	o o	Falls	
Rapids		Intermittent lake	
Channel		Small wash	
Sounding–Depth curve	10	Marsh (swamp)	
Dry lake bed		Land subject to controlled inundation	

Woodland		Mangrove	
Submerged marsh		Scrub	
Orchard		Wooded marsh	
Vineyard		Bldg. omission area	

Note: Many of these symbols are specific colors on topographic maps.

SYMBOLS IN METEOROLOGY

Symbols for Storms, Wind and Fronts

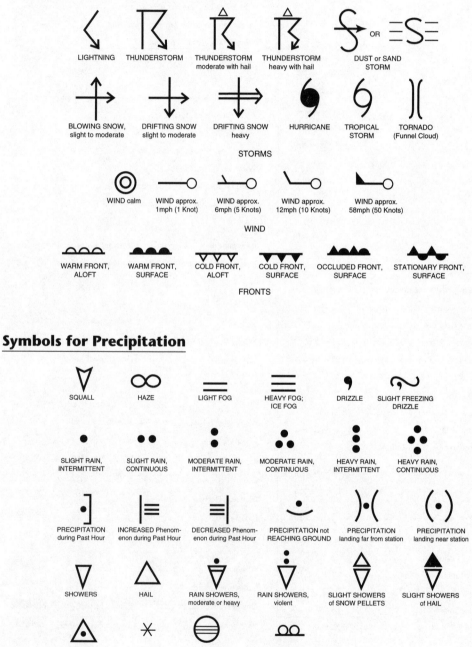

LIGHTNING · THUNDERSTORM · THUNDERSTORM moderate with hail · THUNDERSTORM heavy with hail · DUST or SAND STORM

BLOWING SNOW, slight to moderate · DRIFTING SNOW slight to moderate · DRIFTING SNOW heavy · HURRICANE · TROPICAL STORM · TORNADO (Funnel Cloud)

STORMS

WIND calm · WIND approx. 1mph (1 Knot) · WIND approx. 6mph (5 Knots) · WIND approx. 12mph (10 Knots) · WIND approx. 58mph (50 Knots)

WIND

WARM FRONT, ALOFT · WARM FRONT, SURFACE · COLD FRONT, ALOFT · COLD FRONT, SURFACE · OCCLUDED FRONT, SURFACE · STATIONARY FRONT, SURFACE

FRONTS

Symbols for Precipitation

SQUALL · HAZE · LIGHT FOG · HEAVY FOG; ICE FOG · DRIZZLE · SLIGHT FREEZING DRIZZLE

SLIGHT RAIN, INTERMITTENT · SLIGHT RAIN, CONTINUOUS · MODERATE RAIN, INTERMITTENT · MODERATE RAIN, CONTINUOUS · HEAVY RAIN, INTERMITTENT · HEAVY RAIN, CONTINUOUS

PRECIPITATION during Past Hour · INCREASED Phenomenon during Past Hour · DECREASED Phenomenon during Past Hour · PRECIPITATION not REACHING GROUND · PRECIPITATION landing far from station · PRECIPITATION landing near station

SHOWERS · HAIL · RAIN SHOWERS, moderate or heavy · RAIN SHOWERS, violent · SLIGHT SHOWERS of SNOW PELLETS · SLIGHT SHOWERS of HAIL

ICE PELLETS (Sleet) · SNOW · SMOKY ATMOSPHERE · SKY OBSERVED BY MIST, DUST, ETC.

Cloud Symbols

  CLEAR SKY

OVERCAST, COMPLETE OVERCAST, SKY OBSCURED CLEAR SKY SCATTERED CLOUDS, 0.1 or less SCATTERED CLOUDS, 0.2 or 0.3 SCATTERED CLOUDS, O.4

SCATTERED CLOUDS, 0.5 BROKEN CLOUDS, 0.6 - 0.9 BROKEN CLOUDS, 0.6 BROKEN CLOUDS, 0.7 or 0.8 BROKEN CLOUDS, 0.9

ALTOSTRATUS, thick — STRATOCUMULUS, spreading from cumulus — STRATOCUMULUS, not from cumulus — CUMULUS, little vertical development — CUMULUS and STRATOCUMULUS — CUMULUS, considerable development

CUMULONIMBUS, clear-cut tops lacking — CUMULONIMBUS, clear top — ALTOCUMULUS, thin, semi-transparent — ALTOCUMULUS, thin, patches — ALTOCUMULUS, in bands and thickening — ALTOCUMULUS, double-layered

ALTOCUMULUS, spreading from cumulus — ALTOCUMULUS, tufts or turrents — ALTOCUMULUS, of chaotic sky — CIRRUS filaments (Mare's Tails) high clouds — CIRRUS, dense, patches, tufts — CIRRUS, dense, anvil shaped

CIRRUS, hook-shaped, thickening — CIRRUS and Cirrostratus, over 45° — CIRRUS and Cirrostratus, not 45° — CIRROSTRATUS, not increasing — CIRROSTRATUS, veil covering sky — CIRROCUMULUS

STRATUS and/or FRACTOSTRATUS — FRACTOSTRATUS, Fractocumulus (Scud) — ALTOSTRATUS, thin, semi-transparent

Symbols Used for Weather Station Data

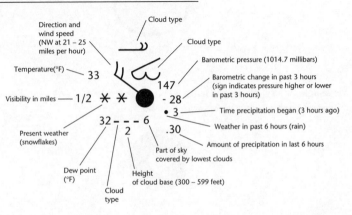

SYMBOLS IN ENVIRONMENTAL SCIENCE

ECOLOGY   WORMICIDE   INSECTICIDE

HERBICIDE   ADHESIVE to
plants (with chemicals)

CHANGING SIGNS

The meanings of signs and symbols are always changing with society's cultural and historical changes. For example, one of the newest signs is for the comet Chiron, found in 1978. It is one of the farthest comets located in the outer solar system, orbiting between the planets Saturn and Uranus.

Chiron

An example of symbol change is the evolution of the recycling sign. Less than 20 years ago, recycling was represented by the following symbol:

Recycling

Now, because of the emphasis of countries to keep our planet clean, there is more than one symbol for recycling. Most of the symbols are very similar, as seen in the following three commonly used signs (the sign for recycled goods resembles the "recyclable" symbol on the left—but with a round, black background).

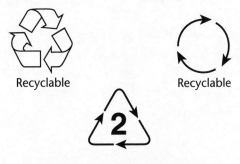

Recyclable   Recyclable

Number is usually from 1 to 7,
and represents the type of plastic.

SYMBOLS IN ELECTRICAL ENGINEERING

Electrical Engineering Symbols

 OR

RESISTOR

DIODE

TRANSISTOR
(p-n-p type)

TRANSISTOR
(n-p-n type)

TRANSISTOR
Field-effect (n-channel)

TRANSFORMER

CIRCUIT BREAKER

 OR

CONNECTOR

CATHODE RAY
TUBE (TV)

LOUDSPEAKER

MICROPHONE

AMPLIFIER

LAMP BULB

CROSSED
CONDUCTORS

JOINED
CONDUCTORS

FUSE

EARTH
(Ground)

 OR

SWITCH

FIXED
CAPACITOR

DIRECT
CURRENT (DC)

ALTERNATING
CURRENT (AC)

ALTERNATING
CURRENT SOURCE

BATTERY (Direct
Current Source)

INDUCTOR

ADDITIONAL SOURCES OF INFORMATION

Adkins, Jan. *Symbols: A Silent Language*. Walker, 1984.

Dreyfuss, Henry. *Symbol Sourcebook: An Authoritative Guide to International Graphic Symbols*. Van Nostrand Reinhold, 1984.

Ford, Brian J. *Images of Science: A History of Scientific Illustration*. Oxford Univ. Press, 1993.

Liungman, Carl G. *Dictionary of Symbols*. ABC-CLIO, 1991.

Shepherd, Walter. *Glossary of Graphic Signs and Symbols*. Dent, 1971.

Tufte, Edward R. *The Visual Display of Quantitative Information*. Graphics, 1983.

Tufte, Edward R. *Envisioning Information*. Graphics, 1990.

Chapter 3 Time

Why Is Time Important to Science?   68

Years, Months, and Days   69

Other Times   74

Moon and Sun Times   78

Time Around the World   81

Worldwide Time Variations   85

Additional Sources of Information   85

WHY IS TIME IMPORTANT TO SCIENCE?

Frequently described as the fourth dimension, time is important to scientific observation because the events that scientists attempt to measure and explain all occur within a time frame. However, we know from Einstein's Theory of Relativity that there is no standard or absolute time frame, because time can be defined only by measurement (for more information on Einstein's theories, see Chapter 7, "Physics").

The measurement of time is based on reoccurring natural phenomena. For example, a year is defined as the amount of time it takes for the Earth to make one complete revolution around the Sun. A day is defined as the amount of time it takes for the Earth to make one complete revolution on its axis. The year and the day are then broken down into more arbitrary units—months, hours, seconds, and so on.

IS TIME TRAVEL POSSIBLE?

According to Einstein's Theory of Relativity, as the speed of an object increases, its physical properties change relative to an observer at rest. And as its mass increases, its size in the direction of travel decreases, and time slows down. This also happens as you travel on a jet, but changes are so small at that speed they go unnoticed. However, the changes become extremely important at very high speeds. (In fact, at the speed of light, time would come to a complete stop.) Take for example a space traveler and his twin on Earth: If the traveler moves at 90 percent the speed of light, he would feel no different from the stationary twin. But the mass of the spacecraft would more than double, its length would be less than half, and a clock on board would take the equivalent of 1 hour on Earth to record 26 minutes. Because of this slowing down of time, the traveler would be aging at less than half the rate of the Earthbound twin (for more information on relativity and time, see Chapter 7, "Physics").

In theory, such conditions near the speed of light may be called a form of "time travel." As to the physical movement back and forth in time—as in H. G. Wells's novel *The Time Machine*—no one knows for sure, but some scientists have serious reservations.

Measured Time

The shortest period ever measured in science (though indirectly) was for the decay of some elementary particles, which lasted for 10^{-24} (0.000000000000000000000001) second. Direct measurements of light bursts in certain lasers have been recorded at about 10^{-15} (0.000000000000001) second. The longest period ever recorded is the age of our universe, which is thought to be between 12 and 18 billion years.

BIOLOGICAL CLOCKS

Most living organisms develop a circadian (sometimes called diurnal) rhythm—a term coined by Frans Halberg in 1959; *circa* means "roughly," and *dian* means "daily"—in which a series of events in the organism are repeated on a regular basis. The rhythms are often synchronized with the natural day-and-night cycle of about 24 hours and are usually independent of other external factors in the environment. For example, certain flowers open and close with the rising or setting Sun, and seas glow with the bioluminescence of single-celled organisms as they swarm every 23 hours.

The human body also follows various rhythms. The body's temperature rises and falls about 1° in about 25 hours, reaching a high at about 4:00 P.M. and a low at about 4:00 A.M. Hormone secretion, blood pressure, and heart rate all vary according to circadian rhythm. Even the excretions of potassium, sodium, and calcium are governed by a daily cycle. The feeling of "jet lag"—fatigue and an out-of-sync feeling experienced by travelers who fly from one time zone to another—is a prime example of our dependence on circadian rhythms.

To find ways to make people more alert—especially for jobs that involve working during the nighttime hours—researchers have been trying to reset the body's internal clock. The pilot project involves a control room that is bright from about 11:00 P.M. to 7:00 A.M. and dark the rest of the day. By reversing normal daylight hours, scientists can trick the part of the brain's hypothalamus (called the suprachiasmatic nucleus) that regulates the normal diurnal cycle.

Common Divisions of Time

Units	Abbreviation	Duration	Examples
Femtosecond	fs	10^{-15} second	burst of type of laser light
Picosecond	ps	10^{-12} second	fastest switch in computers
Nanosecond	ns	10^{-9} second	light travels 1 foot
Microsecond	μs	10^{-6} second	1 millionth of a second
Millisecond	ms	10^{-3} second	neuron fires in brain
Second	sec, s, "		Earth travels 18.5 miles in its orbit
Minute	min, m, '	60 seconds	human heart pumps 12 gallons of blood during physical exertion
Hour	hr, h	60 minutes; 3,600 seconds	adult male sheds 600,000 particles of skin
Day	da, d	24 hours; 1,440 minutes; 86,400 seconds	10 pints of blood makes 1,000 complete circuits in the human body
Week	wk, w	7 days; 168 hours	newborn guppies double in size
Month	mo, m, mon	4.35 weeks (average); 30.44 days (average)	human hair grows an average of 0.5 inch
Year	yr, y	12 months; 365 days (approx.); 52 weeks (approx.)	16 million thunderstorms occur on Earth

YEARS, MONTHS, AND DAYS

The Year

A *tropical year* is the length of time that the Earth takes to make one revolution around the Sun between successive vernal (spring) equinoxes (for more information on the Earth's revolution, see Chapter 9, "Earth Science"). It is equal to 365.2422 mean solar days, or 365 days, 5 hours, 48 minutes, and 46 seconds (it is decreasing at a rate of 0.53 second per century). It is also called the mean solar year, or year of the seasons, and is the basis of the modern calendar used in most countries around the world.

A *sidereal year* is the length of time it takes the Sun to move from a position relative to a fixed star and back to the same position again, as observed from a given point on Earth. It is equal to 365.256636 days, or 365 days, 6 hours, 9 minutes, and 11 seconds. It is longer than the tropical year because it is not affected by the slow wobble in the Earth's rotation that causes the precession of the equinoxes (see "Equinox" later in this chapter).

An *anomalistic year* is the interval between successive passes of the Earth through aphelion and perihelion (the points during orbit at which the Earth is the farthest away from and closest to the Sun, respectively). It is equal to 365.2594 days, or 365 days, 6 hours, 13 minutes, and 53 seconds; this is several minutes longer than a sidereal year, due to the gravitational pull of the other planets.

An *eclipse year* is based on the interval between successive returns of the Sun to the same point (node) in the Moon's orbit, as seen from the Earth. It is equal to 346.6203 days.

The Months

The divisions of the year known as months are loosely based on the revolution of the Moon around the Earth. The months are defined by a calendar, and calendars are based on a culture's preference. Our Gregorian calendar is broken into 12 months, each with 28, 30, or 31 days (see "Calendars," later in this chapter).

Sidereal and Synodic Month

A *sidereal month* is the amount of time it takes the Moon to make one complete revolution around the Earth with respect to a fixed star. The mean sidereal month is equal to 27.3217 days, or 27 days, 7 hours, 43 minutes, and 11.47 seconds. A *synodic month* is the time between two successive conjunctions of the Moon and the Sun, as viewed from the Earth. The mean synodic month is equal to 29.5306 days, or 29 days, 12 hours, 44 minutes, and 2.78 seconds.

Sidereal and Synodic Months

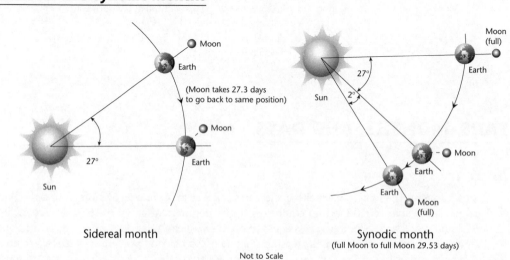

Sidereal month

Synodic month
(full Moon to full Moon 29.53 days)

Not to Scale

Names of the Months

The common names of the Gregorian calendar months have Roman origins.

Month	Origin of Name
January	Janus, god of beginning and endings
February	Februae (Februalia), festival of purification
March	Mars, god of war
April	*Aperio* ("to open," Latin), a reference to plant buds
May	Maia, goddess of fertility (or plant growth)
June	Juno, goddess of women
July	Julius Caesar, Roman ruler (July was originally called Quintilis)
August	Augustus Caesar, Roman ruler (August was originally called Sextilis)
September	*Septum*, "seven," Latin
October	*Octo*, "eight," Latin
November	*Novem*, "nine," Latin
December	*Decem*, "ten," Latin

THE SUN AND THE SUNDIAL

Sundials were the most common way to tell time before the invention of mechanical clocks. The motion of the Sun across the Earth's sky was measured at least as far back as 3500 B.C., using a gnomon (a pointer and pedestal that formed an L-shape)—time is determined by observing the shadow cast by the vertical rod on the horizontal surface. By the eighth century B.C., the Egyptians developed a smaller, crude sundial that was divided into six segments. About 300 B.C., the Babylonian astronomer Berosus built a hemicycle—a wood cube divided into 12 segments, with a pointer at its center—to tell time by the Sun.

The Greeks and Romans developed more elaborate sundials, mainly to keep track of long-term astronomical cycles. The Tower of the Winds in Athens, which dates to about 100 B.C., once housed eight sophisticated sundials with backup mechanisms (usually run by water) in case it was cloudy. As demands for more exact time-keeping increased, sundials made way for sand hourglasses and graduated candles. By the fourteenth century, mechanical clocks had spread throughout Europe—the first clock publicly sounded the hour in 1335, in Milan, Italy.

The Days

Days are measured in two ways:

Because the Earth does not rotate uniformly and its orbital plane is not in line with the plane of the planet's rotation at the equator, the solar day—the period from sunrise to sunset—varies in length. A *mean solar day* is the solar day averaged out to eliminate the Earth's rotational and orbital irregularities. Thus the mean solar day is the average of all solar days in the orbital year, or 24 hours (or 24 hours, 3 minutes, and 56.55 seconds in sidereal time).

The *mean sidereal day* is similar to the solar day. However, instead of being based on our Sun, it is measured by using another star's passage across a particular reference point on the celestial sphere. The mean sidereal day is 23 hours, 56 minutes, and 4.091 seconds (in solar time). The mean solar day is 3 minutes and 55.91 seconds longer than the sidereal day, because Earth must move a little farther in its orbit to get back the point at which the Sun crosses the same meridian. This also varies slightly from day to day because the apparent eastward motion of the Sun is not uniform.

Sidereal and Solar Days

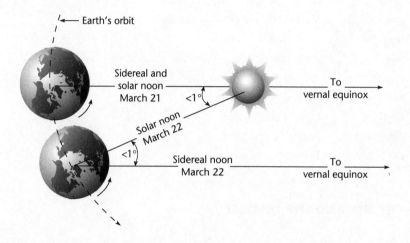

Names of the Days

The English names of the days were derived from either Latin or Saxon. They were derived from the words for the Sun, Moon, the then-known planets, and from the names of mythological gods. The Latin *dies* means "day."

English	Saxon	Latin
Sunday	Sun's day	*Dies solis* ("Sun")
Monday	Moon's day	*Dies lunae* ("Moon")
Tuesday	Tiu's day (Anglo-Saxon god of war)	*Dies Martis* (Mars, Roman god of war)
Wednesday	Woden's day (Anglo-Saxon chief god)	*Dies Mercurii* (Mercury, Roman messenger god)
Thursday	Thor's day (Norse god of thunder)	*Dies Jovis* (Jupiter, the chief Roman god)
Friday	Frigg's day (Norse god of love and fertility)	*Dies Veneris* (Venus, Roman goddess of love and beauty)
Saturday	Saterne's day (from Saturn, Roman god of agriculture)	*Dies Saturni* (Saturn, Roman god of agriculture)

EARLY SCIENTIFIC CLOCK WATCHING

The advent of the mechanical clock was one of the most important technological developments in Western history. Though there were crude mechanical timepieces in China between the eleventh and thirteenth centuries, this type of timepiece rapidly developed in Europe by the fourteenth century.

The mechanical clock gave scientists the ability to quantify their data with new precision, measuring reoccurring time sequences in experiments. Galileo Galilei was one of the first to measure time in a scientific experiment: He explained the motion of falling bodies by carefully timing balls rolling down an inclined plane. Galileo was also the first to suggest that a swinging pendulum could be used to keep time.

The 24-Hour System of Counting Hours

The system of dividing the day into 24 parts may have originated around 3500 B.C. with the Egyptians, who divided the daylight and darkness each into 12 segments, called hours. Because the days and nights naturally lengthened or shortened during the seasons, the length of each "hour" had to be changed to compensate. About 300 B.C., Babylonian astronomers made all 24 hours equal in length during the day, regardless of when the Sun rose or set. Europe did not adapt the equal-hour day until 1350—several decades after the introduction of mechanical clocks.

Today, there are two systems of counting time: the 12-hour system used extensively around the world, and the 24-hour system used mainly by the United States military and throughout much of Europe. In this system, midnight can be designated as 2400 hours of that day, or 0000 hours of the following day. Scientists often use the 24-hour system to keep time. It is especially useful in astronomy to keep track of astronomical locations and events. The Earth has been divided into 24 time zones, and Universal Time (at Greenwich, England) is "0 time," at 0 degree longitude meridian.

Standard and 24-Hour Time Systems

12-Hour (or Standard)	24-Hour
12 midnight	0000 hours (or 2400 of previous day)
1:00 A.M.	0100 hours
2:00 A.M.	0200 hours
3:00 A.M.	0300 hours
4:00 A.M.	0400 hours
5:00 A.M.	0500 hours
6:00 A.M.	0600 hours
7:00 A.M.	0700 hours
8:00 A.M.	0800 hours
9:00 A.M.	0900 hours
10:00 A.M.	1000 hours
11:00 A.M.	1100 hours
12 noon	1200 hours
1:00 P.M.	1300 hours
2:00 P.M.	1400 hours
3:00 P.M.	1500 hours
4:00 P.M.	1600 hours
5:00 P.M.	1700 hours
6:00 P.M.	1800 hours

Standard and 24-Hour Time Systems

12-Hour (or Standard)	24-Hour
7:00 P.M.	1900 hours
8:00 P.M.	2000 hours
9:00 P.M.	2100 hours
10:00 P.M.	2200 hours
11:00 P.M.	2300 hours
12 midnight	2400 hours (or 0000 hours of next day)

Dividing the Solar Day

1 mean solar day = 24 mean solar hours
1 mean solar hour = 60 mean solar minutes
1 mean solar minute = 60 mean solar seconds
1 mean solar day = 86,400 mean solar seconds

Why Do Minutes Have 60 Seconds?

Sixty was the number base used since ancient times. The Sumerians, who lived around the region of Mesopotamia about 5,000 years ago, were the first people known to have recorded a workable counting system, and they also used 60 as a base. Thus hours and degrees of longitude were divided into 60 minutes, and the minutes, into 60 seconds.

What Is a Second?

Before 1956, 1 second (or the mean solar second) was interpreted as $1/86,400$ of a mean solar day (i.e., there are 86,400 seconds in 24 hours). But scientists found that, as the Earth's rotation slowed, each day became about 20 microseconds longer than the corresponding day in the prior year (adding about 0.73 second to each year). They also determined that the year was getting shorter by about 0.53 second each year. To compensate, the second was defined as the ephemeris second, equal to $1/31,556,925.9747$ of the tropical year at 0 hours, 0 minutes, and 0 seconds (00 h, 00 m, 00 s) on December 31, 1899.

Currently, the second is more accurately defined using atomic measurements: 1 second is the duration of 9,192,631,770 periods of the radiation corresponding to the transition between two hyperfine levels of cesium-133 in the ground state (see also "Atomic Time," later in this chapter).

OTHER TIMES

Seasonal Times

The Earth's seasons are caused by the planet's tilted axis (about 23.5°) and its revolution around the Sun. Relative to the stars, the Sun moves about 1° per day, as seen from Earth, and follows a path in the sky called the ecliptic. The celestial equator—or the Earth's geographic equator as projected onto an imaginary celestial sphere—intersects the ecliptic at two points, referred to as the equinoxes.

To an observer on Earth, a measurement of the Sun's height taken each day of the year at the same time seems to follow an asymmetrical figure eight in the sky. When the Sun reaches the highest and lowest points in the figure-eight, the Northern and Southern Hemispheres will experience a corresponding winter or summer solstice; when the Sun reaches the midpoint in the figure eight, both hemispheres experience a corresponding vernal (spring) or autumnal (fall) equinox. Because the Earth slowly wobbles in its orbit (like a top), we experience precession—the occurrences of the equinoxes earlier (by seconds) in each successive sidereal year (for more information on the seasons and precession, see Chapter 9, "Earth Science").

Equinox

The day (actually, the instant) the Sun's direct rays cross the equator and neither the north nor the south pole is inclined to the Sun—or the moment when the Sun's path on the ecliptic crosses the celestial equator—is referred to as an *equinox* (see the figure "The Sun Through the Northern Hemisphere's Seasons"). At an equinox, the day and night are equal in length everywhere. The vernal equinox in the Northern Hemisphere is about March 21, the first day of spring. It also is called the March equinox, spring equinox, or first point of Aries. The autumnal equinox in the Northern Hemisphere is about September 22, the first day of autumn or first point of Libra. The times of the spring and autumnal equinoxes for the Southern Hemisphere are opposite those of the Northern Hemisphere.

Solstice

The day (actually, the instant) that the Sun reaches its northern- or southern-most noontime position for the year—or the moment when the Sun's position on the ecliptic is at its greatest northern or southern declination—is referred to as a *solstice* (see the figure "The Sun Through the Northern Hemisphere's Seasons"). In the Northern Hemisphere, the summer solstice is about June 21, when the Sun's direct rays fall on the Tropic of Cancer (corresponding to 23.5° northern latitude). It also is the first day of summer (or first point of Cancer) and the longest day of the year in the Northern Hemisphere. The winter solstice in the Northern Hemisphere is about December 22, when the Sun's direct rays fall on the Tropic of Capricorn (corresponding to 23.5° southern latitude). It also is the first day of winter (or first point of Capricornus) and the shortest day of the year in the Northern Hemisphere. The times of the summer and winter solstices for the Southern Hemisphere are opposite those of the Northern Hemisphere.

The Sun Through the Northern Hemisphere's Seasons

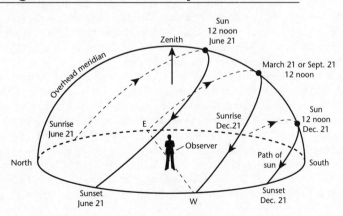

At about 39° northern latitude

Tidal Time

The periodic rise and fall of the Earth's oceans are called tides and are caused primarily by the gravitational attraction of the Moon. The Sun also influences the tides, though its effects are secondary to tides caused by the Moon. Because the Moon's distance from the Earth varies in its orbit around the Earth, the strength of attraction will differ, as do the size and times of the tides (for more information on tides, see Chapter 9, "Earth Science").

Due to other forces, such as those from the rotation of the Earth and the revolution of the Earth–Moon and Earth–Sun systems, tidal prediction is difficult. The high and low tides change each day. The average interval between successive high tides is 12 hours 25.5 minutes, but tidal highs can vary by intervals of less than 12 hours to more than 14 hours.

Average High and Low Tides

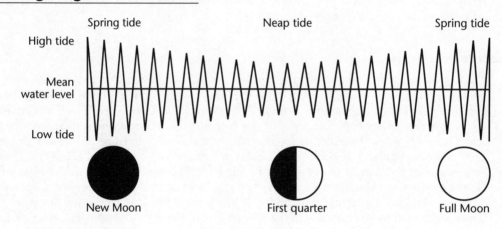

EARTH–MOON FUTURE TIME

Thanks to the action of tidal forces—the gravitational pull between the Earth and the Moon—over the past few billion years, the two bodies are in spin-orbit synchronization. In other words, only one side of the Moon can be seen from the Earth and the Moon's rotation is the same as its revolution—27.32 days, or a lunar month. Originally, both bodies may have been much closer (about 5 to 10 percent of their present distance) and rotating more rapidly, with the Earth's day only a few hours long. The Moon's orbital period was also much shorter.

Even today, the Earth and Moon affect each other: A day on Earth is longer than the following day by 0.00000002 second due to the Moon's pull on the Earth's oceans. The Moon is also affected by the Earth's tidal force, which will eventually slow the Moon's rotation. In addition, because the Earth's rotational energy is transferred to the Moon, our satellite will slowly drift away from us.

Right now, the Moon, at a mean distance of 238,866 miles (384,400 kilometers), moves away from the Earth a few centimeters per year. Some scientists believe that the Moon's rotation and revolution will eventually be 47 days and at a distance of approximately 347,984 miles (560,000 kilometers) from Earth. This should happen in several tens of billions of years—a time that far exceeds estimates of the Earth's and the Moon's probable life spans.

Ephemeris Time

Tables that give the daily positions of the Sun, Moon, and planets are based on *ephemeris time* (ET), which progresses at a precisely uniform rate. Introduced on January 1, 1960, to free astronomical computations from the effect of the Earth's rotational irregularities, ephemeris time is measured from the orbital motion of a planet, such as the Earth, or the motion of the Moon around the Earth (which is the standard for measuring ephemeris time). It is determined from observations of the Sun, Moon, or planets, by calculating when, according to the rate of passage of ephemeris time, one of these objects should reach its observed position among the stars. When using the Moon and Earth system to determine ephemeris time, the position of the Moon with respect to the stars is determined with a transit instrument, from occultations, or by photography.

Atomic Time

Atomic clocks work by measuring how atoms vibrate. Though known for several decades earlier, *atomic time* was not adopted until 1972 as the primary reference for all scientific timing. One of the most accurate and stable time measurements is based on the microwave resonances of certain atoms in a magnetic field, especially by counting the cycles of an electromagnetic signal in resonance with cesium atoms. An atomic second was defined in 1967, by the Thirteenth General Conference of Weights and Measures (under the International Commission on Weights and Measures) as 9,192,631,770 oscillations of the atom cesium-133. Such clocks are accurate to within a few billionths of a second over intervals of a minute or less (or one-thousandth [0.001] of a second in 300 years). Cesium clocks are often referred to as primary clocks because they present extremely precise and accurate time for scientific, research, industrial, defense, and public needs. Secondary clocks are less accurate and must be calibrated from time to time, such as quartz crystal clocks.

A new type of atomic clock is being developed that uses lasers instead of magnets to control and detect the oscillations of cesium atoms. In the future, scientists hope for accuracy of nearly one part in a billion billion—which corresponds to an error of less than 1 second since the Big Bang (the beginnings of our universe) 12 to 18 billion years ago.

KEEPING TRACK OF TODAY'S TIME

One of the most difficult tasks is keeping accurate time around the world. The world's time-keeping network involves atomic clocks in more than 26 countries contributing to the hub located at the International Bureau of Weights and Measures in Sèvres, France. At this center, computers gather information from satellites around the world and formulate the coordinated universal time scale, which is the planet's central time reference. The time is determined by averaging the signals emanating from more than 180 atomic clocks, from 36 laboratories throughout the 26 nations.

One of the main concerns of the international time standard community is the need for better means of transferring time signals out of the world's laboratories to the Sèvres center. One suggestion is to bounce time signals back and forth between laboratories via commercial satellites—which could speed up the precision by one-billionth (0.0001) of a second.

Geologic Time

The geologic time scale is one of the longest timewise and represents the Earth's natural history (more than 4.6 billion years). Radioactive dating, fossil placement within rock layers, and even tree rings are used to place natural objects within this time scale (for the divisions of the geologic time scale, see Chapter 9, "Earth Science").

HOW TREE RINGS KEEP TIME

Trees' annual rings can be used to measure time, since they are formed at the rate of one per year. The ring widths are then converted to relative values called indices, which are averaged for each year to obtain a chronological record. The longest tree-ring record (a sequoia) covers about 8,700 years.

These growth layers can also provide evidence of environmental changes, such as past volcanic and glacial activities, avalanches, flooding, earthquakes, frosts, and tree epidemics. Astronomer Andrew Ellicott Douglass was the first to establish the principles of dendrochronology, by observing that tree rings were wide in wet years and narrow in dry years. In 1937, Douglass established the Laboratory of Tree-Ring Research in Arizona, the largest such research facility in the world.

MOON AND SUN TIMES

Calendars

It is thought that the first calendars were based on movements of the moon. There is evidence from 30,000 years ago or so of marks on bone that some anthropologists have interpreted as calendar marks based on lunar phases. Some more recent cultures, including some Native American groups, are known to have used phases of the moon (which are easily observed) to mark time.

Some archaeologists have argued that many stone structures from early times (e.g., Stonehenge in England) were intended to keep track of a calendar based on the apparent movement of the Sun, but the earliest calendar of which we know for sure was the 365-day Egyptian calendar, based on the rising of the bright star Sirius (it was above the horizon about the same time as the annual flood of the Nile). Early astronomers in Mesopotamia seem to have, at first, used a calendar of 360 days, based on the movement of the Sun among the stars; they later corrected it to 365 days.

Mesoamerican calendars—the best known is the Maya calendar—were probably based on the movement of Venus and the Sun. The Mayans were able to date distant astronomical events by using a combination of a ceremonial calendar of 260 days and an astronomical calendar that, like the Egyptian calendar, had 365 days (they divided their year into eighteen 20-day months, with 5 days left over at the end). Fractions of days were ignored, so an error of about a quarter of a day accumulated every year.

Three Calendars

Gregorian		Hebrew		Muslim	
Month	Number of Days	Month	Number of Days	Month	Number of Days
January	31	Tishri	30	Muharram	30
February	28 (or 29)	Heshvan	29 (or 30)	Safar	29

Gregorian		Hebrew		Muslim	
Month	Number of Days	Month	Number of Days	Month	Number of Days
March	31	Kislev	29 (or 30)	Rabi' I	30
April	30	Tebet	29	Rabi' II	29
May	31	Shebat	30	Jumada I	30
June	30	Adar	29 (or 30)	Jumada II	29
July	31	Nisan	30	Rajab	30
August	31	Iyar	29	Sha'aban	29
September	30	Sivan	30	Ramadhan	30
October	31	Tammuz	29	Shawwal	29
November	30	Ab	30	Dhul Qa'ada	30
December	31	Elul	29	Dhul Hijja	29 (or 30)

Hebrew

The Hebrew calendar is based on the motion of the Moon. The calendar begins at the biblical Creation, which is calculated to have occurred 3,760 years before the modern Christian era (3761 B.C.). In the Hebrew calendar, the new year begins with the month of Tishri, which falls at the same time as our September or October. The Hebrew week lasts for 7 days, following the example of the Babylonian calendar, with the last day of the week being the Sabbath. There are 12 lunar months in a year; every other month is either 30 or 29 days long (see "Three Calendars," earlier in this chapter). Because the Hebrew year is 11 days shorter than the solar year, a 13th month, called ve-Adar, is added seven times during every 19-year cycle.

Muslim (Islam)

The Muslim calendar begins at the day and year when Mohammed fled from Mecca to Medina, July 16, 622, on the Gregorian calendar. As in the Hebrew calendar, the months are based on the motion of the moon, and the number of days in each month alternates between 29 and 30 days (see "Three Calendars," earlier in this chapter). The new year begins with the month of Muharram, which falls during our August or September. This lunar calendar consists of a 354-day year. Leap years (with one extra day) occur often.

Julian

The Romans developed complex lunar–solar calendars that were often influenced by political considerations. The astronomer Sosigenes suggested to Caesar that a calendar of 365 days plus a leap day added every four years would simplify matters. The result is known as the Julian calendar. The year 46 B.C. was given 445 days to compensate for past errors. The new calendar began in 45 B.C., and standardized the year at 365 days and 6 hours.

Gregorian

Although a great improvement over its predecessors, the Julian calendar was slightly longer than the solar year, with the result that the solstices and equinoxes drifted from their calendar dates. This discrepancy also affected certain Christian holy days, such as Easter. Thus, in 1582, Pope Gregory XIII introduced a new calendar, which was developed by astronomer Christopher Clavius.

The Gregorian calendar, a correction of the Julian calendar, added 11 days to restore the date of the actual vernal equinox to March 21 and to reposition ecclesiastical holidays. Thursday, October 4, 1582, was followed by Friday, October 15, 1582. The Gregorian mean year is 11 minutes and 14 seconds longer than the mean solar year, and is equal to 365.2425 days

(365 days, 5 hours, 49 minutes, 12 seconds). It retained the leap year introduced in the Julian calendar but deleted the leap year at the end of the century, unless the year is exactly divisible by 400. The Gregorian calendar was adopted in 1752 by England and its American colonies. Today, it is used by most countries around the world.

The World Calendar

Numerous countries have expressed an interest in a world calendar. In such a calendar, often called the Worldsday calendar, each date would always fall on the same day of the week, and all holidays would occur on the same days each year. There would still be a leap year, with the extra day (or "Worldsday") placed between the months of June and July, or December and January.

Worldsday Calendar

JANUARY

S	M	T	W	T	F	S
1	2	3	4	5	6	7
8	9	10	11	12	13	14
15	16	17	18	19	20	21
22	23	24	25	26	27	28
29	30	31				

FEBRUARY

S	M	T	W	T	F	S
				1	2	3	4
5	6	7	8	9	10	11
12	13	14	15	16	17	18
19	20	21	22	23	24	25
26	27	28	29	30		

MARCH

S	M	T	W	T	F	S
					1	2
3	4	5	6	7	8	9
10	11	12	13	14	15	16
17	18	19	20	21	22	23
24	25	26	27	28	29	30

APRIL

S	M	T	W	T	F	S
1	2	3	4	5	6	7
8	9	10	11	12	13	14
15	16	17	18	19	20	21
22	23	24	25	26	27	28
29	30	31				

MAY

S	M	T	W	T	F	S
			1	2	3	4
5	6	7	8	9	10	11
12	13	14	15	16	17	18
19	20	21	22	23	24	25
26	27	28	29	30		

JUNE

S	M	T	W	T	F	S
					1	2
3	4	5	6	7	8	9
10	11	12	13	14	15	16
17	18	19	20	21	22	23
24	25	26	27	28	29	30 W

JULY

S	M	T	W	T	F	S
1	2	3	4	5	6	7
8	9	10	11	12	13	14
15	16	17	18	19	20	21
22	23	24	25	26	27	28
29	30	31				

AUGUST

S	M	T	W	T	F	S
			1	2	3	4
5	6	7	8	9	10	11
12	13	14	15	16	17	18
19	20	21	22	23	24	25
26	27	28	29	30		

SEPTEMBER

S	M	T	W	T	F	S
					1	2
3	4	5	6	7	8	9
10	11	12	13	14	15	16
17	18	19	20	21	22	23
24	25	26	27	28	29	30

OCTOBER

S	M	T	W	T	F	S
1	2	3	4	5	6	7
8	9	10	11	12	13	14
15	16	17	18	19	20	21
22	23	24	25	26	27	28
29	30	31				

NOVEMBER

S	M	T	W	T	F	S
			1	2	3	4
5	6	7	8	9	10	11
12	13	14	15	16	17	18
19	20	21	22	23	24	25
26	27	28	29	30		

DECEMBER

S	M	T	W	T	F	S
					1	2
3	4	5	6	7	8	9
10	11	12	13	14	15	16
17	18	19	20	21	22	23
24	25	26	27	28	29	30 W

TAKING A LEAP

Leap seconds are ways of making up discrepancies in our time keeping. The major problem is with the Earth—it wobbles as it rotates on its axis, making it impossible to develop a totally accurate time interval. When the majority of time-keeping laboratories around the world agree that the Earth's rotation has slowed by a second, a "leap" second is added to a chosen day. At midnight Greenwich Mean Time, since 1972, there have been more than a dozen leap seconds added to keep the clock synchronized with the Earth's spin.

Because the Earth's revolution around the Sun takes about 365.25 days each year, to keep the calendar in sync with the Earth's orbit, we must add a day (February 29) to the calendar every fourth year. Thus we have 366 days in years divisible by 4 (for example, 1976 and 1984 were leap years). However, because the Earth's revolution actually takes 365.2422 days (not 365.25 days exactly), those years ending in 00 (or century years) must be divisible by 400 to be leap years.

TIME AROUND THE WORLD

Latitude and Longitude

Hipparchus of Nicaea (c. 170–c. 120 B.C.) developed a grid of 360 north-south lines that connected the north and south poles, and 180 lines parallel to the equator. His north-south lines were called *meridians* (from the Latin for "noon"): When it was noon at one point on a meridian it was noon everywhere along that meridian. The east-west lines were called *parallels*, and unlike meridians and as the name implies, these lines were parallel to each other. Meridians measured longitude, or distance east and west; parallels measured latitudes, or distances north and south. Longitude and latitude lines are used today—they are about 69 miles (111 kilometers) apart, as opposed to Hipparchus' average of 70 miles (112.6 kilometers) apart. Latitude is measured from the equator; longitude is measured from the Prime Meridian arbitrarily set to run through Greenwich, England.

Reading Latitude and Longitude

The point on the globe is at 50°N latitude, 60°W longitude.

Standard Time

The world's *standard time* was fixed in 1884, to prevent the time discrepancies that would result if every locality determined its own mean solar time. Today, the Earth is divided into 24 international time zones, measured at about every 15° longitude (24 times 15 equals 360°, a complete circle) with variations that follow geographical or political boundaries. Each time zone differs from the preceding and following zones by 1 hour. Because of political or geographical boundaries, such zone lines often depart from the strict 15° rule. In addition, some zone lines cut a region virtually in half, such as the middle of Australia. To solve this problem, a midzone often differs from its surrounding zones by 0.5 hour on one side and 1.5 hours on the other side.

The continental United States has four zones that determine standard times: 75°, 90°, 105°, and 120° west of Greenwich, England (at the Prime Meridian). Canada has two additional time zones: In the east, Atlantic Standard time, beginning 60° west of Greenwich, and in the west, Yukon Standard Time, starting at 135° west of Greenwich. Alaska-Hawaii Standard time begins at the meridian that runs through Anchorage at 150° and Nome Standard Time begins at the 165° meridian.

Coordinated Universal Time

Coordinated Universal Time coincides with the United States National Bureau of Standard's (NBS) atomic clocks and the United States Naval Observatory's sidereal time. The reference signals are broadcast over the NBS's radio station, WWV, from Boulder, Colorado. Atomic clock ticks are heard on the broadcast every second, and the time is announced every minute.

Universal Time (Greenwich Mean Time) and the Prime Meridian

Greenwich Mean Time (GMT), or *Universal Time* (UT), is the mean solar time at the Greenwich meridian, which runs through Greenwich, England. It is used all over the world in navigation (both air and sea), and for scientific purposes, such as accuracy in astronomical observations. GMT is also nicknamed "Zulu Time" and "Zebra Time." Because worldwide longitudes are measured from Greenwich (0° longitude, or the Prime Meridian), when time there is designated as 0 hours (00^h), the zones to the east are labeled $+1^h$, $+2^h$, and so forth. The zones to the west of the Prime Meridian are labeled -1^h, -2^h, etc. These successive zones meet in the opposite hemisphere at the International Date Line.

International Date Line

The International Date Line is an imaginary line that runs from the north to the south pole at 180° longitude (measured from the Prime Meridian). Though the International Date Line is internationally recognized, it was not officially adopted by the International Meridian Conference in 1884, in which countries around the world developed a system of world time zones and a common zero degree of longitude. In fact, it has never been officially adopted by all countries, but it is usually unofficially accepted.

If you cross the line traveling to the west, you loose a day: for example, if it is Sunday on the east side of the line, it is Monday to the west. The line zigzags around political boundaries. For instance, all of Siberia is on Asia's current day, and Alaska is on North America's current day.

U.S. Time Zones

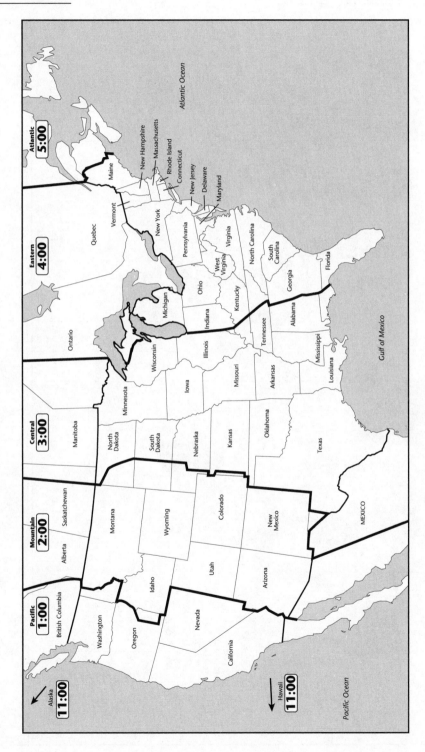

International Time Zones

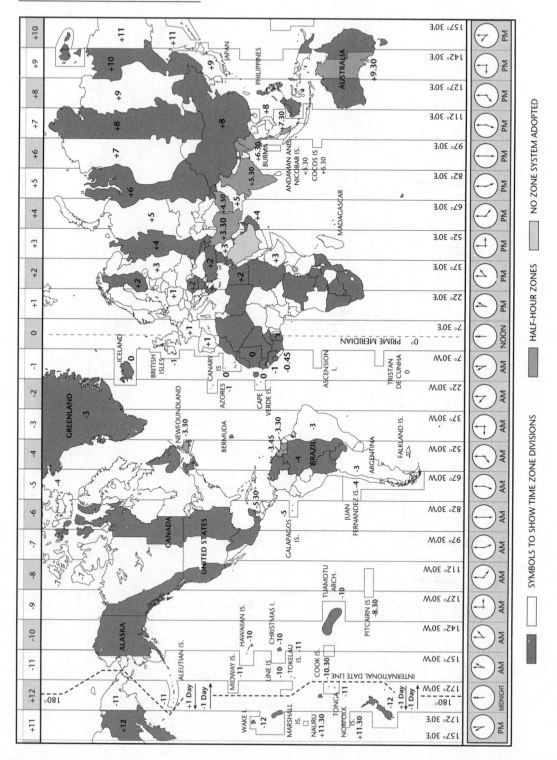

WORLDWIDE TIME VARIATIONS

Daylight Savings Time (United States)

Clock time in most of the continental United States changes two times a year. When the clocks are moved back 1 hour in autumn, the time is referred to as *Standard Time* (ST); when the clocks are moved ahead 1 hour in the spring, it is called *Daylight Savings Time* (DST). DST was originally proposed by Benjamin Franklin to extend the daylight hours later into the evening. In 1967, the Uniform Time Act went into effect in the United States, proclaiming that all states, the District of Columbia, and United States possessions were to observe DST starting at 2:00 A.M. on the last Sunday in April and ending at 2:00 A.M. on the last Sunday in October.

Any state may exempt itself from DST by law. Arizona, Hawaii, part of Indiana, Puerto Rico, the Virgin Islands, and American Samoa are now exempt. The Department of Transportation, which oversees the act, has modified some local zone boundaries in Alaska, Florida, Kansas, Michigan, and Texas over the past several years.

DST was extended by Congress during 1974 and 1975 to conserve energy, but the country returned to the previous end of April to end of October system after those years. In 1987, new legislation went into effect, signed by then-President Reagan on July 8, 1986, to move the start of Daylight Savings Time to the first Sunday in April. The last Sunday in October is still the day to change to Standard Time.

Differences in International Time

It is common throughout the world to adjust clock time to extend the daylight hours during the summer. Generally, western Europe goes on daylight time on the last Sunday in March and changes back on the last Sunday in September. China operates as one time zone even though it should, geographically, be in 11 different time zones. For religious reasons, Israel is approximately 2 hours behind the rest of its time zone, and consequently, the Sun may set as early as 3:30 P.M. Paraguay, Ireland, and the Dominican Republic extend the daylight hours in winter instead of summer; it is known as winter time.

ADDITIONAL SOURCES OF INFORMATION

Coveney, Peter V. *The Arrow of Time: A Voyage Through Science to Solve Time's Greatest Mystery.* Fawcett, 1991.

Fraser, J. T. *Time: The Familiar Stranger.* Univ. Mass. Press, 1987.

Morris, Richard. *Time's Arrows: Scientific Attitudes Toward Time.* Simon & Schuster, 1985.

Sandow, Stuart A., with Bamber, C. and Rioux, J. W. *Durations: The Encyclopedia of How Long Things Take.* New York Times Books, 1977.

Chapter 4

Biology

What Is Biology?   88

Biology and Life   88

Evolution   91

Heredity   93

Classifying Organisms   94

Example of a Five-Kingdom Classification
of Living Organisms   97

Kingdom Descriptions   98

Distinguishing Plants from Animals   101

The Plant Kingdom   104

The Animal Kingdom   120

Major Biologists   136

Significant Scientific Discoveries
in Biology   141

Common Terms in Biology   144

Additional Sources of Information   150

WHAT IS BIOLOGY?

Biology is the "science of life" or the study of living systems. It is concerned with life and its characteristics, including an organism's cellular organization, metabolism, response to stimuli, development and growth, and reproduction. It examines organisms on several levels of organization: atoms, molecules, cells, tissues, organs, organ systems, organisms, and populations.

Biology involves the studies of *zoology* (animals), which includes birds (ornithology), insects (entomology), and animal behavior (ethology); *botany* (plants); *algology* (algae); *mycology* (fungi); *microbiology* (microorganisms such as bacteria and protozoa); and *cytology* (cells). Substudies include evolution, genetics, morphology (anatomy), physiology (processes and mechanisms under which organisms function), taxonomy (classification of organisms), ecology, and embryology (origin and development of embryos).

BIOLOGY AND LIFE

What Is Life?

One of the most difficult definitions in biology is "What is *life?*" There is no simple definition and even the distinction between living and nonliving entities is not definite, though there are certain properties that distinguish animate from inanimate objects. In general, living organisms:

- are highly organized; their various body functions are directly linked together;
- are chemically different from their surrounding environment;
- take in energy from the surrounding environment and use it for their own energy;
- have the capacity to reproduce themselves and to produce offspring that closely resemble the adult;
- can respond to surrounding stimuli;
- are particularly suited to their environment;
- usually can adapt to changes in their surroundings; and
- are composed of carbon-based organic molecules (various combinations of carbon and hydrogen, oxygen, and nitrogen).

In addition, though not all living organisms respond to stimuli, reproduce, grow, or develop, they all possess the capacity to do so.

"NEW" LIFE UNDER THE SEA

Plants and certain algae convert sunlight to chemical energy through photosynthesis. However, in 1977, the research submarine *Alvin*, from Woods Hole Oceanographic Institute, discovered a new type of ecosystem based on chemosynthesis—converting chemicals into food—at volcanic cracks in the crust at the Pacific Ocean's Galapagos Rift.

The deep ocean waters near the rift are close to freezing, but because of the volcanic energy, the water temperature surrounding the rift can reach up to 632°F (350°C). The heat and the hydrogen sulfide from the hot vents (the bacteria use the hydrogen sulfide for energy) make this area a perfect spot for certain chemosynthetic bacteria to live—and make the bacteria a primary link in this deep-ocean food chain.

More than 295 new species have been discovered in the somewhat bizarre Galapagos Rift environment, including giant clams, crabs, and pink brotulid fish. One type of organism, a reddish worm, builds and lives in a tube up to 25 feet (7.6 meters) long—and because it has no organs that correspond to a mouth or intestines, (it is probably nourished by bacteria that live in its cells), it is classified in a phylum by itself. Some scientists speculate that if there are unfrozen oceans on other planets and satellites of the solar system, with even slight volcanic activity, there may be a chance that similar life could exist on other worlds.

Building Blocks of Life

The building blocks of life include carbohydrates, fats, proteins, and nucleic acids—all organic compounds and polymers (organic molecules linked together) synthesized by animals and plants (for more information, see Chapter 5, "The Human Body and Biomedical Science").

Carbohydrates (or saccharides) are the most abundant single class of organic substances found in nature. They are made up of carbon, hydrogen, and oxygen (the hydrogen to oxygen atomic ratio is usually 2 to 1, the same as in water). Single units of carbohydrates are called monosaccharides, such as the simple sugars glucose (dextrose) and fructose (levulose); carbon chains form the sugars and they are classified as trioses, tetroses, and pentoses (based on the number of carbon molecules within the sugar's carbon chain). Cellulose and starch are referred to as polysaccharides, in which two or more monosaccharides join by chemical bonds. Disaccharides, when two or more simple sugars bond together, include sucrose (cane sugar)—when glucose is linked to fructose.

Fats (lipids) are made up of glycerol and fatty acids and are stored by plants and animals as a source of energy. Fats we eat are obtained from animal and plant products. It is generally thought that fats that we eat affect our health (for more information on fats and the body, see Chapter 5, "The Human Body and Biomedical Science").

Proteins are complex polymer molecules that are found in animal tissues. They have a high molecular weight and contain carbon, hydrogen, oxygen, nitrogen, and often sulfur. They are composed of amino acids and are vital to the structure and functioning of all cells. The most abundant protein in mammals (and one that makes up a quarter of their weight), is collagen, the fibrous element found in, for example, hair, nails, teeth, skin, and blood vessels.

Nucleic acids are groups of protein-combined polymers found in both animal and plant cells that carry genetic information in the cell. They include deoxyribonucleic acid (DNA) and ribonucleic acid (RNA).

Theories of the Origin of Life

As the early Earth formed, heavier elements sunk to the planet's core, while the lighter elements—including those important to life, such as hydrogen, oxygen, and carbon—remained closer to the surface (for more information about the early Earth, see Chapter 9, "Earth Science"). Organisms composed of these elements originated and eventually thrived, but the mechanism for how this happened remains a mystery.

Here are two major theories on how life originated.

hydrothermal vents   One theory suggests that warm hydrothermal vents on the early Earth's deep ocean floor gave rise to conditions for life. The early Earth would be a prime place for such vents, as the thin crust had many more breaks than today's thicker crust.

primordial soup   In 1953, chemists Stanley Miller and Harold Urey developed a mixture of molecules thought to be similar to Earth's atmosphere about 4 billion years ago and subjected the mix to an event similar to lightning. When a combination of water vapor, hydrogen, methane, and ammonia was heated to 182°F (100°C) and subjected to an electrical discharge for about a week, four major organic molecules were generated—amino acids, nucleotides, sugars, and fatty acids in their simplest form—possible precursors to the more complex molecules essential for life. Miller and Urey's experiment was later confirmed, though with modifications, by Melvin Calvin and Sydney Fox. In 1979, Allan J. Bard and Harald Reiche produced amino acids by exposing the same solution to the Sun's rays and also adding particles of platinum and titanium oxide.

THE SPACE AND LIFE CONNECTION

The suggestion that life came from space is not new. One of the first proponents of this idea was Sales-Guyon de Montlivault who, in 1821, suggested that early Earth life originated from seeds from the Moon. In the late 1800s, William Thomson (Baron Kelvin) suggested that life arrived here from outer space, perhaps on meteorites. About 1905, Svante Arrhenius, a Swedish chemist, proposed the theory of panspermia, that spores of bacteria could travel great distances in the cold of space, and eventually enter the Earth's (or any other planet's) atmosphere. Scientists now know Arrhenius's theory is probably impossible because the spores would be exposed to deadly cosmic radiation.

Other theories state that elements essential to life (including water, certain gases, and organic molecules) could have been brought to the early Earth by comets and/or asteroids—and helped life to evolve. This theory gained strength when, in 1986, spacecraft flying by Comet Halley showed that the comet contained far more organic material than anticipated. In addition, spectroscopic analysis of asteroids has shown the presence of carbon compounds; carbonaceous meteorites that fall to Earth also have carbon. Titan, Saturn's largest moon and the only one with an atmosphere, has carbon compounds, and even space shows evidence—scientists have identified about 65 molecules in interstellar gases that contain carbon (e.g., hydrogen cyanide and formaldehyde).

Could the large, impacting bodies that struck the Earth early in its history have brought with them key compounds that made it possible for life to evolve? Right now, we can only speculate.

Self-replicating Mechanisms

There had to be a mechanism (or mechanisms) that encouraged early cells to group together and become self-replicating. Several agents have been suggested.

amino acids   How did amino acids link together to form chains of proteins? How did nucleotides (the structural units of nucleic acids) join to form long chains of DNA and RNA (for more information on DNA and RNA, see Chapter 5, "The Human Body and Biomedical Science")? We know that cells link amino acids together into proteins based on instructions carried by DNA (and RNA), and that cells can synthesize DNA and RNA with the aid of enzymes (which are proteins). Recently, scientists have shown that RNA molecules, like enzymes, can catalyze chemical reactions and can produce complementary copies of part of their own nucleotide sequence. If so, nucleotides could have formed from simple gas molecules on the early Earth (as in the Miller-Urey experiment), then assembled spontaneously into self-replicating chains.

bubbles   A recent theory states that the first "cells" self-replicated in ocean foam.

clay   Some scientists suggest that clays may have contributed to the origin of self-replicating systems, as clay can store energy, transform it, and release it in the form of chemical energy. This type of energy contributes to chemical reactions, which may have encouraged the growth of early organisms.

proteinoid spheres   This hypothesis states that the first "cells" were hollow proteinoid spheres—aggregates of proteins (or chains of polypeptides) that formed during the heating of amino acids within the cell's membrane. The groups of protein molecules could have bonded together to form larger molecules called polymers, which in turn could have influenced the formation of other polymers. Eventually, some of the larger molecules could have become self-replicating, leading to collections of organic molecules.

pyrite   Pyrite (fool's gold) has also been pointed to as a possible catalyst to self-replicating systems. Colonies of molecules may have stuck to the surface of pyrite and then started an energy-producing reaction similar to photosynthesis.

EVOLUTION

What Is Evolution?

Evolution is usually defined either as the adaptation of species to their surrounding environment(s) over time or as the theory that life on Earth gradually developed from simple to more complex organisms.

All organisms on Earth today are the products of billions of years of evolution—from single-celled bacteria to the most advanced animals. Life may have started and died out several times—for instance, as a result of the "Late Heavy Bombardment" between 4.5 and 3.8 billion years ago, in which large asteroids and comets struck the planet—before it became permanently established. The oldest known evidence of life has been found in 3.8-billion-year-old Greenland rock; the oldest known fossil evidence—organisms similar to blue-green algae—has been found in Australia and is estimated to be about 3.5 billion years old.

The theory of evolution states that all species have descended from other species and share common ancestors. How evolution occurs is still highly debated, but that it occurs is generally accepted. Paleontological evidence, usually in the form of fossils (for more information on fossils, see Chapter 9, "Earth Science"), is seen as a clue to plant and animal evolution as are comparative studies of animal and plant structures, the biochemistry and embryology of species, and the geographic distribution of flora and fauna.

Over time, living organisms have adapted to physical and chemical processes in their environment to increase their potential for survival and reproduction. As certain traits are passed on from parent to offspring, some organisms prove to be ill-adapted to the environment and disappear, while others increase in number. In general, evolution is a two-part process: It begins with random genetic mutation in an offspring. Then, as proposed by Charles Darwin in his *On the Origin of Species*, evolution is the process of natural selection, in which the unfit organisms are eliminated as a result of selective pressures in the organism's environment. Traditionally, it has been thought that evolution occurs only when natural selection works on a population containing diverse inheritable forms, but some scientists now think that natural selection also works on the genotype, phenotype, DNA, a single gene, etc.

One major unresolved question is the rate of evolution. There are two theories called *gradual evolution* and *punctuated equilibrium*. In the theory of gradual evolution, changes in organisms are, for the most part, the result of a steady accumulation of small modifications. The theory of punctuated equilibrium states that once a species has developed, it remains essentially unchanged for most of its history. But when evolutionary changes occur (usually following a crisis, such as the impact of a large comet), they happen in swift bursts.

WIPING OUT ORGANISMS

Although there are millions of species of fish, amphibians, reptiles, and mammals alive today, these species represent only a small percentage of the organisms that have ever existed on the Earth. What happened to all the others?

Many scientists agree that the Earth's history has been marked by several periods of mass extinction, when large numbers of animals became extinct over a short (geologically speaking) interval of time. For example, at the end of the Permian period, about 250 million years ago, it is estimated that about 96 percent of marine organisms became extinct; one of the most famous mass extinctions occurred at the end of the Cretaceous period, about 65 million years ago, when more than 50 percent of all organisms died off—including the dinosaurs.

The reasons for the mass extinctions are highly debated. One theory is that the impact(s) of a large comet(s) or asteroid(s) threw clouds of dust into the atmosphere, blocking out much of the Sun's light, and changing the climate enough to disrupt the food chain.

Possible Early Evolution

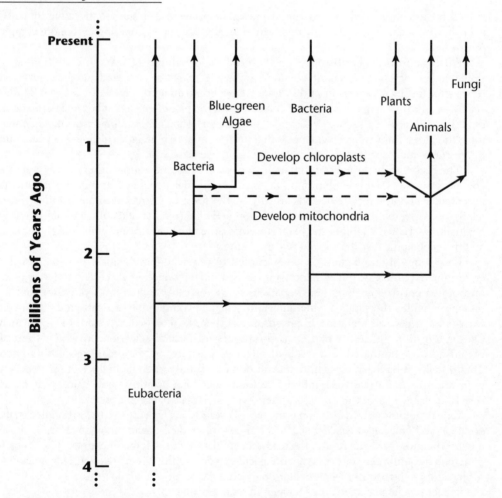

Possible Evolution of Living Organisms

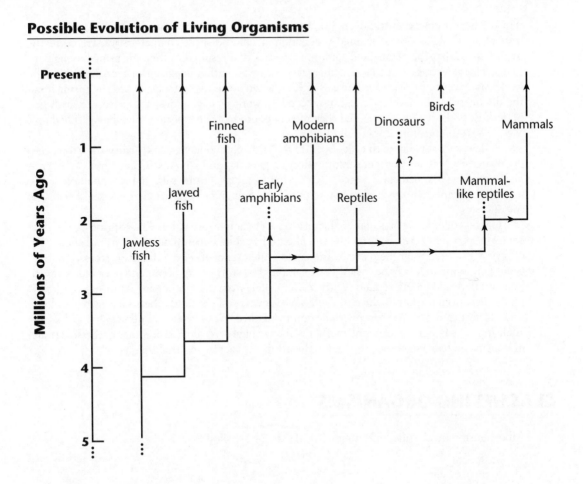

IS EVOLUTION GOING ON TODAY?

Evolution is a process that continues every day, although its results are not always apparent. One classic example of evolution within a short span of time involves the *Biston betularia* moth of England. Before the Industrial Revolution in the 1700s, the moth was mottled with white and brown and easily blended in with the lichen found on trees. But as coal came into widespread use in houses and factories, trees were covered with dark gray soot, making the light-colored moth easy prey for birds. By about 1860, dark gray *Biston betularia* moths were appearing in increasing numbers, as the result of natural selection because these better-camouflaged individuals were no longer easy prey for the birds. By the early 1900s, the dark moths outnumbered the mottled moths. Now England's air is less sooty, however, and since the 1950s, the mottled moths have been making a comeback.

HEREDITY

Gregor Mendel, an Austrian monk, carried out experiments in plant breeding in the 1850s and 1860s. By crossing tall and short pea plants over several successive generations, he demonstrated that the height characteristics were not averaged out in the later generations, as was thought; instead most of the plants retained their original tall and short characteristics. He correctly hypothesized that the plants held certain properties that resulted in their offspring having particular characteristics and that the characteristics were either *dominant* or *recessive*. Mendel's work was finally rediscovered in the early 1900s, when it was used to solve questions arising from the discovery of chromosomes. Because Mendel's work seemed almost too perfect, British geneticist R. A. Fisher once proposed that someone, probably an assistant, may have "tidied up" Mendel's research before it was published.

Today, scientists know that genes and DNA (deoxyribonucleic acid) carry the properties discovered by Mendel (for more information on genetics and DNA, see Chapter 5, "The Human Body and Biomedical Science"). Offspring of all organisms inherit their characteristics from their parents, who each have two sets of genes. Each parent contributes one set of genes to the offspring.

Genes "code" for a particular characteristic, for example, eye color. An offspring carries two copies of each gene (each copy is called an allele). Eye color depends on which pair of alleles the offspring inherited from the parents. In general, alleles are either dominant or recessive—one gene will dominate over the other. For example, brown eyes are dominant over blue eyes in humans. If a child inherits a blue eye (recessive) allele from the mother and a brown eye (dominant) allele from the father, the child will have brown eyes; if a child inherits a brown eye allele from the father and from the mother, the child will have brown eyes. A child who has a blue eye allele from the father and from the mother will have blue eyes. Typical dominant/recessive traits in humans include blue/brown eye color, dwarfism, Rh factor, and thalassemia.

CLASSIFYING ORGANISMS

All organisms are classified into hierarchical categories as follows.*

>   Kingdom
>   Subkingdom
>
>   Phylum (animals); division (plants)
>   Subphylum
>
>   Class
>   Subclass
>   Infraclass
>
>   Order
>   Superfamily
>
>   Family
>   Genus
>   Species
>   Subspecies
>
>   Variety (plants)

*Note: A cultigen (or cultivar) is a cultivated variety or species of organism for which there is no known wild ancestor.

Early classifications divided kingdoms into animals and plants, but most recognized modern systems include five to six divisions. Each division is based on certain characteristics within groups of organisms; these classifications are artificial, and they have no actual existence in nature. For example, *species* is a taxonomic category based on closely related, morphologically similar individuals that interbreed or have the potential to interbreed. In most cases, species of single-celled organisms are divided by their biological niche, the way they generate energy, and the construction of the cell. The species name is italicized and lowercase, and follows the genus name (the first letter of which is capitalized, and the entire word is italicized).

An Example: Human Beings

The science of naming organisms is called taxonomy or systematics. Although taxonomy dates back to Aristotle, modern taxonomy was developed by Carolus Linnaeus in 1735, whose system is still in use. Here is one interpretation of a taxonomic classification for humans.

Taxonomic Level	Name	Example Feature
Kingdom	Animalia	Animal
Phylum	Chordata	Spinal cord
Subphylum	Vertebrata	Segmented backbone
Superclass	Tetrapoda	Four limbs
Class	Mammalia	Suckle young
Subclass	Theria	Live births
Infraclass	Eutheria	Placenta
Order	Primates	Most highly developed
Superfamily	Hominoidea	Humanlike
Family	Hominidae	Two-legged
Genus	*Homo*	Human
Species	*sapiens*	Modern human

Numbers of Species

Over the past 3.5 billion years since life first blossomed on Earth, more than 2 billion species have evolved; however, approximately 90 to 99.9 percent of all species that ever lived are thought to be extinct. It is estimated that between 5 and 30 million different species of organisms now live on the Earth. Groups such as the vertebrates (fishes, amphibians, reptiles, mammals, and birds) and flowering plants have relatively few species, numbering only in the hundreds of thousands; insects account for the greater number of all species.

DIVIDING ORGANISMS

Historically, organisms were classified according to general characteristics within groups of organisms, such as whether they had a spinal cord. After Charles Darwin's theories on evolution were presented, classifications began to reflect evolutionary relationships between organisms. More recent scientific advances in paleontology, genetics, biochemistry, and microscopy have led to even finer classification distinctions between organisms, but not all scientists agree on a standard classification for all Earth's organisms.

The number of divisions vary. There are classification lists with 4 kingdoms: the Monera, Protista, Plantae, and Animalia; and more detailed lists with up to 13 kingdoms for greater distinction. In addition, scientists do not know whether or not viruses are living creatures—and if they are, they will probably need their own kingdom.

The following are the two most well-known classifications—one with five and the other with six kingdoms.

Five-Kingdom Classification

Kingdom Monera   Bacteria that have spherical, rodlike, or spiral forms and blue-green algae that are photosynthetic

Kingdom Protista   Single-celled organisms: photosynthetic organisms; a diverse group, including diatoms, silicoflagellates, coccoliths, and dinoflagellates; parasitic organisms; animal flagellates, similar to euglenoids but lack chlorophyll; amoeba-like forms with an animal-like metabolism, including foraminifera and radiolarians; and ciliated protozoan

Kingdom Fungi   Multinucleated organisms, essentially parasitic: slime molds and *Schizomycophyta* bacteria

Kingdom Plantae   Plants

Kingdom Animalia   Animals

Six-Kingdom Classification

The six-kingdom classification is based on particular characteristics of organisms, for example whether the organism goes through an embryonic stage (for example, fungi do not), the mode by which the organism obtains its nutrients, and the organism's means of mobility.

Kingdom Prokaryotae
    Subkingdom Monera   Blue-green algae and certain bacteria

Kingdom Archaebacteria   Bacteria that produce methane

Kingdom Protista   Single-celled and multicelled eukaryotes, including algae with a nucleus, protozoa, and some fungi and slime molds

Kingdom Fungi   Usually form from spores, including some molds, mushrooms, and lichens

Kingdom Plantae   Plants

Kingdom Animalia   Animals

Groups of Organisms

Ecologists classify organisms according to their function in the environment. Most animals, and some plants, fall into one (sometimes more) of the following categories.

Autotrophs (also called self-nourishers, or producers) manufacture their own food. Green plants are autotrophs, as they manufacture their own food from carbon dioxide, water, minerals, and sunlight.

Heterotrophs do not make their own food and obtain it from other sources. Heterotrophs can be further broken down into:

Herbivores: animals that eat plants

Carnivores (also called predators and meat eaters): animals that eat other animals

Omnivores: animals that eat both plants and animals

Scavengers: animals that eat large, dead organisms

Decomposers: smaller organisms that feed on dead organisms (e.g., bacteria; certain fungi)

Parasites: smaller organisms that eat living organisms, but do not devour them at one time like predators do (e.g., ticks; mistletoe)

EXAMPLE OF A FIVE-KINGDOM CLASSIFICATION OF LIVING ORGANISMS

Note: Common names of all organisms are listed. Examples of organisms within a division are in parentheses. This is only one example of a classification.

Kingdom: Monerans
    Phylum: Bacteria
    Phylum: Blue-green algae (cyanobacteria)
Kingdom: Protists
    Phylum: Protozoans
        Class: Ciliophora
        Class: Mastigophora
        Class: Sarcodina
        Class: Sporozoa
    Phylum: Euglenas
    Phylum: Golden algae and diatoms
    Phylum: Fire or golden brown algae
    Phylum: Green algae
    Phylum: Brown algae
    Phylum: Red algae
    Phylum: Slime molds
Kingdom: Fungi
    Phylum: Zygomycetes
    Phylum: Ascomycetes
    Phylum: Basidiomycetes
Kingdom: Plants
    Phylum: Mosses and liverworts
    Phylum: Club mosses
    Phylum: Horsetails
    Phylum: Ferns
    Phylum: Conifers
    Phylum: Cone-bearing desert plants
    Phylum: Cycads
    Phylum: Ginko
    Phylum: Flowering plants
        Subphylum: Dicots (two seed leaves)
        Subphylum: Monocots (single seed leaves)
Kingdom: Animals
    Phylum: Porifera
    Phylum: Cnidaria
    Phylum: Platyhelminthes
    Phylum: Nematodes
    Phylum: Rotifers
    Phylum: Bryozoa
    Phylum: Brachiopods
    Phylum: Phoronida
    Phylum: Annelids
    Phylum: Mollusks
        Class: Chitons
        Class: Bivalves
        Class: Scaphopoda
        Class: Gastropods
        Class: Cephalopods

Phylum: Arthropods
    Class: Horseshoe crabs
    Class: Crustaceans
    Class: Arachnids
    Class: Insects
    Class: Millipedes and centipedes
Phylum: Echinoderms
Phylum: Hemichordata
Phylum: Cordates
    Subphylum: Tunicates
    Subphylum: Lancelets
    Subphylum: Vertebrates
        Class: Agnatha (lampreys)
        Class: Sharks and rays
        Class: Bony fish
        Class: Amphibians
        Class: Reptiles
        Class: Birds
        Class: Mammals
            Subclass: Monotremes*
            Subclass: Marsupials*
            Subclass: Placentals
                Order: Insectivores
                Order: Flying lemurs
                Order: Bats
                Order: Primates (including humans)
                Order: Edentates
                Order: Pangolins
                Order: Lagomorphs
                Order: Rodents
                Order: Cetaceans
                Order: Carnivores
                Order: Seals and walruses
                Order: Aardvark
                Order: Elephants
                Order: Hyraxes
                Order: Sirenians
                Order: Odd-toed ungulates
                Order: Even-toed ungulates

*Often classifed as orders

KINGDOM DESCRIPTIONS

The kingdoms, except Plantae and Animalia, are described here. The plant and animal kingdoms are described in detail, later in this chapter.

Kingdom: Monera

The organisms found in the Monera kingdom are simple, single-celled, microscopic creatures that have no nucleus. Monera are prokaryotic (meaning the DNA lies loose within the cell) and can be either aerobic or anaerobic. They are considered neither plants nor animals and fall into two groups—bacteria and blue-green algae. There are about 4,000 known species, and they are thought to have been one of the first forms of life to evolve on Earth.

Bacteria

Bacteria are one of the most abundant life forms on Earth, growing on and inside other living things, in every type of environment. They range in size from less than several thousandths of an inch to several hundredths of an inch long. They multiply by simple cell division and are generally spiral, rodlike, or spherical in shape.

Bacteria have no nucleus but have a nucleoid, a single loop of DNA. The DNA carries the genes—about 3,000 of them in one bacterium (humans have about 100,000 genes in a cell). Like most organisms, bacteria need nitrogen, hydrogen, phosphorus, carbon, and oxygen to live, and they are more efficient at obtaining these elements than many other creatures. For example, certain bacteria can break down pesticides and use them as food (for more information about bacteria, see Chapter 5, "The Human Body and Biomedical Science").

Parts of a Bacterium

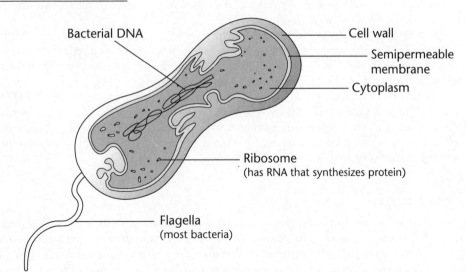

Bacterial DNA

Cell wall

Semipermeable membrane

Cytoplasm

Ribosome
(has RNA that synthesizes protein)

Flagella
(most bacteria)

BACTERIA AND US

Of the approximately 600 million bacteria that live on our skin, four main groups can be found anywhere on the human body: corynebacteria, micrococci, streptococci, and coliform bacteria. Other bacteria are found in specific areas, such as the moisture-loving diphtheroids, one of the bacteria living in the groin and armpits. In fact, the skin of the armpits can carry close to 500,000 bacteria per square inch, while the forearm harbors about 12,000 per square inch.

Inside the human body, bacteria also abound: The large bowel naturally carries coliform bacteria such as *Escherichia coli*, clostridia, and streptococci without any harm to the host—but if certain types of bowel bacteria escape to another part of the body, serious infection or inflammation can occur. Saliva contains about six types of bacteria, including streptococci, spirochetes, fusobacteria, and bacilli—some of which can cause problems such as gum disease.

Blue-Green Algae

Unlike most algae, blue-green algae are not truly plants. They most often colonize on bare rocks and on tree trunks. They can live in extreme temperatures—from hot springs to the harsh environment of the Arctic.

Although their cell structure is similar to bacteria, the blue-green algae carry out photosynthesis similar to other algae and green plants—thus the debate as to the true classification of blue-green algae: Monera or Plantae. They have no chloroplasts that change the sunlight into energy—their mechanism is embedded in lamellalike membranes within the cell. They can be aquatic or terrestrial and may have been the first oxygen-evolving organisms that helped to convert the Earth's atmosphere from anaerobic to aerobic.

Kingdom: Protista

There are about 11 different groups of protists and at least 50,000 species. They are single-celled organisms (with a nucleus) that have their own kingdom because they differ significantly from bacteria, fungi, animals, and plants. Most of the protists, often referred to as protozoa, obtain their nutrition by photosynthesis, absorption, ingestion, or a combination of all three. They reproduce either asexually or sexually. Because they have been so prolific, the protists make up a major part of the fossil record on Earth.

Depending on the phylum, a protozoan can have animal characteristics such as animal flagellates, or plant characteristics, such as the euglena, which is photosynthetic. Protozoa range from the single-celled amoebae to more complex organisms that have special structures for protection, feeding, and catching food.

Most protozoa live in water; others remain relatively static or are parasites. Many are found inside other organisms. For example, protozoa are responsible for various human diseases, such as malaria. Some cause disease in other animals, such as cattle, fish, and poultry. Still others are beneficial, such as the protozoa used in waste treatment plants to remove bacteria during the processing of waste material.

Kingdom: Fungi

Once considered to be plants, fungi are now classified in a kingdom of their own. This kingdom includes the yeasts, mushrooms, mildew, and molds. Fungi obtain their nutrients exclusively by absorption, hence many types are parasitic. Certain fungi play an important role in regulating the environment by decomposing dead plant and animal matter and releasing nutrients that can support the next generations of plant and animal life.

Fungi reproduce both asexually and sexually. Some release a cloud of spores that travel through the air and germinate other fungi. Higher fungi, such as the toadstool and the mushroom, spread the spores on the wind, using their fruiting bodies as carriers. Morels, truffles, and yeast produce their spores internally.

Kingdom: Archaebacteria

The archaebacteria is a kingdom in the six-kingdom classification. This kingdom is made up of single-celled creatures such as the methanogens that create methane. They exist in a warm, oxygen-free environment, ingesting carbon dioxide and hydrogen and producing methane as a byproduct. Other archaebacteria are found in extremely salty or acidic conditions. Because of their hardiness, archaebacteria are also thought to be an important clue to Earth's harsh early environment.

DISTINGUISHING PLANTS FROM ANIMALS

There are several general factors that distinguish plants from animals, though there are numerous exceptions.

locomotion   Most animals move about freely, while it is rare to find plants that can move around in their surrounding environment. Most plants are rooted in the soil, or attached to rocks, wood, or other materials.

food   Green plants that contain chlorophyll manufacture food themselves, but most animals obtain nutrients by eating plants or other animals.

cell structure   Plant cells differ in many ways from animals cells (e.g., the cell wall; there are chloroplasts in the cells of most plants, but not in those of animals).

growth   Plants usually grow from the tips of their branches and roots, and at the outer layers of their stems, for their entire life. Animals usually grow in all parts of their bodies and stop growing after maturity.

method of reproduction   In mosses and ferns, there are several stages of reproduction: the first stage produces eggs and sperm; when an egg is fertilized, the second stage produces a plant that reproduces by spores, which then produce eggs and sperms, and so on. Other plants reproduce with seeds, going through germination, growth, and pollination. Animals reproduce either through sexual means or asexual splitting.

chemical regulation   Though both plants and animals generally have hormones and other chemicals that regulate certain reactions within the organism, the chemical composition of these hormones differ in the two kingdoms.

Composition of Organisms*

Element	Human	Alfalfa	Bacterium
Carbon	19.37	11.34	12.14
Hydrogen	9.31	8.72	9.94
Nitrogen	5.14	0.83	3.04
Oxygen	62.81	77.90	73.68
Phosphorus	0.63	0.71	0.60
Sulfur	0.64	0.10	0.32
Total	97.90**	99.60	99.72

*approximate percents
**see chart below for more detail

Human Elements

Element	Human Body Percent*	Element	Human Body Percent*	Element	Human Body Percent*
Oxygen	63	Potassium	0.4	Iron	trace
Carbon	19	Chlorine	0.2	Cobalt	trace
Hydrogen	9	Sodium	0.2	Copper	trace
Nitrogen	5	Magnesium	0.1	Zinc	trace
Calcium	1.5	Boron	trace	Selenium	trace
Phosphorus	0.6	Fluorine	trace	Molybdenum	trace
Sulfur	0.6	Manganese	trace	Iodine	trace

*approximate percents

GLOWING IN THE DARK: BIOLUMINESCENCE

Many plants and animals, on land and in the oceans, are capable of producing visible light, called bioluminescence. Male and female fireflies of various species flash unique lighting patterns during mating season. Luminous fungi are commonly found growing on rotting trees in tropical forests; they may use light to attract bugs at night—especially insects that can carry away the fungi spores. Flash-light fish can be seen from 100 feet (30 meters) away in dark oceans, making them one of the brightest luminescent organisms known; they use their light to confuse predators. Luminescent algae in comb jellies (genus *Beroe*) give off a yellowish glow from material in their digestive tract, which attracts prey.

The majority of these luminescent animals and plants glow only at night. No one really knows the number of luminescent organisms, though some scientists estimate that more than 50 percent of all animals in the upper layers of the ocean have the characteristic. How do these creatures—including certain species of fish, shrimp, squid, beetles, bacteria, and numerous others—produce light? In most organisms, chemical reactions inside the cells and tissues break down luciferin (a pigment that produces heatless light when combined with oxygen) by luciferase (an enzyme). During this process, energy is released in the form of light. Other organisms also have luminescent proteins that break down and release light in the presence of oxygen or when mixed with calcium or iron ions.

Cells

The study of cells is called *cytology*. The cell theory states that all living things are composed of cells and that all cells arise only from other cells. Most cells have a *cycle*, a regular, timed sequence of events as the cell grows, divides, or dies. All cells exhibit some form of movement—from the active cytoplasm within a plant cell to the amoebae pursuing its prey.

What Is a Cell?

Almost all cells perform biochemical processes, generate and process energy, and store genetic information to be passed down to future generations of cells. Advanced single-celled and multi-celled organisms have nuclei that carry the DNA; primitive cells, such as bacteria, have no nucleus and carry their DNA loosely in coils throughout the cell. The number of cells in an organism varies. For examples, bacteria are single-celled organisms; the average adult human body has about 100 trillion cells.

Cells are the structural unit of all organisms and come in a range of sizes and shapes. Animal cells contain an outside cell membrane only. In most fungi, bacteria, and plants, there is a rigid cell wall outside the membrane. Oxygen, carbon dioxide, ions, food molecules, and waste products enter and leave the cell through the membrane surface. Most animals and plant cells average between 10 and 30 micrometers in diameter. The smallest cells are single-celled microorganisms, which measure only a few thousand atomic diameters across; the largest single cell is the ostrich egg, which can measure about 20 inches (51 centimeters) in diameter.

Cell Comparisons

Cell Part	Prokaryote	Animal	Plant
Nucleus	No	Yes	Yes
Cell membrane	Yes	Yes	Yes
Cell wall	Yes	No	Yes

A Typical Animal Cell

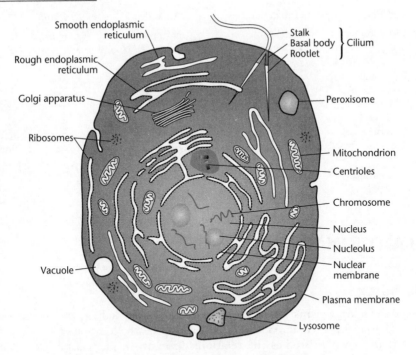

Smooth endoplasmic reticulum

Rough endoplasmic reticulum

Golgi apparatus

Ribosomes

Vacuole

Stalk
Basal body
Rootlet } Cilium

Peroxisome

Mitochondrion

Centrioles

Chromosome

Nucleus

Nucleolus

Nuclear membrane

Plasma membrane

Lysosome

A Typical Plant Cell

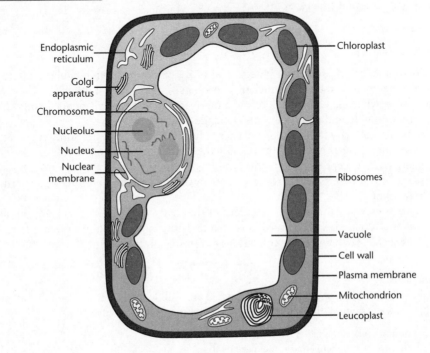

Endoplasmic reticulum

Golgi apparatus

Chromosome

Nucleolus

Nucleus

Nuclear membrane

Chloroplast

Ribosomes

Vacuole

Cell wall

Plasma membrane

Mitochondrion

Leucoplast

Cell Comparisons (cont'd)

Cell Part	Prokaryote	Animal	Plant
Chromosomes	single, with DNA only	multiple, with DNA and protein	multiple, with DNA and protein
Ribosomes	Yes	Yes	Yes
Mitochondria	No	Yes	Yes
Chloroplasts	No	No	Yes, in photosynthetic cells
Golgi bodies	No	Yes	Yes
Lysosomes	No	Often	Similar structures
Vacuoles	No	Small or none	One large single vacuole in a mature cell
Cilia or flagella	No	Often	No
Centrioles	No	Yes	No

THE PLANT KINGDOM

What Is Botany?

Botany is the study of plants. It is divided into many areas, including *plant taxonomy* (describing plants and arranging them into classes); *plant geography* (the location of certain plants); *plant ecology* (part of which studies the relationship between plants and the environment); *paleobotany* (ancient plants); *phytopathology* (plant disease); *economic botany* (how plants can be used as products); and *plant morphology* (the physical structure of plants), including physiology (the function of plant parts), cytology (the study of plant cells and their parts), and anatomy and histology (the internal structure of plants).

What Are Plants?

In the five-kingdom classification system, plants are considered mulitcellular and eukaryotic (there is a membrane around the nucleus of each cell). They have light-absorbing molecules called chlorophyll a and chlorophyll b, and a number of carotenoid pigments. Plants store food in the form of starch; and their cell walls are made of mostly cellulose.

Plants are necessary for the continuation of life on Earth. They are an integral part of the food chain, supplying energy and oxygen for the higher, more complex life forms. They are found everywhere except the polar zones, the highest mountains, the deepest oceans, and the driest parts of the deserts; each plant species has a limited distribution, which principally depends on climate.

Scientists estimate that up to 90 percent of the living mass on Earth is made up of plants. There are an estimated 400,000 species of plants, with Columbia, Equador, and Peru having more plant species than any other collection of countries in the world.

Plant Timetable

The time periods in which certain plants existed are still debated, but in general, the following list represents the general dates in which certain types of plants evolved:

3.5 billion years ago: Blue-green algae evolve
1 billion years ago: Fungi and green algae evolve

600 million years ago : Oxygen from algae plants is sufficient to support life on land and to shield life from the harmful effects of the Sun's ultraviolet rays

500 million years ago: The first land plants appear; marine algae dominate

433 million years ago (perhaps earlier): The earliest vascular plants evolve; the first resemble modern whisk ferns

410 million years ago: The first forests; gymnosperms evolve

350 million years ago: The first seed plants begin to grow (seed ferns, with large fernlike leaves)

285 million years ago: The first conifers evolve

140 to 125 million years ago: The first flowering plants (angiosperms) begin to grow and gymnosperms decline (today, flowering plants include two-thirds of all plants)

Plant Parts

In general, parts of a flowering plant include the following.

The *stem* produces and supports new leaves, branches, and flowers and keeps these features in effective positions to receive light, water, and warmth. The stem's main function is to transport materials (water and nutrients) to and from the roots. It may, in some small way, also contribute to the reproduction of the plant, store food, or help in photosynthesis.

The *root* of a plant is what anchors the organism to a solid surface. The root is also used to absorb nutrients and water, is important in asexual reproduction, and sometimes stores food. Roots range from a single large root (taproot) to a mass of similar-size roots. The roots penetrate the soil by cell division and elongation of the cells just behind the tip.

The *leaf* is the plant's means of intercepting light, obtaining and storing water and food, exchanging gases, and providing a site for photosynthesis.

The *flower* of a flowering plant is the sexual reproductive unit that produces and houses the sex cells (gametes). Flowers also attract pollinators (e.g., insects, birds) that carry off pollen from the stamen and fertilize other plants.

The *fruit* aids in the dispersion of the plant's seeds. After fertilization, the ovary begins to develop into a fruit, and ovules into seeds. The seeds are carried off and will, if conditions are right, eventually start a new plant. The *seeds* are dispersed in several different ways: Light seeds are carried by the wind (e.g., dandelions). Birds are attracted to some fruits and, after eating the fruit, leave seeds in their droppings. Barbed seeds stick to animals as they pass by; the seeds eventually fall off or are scratched off. If some types of fruit are physically shaken (e.g., by the wind), the seeds will drop.

The seeds develop in certain ways, depending on the plant. In general, as the fertilized egg within the ovule develops into an embryo, the ovule walls convert to a seed coat, turning the ovule into a seed (ripened ovule). The seed cover protects the inside from injury or drying and is used as nourishment until the seedling can make food on its own.

The germination of a seed depends on the temperature and moisture of the environment. In particular, warmer temperatures are needed for germination and seedling growth (although for some seeds to germinate, the temperature has to be cool). In the process of germination, the seed takes in water; a root pushes through the seed coating; and finally a shoot pushes up through the soil and forms a tiny leaf. Energy for germination is contained within the seed, but energy for growth after germination comes through the leaf.

The growth of a plant depends on the water, soil conditions, and temperature. After the seed sprouts, energy is derived from photosynthesis, a reaction between the energy from sunlight and the plant's chlorophyll (for more information on photosynthesis, see "Plant Photo-synthesis," later in this chapter). The plant continues to need water for cell enlargement (the result of internal water pressure extending the walls, which is why plants have smaller leaves during a drought); calcium for the regulation of cell division; protein development, auxins and cytokinins (hormones that help with cell elongation and division, respectively); and nitrogen, which helps with the structure of the chlorophyll.

Parts of a Flowering Plant

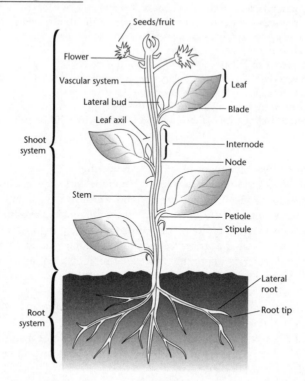

Parts of a Flower

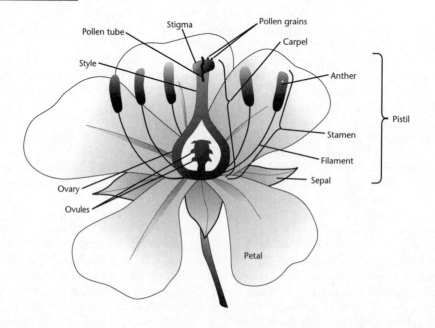

Cross-section of a Leaf

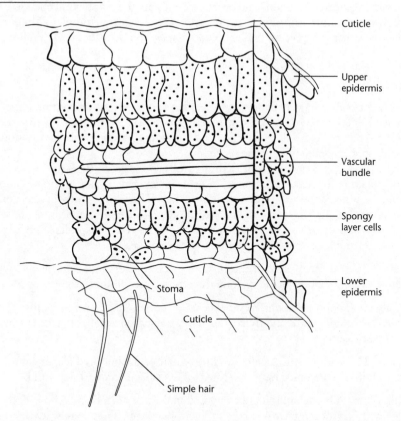

Land Plants

Plants can be generally divided into land plants and water plants (discussed later in this chapter). The first plants to evolve on land were *spore plants*, about 433 million years ago. They are not as prevalent in the modern world. Spore plants produce asexually or sexually with spores, or microparticles, which can grow into new plants. Modern spore plants include ferns, club mosses, liverworts, and horsetails. They are often divided into *vascular plants*, which can survive away from wet habitats and include ferns and their relatives, and *semiterrestrial mosses and other bryophytes*, which absorb nutrients and water from the soil through rootlike hairs and reproduce by motile gametes and small windborne spores.

Seed plants dominate the modern plant world. This group can be divided into gymnosperms and angiosperms. The *gymnosperms* ("naked seeds") are the simplest seed plants and include evergreen trees (there are about 1,000 species of gymnosperms).

The *angiosperms* ("enclosed seeds") are collectively called the flowering plants (flowers are the reproductive structures of the angiosperms). Angiosperms bear their ovules protected inside an ovary; the ovary ripens into seed-bearing fruit. These advanced seed-plants are divided into the monocotyledons (long narrow leaves with parallel veins, including grasses, palms, orchids, and bulbs) and the dicotyledons (multiple-shaped leaves with veins, including broad-leaved trees). Of the more than 250,000 species of flowering plants, the most common angiosperms are wild and garden flowers and hardwood trees.

Flowering plants evolved about 125 million years ago, (they developed in parallel with insects, which aid in pollination) and began to dominate the plant world about 65 million years ago. Flowering plants reproduce by spreading seeds (often found in their fruit). Their reproductive structures have particular colors, shapes, and odors to attract pollinators.

Water Plants

Plant *algae* make up a large portion of mostly aquatic organisms that contain chlorophyll; there are about 15,000 species of algae. They directly absorb water and nutrients into their cells, live close to the surface to be close to light, and reproduce through cellular division and motile gametes or spores (depending on the species).

The majority of algae are green, though often the green pigment is covered by other pigments, making the algae red, brown, or even black. Most algae are single celled, but some seaweeds, sugar kelp, and sea lettuce are multicelled. They vary greatly in size, come in almost every conceivable shape, and are found within almost all water environments: rivers, ponds, lakes, oceans, and estuaries. The photosynthetic algae are the main producers of oxygen in water environments and act as food for many acquatic organisms.

green algae   About 90 percent of the close to 6,000 species of green algae live in fresh water. They have varying shapes, including long threads and green fronds; they have no stem or roots.

brown algae   There are about 2,000 species of brown algae and most live in the oceans, especially the colder oceans and shorelines. They range from small, branching seaweeds to long strings of giant kelp.

red algae   The warmer seas usually hold the small or medium red algae plants, which often grow as frondlike branches. There are close to 4,000 species around the world.

phytoplankton   Phytoplankton are composed mainly of unicellular yellow algae. The oceans are filled with procholorophytes, a type of phytoplankton. They were discovered in 1988 and are now considered the most common plant in the ocean. Most phytoplankton vary regionally and seasonally.

Categories of Plants

Plants fall into many categories, determined by the plant's life cycle in the environment.

Type	Life Cycle
Annual	Completes its life cycle within one growing season—from germination of a seed through growth, flowering, production of seeds, and death
Biennial	Has a natural life cycle of two growing seasons; the seed is sown in the first year and the plant grows, usually with leafy growth; the second year, it flowers and dies
Perennial	Lives for a number of years, and generally flowers each year

Other divisions depend on the hardiness of the plant.

Type	Characteristics
Tender	Sensitive to the cold (can be an annual, biennial, or perennial)
Hardy	Able to withstand frosts (can be an annual, biennial, or perennial)

MEAT-EATING PLANTS

Animals are not the only carnivorous organisms in the world. Certain plants—usually those in nitrate-poor soils—occasionally consume meat to stay alive. One of the best-known is the venus-flytrap, found in the bogs of North Carolina. The inside of the plant's kidney-shaped, slightly hairy lobes is coated with a surgary nectar that attracts smaller animals, such as ants, spiders, flies, and even slugs and snails. If a creature alights on two of the hairs at once, a small electrical current is generated, which causes a change in motor cell water retention. The motor cells, located at the middle of the two lobes, go limp; the plant closes, trapping the creature—all within about two-fifths of a second. Digestive juices in the plant then take over, absorbing the nitrogen and other nutrients from the creature. After the soft parts are digested, the plant opens and drops the skeleton to the ground.

There are several other carnivorous plants. The European butterwort uses a sticky saplike covering on its leaves to trap insects. The pitcher plants of Borneo and Malaysia are large enough to fill with rainwater and drown small birds and mammals ensnared in their hollow, jug-shaped traps. Bladderworts, which hang just below the water's surface, have small, bladderlike traps along their winding stems. When an insect touches a trap, it triggers the bladder to open; the trap fills with water and drowns the victim.

Plant Reproduction

Plants reproduce by *sexual* or *asexual* reproduction, or both, depending on the species. One of the most important factors that aid in plant growth and reproduction is the availability of nitrogen (N_2). Plants use "fixed" nitrogen—nitrogen that has been converted to ammonia (NH_3) by lightning and single-celled organisms that live in the soil. Without such nitrogen "fixers," most plant and animal life would not exist on the Earth.

Sexual Reproduction

Seeds are the focus of sexual reproduction in plants. As a seeded plant grows, it holds an egg within; when the plant matures, the egg is fertilized by sperm (pollen) from itself or another plant. Fertilization from other plants usually takes place by the transfer of pollen grains, which can be carried by wind (such as pine pollen, which has very smooth grains) or by insects, bees, birds, or animals (such as apple pollen, which consists of rough and often sticky grains that cling to the carrier). The fertilized egg (or zygote) remains in the plant and eventually becomes a seed ready to produce another plant.

Asexual Reproduction

Asexual plant reproduction requires only one organism. There is no change in the chromosome number if the new plant is separated from the parent plant; single-cell division in asexual reproduction does not change the chromosome number, as mitosis (cell division that retains the full number of chromosomes) is involved. The new plants have the same genetic structure as the parents.

Asexual reproduction includes plants that grow from bulbs (such as tulips), feelers (long sections of the plant that take root, such as crabgrass), and rhizomes (underground stems, often called sucker roots). Branches grafted to trees (such as certain types of oranges and grapes) can also be classified as asexual reproduction. Single-celled plants such as algae also reproduce asexually, by ordinary cell division.

OF TREES AND SEEDS

Not all common plants are what they seem—and neither are their seeds. Seedless naval oranges are the progeny of a mutant tree that appeared in Brazil in the nineteenth century. The resulting navel oranges we find in the grocery store are all the result of a single branch of that mutant tree grafted to an orange tree; then those branches were grafted to other trees; and so on.

There are other strange seed stories. The oldest seed found so far is from a North American Arctic lupine, thought to be about 10,000 years old: It grew into a plant similar to today's lupine. In fact, the ability of the lupine to survive such a cold and severe environment gave scientists the idea to place rare and endangered plant seeds in cold storage—as stock for the future.

The double coconut is a single-seeded fruit grown only in the Seychelles Islands. It weighs as much as 45 pounds and takes up to 10 years to develop before it is ready to grow into a tree. The seeds of the strawberry are small and yellow, stuck to the side of the stem (the red part we eat). Cherry seeds grow protective coverings to allow them to pass unharmed through the digestive systems of birds—perfect for ensuring that seeds are safely dispersed.

Plant Photosynthesis

Photosynthesis is the process by which plant leaves make carbohydrates. Sunlight, carbon dioxide, and water are converted into carbohydrates, water, and oxygen by the action of chlorophyll in the chloroplasts of the plant. Photosynthesis occurs in most plants, especially those that are green (from chlorophyll), and in some bacteria and protists.

Botanical Names of Plants

Common Name	Botanical Name	Common Name	Botanical Name
Acacia, giraffe	*Acacia giraffae*	Asparagus, garden	*Asparagus officinalis*
Adder's-tongue	*Erythronium sibiricum*	Aspen	
	Ophioglossum vulgatum	European	*Populus tremula*
	islandicum	Quaking	*P. tremuloides*
Alder		Aster	*Aster* sp.
European	*Alnus glutinosa*	Attalea	*Attalea funifera*
Hazel	*A. rugosa*	Avocado, American	*Persea americana*
Red	*A. rubra*	Balloon vine	*Cardiospermum halicacabum*
Alfalfa	*Medicago sativa*	Balsam, garden	*Impatiens balsamina*
Almond	*Prunus amygdalus*	Barley	*Hordeum vulgare*
Aloe	*Aloe* sp.	Bean	
Amaryllis	*Amaryllis* sp.	Broad	*Vicia faba*
Angelica	*Angelica polyclada*	Kidney	*Phaseolus vulgaris*
garden	*A. archangelica*	Sieva	*P. lunatus*
Apple	*Malus pumila*	Beech	
	M. sylvestris	American	*Fagus grandifolia*
Apricot	*Prunus armeniaca*	European	*F. sylvatica*
Arborvitae		Beet, common	*Beta vulgaris*
Eastern	*Thuja occidentalis*	Birch	
Giant	*T. plicata*	European white	*Betula pendula*
Arum, East Asian	*Pinellia ternata*	Paper	*B. papyrifera*
Ash		Sweet	*B. lenta*
European	*Franxinus excelsior*	White	*B. populifolia*
Green	*F. pennsylvanica*	Yellow	*B. lutea*
White	*F. americana*	Blackberry	*Rubus* sp.

Common Name	Botanical Name	Common Name	Botanical Name
Bladderpod	*Lesquerella densipila*	Clubmoss, common	*Lycopodium clavatum*
Blood-lily, Katharine	*Haemanthus katharinae*	Cocklebur, oriental	*Xanthium orientale*
Blueberry, highbush	*Vaccinium corymbosum*	Coconut	*Cocos nucifera*
Brake, sword	*Pteris ensiformis*	Coffee, Arabian	*Coffea arabica*
Bryony, white	*Bryonia alba*	Coneflower, pinewoods	*Rudbeckia bicolor*
Buckwheat	*Fagopyrum sagittatum*	Coreopsis	
Buttercup, creeping	*Ranunculus repens*	Goldenwave	*Coreopsis drummondii*
Cabbage	*Brassica oleracea*	Lance	*C. lanceolata*
	B. oleracea capitata	Plains	*C. tinctoria*
Kerguelen	*Pringlea antiscorbutica*	Corn	*Zea mays*
Cacao	*Theobroma cacao*	Cornflower	*Centaurea cyanus*
Calotrope, fantan	*Calotropis procera*	Coronilla, crownvetch	*Coronilla varia*
Capeberry, South African	*Myrica cordifolia*	Cosmos	*Cosmos sp.*
Carpotroche	*Carpotroche brasiliensis*	Cotton	
Carrot	*Daucus carota*	Levant	*Gossypium herbaceum*
Cashew	*Anacardium occidentale*	Sea Island	*G. barbadense*
Castor bean	*Ricinus communis*	Upland	*G. hirsutum*
Catalpa		Coventry bells	*Campanula trachelium*
Chinese	*Catalpa ovata*	Cowpea	*Vigna glabra*
Northern	*C. speciosa*	Common	*V. sinensis*
Cedar	*Cedrus sp.*	Yard-long	*V. sesquipedalis*
California incense	*Libocedrus decurrens*	Crotalaria	*Crotalaria vitellina*
Celery		Croton, purging	*Croton-tiglium*
Garden	*Apium graveolens dulce*	Cucumber	*Cucumis sativus*
Wild	*A. graveolens*	Currant	
Chaulmoogra tree	*Gynocardia odorata*	European black	*Ribes nigrum*
Common	*Hydnocarpus anthelmintica*	Red	*R. sativum*
Wight	*H. wightiana*	Cypress	
Cherry		Arizona	*Cupressus arizonica*
Black	*Prunus serotina*	Bald	*Taxodium distichum*
Mazzard	*P. avium*	Dahlia	*Dahlia sp.*
Pin	*P. pennsylvanica*	Dandelion	*Taraxacum officinale*
Chestnut		Daphne	*Daphne sp.*
Chinese	*Castanea mollissima*	Date	*Phoenix dactylifera*
Common horse	*Aesculus hippocastanum*	Davallia, Fiji	*Davallia fejeensis*
Chickpea, gram	*Cicer arietinum*	Desert willow	*Chilopsis linearis*
Chinaberry	*Melia azedarach*	Dock, curly	*Rumex crispus*
Chrysanthemum		Dogbane	*Apocynum sp.*
Corn	*Chrysanthemum segetum*	Dogwood	
Pyrenees	*C. maximum*	Cornelian cherry	*Cornus mas*
Cinchona, ledgerbark	*Cinchona ledgeriana*	Flowering	*C. florida*
Clarkia, rose	*Clarkia elegans*	Dollar plant	*Lunaria annua*
Clover		Douglas fir	*Pseudotsuga menziesii*
Alsike	*Trifolium hybridum*	Common	*P. taxifolia*
Burdock	*T. lappaceum*	Eggplant	*Solanum melongena*
Crimson	*T. incarnatum*	Garden	*S. melongena esculentum*
Egyptian	*T. alexandrinum*	Elm, American	*Ulmus americana*
Persian	*T. resupinatum*	Endive	*Cichorium endivia*
Red	*T. pratense*	Erysimum, plains	*Erysimum asperum*
Strawberry	*T. fragiferum*	Eucalyptus	*Eucalyptus sp.*
Subterranean	*T. subterraneum*	Euphorbia,	*Euphorbia marginata*
Suckling	*T. dubium*	snow-on-the-mountain	
Yellow sweet	*Melilotus officinalis*	False-cypress	
White	*Trifolium repens*	Lawson's	*Chamaecyparis lawsoniana*
White sweet	*Melilotus alba*	Nootka	*C. nootkatensis*

Botanical Names of Plants (cont'd)

Common Name	Botanical Name
Fern	
Common staghorn	*Platycerium bifurcatum*
Common sword	*Nephrolepis exaltata*
Filmy	*Hymenophyllum atrovirens*
Grape	*Botrychium virginianum*
Holly	*Cyrtomium falcatum*
Lady	*Athyrium filix-femina*
Maidenhair	*Adiantum pedatum*
Pine	*Anemia adiantifolia*
Royal	*Osmunda regalis*
Tropical	*Gleichenia flabellata*
Water	*Azolla pinnata*
Wood	*Thelypteris normalis*
Fescue	
Alta	*Festuca elatior arundinacea*
Meadow	*F. elatior*
Red	*F. rubra*
Fig	*Ficus carica*
Filbert	*Corylus* sp.
Fir	
Cascades	*Abies amabilis*
Grand	*A. grandis*
Noble	*A. procera*
Red	*A. magnifica*
White	*A. concolor*
Flax, common	*Linum usitatissimum*
Forget-me-not	*Myosotis* sp.
Foxglove	
Common	*Digitalis purpurea*
Grecian	*D. lanata*
Frenchweed	*Thlaspi arvense*
Ginkgo	*Ginkgo biloba*
Gladiolus, common	*Gladiolus hortulanus*
horticultural	
Gooseberry, Chinese	*Actinidia chinensis*
Gourd, snake	*Trichosanthes* sp.
Grape	
European	*Vitis vinifera*
Fox	*V. labrusca*
Roundleaf	*Ribes rotundifolium*
Grass	
Bermuda	*Cynodon dactylon*
Buffalo	*Buchloe dactyloides*
Canada blue-	*Pao compressa*
Canary	*Phalaris canariensis*
Cocksfoot orchard	*Dactylis glomerata*
Colonial bent-	*Agrostis tenuis*
Common carpet-	*Axonopus affinis*
Crested wheat-	*Asgropyron cristatum*
Dallis	*Paspalum dilatatum*
Desert wheat-	*Agropyron desertorum*
Italian rye-	*Lolium multiflorum*
Johnson	*Sorghum halepense*
Kentucky blue-	*Poa pratensis*

Common Name	Botanical Name
Perennial rye-	*Lolium perenne*
Quack	*Agropyron repens*
Reed canary	*Phalaris arundinacea*
Sudan	*Sorghum vulgare sudanense*
Hackberry, common	*Celtis occidentalis*
Hart's-tongue	*Phyllitis scolopendrium*
Hemlock	
Eastern	*Tsuga canadensis*
Western	*T. heterophylla*
Hemp	*Cannabis sativa*
Hibiscus, kenaf	*Hibiscus cannabinus*
Hickory, shagbark	*Carya ovata*
Holly	
American	*Ilex opaca*
English	*I. aquifolium*
Hollyhock	*Althaea rosea*
Horsetail, common	*Equisetum arvense*
Hyssop, hedge	*Gratiola* sp.
Indigo	*Indigofera* sp.
Iris	
Blue flag	*Iris versicolor*
German	*I. germanica*
Grass	*I. graminea*
Ironweed, kinka oil	*Vernonia anthelmintica*
Jacaranda	*Jacaranda* sp.
Jimsonweed	*Datura stramonium*
Juniper, Savin	*Juniperus sabina*
Kale	*Brassica oleracea acepha*
Kamala tree	*Mallotus philippinensis*
Knotweed, prostrate	*Polygonum aviculare*
Lamb's quarter	*Chenopodium album*
Larch, western	*Larix occidentalis*
Larkspur, rocket	*Delphinium ajacis*
Lemon	*Citrus limon*
Lentil	*Lens culinaris*
Lespedeza	
Common	*Lespedeza striata*
Korean	*L. stipulacea*
Wand	*L. intermedia*
Lettuce	*Lactuca sativa*
Licania	*Licania rigida*
Lilac, common	*Syringa vulgaris*
Lily, regal	*Lilium regale*
Linden, American	*Tilia americana*
Litsea	*Litsea* sp.
Locust, black	*Robinia pseudoacacia*
Lotus, East Indian	*Nelumbo nucifea*
Lupine	*Lupinus arcticus*
Tree	*L. angustifolius*
Macadamia, Queenslandnut	*Macadamia ternifolia*
Magnolia	
Great-leaved	*Magnolia macrophylla*
Southern	*M. grandiflora*
Malope	*Malope trifida*

Common Name	Botanical Name	Common Name	Botanical Name
Mango, common	*Mangifera indica*	Persimmon, common	*Diospyros virginiana*
Maple		Petunia	*Petunia* sp.
Red	*Acer rubrum*	Phlox, Drummond	*Phlox drummondii*
Silver	*A. saccharinum*	Pine	
Sugar	*A. saccharum*	Austrian	*Pinus nigra*
Marattia	*Marattia salicina*	Eastern white	*P. strobus*
Marbleseed, western	*Onosmodium occidentale*	Jack	*P. banksiana*
Marigold	*Tagetes* sp.	Loblolly	*P. taeda*
Winter cape	*Dimorphotheca aurantiaca*	Longleaf	*P. palustris*
Meadowrue, Sierra	*Thalictrum polycarpum*	Ponderosa	*P. ponderosa*
Milkweed, common	*Asclepias syriaca*	Shore	*P. contorta*
Millet, pearl	*Pennisetum glaucum*	Shortleaf	*P. echinata*
Morning glory		Slash	*P. caribea*
Common	*Ipomoea purpurea*	Sugar	*P. lambertiana*
Orizaba	*I. orizabensis*	Western white	*P. monticola*
Muskmelon	*Cucumis melo*	Pineapple	*Ananas comosus*
Mustard		Pink, clove	*Dianthus caryophyllus*
Black	*Brassica migra*	Pistachio	*Pistacia* sp.
White	*B. hirta*	Plum	
Nasturtium	*Tropaeolum* sp.	Garden	*Prunus domestica*
Niger seed	*Guizotia abyssinica*	Japanese	*P. salicina*
Oak		Podocarpus	*Podocarpus* sp.
Black	*Quercus velutina*	Polypody, rock	*Polypodium virginianum*
English	*Q. robur*	Pomegranate, common	*Punica granatum*
Scarlet	*Q. coccinea*	Poplar	
Southern red	*Q. falcata*	Eastern	*Populus deltoides*
White	*Q. alba*	Mongolian	*P. suaveolens*
Oat, common	*Avena sativa*	Yellow, or tulip tree	*Liriodendron tulipifera*
Okra	*Hibiscus esculentus*	Poppy	*Papaver rhoeas*
Olive	*Olea europaea sativa*	Corn	
Common	*O. europaea*	Opium	*P. somniferum*
Oncoba, gorli	*Oncoba echinata*	Oriental	*P. orientale*
Onion, garden	*Allium cepa*	Portulaca, common	*Portulaca grandiflora*
Orange		Potato	*Solanum tuberosum*
Sweet	*Citrus sinensis*	Primrose	
Trifoliate	*Poncirus trifoliata*	Evening	*Oenothera biennis*
Palm, African oil	*Elaeis guineensis*	Lemarck	*O. lamarckiana*
Pansy, wild	*Viola tricolor*	Pumpkin	*Cucurbita pepo*
Parinarium	*Parinarium* sp.	Purslane, common	*Portulaca oleracea*
Parsley	*Petroselinum crispum*	Pycnanthus, akomu	*Pycnanthus kombo*
Common curly	*P. latifolium*	Quillwort	*Isoetes braunii*
Parsnip	*Pastinaca sativa*	Radish, garden	*Raphanus sativus*
Pea		Rape	
Field	*Pisum sativum arvense*	Bird	*Brassica campestris*
Garden	*P. sativum*	Winter	*B. napus*
Sweet	*Lathyrus odoratus*	Red cedar, eastern	*Juniperus virginiana*
Peach	*Prunus persica*	Redtop	*Agrostis alba*
Peanut	*Arachis hypogaea*	Redwood	*Sequoia sempervirens*
Pear	*Pyrus communis*	Rhododendron, catawba	*Rhododendron catawbiense*
Peavine, flat	*Lathyrus sylvestris*	Rhubarb	
Pecan	*Carya illinoensis*	Garden	*Rheum rhaponticum*
Peony, fernleaf	*Paeonia tenuifolia*	Medicinal	*R. officinale*
Pepper, bush red	*Capsicum frutescens*	Sorrel	*R. palmatum*
Pepperwort	*Marsilea minuta*	Rice	*Oryza sativa*
Perilla, common	*Pefrilla frutescens*	Rose, cabbage	*Rosa centifolia*

Botanical Names of Plants (cont'd)

Common Name	Botanical Name	Common Name	Botanical Name
Rubber, para	*Havea brasiliensis*	Sweet william	*Dianthus barbatus*
Rutabaga	*Brassica napobrassica*	Tallow wood	*Ximenia americana*
Rye	*Secale cereale*		*X. caffra*
Safflower	*Carthamus tinctorius*	Tara vine	*Taraktogenos kurzii*
Sage		Tetradenia, Asian	*Tetradenia glauca*
Garden	*Salvia officinalis*	Timothy	*Phleum pratense*
Scarlet	*S. splendens*	Tobacco	*Nicotiana glutinosa*
Salsify, vegetable-oyster	*Tragopogon porrifolius*	Common	*N. tabacum*
Scammony, glorybind	*Convolvulus scammonia*	Tomato, common	*Lycopersicon esculentum*
Scarlet runner	*Phaseolus coccineus*	Trefoil, bird's foot	*Lotus corniculatus*
Sequoia, giant	*Sequoiadendron giganteum*	Tulip	*Tulipa sp.*
	Sequoia gigantea	Tung oil tree	*Aleurites fordii*
Sesame, oriental	*Sesamum indicum*	Tupelo, water	*Nyssa aquatica*
Snapdragon, common	*Antirrhinum majus*	Turnip	*Brassica rapa*
Sorghum	*Sorghum bicolor*	Vetch	
	S. vulgare	Common	*Vicia sativa*
Soybean	*Glycine max*	Hairy	*V. villosa*
Spicebush, Japanese	*Lindera obtusiloba*	Hungarian	*V. pannonica*
Spiderwort	*Tradescantia paludosa*	Narrow leaf	*V. angustifolia*
Virginia	*T. virginiana*	One-flower	*V. articulata*
Spikemoss	*Selaginella selaginoides*	Purple	*V. benghalensis*
Spinach	*Spinacia oleracea*	Tiny	*V. hirsuta*
Spruce		Wooly pod	*V. dasycarpa*
Norway	*Picea abies*	Violet, field	*Viola arvensis*
Red	*P. rubens*	Walnut, eastern black	*Juglans nigra*
Sitka	*P. sitchensis*	Waterlily	*Nymphaea alba*
White	*P. glauca*	Watermelon	*Citrullus vulgaris*
Spurge, South American	*Sebastiania fruticosa*	Waterweed, Canadian	*Elodea canadensis*
Spurry, corn	*Spergula avensis*	Wheat	*Triticum aestivum*
Sterculia, hazel	*Sterculia foetida*	Willow	
Stillingia	*Stillingia sp.*	Basket	*Salix viminalis*
Stock, common	*Matthiola incana*	Big catkin	*S. gracilistyla*
Strawberry		Black	*S. nigra*
Chiloe	*Fragaria chiloensis*	Pussy	*S. discolor*
Pine	*F. ananassa*	White	*S. alba*
Strophanthus	*Strophanthus glaber*	Yellow trumpet, Florida	*Stenolobium stans*
Arrow poison	*S. sarmentosus*	Yew	
Sugarcane	*Saccharum officinarum*	English	*Taxus baccata*
Sumac	*Rhus sp.*	Pacific	*T. brevifolia*
Sunflower, common	*Helianthus annuus*	Yucca	*Yucca sp.*
Sweetcane	*Saccharum spontaneum*	Zinnia, oblong leaf	*Zinnia angustifolia*
Sweetgum, American	*Liquidambar styraciflua*		
Sweet potato	*Ipomoea batatas*		

PLANTS AND POLLUTION

One way scientists have been watching the world's pollution problems is by watching plants. Because plants, like humans, "breathe" and use the gases in the atmosphere to survive, they are susceptible to air pollution. One problem is that pollutants, such as those found in smog, reduce the amount of sunlight reaching the plant. This type of pollution may also deter the exchange of gases in the leaf by clogging the stomata and preventing them from functioning. Smog can also increase the production of ozone, which damages the thin-walled (palisade) cells of the plant.

Other damage to plants from pollution includes certain chemicals that are absorbed into the plant. For example, fluorides from the manufacture of phosphates, steel, and aluminum can cause leaf tissue to collapse by inhibiting the enzymes needed for cellulose synthesis. Acid rain, produced especially by the sulfur and nitrous oxides from the burning of fossil fuels, kills plants by burning them with acid-tainted rain.

Poisonous Cultivated and Wild Plants

The following is a list of poisonous plants, including which portions, or areas, of the plant are toxic; the symptoms of the illnesses they cause; and which plants are, or may be, fatal. In addition, apple, cherry, apricot, peach, and plum seeds contain cyanide—the most deadly nonradioactive poison known.

Plants	Toxic Portions	Symptoms of Illness; Degree of Toxicity
Autumn crocus	Bulbs	Nausea, vomiting, diarrhea; may be fatal
Azalea	All parts	Nausea, vomiting, depression, breathing difficulty, prostration, coma; fatal
Belladonna	Young plants, seeds	Nausea, twitching muscles, paralysis; fatal
Bittersweet	Leaves, seeds, roots	Vomiting, diarrhea, chills, convulsions, coma
Bleeding heart (Dutchman's-breeches)	Foliage, roots	Nervous symptoms, convulsions
Buttercups	All parts	Digestive system injury
Caladium	All parts	Intense burning and irritation of the tongue and mouth; can be fatal if the base of the tongue swells, blocking air passage of the throat
Castor bean	Seeds, foliage	Burning in mouth, convulsions; fatal
Cherry	Twigs, foliage	Gasping, excitement, prostration
Daffodil	Bulbs	Nausea, vomiting, diarrhea; may be fatal
Daphne	Berries (red or yellow)	Severe burns to mouth and digestive tract followed by coma; fatal
Death camas (black snakeroot)	All parts	Nausea, severe upset
Delphinium	Young plants, seeds	Nausea, twitching muscles, paralysis; fatal
Dumbcane (dieffenbachia)	All parts	Intense burning and irritation of the tongue and mouth; fatal if the base of the tongue swells, blocking air passage of the throat
Elderberry	Roots	Nausea and digestive upset
Elephant ear	All parts	Intense burning and irritation of the tongue and mouth; fatal if the base of the tongue swells, blocking air passage of the throat
English holly	Berries	Severe gastroenteritis
English ivy	Leaves, berries	Stomach pains, labored breathing, possible coma
Foxglove	Leaves, seeds, flowers	Irregular heartbeat and pulse, usually accompanied by digestive upset and mental confusion; may be fatal
Goldenchain	All parts, especially seeds	Excitement, staggering convulsions, coma; may be fatal
Horse chestnut	All parts	Nausea, twitching muscles, sometimes paralysis
Hyacinth	Bulbs	Nausea, vomiting, diarrhea; may be fatal
Hydrangea	Buds, leaves, branches	Severe digestive upset, gasping, convulsions; may be fatal

Poisonous Cultivated and Wild Plants (cont'd)

Plants	Toxic Portions	Symptoms of Illness; Degree of Toxicity
Iris	Freshly underground portions	Severe but not usually serious digestive upset
Jack-in-the-pulpit	All parts, especially roots	Intense irritation and burning of the tongue and mouth
Jerusalem cherry	All parts (especially the berries)	Nausea, vomiting, often fatal, especially to children
Jimson weed (thorn apple, datura, stinkweed, Jamestown weed)	All parts	Abnormal thirst, distortion of vision, delirium, incoherence, coma; may be fatal
Larkspur	Young plants, seeds	Nausea, twitching muscles, paralysis; fatal
Laurel	All parts	Nausea, vomiting, depression, breathing difficulty, prostration, coma; fatal
Lily of the valley	Leaves, flowers	Irregular heartbeat and pulse usually accompanied by digestive upset and mental confusion; may be fatal
Mayapple	Unripe apples, leaves and roots	Diarrhea, severe digestive upset
Mistletoe	All parts, especially berries	Fatal
Moonseed	Fruits, seeds	Nausea, vomiting; may be fatal
Monkshood	All parts, especially roots	Digestive upset and nervous excitement: juice in plant parts is fatal
Morning glory	Seeds	Large amounts cause severe mental disturbances; fatal
Mushrooms, wild	All parts of many varieties	Fatal
Narcissus	Bulbs	Nausea, vomiting, diarrhea; may be fatal
Nightshade (climbing nightshade, bittersweet nightshade)	All parts, especially unripe berries	Intense digestive disturbances and nervous symptoms; often fatal
Oak	Foliage, acorns	Gradual kidney failure
Oleander	All parts	Severe digestive upset, heart trouble, contact dermatitis; fatal
Philodendron	All parts	Intense burning and irritation of the tongue and mouth; fatal if the base of the tongue swells, blocking air passage of the throat
Poinsettia	All parts	Severe digestive upset; fatal
Poison hemlock	All parts	Stomach pains, vomiting, paralysis of the central nervous system; may be fatal
Poison ivy and oak	All parts	Intense itching, watery blisters, red rash
Poison sumac	All parts	Rash, intense itching; vomiting, may be fatal
Pokeweed	All parts	Severe digestive upset; often fatal
Poppy	Foliage, roots	Nervous symptoms, convulsions
Potato	Foliage, green parts of vegetable	Intense digestive disturbances, nervous symptoms
Privet	Berries, leaves	Mild to severe digestive disturbances; may be fatal

Plants	Toxic Portions	Symptoms of Illness; Degree of Toxicity
Rhododendron	All parts	Nausea, vomiting, depression, breathing difficulty, prostration, coma; fatal (eating honey from flowers may make some ill)
Rhubarb	Leaf blade	Kidney disorder, convulsions, coma; fatal
Rosary pea	Seeds, foliage	Burning in mouth, convulsions; fatal
Snowdrop	Bulbs	Vomiting, nervous excitement
Tomato	Vines	Digestive upset, nervous disorders
White snakeroot	All parts	Nausea, vomiting; may be fatal; one of the most common causes of death among early settlers
Wisteria	Seeds, pods	Mild to severe digestive disturbances
Yellow jessamine	All parts	Nausea, vomiting; often fatal; some may become ill from honey made from the nector of blossoms
Yew	Berry, contains brownish black seed	Seed fatal to eat; die in minutes

Common Herbs

Botanists describe herbs as seed plants with nonwoody stems. Like all plants, herbs can be classified as annuals, perennials, tender perennials, and biennials.

The more popular meaning of *herb* is a plant with culinary, medicinal, and/or other nonfood use. This following is a list of common herbs.

Common Name*	Scientific Name	Common Uses
Angelica (P)	Angelica archangelica	Culinary, tea, fragrance
Anise (A)	Pimpinella anisum	Culinary, tea
Basil (A)	Ocimum sp.	Culinary, ornamental
Bay, laurel (sweet, Grecian) (P)	Laurus nobilis	Culinary, ornamental
Bee balm (bergamot, horsemint, Oswego tea) (P)	Monarda didyma	Ornamental, tea, culinary
Borage (A)	Borago officinalis	Ornamental, culinary, tea
Caraway (A, B)	Carum carvi	Culinary
Catnip (P)	Nepeta cataria	Tea, dye
Chamomile (P, A)	Chamaemelum nobile; Martricaria recutita (German chamomile)	Tea, ornamental, cosmetic
Chervil (gourmet's parsley) (A)	Anthriscus cerefolium	Culinary
Chili peppers (A)	Capsicum sp.	Culinary, medicinal
Chives (P)	Allium schoenoprasum	Culinary, ornamental, flower arrangements
Coriander (A)	Coriandrum sativum	Culinary
Cumin (A)	Cuminum cyminum	Culinary
Dill (A)	Anethum graveolens	Culinary
Fennel (A)	Foeniculum vulgare	Culinary
Fenugreek (TA)	Trigonella foenum-graecum	Culinary, dye
Feverfew (P)	Chrysanthemum parthenium	Ornamental, medicinal
Flax (A)	Linum usitatissimum	Ornamental, oil, fibers
Foxglove (B)	Digitalis sp.	Ornamental, medicinal

Common Name*	Scientific Name	Common Uses
Garlic (P)	*Allium sativum*	Culinary
Geraniums** (TP)	*Pelargonium sp.*	Fragrance, ornamental
Ginger (P)	*Zingiber officinale*	Culinary
Hollyhock (P)	*Alcea rosea*	Ornamental
Horehound (P)	*Marrubium vulgare*	Culinary, ornamental
Horseradish (P)	*Armoracia rusticana*	Culinary
Hyssop (P)	*Hyssopus officinalis*	Aromatic oils, culinary, ornamental, medicinal
Lady's bedstraw (P)	*Galium verum*	Dye, ornamental
Lady's mantle (P)	*Alchemilla mollis*	Ornamental, medicinal
Lavender (P)	*Lavandula angustifolia*	Ornamental, fragrance, culinary
Lemon balm (P)	*Melissa officinalis*	Fragrance, tea, ornamental
Lemongrass (fevergrass) (P)	*Cymbopogon citratus*	Culinary, cosmetic, tea
Lovage (P)	*Levisticum officinale*	Culinary
Marjoram (sweet, garden, annual) (P)	*Origanum majorana*	Culinary, tea, dye, ornamental
Mint†(P)	*Mentha sp.*	Culinary, tea, ornamental
Mustard (A)	*Brassica sp.*	Culinary
Nasturtium (A)	*Tropaeolum majus*	Ornamental, culinary, medicinal
Oregano (wild marjoram) (P)	*Origanum sp.*	Culinary
Parsley (A)	*Petroselinum sp.*	Culinary, ornamental
Peony (P)	*Paeonia officinalis*	Ornamental
Poppy (P)	*Papaver sp.*	Ornamental
Rosemary (P)	*Rosmarinus officinalis*	Culinary, ornamental, cosmetic
Rue (herb o' grace) (P)	*Ruta graveolens*	Ornamental, culinary, dye
Saffron (P)	*Crocus sativus*	Culinary
Sage (P)	*Salvia officinalis*	Culinary, ornamental, fragrance
Savory (P)	*Satureja sp.*	Culinary, ornamental
Sesame (P)	*Sesamum indicum*	Culinary
Shallot (P)	*Allium ascalonicum*	Culinary
Sorrel (P)	*Rumex sp.*	Culinary
Southernwood (P) (old man, lad's love, boy's love)	*Artemisia abrotanum*	Fragrance, ornamental, culinary
Tansy (P)	*Tanacetum vulgare*	Ornamental, dye
Tarragon, French(P)	*Artemisia dracunculus*	Culinary
Thyme‡ (P)	*Thymus sp.*	Culinary, ornamental
Turmeric (P)	*Curcuma domestica*	Culinary, dye
Violet(P)	*Viola odorata*	Ornamental, fragrance, culinary
Watercress (P)	*Nasturtium officinale*	Culinary
Yarrow(P)	*Achillea millefolium*	Ornamental, medicinal, dye

*P, perennial; A, annual; B, biennial; TP, tender perennial; TA, tender annual.

**There are many kinds of scented geranium, including rose, peppermint, lime, apple, lemon, coconut, nutmeg, orange, apricot, and almond.

†There are many kinds of mint, including water, field (corn), Japanese, Scotch, golden, horse (hairy), peppermint, pennyroyal, Corsican, spearmint, curly, apple (woolly), and pineapple.

‡There are many kinds of thyme, including creeping, caraway, lemon, mother of thyme, and woolly.

Germination Tables for Flowers and Vegetables

Annual Flowers

	Approximate Number of Days Until Germination		Approximate Number of Days Until Germination
Acrolinium	8–10	Gaillardia	12–15
Ageratum	7–11	Gomphrena	20–25
Alyssum, sweet	10–13	Helichrysum	5–10
Browallia	18–20	Larkspur	15–20
Cacalia	8–12	Lupine	25–30
Calendula	10–12	Marigold	5–8
California poppy	5–10	Nicotiana	20–25
Candytuft	6–9	Petunia	18–20
Canterburybell	12–15	Phlox Drummondi	20–25
Celosia (coxcomb)	20–25	Pinks	5–8
Centaurea (ragged robin)	5–20	Portulaca	18–20
Chrysanthemum	6–8	Scabiosa	18–20
Cosmos	5–15	Snapdragon	20–25
Cynoglossum	11–15	Sweetpea	15–20
Flax	13–16	Verbena	8–10
Four-o'clock	12–15	Zinnia	5–8

Vegetable Garden Plants

	Approximate Number of Days Until Germination		Approximate Number of Days Until Germination
Asparagus	21–28	Kohlrabi	6–8
Beans, bush	6–10	Lettuce	6–10
Beans, bush lima	6–10	Muskmelon	6–10
Beans, pole	6–10	Mustard	4–5
Beans, pole lima	7–12	Okra	15–20
Beets	7–10	Onion	8–12
Broccoli	6–10	Parsley	18–24
Brussels sprouts	6–10	Parsnip	12–18
Cabbage	6–10	Peas	6–10
Cabbage, Chinese	6–10	Pepper	10–14
Carrots	10–15	Pumpkin	6–10
Cauliflower	6–10	Radish	4–6
Celery	12–20	Rhubarb	12–14
Chard, Swiss	7–10	Rutabaga	4–7
Collards	6–10	Spinach	6–12
Corn, sweet	7–12	Squash, bush	6–10
Cress, garden	4–5	Squash, vine	6–10
Cucumber	6–8	Tomato	6–10
Eggplant	10–15	Turnip	4–7
Endive	8–12	Watermelon	8–12

THE ANIMAL KINGDOM

What Is Zoology?

Zoology is the branch of biological science that studies animal life. It includes the structure, development, classification, physiology, and other characteristics of animal species (for more information on humans, see Chapter 5, "The Human Body and Biomedical Science").

Animal Reproduction

Not all organisms reproduce strictly sexual or asexually. Some species alternate between reproducing sexually and asexually.

Sexual Reproduction

Sexual reproduction in animals generally requires both a male and female to produce offspring. Specialized cells are located in the testes of the male and the ovaries of the female. These cells undergo a type of cell division called meiosis and create gametes. In males, the result is sperm, and in females, ova (eggs). For sexual reproduction to occur, these specialized cells must unite; only one sperm cell can fertilize an egg. When a sperm cell penetrates the egg, it creates a diploid zygote (for a full discussion on human reproduction, see Chapter 5, "The Human Body and Biomedical Science").

Asexual Reproduction

Asexual reproduction in animals is simpler than sexual reproduction because it involves a single organism. Every mature asexual individual can reproduce, often allowing the population of asexual organisms to increase more rapidly than a sexual population.

When an asexual organism divides, it produces two genetically identical replicas of itself (e.g., amoebae). Other organisms produce asexually reproductive cells known as spores that float in the air or water, and eventually produce genetic replicas of the parent. Budding also creates another distinct, yet identical, individual, as the parent spouts smaller offspring that eventually separate from it (e.g., hydras). Still other organisms reproduce by fragmentation—in which pieces of the organism can regenerate into whole organisms (e.g., starfish).

Invertebrates

Any organism that does not have a backbone (spinal column) and is made up of more than one cell is called an invertebrate. Invertebrates make up 95 percent of all animal species; of the 20 phyla, the two largest are Arthropoda and Mollusca. Some of the more well-known invertebrate phyla are discussed below (in alphabetical order).

Phylum: Annelida

Annelids, or segmented worms, include earthworms, leeches, and marine worms. These worms have soft bodies, are symmetrical, and can be anywhere from $1/32$ inch (0.5 millimeter) to 10 feet (3 meters) in length. Earthworms are seen on sidewalks and driveways during periods of heavy rain because the water seeps into the soil and cuts off their oxygen.

Phylum: Arthropoda

Arthropods, or animals with multi-jointed segmented limbs, are the largest group of invertebrates and comprise almost 80 percent of all animal species. They have segmented bodies covered by exoskeletons (or external skeletons) that are molted from time to time to allow the arthropod to grow. They have paired appendages for increased mobility, protection, and feeding. This group includes spiders, horseshoe crabs, crustaceans, insects, and centipedes. It is thought that arthropods were some of the first animals to adapt to land millions of years ago.

Insects are the most successful arthropods. It is estimated that the total number of insects on Earth is close to 10^{18}—or 1 billion insects for every human being. Within the insects, the order Coleoptera (beetles) is the largest; there are more species of beetles than of any other species on Earth.

THE REAL KILLER BEES

Killer bees (officially called Africanized honeybees) originated in Brazil in 1956 as an experiment to mate the African honeybee with local bees. The breeders were hoping to get a bee that would produce more honey in the tropics. Instead, they produced aggressive bees that have been known to attack people and animals. Each year, the bees move about 350 miles (563 kilometers) north; in 1990, they came over the U.S. border and into Hidalgo, Texas.

The popular name "killer bee" has not been beneficial to the insects. In fact, there are many myths about these bees. For example, they do not fly faster than other domestic (usually European) honeybees (they all average between 12 and 15 miles, or 19 and 24 kilometers, per hour), their sting has less venom than that of a domestic honeybee, and they are smaller than domestic honeybees.

Killer bees do have some features that make them an insect to watch. When a bee's body is crushed, from a swat, for example, it releases an odor that incites other bees to attack. Although these bees do not seek out victims, they will protect their hive vigorously (about 10 times as many African bees as European bees will sting when the colonies are equally disturbed). However, scientists also believe that the killer bees' aggressiveness will eventually diminish as they interbreed with the more placid European bees to the north.

Phylum: Coelenterata

Coelenterates are mostly marine invertebrates, including jellyfish, sea anemones, and corals. They are characterized by three-layered body walls, tentacles, primitive nervous systems, and special stinger cells (used for protection). Some coelenterates, such as corals, are zoophytes, or animals that resemble plants.

Phylum: Echinodermata

Echinoderms are marine invertebrates that live on the ocean floor. They have no head, and have tube feet and skeletons that are just below the surface of the outer layer. If any part of an echinoderm's body is cut off, the individual can regenerate that part. Members of this phylum include starfish, sea urchins, sand dollars, and sea cucumbers.

Phylum: Mollusca

Most mollusks live in water or at the tidal zone of a shoreline. They live inside shells and have soft, unsegmented bodies and a powerful foot that enables them to move around. Mollusks include clams, oysters, scallops, bivalves (whose shells have two similar halves, or valves; e.g., mussels), gastropods (both land and sea snails), and squid. Octopuses and cuttlefish, whose shell is enclosed by the body, are two of the most advanced mollusks. One of the largest marine invertebrates known is the squid of the genus *Architeuthis*: The largest ever found measured 70 feet (21.3 meters) long; some may even be longer.

Phylum: Nematoda

Roundworms, with about 10,000 known species, are wormlike animals that have an outer coat made of noncellular material and a fluid-filled chamber that separates their body walls from their insides. They live both in water and on land. This phylum includes rotifers (although in some classifications, rotifers are a separate phylum), nematodes, and horsehair worms.

Phylum: Platyhelminthes

Flatworms are primitive organisms that are flat, soft-bodied, and symmetrical. There are four classes of flatworms: one aquatic class (planarians), two parasitic classes (flukes), and one class of tapeworms.

Phylum: Porifera

In the eighteenth century, sponges were thought to be plants, but we now know that they are animals. They live mostly in colonies in the water, attached to rocks. They look similar to a sack, and take in water through small holes in their body. A hard skeleton is formed by substances that become stuck to their body walls.

The Vertebrates

Vertebrates are animals that have a backbone (spinal cord). They include the following classes: amphibians, birds, fish (three classes), mammals, and reptiles. Scientists believe that the first vertebrate was the conodont, an eel that was 1 to 2 inches (2.5 to 5 centimeters) long and lived between about 515 and 200 million years ago. Conodonts had sawlike teeth and a finned tail; the presence of the bone cells, but no true bone structure, makes it one the first vertebrates.

Class: Amphibia

There are about 4,000 known species of amphibians. Millions of years ago, amphibians were the first animals to leave the oceans and move to land. They were also the first vertebrates to have lungs, true legs, tongues, ears, and voice boxes.

Amphibians are usually streamlined and cold-blooded (poikilothermic), with moist, scaleless skin (which is not waterproof). They lay their eggs in water, where the young hatch. When—as adults—they loose the ability to breathe under water, they live both on land and in the water. (There are exceptions: More than 60 species of South and Central American tree frogs are marsupials—the eggs develop on the mother's back, often in pouches.) The majority of amphibians breathe with gills as larvae and with lungs as adults. Amphibians include frogs, toads, newts, salamanders, mudpuppies, sirens, and caecilians.

The largest amphibian is the giant salamander, *Andrias japanicus*, which can grow to about 6 feet (1.8 meters) long, and lives in mountain streams in Japan. The shortest amphibian (and the smallest frog) is the *Sminthillus limbatus*, from Cuba, and is only $1/2$ inch (1.2 centimeters) in length.

Class: Aves

Birds are controversial animals: No one really knows how the 28 orders of birds are related in evolutionary terms. One of the oldest ancestors of the bird, dating to about 150 million years ago, is thought to be the *Archaeopteryx* (some scientists, however, believe that this fossil animal was a small dinosaur). The *Archaeopteryx* had teeth, a reptilian tail, and three claws on each wing like a reptile. It had feathers and a distinct wishbone (an indicator of flight, though it probably was not a strong flier). The origins of the creature are still debated, as only five fossils have been found. Two other birdlike fossils were found in 1990, in Texas, called *Protoavis texensis*. They are thought to be ancestors of birds and are 75 million years older than the *Archaeopteryx*.

Because of the fossil evidence, many scientists believe that birds are descendants of reptiles. Similar to modern birds, ancient birds had scales on their feet, a single ball-and-socket articulation between the skull and neck, a simple middle ear of just one bone (mammals have three bones), and reproduced by laying eggs.

Modern birds vary widely in the foods they eat, nesting sites, migratory paths, calls and songs, and ability to survive habitat changes. Generally, though, most birds have some similar characteristics: a fast metabolism (most birds eat high-energy food such as fruits, seeds, insects, and fish, and digest it quickly), light bones and overall body weight (birds' bones have a honeycomb structure that reduces weight), wings (which are highly modified forelimbs), feathers (for flight, insulation, display, and camouflage), and streamlining (including contoured feathers, flying with the feet close to the body, and lack of external ears).

Classes: Agnatha, Chondrichthyes, and Osteichthyes

Agnatha are the most primitive of fish and are jawless. Chondrichthyes are animals with cartilage but no true bones, such as sharks and rays. Osteichthyes are bony fish.

There are close to 21,000 different species of fish. Fish are probably descendants of the jawless fishes that lived about 425 million years ago (there is disagreement because of a lack of fossil evidence). About 400 million years ago, fish (with and without backbones) were the most plentiful and advanced forms of life. Bony fish are thought to have evolved in freshwater rivers and lakes, then later moved to the ocean.

Fish are very adaptable to their surrounding environment and have retained, in general, the same shapes throughout Earth's history. They breathe dissolved oxygen from water with the use of gills. They have mostly translucent scales arranged in rows along the length of their bodies and have eyes that are adapted to see underwater (some surface fish can see both in water and air). Fish diets vary, depending on the species—from suspended particles of plant and animal material, seaweeds, and other fish to marine mammals. Their method of obtaining food is also species dependent. For example, most sharks depend on smell to find food while some fish even use electric fields to detect prey.

Class: Mammalia

The class Mammalia is a large group of warm-blooded vertebrates often characterized by mammary glands, a covering of hair, and special characteristics of the middle ear, red blood cells, and embryonic development. Mammals first developed from reptiles around 200 million years ago and now include about 4,000 species (see also "Orders of Mammals," later in this chapter).

Class: Reptilia

Reptiles ruled the Earth about 300 million years ago. The first true reptile is thought to have been the *Hylonomus*, a lizardlike creature about 27 inches (70 centimeters) long. About 65 million years ago, many of the larger reptiles became extinct because of natural disasters. Today, there are close to 6,000 species of reptiles living on Earth. They include turtles, lizards, tuatara, worm lizards, snakes, and crocodiles.

Modern reptiles are much smaller than some of their largest ancestors. For example, dinosaurs and pterosaurs were as long as 80 to 90 feet (24 to 27 meters). The largest reptiles today are the crocodiles (including gavials, caimans, and alligators) and certain pythons (including the reticulated python, *Python reticulatus*)—none of which usually measures more than 33 feet (10 meters) in length.

Reptiles are considered cold blooded, or poikilothermic (the temperature of their bodies vary with the temperature of the environment), and ectothermic (the reptile's body warmth depends on an external source, such as the Sun). In reality, most reptiles are not truly cold blooded. They are able to regulate their body heat to some extent; their body processes generally operate under optimum temperature ranges. For example, snakes need heat to digest food. If the snake gets too cold it can die because the food rots in its stomach.

Generally, reptiles have five-toed limbs, eyelids, and external ears; they are covered with small scales on top and underneath. Their legs protrude outward, resulting in a waddle and twist when they walk. Most are carnivorous, but some are herbivores.

Generally, snakes are legless, have transparent and permanently closed eyelids, and a row of ridged scales underneath their bodies. They swallow their prey whole and are all carnivorous.

ANIMAL PATTERNS

Animals follow daily patterns, much as humans do, but these patterns are set by the rhythms of nature. For example, various animals tend to be active at a certain time of day, especially in their search for food. *Diurnal* animals, such as songbirds, bears, and rabbits, are active during the daytime. *Nocturnal* animals, such as owls, certain mice, and raccoons, are more active at night. *Crepuscular* animals, such as deer and certain birds (nighthawks), are active in the twilight hours.

There is a distinct advantage in these staggered schedules, since they allow several species to occupy the same site without interfering with one another. This allows for a greater diversity of species within a particular area and increases the chances of survival by adding to the number of occupants in the local food chain.

Orders of Mammals

Animals with backbones are chordates—that is, they belong to the phylum Cordata. Their subphylum is Vertebrata (segmented backbones) and below that, is the class Mammalia. Mammals are the most highly advanced organisms on Earth. They are warm blooded, suckle their young, have relatively large brains, and have four-chambered hearts.

The various orders of mammals are discussed (in alphabetical order) in the paragraphs that follow. Orders are made up of families, and the Latin names of these families, along with some representative animals, are provided. (**Note:** Not all classifications include the same orders; for example, some classifications list pouched and egg-laying mammals as orders.)

Order: Artiodactyla

The order Artiodactyla is made up of the even-toed ungulates. Both ruminators (animals that chew a cud and have a stomach with three or four cavities) and nonrumiators fall into this order. Ruminators include the families Girrafidae (giraffes), Cervidae (deer, moose, elk, reindeer), Antilocapridae (pronghorn antelope), and Bovidae (cattle, bison, waterbucks, gazelles, yaks, sheep, wildebeest, springboks, musk oxen, goats). Nonruminators include the families Suidae (pigs), Tayassuidae (peccaries), Hippopotamidae (hippopotamuses), and Camelidae (camels, llamas).

Order: Carnivora (meat-eaters)

Two of the infraorders under Carnivora (the meat eaters) divide the land carnivores into the Arctoidea (relatives of dogs) and the Aeluroidea (relatives of cats). The first is characterized by long snouts and unretractable claws and includes the following families: Canidae (wolves, dogs, jackals, foxes), Ursidae (bears, giant pandas; there is some disagreement to the ancestry of the giant panda), Procyonidae (raccoons, coatis, lesser pandas), and Mustelidae (weasels, skunks, otters, martens). The second infraorder, characterized by retractable claws, includes the Felidae (cats, lions, cheetahs, leopards), Hyaenidae (hyenas), and Viverridae (mongooses, civets).

Order: Cetacea (whales and porpoises)

The order Cetacea includes some of the marine mammals and is divided into two suborders. The first is made up of the toothed whales (with regular conical teeth): Physeteridae (sperm whales), Monodontidae (belugas, narwhals), Phocoenidae (porpoises), and Delphinidae (dolphins, orcas). The second suborder is made up of the baleen, or whalebone, whales (with baleen instead of teeth): Balaenoptridae (fin-backed whales, humpback whales), Balaenidae (right whales), and Eschrichtiidae (gray whales).

Order: Chiroptera (bats)

Bats, the only mammals that can truly fly, fall into two suborders. Megachiroptera contains one family, the Pteropodidae (flying foxes, Old World fruit bats). Microchiroptera has 17 families, including Rhinopomatidae (mouse-tailed bats), Emballonuridae (sheath-tailed bats), Craseonycteridae (hog-nosed or butterfly bats), Noctilionidae (bulldog or fisherman bats), Nycteridae (slit-faced bats), Megadermatidae (false vampire bats), and Rhinolophidae (horseshoe bats). The greatest difference in flying technique between bats and birds is that birds use two large pairs of muscles to fly; the more acrobatic bats use four large pairs and several smaller muscles to fly.

Order: Dermoptera (colugos or flying lemurs)

The order Dermoptera includes the Asian animals colugos and flying lemurs, although these gliding tree mammals do not truly fly and are not lemurs. The family is Cynocephalidae.

Order: Edentata (toothless mammals)

Families of Edentata (mammals without teeth) include Dasypodidae (armadillos), Bradypodidae (sloths), and Myrmecophagidae (hairy anteaters).

Order: Hyracoidae (hyraxes and dassies)

The Hyracoidae are small hoofed animals, including the hyraxes and dassies in the family Procaviidae. It is one of three orders of mammals that has only one modern family remaining. The African rock hyrax (*Procavia capensis*) is one of nine living species in this family.

Order: Insectivora (insect-eaters)

There are three families of Insectivora (the insect eaters): Talpidae (moles), Soricidae (shrews), and Erinaceidae (hedgehogs).

Order: Lagomorpha (pikas, hares, and rabbits)

The families Ochotonidae (pikas) and Leporidae (hares and numerous types of rabbits) make up the order Lagomorpha.

Order: Perissodactyla

The order Perissodactyla (odd-toed ungulates) include these families: Equidae (horses, donkeys, zebras), Tapiridae (tapirs), Rhinocerotidae (rhinoceroses). There are two suborders: Hippomorpha and Ceratomorpha.

Order: Pholidata (pangolins)

The only family in the order Pholidata is the Manidae (pangolins).

Order: Pinnipedia (seals and walruses) (sometimes a suborder)

These fin-footed mammals include the families of Otariidae (eared seals, sea lions), Odobenidae (walruses), and Phocidae (earless seals).

Order: Primates (primates)

The order Primates is divided into two suborders: Prosimii (primates with longer snouts) includes the families Tupalidae (tree shrew), Lemuridae (lemurs), Daubentonlidae (aye-ayes), Lorisidae (lorises, pottos), and Tarsiidae (tarsiers). The other suborder is the Anthropoidea, which have shorter snouts; it includes the families Callitrichidae (marmosets), Cebidae (New World monkeys), Cercopithecidae (Old World monkeys), Hylobatidae (gibbons), Pongidae (gorillas, chimpanzees, orangutans), and Hominidae (human beings).

Order: Proboscidea (elephants)

The order Proboscidea includes the family *Elephantidae* (elephants).

Order: Rodentia (gnawing mammals)

The Rodentia is the most prolific mammalian order and is divided into three suborders. The families include Aplodontidae (mountain beavers), Sciuridae (chipmunks, squirrels, marmots), Cricetidae (field mice, lemmings, muskrats, hamsters, gerbils), Muridae (Old World mice, rats), Heteromyidae (New World mice), Geomyidae (gophers), and Dipodidae (jerboas).

Order: Sirenia (dugongs and manatees)

The order Sirenia is divided into two families: Trichechidae (manatees) and Dugongidae (dugongs and other sea cows).

Order: Tubulidentata (aardvarks)

The order Tubulindentata is made up of the family Orycteropodidae (aardvarks).

*Subclasses of Mammals**

Subclass: Marsupialia (pouched mammals)

Marsupials, mammals that carry their young in a pouch, include the following families: Caenolestidae (rat opossums), Diddeelphidae (true opossums), Dasyuridae (native cates, native mice), Notoryctidae (marsupial moles), Myrmecobiidae (numbats), Peramelidae (bandicoots), Phalangeridae (koalas), Vombatidae (wombats), and Macropodidae (kangaroos, wallabies).

Subclass: Monotremata (egg-laying mammals)

The Monotremata are the rare, egg-laying mammals. Families in this order include Tachyglossidae (echidnas, or spiny anteaters) and Ornithorhynchidae (platypuses).

These subclasses are considered orders in some classifications.

Mammal Gestation Periods

Note: The first chart is listed alphabetically by animal; the second chart is listed from shortest to longest gestation periods.

Mammal	Gestation Period	
	Months	Days
Armadillo	2 to 4	60 to 120
Ass	11.5	340
Baboon	5 to 6	150 to 183
Bear		
Grizzly	7	210 to 265
Polar	8	240
American black	7	210 to 215
Beaver	3.5	105
Bobcat	2	60 to 63
Cat	2	52
Cattle	9.25	238
Cheetah	3	91 to 95
Chimpanzee	7.5	230 to 240
Dog	2	53 to 71
Dolphin	10 to 12	305 to 365
Dormouse	—	21 to 32
Elephant	21.7	650 to 660 days
Fox, red	2	60 to 63
Gerbil	—	21 to 28
Giraffe	15.25	453 to 464
Goat	5	150
Gopher	—	12 to 20
Guinea pig	2	63
Hamster	—	15 to 37
Hippopotamus	8	240
Horse	11.5	340
Kangaroo	6 to 11	183 to 325
Koala	1.25	34 to 36
Lion	3.5	100 to 119
Llama	11.5 to 12.25	348 to 368
Mouse	—	20 to 30
Opossum, American	—	12 to 13
Panda	4.5	125 to 150
Pig	3.25	101 to 129
Rabbit	1	30
Raccoon	2	63
Rat	—	23 to 25
Reindeer	7 to 8	210 to 240
Rhinoceros, black	15	450
Sheep	4.5 to 5	135 to 160
Skunk	2	62 to 66
Squirrel	1.33	40
Tiger	3.5	103
Whale, most	10 to 12	305 to 365
Beluga	14 to 15	420 to 450
Sperm	14 to 15	420 to 450
Wolf	2	61 to 63
Zebra	11.5	340

Mammal Gestation Periods (cont'd)

Gestation Period		Mammal
Months	**Days**	
—	12 to 13	American opossum
—	12 to 20	Gopher
—	15 to 37	Hamster
—	20 to 30	Mouse
—	21 to 28	Gerbil
—	21 to 32	Dormouse
—	23 to 25	Rat
1	30	Rabbit
1.25	34 to 36	Koala
1.33	40	Squirrel
2	52	Cat
2	53 to 71	Dog
2	60 to 63	Bobcat
2	60 to 63	Fox, red
2	61 to 63	Wolf
2	62 to 66	Skunk
2	63	Guinea pig
2	63	Raccoon
2 to 4	60 to 120	Armadillo
3	91 to 95	Cheetah
3.25	101 to 129	Pig
3.5	100 to 119	Lion
3.5	103	Tiger
3.5	105	Beaver
4.5	125 to 150	Panda
4.5 to 5	135 to 160	Sheep
5	150	Goat
5 to 6	150 to 183	Baboon
6 to 11	183 to 325	Kangaroo
7	210 to 215	American black bear
7	210 to 265	Grizzly bear
7 to 8	210 to 240	Reindeer
7.5	230 to 240	Chimpanzee
8	240	Hippopotamus
8	240	Polar bear
9.25	238	Cattle
10 to 12	305 to 365	Dolphin
10 to 12	305 to 365	Most whales
11.5	340	Ass
11.5	340	Horse
11.5	340	Zebra
11.5 to 12.25	348 to 368	Llama
14 to 15	420 to 450	Beluga whale
14 to 15	420 to 450	Sperm whale
15	450	Black rhinoceros
15.25	453 to 464	Giraffe
21.7	650 to 660	Elephant

ANIMAL NAVIGATION

How do animals navigate over long distances, such as birds migrating south for the winter or salmon returning to their spawning grounds to breed? Apparently, each creature finds its way in a different manner.

For example, some animals may use the Earth's magnetic field to find their way around. Scientists note that birds often find it difficult to migrate in times of high sunspot activity, when the Sun's magnetic field is extremely active. Birds are apparently born with a magnetic sense—thanks to particles of the magnetic mineral magnetite in their brain cells that may help them to "set" their internal compasses for migration. Some scientists believe that pilot whales also have magnetite in their brain cells—and beachings occur near rock formations that distort the local magnetic fields, fouling the creatures' navigational abilities. Even bacteria in the oceans orient themselves by forming iron minerals that act as a compass, pointing to the North or South Pole (depending on which ocean they inhabit).

Other animals, such as bees and salmon, seem to navigate by the Sun's position in the sky. Some animals, such as birds, may find their way by noting landmarks or, like many mammals, with the help of scent trails. Other birds, such as the shearwaters and petrels, can hear infrasounds—made by ocean waves or wind blowing over sand dunes—which may be how they navigate back to nesting sites.

Poisonous Animals

Numerous animals use poison for protection or to capture their prey. Animal venoms are divided into two types (venom usually contains both types, but one dominates). The *neurotoxic* type acts on the victim's nervous system (the venom stops the heart or lungs), causing little tissue damage. The *hemotoxic* type breaks down the victim's tissues, usually by an acid or a toxin that prevents or causes blood clotting, or destroys red or white blood cells.

black widow spider   The black widow spider is found in Europe, Africa, Asia, Australia, New Zealand, and the Americas; it uses a neurotoxic venom that is about 15 times more toxic than that of a rattlesnake. In humans, the bite causes severe nausea, vomiting, and paralysis, but it is rarely fatal, because only a small amount of poison is injected.

brown spider   The brown spider is found in Europe, Asia, and the Americas; it uses a hemotoxic venom that causes a stinging or burning pain, bleeding, blistering, and ulceration. In extreme cases, the venom causes fever, vomiting, and possible convulsions and heart attack.

cobra   The cobra is found in Asia, Africa, and India; it primarily uses a neurotoxic venom that causes paralysis and then respiratory failure.

European earth salamander   The earth salamander of Europe uses a neurotoxic venom, but its effects on humans are unknown. Its prey experience cardiac arrhythmia, convulsions, paralysis, and death.

puffer fish   The puffer fish is found in the Indian and Pacific Oceans; it uses a neurotoxic poison. A puffer fish is poisonous only when eaten, causing tingling lips and tongue, salivation, vomiting, numbness, muscular paralysis, mental confusion, and in extreme cases, convulsions and death.

short-tailed shrew   The short-tailed shrew is found in North America. There is a neurotoxic venom present in its saliva. The effects are a localized pain or discomfort and a reddening at the wound.

snakes Poisonous snakes are found all over the world. In North America, timber rattlesnakes (most of North America), copperheads (from Massachusetts to Florida, west to Illinois), water moccasins (Virginia to Florida, west to the Gulf of Mexico), and coral snakes (South Carolina to Florida, west to the Gulf) are poisonous. Most snakes carry a hemotoxic poison, but some use a neurotoxic poison (in some species the type of poison depends on the individual). See also *cobra* and *viper*.

viper Vipers are found in Europe, Asia, and Africa. They primarily use a neurotoxic venom that causes a stinging and burning pain, tissue damage, and in extreme cases blood poisoning or heart failure.

Animal Lists

Animal Records

Modern animals come in all sizes—even within the same species—and several species have been on Earth for millions of years. Here are some animal records.

- *Chlamydia* and *Rickettsia* bacteria are the smallest living things and are only a few hundred atoms in diameter.
- The smallest known sea mammal is the Commerson's dolphin (*Cephalorhynchus commersonii*) which averages 50 pounds (237 kilograms). The smallest known land mammal is a virtual tie between the bumblebee (or Kitti's) hog-nosed bat (*Craseonycteris thong longyai*), at 1 inch (2.54 centimeters) long and 0.06 ounces (1.6 grams), and the pygmy shrew (*Suncus erruscus*), which averages about 1.5 inches (3.8 centimeters) long and weighs 0.05 ounces (1.5 grams).
- The deepest mammal divers are the northern elephant seals (*Mirounga angustirostris*), which have reportedly dove to depths of ⁴/₅ mile below the ocean surface.
- The world's longest insect is the *Pharnacia serratipes* of Indonesia. The female can reach up to 13 inches (33 centimeters).
- The longest worms are ribbon worms. The bootlace worm (*Lineus longissimus*) averages about 15 feet (4.6 meters) in length, and some have been reported as large as 100 feet (30.5 meters). In Scotland in 1864, one worm measured more than 180 feet (54.9 meters)—one of the longest animals ever found.
- The oldest inhabitants on Earth are the deep-sea snails (*Neopilina galatheae*). The species is reported not to have changed over the last 500 million years.
- The fastest long-distance animal is the Proghorn American antelope, which averages 45 miles (72 kilometers) per hour; it is able to go longer distances because its lungs and heart are three times the size of a comparable animal. The cheetah is still the fastest land animal on Earth.
- The largest land mammal is the African Bush elephant (*Loxodonta africana*). The elephant averages 10 feet (3.1 meters) tall and weighs about 5.25 tons (4.8 tonnes).
- The baleen whales are the world's largest animals, and include the finback and blue whales. The largest blue whale known was found off the south Atlantic island of South Georgia and measured 110 feet 2 inches (33.6 meters) in length.
- Sperm whales have two records: they have the heaviest brain of any living animal (it weighs more than 20 pounds [9 kilograms] which is about 4 times heavier than the average human brain) and are the world's largest carnivores.
- The world's only cold-blooded adult mammal is the naked mole rat (they are not naked, a rat, or a mole). They live in colonies of about 70 animals in the desert fringes of Somalia, Ethiopia, and Kenya.
- The only cold warm-blooded mammal is the Arctic ground squirrel (*Spermophilus parryii*), which can lower its body temperature below freezing.

FASTEST OF ALL

There are many animals on Earth that hold land and ocean speed records. Some records of species are, for example, the swooping dive of a peregrine falcon that reaches close to 180 miles (290 kilometers) per hour and some species of flying fish that glide up to 32 miles (50 kilometers) per hour. The fastest humans run a maximum of about 23 miles (37 kilometers) per hour.

Other records are held by animals that have developed special abilities.

- Fastest avian swimmer: penguin at 33 feet per second (10 meters per second)
- Fastest known reptile: leatherback turtle at 33 feet per second (10 meters per second)
- Fastest land animal: cheetah at 92 feet per second (28 meters per second)
- Fastest bird (level): spin-tailed swift at 156 feet per second (48 meters per second)
- Fastest diving bird: peregrine falcon at 318 feet per second (97 meters per second)

Animal Lives

How long do animals live? Most animals die from disease, violence, or accident, not from old age—so no one really knows the life span of most animals living in the wild. Some scientists believe that marine animals may have a much longer life span than land animals, because they are supported by water all their lives, while land animals are "worn down" by the effects of gravity.

Currently, the life expectancy at birth for humans in the United States is about 78 years for females and 76 years for males, but that, too, depends on many cultural and health factors. Humans are thought to have an inherited potential to live 150 years; the longest authenticated human life span reached about 120 years (as of 1995). Here are the longest recorded life spans for other species.

Housefly, 0.2 years	Lobster, 50 years
House mouse, 6 years	Termite, 50 years
Golden hamster, 10 years	Horse, 62 years
Goat, 18 years	Ostrich, 62 years
Rabbit, 18 years	Cockatoo, 70 years
Sheep, 20 years	Condor, 70 years
Budgerigar, 28 years	Indian elephant, 70 years
Dog, 29 years	Freshwater oyster, 80 years
Domestic cat, 34 years	Orcas, 90 years
Pigeon, 35 years	Deep-sea clam, 100 years
Cow, 40 years	Fin whale, 115 years
Goldfish, 41 years	Common box tortoise, 138 years
Chimpanzee, 50 years	Marion's tortoise, 150+ years

AMBER AND THE PITS

How do we know about some of the creatures that lived millions of years ago? There are fossils, but scientists have also been helped by two of nature's own preservation substances: tar pits and amber.

Tar pits, especially those at La Brea near Los Angeles, California, have preserved animals such as 14,000-year-old mammoths, saber-toothed cats, and dire wolves. Caught in the mire of the tar, the animals were trapped and sank below the surface; their bones were preserved because the tar pits have little oxygen (that would decay the animals' bones) and because they were protected from erosion.

Amber is actually hardened tree resin (a thick saplike substance) that is found mostly around the Baltic Sea; it is yellow to reddish brown and can be clear to opaque. Amber has been known for 2,000 years, because of its property of producing an electric charge when rubbed. More recently, it has been used for gemstones. But the real interest in amber comes from what is often encased inside: Some of the ancient resin trapped whole anthropods and plant pollens. Besides extracting DNA from the pollen of a 25- to 40-million-year-old now-extinct tree, scientists have extracted some of the oldest fossil DNA from what was inside one of the chunks of hardened resin—a 120 to 135-million-year-old weevil.

Extinct Animals

In the late twentieth century, extinctions are often likely to be the result of human activity. Rural landfills take in urban garbage, open land is blacktopped, factories produce toxins as by-products, and engineers alter waterways. In the tropical forests, the clearing of forests for farming, housing developments, and cattle grazing has contributed to the extinction of numerous species.

These and other activities all have a direct impact on the ecosystems that support animal life. Although there are natural extinctions of organisms, an increased awareness of the impact of human activities and of the fragile links of interdependence among all of Earth's creatures may eventually allow extinctions to level off.

The following lists comprise the number of different animals thought to be extinct since 1500, along with the popular names of those animals. Exact figures are difficult to determine, because endangered species often make the transition to extinction quickly and without notice. Occasionally, populations of animals thought to be extinct are discovered to be extant. In these lists, numbers of varieties are in parentheses.

AMPHIBIANS

Palestinian painted frog   Vegas Valley leopard frog

BIRDS

Akioloa (4)   Gadwall
Alauwahio (2)   Great amakihi
Amazon (3)   Great auk
Bonin night heron   Grosbeak (2)
Caracara   Guadalupe Caraca
Chatham Island bellbird   Guadalupe flicker
Chatham Island fernbird   Guadeloupe rufous-sided towhee
Conure (2)   Heath hen
Courser   Huia
Delalande's coucal   Ivory-billed woodpecker
Dodo (2)   Jamaican pauraqué
Duck (2)   Kioea
Dusky Seaside Sparrow   Laysan apapane
Elephant bird   Laysan millerbird
Emu (2)   Lord Howe Island blackbird
Eskimo curlew   Lord Howe Island fantail
Finch (5)   Macaw (4)
Flycatcher (2)   Mamo (2)

BIRDS (cont'd)

Merganser
Moas (15)
New Caledonian lorikeet
Norfolk Island kaka
Nukupuu (3)
O-O (3)
Oahu akepa
Omao (3)
Ostrich, Arabian
Owl (10)
Painted vulture
Parakeet (8)
Parrot (3)
Petrel
Pigeon (7)
Quail (2)
Quelili
Rail (17)

Réunion fody
Ryukyu kingfisher
Saint Kitts Puerto Rican bullfinch
Sandpiper (2)
São Tomé grosbeak
Serpent eagle
Shelduck
Solitaire (2)
Sparrow (3)
Spectacled cormorant
Starling (6)
Tanna dove
Thrush (2)
Towhee
Ula-ai-hawane
White eye (2)
White gallinule
Wren (6)

FISH

Cisco (2)
Killifish (2)
Lake Titicaca orestias
Minnow (2)
New Zealand grayling
Pupfish (2)

Speckled dace
Spinedace (2)
Sucker (4)
Thicktail chub
Utah Lake sculpin

MAMMALS

Agouti (2)
Arizona jaguar
Aurochs
Badlands bighorn sheep
Bali tiger
Bandicoot (4)
Bat (6)
Bear (3)
Blue buck
Buffalo (2)
Burchell's zebra
Caribbean monk seal
Caucasian wisent
Christmas Island musk shrew
Dawson's caribou
Elk (2)
Greenland tundra reindeer
Hartebeest (2)
Hispaniolan hexolobodon
Hutia (5)

Ibex (2)
Isolobodon (2)
Lion (2)
Nesophont (6)
Potoroo (3)
Puerto Rican caviomorph
Quagga
Quemi (2)
Rat (12)
Rufous gazelle
Schomburgk's deer
Sea mink
Shamanu
Steller's sea cow
Syrian onager
Tarpan
Wallaby (2)
Warrah
Wolf (10)

REPTILES

Ameiva (2)
Galliwasp
Gecko (2)
Iguana (2)
Lizard (4)

Racer snake (2)
Round Island boa
Skink (3)
Tortoise (11)
Tree snake (2)

Endangered Animals

Common Name	Scientific Name	Range
MAMMALS		
Asian wild ass	*Equus hemianus*	Southwestern and Central Asia
Point Arena mountain beaver	*Aplodontis rufa nigra*	United States (Calif.)
Bobcat	*Felis rufus escuinapse*	Central Mexico
Ozark big-eared bat	*Plecotus townsendii ingens*	United States (Mo., Okla., Ariz.)
Brown or grizzly bear	*Ursus arctos horribilis*	United States (48 conterminous states)
Cheetah	*Acinonyx jubatus*	Africa to India
Eastern cougar	*Felis concolor cougar*	Eastern North America
Columbian white-tailed deer	*Odocoileus virginianus leucurus*	United States (Wash., Ore.)
Chinese river dolphin	*Lipotes vexillifer*	China
Asian elephant	*Elephas maximus*	Southcentral, Southeast Asia
San Joaquin kit fox	*Vulpes macrotis mutica*	United States (Calif.)
Gorilla	*Gorilla gorilla*	Central and West Africa
Leopard	*Panthera pardus*	Africa and Asia
Asiatic lion	*Panthera leo persica*	Turkey to India
Howler monkey	*Alouatta pigra*	Mexico to South America
Southeastern beach mouse	*Peromyscus polionotus phasma*	United States (Fla.)
Ocelot	*Felis pardalis*	United States (Texas, Ariz.)
Southern sea otter	*Enhydra lutris hereis*	United States (Wash., Ore., Calif.)
Giant panda	*Ailuropoda melanoleuca*	China
Florida panther	*Felis concolor coryi*	United States (La., Ark. east to S.C., Fla.)
Utah prairie dog	*Cynomys parvidens*	United States (Utah)
Morro Bay kangaroo rat	*Dipodomys heermanni morroensis*	United States (Calif.)
Black rhinoceros	*Diceros bicornis*	Subsaharan Africa
Carolina northern flying squirrel	*Glaucomys sabrinus coloratus*	United States (N.C., Tenn.)
Tiger	*Panthera tigris*	Asia
Hualapai Mexican vole	*Microtus mexicanus hualpaiensis*	United States (Ariz.)
Wild yak	*Bos grunniens*	China (Tibet), India
Mountain zebra	*Equus zebra zebra*	South Africa
Red wolf	*Canis rufus*	United States (southeast to central Tex.)
BIRDS		
Masked bobwhite (quail)	*Colinus virginianus ridgwayi*	United States (Ariz.)
California condor	*Gymnogyps californianus*	United States (Ore., Calif.)
Hooded crane	*Grus monacha*	Japan, Russia

Common Name	Scientific Name	Range
BIRDS (cont'd)		
White-necked crow	*Corvus leucognaphalus*	United States (P.R.), Dominican Republic, Haiti
Eskimo curlew	*Numenius borealis*	Alaska and North Canada
American peregrine falcon	*Falco peregrinus anatum*	Canada to Mexico
Hawaiian hawk	*Buteo solitarius*	United States (Hawaii)
Indigo macaw	*Anodorhynchus leari*	Brazil
West African ostrich	*Struthio camelus spatzi*	Spanish Sahara
Golden parakeet	*Aratinga guarouba*	Brazil
Australian parrot	*Geopsittacus occidentalis*	Australia
Attwater's greater prairie-chicken	*Tympanuchus cupido attwateri*	United States (Tex.)
Bachman's warbler (wood)	*Vermivora bachmanii*	United States (southeast), Cuba
Kirtland's warbler (wood)	*Dendroica kirtlandii*	United States, Canada, Bahama Island
Ivory-billed woodpecker	*Campephilus principalis*	United States (southcentral and southeast), Cuba
REPTILES		
American alligator	*Alligator mississippiensis*	United States (southeastern)
American crocodile	*Crocodylus acutus*	United States (Fla.)
Atlantic salt marsh snake	*Nerodia fasciatia taeniata*	United States (Fla.)
Plymouth red-bellied turtle	*Pseudemys rubiventris bangsi*	United States (Mass.)
FISHES		
Yaqui catfish	*Ictalupus pricei*	United States (Ariz.)
Bonytail chub	*Gila elegans*	United States (Ariz., Calif. Colo., Nev., Utah, Wyo.)
Gila trout	*Salmo gilae*	United States (Ariz., New Mex.)

SOURCE: *Fish and Wildlife Service, U.S. Department of Interior; as of July 30, 1992*

THE NEW ZOOS

Zoos are not new: they were reportedly in existence in China about 1100 B.C., when the first emperor of the Chou Dynasty created the first known zoo. Only a few decades ago, most zoos confined animals in small cages with little thought to their natural habitat. But today is the era of the new zoos—habitats that simulate an animal's real environment.

Zoos, also called natural wildlife parks or wildlife conservation parks, encourage animals to behave more like they do in the wild by creating conditions as close as possible to the natural habitat. The animals are given healthier diets, similar to what is found in the wild, and often they are set up to live with others of their species. Even hurt animals that will be returned to the wild are secluded so there is no human imprinting (when exposure to humans makes the animal prefer human company over its own species). The new natural environments give humans an idea of how animals live in the wild—and give the animals a chance to nurture in a more natural habitat.

Zoos are also places where certain endangered species are brought to encourage species preservation. For example, the last of the California condors were captured and taken to a zoo to breed. Recently, as the result of the breeding, condors were released into the wild in the hopes that they will increase in numbers.

MAJOR BIOLOGISTS

Arber, Werner (1929–)   Swiss microbiologist who discovered restriction enzymes (enzymes able to cut DNA at certain sites).

Audubon, John James (1785–1851)   French-American ornithologist and naturalist who is known for his bird drawings and paintings.

Baer, Karl Ernst von (1792–1876)   Estonian-born German biologist, comparative anatomist, and embryologist who was the first to identify the egg cell. He also worked on comparative studies of embryos.

Balfour, Francis Maitland (1851–1882)   British zoologist who made several suggestions for animal classification, including that animals with backbones be classed as Chordata, a term that is still used today.

Banks, Sir Joseph (1743–1820)   British botanist and long-time president of the Royal Society of London. Though he conducted little research of his own, he was influential in promoting scientific investigation in Europe.

Bates, Henry Walter (1825–1892)   British naturalist and explorer whose work in insect mimicry allowed for the acceptance of the theory of evolution suggested by Charles Darwin and Alfred Wallace.

Bateson, William (1861–1926)   British biologist who coined the term *genetics* (the causes and effects of heritable characteristics). He was a strong proponent of Gregor Mendel's work on heredity.

Bauhin, Caspar (1560–1624)   Swiss botanist who developed the use of genus and species names for classification.

Belon, Pierre (1517–1564)   French naturalist who determined that many species had skeletal similarities. He also classified more than 200 species and compared the bones of humans and birds.

Bentham, George (1800–1884)   British botanist and taxonomist who compiled one of the first books on British flora. He collected more than 100,000 specimens of plants in his early years, giving them to London's Kew Gardens in 1854.

Bilharz, Theodor (1825–1862)   German anatomist and zoologist whose work introduced a new era of tropical parasitology.

Bock, Jerome (1498–1554)   German botanist (also known as Hieronymus Tragus) who was one of the three German fathers of modern botany, and who represented the transition between medieval and modern botany (O. Brunfels and L. Fuchs were the other two).

Borlaug, Norman Ernest (1914–)   American agronomist and plant breeder who was one of the creators of the green revolution in agriculture. He won the Nobel Peace Prize in 1970 for his work on breeding "miracle" wheat for India and Mexico.

Bose, Sir Jagadis Chandra (Jagadischandra) (1858–1937)   Indian plant physiologist and physicist who was the first modern Indian scientist to gain an international reputation. In plant physiology, he recorded the responses of plants to electrical and mechanical stresses.

Brown, Robert (1773–1858)   British botanist who discovered the nucleus of the cell.

Brunfels, Otto (1489–1534)   German botanist who was one of the three German fathers of modern botany and who represented the transition between medieval and modern botany

(J. Bock and L. Fuchs were the other two). He also created accurate and detailed illustrations, the first printed to have scientific value.

Burbank, Luther (1849–1926)   American plant breeder who developed new varieties of many plants, including the Burbank potato, berries, and plums.

Camerarius, Rudolph Jacob (1665–1721)   German botanist who was the first to identify the male and female reproductive organs of plants.

Candolle, Augustin Pyrame de (1778–1841)   Swiss botanist who was one of the most distinguished taxonomists of his time. He accurately described the relationships between plants and soils, which affect geographical plant distribution. More than 300 plants, one family, and two genera are named after him.

Claude, Albert (1898–1983)   Belgian-born American cell biologist whose studies with the electron microscope showed structures never seen before, such as the details of the cell mitochondria.

Cohen, Stanley H. (1922–)   American biochemist who determined that DNA molecules could be cut, separated, and joined, thus paving the way for genetic engineering. He also worked on the mechanisms responsible for cell and organ growth, sharing the Nobel Prize in 1986.

Cohn, Ferdinand Julius (1828–1898)   German botanist and bacteriologist who determined that cytoplasm in plants and animals was virtually the same. He also performed detailed studies on bacteria, including categorizing them by genus and species.

Correns, Karl Franz Joseph Erich (1864–1933)   German botanist and geneticist who promoted the works of Gregor Mendel, which had been ignored for four decades.

Cuvier, Georges Léopold Chrétien Frédéric Dagobert (1769–1832)   French comparative anatomist, paleontologist, and taxonomist who developed the first method of classifying mammals, and founded the science of comparative anatomy.

Darwin, Charles Robert (1809–1882)   British naturalist who revolutionized biology with his theory of evolution through the process of natural selection. He also provided geological evidence for evolution and made detailed observations of volcanoes and earthquakes.

Davenport, Charles Benedict (1866–1944)   American zoologist and geneticist who introduced statistics into evolutionary studies. He also studied the genetic relationships of skin pigmentation.

de Vries, Hugo Marie (1848–1935)   Dutch plant physiologist and geneticist who promoted the works of Gregor Mendel, which had been ignored for four decades. He also determined that mutations occur in organisms.

Duggar, Benjamin Minge (1872–1956)   American plant pathologist who discovered the first antibiotic. He found the first of the tetracyclines when examining soil samples.

Dujardin, Félix (1801–1860)   French biologist and cytologist who discovered that protists do not have organ systems similar to those of multicellular organisms.

Eichler, August Wilhelm (1839–1887)   German botanist who was one of the most prominent systematic and morphological botanists of his time. He worked on the taxonomy of the higher plants and studied flower symmetry.

Engelmann, George (1809–1884)   American botanist who, besides working on the taxonomy of plant groups, studied plant pollination and grape disease.

Engler, (Gustav Heinrich) Adolf (1844–1930)   German botanist who was one of the most influential systematic botanists of his time. He also worked on genetic theory to explain floral diversity in the Northern Hemisphere.

Forbes, Edward (1815–1854)   British naturalist who was the first to propose that living organisms exist deep in the oceans, below where light penetrates.

Frisch, Karl von (1886–1982)   Austrian zoologist, entomologist, and ethnologist who studied animal behavior, especially communication among bees.

Fuchs, Leonhard (1501–1566)   German botanist and physician for whom the fuchsia is named; he also described hundreds of German and foreign plants known at the time. He was one of the three German fathers of modern botany, representing the transition between medieval and modern botany (O. Brunfels and J. Bock were the other two).

Gaertner, Karl Friedrich von (1772–1850)   German botanist who wrote the first comprehensive treatment of the problems of plant hybridization.

Geoffroy Saint-Hilaire, Étienne (1772–1844)   French naturalist who described most of the known animals of his time.

Gerard, John (1545–1612)   British herbalist who wrote the book *Herbal*, which described most of the botanical knowledge of the time.

Gesner, Conrad (1516–1565)   Swiss naturalist, encyclopedist, and physician who published the first volume on zoology. He was the first to illustrate fossils.

Gill, Theodore Nicholas (1837–1914)   American ichthyologist who was an outstanding taxonomist of his time. His writings also had a major influence on the field of ichthyology.

Grassi, Giovanni Battista (1854–1925)   Italian zoologist who proved that the *Anopheles* mosquito carried the malaria organism in its digestive tract, the first step toward understanding the disease.

Grew, Nehemiah (1641–1712)   British botanist who conducted some of the earliest studies of the anatomy of plants.

Hales, Stephen (1677–1761)   English plant physiologist and chemist who established the study of plant physiology, and was one of the first to use instruments to measure the nutrition and movement of liquids within plants.

Hooker, Sir Joseph Dalton (1817–1911)   British plant taxonomist and explorer (son of William Hooker). His studies in botany sent him around the world. From one trip to the Himalayas, he introduced the rhododendron to Europe. He was good friends with Charles Darwin.

Hooker, Sir William Jackson (1785–1865)   British botanist (father of Joseph Hooker) who helped found and direct the Royal Botanical Gardens at Kew. His private collection was once one of the finest herbariums in Europe.

Jussieu, Antoine Laurent de (1748–1836)   French plant taxonomist who determined that a plant's traits are the best way to classify it. Most of his classifications are still used today.

Knight, Andrew (1758–1838)   English botanist who studied the way plant roots and stems grow, including some of the first work in how plants respond to an outside stimulus (tropism).

Lamarck, Jean Baptiste Pierre Antoine de Monet, Chevalier de (1744–1829)   French biologist, responsible for an early theory of evolution. He also developed a classification system for invertebrates and was the first to distinguish between invertebrates and vertebrates.

Leeuwenhoek, Anton van (1632–1723)   Dutch microscopist who discovered numerous organisms, including protists, sperm (which he correctly assumed as the source of reproduction), and bacteria.

Leuckart, Karl Georg Friedrich Rudolf (1822–1898)   German zoologist who investigated many of the parasites of human beings.

Linnaeus, Carolus (Carl von Linné) (1707–1778)   Swedish naturalist who introduced certain classifications of organisms that are still in use today.

Lorenz, Konrad Zacharias (1903–1989)   Austrian zoologist and ethologist who is considered the founder of ethology.

Malpighi, Marcello (1628–1684)   Italian botanist who was one of the first to study the anatomy of plants.

Mayr, Ernst Walter (1904–)   German-born American zoologist who performed numerous studies on classification of organisms, evolution, and population genetics.

Mendel, Gregor Johann (1822–1884)   Austrian monk and botanist who introduced the idea of heredity, based on his studies of pea plants.

Miller, Stanley Lloyd (1930–)   American chemist who, along with Harold Urey, developed a methodology to create a primitive atmosphere, thought to be similar to Earth's early atmosphere.

Mohl, Hugo von (1805–1872)   German botanist who was the first to discover protoplasm (now called cytoplasm) as the principal living substance of cells.

Naudin, Charles (1815–1899)   French experimental botanist and horticulturist who experimented with hybridization of plants. He found that certain characteristics were inherited on a regular basis.

Needham, John (1713–1781)   British naturalist who tried to prove the existence of spontaneous generation, by which organisms were thought to spring to life spontaneously.

Pringsheim, Nathanael (1823–1894)   German botanist who was one of the first scientists to study algae.

Ray, John (1628–1705)   British naturalist and taxonomist who first proposed the concept of species. His work helped to lay the groundwork for classification systems.

Réaumur, René Antoine Ferchault de (1683–1757)   French entomologist, physicist, and metallurgist who wrote *The History of Insects*, which laid the foundation for the study of entomology.

Sachs, Julius von (1832–1897)   German botanist who discovered that chlorophyll is responsible for turning carbon dioxide and water into starch and releasing oxygen. He also was the first to find chlorophyll in chloroplasts.

Schleiden, Matthias Jakob (1804–1881)   German botanist who was the first to discover that cells were the chief components of plants.

Schultze, Max Johann Sigismund (1825–1874)   German zoologist who studied cytoplasm (then called protoplasm) and noted that it is consistent for all organisms.

Schwann, Theodor (1810–1882)   German physiologist who discovered the first animal enzyme, pepsin. He was also famous for his cell theory, along with M. J. Schleiden.

Siebold, Karl Theodor Ernst von (1804–1885)   German zoologist and parasitologist who was the first to note that protists (protozoa) were single cells.

Steller, Georg Wilhelm (1709–1746)   German naturalist and explorer who studied numerous species, including the Steller jay, sea lion, and eider duck.

Strasburger, Eduard Adolf (1844–1912)   German botanist who was one of the first to describe the movement of chromosomes and cellular division. He is also responsible for coining the terms *cytoplasm* and *nucleoplasm*.

Tansley, Sir Arthur George (1871–1955)   British plant ecologist who pioneered the science of plant ecology. He also was instrumental in the formation of organizations devoted to the study of wildlife preservation and ecology.

Theophrastus (c. 372–c. 287 B.C.)   Greek botanist and philosopher who described some 500 species of plants; he was one of the first to describe regional plants.

Thomson, Sir Charles Wyville (1830–1882)   British marine biologist who determined that life does exist deep in the oceans. He also contributed many theories that are the basis for modern oceanography.

Thunberg, Carl P. (1743–1828)   Swedish botanist who had one of the most extensive collections of botanical specimens of his time. He was also the first Western botanist to investigate Japanese plants and wrote extensively on the subject.

Tinbergen, Nikolaas (1907–1988)   Dutch-born British zoologist and ethnologist who studied animal behavior under natural conditions.

Tradescant, John (1570–1633)   British gardener and botanist (father of John Tradescant) who was a pioneer in the collection and cultivation of plants.

Tradescant, John (1608–1662)   British botanist and plant collector (son of John Tradescant) who was a collector and cultivator of plants.

Trembley, Abraham (1710–1784)   Swiss naturalist who studied grafting and regeneration of animal tissue.

Tschermak von Seysenegg, Erich (1871–1962)   Austrian botanist who popularized the works of Gregor Mendel, whose work had been ignored for four decades.

Tull, Jethro (1674–1741)   British agriculturist, writer, and inventor who invented a machine for planting seeds. He is best-known for his suggestions on plant cultivation, such as the use of manure and hoeing around crops to remove weeds.

Urey, Harold Clayton (1893–1981)   American physical chemist who, along with Stanley Miller, developed a methodology to create a primitive atmosphere, thought to be similar to Earth's early atmosphere. He also discovered heavy hydrogen, or deuterium.

Wallace, Alfred Russel (1823–1913)   British naturalist who formulated the theory of evolution by natural selection independently from Charles Darwin.

Went, Friedrich August Ferdinand Christian (1863–1935)   Dutch botanist who specialized in tropical agriculture. His Utrecht School was renowned for research in plant physiology and tropisms.

White, Gilbert (1720–1793)   British naturalist who is called the father of ecology. His book on animal and plant life in Selborne, England, was a best-seller of its time.

Willughby, Francis (1635–1672)   British naturalist who presented a systematic work on birds and fish, paving the way for Linnaeus's classification.

Wilson, Alexander (1766–1813)   British-born American ornithologist who was the founder of ornithology in America. He drew and wrote about birds and noted 48 species previously unknown in the United States.

Wilson, Edmund Beecher (1856–1939)   American biologist and zoologist who studied how fertilized eggs develop into embryos. He was the first to note the X and Y chromosomes of animals.

SIGNIFICANT SCIENTIFIC DISCOVERIES IN BIOLOGY

B.C.	c. 10000	The dog domesticated in Mesopotamia (Iraq) and Canaan (Israel)
	c. 8000	Potatoes and pumpkins domesticated
	c. 7000	Flax cultivated
	c. 5000	The horse domesticated in Ukraine
	c. 2700	Silkworm cultivation started in China
	c. 1100	First zoo founded in China, the Park of Intelligence
	c. 350	Aristotle grouped 500 known species of animals into eight classes
	c. 300	Theophrastus of Eresus (Aristotle's student) described more than 550 plants
A.D.	c 40.	The medical properties of about 600 plants was included in *De Materia Medica* by Greek physician Pedanius Dioscorides of Anazarbus
	c. 50	Pliny the Elder wrote *Naturalis Historia*, describing all that was known about zoology (and other facets of science) at that time
	1333	First botanical garden founded in Venice, Italy
	1517	Naturalist Pierre Belon was first to note similarities between certain bones from fish and mammals
	1551	Swiss naturalist Konrad von Gesner wrote a book that begins the science of zoology
	1555	One of the first books written that classifies species (about 200 species) and compared the bone anatomy of birds and humans
	1580	Plants found to have male and female sex by Prospero Alpini
	1596	John Gerard wrote *Herbal*, an important text on botanical knowledge Li Shi-Chen described more than 1,000 plants and 1,000 animals and 8,000 medicinal uses for them
	1599	First serious book on zoology by Ulisse Aldrovani
	1621	Hieronymus Fabricius's *On the Development of Eggs and Chickens*, elevated embryology to a science
	1623	The use of genus and species names developed by Caspar Bauhin
	1665	Robert Hooke described cells for the first time
	1668	The idea that maggots arise spontaneously was disproved by Francesco Redi
	1677	Sperm discovered as a source of reproduction by Anton van Leeuwenhoek, but are described as human larva (fertilization was not known)
	1682	Nehemiah Grew described the different types of plant stem and root tissues and noted male and female parts of flowering plants
	1683	Bacteria first observed by Anton van Leeuwenhoek, but will not be observed by scientists again until the next century
	1693	John Ray writes a book that includes the first important classification of animals (he first proposed the term *species* in 1686)

1694	Rudolph Jakob Camerarius determined the male and female plant reproductive organs
1696	Microorganisms, mainly protists (called *animalculae*), discovered by Anton van Leeuwenhoek
1711	The animal, not plant, nature of corals discovered by Luigi Marsigli
1730	Bacteria "discovered" again by Otto Müller
1734	*The History of Insects* by René de Réaumur laid the foundation for entomology
1735	Carolus Linnaeus introduced a classification of organisms (still in use today)
1742	First graft made of animal tissue using the hydra by Abraham Trembley
1744	Trembley discovered regeneration in polyps
1748	Famous experiment by John Needham seemed to prove spontaneous generation, as "little animals" are observed in sealed flasks of broth
1753	Carolus Linnaeus uses binary nomenclature in botany, laying the foundation for today's classification system of species
1761	First veterinary school founded in Lyons, France
1763	First fertilization experiments on plants using animal pollinators by Joseph Gottlieb Kölreuter
1767	Lazzaro Spallanzani offered evidence that disproves Needham's ideas of spontaneous generation
1779	Jan Ingenhousz discovered that plants absorb oxygen at night and carbon dioxide during the day—now called the plant respiratory cycle
1794	One of the first standard works written on fungi by Elisa Mangus Fries
1795	George Cuvier developed a method of classifying mammals
1803	First wild bird banding studies conducted in America by John Otto
1804	Rotation of crops introduced by A. D. Thaer
	Plants found to require carbon dioxide from the air and nitrogen from the soil is discovered by Nicholas de Saussure
1813	The term *taxonomy* introduced by Augustin de Candolle
1817	Chlorophyll was isolated by Pierre Pelletier and Joseph Bienaimé Caventou
1822	Jean Lamarck distinguished between invertebrates and vertebrates
1831	Robert Brown discovered the nucleus in the cell
1836	First known animal enzyme, pepsin, discovered by Theodor Schwann
1840	Jean-Baptiste-Joseph-Dieudonné Boussingault discovered that nitrogen absorbed by plants comes from nitrates in the soil
1844	Rudolf Albert von Kölliker discovered that the egg is a cell, and an organism originates by divisions of the egg cell
1856	Edmund Wilson noted X and Y chromosomes of mammals
1857	Gregor Mendel started experiments with peas in his garden, leading to his laws of heredity
1858	Three communications to the Linnean Society described the theory of evolution by natural selection, including reports from Charles Darwin and Alfred Wallace
1859	Charles Darwin published his *On the Origin of Species by Means of Natural Selection or the Preservation of Favoured Races in the Struggle for Life*, detailing natural selection and evolution
1865	Chloroplasts found in plants by Julius von Sachs
	Gregor Mendel introduced his work in heredity
1875	Ernst Hoppe-Seyler developed a method to classify proteins that is still used today
1879	Discovery of nucleic acids by Albrecht Kossel
1883	Camillo Golgi found specific cells of the nervous system, now called Golgi cells
1887	Edouard-Joseph-Louis-Marie van Beneden finds that each species has a fixed number of chromosomes

1888	An improved method of obtaining yeast was found by Emile Hansen; it is adopted by breweries
1898	First know virus found (affecting tobacco) was discovered by Martinus Willem Beijerinck
	First known virus detected in animals (foot-and-mouth disease) by Friedrich Löffler and Paul Frosch
1900	First known essential amino acid found in an experiment with rats by Frederick Hopkins
	Gregor Mendel's work on the heredity of plants rediscovered by three German scientists
1901	Hugo De Vries determined that changes in a species occur in jumps, which he calls mutations
1905	Richard Willstätter discovered the structure of chlorophyll
1915	Viruses discovered that prey on bacteria by Frederick William Twort
1944	R. B. Cowles and C. M. Bogert find that desert reptiles regulate their body temperature by specific behavior patterns
1945	Melvin Calvin uses carbon-14 isotope to study photosynthesis
1946	Genetic material from different viruses were combined to form a new type of virus independently by Max Delbrück and Alfred Day Hershey
1952	Joseph Lederberg finds that viruses that attack bacteria transmitted genetic material from one bacterium to another, a step toward genetic engineering
1953	A supposedly extinct fish, known as a coelacanth, turned out to be common around the Comoro Islands
1954	Arctic lupine seeds found that had been buried in burrows in the Yukon Territory of Canada since the end of the last ice age; they are still viable
1958	A species of lizard discovered in Armenia that consists entirely of females who reproduced by parthenogenesis—without fertilization by male sperm—the first known all-female vertebrate species
1960	Kenneth Norris and John Prescott find that bottlenose dolphins use echolocation (similar to sonar) to locate objects in water
1965	Artificial sex attractants, or pheromones, for cockroaches and other insects were developed by W. A. Jones, Morton Beroza, and Martin Jacobson
	DNA discovered in the chloroplasts of algae by Hans Ris and Walter Plaut
1968	Werner Arber finds a bacteria that fights against viruses by producing an enzyme that cuts viral DNA at a specific point; eventually used in genetic engineering
1973	The first calf was produced from a frozen embryo
1980	A gene was transferred from one mouse to another and still functioned
1981	Chinese first to clone an animal, the golden carp (fish)
	First genes transferred from one animal to another by transferring genes from one species of mice to another at Ohio University
1982	The first foreign DNA (to correct mouse dwarfism) is injected into an embryo of a mouse and becomes part of the mouse's genetic makeup (called the "supermouse")
1983	Walther Gehring and co-workers discovered the homeobox—the common sequence of genes in a variety of organisms that directs development of the organisms, most of which (organisms such as insects, worms, vertebrates, etc.) are segmented; it was speculated that the homeobox may control segmentation
	First artificial chromosome created with yeasts by Andrew W. Murray and Jack W. Szostak
1984	First genes cloned from an extinct species by Allen Wilson and Russell Higuchi
1986	First genetically engineered organisms grown (tobacco), in Wisconsin
1988	First patent issued for a vertebrate, a mouse developed by genetic engineering at Harvard Medical School

1991	Rat muscle was turned to bone in an experiment that may pave the way for the production of spare body parts
1992	Scientists reported that two light-sensitive genes may help mammals to reset their biological clocks
	Nickel was added to the required plant nutrition list, the first to be added in 38 years
	Antioxidant vitamins found to help plants withstand stress
	The oldest organism known to exist is discovered in Michigan: a 1,500 year-old fungus covering 30 acres underground (*Armillaria bulbosa*)
1993	The first successful cloning of a human embryo took place

COMMON TERMS IN BIOLOGY

abiogenesis   The theory that living things can develop from nonliving material, e.g., by spontaneous generation. This theory is generally obsolete.

absorption   The process by which the end products of digestion (and other dissolved liquids and gases) are eventually absorbed by the organism's fluids and cells.

adenosine triphosphate (ATP)   A chemical compound that is present in all living cells. It is the immediate provider of energy to muscles.

aerobic   Occurring in or having to do with the presence of oxygen. Certain bacteria in waste-treatment plants are aerobic, using the oxygen present to convert waste matter into harmless liquids or gases.

algology   The study of algae; also called phycology.

amino acids   Basic chemical units from which proteins are synthesized by the body. They are essential to all forms of life.

anaerobic   Occurring in or having to do with the absence of oxygen. Anaerobic bacteria get their oxygen by decomposing compounds that contain oxygen. For example, in swamps and peat bogs, certain bacteria remove an atom of oxygen from the surrounding nitrates (NO_3), changing them to nitrites (NO_2).

anther   The pollen-bearing part of a stamen.

asexual   An organism that has no sex and is independent of sexual processes. Asexual reproduction is usually accomplished by budding or fission.

atavism   An apparent "throwback" characteristic of an organism that shows a feature of an earlier ancestor. Though not truly correct, it is often called an evolutionary reversal. For example, modern horses have a single hoof; occasionally, one will be born with an extra two or three toes, similar to an ancestor of the horse, *Hyracotherium*, that had four toes in front and three in back.

bark   The covering of the stems, branches, and roots of a tree or certain other plants.

bigeneric   A plant whose parents are from two different genera.

binary fission   The splitting of a cell into two parts. For example, a single-celled paramecium reproduces by binary fission.

biogenesis   The origin of life from preexisting life. The term is more commonly used to refer to the origin of life without regard to the process.

biosphere   All of the life on Earth, usually discussed as an interdependent system.

biosynthesis   The formation of chemical compounds by a living organism.

biota   The animals (fauna) and plants (flora) at a particular time and place.

blade   The flat part of a leaf or petal.

bog plant   A plant that lives in a soil that is constantly wet but not submerged under water.

bolting   The premature formation of flowers and seeds by a vegetable plant.

bud   The undeveloped appendage, or contracted shoot containing immature leaves and/or flowers, of a plant. It usually blossoms into a flower or leaves.

bulb   A swollen, underground bud formed from the plant's scales or leaves. It allows a plant to survive the rigors of lying dormant, especially in winter.

calyx   The cup-shaped outer leaves (sepals) that surround an unopened flower bud.

cellulose   The chemical compound, called a polysaccharide, that forms the skeletal structure of a plant cell wall.

chlorophyll   About a dozen kinds of green pigments present in most plant cells, giving plants their characteristic green color. It is able to use energy from sunlight, carbon dioxide, and water to form carbohydrates.

chloroplasts   The cell bodies that contain chlorophyll. The place where sugar is synthesized; an average leaf cell contains about 50 chloroplasts.

chromosome   The threadlike structures in the nucleus of a cell that appear when the cell divides. Chromosomes carry the strands of genetic material called deoxyribonucleic acid (DNA) that determines an organism's characteristics.

cilia   Tiny hairlike structures on certain cells and organisms.

clone   A cell or organism produced asexually from a single cell. Clones are genetically identical. Certain organisms clone by budding, such as hydras, or fission, such as single-celled paramecia.

commensalism   A one-sided relationship, when an organism gains food in the presence of another organism, without harming the other. For example, there are bacteria in the human intestines that help to break down food but do no harm to the human host.

compost   The decayed remains of plants used for conditioning and fertilizing the soil.

cross-pollination   The pollination of a flower by pollen from a different plant. Bees are often considered the best cross-pollinators.

cuticle   The transparent film covering a plant, formed by the epidermal cells.

cytology   The study of the structure, growth, behavior, and reproduction of cells.

cytoplasm   The part of an animal or plant cell that is within the membrane but outside the nucleus; it was formally referred to as protoplasm.

deciduous   Describes a plant that sheds all its leaves, usually in the autumn. The term usually refers to trees and shrubs.

diffusion   The transferring of gases, liquids, or solids in or out of the cell walls.

dormancy   The temporary cessation of growth and activity in a plant or its seeds. A plant usually goes dormant during the winter months.

dwarf   A plant that is shorter or slower growing than the normal forms of the plant. Dwarf plants are usually hybrids that are similar to the larger plants in all but size.

embryo   In animals, an embryo is the group of living cells that form from a fertilized egg; an embryo develops into a fetus, which is eventually born or hatched as an infant. Plant embryos are in the seeds.

endogenous   Relating to factors influencing an organism that originate within the organism. For example, an organism's hormone secretions are endogenic factors (see *exogenous*).

enzymes   Often called organic catalysts, enzymes are complex protein substances that accelerate chemical activities in a living organism (the human body has more than 1,000 enzymes).

epidermis   The outer layer of a plant or animal that is essentially waterproof and provides protection.

epiphytic   Describes a plant that lives on another plant without being a parasite.

epizoic   A type of relationship in which one organism dwells on the body of another to aid its own movement. For example, the remora "sucker" fish attaches itself to a larger fish to hitchhike about the oceans. It refers only to animals.

ethnology   A branch of archaeology that includes the study of how ancient civilizations used plants in their everyday life.

eukaryotic   Describes a cell or organism that has a distinct nucleus or a nucleus bound by a membrane.

exogenous   Relating to factors influencing an organism that originate outside the organism. For example, environmental influences on an organism are exogenic factors (see *endogenous*).

exotic   A plant that is not native to the area in which it is growing.

extinction   The passing of a species or other taxonomic group out of existence. Extinction is the normal evolutionary path for most organisms.

extracellular   Outside the cell of an organism.

fauna   The animal life of a certain region or time period.

fermentation   The process of converting carbohydrates of other organic substances into complex carbohydrates. Enzymes of yeasts, molds, or bacteria are often involved in fermentation processes, such as the conversion of sugar to alcohol.

fertile   Describes plants that can produce seeds, fruits, pollen, spores, etc. The term also refers to soils that contain abundant plant nutrients.

filament   The stalk of a flower's stamen bearing the anther.

flagella   Long, thin organelles that extend from the surface of some protist, animal, and plant cells. They often move back and forth in a wavy or spiraling motion, propelling the cell through a fluid or moving water past the organism.

flora   The plant life of a certain region or time period.

fruit   The entire seed-bearing organ of a plant. Tomatoes, seeds from a poppy, and pea pods are all fruit.

gene   A unit of a chromosome that codes for a specific hereditary trait.

germination   The first stage in the development of a plant seed.

glucose   A six-carbon sugar molecule that is the most common simple sugar. It is important in animal respiration and other processes in organisms.

glycolysis   The first series of chemical reactions that take place during cellular respiration. It converts glucose to pyruvate (an acid).

gymnosperm   A class of plants in which ovules and seeds are not enclosed in the ovary (e.g., evergreens).

hand-pollination   The transfer of pollen by manual means from one flower to another (from stamen to stigma). Many vegetables can be encouraged to pollinate in this way.

herbicide   A chemical that kills certain plants, usually used for weed control.

homeostasis   The state of organisms that allows them to maintain a stable internal environment, usually by regulating the fluids inside and outside their cells.

humus   The dark, thick material that is produced when organic matter decays. It is necessary for good soil structure when growing plants.

hybrid   A plant that is produced by the crossing parents of different varieties, species, or genera. Hybrids are usually grown to produce new types of plants with desirable traits.

inbreeding   The mating of closely related individuals, such as brothers and sisters.

inflorescence   A group of flowers on a plant.

instars   The stage between molts as an insect metamorphoses into adulthood.

instinct   An organism's inborn drive or its natural tendencies toward life, the environment, sexual reproduction, and death. In zoology, instinct is often described as an animal's reaction to specific stimuli.

kernel   The entire grain or seed of a cereal plant, such as corn or wheat.

larva   In the life cycle of an animal or insect, the young, immature form that undergoes a change in structure as it becomes an adult. For example, moths and mosquitoes have a larval stage.

leaf   An outgrowth of a plant stem in which many plant functions take place, including photosynthesis, respiration, and the storage of food and water. Leaves are usually green because they contain chlorophyll.

life cycle   The successive stages, usually functional and morphological, through which an organism passes.

meiosis   A process of cell division by which the number of chromosomes is reduced to half the original number, resulting in the production of gametes or spores. It is sometimes called reduction division.

metamorphosis   The change from one stage in an organism's life cycle to another, for example, from the pupal to adult stages of an insect.

microbe   A microorganism, especially a bacterium that causes disease. Microbes are also used in fermentation processes.

microorganism   A microscopic or submicroscopic organism, for example, yeasts, viruses, bacteria, protozoan, and algae.

mitosis   A process of cell division that forms two new nuclei, each containing the same number of chromosomes. It is sometimes called nuclear division.

molt   When an organism periodically sheds its skin, feathers, or exoskeleton; it is usually part of the organism's growth process.

monocarpic   Plants that flower once and then die; annual and biennial plants are monocarpic.

mulch   A covering of garden compost, peat, wood chips, plastic sheeting, etc., that covers the soil around plants. Mulching discourages weeds; increases water retention; and, depending on the material used, adds nutrients to the soil.

mutation   Any spontaneous change in organisms' inherited characteristics.

mutualism   Relationships between organisms in which both partners benefit. For example, cleaner fish pick food morsels from the teeth of sharks.

nucleoplasm   The material within the nucleus of a cell.

organelles   A specialized structure or part of a cell that has a certain function. For example, the nucleus, ribosome, and mitochondrion within a cell are all organelles.

organism   An individual living entity.

osmosis   The diffusion of water or other liquids through a semipermeable membrane. The water usually travels from the side with the greater concentration of a solution to the side with the lesser concentration.

ovary   In angiosperm plants, the portion of the pistil where the ovules are held. In animals, the reproductive glandular organ that produces sex hormones and eggs (ova) in female vertebrates.

ovules   The structures that grow into seeds after the fertilization of a plant.

parasitism   A relationship between two organisms in which one organism (the parasite) benefits and the other (the host) is usually harmed. For example, mistletoes are parasitic.

peat   The partially decomposed remains of mosses and sedges dug from boggy areas. Peats are used for mulching and as a soil additive. It is also called peat moss.

photosynthesis   The process by which plants use light to convert water and carbon dioxide into sugar. Photosynthesis occurs only during the daylight hours; special indoor lights can also encourage plant photosynthesis.

phyletic evolution   The progression of evolution of a particular species or other group.

pistil   The seed-bearing organ of the flower.

plankton   Single-celled organisms, either plant (phytoplankton) or animal (zooplankton), that float usually at or near the surface of the oceans, including small crustaceans, algae, and protozoan. Plankton is one of the most important types of organisms in the ocean food chain.

pollen grain   Dust-size particles produced by the male part of a flower that carry the male sex cells. Most flowers depend on wind or other organisms, such as bees, to carry the pollen to the female part of another flower for fertilization.

pollination   The transfer of pollen from the male anther to a female stigma of a flower. It is the first step in flower reproduction.

polycarpic   A plant that grows and flowers for several seasons; perennial plants are polycarpic.

polyp   A sessile (stationary) coelenterate that is usually attached to an object at one end, with tentacles at the unattached end (e.g., hydras).

prokaryotes   A cell or organism that does not have a distinct nucleus and in which the DNA lies loose within the cell. For example, bacteria and blue-green algae are prokaryotes.

protoplasm   An older term meaning the principal living substance of a cell, made up of protein (see also *cytoplasm*).

regeneration   The ability of some organisms—either plant or animal—to regenerate a lost part. For example, some species of starfish are able to regenerate a lost limb.

rhizoid   Certain plants' rootlike hairs that absorb nutrients and water, plus anchor the plants to a solid surface.

root   The organ that anchors a plant to the ground. They are responsible for absorbing water and minerals from the soil.

runner   A shoot of a plant that runs along the ground or just beneath the ground and roots to form other plants. It is also called a stolon.

seed   The fully developed ovule containing a dormant embryo plant. Under the right conditions of temperature, moisture, and time, a seed has the potential to germinate and grow into an adult plant.

seedling   A young plant.

self-pollination   Occurs when a plant is fertilized by its own pollen.

sepal   A leaflike structure just below the base of a flower's petals.

sessile   Relating to an organism that is fixed to one spot. For example, a goose barnacle is sessile.

shoot   A bud or sprout of a plant.

shrub   A low, woody plant that has no distinct trunk.

spores   Dust-size particles that are the reproductive bodies of ferns, mosses, and some other lower plants.

stamen   The male part of a flower. The pollen-bearing anther is at its tip.

stem   The major structural part of a plant. The stem transports water and minerals from the roots to the leaves, and the food made in the leaves to other parts of the plant.

stigma   The female part of a flower. Part of the pistil, it is where the pollen from the male's stamen is deposited.

stoma   Small pores in the epidermis of a plant's leaves and stems. They are responsible for the exchange of gases in the plant leaves or stems.

style   The part of the plant ovary bearing the stigma.

succulent   A plant with fleshy stems or leaves that store water. It usually grows in arid regions.

symbiosis   Cooperation between organisms, to the benefit of both. For example, the intestines of Australian termites contain protozoa that break down pulverized wood, providing food for both themselves and the termites.

taproot   The main root of a plant that reaches deep underground.

tissue   A group of cells with similar functions and internal structures.

transpiration   The process of giving off moisture through the pores in plant leaves.

tuber   A swollen underground plant food storage organ that is similar to a bulb; a potato is a tuber.

zoophyte   Any invertebrate animal that resembles a plant. For example, coral, sponges, and sea anemones are zoophytes.

zygote   The fertilized egg cell of a plant or animal.

ADDITIONAL SOURCES OF INFORMATION

Bodanis, David. *The Secret Garden: Dawn to Dusk in the Astonishing Hidden World of the Garden*. Simon & Schuster, 1992.

Durrell, Gerald. *A Practical Guide for the Amateur Naturalist*. Knopf, 1986.

Johnson, George B. *Biology: Visualizing Life*. Holt, 1986.

Levy, Charles K., and Primack, Richard B. *A Field Guide to Poisonous Plants and Mushrooms of North America*. Stephen Greene, 1984.

Lincoln, R. J., and Boxshall, G. A. *The Cambridge Illustrated Dictionary of Natural History*. Cambridge Univ. Press, 1990.

Moore, John A. *Science as a Way of Knowing: The Foundations of Modern Biology*. Harvard Univ. Press, 1993.

Smoot, O. H. *Biology Living Systems*. Merrill, 1986.

The Way Nature Works. Macmillan, 1992.

The Human Body and Biomedical Science

Human Blood   *152*

Nonblood Components and Needs
of the Human Body   *156*

Human Cells   *160*

Systems of the Human Body   *161*

Genetics   *178*

Types of Health Care Providers   *184*

Common Medical Problems   *187*

Biomedical Laboratory Technology   *201*

Dental Technology   *209*

The Human Mind and Psychology   *209*

Major Biomedical and Biological Scientists   *212*

Significant Scientific Discoveries
in Biomedical Science   *217*

Common Terms in Biomedical Science   *219*

Additional Sources of Information   *223*

Editor's note: *This text is not meant as a substitute for professional medical advice. If you have any questions regarding your health, consult your physician.*

HUMAN BLOOD

What Is Blood?

Blood is a major body tissue (also called the body's only liquid organ) that carries food and oxygen to other tissues, removing waste products at the same time. It is somewhat viscous, being between 4.5 and 5.5 times more dense than water (at the same temperature). Blood tastes salty and smells metallic. It is slightly alkaline, with a pH range from 7.35 to 7.45 (blood in the veins and blood in the arteries, respectively). At any one time, an average adult human has about 12 pints (5.5 liters) of blood circulating throughout the body. The blood is circulated through a series of vessels—arteries, veins, and capillaries—by the pumping action of the heart. Blood carries waste products away from various body tissues to specific organs, where the wastes are disposed; it also carries and delivers oxygen and certain needed chemicals to all cells.

Composition of Blood

About 60 percent of the blood is composed of plasma. The remainder of the blood is made up of red blood cells, (erythrocytes), white blood cells (leukocytes and phagocytes), and platelets.

Plasma

Plasma is a yellow-colored liquid made of about 90 percent water that carries various molecules throughout the bloodstream. These include fibrinogen, the plasma protein that helps the blood to clot, various inorganic ions, dissolved gases (such as oxygen and carbon dioxide), organic nutrients (such as amino acids and fats), hormones, antibodies, enzymes, and waste materials (such as uric acid).

Red Blood Cells

Red blood cells (*erythrocytes*) are concave, disc-shaped cells that transport oxygen to all the tissues of the body; they have no nuclei or internal structure. There are about 25 trillion red blood cells in the average adult body (the number is slightly lower in human females than in males). Their number remains amazingly constant from day to day: Red blood cells form in the bone marrow at a rate of approximately 2 million per second, while the same number of cells are destroyed in the liver and spleen. An average healthy red blood cell lives about 120 days.

As the red blood cell matures, it becomes filled with *hemoglobin*, a protein (with a red pigment that gives the cell its characteristic color) that attracts and then transports oxygen from the lungs to the tissues, and contains vital iron. There are close to 280 million molecules of hemoglobin in a single human red blood cell.

Red blood cells differ among species; for example, the mollusk has a pigment called hemocyanin, which contains copper instead of iron in its bloodstream. Hemoglobin also can vary among individuals within a single species; for example, the hemoglobin of a human embryo is slightly different from that of an adult.

White Blood Cells

White blood cells (*leukocytes*) are larger than red blood cells; and for every 1,000 red blood cells, there is only 1 or 2 white blood cells. Unlike red blood cells, the white blood cells can migrate not only to the blood vessels but into the nearby tissues as well. Apparently, both damaged tissues and invading bacteria release chemicals that attract white blood cells. White blood cells destroyed during a fight against infection, along with dead tissue, bacterial cells, and living white blood cells, can be seen as pus at the wound site. New white blood cells are formed in the bone marrow and in other specific tissues, including the lymphoid and myeloid tissues.

White blood cells are responsible for defending the body against invaders such as viruses and bacteria; within this group of cells are the *lymphocytes*, which play an important role in the body's immune system. These cells include *T lymphocytes* (the "T" stands for thymus, where the cells mature), which fight bacteria, fungi, and other foreign bodies in the body. They are the primary cells that cause the rejection of transplanted organs. In addition, one of the major symptoms of the disease AIDS is the lack of T-cells. The *B-lymphocytes* (the "B" stands for bursa, but the cells actually mature in the bone) are responsible for releasing antibodies that fight foreign bodies (antigens) in the body.

Other types of white blood cells include the *phagocytes*, which ingest and destroy bacteria and cell fragments in the blood. Phagocytes include the macrophages, which are large phagocytes that ingest cells, and neutrophils, which are smaller cells that eat other cells.

Platelets

Platelets (*thrombocytes*) are the smallest blood cells. They are round, colorless cells found in the bloodstream and are thought to be fragments of megakarocytes (giant bone marrow cells). Around half the size of red blood cells, they are important in blood clotting, which controls bleeding, and in helping to repair damaged blood vessels.

Blood Types

The *blood type* of a person is genetically determined, as are the characteristics of the red blood cells' surfaces and plasma antibodies. The red blood cell surfaces are composed of proteins, polysaccharides, and lipids, many of which are *antigens* (also called protein markers). A person's blood type is determined based on the antigens. The immune system uses the antigens to determine which substances belong in the body and which are foreign substances that need to be attacked and eliminated from the body.

Groups of antigens (also called blood group substances) form the ABO, Rh (or Rhesus), and other human blood type groups. Of the 300 known human blood groups, the ABO blood system is the most commonly used. (The incidence of various blood types in the population varies greatly by race.) The ABO blood group divides all humans into four blood types: A (A antigens only), AB (both A and B antigens), B (B antigens only), and O (neither A nor B antigens). Nonhuman animals also have various numbers of blood antigen systems (blood types). For example, pigs have 16, cows have 12, dogs have 7, and cats have 2. The most common human blood type in the world is type O; the rarest is from a different blood group system called Bombay (symbolized *hh*).

ABO Blood Type Relationships

In the ABO blood group, some blood types are compatible, depending on whether the blood is received or donated. When someone is given blood of an incompatible blood type, antigens cause the blood to clot. These clots could clog important blood vessels and lead to complications such as a stroke. In addition, the red blood cells may be destroyed by antibodies, which naturally attack the offending antigen. This can lead to shock, kidney failure, and possibly death.

Blood Type	Can Receive From	Can Be Donor To
A	A, O	A, AB
B	B, O	B, AB
AB	A, B, AB, O	AB
O	O	A, B, AB, O

People with blood type O are called *universal donors*; and if the person is also Rh– (see below), their blood can be transfused into almost anyone.

Inheritance of Human ABO Blood Groups

Parents	Children Possible	Children Not Possible
A×A	A, O	AB, B
A×B	A, B, AB, O	
A×AB	A, B, AB	O
A×O	A, O	AB, B
B×B	B, O	A, AB
B×AB	A, B, AB	O
B×O	B, O	A, AB
AB×AB	A, B, AB	O
AB×O	A, B	O, AB
O×O	O	A, B, AB

Rh Blood Type

The *Rhesus (Rh) blood type* (also called the *Rh factor*) is another blood group, based on certain genetically determined types of protein on the surface of red blood cells. Those with this type of protein are called Rh+; those without it are Rh–. The Rh type is often represented with the ABO blood group by a + or – sign, for example, A+ or B– blood type.

Rh incompatibility in a transfusion can cause a severe reaction. Rh type is particularly important to childbearing: For example, when the father is Rh+ and the mother is Rh–, the fetus may be Rh+. If that's the case, when the baby is delivered, the mother may produce anti-Rh antibodies if the baby's blood enters her circulatory system. The mother's next baby could react to the antibodies, resulting in *erythroblastosis fetalis*, which could be fatal to the baby. Years ago, doctors would replace the baby's blood immediately with antibody-free blood. Today, an anti-Rh preparation is injected into the Rh– mother right after delivery or an abortion, ridding her body of the fetal proteins that produced the anti-Rh antibodies.

DONATING BLOOD

The procedure of donating blood has been in use since World War I. Blood is needed for transfusion, mainly for surgical procedures and for accident victims. Donors usually give a pint of whole blood, which is then divided into platelets, white blood cells, and red blood cells.

One can donate blood (for red blood cells) about once every two months. Another form of donation called pheresis is just for donating platelets, which are separated from the blood and used for patients going through bone marrow transplants or chemotherapy. A pint of blood is collected, the platelets are removed, and then the processed blood is transfused back to the donor. This process takes place eight times to get the amount of platelets needed. Pheresis donors can give platelets every two weeks, because the body replaces the platelets more quickly than it replaces red blood cells. In addition, this method yields as many platelets as ten normal whole blood donations.

Donated blood is routinely tested for a multitude of foreign bodies, such as HIV (which causes AIDS), hepatitis B, and syphilis. In addition, blood that will be used by newborns and infants is usually irradiated to eliminate harmful elements in the blood.

Common Blood Disorders

Name	Description
Anemia	Too few red blood cells
Aplastic anemia	Too few of all types of blood cells; the bone marrow is usually damaged
Megaloblastic anemia	Deformed red blood cells; often caused by poor nutrition and associated with vitamin deficiency
Sickle-cell anemia	Abnormal hemoglobin; red blood cells distort and are unable to carry sufficient oxygen to the tissues; can also block smaller blood vessels
Hemophilia	A group of bleeding disorders; bleeding is caused by defective platelets and poor clotting ability
Leukemia	A form of cancer; too many white blood cells produced in the bone marrow
Polycythemia	Too many red blood cells
Thrombosis	Excessive clotting; often results in circulatory problems

Disease Carriers in the Blood

Bacteria

Bacteria are one of the most abundant life forms on Earth, growing and living on and inside other living things. They range in size from less than several thousandths to hundredths of an inch long (for more information on bacteria, see Chapter 4, "Biology"). Bacteria have a nucleoid that contains DNA, but they have no nucleus. Many types of bacteria release toxins when they enter the human bloodstream. For example, one type of food poisoning is caused by *Clostridium botulinum;* and tetanus is caused by the bacterium *Clostridium tentani*, which can invade the bloodstream via deep, unclean wounds.

Viruses

Viruses and subviruses are sometimes called nonliving molecules. They are 10 to 100 times smaller than the typical bacterium; for example, the herpes virus measures 100 nanometers or 100 billionth of a meter across, whereas a typical bacterium measures 1,000 nanometers (for more information on viruses, see Chapter 4, "Biology").

Viruses are usually parasitic and show no signs of life until they enter a living cell. They are made up of genetic material wrapped in protein. When a virus enters a cell (called the host), it sheds its protein cover. Then the virus tricks the host cell into duplicating the virus's nucleic acid instead of its own. In most cases, as the virus is duplicated, the cell is destroyed.

Human diseases caused by viruses include AIDS, the common cold, influenza, smallpox, rabies, polio, measles, mumps, cold sores, genital sores, shingles, and Epstein-Barr syndrome. There are about 200 known common cold viruses. The abundance of influenza types is caused by rapid mutations of the influenza viruses.

Vaccinations can be helpful in controlling some of these diseases by allowing the body's immune system to generate antibodies against the virus. For most vaccinations, a dead virus is injected into the bloodstream. Today, live-virus vaccines are also being used for diseases such as polio, measles, and chicken pox. It is often difficult to develop a vaccine against a certain virus. For example, the human immunodeficiency virus (HIV) that causes AIDS attacks the immune system. This makes it more difficult to develop a vaccine, since the immune system itself is involved.

KEEPING IT COLD

The idea of freezing red blood cells started in the early 1950s. One of the major problems with the first frozen blood supplies was that it was assumed that freezing eradicated any infectious agents in the blood. But in 1978, it was demonstrated that hepatitis B virus, a highly infectious disease, was still active after the blood was processed. And since then, other diseases have been found to be active in the blood after freezing. Today, there is an intense effort to screen each blood donor as well as his or her blood.

Donated blood is washed, and the white blood cells and platelets are removed. To freeze the red blood cells, a glycerol solution is added. To unfreeze, the glycerol is removed. The ability to store blood for long periods has been a boon to human health: Not only are rare blood types available for emergency transfusions, but people can also store their own blood before surgery.

Storing blood will also help our future space endeavors. When astronauts return to Earth—especially on longer flights—it takes time for the red blood cell count to return to normal levels. Frozen blood could be stored onboard the space stations, and astronauts who have been in space for a long stay could have a blood transfusion—called autodonation—to raise their red cell mass before they return to Earth. In the far future, space colony astronauts will be able to freeze their own blood in case it is needed for an emergency transfusion.

NONBLOOD COMPONENTS AND NEEDS OF THE HUMAN BODY

Proteins

Proteins are organic compounds that contain oxygen, carbon, nitrogen, hydrogen, and often sulfur atoms. Some of the largest molecules that naturally exist in living organisms, they are composed of amino acids arranged in a pattern specific to a protein type. The various amino acid arrangements create thousands of proteins, including enzymes, globulins, and antibodies. Approximately 80 amino acids are found in nature; of these, humans need 20 for metabolism or growth of body tissues. The human body can manufacture 9 of the amino acids; the rest (called *essential amino acids*) are obtained from animal or plant tissues in the diet.

Proteins are essential for the functioning of cells. They are used as structural materials for muscles and organs and help form hair and fingernails. Some proteins work in harmony with other materials. For example, clotting proteins work with platelets to control bleeding, and antibodies help white blood cells fight infections.

Carbohydrates

Carbohydrates are organic compounds that contain oxygen, carbon, and hydrogen atoms. Produced in green plants by photosynthesis, carbohydrates are a necessary food for animals (even carnivores). Carbohydrates include the small molecules of simple sugars (monosaccharides), such as fructose and glucose; the disaccharides, such as lactose and sucrose; and larger molecules called polysaccharides, such as starch and cellulose. Though carbohydrates are rich in energy, no animal can survive on only carbohydrates, since they do not contain nitrogen, which is necessary for production of amino acids for protein synthesis.

Minerals

Minerals are necessary for chemical reactions and for building some important molecules in the body. For example, iron is a necessary component of red blood cells, and calcium is essential to maintain the skeleton. There are at least 25 different minerals that help maintain human health, including calcium, iron, chlorine, cobalt, copper, iodine, manganese, phosphorus, potassium, and sodium; generally, only small amounts are needed for good health.

Minerals for Health

Minerals	Sources	Symptoms of Deficiency
Iron	Liver, lean meats, nuts, dried beans, peas, dried fruits, whole grains, leafy green vegetables	Bad digestion, anemia (including smaller red blood cells), changes in body enzymes that contain iron
Iodine	Iodized salt, seafood, butter, milk, cheese, eggs (especially if the animals' feed was rich in iodine)	Goiter (enlarged thyroid), cretinism in infants
Manganese	Abundant in most animal and plant food, especially whole grains, nuts, and legumes	Sterility and abnormal fetuses (in animals), bone deformation
Copper	Found in most food; organ meats, shellfish, nuts, peas, dried beans, cocoa (not in dairy products)	Can cause anemia in infants fed cow's milk, unknown affect in adults (excess leads to Wilson's disease, a rare metabolic disease)
Zinc	Wheat germ, bran, whole grains, peas, fish, lean meats, poultry	Retarded growth, anemia, poor wound healing (although such a deficiency is rare in the United States)
Fluorine	Water (either naturally or added)	Tooth decay in young children, possibly osteoporosis in adults (excess can cause teeth mottling and deformed bones)
Chromium	Corn oil, whole grains, meats	Poor metabolism of glucose

Vitamins

Vitamins are organic molecules necessary for maintaining certain chemical reactions and for building various molecules in the body. Most vitamins participate in biochemical reactions; some, called coenzymes, activate specific enzymes in the body. Vitamins are divided into the fat- and water-soluble vitamins. If too much of a water-soluble vitamin is consumed, the excess amount is excreted in the urine.

List of Vitamins

Vitamin	Sources	Symptoms of Deficiency
WATER SOLUBLE		
Thiamin (B_1)	Liver, milk, bread, lima beans, pork, pasta, wheat germ, oysters, enriched cereal	Beriberi (nausea, severe exhaustion, paralysis), heart swelling, leg cramps
Riboflavin (B_2)	Red meat, liver, milk, dark green vegetables, eggs, pasta, bread, mushrooms, peas, whole grains, and enriched cereal	Severe skin problems (especially around mouth and nose), sensitivity to light
Niacin (B_3)	Red meat, poultry, beans, peas, tuna, whole grains, enriched cereal, nuts, dried beans and peas; manufactured in the body from the amino acid tryptophan	Pellagra (weak muscles, no appetite, diarrhea, skin blotches, mental confusion, irritability)
Pyridoxine (B_6)	Muscle meats, liver, fish, poultry, whole grains, avocados, spinach, green beans, bananas	Depression, nausea, vomiting, skin disorders, anemia, kidney stones
Cobalamin (B_{12}, folate)	Liver, red meat, kidneys, fish, eggs, milk, oysters	Pernicious anemia, exhaustion, degeneration of peripheral nerves
Folic acid (folacin)	Liver, kidneys, leafy dark green vegetables, beans, peas, wheat germ, brewer's yeast	Anemia, smooth tongue, diarrhea
Pantothenic acid	Liver, kidneys, nuts, eggs, dark green vegetables, whole grain bread, cereal, yeast	Anemia, vomiting, abdominal pain, fatigue, sleep problems
Biotin	Egg yolk, kidneys, liver, yeast, nuts, green beans, dark green vegetables; manufactured in the intestinal tract	Dermatitis, fatigue, depression, loss of appetite, nausea
C (ascorbic acid; antioxidant)	Citrus fruits, melons, tomatoes, green peppers, strawberries, potatoes	Scurvy (bleeding gums, degenerated muscles, swollen joints, tender skin, loose teeth), wounds do not heal
FAT SOLUBLE		
A (retinol)	Liver, eggs, dark green and deep orange vegetables (spinach, squash, carrots), butter, cheese, milk	Inflamed eye membranes, night blindness, rough skin, no bone growth, cracked and decayed teeth

Note: *beta-carotene is a precursor of vitamin A and is an antioxidant.*

D (calciferol)	Fortified milk, fish-liver oil, tuna, salmon, egg yolk; production triggered by ultraviolet rays of the sun on the skin	Rickets (soft bones—especially children—bowed legs, malformed teeth, protruding abdomen), osteomalacia (in adults)

Vitamin	Sources	Symptoms of Deficiency
E (tocopherol; antioxidant)	Liver, wheat germ, margarine, whole grain cereals, vegetable oils, leafy green vegetables, dried beans, olives, seeds, corn	Breakage of red blood cells in premature infants
K (menaquinone)	Liver, potatoes, cabbage, peas, leafy green vegetables	Hemorrhage in newborns, anemia

Fats

Fats are the best-known group of lipids. They are composed of glycerol and fatty acid subunits. Glycerol is similar to the simple sugars; fatty acids are commonly broken down into saturated and unsaturated.

Fats in food and in the body usually occur as triglycerides. They travel through the blood and are broken down by enzymes, which produces energy. Because the fats do not mix with the water of the blood, they are packaged into special particles to keep them intermixed in the bloodstream. These particles, called lipoproteins, include very low density lipoproteins (VLDL), low-density lipoproteins (LDL), and high-density lipoproteins (HDL).

All the lipoproteins contain cholesterol. Cholesterol is a powdery, odorless, white, fatlike substance that is derived from food and manufactured by the liver and intestine. Cholesterol is an essential ingredient of cell walls; it also slows down water loss due to evaporation through the skin. It is used in the formation of steroids and sex hormones and also covers the nerves, allowing for transmission of nerve impulses.

The liver uses excess carbohydrates and fats from food to make triglycerides, which are then packaged in the VLDLs and travel from the liver to the rest of the body. The VLDL contains not only the triglycerides but also cholesterol, protein, and other fats; when the triglycerides from the VLDLs are extracted and enter the cells, the fat-depleted particles are then called LDL, which contain mostly cholesterol and protein.

The LDL particles can remain in the blood for long periods of time. In some people, the LDL is carried from the bloodstream by LDL receptors on cell surfaces (the amount of LDL receptors in the body is thought to be genetically determined). Once inside the cells, the LDL is broken down. HDL, the smallest lipoprotein, removes cholesterol from the LDL and cells. The cholesterol is sent to the liver where it is broken down into bile acids and excreted into the small intestine or reprocessed into new VLDL particles.

THE PROBLEM WITH LIPOPROTEINS

Not all lipoproteins are helpful to the body. In recent years, researchers have discovered that the levels of cholesterol, in the form of high-density lipoproteins and low-density lipoproteins, can affect one's susceptibility to heart disease—but the debate continues as to how much and why.

LDL is considered the "bad" cholesterol. If LDL stays in the body for long periods, the cholesterol contained in the LDL package can add to the plaque on artery walls. Individuals with relatively more LDL receptor cells (which carry away and break down the LDL) have lower serum LDL levels and, generally, less chance of developing coronary disease. The "good" cholesterol is the HDL. Because these particles remove the cholesterol from the LDL, they prevent the buildup of plaque in the arteries.

There may be more culprits in the plaque buildup arena: Recently, researchers found that high concentrations of the cholesterol-carrier lipoprotein-a (Lp-a) in the blood may contribute to heart disease. The Lp-a—a close cousin of LDL—may help to deposit cholesterol on artery walls. Another new study suggests that Lp-a may also cause smooth muscle cells in the arteries to grow faster than usual, thus clogging the arteries even more.

The Food Pyramid—A Guide to Daily Food Choices

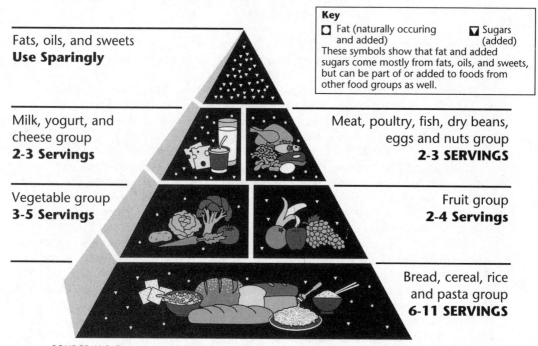

Key

☐ Fat (naturally occuring and added)   ☑ Sugars (added)

These symbols show that fat and added sugars come mostly from fats, oils, and sweets, but can be part of or added to foods from other food groups as well.

Fats, oils, and sweets
Use Sparingly

Milk, yogurt, and cheese group
2-3 Servings

Meat, poultry, fish, dry beans, eggs and nuts group
2-3 SERVINGS

Vegetable group
3-5 Servings

Fruit group
2-4 Servings

Bread, cereal, rice and pasta group
6-11 SERVINGS

SOURCE: U.S. Department of Agriculture/U.S. Department of Health and Human Services

HUMAN CELLS

Cell Comparisons

There are between 50 and 75 trillion cells in the body; each second there are about 6 trillion reactions taking place within each cell. The size of each cell varies greatly; most of them are extremely small, and a million such cells would occupy a space no larger than the dot at the end of this sentence. The majority of cells work to transform energy for the body. When a number of similar cells work together, they are called a *tissue* (blood is considered a tissue type); a collection of tissues is called an *organ*.

Each type of cell has its own life span, and when a human dies, it may take hours or days before all the cells in the body die. Human cells include blood, bone, brain, colon, liver, skin, stomach, ova, and spermatozoa. The following list indicates how long it takes each type of cell to replace itself.

Cell	Approximate Life Span
Red blood cells	120–130 days
White blood cells	> 1 year
Platelets (blood)	10 days
Bone (skeleton)	3 months
Brain	90+ years (an entire lifetime)
Colon	4 days
Liver	6 weeks
Skin	1 month
Stomach	5 days
Spermatozoa	3 days

THEORIES ON AGING

Every human body ages over time. The human life span varies from person to person. On average, a newborn today can expect to live to the age of about 75. Scientists believe that the probable maximum human life span is about 150 years; the record of the oldest person to date is Shigechiyo Izumi (1871–1986) of Japan, who lived to be 120 years and 237 days.

There are a variety of theories as to why all living things grow old and die. The free-radical theory states that free radicals, certain chemicals produced as a by-product of biological activity, are particularly harmful to healthy cells. As a person ages, free radicals gradually destroy cells until they can no longer function properly, causing the entire body (especially whole organ systems such as the kidneys or heart) to break down and die. The programmed senescence theory suggests that the rate at which we age is predetermined, and that our genetic makeup controls the aging and death of the cells. After enough of the cells die, the organs cease to function and death occurs.

Many researchers also believe that the average life spans of most species are predetermined. If this is true, it may be that a species' life span encourages the survival of that species. For example, humans may live only a certain length of time so that the young can introduce new combinations of traits, thereby strengthening the human gene pool.

SYSTEMS OF THE HUMAN BODY

There are nine major systems in the human body: hormonal, circulatory, digestive, muscular, nervous, reproductive, respiratory, skeletal, and immune.

The Hormonal System

The *hormonal system* consists of a series of tissues, glands, and cells. The glands produce chemicals, called hormones, that are secreted into the bloodstream, by releasing the chemicals either directly into the bloodstream (*endocrine glands*) or through tubes called ducts (*exocrine glands*).

The *hormones* stimulate other cells or a particular organ or a group of organs. They regulate many of the body's activities, including growth, development, and homeostasis. There may be as many as 100 hormones in the human body, but not all have been determined. The hormones are similar in human males and females, with the exception of the sex hormones.

The major exocrine glands are all associated with the digestive system (see "The Digestive System," later in this chapter). The major hormone-secreting endocrine glands in the human body are the thyroid, adrenal, pituitary, pineal, parathyroid, and pancreas (although some glands, e.g., the pancreas, are considered to be crosses of both exocrine and endocrine glands). There are two gender-specific endocrine glands: the ovary in females and the testis in males.

Important Hormones

Hormone	Function(s)	Source
Adrenocorticotropic hormone (ACTH)	Stimulates the adrenal cortex	Pituitary (anterior)
Calcitonin	Lowers the blood calcium	Thyroid
Chorionic gonadotropin	Stimulates the ovaries to continue producing estrogen and progesterone during the early stages of pregnancy	Placenta
Cortical sex hormones	Stimulates secondary sex characteristics (especially in males)	Adrenal (cortex)
Digestive hormones (e.g., gastrin)	Aids in the digestion of food	Gut wall
Epinephrine (adrenaline)	Rapidly stimulates the metabolism in emergencies, decreases insulin secretion, and stimulates pulse and blood pressure	Adrenal (medulla)
Erythropoietin	Stimulates the production of red blood cells	Kidney
Estrogens	Stimulates secondary sex characteristics in females	Ovary
Follicle-stimulating hormone (FSH)	Stimulates the growth of ovarian follicles and seminiferous tubules of the testes	Pituitary (anterior)
Glucagon	Raises the blood glucose in the body (changes glycogen into glucose)	Pancreas (islet of Langerhans)
Glucocorticoids (e.g., cortisone)	Controls the balance of the body's carbohydrates, proteins, salts, water metabolism, and minerals	Adrenal (cortex)
Gonadrotropic hormones	Stimulates gonads	Pituitary (anterior)
Growth hormone	Stimulates body growth	Pituitary (anterior)
Histamine	Increases the permeability of capillaries	Damaged tissues
Hypothalamic-releasing and inhibiting hormones	Causes the release and inhibition of hormones from the anterior pituitary gland	Hypothalamus
Insulin	Lowers the blood glucose in the body	Pancreas (islet of Langerhans)
Melatonin	May assist in regulating the pituitary	Pituitary (posterior)
Mineralcorticoids	Regulates sodium and potassium metabolism	Adrenal (cortex)
Norepinephrine (noradrenaline)	Rapidly stimulates the metabolism in emergencies, mobilizes the body during stress	Adrenal (medulla)

Hormone	Function(s)	Source
Oxytocin	Stimulates milk production and uterine contractions	Pituitary (posterior)
Parathormone	Increases blood calcium and decreases phosphate	Parathyroid
Progesterone	Allows the uterus to prepare for pregnancy	Ovary
Prolactin	Stimulates milk secretion	Pituitary (anterior)
Renin	Helps with the flow of blood	Kidney
Testosterone (androgens)	Sperm production, stimulates secondary sex characteristics in males	Testis
Thymosin	Allows the maturation of the white blood cells	Thymus
Thyroid-stimulating hormone (TSH)	Stimulates the thyroid gland	Pituitary (anterior)
Thyroxine	Stimulates body metabolism, helps regulate body growth and development	Thyroid
Vasopressin (ADH)	Allows the kidneys to retain water, stimulates constriction of blood vessels; it is stored in the posterior pituitary but made in the hypothalamus	Pituitary (posterior)

The Circulatory System

The circulatory system circulates the blood and associated chemicals throughout the body (see also "Human Blood," earlier in this chapter). Organisms such as insects have open circulatory systems; higher animals, such as humans and other mammals, have closed circulatory systems. The closed circulatory system is composed of the heart, connected vessels, and the spleen; the urinary tract is also often included in this system. (The term *cardiovascular system* is also often used to describe the heart and connected vessels of the body.)

The *heart,* a rhythmically contracting muscle, is the major organ of the cardiovascular system. It has two separate sides—one that carries the oxygen-rich blood returning from the lungs, and the other that carries the oxygen-poor blood returning from the tissues. The body's heart rate is controlled by cells in the heart's sinus node, which regulate the electrical system of the heart and its contractions. The average heart beats 70 to 80 times and pumps 5 quarts of blood per minute; this is equivalent to about 100,000 beats and 1,800 gallons of blood pumped per day. During vigorous exercise, the heart increases its output nearly fivefold.

The blood is pumped through a series of branching *blood vessels,* in the following sequence: From the heart to the large arteries, to the smaller arteries (arterioles), and to the capillaries. Nutrients, gases, hormones, and other molecules in the blood pass through the thin capillary walls to the interstitial fluids that surround the body's cells, while waste products such as carbon dioxide are picked up by the blood. From there, the blood travels through small veins (venules), into larger veins and back to the heart.

The *spleen* is where the body's blood is filtered and stored. The spleen stores red blood cells until they are needed and removes the damaged cells, including old red blood cells, platelets, and damaged or fragments of cells. (For the location of the spleen, see the illustration "The Digestive System," later in this chapter.)

The *urinary tract*—which includes two kidneys, the bladder, two ureters, and the urethra— is also considered part of the circulatory system, because it cleanses the blood of waste products. As a result of metabolism, cells produce chemical wastes, which can be toxic if not removed from the body. Each *kidney's* more than 1 million small filtering units, called *glomeruli*, process chemical wastes and excess water in the body, which produces urine. The two *ureters*, muscular tubes that lead from the kidneys, carry the urine to the *bladder*, a temporary holding place in the lower abdomen. The urine is eventually expelled from the bladder through the urethra. The lower urinary tracts of females and males differ in structure and are each closely related to the reproductive organs. The female urethra is about 1 inch (25 millimeters) long and is located in front of the reproductive organs. The male urethra is about 10 inches (25 centimeters) long and is the outlet for both urine and semen.

The Circulatory System

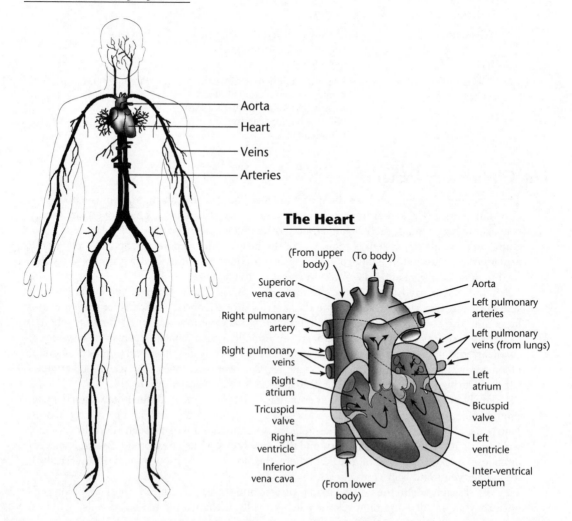

Aorta
Heart
Veins
Arteries

The Heart

(From upper body)   (To body)

Superior vena cava

Right pulmonary artery

Right pulmonary veins

Right atrium

Tricuspid valve

Right ventricle

Inferior vena cava

(From lower body)

Aorta

Left pulmonary arteries

Left pulmonary veins (from lungs)

Left atrium

Bicuspid valve

Left ventricle

Inter-ventrical septum

The Urinary Tract

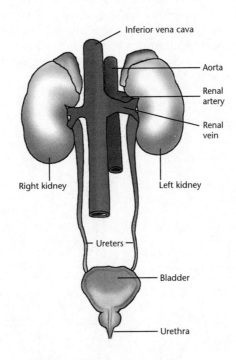

WHAT DOES YOUR BLOOD PRESSURE MEAN?

When you or your doctor takes your blood pressure, it is truly the measure of the blood's pressure. As the heart pumps blood through the body, there is a pressure, or force, exerted against the arterial walls. The *systolic* blood pressure is when the heart muscle contracts in the cardiac cycle; the *diastolic* pressure is the relaxation or dilation phase of the heart muscle in the cardiac cycle. Blood pressure is not strictly a function of how the heart pumps. It is also somewhat controlled by hormones secreted by the kidneys and by the sympathetic nervous system, which controls the dilation and constriction of blood vessels throughout the body.

When your blood pressure is taken with a sphygmomanometer (the manual instrument used to measure blood pressure), a cuff is placed around your upper arm and inflated until the blood in your artery stops. Gradually, the air is let out of the cuff. The person taking the blood pressure reading listens through a stethoscope (placed over the artery at your inside elbow) for a thumping sound, which represents the systolic pressure. When the thumping starts to fade, that is the diastolic pressure. At both these points, the level of the mercury (in millimeters) in the sphygmomanometer is read. Your blood pressure reading is represented by the two numbers—the first number (and normally the larger number) is the systolic reading, and the second number is the diastolic reading.

The Digestive System

The *digestive system* (also called the gastrointestinal system) breaks down food, which is used for energy, and eliminates wastes. As food enters the mouth, chewing and enzymes in the saliva begin to break it down. As the *esophagus* contracts in waves, it pushes the food to the *stomach*, where muscles, enzymes, and digestive acids break the food down further into a liquid. The stomach slowly empties into the *small* and *large intestines*. The food's acidity is neutralized in the small intestine and most of its nutrients are absorbed. In the large intestine, water is removed from the mostly digested food, turning the waste into semisolid feces, or stool. The last of the water is removed at the *sigmoid colon* and *rectum*, where waste accumulates until its volume stimulates a bowel movement.

The Digestive System

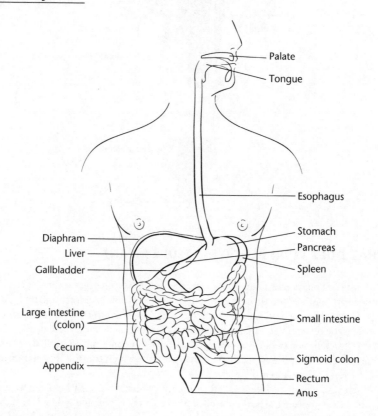

The Muscle System

The *muscle system* is responsible for the body's flexibility and movement. All movement is caused by the muscles, which are composed of contracting tissues. There are three major types of muscles.

voluntary (skeletal)   The voluntary muscles consists of the muscles in the body that respond to conscious control from the brain, i.e., the muscles contract or lengthen, depending on the chemical messages they receive from the brain. These muscles usually look striated or striped when viewed under a microscope. They are attached to the bones by tendons.

involuntary (visceral, smooth)   Involuntary muscles are in the stomach and intestines, the walls of arteries and veins, and several other places in the body. They respond automatically, without conscious control (although a person does have partial control over some of these muscles). They are usually unstriated and smooth, especially those muscles in the gut.

cardiac muscles   The cardiac muscles make up the heart muscles and are striated and smooth. These muscles are responsible for the involuntary beating of the heart.

The Muscle System

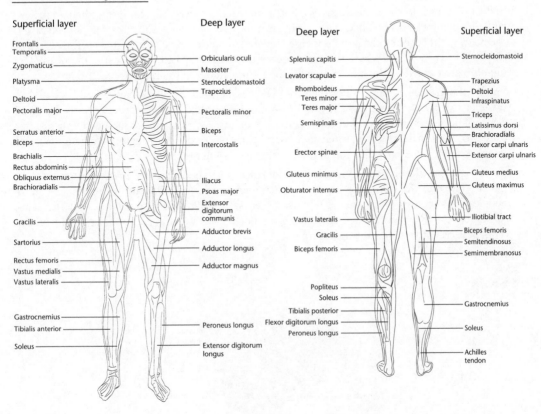

Superficial layer	Deep layer	Deep layer	Superficial layer

Frontalis
Temporalis
Zygomaticus
Platysma
Deltoid
Pectoralis major
Serratus anterior
Biceps
Brachialis
Rectus abdominis
Obliquus externus
Brachioradialis
Gracilis
Sartorius
Rectus femoris
Vastus medialis
Vastus lateralis
Gastrocnemius
Tibialis anterior
Soleus

Orbicularis oculi
Masseter
Sternocleidomastoid
Trapezius
Pectoralis minor
Biceps
Intercostalis
Iliacus
Psoas major
Extensor digitorum communis
Adductor brevis
Adductor longus
Adductor magnus
Peroneus longus
Extensor digitorum longus

Splenius capitis
Levator scapulae
Rhomboideus
Teres minor
Teres major
Semispinalis
Erector spinae
Gluteus minimus
Obturator internus
Vastus lateralis
Gracilis
Biceps femoris
Popliteus
Soleus
Tibialis posterior
Flexor digitorum longus
Peroneus longus

Sternocleidomastoid
Trapezius
Deltoid
Infraspinatus
Triceps
Latissimus dorsi
Brachioradialis
Flexor carpi ulnaris
Extensor carpi ulnaris
Gluteus medius
Gluteus maximus
Iliotibial tract
Biceps femoris
Semitendinosus
Semimembranosus
Gastrocnemius
Soleus
Achilles tendon

The Nervous System

The *nervous system* controls the flow of information in the body. It is also includes the nerves, brain, and indirectly, the sense organs—especially those responsible for sight, sound, smell and taste.

The nervous system is divided into two parts: The *central nervous system* includes the brain and the spinal cord and the *peripheral nervous system* includes the rest of the neural network found throughout the body—the cervical (neck), thoracic (chest), lumbar (lower back), and sacral (pelvis) nerves, which branch from the spine at their respective areas.

The *brain*—the main control center of the nervous system—is contained in a rigid bony case called the skull and has three parts: *cerebral hemispheres*, *cerebellum*, and *brainstem*. The cerebral hemispheres control the higher functions, such as speech and hearing; the cerebellum controls the subconscious activities and some balance functions; and the brainstem maintains the necessary functions of the body, such as breathing and circulation.

The *senses* function through specialized organs, all of which are directly related to the nervous system.

Hearing   Hearing is the ability to detect and interpret sound waves. Mammals have the most highly developed ears in the animal kingdom. The ear is the major organ used for hearing: The outer ear captures the sound, which then travels down the auditory canal. The sound waves strike the eardrum, transmitting the waves to the ossicles, then to the cochlea. The cells in the cochlea then translate the sound to the otic nerve, which carries the information to the brain.

Sight   Though most animals do not see in the same manner as we do, most have light-sensitive cells grouped into organs called eyes. In humans, the eyes are one of the most complex organs in the body. Light entering the pupil is focused by the lens. The image is projected on the retina, at the back of the eyeball, where the light energy is converted to electrical nerve impulses. The impulses are carried by the optic nerve to the brain, where the brain interprets the image.

Smell   The olfactory organs are responsible for the sense of smell. Receptor cells, located in two clefts in the upper part of the nasal passages, have cilia that project down into the nasal cavity. The receptors respond quickly to minute quantities of smell-producing chemicals, but they also adapt so that half the intensity is lost within a second. The receptors produce electrical impulses, which are carried to the brain by the olfactory nerves.

Taste   Taste is closely related to the sense of smell; taste buds, located on the tongue, detect flavors. There are four kinds of taste buds, each located on a specific part of the tongue. These buds can distinguish four types of flavors: sweet, salty, sour, and bitter. Note that the same substances can give rise to sour sensations in one person and sweet in another, depending on the dominant receptors on each person's tongue.

The Brain

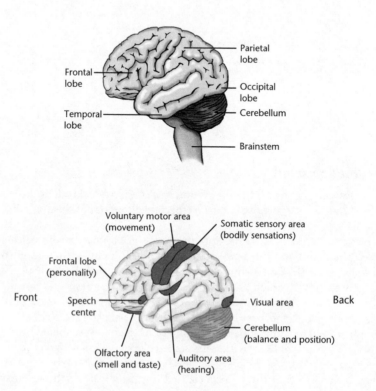

The Nervous System

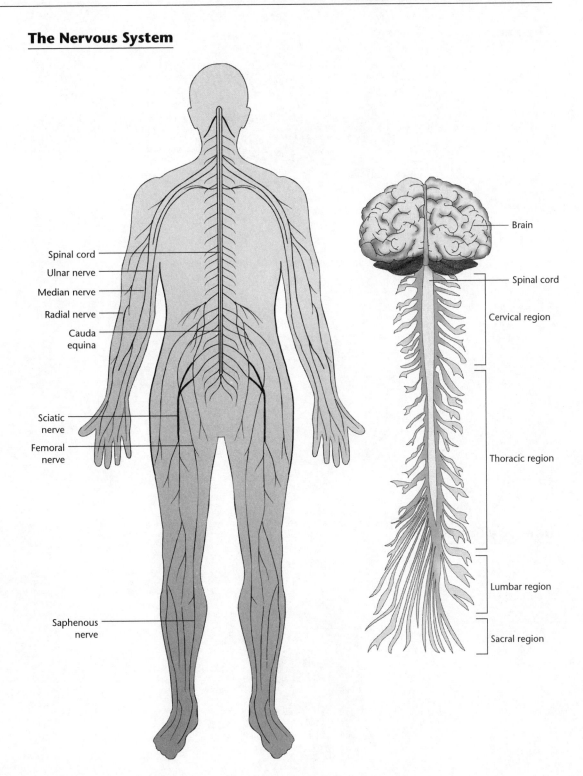

Spinal cord
Ulnar nerve
Median nerve
Radial nerve
Cauda equina

Sciatic nerve
Femoral nerve

Saphenous nerve

Brain
Spinal cord
Cervical region
Thoracic region
Lumbar region
Sacral region

The Ear

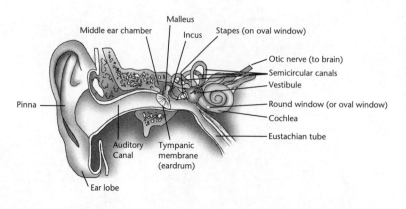

Ossicles include the malleus, incus, and stapes.

The Eye

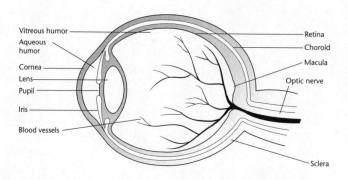

Olfactory System

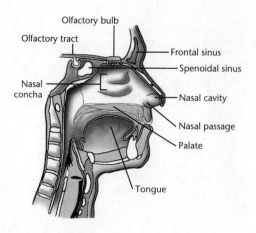

Areas of Taste on the Tongue

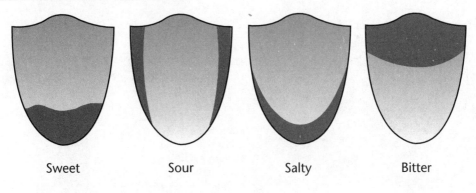

Sweet   Sour   Salty   Bitter

The Reproductive System

The major parts of the *male reproductive system* include the two testes, which are suspended in a sac (scrotum) that hangs below the groin, and the penis. The testes produce sperm and the male sex hormone testosterone. Behind each gland is a tube called the epididymis, which transports the sperm to the urethra for ejaculation through the penis. The prostate and Cowper's gland create the sperm; the sperm is carried in seminal fluid through the urethra from the male to the female reproductive tract during intercourse.

The *female reproductive system* consists of the ovaries, uterus, vagina, and related organs. The two ovaries contain thousands of eggs, and approximately once a month during a female's fertile years, an egg is released by one of the ovaries into the fallopian tube. If the egg is fertilized, it implants on the wall of the uterus.

The Male Reproductive System

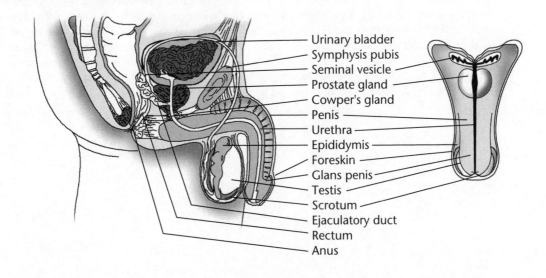

- Urinary bladder
- Symphysis pubis
- Seminal vesicle
- Prostate gland
- Cowper's gland
- Penis
- Urethra
- Epididymis
- Foreskin
- Glans penis
- Testis
- Scrotum
- Ejaculatory duct
- Rectum
- Anus

The Female Reproductive System

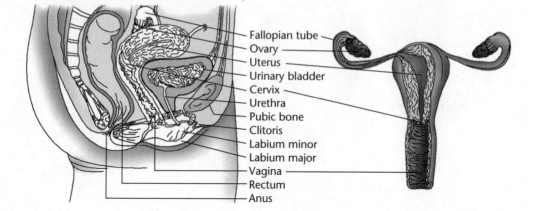

Fallopian tube
Ovary
Uterus
Urinary bladder
Cervix
Urethra
Pubic bone
Clitoris
Labium minor
Labium major
Vagina
Rectum
Anus

Menstruation and Menopause

During a woman's fertile years, she goes through a monthly cycle of *menstruation*—a combination of physical processes and hormone reactions (mostly from the hypothalamus, pituitary gland, and ovaries). A few days before menstruation, a woman experiences *ovulation* (or the release of an egg from one of the ovaries) and the lining of the uterus becomes engorged with blood to prepare for the possibility of fertilization by a sperm cell. If fertilization does occur, the egg burrows into the lining of the uterus and starts to grow, developing into an embryo. If the egg is not fertilized, the uterine lining is not needed and is shed, resulting in the release of blood passing through the cervix, to the vagina, and then out of the body. The result is the five-day (on average) "period"; approximately nine days later, a new lining begins to develop in the uterus, which starts the 28-day cycle all over again. The number of days of menstruation and the number of days between periods vary with the individual woman.

When ovulation begins to occur at irregular intervals, usually after age 45, a woman begins to experience *menopausal* symptoms. Menopause results in eventual cessation of periods. About 25 percent of women do not notice any physical or mental symptoms during menopause, and another 50 percent notice slight changes. The rest notice inconvenient physical symptoms, including hot flashes, sweating, dryness of the vagina, headaches, and heart palpitations. Some women also experience psychological symptoms, such as depression, irritability, anxiety, sleep disturbances, and difficulty concentrating. Most of the symptoms are caused by hormonal imbalances.

The Respiratory System

The purpose of the *respiratory system* is to take oxygen into the body and to get rid of carbon dioxide (a waste product). As oxygen is picked up by the blood, carbon dioxide is released.

The center of the respiratory system is the *lungs*. The respiratory tract, or the channel that air follows in and out of the lungs, includes the nose, throat, and trachea (or windpipe). The *trachea* divides into two tubes called bronchi, one of which travels to each lung (in addition,

The Respiratory System

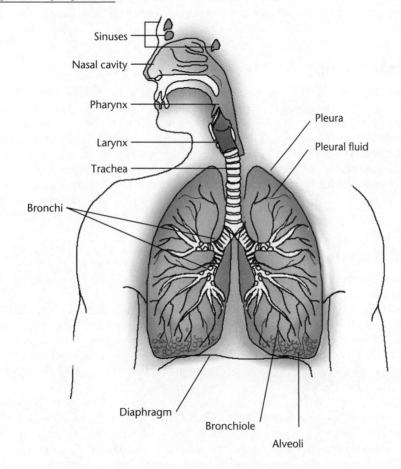

Sinuses

Nasal cavity

Pharynx

Larynx

Trachea

Bronchi

Pleura

Pleural fluid

Diaphragm

Bronchiole

Alveoli

at the top of the trachea is the *larynx*, or voicebox, which has membranes that tighten as air is exhaled, producing sound). The bronchi branch into smaller air passages called *bronchioles*. At the tip of each bronchiole is a balloonlike cavity called an *alveolus*. Each lung contains about 300 million alveoli. Tiny blood vessels in the thin walls of the alveoli exchange oxygen for carbon dioxide.

The *diaphragm*, a dome-shaped muscle (when relaxed) attached to the lower ribs, contracts and flattens when we inhale. The muscles between the ribs also contract, allowing the chest to expand upward and outward. The lungs expand, taking in air. When air is expelled from the lungs, the chest muscles and diaphragm relax, and the lungs contract, squeezing out the air. Not all the air released is carbon dioxide—there is still some oxygen mixed in the air from the lungs. This is why artificial respiration can restore a person's breathing in an emergency.

The Skeletal System

There are 206 *bones* that make up the human skeleton, most of which allow the body to move (as muscles contract, they pull on bones); store necessary calcium; and contain bone marrow, which produces the body's red and white blood cells and platelets. There are three types of bone: *long*, or cortical, bones (the leg and arm bones, which are capable of supporting great weights); *flat*, or compact, bones (like the skull and hip, which are stacked for strength); and *trabecular* bones (the vertebrae of the spine, which have features that fall somewhere in between the long and flat bones). *Cartilage* is a flexible but strong substance found at the joints and in the nose and ears; *ligaments* are the softer, more flexible tissues that attach the bones to each other.

The Immune System

The *immune system* protects the body from infections, diseases, and injury-causing agents. It is made up of the lymphatic system and the skin.

The *lymphatic system* is composed of lymph nodes and small vessels (lymphatics). The nodes are usually about 0.5 to 10 inches (1 to 25 centimeters) across. Medium-size nodes are located in the groin and armpits; smaller nodes are located in the throat and the trunk. They act in coordination with the body's immune system to fight off infectious agents (such as bacteria); the lymph nodes often swell in response to infection. The system is found throughout the entire body, and the nodes are connected to each other via the lymphatics.

Lymphocytes are also found in the lymph system and are known as white blood cells. These cells defend the body against foreign agents. *Phagocytes* are also a type of white blood cell. These cells filter and cleanse the lymph system by ingesting bacteria and cell fragments. (For more information on lymphocytes and phagocytes, see "White Blood Cells," earlier in this chapter.)

The *skin* is part of the immune system because it protects the body from physical injury. Hundreds of small nerves in the skin send impulses to the brain, which are felt as physical pressure, pain, or other associated sensations. It is the body's largest organ, with its total surface area being about 20 square feet (1.9 square meters) for an average-size person. It weighs about 5.6 pounds (2.7 kilograms).

The skin serves as a barrier to prevent injury to organs, repel dirt and water, and stop the entry of most harmful chemicals—all in one package. It has sweat glands that cool the body and glands that lubricate the body with necessary oils—both of which kill or retard the growth of certain harmful bacteria. It also has hair follicles that provide hair for protection of the skull and other parts of the body.

The Skeletal System

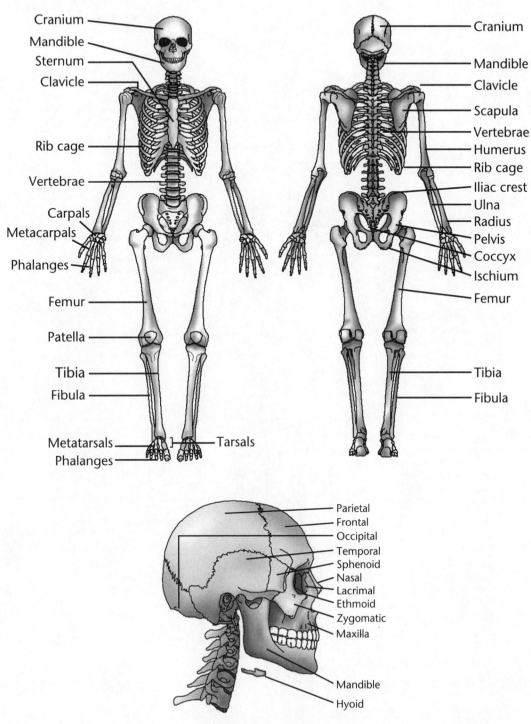

Cranium
Mandible
Sternum
Clavicle
Rib cage
Vertebrae
Carpals
Metacarpals
Phalanges
Femur
Patella
Tibia
Fibula
Metatarsals
Phalanges

Cranium
Mandible
Clavicle
Scapula
Vertebrae
Humerus
Rib cage
Iliac crest
Ulna
Radius
Pelvis
Coccyx
Ischium
Femur
Tibia
Fibula

Tarsals

Parietal
Frontal
Occipital
Temporal
Sphenoid
Nasal
Lacrimal
Ethmoid
Zygomatic
Maxilla
Mandible
Hyoid

Skull Bones

The Lymphatic System

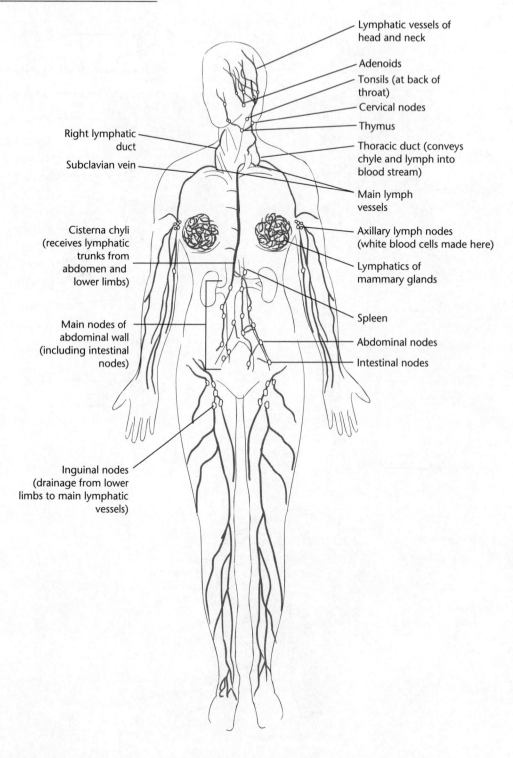

Lymphatic vessels of head and neck

Adenoids

Tonsils (at back of throat)

Cervical nodes

Thymus

Thoracic duct (conveys chyle and lymph into blood stream)

Main lymph vessels

Axillary lymph nodes (white blood cells made here)

Lymphatics of mammary glands

Spleen

Abdominal nodes

Intestinal nodes

Right lymphatic duct

Subclavian vein

Cisterna chyli (receives lymphatic trunks from abdomen and lower limbs)

Main nodes of abdominal wall (including intestinal nodes)

Inguinal nodes (drainage from lower limbs to main lymphatic vessels)

The Skin

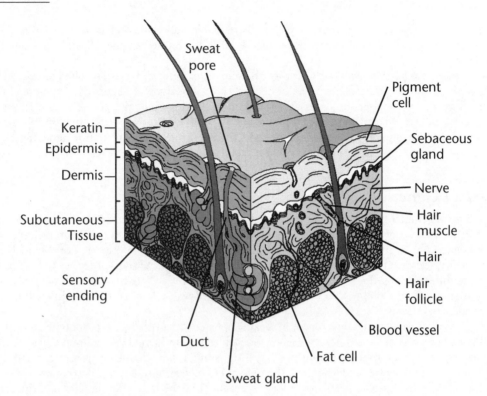

Sweat pore

Pigment cell

Keratin
Epidermis
Dermis

Sebaceous gland

Nerve

Subcutaneous Tissue

Hair muscle

Sensory ending

Hair

Hair follicle

Duct

Blood vessel

Fat cell

Sweat gland

WHAT IS SKIN CANCER?

Although the skin is an excellent protector, it can also be a fragile organ, especially when exposed to ultraviolet rays from the Sun. One result of exposure is the burning of the skin—another is the possible development of skin cancer after successive exposures to the Sun.

Skin cancer is one of the most common of cancers, and one of the most curable if treated early. There are three types of skin cancer. Squamous and basal cell (the two most common) skin cancers are usually caused by excessive exposure to the Sun and occur most often on the face, shoulders, and arms—or the areas most exposed to sunlight. They are usually eliminated by the removal of the affected areas. Melanomas, the least common, are cancers of the pigment-producing cells of the skin. They can grow into the deeper layers of the skin, and if unchecked, can metastasize—spread to other parts of the body—making it the most dangerous of the skin cancers.

Statistics show that there has been an increase in skin cancer over the past half century. Researchers theorize that an increase in skin cancer may be the result of two events: the increase in leisure activity (thus an increase in the number of hours we spend in the Sun) and the decrease the Earth's ozone layer, which protects us from the ultraviolet rays (for more information on the ozone layer, see Chapter 11, "Environmental Science").

What are the best ways to reduce your chances of skin cancer? Doctors recommend a sunscreen lotion or cream with a Sun protection factor (SPF) rating of 15 or more. All people, especially the fair skinned, should avoid excessive exposure to the Sun, using sunscreen or clothing that covers the skin. Be sure to have your doctor check any suspicious dark spot or growth on your skin.

GENETICS

It is *heredity* that causes offspring to physically resemble their parents. Heredity makes it likely that tall parents with blue eyes will have blue-eyed children who become tall adults in a suitable environment.

Since early in the twentieth century, the science of heredity has been called *genetics*. The agents of heredity were named *genes*, and genetics is the study of genes. But for most of the century, the physical nature of genes was unknown. During that time, the science of classical genetics developed explanations of how combinations of genes produce traits in offspring. Later, when genes themselves had been located, modern genetics arose to explain how genes function, and to identify the chemical and physical makeup of particular genes.

Classical Genetics

Classical genetics began with the work of Gregor Mendel, a monk in the nineteenth century, but his discoveries about heredity were unknown until 1900, when three different biologists recognized his contribution and gave it wide publicity (for more information on Mendel and heredity, see Chapter 4, "Biology"). Mendel had shown that some traits are inherited in an all-or-nothing fashion. If a white-flowered pea plant is bred with a red-flowered variety, the offspring are all pure red, not pink. Mendel said that red was a dominant trait, while white was hidden, or recessive.

As classical genetics developed, it became apparent that usually every individual has two copies of each gene (you inherit one gene for each trait from each of your parents). Gene codes are responsible for all the different biological traits in an individual (they *generate* traits). For example, in the peas Mendel studied, the red variety of peas normally has two copies of a gene for color. In this case, the gene for color is symbolized by the letters *Rr*. The form of the color gene that makes the flowers red is called *R*. The color gene that makes the pea flowers white is called *r*. The capital letter *R* means that the trait "red flowers" is the *dominant* form of this gene; the lower-case letter *r* means that the trait "white flowers" is the *recessive* form of this gene. The different forms for a particular gene are called *alleles*; the gene is for "color" and the allele codes for the "particular color." Thus a pure-bred red-flowered pea has the alleles *RR* for the genetic trait of color; a white-flowered pea has the alleles *rr*.

The situation becomes more complicated when the pea plant has mixed alleles: *Rr*. Because the *R* allele is the dominant one, an *Rr* plant will have red flowers. It takes only one copy of a dominant allele to have that trait show up in the individual, which is why it is called "dominant." Because the *r* allele is recessive, an individual plant must have two copies of this allele (*rr*, or no copies of the *R* allele) to have white flowers.

When two plants with the allele combination *Rr* are bred with each other, probability statistics must be used to predict the type of offspring that will occur from each breeding. Each parent contributes one allele to each offspring. Thus four different types of offspring arise from the breeding of an *Rr* plant with an *Rr* plant:

Parents	*Offspring*
Plant 1's *R* with Plant 2's *R*	*RR* (red flowers)
Plant 1's *R* with Plant 2's *r*	*Rr* (red flowers)
Plant 1's *r* with Plant 2's *R*	*rR* (red flowers)
Plant 1's *r* with Plant 2's *r*	*rr* (white flowers)

Thus for any given mating, the offspring has a 75 percent chance (three combinations out of four) of having red flowers. This probability applies to each individual offspring separately. In the case of plants, when hundreds of seeds might be produced, each seed from this type of breeding has a 75 percent chance of producing a plant with red flowers.

Heredity is usually more complex than the case of flower color in pea plants. Snapdragons, for example, have what is called *incomplete dominance* with respect to the gene for flower color. If R is the allele for red flowers and W is the allele for white flowers in the snapdragon, the allele combinations RW and WR are pink; when two pink snapdragons are crossed, their offspring can be either RR, RW, WR, or WW. Thus each individual plant from this cross has a 25 percent chance (one combination out of four) of having red flowers, a 50 percent chance (two combinations out of four) of having pink flowers, and a 25 percent chance (one combination out of four) of having white flowers.

The situation is complicated further because most traits in living organisms are the result of a complex mixture of several different genes, some of which may also be influenced by the environment. Height in humans is a typical example of such a trait. Although the alleles of several different genes of the parents influence height in offspring, there is no single gene for tallness. Diet affects height, and well-fed children of short parents are often taller than either parent, especially if the parents grew up in poverty. Certain childhood illnesses can also affect the individual's final adult height.

Modern Genetics and Chromosomes

Classical geneticists recognized that genes are located on rod-shaped structures in the body's cells. These structures can be observed only by staining a cell that is about to divide. Because the structures become colored by the stain, they are called *chromosomes*.

Most organisms have pairs of chromosomes, although sometimes there are four matched chromosomes or another type of grouping. Humans have 23 pairs of chromosomes, or a total of 46 individual chromosomes. Within each pair of human chromosomes—except for one pair in males—the same genes appear in the same order on each structure, but the alleles are not necessarily the same on both chromosomes. For example, a gene that controls eye color can be found at the same location on each one of a pair of chromosomes, but the allele may be for blue eyes on one chromosome and for brown eyes on the other.

The exception to pairing of chromosomes is the pair that controls the sex of an individual. In general, each member of the pair in male humans is very different from the other, with a sex chromosome called X and a small one called Y; female humans have two X chromosomes.

Sometimes, an individual has an unusual combination of chromosomes, which usually is manifest by a variety of disorders. The most well known disorder of this type is Down's syndrome. Down's syndrome individuals have three copies of chromosome number 21, and in fact, the disorder is quite often referred to as trisomy 21. Although a few other unusual chromosome combinations have been described, such individuals usually are not born alive.

The exact number of genes in any given living organism is not known, but there are probably about 100,000 different genes in a human being. There are two copies of each gene (the alleles) in each body cell—one copy on each chromosome of a matched pair. The best available evidence supports a theory that can be called "one gene, one protein." That means that each gene carries out its function by directing the manufacture of a single protein. The protein product may have a directly observable effect: for example, the gene that causes the production of blue pigment in the eyes. More often, however, a gene does not have a direct observable effect: for example, a gene that codes for a protein that is then modified by other chemicals in the body.

Most genes work together this way to build and maintain all the structures and functions of all the cells that make up the body.

Chromosomes copy themselves when a body (somatic) cell reproduces by division (splits into two new cells). Each of the new cells obtains either an original chromosome or a copy. In that way, each of the daughter cells has the same genes as the original cell. This process is called *mitosis*.

Egg and sperm cell chromosomes undergo a different process, called *meiosis*. Egg and sperm cells receive half the chromosomes of each parent cell. Members from each pair are taken at random to produce the set of 23 individual chromosomes in an egg or sperm cell, but because all the pairs are represented, there is a full set of genes. When the egg and sperm unite to initiate a new individual, the allele combinations for that individual are different from either parent, although all the alleles come from the parents. In that way, the gene combinations carry both the hereditary traits of the parents and also provide variation, since the offspring often has a different set of alleles than either parent.

What Is DNA?

The part of each chromosome that includes the genes is a single giant molecule of a chemical called *deoxyribonucleic acid* (DNA). Most of the rest of the chromosome consists of proteins that hold the DNA and aid the functioning of the genes and the whole chromosome. The DNA itself is a long coil called a *double helix*, which is often compared to a twisted ladder. The opposite sides of the ladder are spirals of a *sugar-phosphate* combination. The rungs of the ladder represent a pair of molecular subgroups called *bases*; a combination of one base with the sugar-phosphate section of the side is called a *nucleotide*. Technically, DNA is a polymer (like a plastic), since it is formed by stringing together nucleotides at any length.

There are four different bases in DNA—*adenine* (A), *thiamin* (T), *guanine* (G), and *cytosine* (C). The bases are linked to each other to form a "rung," but because of their structure, the bases can only link in certain pairs. A always links with T, and G links with C (for more information on DNA, see Chapter 4, "Biology"). When a chromosome divides as part of cell reproduction, a special enzyme gradually takes the two halves of the twisted ladder apart; each half is called a strand of DNA. During cell division, there are many free-floating nucleotides in the cell that are attracted to the nucleotides in the separated DNA strands. But because A can only go with T (and not with G or C), two copies of double-stranded DNA are formed, each exactly like the original. In this way heredity traits are carried from cell to cell and from parent to child.

The pattern of bases along one strand of DNA contains the information needed to build a whole group of proteins. The recipe for each protein is encoded in a sequence of bases. An analogy is the way letters form written words; but a protein is more like a long sentence than a single word, since it may be formed from hundreds of building blocks, called *amino acids*. The gene is a coded recipe for building a protein. One strand of DNA (called the "sense" strand) contains the recipe for the protein; the complementary strand of DNA contains the recipe for the recipe and is used only when cells divide.

A total of 20 different amino acids are used in building proteins, and each one can be represented by three bases in a row—a triplet that is called a *codon* (for more information on amino acids, see Chapter 4, "Biology"). Since there are 64 combinations of the four bases taken three at a time, and only 20 amino acids are created, most amino acids can be encoded in two or as many as four different codons. Also, there are three codons that mean "stop" (like a period at the end of the sentence), and one that means "start" (like a capital letter at the start of the sentence).

DNA

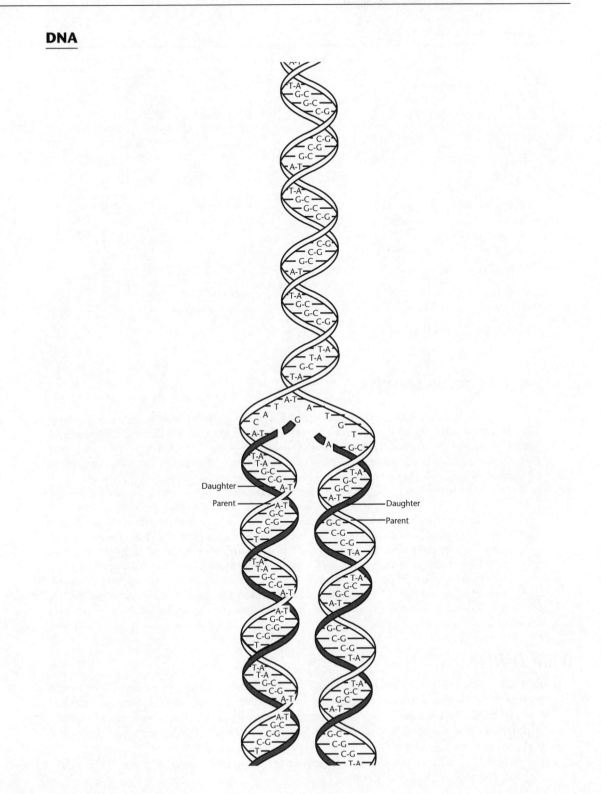

The Genetic Code in DNA

Codon	Amino Acid	Codon	Amino Acid	Codon	Amino Acid	Codon	Amino Acid
UUU UUC	} Phenylalanine*	UCU UCC	}	UAU UAC	} Tyrosine*	UGU UGC	} Cysteine*
UUA UUG	} Leucine	UCA UCG	} Serine	UAA UAG	} Terminate	UGA	Terminate
						UGG	Tryptophan*
CUU CUC CUA CUG	} Leucine*	CCU CCC CCA CCG	} Proline	CAU CAC	} Histidine*	CGU CGC CGA CGG	} Arginine
				CAA CAG	} Glutamine		
AUU AUC AUA	} Isoleucine*	ACU ACC ACA ACG	} Threonine*	AAU AAC	} Asparagine	AGU AGC	} Serine
AUG	Methionine*			AAA AAG	} Lysine*	AGA AGG	} Arginine
GUU GUC GUA GUG	} Valine*	GCU GCC GCA GCG	} Alanine	GAU GAC	} Aspartic acid	GGU GGC GGA GGG	} Glycine
				GAA GAG	} Glutamic acid		

Essential amino acid for humans.

GENETIC FINGERPRINTS

In several recent famous criminal cases, DNA has been featured because it can be used to help identify persons. The DNA in each one of your body cells is identical, whether the cell comes from blood, saliva, skin, or hair follicles. Another reason for the use of DNA in criminal cases is that statistically, only 1 in 3 million individuals will have the same DNA profile (with the exception of identical twins, who have matching DNA because they came from the same fertilized egg).

Here's how the DNA is used to identify an individual. First, DNA is extracted from cells found at a crime scene and also from the suspect's blood. To make a DNA profile, chemicals are used that break the long strands of DNA at specific places. The fragments are then separated by size and other characteristics and specially treated so that the fragments form a pattern of lines of various thicknesses. This pattern is the DNA profile. Because there is such a low statistical probability that two individuals chosen at random will have the same profile, many courts allow DNA profiles to be used as evidence in criminal cases. When DNA is used this way, it is sometimes called a "genetic fingerprint." In addition, a DNA profile from the badly decomposed body of a murder victim has often been compared with a parent's blood DNA profile for purposes of identification.

What Is RNA?

Ribonucleic acid (RNA) is the chemical that translates the genetic code of the DNA into a protein. RNA is also a polymer whose parts are phosphate, sugar, and the base nucleotides. Unlike DNA, RNA is formed as a single strand, and its sugar is different from that in DNA. Furthermore, one of the four bases in RNA is different from DNA's: RNA links together guanine (G) and cytosine (C); adenine (A) links with a base called uracil (U).

When a cell makes a protein, the recipe is coded in the DNA, but the "cook" is the RNA. Here are the steps of protein synthesis.

1. The first step is *transcription*, in which a type of RNA called *messenger* RNA (mRNA) forms along the DNA and matches it base for base—that is, each C on the DNA matches a G on the RNA and vice versa, while each A on the DNA matches a U on RNA and each T on DNA matches an A on RNA.

2. The mRNA then moves to a structure in the cell called a ribosome, where the second process, *translation*, takes place. In the ribosome, the mRNA is pulled through the ribosome one codon at a time. As each codon passes through, it is matched with a small molecule of RNA called *transfer RNA* (tRNA).

3. The tRNA picks up an amino acid from among those that are naturally floating around in the cell. There are 20 special proteins in the cell that match the appropriate tRNA and amino acid.

4. The tRNAs drop off their amino acids in the ribosome. The amino acids are then added one at a time to the new protein chain that is being formed there.

5. As the ribosome pulls along the mRNA strand, the protein chain grows to a length of perhaps 100 or even 500 amino acids. When a "stop" codon is reached on the RNA, the protein chain pops out and the mRNA leaves the ribosome.

6. Left to its own devices, the protein folds itself into a characteristic shape and begins to interact with other molecules in the cell.

Genetic Engineering

New details are still being learned about how genes work, but by the early 1970s enough was known about genes that it became possible to manipulate genes in simple organisms, such as bacteria. Inserting new genes into DNA, removing existing genes, or changing part of a gene is called *genetic engineering*. By 1974, scientists and others had begun to worry that genetic engineering might produce dangerous new life forms. Scientists soon set up special committees to oversee experiments in genetic engineering.

For practical purposes, genetic engineering began when scientists added the gene for human insulin to the DNA of a common bacterium in such a way that the bacterium could then produce insulin. Insulin is an important hormone, and the lack of insulin causes a form of diabetes. The only treatment for this form of diabetes is regular injections of insulin, most of which comes from pigs. But some diabetics are allergic to this type of insulin. Genetic engineering has allowed human insulin to be manufactured in large amounts simply by growing the bacteria in tanks and removing the insulin. Today, many other human proteins are made in the same manner. These proteins (hormones, enzymes, and other biological chemicals) have helped to treat growth deficiencies, hemophilia, multiple sclerosis, and many other diseases for which there was previously no known treatment.

Since the 1970s, scientists have learned how to introduce new genes into higher organisms, including yeasts, human cells kept alive in laboratories, farm animals, and plants. While such genetic engineering is often used to manufacture proteins for use separately, the new genes can also be used to change an organism. For example, farm animals have been genetically engineered to be larger. Plants have also been genetically engineered to resist diseases or insects; and in 1994, tomatoes that were genetically engineered to ripen more slowly were introduced in the marketplace.

TYPES OF HEALTH CARE PROVIDERS

allergist   A physician specializing in the diagnosis and treatment of allergies.

anesthesiologist   A physician who is concerned with the administration of anesthesia and then the condition of the patient who is under anesthesia.

audiologist   A specialist who evaluates hearing problems and advises on the possible use of hearing aids.

cardiologist   A physician who specializes in cardiovascular problems; although a cardiologist is not a surgeon, he or she often performs invasive procedures such as angioplasty (see also *cardiovascular surgeon*).

cardiovascular surgeon   A physician who operates on the cardiovascular system.

chiropractor   A health care professional who concentrates on nonsurgical, drugless treatments for patients and uses physical manipulation. Chiropractic work centers on the idea that unaligned vertebrae and their surrounding ligaments put pressure on spinal nerves, causing pain and a variety of internal disorders.

dentist   A doctor who specializes in teeth and associated structures of the oral cavity; dentists may specialize in operative (restoring parts of the teeth), preventive (maintenance of the structures in the mouth), and prosthetic (artificial appliances to replace missing teeth) dentistry.

dermatologist   A physician who evaluates and treats diseases of the skin.

electrophysiologist   A specialist who works with electrical phenomena involved in physiological processes, such as those used in cardiology, neurology, and sleep studies.

endocrinologist   A physician who in the endocrine system, or the glands that regulate body activity by special secretions, such as the thyroid, pituitary, and adrenal glands.

epidemiologist   A physician or scientist who studies the incidence of disease in populations and the influence of the environment and lifestyle on disease patterns, for example, how tobacco (in association with smoking) has affected the health of a particular population.

gastrointerologist   A physician who specializes in digestive and intestinal problems.

general (or family) practitioner   A physician who treats patients for a multitude of diseases and disorders; cases that he or she does not feel qualified to handle are sent to specialists.

geriatrician   A physician who specializes in the care and medical problems of older people.

gynecologist   A physician who specializes in the health and diseases of the female reproductive organs.

hematologist   A physician who specializes in blood problems, especially those involving the bone marrow.

histologist   A physician or scientist who studies the form and structure of various tissues in the body.

immunologist   A physician who specializes in the body's natural defense mechanism against disease (or immunity).

naturopathologist   A health care professional who uses a drugless system of healing, which is based on the principle that waste products and toxins build up in the body and cause disease. The naturopathologist uses natural foods and physical methods of treatment (air, water, and light) to treat disease.

nephrologist   A physician who specializes in the diseases of the kidneys.

neurologist   A physician who specializes in the functions and disorders of the nervous system.

nurse practitioner   A health care professional who takes care of the sick and injured; a nurse practitioner is not licensed to prescribe certain treatments.

obstetrician   A physician who deals with pregnancy and delivery (obstetrics).

oculist   See *ophthalmologist*

oncologist   A physician who studies the causes, development, characteristics, and treatment of tumors; usually associated with cancer treatment.

ophthalmologist   A physician who specializes in the anatomy, physiology, and diseases of the eye (also called an oculist).

optician   A technician who makes glasses and contact lenses.

optometrist   A doctor who measures a patient's visual powers and acuity, prescribes corrective lenses, and diagnoses and treats diseases of the eye.

oral and maxillofacial surgeons   Physicians who specialize in problems of the jaw and mouth. The oral surgeon usually extracts teeth, and the maxillofacial surgeon often treats patients with facial problems associated with the upper and lower jaw areas.

orthodontist   A doctor who specializes in the bite and tooth alignment of the mouth.

orthopedic surgeon   Physicians who specializes in the corrective treatment of musculo-skeletal deformities, diseases, and ailments.

osteopath   A physician who sometimes uses manipulation of the neuromusculoskeletal system (bones, muscles, tendons, nerves, spinal cord, tissues, and brain) to determine and treat health problems.

otolaryngologist   A physician who specializes in problems of the ears, nose, and throat (also called an otorhinolaryngologist).

pathologist   A physician or scientist who specializes in the causes, processes, and alterations of organs and tissues produced by disease.

pediatrician   A physician who specializes in the health problems and medical treatment of children and adolescents.

periodontist   A doctor who specializes in gum and bone problems of the mouth, especially gum disease.

pharmacist   A health care professional who compounds and dispenses medications prescribed by physicians, dentists, and optometrists.

pharmacologist   A scientist who studies all aspects of drugs.

physiatrist   A health care professional who specializes in rehabilitation, using heat, light, water, and electricity to diagnose and treat a wide variety of physical problems.

physical therapist   A health care professional who uses heat, cold, physical manipulations, and so on to treat a wide array of physical health problems.

physiologist   A physician or scientist who studies the functions of an organism and its parts by chemical and physical methods.

podiatrist   A physician who specializes in foot problems, such as corns, bunions, and bone spurs; also called a chiropodist.

primary care physician   A physician who plans and provides comprehensive primary health care to all members of a family, regardless of age or sex, on a continuing basis (similar to a family practitioner).

prosthodontist   A doctor who specializes in the construction of appliances to replace missing or broken teeth, and sometimes other parts of the face and oral cavity.

psychiatrist   A physician who specializes in the diagnosis, treatment, and prevention of mind disorders.

psychologist   A health care professional who deals with mental processes and behavior.

pulmonologist   A physician who specializes in lung problems.

radiologist   A technician who specializes in the use of such diagnostic techniques as x-rays, CT scans, and MRI for the diagnosis and treatment of diseases (see "Biomedical Laboratory Technology" later in this chapter).

radiotherapist   A health care professional who detects and treats disease using radiation therapy, such as x-ray treatments for breast cancer.

rheumantologist   A physician who specializes in the diagnoses and treatment of rheumatic diseases, such as arthritis, vasculitis, and lupus.

traumatologist   A physician who specializes in trauma injuries, especially damage caused by violent external forces (e.g., from automobile accidents).

urologist   A physician specializing in problems of the urinary tract, including urine problems, prostate conditions, impotence, and incontinence.

virologist   A physician or scientist who specializes in viruses.

HOW DO WOUNDS HEAL?

If you cut your hand, the body's first response is to stop the bleeding. Blood-borne cells known as platelets move through the arteries to reach the injured site; once there, they secrete a sticky substance that "glues" the cells together. This plug seals the leaking blood vessels until the liver can secrete chemicals into the blood to cause it to clot. Threadlike fibers called fibrin form a web in the gelled blood, holding together the sides of the cut. As the platelets accumulate, they put more pressure on the web, causing a clot to form and harden on the surface of the skin. As this dries, a scab forms—a natural cover to protect the area.

Next, phagocytosis, a cleaning process, begins. White blood cells are sent into the area to "eat" any bacteria, dirt, or dead cells in the wound. Within 6 to 12 hours, after the white blood cells have done their job, a stronger type of white blood cell enters the area to attack harmful microbes, dead tissue, and spent white blood cells. These all form pus, evidence of an infection and the body's reaction to that infection.

Approximately 24 hours later, cells in the injured skin and blood vessels begin to reattach themselves. Small blood vessels send out tendrils that spread through gelled blood and reestablish blood flow. Meanwhile, the surface skin cells grow together to close the outside of the wound. Below the surface of the scab, fibroblasts ("builder cells") move along capillaries and fibrin strands to bridge the wound. As they move, the fibroblasts release a chemical that combines with other chemicals in the wound to create collagen, the basic structural material of skin, cartilage, ligaments, and tendons. Collagen closes the wound and completes the tissue repair.

COMMON MEDICAL PROBLEMS

Common medical problems include communicable, hereditary and genetic, chronic, and other diseases.

Communicable Diseases

The majority of communicable (or contagious) diseases are those thought to be spread from human to human. Not all communicable diseases are spread by direct contact. For example, Legionnaire's disease is communicable because it is contracted from air-conditioning systems, but it is doubtful that one person can give it to another.

acquired immunodeficiency syndrome (AIDS)   AIDS was first reported in 1981, by the United States Centers for Disease Control and Prevention. The condition is caused by the human immunodeficiency virus (HIV), which attacks the T-cell lymphocytes of the immune system, leaving the body vulnerable to serious illnesses that are normally repelled by a healthy immune system. HIV is transferred through blood and other body fluids. It is not spread by casual contact. Three main groups appear to be at risk: those engaging in unprotected sexual contact, those sharing unsterilized drug needles, and hemophiliacs receiving regular blood transfusions (this is rare, as blood transfusions have been tested for HIV and AIDS for the past decade).

chicken pox (herpes zoster)   The virus that causes chicken pox (vericella) is called herpes zoster; it is highly contagious. It is acquired through the respiratory system and is then carried by the bloodstream to all parts of the body. Chicken pox symptoms do not usually appear until about two weeks after exposure. The first symptoms include fever, headache, and loss of appetite; an itchy rash of small blisters develops in about two days, and after a few days, the blisters break and scab over. There is a vaccine for high-risk patients (usually those with suppressed immune systems); in the 1990s, a new vaccine was being tested.

colds   There are close to 200 known cold viruses that cause the so-called common cold. Symptoms include runny nose, slight fever, muscle ache, slight cough, and nasal congestion. It is also called an upper respiratory infection. Colds can lead to ear infections or pneumonia.

diphtheria   Diphtheria is a highly contagious childhood disease that often affects the throat and, less commonly, the nose. It is caused by the bacterium *Corynebacterium diphtheriae* and is characterized by a severe sore throat, fever, headache, and nausea. In later stages of the disease a membrane can develop in the throat, which, along with swelling, can cause breathing problems. Diphtheria is all but eradicated from the United States but is still widespread in some countries. It is treated with a diphtheria antitoxin and antibiotics.

Epstein-Barr virus   See *mononucleosis*

hepatitis   Hepatitis, an inflammation of the liver, can occur in several ways. Hepatitis is caused by a virus and is commonly divided into A and B types, although there are other types. Both the A and B types can be either mild or serious. Hepatitis A virus (HAV) is transmitted by the fecal-oral route, and hepatitis B virus (HBV) is transmitted by sexual contact (making it a sexually transmitted disease). Hepatitis C was recognized as a separate disease in 1975 (although it was isolated in 1987); it is a blood-borne disease.

herpes simplex   There are two types of herpes simplex: type I (nongenital) and type II (primarily genital). Type I—contagious and commonly noticed as cold sores around the mouth—is an inflammation of the skin caused by a virus, which creates groups of small, painful blisters. Type II is usually found in the genital area and can be passed from person to person through sexual contact. It is an inflammation of the skin that causes groups of small, fluid-filled blisters. Accompanying flu symptoms are also common. It is possible to have a combination of types I and II on the mouth.

influenza   Influenza is an infectious disease caused by a virus. After a brief incubation period, the most common symptoms include fever, chills, sore throat, headache, cough, and achiness. There are no medications to cure influenza, but drugs are often taken to reduce the discomfort. There are also influenza vaccines. Unfortunately, they will not guard against all of the influenza viruses.

leprosy (Hansen's disease)   Leprosy is a communicable disease characterized by the presence of lesions of the skin, of some mucous membranes of the respiratory system, and of the peripheral nerves. It is believed to be caused by the bacterium *Mycobacterium leprae* (Hansen's bacillus), which is known to attack the skin and nerves, excluding the brain. How leprosy is transmitted is unknown; it is rare and considered the least contagious of the infectious diseases.

measles   Measles is an infectious disease caused by a virus. Initially, it is characterized by a runny nose, cough, slight fever, and aches in the head, neck, and back. By the third or fourth day, the fever ranges between 103° and 104°F, and a rash appears. It is primarily a childhood disease, but can be contracted at any time, usually by breathing airborne droplets or contacting an object touched by an infected person. The incubation period is about 11 days, and the infected person can transmit the disease three to four days before the rash appears. Measles is not as prevalent now as it was a few decades ago, though there are occasional outbreaks of the disease. A vaccine is available. (See also *rubella*.)

meningitis   Meningitis is an infectious disease that is either bacterial or viral. It is characterized by the inflammation of the membranes that cover the brain and spinal cord. The most common form of bacterial meningitis is called meningococcal meningitis, transmitted by airborne droplets and by contact; the incubation period is 2 to 10 days. The most common symptoms are a stiff neck, violent persistent headache and vomiting, and later, convulsions and delirium. Bacterial meningitis is treated with antibiotics. Viral meningitis produces milder symptoms.

mononucleosis (infectious mononucleosis; Epstein-Barr virus)   Mononucleosis (mono) is caused by a virus. Symptoms include severe sore throat, swollen glands in the neck, armpits, and groin, swollen tonsils, and prolonged fatigue.

mumps   Mumps is a viral infection that attacks and enlarges the parotid glands, which are located just below and in front of the ears. It is highly contagious.

pneumonia   Infectious pneumonia is caused by a bacterium or virus, and there are many types of pneumonia (e.g., lobar, bronchial, primary atypical, and chemical). It is characterized by an acute inflammation or infection of the lung and is generally found in children and older adults. The microorganisms that cause pneumonia are always present in the lungs; it is the lowering of resistance—by a severe cold, alcoholism, disease, or general poor health—that triggers an attack. Pneumonia may also be caused by exposure to certain irritating chemicals. Bacterial pneumonia can be treated with antibiotics; viral pneumonia usually has to run its course.

poliomyelitis (polio; infantile paralysis)   Polio is a contagious disease caused by a virus that attacks the central nervous system, injuring or destroying nerve cells that control the muscles. Polio often leads to paralysis (mostly in the legs) and to problems with muscles, including those involved in swallowing and breathing. Poliomyelitis is now rare in the United States, thanks to vaccination programs.

rubella (German measles)   Not as infectious as measles, rubella is a childhood disease caused by a virus that is spread from the nose and throat of an infected person. The incubation period is

14 to 21 days; it is characterized by a sore throat, swollen glands (behind the ears), slight fever, and pink spots all over the body. One bout with rubella usually builds up immunity to the disease for life. It is of particular concern to pregnant women, because rubella during the first three or four months of pregnancy can cause birth defects.

sexually transmitted diseases (STDs)   See also *acquired immunodeficiency syndrome, hepatitis* (HBV form), and *herpes simplex*

> **chlamydia**   Chlamydia is an infectious disease that may be a more prevalent STD than gonorrhea. It is caused by the bacterium *Chlamydia* and is transmitted by sexual contact. It is often discovered during a routine exam. Symptoms in women include a green vaginal discharge, but in most cases, it goes unnoticed until internal pain develops. Undetected, chlamydia can lead to infertility and can infect a newborn during birth. It is treated with antibiotics.

> **gonorrhea**   Gonorrhea was once called a venereal disease but is now classified as an STD. This is an infectious disease that is contracted from an infected partner during sexual intercourse and is caused by the gonococcus bacterium. The incubation period is 2 to 10 days. In males, symptoms include a burning sensation during urination and an irritation of the penis (caused by the infection at the end of the urethra). If the infection continues up the urethra, it can lead to urethritis, or an inflammation of the urethra. Symptoms in females include a burning sensation during urination and a milky discharge from the vagina. Untreated cases can often lead to complications, such as arthritis, conjunctivitis (eye inflammation), and endocarditis (heart inflammation); it can also cause infertility in women. Antibiotics are used to treat gonorrhea.

> **human papillomavirus (HPV; genital warts)**   Genital warts, an STD, are caused by HPV; the condition is also called *condylomata acuminata* or venereal warts. There are few symptoms to genital warts, which is why it is easily spread through sexual contact. Small, hard spots appear three weeks to three months after exposure around all parts of the groin area. In women, the spots can appear around and in the vagina, around the anus, and on the cervix; in men, the spots appear on the tip of the penis, although the shaft, scrotum, and anus may also be involved. The warts may also appear on the mouth if a person has had oral sex. Genital warts in women is thought to increase the risk of cervical cancer. Treatment consists of removal of the warts, although the warts often reappear.

> **pelvic inflammatory disease (PID)**   PID is the inflammation of the upper female reproductive system, including the uterus, ovaries, fallopian tubes, and nearby structures. It is most often caused by gonorrhea or chlamydia, as the infection travels up the reproductive tract, and thus is classified as an STD. The symptoms include fever or sharp pain in the genital area. PID can also be chronic, remaining undetected over a long period. It often leads to infertility, as the fallopian tubes become scarred. It is usually treated with antibiotics and other medications.

> **syphilis**   Syphilis was once called a venereal disease but is now classified as an STD. It is an infectious disease contracted from an infected partner during sexual intercourse. Also, an infected mother can infect her unborn child during the later stages of pregnancy. It is caused by the spiral-shaped bacterium *Treponema pallidum*, which needs a moist environment to survive. Hard sores appear in the groin area about three weeks (though it can vary from 10 to 90 days) after the initial contact. Six weeks later, the bacteria have entered the bloodstream, affecting all parts of the body. The most common symptoms include a skin rash and sores, low-grade fever, sore throat, enlargement of the lymph glands, and sores on the mouth—all lasting for a short time. Untreated cases allow the bacterium

to invade organs and tissues of the body, which may lead to serious complications years after the initial infection. The last stage of syphilis is characterized by rubbery growths anywhere in the body, including membranes of the nose and throat and in the liver, lungs, or stomach. Syphilis can lead to a number of conditions, including heart disease, inflammation of the bones, degeneration of the spinal cord, blindness, and in the latter stages, mental illness. In women, it can also cause infertility. It is treated with antibiotics.

trichomoniasis   Trichomoniasis is an STD caused by the parasite *Trichomonoas vaginalis*. Trich has few symptoms; when the infected individual does show symptoms, it is often 4 to 20 days after exposure (although some symptoms may not show up until years later). In women, the symptoms include painful urination, vaginal discharge, abdominal pain, and itching in the genital region (it is usually discovered during a routine Pap smear). Men experience painful urination and an unusual whitish discharge from the penis. Although not serious in itself, it can lead to chronic inflammation of the urinary tract and may make a person more susceptible to other types of infection.

shingles   After contracting chicken pox, either in childhood or adulthood, herpes zoster (the same virus that causes chicken pox) can erupt as shingles. Like chicken pox, shingles erupts as small blisters and usually follows a nerve or a swath across the midsection. Shingles occur because a person's built-up immunity to the chicken pox virus decreases with age. Because the nerves and skin are inflamed, shingles can lead to a type of neuralgia, resulting in a sharp, burning pain where the shingles blisters occurred.

smallpox (variola)   Smallpox is one of the most infectious diseases known. Caused by a virus that is present in the nose and throat of an infected person, it is characterized by blisters on the skin, headache, chills, and a high fever; the blisters may eventually leave disfiguring pits in the skin, especially in the face. Smallpox has been extinct worldwide since 1977 (although the smallpox virus is still kept in certain medical research labs).

tuberculosis (TB)   Tuberculosis is an infectious disease that is usually passed through sputum of an infected person or carried in the air. TB usually affects the lungs and is accompanied by fever, night sweats, weight loss, and coughing up blood. It is caused by the bacterium *Mycobacterium tuberculosis*, which generally attacks the lungs, although it may occur in almost any other part of the body. TB has increased recently, in association with AIDS. It is treated by drugs that keep the bacteria from multiplying and that allow the body's immune system to fight the disease over the long term.

whooping cough (pertussis)   Whooping cough is an infectious disease that is often accompanied by bronchitis and violent attacks of coughing. This respiratory infection usually occurs in children and is caused by the *Hemophilus pertussis* bacterium. It is spread by the victim's coughing and sneezing or by handling items that an infected patient has touched. Whooping cough is not as prevalent as it was decades ago, because a vaccine is now available.

Hereditary or Genetic Diseases

Hereditary or genetic diseases are those that are often passed from one generation to another and/or are usually caused by defects or abnormalities in genetic material. They include the following disorders.

cystic fibrosis   Cystic fibrosis is a rare disease of the endocrine glands that affects the pancreas, sweat glands, and respiratory system. It is caused by a genetic defect that results in the impaired chloride passage through cell membranes. Cystic fibrosis occurs most frequently in Caucasian Europeans and is the most common fatal genetic disease of Caucasian children. As yet, there is no cure, and treatment concentrates on alleviating the symptoms, which include respiratory and digestive problems.

Down's syndrome   Down's syndrome occurs when an individual is born with an extra copy of chromosome number 21. The extra genetic material causes mental retardation, distinctive facial features, and abnormalities of some systems of the body. The syndrome is caused by a defect in the separation of the chromosomes, called *nondisjunction*. Most scientists do not consider Down's syndrome hereditary, because both parents usually have the normal number of chromosomes. The risk of bearing a Down's syndrome child appears to go up sharply after maternal age 35; recent studies indicate that the syndrome may actually correlate with fraternal age.

hemophilia   Hemophilia is found in four hereditary forms. Two are transmitted genetically as X-linked (carried on the X chromosome) abnormalities, passed from unaffected carrier mothers to their sons; one inherited from two carrier parents (affecting both males and females equally); and the final form, called von Willebrand's disease, comes from one affected parent (affecting both males and females equally). (A *carrier* is a person who is not always affected by a disease but can carry and transmit the disease to offspring.) A hemophiliac will bleed easily, even internally from a minor fall, causing large, often harmful accumulations of blood in the tissues. Treatment is usually transfusions of whole blood at the hospital; more recently, only the missing blood factor is transfused, which involves techniques that allow the patient to be treated at home.

Huntington's disease   Huntington's disease is a rare hereditary disease of the nervous system that appears in early adult life or middle age. It is characterized by involuntary muscular twitching. It is a degenerative disease that eventually affects the entire body and causes mental deterioration, and eventual death. No medical treatment exists, though certain sedatives minimize the symptoms.

muscular dystrophy   A relatively rare hereditary disease, muscular dystrophy usually starts during early or late childhood. It is characterized by a progressive weakness and deterioration of the muscles. It is caused by an inherited enzyme deficiency, resulting in a defect in the muscles' ability to use certain amino acids to make proteins.

sickle-cell disease (anemia)   Sickle-cell disease is a condition in which certain red blood cells (the carriers of oxygen throughout the body) become rigid, elongated, and sickle-shaped. As the stricken cells move through the body, they become lodged in tight spots, cutting off the flow of blood—and thus oxygen. The oxygen-starved area becomes swollen and tender, and causes a throbbing pain. Sickle-cell disease often affects people of African descent and less frequently people of Mediterranean, Greek, Italian, Arabian, or Indian decent. It is thought that sickle-cell disease can shorten a person's life because of the chronic damage to the tissues.

Tay-Sachs disease   Tay-Sachs is an inherited disease that usually affects Jewish children of eastern European background. It is caused by the transmission of an abnormal gene that causes a lack of the enzyme hexosaminidase. It is characterized, usually from ages four to six months, by progressive mental and physical retardation, paralysis, blindness, red spots, and other symptoms; it is eventually fatal. Because parents' genes can indicate the probability of a parent being a carrier of Tay-Sachs, the disease can be discovered by examining the amniotic fluid surrounding the fetus (or other tests).

thalassemia   Common among Mediterranean people, thalassemia is an inherited blood disorder that causes anemia. It is thought to be caused by a defect in hemoglobin synthesis.

Chronic Diseases

Chronic (or long-duration and/or reoccuring) diseases include the following.

arthritis   An inflammation that leads to pain, redness, and swelling in the joints. The most common form is *osteoarthritis* (or degenerative joint disease), which affects about 16 million people in the United States alone. It is caused by the wearing away of the cartilage at the bone ends, causing the bones to rub and cause pain. Approximately 3 million people in the United States have *rheumatoid arthritis*, in which the body's own immune system attacks the tissue in the joints, causing inflammation and swelling. Other types of arthritis include *juvenile rheumatoid arthritis*, an autoimmune disorder that affects young children; *lupus* (also see *systemic lupus erythematosus*), an autoimmune, arthritic disorder that affects mostly women; and arthritis associated with such diseases as Lyme disease, Kawasaki disease, and strep A infection. Arthritis is usually treated with physical therapy, corticosteroidal drugs (although they usually have side effects), and nonsteroidal antiinflammatory drugs (NSAIDs); for more advanced cases, joints are sometimes replaced with artificial implants.

cancer   When normal cells suddenly become abnormal, grow too quickly, consume large amounts of the body's energy, and produce toxic substances, they are often referred to as cancer cells. Cancer is not a single disease, but more than 100 different diseases, with the common characteristic of the abnormal growth of cells. They can occur in any part of the body and are most frequently found in older people. They are caused by defective DNA, which can be from environmental factors (such as certain skin and lung cancers); by ingestion of a substance (such as the ingestion of a carcinogen); or hereditary (such as possibly breast and bowel cancer). There are two basic types of cancer: A *carcinoma*, the most common, starts in the glands and surface tissues of the body, such as skin, colon, breast, and prostate. A *sarcoma* starts in the connective tissues, such as bones and muscles. Lymphoma, or cancer of the lymph glands, is a sarcoma.

cardiac problems   Many scientists believe that heart problems may run in families. Here are some types of chronic heart problems.

angina pectoris   Angina is the chest pain caused by coronary artery disease. It usually occurs suddenly and lasts for only short periods, especially upon exertion. It occurs when not enough blood travels through a semiblocked (or fully blocked) artery, cutting the supply of oxygen to the heart muscle.

atrial fibrillation   Atrial (or auricular) fibrillation is a kind of abnormal heartbeat in which one of the two chambers of the heart does not properly contract. It is usually caused by a problem in the sinus node (the area of the heart that coordinates the action of the muscle).

bradycardia   Bradycardia is a slow heart beat, usually caused by a problem in the heart's electrical system.

congestive heart failure   Congestive heart failure is a condition that occurs when the heart cannot remove enough blood from the veins. The blood backs up and overfills the vascular system, and the body begins to retain too much fluid. This often results in the lungs filling with fluid (pulmonary edema) and swelling (edema), usually in the feet and lower legs. Diuretics are usually used to treat congestive heart failure. Other medications are used for more severe cases.

endocarditis   Endocarditis is the inflammation of the heart's lining membrane and its valves. It is usually the result of an infection surrounding the area.

heart attack   See *infarction*

infarction (myocardial infarction, heart attack)   The death of heart tissues caused by blockage of their blood supply. Once a heart attack occurs, the affected part of the heart muscle is not replaced. In most cases, scar tissue builds up, permanently reducing the pumping action of the heart.

ischemia   Ischemia is the reduction in blood circulation in a tissue caused by blockage of its blood vessels; it is a condition that often results from atherosclerosis. Ischemia usually produces arrhythmia in the heart and causes the affected heart tissue to become starved for oxygen, which builds up toxins. If the condition persists or if a vessel suddenly becomes completely blocked, a myocardial infarction (or heart attack) will occur.

diabetes (Type I and Type II)   Diabetes is a condition in which there is an uncontrolled level of sugar in the blood, which is caused by the body's inability to use insulin. Sugars from digested food usually stimulate the pancreas to produce insulin; the insulin allows the cells to use the sugar as a source of energy for their normal functions. A person with diabetes cannot use the insulin, causing the sugar in the bloodstream to rise dramatically. Hyperglycemia is caused by too much sugar in the blood; hypoglycemia is caused by low blood sugar levels. *Type I diabetes* (often called juvenile diabetes) usually affects young people, in whom the pancreas produces no insulin. *Type II diabetes* (often called adult-onset diabetes) can affect any age group, but mostly older adults. In adult-onset diabetes, the pancreas gradually loses its ability to produce enough insulin over the years. Risk factors include obesity (fat cells use up insulin), decrease in exercise (sugar is used by the muscles), and heredity (adult-onset diabetes often runs in families). The blood sugar levels are usually kept in check with oral medications, exercise, and diet, but left unchecked, they could lead to complications such as diabetic retinopathy (or vision loss due to elevated blood sugar level, which is harmful to the small blood vessels that bring nutrients and oxygen to the eyes), kidney failure, and impotence; poor circulation in the extremities sometimes causes gangrene, creating the need to amputate to save the patient's life.

migraines   Migraine headaches strike with a severe, throbbing pain, usually on one side of the head. They are sometimes accompanied by nausea. There may also be neurological symptoms, such as spots or flashing lights in front of the eyes, dizziness, or numbness. A migraine attack may last from 1 hour to four days. No one knows the causes of migraines, but patients are often advised to avoid certain foods or conditions that have been known to trigger an event, such as sunlight, chocolates, red wine, or citrus fruits.

systemic lupus erythematosus (lupus)   Lupus is a chronic, arthritic autoimmune disease affecting the skin, blood vessels, joints, and various internal organs. It is found more in women than in men, and there is no known cure. It can be fatal.

Other Medical Problems

Other medical problems include diseases and conditions that are caused by various factors such as poor diet and nutrition, viruses, and subviruses. These include the following:

allergies   Allergies are hypersensitivity to various substances, causing the body's immune system to respond to the foreign substance (allergen). The number of substances that triggers an allergic response is long, and includes bee and insect stings, food and food additives, animal dander, drugs, pollen, and dust. Reactions range from mild to severe and can be any type of response, such as upper respiratory problems (sneezing and stuffy nose) to breaking out in a rash. Although it is often disputed, there may be a hereditary predisposition that can make people more susceptible to allergies, but the actual substance that triggers the reaction can vary from generation to generation. In general, children have a one-in-four chance of developing an allergy if one parent is allergic.

YOUR TYPE OF ALLERGY

When we think of allergies, we often picture a runny nose and sneezing. But there are at least four types of allergic reactions:

Type I allergies are characterized by the production of immunoglobulin E (IgE) and are the most prevalent kind of allergic response. This category includes allergic asthma and allergic rhinitis (hay fever). Once the immune system "thinks" that an innocuous substance is threatening, it sends IgE (a type of antibody) to coat certain cells, releasing chemicals called mediators. One mediator is histamine, which causes the blood vessel to dilate and release fluid into the surrounding tissues. This causes the usual runny nose and sneezing. Type I allergies are also responsible for the reactions caused by pet dander, insect stings, dust, and some foods and drugs.

Type II allergies are rare reactions in which the allergens bind to red blood cell and platelet surfaces. The response of the body is to send in immunoglobulin M (IgM) and immunoglobulin G (IgG) to fight the perceived infection. Type II allergies, which can cause liver and kidney damage or a type of anemia, are usually reactions to medications, such as sulfa.

Type III allergies are usually caused by drug reactions, such as to penicillin. Instead of the IgG and IgM binding with the allergen on the cell surface, the antibodies bind away from the cell's surface, causing clumps of allergens and antibodies. These collections get caught in the tissues and cause swelling, which often affects the kidneys, joints, and skin.

Type IV allergies include skin reactions to poison ivy, detergent, cosmetics, and other contact allergens. The T-lymphocytes and macrophages (types of white blood cells, or immune cells) react with the allergens, releasing mediators, which cause swelling and itchy rashes.

Alzheimer's disease   Alzheimer's is a progressive disease that affects a person's mental state. Its cause is unknown. Some studies suggest a deficit of the enzyme needed to produce the neurotransmitter acetylcholine, a key element in memory formation; or possibly a virus, genetics, or environmental toxin, but no cause has actually been proven. It is the leading cause of dementia in older people and occurs in about 11 percent of the elderly population.

anemia   Anemia is a condition in which the number of red blood cells is too low (or are damaged by disease), causing a decrease in oxygen to all the tissues of the body. An anemic person may appear pale and be tired or listless, because the body lacks oxygen. It may be caused by several conditions, including loss of blood, a decrease in iron levels in the bloodstream, or a problem with the bone marrow (where red blood cells are produced).

aneurysm   The swelling or bulging of a blood vessel is called an aneurysm. The term usually refers to cerebral arteries and the abdominal aorta, in which the bulging wall may eventually burst or rupture.

anorexia nervosa   Anorexia nervosa is an eating disorder, usually associated with people obsessed with thinness, that causes a person to fast compulsively in order to lose weight. It involves self-starvation and obsessive exercise to burn up calories. It is also often linked with induced vomiting and the use of laxatives (see also *bulimia*). It is believed that dieting early in life may cause a disturbance in the hypothalamus area of the brain, which regulates the body's water balance, temperature, endocrine secretions, and sugar and fat metabolism. Anorexia is most common in adolescent girls.

appendicitis   Appendicitis is a life-threatening inflammation of the pouchlike appendix that lies at the end of the large intestine (on the right side of the body). It is most often caused by hard pieces of waste or foreign matter lodging in the pouch, creating an obstruction that leads to inflammation. If left untreated, the appendix can rupture, sending harmful poisons into the body.

arrhythmia Arrhythmia is an abnormal beating of the heart (see also *cardiac problems*, in "Chronic Diseases," earlier in this chapter).

asthma Asthma involves sudden spasms of the bronchi (smaller air passages) of the lungs, swelling of the bronchial tubes, and production of a thick mucus. It is characterized by breathlessness (dyspnea) and wheezing; it can be brought on by an allergy, emotional stress, or an infection.

atherosclerosis Atherosclerosis is a buildup of plaque in the arteries that can block the flow of blood in various parts of the body (the resulting condition in the heart goes by various names, including arteriosclerotic, ischemic, or coronary heart disease). Such a blockage may be slight or can completely block the artery, depending on the progression of the disease. When associated with the heart (coronary) arteries, it is often treated by angioplasty or bypass surgery.

benign prostatic hypertrophy Benign prostatic hypertrophy (BPH) is a noncancerous enlargement of the prostate gland.

bronchitis Bronchitis is the inflammation of the lungs' air passages, usually from an infection or chemical irritation. It often leads to coughing and spitting, as the alveoli (the ends of the bronchiole that normally only contain air) secrete mucous.

bulimia Bulimia is an abnormal condition that is characterized by the increased urge to eat. After the person is satiated by food, vomiting is induced. Most common in women, it is thought to be caused by underlying psychological or sociological factors.

bursitis Bursitis is an inflammation of a bursa, which is a sac found between the tendon and the bone or the between the tendon or bone and the skin. When the tendon is irritated, the bursa fills with fluid to protect the tendon from the source of irritation. Bursitis often affects the shoulders, knees, and pelvic bones.

carpal tunnel syndrome Carpal tunnel syndrome occurs when the tissues in the carpal tunnel—a passage through the wrist protecting the median nerve that gives sensation to the fingers—become inflamed and irritate the median nerve. It is often described as a tingling in the fingers. It is caused by the repeated motions made with the fingers and the wrist (such as gripping, rotating, and typing) that puts a strain on the wrist. A surgical procedure, in which the ligament at the wrist is cut, can relieve the pressure on the median nerve.

cataract A cataract is an opaqueness or clouding of the eye's lens that occurs either in one portion or in the entire lens. It can be caused by diabetes, the use of some types of steroids, an eye injury, aging, or years of exposure to sunlight.

chronic rheumatic heart disease Chronic rheumatic heart disease is damage to the heart thought be the result of a streptococcus infection (especially from strep throat) when young. It is thought that the body, in attacking the infection with antibodies, also attacks the heart, usually the valves. In many people, the condition causes no symptoms. It is not infectious.

colitis Colitis is an inflammation of the colon (large bowel).

conjunctivitis Conjunctivitis is the inflammation of the membrane that lines the eyelids and covers the eyeball.

constipation Constipation is the inability to eliminate feces from the body on a regular basis.

Crohn's disease Crohn's disease is an inflammation of the intestinal tract.

cystitis Cystitis is an inflammation of the bladder caused by a bacterial infection; it is usually caused by the spread of infection from the urethra (urethritis). Symptoms are often similar to urethritis, including pain on urination, urgency to urinate (although little is passed), and general fatigue. It is usually treated with antibiotics (see also *interstitial cystitis*).

dermatitis An inflammation of the skin is called dermatitis, which is characterized by redness, irritation, itching, swelling, and often the formation of small blisters. The inflammation can be caused by many factors, including allergy to a chemical substance, plants, animal hair, or soap. It is not a disease or disorder, but is a symptom of a problem.

diarrhea Diarrhea is watery or loose stools, usually from a disorder in the digestive tract; it can be caused by a multitude of ailments. The inflammation or irritation of the intestines, usually from an infection, causes an abnormally quick movement of waste material to the colon, as the body tries to flush the offending microorganism from the body. Diarrhea can cause severe dehydration because of the loss of body fluids.

diplopia Diplopia is a visual disorder that causes a person to see double. It is also called double vision.

diverticulitis Diverticulitis is an inflammation of an outpouching (or abnormal saclike area) protruding from the lining of the intestines. Pain is often felt in the lower abdomen; it is often treated with antibiotics.

dyspepsia Dyspepsia is indigestion.

emphysema Emphysema is characterized by enlarged lungs and breathing difficulties, such as breathlessness and coughing. It is often found in smokers, in which the lung tissue is destroyed, causing scarring of the air sacs, or bronchioles.

encephalitis (sleeping sickness) See entry under "Animal- and Insect-Borne Diseases," later in this chapter.

endometriosis Endometriosis is a condition in which material similar to the lining of the uterus (or womb) is present at other sites outside the womb, especially in the pelvic cavity (although other sites, such as the intestines and colon, can be effected). Like the uterus, the sites respond to the menstrual cycle, but the buildup of blood has no place to drain and causes pain.

epilepsy A group of brain disorders that are triggered by sudden and uncontrollable electrical discharges in the brain's cerebrum is called epilepsy. Symptoms include mild to violent muscular seizures. It occurs in 1 out of every 200 people. The cause of most epilepsy is unknown, though it is often associated with an injury to the head, a brain tumor, or diseased blood vessels in the brain. *Grand mal* seizures are usually dramatic and often accompanied by blackouts and convulsions; *petit mal* seizures, which usually disappear after puberty, occur many times a day and are characterized by a brief disruption of consciousness.

fibroid tumors Fibroid tumors are benign tumors that usually develop in the smooth muscular wall of the uterus. They are usually harmless growths and vary in size and shape; it is estimated that 20 to 50 percent of all women over 30 years of age have at least some evidence of fibroids.

gall stones Stones in the gallbladder are generally a disorder of cholesterol metabolism. The excess cholesterol, which is mixed with the liver's bile and stored in the gallbladder, develops into soft clumps that can eventually harden. A gall stone attack occurs when a stone enters or gets stuck as it travels through the bile duct connecting the gallbladder and intestines. There may be a genetic predisposition to gall stones.

ganglion A ganglion is a cyst that occurs on either side of the wrist, knee, or ankle. It is caused by the leaking of a jellylike substance from a joint or tendon sheath.

gastritis Gastritis is the superficial irritation or inflammation of the stomach lining. It is thought that gastritis can lead to chronic stomach problems.

gastroenteritis   Gastroenteritis, the inflammation of the stomach and/or intestines, is usually caused by bacteria (often from food poisoning, in which food is contaminated with staphylococcus bacteria), parasites, viruses, or certain medications (such as antibiotics or cancer drugs). It is often accompanied by intestinal contractions and diarrhea, as the intestinal tract attempts to fight off the inflammation.

glaucoma   Glaucoma is the progressive narrowing of the visual field. It is actually a group of disorders characterized by increased pressure of the fluid in the eyeball. Such pressure can kill cells located near the optic nerve—the nerve that carries the visual signals from the back of the eye to the brain.

gout   Gout is a form of arthritis caused by the buildup of too much uric acid in the blood, which then becomes deposited around the joints.

heartburn   Heartburn is caused by the production of excess acid in the stomach; the acid is refluxed, or released backward, into the esophagus, causing a bile taste and/or burning sensation in the mouth and throat. It is often caused by eating heavy or spicy foods. It is usually treated with antacids.

hemorrhoids   Dilated veins in the anus, or hemorrhoids, cause considerable discomfort. There are three elastic cushions of fibrous tissue attached to the sphincter muscle that act as "stoppers" at the anal opening. When the tissue grows larger, usually because of straining, the fibers break or stretch, causing the cushions to slide outside the anus. The external sphincter traps the cushions by closing behind them, resulting in protruding hemorrhoids. No one really knows what causes hemorrhoids to appear in the first place, but it is thought there may be a genetic predisposition to the condition.

hernia   An example of a hernia occurs when a portion of the intestinal tract pushes through a weak part in an abdominal muscle (hiatus hernia). Hernias can occur elsewhere, including the groin.

high blood pressure (hypertension)   High blood pressure is the continual high level of the blood's pressure (also see "The Circulatory System," earlier in this chapter). It can lead to an increased risk of heart attacks and stroke as well as kidney damage and eye problems (retinopathy). High blood pressure appears to run in families; it has also been linked to excessive intake of salts, smoking, birth control pills, obesity, heart disorders, stress, and adrenal gland problems. It is most often controlled by changes in diet and lifestyle (including exercise), and/or via drug therapy.

hyperthyroidism   Hyperthyroidism is the overactivity of the thyroid gland, which causes excessive secretion of the thyroid hormones. Symptoms include jumpiness, irritability, excessive sweating, heart palpatations, and often protruding eyes.

hypothyroidism   Hypothyroidism is the underactivity of the thyroid gland, which causes insufficient secretion of the thyroid hormones. Symptoms include fatigue, inability to get warm, and lack of energy.

incontinence   Incontinence is the inability to control urination or bowel movements. It is caused by a multitude of conditions—factors often differ between males and females.

interstitial cystitis   Interstitial cystitis (IC) is an inflammation of the bladder wall that causes its sufferers to go to the bathroom as many as 70 times per day. It destroys the lining and the elasticity of the bladder, diminishing the organ's ability to hold urine. It affects mostly women over 40; the cause is still unknown, but it is thought to be an autoimmune disease (as it is often associated with people who have numerous allergies).

kidney stones   Any stone in the urinary tract is called a kidney stone. The stones either pass through the tract or can become stuck in the ureter (the duct that carries urine from the kidney to the bladder). It is commonly caused by too much calcium in the body.

low blood pressure (hypotension)   Low blood pressure is generally defined as a systolic pressure less than 100 (see "The Circulatory System," earlier in this chapter).

malnutrition   Malnutrition is the result of an improper diet or a defect in the body's metabolism that causes the body not to use food properly. Poor nourishment can lead to health problems, e.g., lack of vitamin C can cause scurvy, or excessive bleeding of the gums and easily bruised skin (see "Nonblood Components and Needs of the Human Body," earlier in this chapter).

myopia   Myopia is nearsightedness, or difficulty seeing objects at a distance.

obesity   Obesity is an excessive accumulation or high percent of fat in the body. Obesity can often shorten life and lead to several diseases, including heart problems and diabetes.

osteoporosis   Osteoporosis is the weakening of the bone as a result of a decrease in bone density. It often leads to broken bones, even under minor stresses. It is caused by a loss of minerals and of the matrix that surrounds the bone's minerals. Age is often a factor, as are lack of exercise and a decrease in calcium consumption. Women often experience osteoporosis after menopause, as levels of the hormone estrogen decline.

Parkinson's disease   With symptoms that include tremors, stiffness, and slowed movements, Parkinson's disease usually occurs in older adults. It is caused by the degeneration of the part of the brain that releases dopamine, a neurotransmitter. It is not known why this part of the brain deteriorates.

phlebitis   Phlebitis occurs when a clot forms in an unbroken blood vessel; it is usually accompanied by swelling (see also *thrombosis*). The causes of phlebitis are not known, but it is often accompanied by inflamed varicose veins. It sometimes occurs in patients receiving intravenous fluids.

prostatitis   Prostatitis is the inflammation of the prostate gland.

psoriasis   Psoriasis is a chronic condition in which the skin has itchy, scaly, dry, and red skin patches.

Raynaud's disease   Raynaud's disease is a condition marked by paleness, numbness, redness, and discomfort in the extremities—the toes and fingers—when they are exposed to the cold. It is caused by the contraction of blood vessels that feed the skin. The restricted blood flow causes the extremities to turn white, then blue. It usually occurs in females between the ages of 15 and 50 and is rarer in males.

rhinitis   Rhinitis is the inflammation of the nose's mucous membranes caused by viruses, bacteria, or allergies. Acute rhinitis can be caused by the common cold.

sarcoidosis   Sarcoidosis is a chronic disorder in which the lymph nodes in many parts of the body are enlarged and small fleshy swellings develop in such locations as the lungs, liver, and spleen. It is rare, and there is no known cause. The condition is not considered serious in most cases.

sinusitis   Inflammation of the sinuses is called sinusitis, which commonly occurs when a person has a cold, the flu, or allergies. It can be exacerbated as the result of air pressure changes on airplane flights or by inhaling environmental irritants.

strep throat   Strep throat is an infection of the throat caused by a strain of the streptococcus bacteria. It is of particular concern, especially in children, because it can lead to rheumatic fever (see also *chronic rheumatic heart disease*).

stroke   A stroke (or cerebrovascular accident) is a sudden disturbance in brain activity through the disruption of part of its blood supply (it is classified as a circulatory problem). An embolic stroke is caused by a circulating clot called an *embolism*. A *cerebral infarction* occurs when an artery to the brain becomes clogged; a *cerebral hemorrhage* occurs when a blood vessel in the brain ruptures. A *lacunar infarction* is a small stroke from the blockage of the smallest blood vessels in the brain.

sty   A sty is an inflammation of the eyelid's edge, usually caused when an eyelash follicle gets infected.

sudden infant death syndrome   Sudden infant death syndrome (SIDS) is one of the leading causes of infant death in the United States, striking babies between two and four months of age. The deaths are unexpected, with the infant showing no indication of any disease. The cause of SIDS is unknown. It is thought to be related to immaturity on the part of the brain that controls breathing; sleep apnea and the child's sleeping position have also been sighted as possible causes.

temporomandibular disorder (TMD)   TMD is also called temporomandibular joint (TMJ) disorder and is caused by the cramping of the jaw muscles, which leads to aching around the jaw joint. It has also been linked to several other medical problems, including degenerative arthritis. TMD is associated with headaches and ringing in the ears, though the connection between it and these conditions is often debated. It is often called the "great mimicker" because its symptoms imitate the symptoms of many other medical conditions.

tendonitis   An inflammation of the tendon, the soft tissue structure connecting muscle to bone, is called tendonitis. It usually occurs in the elbows (commonly called tennis elbow), shoulders, and knees and is often brought on by certain types of strenuous activity.

thrombosis   Thrombosis is a clot that forms in an unbroken blood vessel; it is not accompanied by swelling (see also *phlebitis*). It is often caused by an injury to a vein or as a complication of phlebitis. Patients who are bedridden for long periods of time may also develop this condition.

tonsillitis   An inflammation of the tonsils, the lymph nodes at the back of the throat, is called tonsillitis. It is treated with antibiotics. In extreme cases, the tonsils are surgically removed.

trigeminal neuralgia   Trigeminal neuralgia is a rare, intense pain on only one side of the face, which follows the path of the trigeminal nerve. Like other neuralgias (or nerve pains), it is often sudden and severe. It is thought that a sagging artery at the base of the brain pushes against the nerve, causing it to throb.

tumor   A tumor is a mass of tissue growth with no physiologic function. Tumors can be either malignant (cancerous) or nonmalignant (benign or not cancerous).

typhoid fever   Typhoid is an infection caused by a form of salmonella bacteria (*Salmonella typhosa*) which mainly causes gastrointestinal symptoms (nausea, vomiting, and diarrhea). It is usually spread through water supplies contaminated by sewage. It is treated with antibacterial drugs, and a vaccine is available.

ulcer   An ulcer is an open lesion of the skin or a mucous membrane, with loss of substance or necrosis (the death of cells) of the tissue. Peptic (gastrointestinal or stomach) ulcers are found mainly in the stomach, and were once thought to be brought on by stress. They are now believed to often be caused by a particular bacteria.

urethritis   Urethritis is an inflammation of the urethra caused by a bacterial infection. If allowed to get worse, it can spread to the bladder, causing cystitis. Symptoms are often the same as cystitis, including pain on urination, urgency to urinate (although little is passed), and general fatigue. It is usually treated with antibiotics.

uterine prolapse   A uterine prolapse occurs when the ligaments holding the female uterus weaken, which causes the organ to shift position. In more severe cases, the uterus protrudes through the vagina and must be put back in place surgically.

varicose veins   Veins close to the surface of the skin that become twisted and enlarged are called varicose veins. They occur because the valves, which usually help push blood back up to the heart, weaken or malfunction, causing the blood to pool in the veins, especially in the legs. The weakened vessels bulge under the pressure of the pooling blood. They are more common in females than in males.

warts   Warts are caused by 30 different types of papillomaviruses, which cause skin cells to multiply rapidly. There are many different types, such as common warts (usually around injured sites), flat warts (on the hands), filiform (on eyelids, armpits, and necks), and plantar warts (on the bottom of the feet). They are eliminated in several ways, such as removal by burning or freezing. The wart virus can be spread by touch (especially from a broken wart) or skin shed by a wart (see also *human papillomavirus* under "Communicable Diseases," earlier in this chapter).

Animal- and Insect-Borne Diseases

encephalitis (sleeping sickness)   The inflammation of the brain and its coverings, encephalitis, can lead to persistent drowsiness and delirium. It is caused by a virus, and there are many forms of the disease (most of them are rare). The virus is commonly transmitted to humans by the bite of mosquitoes and ticks; other forms of the disease can be caused by lead poisoning or infection. There are no medications for encephalitis, and drugs administered are meant to relieve only the symptoms.

Lyme disease   Lyme disease was first reported in 1975 in Old Lyme, Connecticut. It is caused by a spirochete, *Borrelia burgdorferi*, a bacterium that is carried by the deer tick. The disease can mimic other conditions, but in general, its symptoms include various combinations of fever, headache, stiff neck, fatigue, swollen lymph glands, and a rash. If not treated early, weeks or months later, the patient can develop heart difficulties, swollen joints, and arthritic symptoms. It is treated in its early stages with antibiotics (such as penicillin or tetracycline).

malaria   Malaria is a sometimes chronic infectious disease caused by one of four species of parasitic protozoa. Malaria is fairly widespread in the tropics and subtropics and is passed to humans by the bite of an infected female mosquito of the genus *Anopheles*. The symptoms include headache, chills, pains in the joints, and a slight fever. The infected person alternates between chills and fever, with sweating as the fever decreases. Malaria's incubation period is about 35 days. Relapses are common, even several years later. It is treated by drugs to relieve some of the symptoms. Persons traveling to malaria-infested areas can obtain pills such as chloroquine to prevent infection.

rabies (hydrophobia)   Rabies is an infectious disease caused by a virus. It is most often spread to humans by the bite of an infected warm-blooded animal (the virus is usually carried in the saliva). Rabies affects the brain and nervous system. Domesticated animals can be vaccinated against rabies. An antirabies vaccine and serum must be administered to infected humans as soon as possible; if untreated, rabies is fatal to humans.

rickettsal diseases   Rickettsal diseases are caused by bacterial microorganisms found within certain disease-carrying animals and associated insects. The major rickettsal diseases are as follows.

> **Q fever**   Q fever infection is caused by the rickettsia *Coxiella burnetii*; it is not common. Generally, it is found in areas where cattle, sheep, and goats are raised; the infection is usually airborne, found in the dust around these areas. It is characterized by headache, chills, fever, anorexia, and malaise. It also affects the lungs and can lead to other complications such as jaundice, hepatitis, and abnormal liver function. Treatment includes antibiotics.

Rocky Mountain spotted fever   Rocky Mountain spotted fever is carried by ticks that are infected by feeding on infected rodents and other small animals. This disease is characterized by severe headache, nausea, and high fever. A rash usually starts on the wrists and ankles, then spreads; lesions eventually occur on the palms and soles. It is often treated with antibiotics such as tetracycline.

typhus   There are many forms of typhus found worldwide. For example, typhus can be carried by rats and spread by rat fleas; body louse–borne typhus includes Brill-Zinsser disease. Symptoms vary widely but most include chills, fever, severe headache, vomiting, and nausea. Most types of typhus are usually treated with antibiotics and extermination of the insects is carried out.

EPIDEMICS OF THE PAST

Epidemics have decimated ancient peoples throughout history. Today, with the advent of better nutrition, hygiene, and inoculations, epidemics are often easier to contain and localize. Epidemiological theory holds that major infectious diseases of humankind became important about 5,000 years ago, when dense populations, often the result of growing cities, made microparasitic diseases easily transmitted. Major epidemics of the past are listed below.

Date	Epidemic
162	Eurasian epidemics of "new" diseases, possibly measles and smallpox
542	Bubonic plague in the Mediterranean, reaching China by A.D. 610
1331	Bubonic plague in China, reaching western Eurasia by 1346 and northern Europe thereafter (1347–1351)
1494	
	Global epidemic of syphilis that may have started in Italy (although some researchers believe it was brought from the new world)
1520	Smallpox spread throughout the Americas, from Hispaniola, reaching Peru by 1525
1556	Influenza in Europe and the Americas
1648	Yellow fever spread from South America to the Caribbean and Middle America
1817	Cholera spread all over the world; the epidemic may have originated in Bengal
1918	Influenza killed 20 million as it spread around the world from northern France

BIOMEDICAL LABORATORY TECHNOLOGY

Technology has burgeoned in the medical field, helping to make diagnosis, surgical procedures, and health maintenance easier for doctors and patients.

Invasive Techniques

angioplasty   Angioplasty is a procedure that uses a catheter and a balloon to open up blocked arteries, usually those of the heart. The balloon pushes the plaque buildup in the artery against the vessel's wall, allowing a freer flow of blood. It is often used as an alternative to open heart/ bypass surgery.

arthroscopic surgery   Arthroscopic surgery is done with an instrument that looks into a joint, especially the knee. The instrument has its own light source and lens, to allow the surgeon to magnify the joint; the images are recorded with a television camera and displayed on a screen. The surgeon corrects the cartilage, bone, or tendon problem without having to make a large incision.

automatic implantable cardiac defibrillator (AICD)   The AICD is a device that automatically administers a form of CPR when a person's heart gives indications that it is about to stop.

autoradiography   Autoradiography is a recording of radiation emitted by the tissue itself, usually after the purposeful injection of a radioactive isotope into the body. It is used to diagnose such disorders as tumors.

chemotherapy   Chemotherapy is the application of chemical (nonnuclear) agents that have a specific, toxic effect on disease-causing factors. It is mainly used for the treatment of cancer and aims to shrink tumors and destroy metastases.

computerized axial tomography (CT or CAT scan)   CT scans create an image of the internal structures of the body and are usually used for diagnostic purposes. Tomography is a sectional x-ray; as the purposeful injection of radiation passes through the body, a computer converts data on the amount of radiation absorbed by each tissue into a three-dimensional picture.

coronary artery bypass graft (CABG)   CABG is an operation performed to treat coronary artery disease. It is a procedure by which the surgeon bypasses the blockage in a coronary artery by grafting a new vessel and diverting the flow of blood through it instead of the old vessel. The surgeon often uses a vein from the patient's leg or an artificial vein.

cryosurgery   Cryosurgery is a technique that uses cold temperatures to freeze tissues on certain parts of the body. An example is the use of liquid nitrogen to destroy tissues, such as warts.

endoscope   An endoscope is an instrument that has flexible exploratory "tubes" that use fiber optics for its light source. Some specific endoscopes are a *laparoscope* to look into the abdomen, a *colonoscope* to look into the colon (the medical procedure is called a colonoscopy), and a *cystoscope* to look into the bladder.

laser surgery   Laser surgery uses a highly energetic laser beam to cut tissue with limited bleeding. It is being used in many types of operations, including the removal of tumors and gallbladder surgery. Lasers are also used for microsurgery because the beam can be focused with great precision in small areas, as in certain types of delicate eye surgery.

position emission transaxial tomography (PETT or PET scan)   PETT is an x-ray scan that produces images of the brain's activity. Glucose and other substances are tagged by radioactive isotopes, then tracked as they move through the brain. The scan allows the visualization of certain metabolic processes in the brain, such as changes that occur during a migraine headache.

radioactive isotopes   Radioactive isotopes are forms of chemical elements that emit radioactive particles. They are used in diagnosing some illnesses. For example, to determine the condition of the thyroid gland, the patient is given a radioactive iodine pill. Hours later, a scanner determines the amount of radioactive iodine that has been taken up by the thyroid.

Noninvasive Techniques

There are several ways to look into a patient—and even operate on a patient—without "invading" the body. The techniques, called noninvasive, are being used more and more, allowing for greater safety, less discomfort, and faster recovery. These methods include those that do not require the patient to ingest a substance, such as a radioactive tracer or dye, to obtain results.

echocardiogram   Echocardiograms use ultrasonic waves to measure the heart and its function, including the position and motion of the heart and valves.

electrocardiograph (ECG or EKG)   The ECG records the electrical changes in the heart that accompany the cardiac cycle.

electroencephalograph (EEG)   The EEG traces the electrical impulses in the brain.

lithotripsy   Lithotripsy is a high-pressure shock wave treatment in which the waves are transmitted through water and focused on the affected body part. This technique is often used to break up kidney stones. Electrodes are directed by computer; the shock waves converge from all directions to break up the offending stones even if they are located behind bones.

magnetic resonance imaging (MRI)   MRI (sometimes called nuclear magnetic resonance [NMR] imaging) uses a scanner that can perform diagnostic functions and quantitative analysis on a tissue sample. It uses a large, circular magnet (not nuclear radiation) to determine the magnetic bearings of a number of atom nuclei in the patient's body. As the magnet is switched on, the atoms in the body are excited by radio waves; the atoms move into a high-energy state and give off weak radio signals, which are converted into images of tissues. Each radio wave frequency represents a certain element in the tissues. For example, the MRI can search for carbon, which represents bone.

mammography   An x-ray of a woman's breast is called mammogram. Mammography determines the internal structure of the breast and is used to screen for breast cancer.

ultrasound   Ultrasound is one way of looking inside a patient. It is used during pregnancy to determine the fetus's position and condition. It is also used to determine whether certain tissues are fluid or solid, as in the imaging of the gallbladder and breasts (the latter to clarify a mammogram). High-frequency sound waves are bounced off an internal region of the patient's body; the data are sent to a computer, which interprets the sound waves and displays them as images on a monitor. The method allows the visualization of internal body structures in real time, or as things are actually happening.

FROZEN ORGAN ASSETS

Organ transplants are necessary when an organ becomes impaired in an otherwise healthy body. Transplanted organs include, in the order of the number of transplants per year, kidneys, liver, heart, pancreas, lung, and heart-lung. Organs are not easy to transplant, and for example, heart transplants have only a 35 to 40 percent chance of extending a patient's life for 5 years. One difficulty with transplants is that the new organ may be rejected by the recipient's body because of tissue incompatibility.

Researchers are trying to increase the number of organs available for transplant, however, because there are successes. But hearts live only a few hours and kidneys only a few days under cold conditions. They have long known that it is possible to freeze blood, sperm cells, and other tissues. But what about the larger organs of the body? Is it possible to freeze a heart or kidney for a long period to preserve it for transplant?

Unfortunately, not yet—the major reason is that organs, unlike blood or tissues, contain a multitude of different cells, each of which responds to freezing differently. In addition, certain cells react adversely to being frozen. Ice crystals from the freezing of liquids within the cell can grow too fast and too large, tearing the delicate outside membrane and destroying the structures within the cell.

This does not mean, however, that researchers have stopped trying. Cryobiologists (scientists who study life systems at low temperatures) are trying to solve the problems of freezing whole organs. So far, they are looking at the special fluids that keep an insect alive during subfreezing weather.

Other Methods for Maintaining Health

Through the centuries—and even more recently—there have been numerous natural methods for maintaining health, treating disease, and relieving pain. Most of these types of treatment are used today in conjunction with (or in replacement of) modern medical techniques.

acupressure   Acupressure (also often called pressure-point massage) uses pressure along specific meridian points of the body to eliminate pain and stress. According to practitioners, acupressure also opens up the body's energy pathways (see also *acupuncture*).

acupuncture   Acupuncture is an ancient therapeutic technique developed in China. It uses 0.5- to 5-inch-long needles placed in specific parts in the body to relieve such conditions as trigeminal neuralgia, tennis elbow, lower back pain, gastritis, toothache, and headaches. The Chinese believe that the body contains a number of meridians, or pathways, along which the life energy (*chi*) flows. The acupuncture needles placed at particular points along the meridians can unblock the *chi* to restore health or reduce pain. Acupuncture is gaining increasing acceptance in Western medicine.

biofeedback   Biofeedback is a technique that helps a person gain conscious control of certain body functions, such as heart rate, blood pressure, and responses to stress; it is also used to manage pain. The technique uses instruments that provide visual or auditory feedback as the patient attempts to control a specific body function. The method is not learned in one session, and may take weeks, months, or years of practice to get positive results. Biofeedback is often used in conjunction with meditation techniques.

homeopathy   Homeopathy was developed by Samuel Hahnemann (1753–1843), a German physician and chemist. In particular, practitioners believe that the symptoms of a disease are evidence of the body's own curative process in response to the disease. Homeopathic practitioners, therefore, enhance the development of symptoms to accelerate the body's ability to cure itself, using minute quantities of drugs that would normally bring on the same symptoms. Homeopathy is often thought to work best for chronic symptoms.

massage   Massage is often used to soothe muscles, relieve stress, and produce a sense of well-being. It works on the principle that muscles that are overworked and stressed build up lactic acid, causing soreness, stiffness, and spasms. Massage improves the circulation into and out of the muscles, thus removing the lactic acid toxins. Massage can also stretch the muscles (making them more flexible), improve circulation, and relieve some types of pain.

meditation   Meditation has been practiced for centuries by numerous cultures. It is a relaxation technique that lowers the blood pressure in some people. There are numerous types of meditation techniques. The common theme in all of them is to relax the muscles of the body, clear the brain of extraneous thoughts, and concentrate on deep breathing.

naturopathy   Naturopathy is a drugless system of healing that is based on the principle that waste products and toxins build up in the body and cause disease. It uses natural foods and physical methods of treatment (air, water, and light) to treat diseases.

osteopathy   Osteopathic medicine involves the manipulation of the musculoskeletal system to maintain the health of the body. It includes the manipulation procedures in conjunction with traditional therapeutic and diagnostic techniques to treat diseases.

pain oncology nursing   Pain oncology nursing is a relatively new area, although it is based on the familiar idea of tender loving care. It employs skilled health professionals who support and educate cancer patients and who are committed to relieving their patients' cancer pain. Though narcotics, steroids, and anti-inflammatory drugs are used to alleviate pain, oncology nursing also uses relaxation exercises, music therapy, and guided imagery.

Life Expectancy by Race, Sex, and Age[1]

Age (years)	Expectation of Life in Years					Expected Deaths per 1,000 Alive at Specified Age [2]				
		White		All Other			White		All Other	
	Total	Male	Female	Male	Female	Total	Male	Female	Male	Female
At birth	75.3	72.7	79.2	64.8	73.5	9.86	9.08	7.15	20.04	17.17
1	75.0	72.3	78.8	65.2	73.8	0.69	0.69	0.53	1.18	0.91
2	74.1	71.4	77.8	64.2	72.9	0.52	0.50	0.41	0.91	0.75
3	73.1	70.4	76.9	63.3	71.9	0.40	0.38	0.32	0.72	0.61
4	72.1	69.5	75.9	62.3	71.0	0.33	0.32	0.27	0.59	0.49
5	71.7	68.5	74.9	61.4	70.0	0.29	0.29	0.23	0.51	0.40
6	70.2	67.5	73.9	60.4	69.0	0.26	0.27	0.21	0.45	0.32
7	69.2	66.5	73.0	59.4	68.0	0.24	0.26	0.19	0.40	0.27
8	68.2	65.5	72.0	58.5	67.1	0.21	0.23	0.17	0.34	0.23
9	67.2	64.5	71.0	57.5	66.1	0.18	0.20	0.15	0.28	0.22
10	66.2	63.6	70.0	56.5	65.1	0.16	0.17	0.13	0.24	0.23
11	65.2	62.6	69.0	55.5	64.1	0.17	0.17	0.13	0.24	0.25
12	64.3	61.6	68.0	54.5	63.1	0.22	0.24	0.16	0.34	0.27
13	63.3	60.6	67.0	53.5	62.1	0.32	0.39	0.22	0.55	0.30
14	62.3	59.6	66.0	52.6	61.2	0.47	0.59	0.30	0.83	0.33
15	61.3	58.6	65.1	51.6	60.2	0.63	0.82	0.39	1.16	0.37
16	60.4	57.7	64.1	50.7	59.2	0.79	1.03	0.48	1.47	0.42
17	59.4	56.8	63.1	49.8	58.2	0.91	1.21	0.53	1.78	0.48
18	58.5	55.8	62.1	48.8	57.3	0.99	1.31	0.55	2.07	0.54
19	57.5	54.9	61.2	47.9	56.3	1.03	1.37	0.53	2.33	0.63
20	56.6	54.0	60.2	47.1	55.3	1.06	1.42	0.50	2.61	0.70
21	55.6	53.0	59.2	46.2	54.4	1.10	1.47	0.48	2.89	0.79
22	54.7	52.1	58.3	45.3	53.4	1.13	1.51	0.47	3.10	0.88
23	53.8	51.2	57.3	44.4	52.4	1.15	1.53	0.47	3.23	0.95
24	52.8	50.3	56.3	43.6	51.5	1.17	1.55	0.49	3.28	1.03
25	51.9	49.4	55.3	42.7	50.6	1.18	1.55	0.49	3.28	1.10
26	50.9	48.4	54.4	41.9	49.6	1.20	1.56	0.52	3.38	1.18
27	50.0	47.5	53.4	41.0	48.7	1.23	1.58	0.54	3.50	1.28
28	49.1	46.6	52.4	40.2	47.7	1.27	1.62	0.56	3.69	1.39
29	48.1	45.7	51.5	39.3	46.8	1.32	1.67	0.59	3.94	1.51
30	47.2	43.8	49.5	37.6	44.9	1.45	1.79	0.66	4.47	1.78
32	45.3	42.9	48.6	36.8	44.0	1.51	1.86	0.70	4.78	1.91
33	44.4	42.0	47.6	36.0	43.1	1.59	1.93	0.73	5.14	2.02
34	43.5	41.0	46.6	35.1	42.2	1.66	2.02	0.76	5.53	2.13
35	42.5	40.1	45.7	34.3	41.3	1.75	2.11	0.80	5.96	2.25
36	41.6	39.2	44.7	33.5	40.4	1.85	2.22	0.85	6.39	2.37
37	40.7	38.3	43.7	32.7	39.5	1.94	2.32	0.91	6.79	2.53
38	39.8	37.4	42.8	32.0	38.6	2.04	2.42	0.99	7.11	2.71
39	38.8	36.5	41.8	31.2	37.7	2.14	2.52	1.09	7.40	2.92
40	37.9	35.6	40.9	30.4	36.8	2.25	2.63	1.20	7.69	3.16
41	37.0	34.7	39.9	29.7	35.9	2.38	2.76	1.33	8.02	3.40
42	36.1	33.8	39.0	28.9	35.0	2.53	2.93	1.46	8.38	3.65
43	35.2	32.9	38.0	28.1	34.1	2.71	3.13	1.59	8.78	3.90
44	34.3	32.0	37.1	27.4	33.3	2.92	3.38	1.73	9.23	4.15
45	33.4	31.1	36.1	26.6	32.4	3.15	3.66	1.89	9.69	4.43
46	32.5	30.2	35.2	25.9	31.5	3.41	3.98	2.07	10.19	4.74
47	31.6	29.3	34.3	25.1	30.7	3.71	4.33	2.29	10.80	5.07

Life Expectancy by Race, Sex, and Age[1]

Age (years)	Expectation of Life in Years					Expected Deaths per 1,000 Alive at Specified Age [2]				
	Total	White		All Other		Total	White		All Other	
		Male	Female	Male	Female		Male	Female	Male	Female
48	30.7	28.4	33.4	24.4	29.8	4.05	4.71	2.54	11.53	5.43
49	29.8	27.5	32.4	23.7	29.0	4.43	5.12	2.84	12.37	5.83
50	28.9	26.7	31.5	23.0	28.2	4.85	5.58	3.16	13.30	6.27
51	28.1	25.8	30.6	22.3	27.3	5.31	6.10	3.51	14.25	6.75
52	27.2	25.0	29.7	21.6	26.5	5.84	6.73	3.90	15.21	7.30
53	26.4	24.2	28.8	20.9	25.7	6.43	7.49	4.32	16.14	7.91
54	25.6	23.3	28.0	20.3	24.9	7.08	8.35	4.76	17.07	8.59
55	24.7	22.5	27.1	19.6	24.1	7.79	9.29	5.24	18.04	9.31
56	23.9	21.7	26.2	18.9	23.4	8.55	10.29	5.77	19.09	10.09
57	23.1	21.0	25.4	18.3	22.6	9.37	11.37	6.34	20.27	11.01
58	22.3	20.2	24.6	17.7	21.8	10.27	12.55	6.97	21.61	12.12
59	21.6	19.4	23.7	17.1	21.1	11.23	13.81	7.64	23.10	13.38
60	20.8	18.7	22.9	16.4	20.4	12.27	15.18	8.39	24.68	14.76
61	20.1	18.0	22.1	15.9	19.7	13.37	16.63	9.18	26.36	16.17
62	19.3	17.3	21.3	15.3	19.0	14.52	18.12	10.02	28.15	17.51
63	18.6	16.6	20.5	14.7	18.3	15.69	19.62	10.91	30.07	18.72
64	17.9	15.9	19.7	14.1	17.7	16.91	21.18	11.84	32.12	19.85
65	17.2	15.2	19.0	13.6	17.0	18.20	22.80	12.85	34.31	21.00
70	13.9	12.1	15.3	11.0	13.9	27.31	34.77	20.03	47.63	29.38
75	10.9	9.4	11.9	8.8	11.0	41.31	53.66	31.61	65.79	42.53
80	8.3	7.1	8.9	6.9	8.5	63.71	82.84	51.62	94.32	65.05
85 and over	6.2	5.3	6.5	5.6	6.7	1,000.00	1,000.00	1,000.00	1,000.00	1,000.00

[1] *The data are based on statistics published in the late 1980s.*

[2] *Based on the proportion of the cohort who are alive at the beginning of an indicated age interval who will die before reaching the end of that interval. For example, out of every 1,000 people alive and exactly 50 years old at the beginning of the period, between 4 and 5 (4.85) will die before reaching their 51st birthday.*

Deaths and Death Rates, by Selected Causes (1970–1990)[1]

Cause of Death	Deaths (1,000)					Crude Death Rate Per 100,000 Population[2]				
	1970	1980	1985	1989	1990[3] prel.	1970	1980	1985	1989	1990[3] prel.
All causes	1,921.0	1,989.8	2,086.4	2,150.5	2,162.0	945.3	878.3	873.9	866.3	861.9
Major cardiovascular diseases	1,008.0	988.5	977.9	931.8	920.4	496.0	436.4	409.6	375.4	366.9
Diseases of the heart	735.5	761.1	771.2	733.9	725.0	362.0	336.0	323.0	295.6	289.0
Percent of total	38.3	38.3	37.0	34.1	33.5	38.3	38.3	37.0	34.1	33.5
Rheumatic fever and rheumatic heart disease	14.9	7.8	6.6	6.1	6.3	7.3	3.5	2.8	2.5	2.5
Hypertensive heart disease[4]	15.0	24.8	23.7	23.3	23.6	7.4	10.9	9.9	9.4	9.4

Cause of Death	Deaths (1,000)					Crude Death Rate Per 100,000 Population[2]				
	1970	1980	1985	1989	1990[3] prel.	1970	1980	1985	1989	1990[3] prel.
Ischemic heart disease	666.7	565.8	536.8	498.0	489.3	328.1	249.7	224.8	200.6	195.1
Other diseases of endocardium	6.7	7.2	9.5	12.2	12.3	3.3	3.2	4.0	4.9	4.9
All other forms of heart disease	32.3	155.5	194.6	193.5	15.9	68.7	81.5	78.2	77.1	—
Hypertension[4]	8.3	7.8	7.8	8.8	9.2	4.1	3.5	3.2	3.5	3.7
Cerebrovascular diseases	207.2	170.2	153.1	145.6	145.3	101.9	75.1	64.1	58.6	57.9
Atherosclerosis	31.7	29.4	23.9	19.4	16.5	15.6	13.0	10.0	7.8	6.6
Other	25.3	20.0	22.0	24.3	24.4	12.5	8.8	9.2	9.8	9.7
Malignancies[5]	330.7	416.5	461.6	496.2	506.0	162.8	183.9	193.3	199.9	201.7
Percent of total	17.2	20.9	22.1	23.1	23.4	17.2	20.9	22.1	23.1	23.4
Of respiratory and intrathoracic organs	69.5	108.5	127.3	142.3	143.8	34.2	47.9	53.3	57.3	57.3
Of digestive organs and peritoneum	94.7	110.6	116.6	119.7	121.3	46.6	48.8	48.8	48.2	48.4
Of genital organs	41.2	46.4	49.7	55.0	58.0	20.3	20.5	20.8	22.1	23.1
Of breast	29.9	35.9	40.4	43.1	45.1	14.7	15.8	16.9	17.4	18.0
Of urinary organs	15.5	17.8	18.9	20.2	20.4	7.6	7.9	7.9	8.2	8.1
Leukemia	14.5	16.5	17.3	18.2	18.7	7.1	7.3	7.3	7.4	7.4
Accidents and adverse effects	114.6	105.7	93.5	95.0	93.6	56.4	46.7	39.1	38.3	37.3
Motor vehicle	54.6	53.2	45.9	47.6	47.9	26.9	23.5	19.2	19.2	19.1
All other	60.0	52.5	47.6	47.5	45.7	29.5	23.3	19.9	19.1	18.2
Chronic obstructive pulmonary diseases and allied conditions[6]	30. 9	56.1	74.7	84.3	89.0	15.2	24.7	31.3	34.0	35.5
Bronchitis, chronic and unspecified	5.8	3.7	3.6	3.8	3.4	2.9	1.6	1.5	1.5	1.3
Emphysema	22.7	13.9	14.2	15.5	16.5	11.2	6.1	5.9	6.2	6.6
Asthma	2.3	2.9	3.9	4.9	4.6	1.1	1.3	1.6	2.0	1.8
Other	([6])	35.6	53.0	6.02	64.6	([7])	15.7	22.2	24.3	25.7
Pneumonia and influenza	62.7	54.6	67.6	76.6	78.6	30.9	24.1	28.3	30.8	31.3
Pneumonia	59.0	51.9	65.6	75.0	76.7	29.0	22.9	27.5	30.2	30.6
Influenza	3.7	2.7	2.1	1.6	1.9	1.8	1.2	0.9	0.6	0.8
Diabetes mellitus	38.3	34.9	37.0	46.8	48.8	18.9	15.4	15.5	18.9	19.5
Suicide	23.5	26.9	29.5	30.2	30.8	11.6	11.9	12.3	12.2	12.3
Chronic liver disease and cirrhosis	31.4	30.6	26.8	26.7	25.6	15.5	13.5	11.2	10.8	10.2
Other infective and parasitic diseases	6.9	5.1	8.1	29.2	32.2	3.4	2.2	3.4	11.8	12.8
Human immunodeficiency virus (HIV) infection (AIDS)	([8])	([8])	([8])	22. 1	24.1	([8])	([8])	([8])	8.9	9.5
Homicide and legal intervention	16.8	24.3	19.9	22.9	25.7	8.3	10.7	8.3	9.2	10.2
Nephritis, nephrotic syndrome, and nephrosis	8.9	16.8	21.3	21.1	20.9	4.4	7.4	8.9	8.5	8.3
Septicemia	3.5	9.4	17.2	19.3	19.8	1.7	4.2	7.2	7.8	7.9
Certain conditions originating in the perinatal period	43.2	22.9	19.2	18.8	17.5	21.3	10.1	8.1	7.6	7.0

Deaths and Death Rates, by Selected Causes (1970–1990)[1] (cont'd)

Cause of Death	Deaths (1,000)					Crude Death Rate Per 100,000 Population[2]				
	1970	1980	1985	1989	1990[3] prel.	1970	1980	1985	1989	1990[3] prel.
Congenital anomalies	16.8	13.9	12.8	12.9	13.4	8.3	6.2	5.4	5.2	5.3
Benign neoplasms[9]	4.8	6.2	6.7	6.7	7.0	2.4	2.7	2.8	2.7	2.8
Ulcer of stomach and duodenum	8.6	6.1	6.6	6.5	6.2	4.2	2.7	2.8	2.6	2.5
Hernia of abdominal cavity and intestinal obstruction[10]	7.2	5.4	5.4	5.5	5.6	3.6	2.4	2.2	2.2	2.2
Anemias	3.4	3.2	3.7	4.0	4.2	1.7	1.4	1.5	1.6	1.7
Cholelithiasis and other disorders of gall bladder	4.0	3.3	3.0	3.0	3.0	2.0	1.5	1.2	1.2	1.2
Nutritional deficiencies	2.5	2.4	2.9	3.0	3.1	1.2	1.0	1.2	1.2	1.2
Tuberculosis	5.2	2.0	1.8	2.0	1.8	2.6	0.9	0.7	0.8	0.7
Infections of kidney	8.2	2.7	2.0	1.4	1.1	4.0	1.2	0.8	0.6	0.4
Viral hepatitis	1.0	0.8	0.9	1.5	1.7	0.5	0.4	0.4	0.6	0.7
Meningitis	1.7	1.4	1.2	1.1	1.2	0.8	0.6	0.5	0.4	0.5
Acute bronchitis and bronchiolitis	1.3	0.6	0.6	0.6	0.6	0.6	0.3	0.3	0.3	0.2
Hyperplasia of prostate	2.2	0.8	0.5	0.4	0.3	1.1	0.3	0.2	0.2	0.1
Symptoms, signs, and ill-defined conditions	25.8	28.8	31.0	27.0	26.3	12.7	12.7	13.0	10.9	10.5
All other causes	108.8	120.0	153.0	171.5	174	53.5	53.0	64.4	69.1	69.4

[1]This table excludes deaths of nonresidents of the United States. The standard population used for this table is the total population of the United States enumerated in 1940. Beginning in 1979, deaths are classified according to the 9th revision of the International Classification of Diseases; for earlier years, they are classified according to the revision in use at that time.

[2]For the years 1970, 1980, and 1990, data are based on the resident population enumerated as of April 1; for 1985 and 1989, data are based on the resident population estimated as of July 1. Estimates do not reflect revisions based on the 1990 Census of the Population.

[3]Based on a 10 percent sample of deaths; includes nonresidents.

[4]With or without renal disease.

[5]Includes other types of malignancies not shown separately.

[6]Before 1980, data are shown for bronchitis, emphysema, and asthma.

[7]Included in "All other causes." Comparative data not available separately.

[8]Data are included in several other categories.

[9]Includes neoplasms of unspecified nature; beginning 1980 also includes carcinoma in situ.

[10]Without mention of hernia.

DENTAL TECHNOLOGY

Fluoridated water and other advances have made tooth decay far less common than in the past. Decay usually begins as a pit or fissure near the biting and chewing surfaces of the tooth, between the teeth, or at the lower part of the tooth's crown (at the start of the root) where plaque builds up. Tooth decay usually begins in childhood and adolescence; adults develop fewer cavities because of better eating habits and hygiene.

Dental technology concentrates on maintaining not only the teeth but, in particular, the gums. Gum (or periodontal) disease is one of the major problems seen by dentists. It is caused by a combination of and reactions between a certain bacteria and white blood cells. Poor oral hygiene or health, or excessive sugar in the diet can exacerbate the problem. The early stages of gum disease, called gingivitis, include puffy gums and often bad breath (halitosis). The second stage, called periodontitis, includes the inflammation of the gums, in which pockets form between the gum tissue and the tooth. The final stages of gum disease includes the loss of vital bone, which can lead to loss of teeth. Gum disease from severe neglect or malnutrition can lead to gangrene of the mouth.

The Teeth

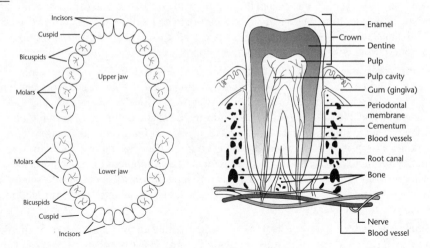

THE HUMAN MIND AND PSYCHOLOGY

Psychoses and Major Mood Disorders

Psychosis is not a specific diagnosis but a descriptive term used for a class of mental disorders that includes *delusions* (false beliefs in the face of compelling evidence to the contrary) and *hallucinations* (sounds or sights perceived while awake in the absence of any external stimulus). Thus psychosis is often described as loss of contact with reality.

There is strong evidence that psychoses and persistent mood disorders result from chemical imbalances in the brain. Psychotic states can be caused by drugs, such as LSD or prolonged use of amphetamines; psychotic illnesses are often successfully treated by drugs. Psychiatrists (physicians who treat mental disorders) use several different categories to describe psychoses, which can be short episodes or lifelong illnesses.

Excluding psychoses caused by drug abuse, psychotic illnesses fall into three major categories: schizophrenia, major depression, and manic syndrome. Bipolar disorder combines depression and mania. A fifth category is delusional disorder, which is considered psychotic behavior (not a psychosis). Except for schizophrenia, these illnesses are primarily severe mood disorders.

schizophrenia   Symptoms vary from person to person and from time to time, making schizophrenia difficult to diagnose. Many of the symptoms are not psychotic, such as a flat emotional response, disconnected conversation, and lack of will to initiate acts. All possible psychotic symptoms may be present from time to time as well. Delusions are common, especially about thought control; hallucinations are also frequent, especially hearing voices. Sometimes schizophrenia can affect body movements; for example, the schizophrenic may be catatonic, rigidly holding one position. Schizophrenia rarely develops in children or in older adults. It most often occurs in an adolescent or young adult, who develops a mental disorder that persists beyond six months. One criterion for schizophrenia is that the underlying disease continues for the remainder of a person's life; and like diabetes, it can be managed but not cured.

major depression   Often known as *clinical depression*, major depression is far more than being merely sad. Physical symptoms are often present, including insomnia and loss of appetite. Feelings of confusion, indecision, and lethargy can interfere with all aspects of life. Mental symptoms are often severe enough to interfere with work, sex, and other aspects of intrapersonal relationships; it often affects feelings of pleasure in general. Feelings of unworthiness, self-pity or self-blame, hopelessness, and agitation can lead to suicide. Psychotic symptoms may not be present, but when they are, the most common is a delusion of utter worthlessness.

manic syndrome   Just as major depression is far more than feeling sad, manic syndrome goes well beyond an elevated or irritated mood. During a manic episode a person may have psychotic delusions of grandeur, such as a belief that he or she has a special relationship to God. Sometimes people suffering from this syndrome have the hallucination that God has spoken to them or that they have heard from a messenger from God. But, like major depression, manic syndrome is primarily a mood disorder, characterized by racing and wandering thoughts, incessant talkativeness, risk-taking behavior, and development of grandiose schemes and plans. Almost always the manic individual has a reduced need to sleep. While suicide is the worst complication of depression, the manic is most likely to abuse drugs and alcohol, sometimes leading to a fatal overdose.

bipolar disorder   Bipolar disorder was once called manic depression or manic-depressive disease. This condition is marked by periodic crossovers between two poles of personality— manic episodes alternating with depressive episodes. Bipolar disorder can sometimes include psychosis in either phase.

delusional disorder   Delusions can occur in the absence of schizophrenia or mood disorders. The most common pattern is often called *paranoia*, in which a person has the delusion that other people are trying to do him or her harm, often in a grand conspiracy. Exaggerated jealousy and "stalking" a person are also common forms of delusionary thoughts and behavior.

Neuroses

The general term for mental illnesses that do not have strictly psychotic symptoms is *neurosis*, but there is a wide range of such disorders. Classification of some of these disorders as illnesses is often controversial: Sexual behavior that may seem to be mental illness to our society at large can, in other cultures, be considered part of normal behavior. Often a neurosis is merely an exaggerated form of normal behavior or feelings. At the other end of the spectrum, certain personality disorders are as bizarre as the delusions and hallucinations of psychotics.

dissociative disorders The rare multiple personality disorder, in which a person assumes different identities, is a dissociative disorder (as is amnesia) that is not caused by brain damage. Trances that are not deliberately induced also fall into this category. A characteristic of most dissociative disorders is memory impairment of one form or another, although it is not known whether there is an underlying physical cause for memory loss.

obsessive-compulsive disorder Although classed by psychiatrists as an anxiety disorder, obsession—like psychosis and multiple personality disorder—is often a serious mental illness. This category ranges from serious compulsions to violent behavior to obsessive doubts about the consequences of past events (e.g., excessive wondering whether one has accidentally injured another person). Frequently, an obsession concerns cleanliness. Compulsions may require repeating some act, such as returning home over and over to make certain that the door is locked, or always performing an act in exactly the same way. Appropriate drugs can effectively treat obsessive-compulsive disorders, suggesting that there is a physical cause.

sexual disorders Sexual disorders include exhibitionism (displaying genitals), pedophilia (having children as sex objects), masochism and sadism (desire to receive or inflict pain to achieve sexual satisfaction), and similar behavior.

anxiety disorders Free-floating anxiety is simply excessive worry about various life circumstances, but it may also have such physical symptoms as chest pain, shortness of breath, and muscle tension. A more severe anxiety of the same nature is a panic attack, which begins with terror and may include faintness, sweating, nausea, hot flashes or chills, and fear of losing control of oneself.

PHOBIC NEUROSES

A large group of anxiety disorders are also known as phobic neuroses, characterized by such fears as the following.

Acrophobia Fear of high places	*Graphophobia* Fear of writing
Agoraphobia Fear of open or public spaces	*Gynophobia* Fear of women
Aichinophobia Fear of sharp objects	*Haptophobia* Fear of being touched
Ailurophobia Fear of cats	*Harpaxophobia* Fear of robbers
Amathophobia Fear of dust	*Heliophobia* Fear of the Sun
Androphobia Fear of men	*Hemophobia* Fear of blood
Anthophobia Fear of flowers	*Homichlophobia* Fear of fog
Astraphobia Fear of lightning and thunder	*Hydrophobia* Fear of water
Astrophobia Fear of stars	*Hypnophobia* Fear of sleep
Autophobia Fear of being alone	*Kakorrhaphiophobia* Fear of failure
Ballistophobia Fear of missiles	*Lalophobia* Fear of speaking
Basiphobia Fear of walking	*Limnophobia* Fear of lakes
Batrachophobia Fear of frogs	*Linonophobia* Fear of string
Bibliophobia Fear of books	*Musicophobia* Fear of music
Chionphobia Fear of snow	*Musophobia* Fear of mice
Chrometophobia Fear of money	*Necrophobia* Fear of dead bodies
Demophobia Fear of crowds	*Neophobia* Fear of new things
Dendrophobia Fear of trees	*Nosemaphobia* Fear of infection
Ecclesiaphobia Fear of churches	*Nyctophobia* Fear of night
Ergophobia Fear of work	*Ombrophobia* Fear of rain
Erythrophobia Fear of the color red	*Ophidiophobia* Fear of reptiles
Gamophobia Fear of marriage	*Panphobia* Fear of everything
Genophobia Fear of sex	*Pediophobia* Fear of children (or dolls)
Gephyrophobia Fear of bridges	*Phagophobia* Fear of eating

Pharmacophobia   Fear of taking medications
Phasmophobia   Fear of ghosts
Phonophobia   Fear of noise
Phyllophobia   Fear of leaves
Pogonophobia   Fear of beards
Psychrophobia   Fear of cold
Pyrophobia   Fear of fire
Sciophobia   Fear of shadows

Siderodromophobia   Fear of trains
Sitophobia   Fear of food
Taphephobia   Fear of being buried alive
Thalassophobia   Fear of the oceans
Thanatophobia   Fear of death
Triskaidekaphobia   Fear of the number 13
Zoophobia   Fear of animals

Other Mental Disorders

Among the other disorders recognized by psychiatrists are hypochondria of various types (in which a person imagines an illness or pain); sleep disorders, from insomnia to sleepwalking; and adjustment disorders, such as personality problems that interfere with work or friendships.

MAJOR BIOMEDICAL AND BIOLOGICAL SCIENTISTS

Adler, Alfred (1870–1937)   Austrian psychiatrist who introduced the term *inferiority feeling* (later *inferiority complex*). He also suggested a more supportive psychotherapy.

Avery, Oswald Theodore (1877–1955)   American bacteriologist who showed that DNA was involved in heredity. His work led to a push for more involved DNA studies.

Avicenna (980–1037)   Persian physician who wrote several volumes in the *Canon of Medicine*, which was the authoritative treatise on medicine until the seventeenth century.

Baltimore, David (1938–)   American molecular biologist who discovered that some cancer RNA can transfer genetic information to DNA within a healthy cell, turning it cancerous. He shared the Nobel Prize in 1975 with Howard Temin and Renato Dulbecco, for their work on interactions between tumor viruses and genetic material within cells.

Bartholin, Caspar (1585–1629)   Danish anatomist whose book on human anatomy was the best known of his time. He also wrote on physics, logic, and ethics.

Beaumont, William (1785–1853)   American physician who was one of the first to study digestion. He treated a patient who was wounded by a shotgun to the stomach. After treatment, the open wound was covered by a thin layer of flesh that could be pushed back. Beaumont's observations on the digestive processes contributed to the modern studies on digestion.

Bernard, Claude (1813–1878)   French physiologist who is called the father of physiology; he introduced several concepts in the field, including that the functions of the various organs within the body are closely interrelated and that the body maintains a constant internal environment despite external changes.

Black, James (1787–1867)   Scottish physician who studied circulation, mainly of ducks and frogs, and applied the information to humans. He was also an amateur geologist and paleontologist.

Black, Sir James Whyte (1924–)   British pharmacologist who developed two important drugs: cimetidine (to treat ulcers) and propranolol (to block beta-receptors and relieve angina pectoris). He shared the Nobel Prize in 1988.

Blackwell, Elizabeth (1821–1910)   American who received her degree from Geneva Medical College in New York in 1894 and was the first woman physician in the United States.

Her small practice in New York expanded into the New York Infirmary for Women and Children, which had an all-female staff.

Bowman, Sir William (1816–1892)   British physician who is known as the father of histological anatomy and ophthalmic surgery. He worked with the microscope, making detailed descriptions of nerves, skin, muscles, etc. and did major work in eye disease.

Broca, Pierre Paul (1824–1880)   French physician and anthropologist; he was an outstanding surgeon and was the first to identify the speech center in the brain.

Brown, Michael Stuart (1941–)   American geneticist who, with J. L. Goldstein, discovered how cholesterol is metabolized in the body. He shared the Nobel Prize with Goldstein in 1985.

Chain, Ernst Boris (1906–1979)   German-born British biochemist who shared the Nobel Prize in 1945 with Sir Alexander Fleming and Sir Howard Florey for the discovery of penicillin.

Chittenden, Russell Henry (1856–1943)   American physiologist and biochemist who was the first to observe free glycine in nature. He discovered the nature of proteins, and his digestive studies led to the discovery of the role of enzymes.

Corti, Alfonso Giacomo Gaspare (1822–1888)   Italian anatomist and histologist who first explained the fine structure of organs. He also was one of the first to stain objects on a slide, improving microscope technology.

Crick, Francis Harry Compton (1916–)   British molecular biologist who, with James Watson, Maurice Wilkins, and Rosalind Franklin, discovered the structure of DNA. Only three shared the Nobel Prize in 1962 (Franklin died before the award was presented).

Cushing, Harvey William (1869–1939)   First American to specialize in neurological surgery. His important contributions included work on intercranial tumors.

Cuvier, Baron Georges Léopold Chrétien Frédéric Dagobert (1769–1832)   French comparative anatomist, paleontologist, and taxonomist who founded the science of comparative anatomy.

Darlington, Cyril Dean (1903–1981)   British geneticist whose work on chromosomes influenced ideas on hereditary mechanisms and evolution.

Darwin, Erasmus (1731–1802)   British physician who developed ideas on animal causation, and classification of disease. He also worked out a theory of biological evolution, somewhat similar to the one his grandson (Charles Darwin) developed years later.

Dausset, Jean Baptiste Gabriel (1916–)   French physician and immunologist who worked on the genetic basis for immunological reactions. He shared the Nobel Prize in 1980 with George Snell and Baruj Benacerraf.

Davaine, Casimir Joseph (1812–1882)   French physician and microbiologist whose greatest contribution was to medical microbiology. He also was the first to recognize the pathogenic role of bacteria and he advanced the study of spread of infection.

Ehrlich, Paul (1854–1915)   German physician, bacteriologist, and chemist who discovered numerous bacterial toxins and antitoxins; he was also the first to use chemotherapy in medicine. He shared the 1908 Nobel Prize with Ilja Mecnikov for their immunity studies.

Enders, John Franklin (1897–1985)   American microbiologist who developed a virus in nonnervous tissue cultures. His work was the preliminary step toward a polio vaccine. He won the Nobel Prize in 1954.

Erasistratus of Chios (c. 276–c. 194 B.C.). Greek anatomist and physician whose work was the most respected of his time (though none of his writings survive). Studies by Herophilus of

Chalcedon and Erasistratus laid the foundation for anatomy and physiology. He also was one of the first to discover that the brain was the center of intelligence.

Fabricius ab Aquapendente, Hieronymus (or Fabrici, Girolamo) (1537–1619)   Italian anatomist and embryologist who did detailed work on blood vessels.

Fallopius, Gabriel (1523–1562)   Italian anatomist whose work centered on the anatomy of young children and on female reproduction. The fallopian tube was named after him.

Fleming, Sir Alexander (1881–1955)   British bacteriologist who discovered how the human body defends itself against bacterial infection. He also worked on eradicating syphilis. He shared the Nobel Prize in 1945 with Sir Howard Florey and Ernst Chain for the discovery of penicillin.

Florey, Sir Howard Walter (1898–1968)   Australian pathologist who shared the Nobel Prize in 1945 with Sir Alexander Fleming and Ernst Chain for the discovery of penicillin.

Flourens, Jean Pierre Marie (1794–1867)   French physician and anatomist who studied the physiology of the nervous system and the formation and growth of bones. He also discovered chloroform's anesthetic properties.

Franklin, Rosalind (1920–1958)   British crystallographer who, with James Watson, Maurice Wilkins, and Francis Crick, worked to discover the structure of DNA. She used x-ray diffraction studies of DNA to determine its structure. Three of the scientists shared the Nobel prize in 1962; Franklin died before the award was presented, thus disqualifying her.

Freud, Sigmund (1856–1939)   Austrian psychoanalyst who laid the foundation for modern psychoanalysis. He introduced the importance of dreams as well as the unconscious and the ego, superego, and id to the human psyche.

Galen (c. 130–c. 200)   Turkish physician who became one of the most famous and influential doctors of Rome. He developed a physiological model of the human body that was held as the standard for anatomy for centuries.

Goldstein, Joseph Leonard (1940–)   American physician and geneticist who with M. S. Brown, discovered how cholesterol is metabolized in the body. He shared the 1906 Nobel prize with Brown in 1985.

Golgi, Camillo (1843–1926)   Italian cytologist and histologist who did extensive research in malaria. He also discovered the Golgi bodies on cells. He shared the Nobel Prize with Santiago Ramón.

Hansen, Armauer Gerhard Henrik (1841–1912)   Norwegian bacteriologist who discovered the bacterium responsible for leprosy. Hansen's disease is the alternative name for leprosy.

Harvey, William (1578–1657)   British physician who studied physiology, anatomy, embryology, and medicine, advancing each field. He also examined the reproduction of numerous species. His work included the study of nutrition to improve the health of the general public.

Hashimoto, Hakaru (1881–1934)   Japanese surgeon who determined the cause of thyroiditis, which was then named Hashimoto's disease.

Heidenhain, Rudolf Peter Heinrich (1834–1897)   German physiologist who performed extensive studies of muscles and nerves. He also advanced ideas on the physiology (secretion and absorption) of glands.

Herophilus of Chalcedon (c. 335–c. 280 B.C.). Greek doctor who, though all of his writings are gone, was the most respected anatomist and physician of his time. Studies by Herophilus and Erasistratus laid the foundations for anatomy and physiology.

Hippocrates of Cos (c. 460–c. 370 B.C.)   Greek physician who developed ideas that led to the Hippocratic oath; he is called the father of medicine. He started a school of medicine at Cos, where he encouraged the separation of medicine and religion.

Huxley, Sir Andrew Fielding (1917–)   British physiologist who studied nerve and muscle fibers. He shared the 1963 Nobel Prize with Sir John C. Eccles and Alan L. Hodgkin.

Jenner, Edward (1749–1823)   British physician who discovered the smallpox vaccine. He was also the founder of immunology and pioneer of modern virology.

Jung, Carl Gustav (1875–1961)   Swiss psychologist and psychiatrist who, as one of the most influential psychologists of his time, founded analytic psychology. His work contradicted many of the ideas of Sigmund Freud.

Kitasato, Baron Shibasaburo (1852–1931)   Japanese bacteriologist who was the first to derive a culture of bacillus that caused tetanus. His work opened the field of serology.

Malpighi, Marcello (1628–1694)   Italian histologist who was a master at microscopy techniques. He also studied the movement of blood through capillaries and described lung structure using microscopy.

Meckel, Johan Friedrich (1724–1774)   German anatomist and botanist who was one of the most influential anatomists of his time. He was also the grandfather of Johann Meckel.

Meckel, Johann Friedrich (1781–1833)   German anatomist and surgeon who was one of the greatest anatomists of his time. He was also the first to write a comprehensive description of birth defects.

Müller, Johannes Peter (1801–1858)   German who founded the modern science of physiology.

Papanicolaou, George Nicholas (1883–1962)   Greek-born American anatomist who developed a test to diagnose diseases, such as cervical cancer and certain types of sexually transmitted diseases in women. The test is commonly called the Pap test.

Parkinson, James (1755–1824)   British surgeon who made the first clinical description of the disease now known as Parkinson's disease. He also was a popular medical writer and had side interests in geology and paleontology (he was the first to suggest that coal derived from fermented plants).

Pasteur, Louis (1822–1895)   French chemist and microbiologist who developed the germ theory of disease. He also developed the first vaccine against rabies and was the founder of microbiology.

Pavlov, Ivan Petrovich (1849–1936)   Soviet physiologist who worked on blood circulation, digestion, and the physiology of the brain and nervous system. He was a student of Heidenhaim and is famous for his studies that demonstrated the phenomenon of the conditioned reflex.

Raynaud, Maurice (1834–1881)   French physician who discovered Raynaud's disease, in which spasms in the arteries to the fingers and toes cause the digits to turn blue and cold.

Reye, Ralph Douglas Kenneth (1912–1978)   Australian pediatrician and the first to describe the occurrence of an acute neurological illness in children following certain viral infections; it is known as Reye's syndrome.

Sabin, Albert Bruce (1906–1993)   Polish-born American microbiologist who invented the first oral polio vaccine called the Sabin vaccine.

Salk, Jonas Edward (1914–1995)   American microbiologist who formulated a polio vaccine. His final research work dealt with searching for a cure for AIDS.

Salmon, Daniel Elmer (1850–1914)   American pathologist who discovered *Salmonella* bacteria.

Spemann, Hans (1869–1941)   German zoologist, embryologist, and histologist who discovered that embryo development is determined by the interactions among various parts of the embryo and that certain areas acted as organizers for the development of tissues.

Sperry, Roger Wolcott (1913–1994)   American neurobiologist who discovered certain brain functions, especially the specialization of the hemispheres. He shared the Nobel Prize in 1981 with David Hubel and Rorsten Wiesel for their work in information processing in the visual system.

Stokes, William (1804–1878)   Irish physician who advanced the fields of cardiac and pulmonary disease. He was the leading Irish physician of his time.

Sydenham, Thomas (1624–1689)   English physician who is called the English Hippocrates because he reintroduced the Hippocratic methods. He was one of the founders of epidemiology and thus is also called the father of modern medicine. He was instrumental in describing numerous diseases, including measles and scarlet fever.

Temin, Howard Martin (1938–)   American molecular biologist who discovered a process in which an enzyme causes RNA to be transcribed onto DNA, a key bit of knowledge for genetic engineering. He shared the Nobel Prize in 1975 with David Baltimore and Renato Dulbecco for their work on interactions between tumor viruses and genetic material within cells.

Theiler, Max (1899–1972)   South African-born American virologist who discovered how mice became susceptible to yellow fever, thus laying the groundwork for the development of a human vaccine. He won the Nobel Prize in 1951.

Vallisneri, Antonio (1661–1730)   Italian physician and biologist who disagreed with the spontaneous generation theory popular among his contemporaries. He believed that contagious diseases were caused by microscopic parasites.

Vesalius, Andreas (1514–1564)   Flemish anatomist who found discrepancies in Galen's texts, noting that most of Galen's work was probably based on animal anatomy. Vesalius was the first to call for the use of human cadavers to understand human anatomy; he wrote some of the major anatomy books of his time.

Waddington, Conrad Hal (1905–1975)   British embryologist and geneticist who wrote the first notable work on the development of bird and mammal embryos. He also discovered that chemical messengers from particular tissues were responsible for inducing development of other tissues.

Warburg, Otto Heinrich (1883–1970)   German biochemist who discovered iron oxygenase, a respiratory enzyme, and a method for studying respiration of tissues in thin section. He was one of the most accomplished biochemists of his time, and won the Nobel Prize in 1931.

Wassermann, August von (1866–1925)   German bacteriologist who developed a test for syphilis. He also studied immunology, serology, bacteriology, and cancer therapy.

Watson, James Dewey (1928–)   American biochemist who, with Francis Crick, Maurice Wilkins, and Rosalind Franklin, discovered the structure of DNA. He shared the Nobel Prize with Crick and Wilkins (Franklin died before the award was presented).

Wharton, Thomas (1614–1673)   British physician who wrote one of the first accounts of the glands in the human body.

Wilkins, Maurice (Hugh Frederick) (1916–)   New Zealand-born British biophysicist who, with James Watson , Francis Crick, and Rosalind Franklin, discovered the structure of DNA. He shared the 1962 Nobel Prize with Watson and Crick (Franklin died before the award was presented).

Willis, Thomas (1621–1675)   British anatomist and physician who was the first to clinically describe typhoid fever. He also described other contagious diseases (including plague and measles) as well as several basic processes of human chemistry and blood.

Wilson, Edmund Beecher (1856–1939)   American cytologist and embryologist whose work on cell development and embryology led to the discovery of the X and Y chromosomes.

Winslow, Jakob Benignus (1669–1760)   Danish anatomist who was the greatest anatomist of his day. He concentrated on muscular movement.

Young, Thomas (1773–1829)   British physicist, physician, and Egyptologist who extensively studied the lens of the eye. His work also led to major discoveries concerning light in the field of physics.

Zinder, Norton David (1928–)   American geneticist who discovered genetic transduction, the carrying of hereditary material from one strain of microorganism to another by a filterable agent (e.g., a bacterial virus) in species of *Salmonella* bacteria.

SIGNIFICANT SCIENTIFIC DISCOVERIES IN BIOMEDICAL SCIENCE

B.C.	~3000	Tooth filling performed in Sumer
	~2500	Egyptian carvings depicted surgery
	~2000	Egyptians introduced a form of contraceptive
	~1550	Inscriptions from the papyrus Ebers described 700 medications and indicated the physicians of the time prescribed diets, massage, and fasts
	~535	A human cadaver was dissected for scientific study by Greek physician Alcmaeon of Croton (Italy)
	~500	First known cataract operation performed in India
	~400	Hippocrates founded the profession of medicine, separated medicine from religion, and developed the Hippocratic oath
	~300	First anatomy book written by Greek physician Diocles, a student of Aristotle
	~170	Pulse first used as a diagnostic aid by Galen
	~180	Galen accumulates all known medical knowledge of the time in a treatise; it was used until the end of the Middle Ages
A.D.	541	A bubonic plague struck Europe (it continued until 544)
	~640	Diabetes first noted by Chinese physician Chen Ch'üan
	977	First known hospital founded in Baghdad
	~1000	*Canon of Medicine* written by Avicenna; it was a five-volume compilation of Greek and Arabic medicine that was used until the seventeenth century
	1414	First case of influenza reported in France
	1460	First book on surgery written by Heinrich von Pfolspeundt
	1500	First recorded cesarean operation
	1518	Smallpox reaches the Americas
	1520	Smallpox decimates the Aztec people, allowing Hernando Cortes and his men, who had childhood immunity to the disease, to overrun the empire
	1559	Galen's ideas on heart flow were proven incorrect by Italian anatomist Realdo Columbo

1624	Thomas Sydenham identifies scarlet fever and measles and uses iron to relieve anemia
1647	First records of yellow fever in the Americas
1659	Typhoid fever first described by Thomas Willis
1709	George Berkeley made one of the most significant contributions to psychology in the eighteenth century, in his *New Theory of Vision*
1752	René Antoine Ferchault de Réaumur discovers the role of gastric juices
1805	Georges Cuvier founded the science of comparative anatomy
1825	First tracheotomy performed by Pierre Bretonneau
1831	Chloroform discovered independently by Eugène Soubeiran, Justin von Liebig, and Samuel Guthrie
1832	Thomas Hodgkin describes Hodgkin's disease, a cancer of the lymph nodes
1834	First mercury dental filling used
1842	First use of ether in surgery by Crawford W. Long; he did not publish his work, thus credit for the first use of ether is often given to William Morton (1846)
1844	First discovery that an egg is a cell and that all cells in an organism originate by divisions from the egg
	Discovery of bacillus that causes diphtheria
1858	Experimental psychology introduced by Wilhelm Wundt
1865	Tuberculosis determined to be a contagious disease by Jean-Antoine Villeman
1877	Louis Pasteur noted that some bacteria die when cultured with certain other bacteria (which eventually led to the first antibiotics in 1939)
1879	Pasteur's discoveries led to the development of vaccines against many diseases, including smallpox
1883	First book on comparative psychology, written by George John Romanes
1885	Sigmund Freud started to develop psychoanalysis
	Pasteur developed a vaccine against rabies
1887	First type of contact lens developed
1890	The field of immunology developed by Paul Ehrlich
1893	First open heart surgery performed by American Daniel Williams
1896	First diagnostic x-ray taken in the United States by Michael I. Pupin
1897	English physician Ronald Ross determined that *Anopheles* mosquitoes transmit the malaria parasite in humans
1900	Walter Reed determined that mosquitoes of the genus *Aedes* spread yellow fever
1902	Ivan Petrovich Pavlov formulated the theory of reinforcement, or learning by conditioning
	Walter Stanborough Sutton determined that chromosomes may be the carriers of inherited characteristics
1905	Female mammals found to have two X chromosomes; males to have an XY pair
1910	First types of chemotherapy used by Paul Ehrlich (to cure syphilis)
1926	X-rays found to induce genetic mutations by Hermann J. Muller
	Enzymes established to be proteins by James B. Sumner
1929	First DNA found by Phoebus Levene, although it was not isolated until 1936
	Manfred Sakel is the first to use electroshock to treat schizophrenia
1936	Andrei Nikolaevitch Belozersky isolates DNA in its pure state
1937	RNA discovered in tobacco leaves by Frederick C. Bawden and coworkers
1940	Rh factor discovered by Karl Landsteiner and Alexander S. Wiener
1943	First dialysis machine developed by Wilhelm Kolff
1945	First fluoridation of water supplies to prevent dental decay
1953	DNA structure discovered by James Watson and Francis Crick, based on x-ray work by Rosalind Franklin and Maurice Wilkins
1954	First hormone (called oxytocin) synthesized by Vincent Du Vigneaud
	J. H. Tjio and Albert Levan show that humans have 46 chromosomes

1955	The Salk vaccine for polio came into use (it was introduced in 1952), developed by Jonas Salk
1962	Lasers used for eye surgery for the first time
1965	Vaccine for measles available
1966	Vaccine for rubella (German measles) developed
1967	First use of mammography to check for breast cancer
	First successful heart transplant, done in South Africa by surgeon Christiaan Neelthing Barnard
	Coronary bypass surgery developed by Rene Favaloro
1969	First single gene isolated by Jonathan Beckwith and coworkers
1972	First CT scan introduced
1973	First NMR (or more recently, called MRI) developed
1977	The first probable cases of AIDS (acquired immune deficiency syndrome); the disease was not recognized until 1981
	Smallpox virus is believed to be extinct in the world (although samples of the virus are retained in laboratories for research purposes)
	Angioplasty invented by Andreas R. Gruentzig
1978	First human egg fertilized outside the body (called a test tube baby) results in birth of girl to Lesley Brown in the United Kingdom
1981	AIDS recognized for the first time
1982	First commercial product of genetic engineering released: human insulin from a bacteria (produced by Eli Lilly & Co.)
1982	William DeVries and coworkers perform first artificial heart transplant: Patient Barney Clark lived 112 days
1983	First artificial chromosome developed
1984	Techniques of genetic fingerprinting developed by Alec Jefferys, using specific core sequences of DNA unique to each person (although there are overlaps)
	First animals (sheep) successfully cloned by Steen A. Willadsen
	First genes cloned from an extinct species by Allan Wilson and Russell Higuchi
1988	First mouse developed by genetic engineering is patented (the first for a vertebrate); the patent is issued to Harvard Medical School

COMMON TERMS IN BIOMEDICAL SCIENCE

ACE inhibitors   Sometimes administered to lower blood pressure.

adrenaline   A hormone excreted by the adrenal glands that increases heart rate, energy, and resistance to fatigue.

allergen   Substances that cause adverse reactions, such as sneezing, in sensitive individuals, e.g., certain pollens and foods are allergens to some people.

amino acids   The basic organic chemical units from which proteins and peptides are synthesized by the body. All amino acid molecules contain one amino group and a carboxyl group held by a bond (see *peptide*). They are essential to all forms of life.

analgesics   Painkilling medications, such as aspirin, acetaminophen, nonsteroidal anti-inflammatory drugs, and narcotics.

anesthetics   Substances that dull bodily sensations, especially pain; they may be local or general.

antacids   Compounds that contain one or more minerals, such as calcium, sodium and magnesium, that neutralize excess stomach acid.

antibiotics   Chemicals used as drugs to kill or inhibit the growth of microorganisms. The drugs are derived from molds or bacteria and are used to treat bacterial infections (they do not work on viral infections).

antibodies   Proteins made by the body's immune system that help fight off foreign substances, such as viruses, bacteria, and other microorganisms.

anticoagulant   Medications that prevent blood clots from forming.

antidepressant   A drug used to treat mental depression.

antigen   Any foreign substance in the body that provokes the production of antibodies.

antihistamines   Drugs that are principally used to relieve allergy and hay fever symptoms. Once absorbed into the bloodstream, antihistamines attach themselves to the histamine receptors; in the nose, they block histamines from dilating the nasal vessels, which cause a runny nose.

anti-inflammatories   See *nonsteroidal anti-inflammatory drugs*.

antipsychotic drugs   Drugs used to treat certain serious mental conditions, such as schizophrenia.

antiseptic   Any chemical used to destroy harmful microorganisms.

arterioles   The smaller arteries in the circulatory system.

autoimmune disease   An illness that involves the formation of autoantibodies that appear to damage or attack the host's own tissues.

barbiturate   Drugs that produce drowsiness and/or a hypnotic state; they can be addictive.

benign   In reference to tumors, benign means not malignant.

benzodiazepines   Drugs prescribed for nervousness, sleeping problems, and to relax muscles or control seizures; they can be addictive if taken for long periods.

beta-blockers   Medications that reduce heart rate and force contraction as well as dilate blood vessels, lowering blood pressure. They are prescribed for coronary artery disease (including angina, irregular heart rhythms, and a history of heart attack) and to prevent migraine headaches.

biopharmaceuticals   Drugs that mimic the action of compounds that usually occur naturally in the body. They are usually produced by cloning or by the chemical synthesis of proteins.

biopsy   The removal of living tissues for laboratory examination.

bone marrow   The soft, pulpy center of the bone that produces the body's red blood cells, white blood cells, and platelets.

calcium channel blockers   Medications that help prevent ischemia, by maintaining the blood flow through the body's arteries and reducing the heart's work. They lower the calcium concentration in the blood vessels' smooth muscles, thus dilating the vessels, decreasing the heart rate, and lowering the blood pressure.

carcinogen   Any substance that can cause cancer, such as a chemical.

carcinoma   A cancer that appears on the skin, glands, and other tissues; it is derived from epithelial tissue.

catheter   A tube that maintains an opening to the body, e.g., a catheter can be inserted into the bladder after surgery to remove urine without disturbing the patient.

chemotherapy   A treatment that uses specific chemicals to destroy disease; it is most frequently used as a treatment to eliminate cancerous growths.

contraceptives   Drugs and physical devices that diminish the possibility of pregnancy, including the birth control pill and the condom.

coronary arteries   Arteries that supply blood to the heart.

cytoplasm   The substance of a cell outside the nucleus; the older term is protoplasm.

delirium   The sudden onset of confusion (including the inability to pay attention to one's surroundings and environment), usually caused by a serious illness.

diuretic   Also often called water pills, they are drugs that increase the amount of urine produced to help the kidneys get rid of salt and water.

endemic   The presence of disease within a given population.

endorphins   Natural painkillers and important neurotransmitters, especially for emotions, endorphins react with opiate receptor sites in a cell (the same area in which opiate drugs react), binding with the sites to reduce pain. Beta-endorphins, also natural painkillers, are often released during exercise.

enzyme   A protein that acts as an organic catalyst, affecting the speed of a metabolic reaction.

fiber   The indigestible part of vegetable matter. It is found in fruits, cereals, and vegetables and consists mostly of two indigestible polymers: cellulose and lignin.

gamma globulin   A type of blood protein that includes antibodies. It is extracted from donated blood and is used to fight infections such as hepatitis A.

homeostasis   An organism's body's state that maintains internal stability by compensating for environmental changes, e.g., without homeostasis, our body temperature would match the ambient temperature.

hormones   Chemicals produced in an organ of the body that are carried in a bodily fluid to another organ or tissue, where they have specific effects.

immune system   The body's defense against infection and disease. It may also trigger an allergic reaction.

immunization   The process of rendering the body resistant to a disease, as by inoculating with a vaccine.

in vitro   The reaction of tissues that have been removed from an organism, taking place in a laboratory, as in a petri dish.

in vivo   The reaction that takes place in a living organism.

inoculation   The introduction of a pathogen (orally or by injection) to allow the body to build up immunity to the pathogen.

interferon   A natural protein produced by animal cells when they are invaded by viruses, inducing the healthy cells to manufacture an enzyme that counters the infection. Through genetic engineering, it has been developed as a drug that is used to inhibit some cancers and some viruses.

laxative   A substance used to encourage bowel movements.

lipids   Organic compounds that include fats, oils, steroids, and waxes. The major types are fatty acids, triglycerides, phospholipids, and steroids.

lumen   The part of an artery where the blood flows; when it is blocked by plaque, the condition is often referred to as atherosclerosis.

malocclusion   When the upper and lower teeth do not meet properly.

metabolism   The sum of all biochemical reactions in the body, including anabolism (where more complex chemicals are built up from less complex ones) and catabolism (the breakdown of complex substances into simpler ones).

metastasis   The spread of disease from one part of the body to an unrelated part, as when cells from a malignant tumor are transferred through the bloodstream.

narcotics   Drugs used to relieve pain and induce sleep; they are often addictive.

nausea   The feeling that vomiting may occur; it is caused by a number of disorders, both minor and serious.

nerve   A cordlike fiber that carries electrochemical impulses throughout the body, such as to and from the brain.

neuron   The structural and functional unit of the nervous system; it is a specialized cell that is capable of being stimulated and of conducting impulses. It consists of an axon and one or more dendrites.

neurotransmitter   A chemical that either transmits or inhibits nerve impulses at a synapse.

nitroglycerin   A medication often used to treat angina and coronary artery disease. It dilates the small arteries of the body, allowing the heart to pump more blood into vessels that may be restricted. It is placed under the tongue and absorbed directly into the bloodstream.

nonsteroidal anti-inflammatory drugs (NSAIDs)   Medications that decrease inflammation in the body and control pain, without the use of steroids, e.g., aspirin and ibuprofen.

pain   Physical pain is described as one of the senses of the skin; it is a physical reaction, either from internal or external stimuli, to a stimulus that overloads the nerves. It is defined as an unpleasant sensory and emotional experience associated with the actual physical or potential tissue damage. Pain is a subjective experience that cannot be measured in any quantifiable way.

pandemic   An outbreak of a disease, usually worldwide or hemispherewide.

pathogen   Any disease-producing microorganism or agent, e.g., a germ.

penicillin   An antibiotic that is active against certain types of bacteria and cocci. It consists of the salts of a series of antibiotic organic acids produced by *Penicillium* and *Aspergillus* species.

peptide   A compound of two or more amino acids that has one carboxyl group of one acid joined with the amino group of the other. (See also *amino acids*.)

peristalsis   The wavelike muscular contractions along the wall of a hollow muscular vessel that move the contents along. The word is usually used in reference to the esophagus and the digestive system (the intestines).

plaque   A fatty, fibrous, cholesterol-containing mass in the lining of the arteries. The term is also used to describe a mass of bacterial cells and other debris that accumulates on the surfaces of teeth.

polypeptides   A substance containing two or more amino acids in the molecule, joined together by peptide linkages.

polyps   Swollen or tumorous tissues that may or may not be cancerous. They are found in various parts of the body, such as the lining of the digestive tract, nose, bladder, and throat.

presbyopia   The eye condition, mostly in older adults, in which it becomes difficult to focus on close objects. It is caused by the lens of the eye becoming less elastic with age.

prosthesis   An artificial substitute for a missing human part, such as a leg, breast, hip, or knee.

proteins   Complex organic compounds made up of amino acids. (See also *enzyme*.)

puberty   The stage of the human life cycle at which the reproductive organs become capable of functioning.

somnolence   Sleepiness or an unnatural drowsiness.

spasm   A sudden, and often continuous, contraction of a muscle that can cause pain and restrict movement.

synapse   The point at which a nerve impulse is transmitted from one neuron to another.

tissue plasminogen activator (tPA)   A drug that dissolves a clot and restores the heart's blood and oxygen supply very quickly. It is most often given to patients at the first sign of a heart attack.

tissue   A group of similar cells and the intercellular substance that perform a specific function within an organ of the body.

trauma   A sudden injury, either physical or psychological.

uric acid   A waste product of the metabolism of proteins. The kidney eliminates uric acid from the body; too high levels in the body may result in gout.

vaccinate   To render immune by inoculation with a vaccine, which is used to stimulate the production of particular antibodies.

vascular system   Composed of the blood vessels, which run through the entire body.

vertigo   A feeling of dizziness or loss of balance caused by numerous reasons. It can be caused by inner-ear or blood-pressure problems, or adverse drug reactions.

ADDITIONAL SOURCES OF INFORMATION

Bunch, Bryan. *Current Health and Medicine*. Gale Research, 1995.

Chiras, Daniel D. *Human Biology*. West, 1991.

Dox, Ida G., Melloni, B. John, and Eisner, Gilbert M. *The HarperCollins Illustrated Medical Dictionary*. HarperCollins, 1993.

Humphrey, Nicholas. *A History of the Mind: Evolution and the Birth of Consciousness*. Simon & Schuster, 1992.

Kass, Frederic I., Oldham, John M., and Pardes, Herbert, eds. *The Columbia University College of Physicians and Surgeons Complete Home Guide to Mental Health*. Holt, 1992.

Moore, Thomas J. *Lifespan: Who Lives Longer and Why*. Simon & Schuster, 1993.

Reader's Digest. *Family Guide to Natural Medicine: How to Stay Healthy the Natural Way*. Reader's Digest, 1993.

Thomas, Lewis. *The Fragile Species*. Scribner's, 1992.

Vogel, Steven. *Vital Circuits: On Pumps, Pipes, and the Workings of Circulatory Systems*. Oxford Univ. Press, 1993.

Chapter

6

Chemistry

What Is Chemistry?   226

Classifying Matter: Elements, Compounds, and
Mixtures   227

Atomic Structure   230

Matter as a Solid, Liquid or Gas   235

The Periodic Table of the Elements   238

Chemical Formulas and Equations   244

Chemical Kinetics   245

Chemical Bonding and Reactions   246

Organic Chemistry   249

Acids and Bases   251

Electrochemistry of Batteries   253

Radiochemistry   255

Chemical Laws and Rules   257

Major Chemists   259

Significant Scientific Discoveries
in Chemistry   263

Common Terms in Chemistry   266

Additional Sources of Information   270

WHAT IS CHEMISTRY?

Chemistry is the scientific study of the composition, structure, and properties of matter and its changes. Chemistry is important to the other sciences, as it encompasses all materials in the universe, whether the composition of gases in far-off stars or the complex structures of the components within living cells.

Early Chemical Studies

Chemistry has its roots in alchemy, a practice that probably started with the Taoists in China and the Pythagoreans in Greece after the sixth century B.C., in which, in general, people sought ways to change or transmute one substance into another substance, such as ordinary metals into gold. For centuries, alchemists looked for the Philosopher's Stone, a substance that could not only change other metals into gold but cure people of illness. Alchemists worked in secret, learning much about the nature of substances. They heated liquids into gases and then turned them back into liquids again, inventing the chemical process of *distillation*. In addition, many of the specially shaped bottles, flasks, and funnels seen in a modern scientific laboratory were invented by alchemists.

Alchemists based their work on the Chinese and Egyptians, and later the ancient Greeks who believed that the four elements of fire, air, water, and earth combine to make everything in the world (although Democritus, a Greek, believed that everything was made of tiny particles that he called "atoms"). By the Middle Ages, there were many famous alchemists in European, Arab, and Chinese cultures.

The decline of alchemy apparently started with Paracelsus (born 1493), a Swiss doctor who believed that alchemy should be used to find a cure for disease, not just change metals into gold. Paracelsus believed that there were many kinds of metals and hence many kinds of elements. He successfully cured some patients, but was rather arrogant and made many enemies. After Paracelsus, alchemy was on the decline, as many alchemists resorted to tricks and fraud. However, one of Paracelsus's followers, Libavius, wrote the first real text on chemistry.

In 1660, King Charles II of England founded the Royal Society of London. This group of thinkers set the stage for the field of chemistry, a new science to study the structure and properties of substances based on sound experiments and observations—rather than magic (the word *chemistry* is derived from the Arabic for "gold cooking"). The scientists wanted to share information and not work in secret like their predecessors. Yet the methods and observations of 2000 years established by alchemists had an important influence on the growth of the new science of chemistry.

By the late eighteenth and early nineteenth centuries, people such as French scientist Antoine Lavoisier, British chemist Joseph Priestley, and Swedish scientist Karl Scheele were identifying elements and discovering the nature of important chemical reactions such as combustion. Even practical activities, such as evaporating sea water for preserving fish and making candles and soap from animal fats, reflected advances in chemistry and technology.

At the beginning of the nineteenth century, English scientist John Dalton announced his atomic theory to explain the formation of compounds by elements. He revised the ideas of Democritus by describing chemical behavior in terms of atoms, stating that all elements are composed of atoms that can be neither created nor destroyed. Furthermore, Dalton proposed that all atoms of the same element are identical and combine to form "compound atoms" (or molecules) in simple ratios. By the end of the nineteenth century, many elements had been identified and placed in the newly developed Periodic Table of the Elements.

In the twentieth century, probing matter with more advanced techniques has led scientists to a greater understanding of the structure of the atom, but it has also led to larger questions about the nature of matter itself. Now the lines between chemistry and physics, and chemistry and biology have crossed, as physicists collide nuclei of atoms at high speeds and biochemists use crystallography to determine the structure of complex molecules like DNA. Yet whatever the application, an understanding of chemistry is the underpinning of all sciences.

Branches of Chemistry

The field of chemistry includes numerous branches and specialized subdivisions that involve other sciences.

Branch	Study
Analytical chemistry	Detailed analysis of chemical substances and their individual components
Astrochemistry	Analysis of substances from other bodies in space, such as asteroids
Biochemistry	Compounds and chemical reactions in living systems
Electrochemistry	Relationship between flow of electricity and chemical changes
Environmental chemistry	Chemical changes in the natural environment and how they affect living organisms
Geochemistry	Analysis of rocks and minerals
Inorganic chemistry	Compounds generally not containing carbon and usually derived from minerals
Nuclear chemistry	Changes in the atomic nucleus
Organic chemistry	Compounds from living organisms, and hydrocarbons and their derivations
Photochemistry	Reactions caused by light or ultraviolet radiation on chemical elements
Physical chemistry	Application of physical principles to describe chemical processes
Radiochemistry	Radioactive isotopes of chemical elements
Stoichiometry	Mathematical relationships among components of chemical reactions and formulas

CLASSIFYING MATTER: ELEMENTS, COMPOUNDS, AND MIXTURES

Elements, Compounds, and Mixture Relationships

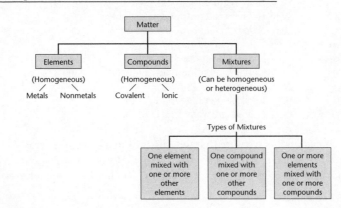

Elements and Compounds

Chemists study and classify *matter*—the endless array of materials that we come into contact with each day. Matter can be defined as anything that has mass and takes up space; it can be classified into three groups: elements, compounds, and mixtures.

An *element* is a substance that cannot be broken down into other substances. Some of the elements that are part of everyday life include oxygen, gold, iron, and nitrogen. (See also "The Periodic Table of the Elements," later in this chapter.)

A *compound* is a substance composed of two or more elements chemically combined in a definite proportion. There are about 10 million compounds known, including water, sand, ammonia, and table salt. They can be broken down into their constituent elements only by chemical change and not by physical means. For example, using electricity, you can separate water into the elements hydrogen and oxygen. A compound has properties separate and distinct from its constituent elements. Water, a liquid at room temperature, has chemical and physical properties different from either of its constituents, hydrogen or oxygen—both flammable gases.

Mixtures: Solutions and Suspensions

A *mixture* is a combination of two or more substances that retain their individual properties. They are held together by physical rather than chemical means and include soil, most rocks, milk, and saltwater. Mixtures that are uniform throughout are *homogeneous*. Those that are non-uniform (one part of the mixture has a composition that is different from another part) are *heterogeneous*.

A *solution* is a mixture that is uniform throughout, such as salt water, and contains a mixture of the very smallest particles—ions, atoms, or molecules of two or more substances. The dissolved salt in saltwater is commonly referred to as the *solute* and the water is the dissolving agent, or *solvent*. Saltwater is a stable, homogeneous mixture in which tiny particles of one compound (salt) is distributed evenly in another compound (water).

Kinds of Solutions

Solutions in which the solvent is water are known as *aqueous solutions*. When the solvent is alcohol, the solution is known as a *tincture*. Solutions are not limited to liquids. Gas solutions include air, which is made up primarily of oxygen and nitrogen; solid solutions also exist, in which one solid is mixed with another on the molecular level, such as in alloys of metals.

Kinds of Solutions	*Example*
Solid in solid	Steel (carbon in iron)
Liquid in solid	Rubber cement (benzene in rubber)
Gas in solid	Alloy of palladium and hydrogen
Solid in liquid	Saltwater (salt in water)
Liquid in liquid	Vinegar (acetic acid in water)
Gas in liquid	Carbonated drink (carbon dioxide in water)
Gas in gas	Air
Solid in gas	Perfume (perfume particles in air)
Liquid in gas	Humid air (water in air)

In general, the amount of a solute that will dissolve in a solvent increases with an increase in temperature. The number of grams of a solute that will dissolve in a solvent may be plotted on a graph and shown as a solubility curve (see figure "Solubility Curves for Selected Solutes in Water").

Solubility Curves for Selected Solutes in Water

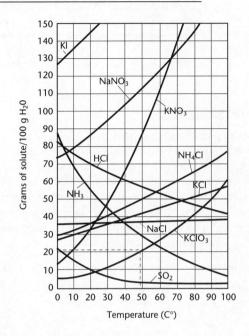

Some Common Solutes

A *concentrated solution* is one in which there is a relatively large amount of solute dissolved in solution. When a solution contains as much of a solute as it can hold at that temperature, the solution is *saturated*; if the solution has less solute than it can hold it is said to be *unsaturated*. An unsaturated solution is likely to be a dilute solution, one that has a relatively small amount of solute compared with the solvent.

A *supersaturated solution* is one in which a cooling solution has an excess of solute. Such solutions are unstable. For example, as water evaporates from the solution, molecules of the solute stick together and form crystals. The slower the crystal forms, the larger and more perfect the shape.

Solutions with the ability to conduct an electric current are known as *electrolytes*. Electrolytes contain charged particles, or ions, which allow the free flow of electrons from one terminal, through the solution, to the other terminal (see also "Atoms, Ions, and Molecules" later in this chapter). Thus electrolytes make industrial processes such as electroplating possible, in which thin layers of metal are deposited onto objects.

WHY DOES ANTIFREEZE WORK IN YOUR AUTOMOBILE?

Properties that are characteristic of a solvent and depend on the concentration but not on the nature of the dissolved solute are known as the solvent's *colligative properties*. One such property is the depression of the freezing point. When a solute is dissolved in a liquid, the freezing temperature of the solution will be lower than the freezing point of the pure liquid alone.

For example, when your car's radiator is filled with a mixture of water and antifreeze, the mixture prevents the water from freezing at a temperature of 32°F (0°C). You could actually use saltwater in the radiator to lower the freezing point, but the salt would cause damage to the metal components. Rather, ethylene glycol is the most common antifreeze. A solution of half water and half antifreeze does not freeze above about −35°F (−37°C). The coolant has a higher specific gravity than water; an indicator gauge with a float will indicate the amount of the antifreeze in the radiator.

Colloidal Dispersions

Mixtures in which small particles are permanently dispersed throughout a solvent are *colloidal dispersions* (or *suspensions*). For example, milk is a colloidal suspension of fats, proteins, and milk sugar dispersed in a liquid (water). The particles dispersed in milk are submicroscopic clumps (known as *colloidal micelles*) that range from 0.000000039 to 0.00003937 inch (0.0000001 to 0.0001 centimeter) in diameter. The way the particles scatter light gives a suspension such as milk its cloudy appearance in contrast to the clear appearance of a solution. Blood is a colloidal dispersion made of clumps of ions, molecules, and cellular bodies in water. Mayonnaise, butter, and jelly are also colloidal dispersions.

Kind of Colloidal System	Description	Example
Foam	Gas dispersed in liquid	Whipped cream
Solid foam	Gas dispersed in solid	Marshmallow
Liquid aerosol	Liquid dispersed in gas	Fog, mist
Sol	Solid dispersed in a liquid	Jelly
Solid sol	Solid dispersed in a solid	Pearls, opals
Smoke	Solid dispersed in a gas	Dust in air
Emulsion	Liquid dispersed in a liquid	Cream, mayonnaise
Solid emulsion	Liquid dispersed in a solid	Butter, cheese

ATOMIC STRUCTURE

What Are Protons, Neutrons, and Electrons?

Matter is composed of minute particles called *atoms*. Atoms are the smallest particles possessing the properties of an element that can enter into a chemical combination. They are made up of protons, neutrons, and electrons, which are called *elementary*, or *subatomic, particles*. *Protons* are particles with a positive charge; *neutrons* are particles with no charge. Together, the proton and the neutron make up the nucleus of most atoms. For years, protons and neutrons were thought to be fundamental particles; however, protons and neutrons are now known to be triplets of more basic particles called *quarks* (for more information on quarks, see Chapter 7, "Physics"). *Electrons* are the negatively charged fundamental particles found around the nucleus of an atom.

The Three Major Subatomic Particles

Name	Charge	Mass (grams)*	Symbols
Electron	−1	9.1091×10^{-28}	β, e^-
Proton	+1	1.67252×10^{-24}	p, p^+
Neutron	0	1.67482×10^{-24}	n

Values for particles at rest.

Atoms, Ions, and Molecules

Atomic Number and Mass

The atoms of each element have a specific atomic number and atomic mass. The *atomic number* is the number of protons in the nucleus of an atom; the *atomic mass* is the combined mass of its protons and neutrons. Do not confuse the mass number with atomic mass. The *mass number* is the total number of nucleons (the particles in the nucleus of an atom) and is the integer closest to the observed mass of an isotope.

Atomic Nomenclature

Here is the written symbol for the isotope oxygen-16.

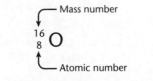

$$^{16}_{8}O$$

Mass number
Atomic number

(Neutron number = mass number – atomic number)

Formation of Ions

When an atom gains or loses electrons, it acquires a *net electric charge*, which is the number of protons minus the number of electrons. For example, if there are 6 protons and 8 electrons, the net charge is –2 (written as 2^- and often referred to as the *valence*).

An *ion* is an atom, or group of atoms, with a net electric charge. An ion can be positive (known as a *cation*) or negative (known as a *anion*). For example, magnesium has an atomic number of 12, meaning it has 12 protons and 12 electrons with a net electric charge of 0. If two of its outermost electrons are lost, the atom becomes an ion with a net charge of 2^+.

Valence involves the number of chemical bonds that an atom may form; this determines how chemical formulas are written for various compounds. The *valence number* is the number of electrons an atom can give up or acquire to achieve a filled outer shell (the orbits in which the electrons revolve around the nucleus are called *shells*). A *valence electron* is one that belongs to the outermost shell of an atom.

Oxygen Atom

Naturally occurring oxygen includes three isotopes: oxygen-16 ($^{16}_{8}O$), oxygen-17 ($^{17}_{8}O$), and oxygen-18 ($^{18}_{8}O$). Of nearly all the oxygen atoms, 99.76% of the total are oxygen-16 atoms.

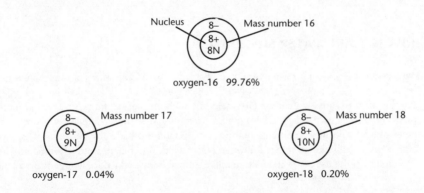

Names and Charges of Common Ions

Cations

1+

Ammonium (NH_4^+)
Cesium (Cs^+)
Copper(I) (Cu^+)
Potassium (K^+)
Silver (Ag^+)
Sodium (Na^+)

2+

Barium (Ba^{2+})
Beryllium (Be^{2+})
Cadmium (Cd^{2+})
Calcium (Ca^{2+})
Cobalt (II) (Co^{2+})
Copper (II) (Cu^{2+})
Iron (II) (Fe^{2+})
Lead (II) (Pb^{2+})
Magnesium (Mg^{2+})
Mercury (I) (Hg_2^{2+})
Mercury (II) (Hg^{2+})
Nickel (Ni^{2+})
Strontium (Sr^{2+})
Zinc (Zn^{2+})

3+

Aluminum (Al^{3+})
Chromium (III) (Cr^{3+})
Iron (III) (Fe^{3+})

Anions

1−

Acetate ($C_2H_3O_2^-$)
Bromide (Br^-)
Chlorate (ClO_3^-)
Chlorite (ClO_2^-)
Chloride (Cl^-)
Cyanide (CN^-)
Fluoride (F^-)
Hydrogen carbonate or
  bicarbonate (HCO_3^-)
Hydrogen sulfate (HSO_4^-)
Hydrogen sulfide (HS^-)
Hydroxide (OH^-)
Iodide (I^-)
Nitrate (NO_3^-)
Nitrite (NO_2^-)

2−

Carbonate (CO_3^{2-})
Chromate (CrO_4^{2-})
Dichromate ($Cr_2O_7^{2-}$)
Oxide (O^{2-})
Oxalate ($C_2O_4^{2-}$)
Peroxide (O_2^{2-})
Sulfate (SO_4^{2-})
Sulfide (S^{2-})

Sulfite (SO_3^{2-})
Tartrate ($C_4H_4O_6^{2-}$)

3−

Phosphate (PO_4^{3-})

HOW IS YOUR WATER SOFTENED?

Many people live in regions where water is considered "hard," that is, it contains numerous metallic ions, especially those of iron (Fe^{2+} or Fe^{3+}) or calcium (Ca^{2+}). These positively charged cations combine with negatively charged fatty acid anions from soap to form a waxy, insoluble salt. So instead of forming soap suds, the two combine to form soap scum. Where ion concentration is high, the insoluble molecules precipitate out of solution and onto bathtubs and sinks. This process may form a crusty, chalklike substance known as boiler scale. When hard water is a mild problem, it can be abated with the use of a water softener, like sodium borate added to detergents and soap.

If the hard water problem is severe, it may be necessary to install a water softener in the home. Most water softeners work as ion exchangers. As the hard water flows though a tank, it passes though an ion-exchange resin that contains millions of tiny, insoluble, porous beads that are filled with sodium cations (positive ions). As the sodium dissolves in the water, the resin attracts the iron and calcium ions in the water. They enter the exchanger to replace the dissolved sodium. This release of sodium gives softened water its characteristic high sodium content. The resin eventually has to be regenerated by pumping concentrated sodium chloride (saltwater) through it, exchanging the hard water ions for more sodium ions—typically using 5 to 6 pounds of sodium chloride for one regeneration.

Atomic Models

At the beginning of the nineteenth century, John Dalton theorized that an atom was an indivisible particle of an element. However, after the electron (a negatively charged particle with very little mass) was discovered in 1897, and then the proton several years later, the atom model was revised. In 1909, Ernest Rutherford showed that atoms were mostly space, revising the model of an atom to a tight positive nucleus containing the protons and neutrons with electrons around it; by 1913, Danish physicist Neils Bohr envisioned a planetary arrangement in which the electrons orbited the nucleus at different energy levels.

The current way of describing an electron is a model referred to as the *charge-cloud model*, *quantum-mechanical model*, or the *orbital model*. This model is based on the idea of Heisenberg's Uncertainty Principle, which states that we do not know the precise location or the velocity of any given electron. The model uses indistinct and overlapping "probability clouds" to approximate the position of an electron. Where a cloud is dense, the probability of finding an electron in that vicinity is high; where the density is low, the probability of finding an electron in that vicinity is low. In this model, each electron energy level is denoted by numbers that take into account its angle and velocity. The system is more complex than the arrangement of concentric shells as suggested by the Bohr model because there are overlaps in the ordering of the energy levels.

Atomic Models Over Time

Evolving ideas about the structure of the atom:

1803	Dalton	Indivisible particle
1897	Early atom	"Plum pudding"
1909	Rutherford	Positively charged nucleus surrounded by mostly empty space
1913	Bohr	Electrons in energy levels
1950s	Many researchers	Charge-cloud model (present model)

Electron Models

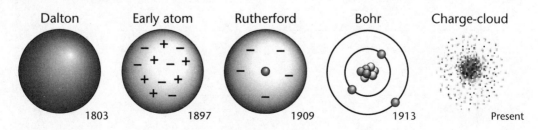

Dalton	Early atom	Rutherford	Bohr	Charge-cloud
1803	1897	1909	1913	Present

Electron Configurations of the Elements

Z* Element	Shell 1 (s)	Shell 2 (s p)	Shell 3 (s p d)	Shell 4 (s p d f)	Shell 5 (s p d f)	Shell 6 (s p d f)	Shell 7 (s)
1 H	1						
2 He	2						
3 Li	2	1					
4 Be	2	2					
5 B	2	2 1					
6 C	2	2 2					
7 N	2	2 3					
8 O	2	2 4					
9 F	2	2 5					
10 Ne	2	2 6					
11 Na	2	2 6	1				
12 Mg	2	2 6	2				
13 Al	2	2 6	2 1				
14 Si	2	2 6	2 2				
15 P	2	2 6	2 3				
16 S	2	2 6	2 4				
17 Cl	2	2 6	2 5				
18 Ar	2	2 6	2 6				
19 K	2	2 6	2 6	1			
20 Ca	2	2 6	2 6	2			
21 Sc	2	2 6	2 6 1	2			
22 Ti	2	2 6	2 6 2	2			
23 V	2	2 6	2 6 3	2			
24 Cr	2	2 6	2 6 5	1			
25 Mn	2	2 6	2 6 5	2			
26 Fe	2	2 6	2 6 6	2			
27 Co	2	2 6	2 6 7	2			
28 Ni	2	2 6	2 6 8	2			
29 Cu	2	2 6	2 6 10	1			
30 Zn	2	2 6	2 6 10	2			
31 Ga	2	2 6	2 6 10	2 1			
32 Ge	2	2 6	2 6 10	2 2			
33 As	2	2 6	2 6 10	2 3			
34 Se	2	2 6	2 6 10	2 4			
35 Br	2	2 6	2 6 10	2 5			
36 Kr	2	2 6	2 6 10	2 6			
37 Rb	2	2 6	2 6 10	2 6	1		
38 Sr	2	2 6	2 6 10	2 6	2		
39 Y	2	2 6	2 6 10	2 6 1	2		
40 Zr	2	2 6	2 6 10	2 6 2	2		
41 Nb	2	2 6	2 6 10	2 6 4	1		
42 Mo	2	2 6	2 6 10	2 6 5	1		
43 Tc	2	2 6	2 6 10	2 6 6	1		
44 Ru	2	2 6	2 6 10	2 6 7	1		
45 Rh	2	2 6	2 6 10	2 6 8	1		
46 Pd	2	2 6	2 6 10	2 6 10			
47 Ag	2	2 6	2 6 10	2 6 10	1		
48 Cd	2	2 6	2 6 10	2 6 10	2		
49 In	2	2 6	2 6 10	2 6 10	2 1		
50 Sn	2	2 6	2 6 10	2 6 10	2 2		
51 Sb	2	2 6	2 6 10	2 6 10	2 3		
52 Te	2	2 6	2 6 10	2 6 10	2 4		
53 I	2	2 6	2 6 10	2 6 10	2 5		
54 Xe	2	2 6	2 6 10	2 6 10	2 6		
55 Cs	2	2 6	2 6 10	2 6 10	2 6	1	
56 Ba	2	2 6	2 6 10	2 6 10	2 6	2	
57 La	2	2 6	2 6 10	2 6 10	2 6 1	2	
58 Ce	2	2 6	2 6 10	2 6 10 2	2 6	2	
59 Pr	2	2 6	2 6 10	2 6 10 3	2 6	2	
60 Nd	2	2 6	2 6 10	2 6 10 4	2 6	2	
61 Pm	2	2 6	2 6 10	2 6 10 5	2 6	2	
62 Sm	2	2 6	2 6 10	2 6 10 6	2 6	2	
63 Eu	2	2 6	2 6 10	2 6 10 7	2 6	2	
64 Gd	2	2 6	2 6 10	2 6 10 7	2 6 1	2	
65 Tb	2	2 6	2 6 10	2 6 10 9	2 6	2	
66 Dy	2	2 6	2 6 10	2 6 10 10	2 6	2	
67 Ho	2	2 6	2 6 10	2 6 10 11	2 6	2	
68 Er	2	2 6	2 6 10	2 6 10 12	2 6	2	
69 Tm	2	2 6	2 6 10	2 6 10 13	2 6	2	
70 Yb	2	2 6	2 6 10	2 6 10 14	2 6	2	
71 Lu	2	2 6	2 6 10	2 6 10 14	2 6 1	2	
72 Hf	2	2 6	2 6 10	2 6 10 14	2 6 2	2	
73 Ta	2	2 6	2 6 10	2 6 10 14	2 6 3	2	
74 W	2	2 6	2 6 10	2 6 10 14	2 6 4	2	
75 Re	2	2 6	2 6 10	2 6 10 14	2 6 5	2	
76 Os	2	2 6	2 6 10	2 6 10 14	2 6 6	2	
77 Ir	2	2 6	2 6 10	2 6 10 14	2 6 7	2	
78 Pt	2	2 6	2 6 10	2 6 10 14	2 6 9	1	
79 Au	2	2 6	2 6 10	2 6 10 14	2 6 10	1	
80 Hg	2	2 6	2 6 10	2 6 10 14	2 6 10	2	
81 Tl	2	2 6	2 6 10	2 6 10 14	2 6 10	2 1	
82 Pb	2	2 6	2 6 10	2 6 10 14	2 6 10	2 2	
83 Bi	2	2 6	2 6 10	2 6 10 14	2 6 10	2 3	
84 Po	2	2 6	2 6 10	2 6 10 14	2 6 10	2 4	
85 At	2	2 6	2 6 10	2 6 10 14	2 6 10	2 5	
86 Rn	2	2 6	2 6 10	2 6 10 14	2 6 10	2 6	
87 Fr	2	2 6	2 6 10	2 6 10 14	2 6 10	2 6	1
88 Ra	2	2 6	2 6 10	2 6 10 14	2 6 10	2 6	2
89 Ac	2	2 6	2 6 10	2 6 10 14	2 6 10	2 6 1	2
90 Th	2	2 6	2 6 10	2 6 10 14	2 6 10	2 6 2	2
91 Pa	2	2 6	2 6 10	2 6 10 14	2 6 10 2	2 6 1	2
92 U	2	2 6	2 6 10	2 6 10 14	2 6 10 3	2 6 1	2
93 Np	2	2 6	2 6 10	2 6 10 14	2 6 10 4	2 6 1	2
94 Pu	2	2 6	2 6 10	2 6 10 14	2 6 10 6	2 6	2
95 Am	2	2 6	2 6 10	2 6 10 14	2 6 10 7	2 6	2
96 Cm	2	2 6	2 6 10	2 6 10 14	2 6 10 7	2 6 1	2
97 Bk	2	2 6	2 6 10	2 6 10 14	2 6 10 8	2 6 1	2
98 Cf	2	2 6	2 6 10	2 6 10 14	2 6 10 10	2 6	2
99 Es	2	2 6	2 6 10	2 6 10 14	2 6 10 11	2 6	2
100 Fm	2	2 6	2 6 10	2 6 10 14	2 6 10 12	2 6	2
101 Md	2	2 6	2 6 10	2 6 10 14	2 6 10 13	2 6	2
102 No	2	2 6	2 6 10	2 6 10 14	2 6 10 14	2 6	2
103 Lr	2	2 6	2 6 10	2 6 10 14	2 6 10 14	2 6 1	2
104 Unq	2	2 6	2 6 10	2 6 10 14	2 6 10 14	2 6 2	2
105 Unp	2	2 6	2 6 10	2 6 10 14	2 6 10 14	2 6 3	2
106 Unh	2	2 6	2 6 10	2 6 10 14	2 6 10 14	2 6 4	2
107 Uns	2	2 6	2 6 10	2 6 10 14	2 6 10 14	2 6 5	2
108 Uno	2	2 6	2 6 10	2 6 10 14	2 6 10 14	2 6 6	2
109 Une							

*Z, atomic number.

Measuring Molecules

A molecule is the smallest unit of a substance that retains the properties of that substance. For example, a molecule of sodium chloride is represented by NaCl; a molecule of water is represented by H_2O. The average molecule diameter is 0.5 to 2.5 angstroms (Å), with 1 Å equaling 3.937×10^{-9} inch (10^{-8} centimeter).

The unit of measurement for molecules is the *mole* (abbreviated mol). This represents the number of atoms, molecules, or formula units large enough to be easily measured in the laboratory. One mole is the amount of a substance that contains Avogadro's constant of particles, or 6.02×10^{23}. For example, the number of carbon atoms in 12 grams of carbon-12 (C^{12}) is equal to Avogadro's constant.

The measurement of atomic masses of elements can be used to find the mass of 1 mole of any substance, or its *molar mass*. For example, carbon's atomic mass is 12.01; therefore, 1 mole of carbon is equal to 12.01 grams. The molar mass of a compound is the sum of the molar masses of its component atoms.

MATTER AS A SOLID, LIQUID, OR GAS

Under most conditions, matter exists as a solid, liquid, or gas, each of which have certain characteristics. Under extraordinary conditions, such as the extreme heat associated with the Sun's interior, matter exists as plasma. There are the four phases, or states, of matter.

Solids

Molecules in solids maintain fixed positions, giving the substance a definite shape. The tightly packed particles are held together by bonding, usually covalent or ionic (see "Bonding," later in this chapter). The strength of a solid depends on the elements in the solid and the types of bonding. The molecules within a solid may form within an orderly pattern known as a crystal lattice, a structure typical of such solids as metals and gems. The temperature at which a solid becomes a liquid is called its *melting point*. At this point, the random motion of molecules increased by heat, causes them to become excited and break loose the bonds that keep them in place.

Liquids

A liquid has a definite volume but no definite shape. It is a state of matter in which the molecules are loosely bound by intermolecular forces. Because these forces are weak, the liquid is able to change its shape to conform to its container. Familiar liquids include water and alcohol. The temperature at which a liquid becomes a solid is its *freezing point*. The temperature at which a liquid becomes a gas is its *boiling point*.

Gases

Gases have no fixed shape or volume. The force of attraction between the gas's molecules is small because of the relatively large distances between molecules. As a result, the molecules are always in motion and continually collide with each other and the container, creating what is known as *gas pressure*. The volume of a gas is affected by changes in temperature and pressure. The temperature at which a liquid becomes a gas is called its *boiling point*; the boiling point also depends on the pressure exerted. The temperature at which a gas becomes a liquid is its *condensation point.*

Plasma

Plasma is a form of matter that starts out as a gas and then becomes ionized, and consists of free moving ions and electrons. It exhibits different properties than a gas, liquid, or solid; it obtains those properties by taking on an electric charge. Plasmas are found in interstellar gases and stars. They are affected by electric and magnetic fields.

GLASS: A SUPERCOOLED LIQUID

Glass is an amorphous substance that contains particles that move relative to each other over time—though much more slowly than in most liquids. For this reason, glass is referred to as a supercooled liquid. Glass has no ordering of the atoms or crystal pattern (its structure is called amorphous). It softens easily on heating and has no definite melting point like true solids; it is also known to "run" or deform like a liquid over long periods (the "sagging" effect often seen in the windows in very old buildings is the result of this property). Glasslike characteristics can even be seen in the mineral quartz, an impure variety of sand with the same molecular composition as glass. If quartz is heated above its melting point and rapidly cooled, the silicate chains do not have time to form characteristic quartz crystals; instead, glass forms, hardening into a disordered structure.

Commercial glass is made in various ways. For example, heating lime (calcium oxide), sodium carbonate, and sand, produces calcium silicate, or soda glass; boron oxide mixed with sand is used for glass laboratory apparatus. The different combinations of elements give the glass special properties, such as softness or a lower melting point.

Physical Properties of Matter

Physical properties of solids, liquids, and gases are those characteristics that can be observed and those that describe its behavior under certain conditions. Properties such as volume and mass depend on the amount of a substance that is being observed. Properties that do not depend on the quantity include the melting point of a solid and the boiling point of a liquid as well as density, color, hardness, odor, taste, elasticity, and tensile strength.

Freezing and Boiling Points of Common Substances

Substance	Freezing Point (°F/°C)	Boiling Point (°F/°C)
Iron	2,795/1,535	4,982/2,750
Mercury	–38/–39	675/357
Nitrogen	–344/–209	–321/–196
Oxygen	–360/–218	–297/–183
Water	32/0	212/100

Densities of Common Substances at 68°F (20°C)

Density is a measurement of the quantity of mass per unit of volume.

Solids	Density ($\times 10^3$ kilogram/meter^3)	Solids	Density ($\times 10^3$ kilogram/meter^3)
Aluminum	2.70	Iron	7.87
Copper	8.96	Lead	11.35
Gold	19.32	Silver	10.50

Liquids	Density
Chloroform	1.49
Ethyl alcohol	0.79
Mercury	13.55
Water	1.00

Gas	Density (under normal atmospheric pressure)
Helium	0.0001663
Hydrogen	0.0000837
Nitrogen	0.001165
Oxygen	0.001331

UNUSUAL PROPERTIES OF WATER

Water is essential to life; it is the most common solute and the only compound that changes to and from the solid, liquid, and gas states at temperatures we commonly experience. It also has the particular feature of being densest at a temperature above its freezing point, which is why ice floats and lakes freeze from the top down. The water molecule connects hydrogen and oxygen atoms at such an angle as to cause its crystal lattice to form a solid less dense than its liquid state.

The following figure illustrates water at different temperatures.

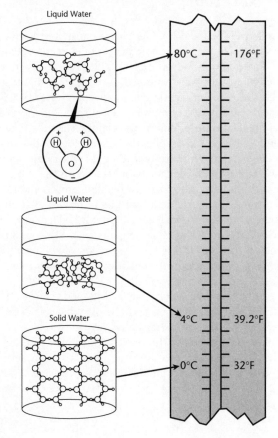

THE PERIODIC TABLE OF THE ELEMENTS

What Is the Periodic Table of the Elements?

The Periodic Table of the Elements is a listing of the chemical symbols (and often many of their physical characteristics) of 109 elements. The first 92 elements occur in nature (with a few exceptions: astatine, atomic number 85; technetium, atomic number 43; and some other elements are artificial although their artificiality is debated); the remaining elements have been artificially created in laboratory particle accelerators. The chemical elements exist in a free state or combined with another element.

In the Periodic Table, the elements are arranged in order of increasing atomic number from left to right and from top to bottom. The horizontal rows of elements are called *periods*; the vertical columns of related elements are called *groups*. Across the table, there is a general trend from metallic to nonmetallic elements; down a group, there is an increase in atomic size and in electropositive behavior. The members of a group have similar behavior because of similarities in their electron configurations.

History of the Periodic Table

Both Johann Dobereiner (1780–1849), a German chemist, and John Newlands (1837–1898), an English scientist, observed that the atomic masses of elements seemed to be related to their chemical properties. Later, Lothar Meyer (1835–1895) proposed there was some repeating pattern of the properties when they were arranged in order of atomic masses. But the systematic placing of the elements into an organized table was accomplished by a Russian chemist, Dmitri Mendeléev, who stated in 1869 that the properties of the elements are a periodic function of their atomic masses; the relationships among the elements is called the *periodic law*.

Mendeléev found that he could simplify the descriptions of the elements if he put them in order. He arranged the elements in horizontal rows of eight using cards with the names of the elements, making it into a game he called "patience." With the 9th element he started a new row. He found that with the repeating rows, vertical columns contained elements with similar properties. He called these related elements families or groups. Not all the elements had been discovered at that time, but once Mendeléev had established a pattern, he left spaces for undiscovered elements, correctly predicting that elements would be found to fill those spaces. This arrangement of elements shows that there is a repetition of chemical properties in a cycle of 8 elements. This periodicity is not true for the entire chart of elements; with the heavier elements, there is a change from a cycle of 8 to one of 18.

The modern periodic law proposed by Henry Moseley (1887–1915) better explained the gaps in the table, and stated that physical and chemical properties are a periodic function of their atomic number rather than mass. (Tragically, Moseley was killed in action as a young man in World War I, which, in part, lead to the British policy of exempting scientists from combat duty.) Today, we know that it is the electron that determines properties, with the number of electrons directly related to the atomic number and not the mass. Curiously, Mendeléev had some correct ideas about the formation of chemical compounds but adamantly refused to accept the concept of the electron.

Mendeléev's Periodic Table

[as published in Volume I of the first English edition of his Principles of Chemistry*]*

Groups	Higher salt-forming oxides	Typical or 1st small period	LARGE PERIODS				
			1st	2nd	3rd	4th	5th
I.	R_2O	Li = 7	K 39	Rb 85	Cs 133	—	—
II.	RO	Be = 9	Ca 40	S 87	Ba 137	—	—
III.	R_2O_3	B = 11	Sc 44	Y 89	La 138	Yb 173	—
IV.	RO_2	C = 12	Ti 48	Zr 90	Ce 140	—	Th 232
V.	R_2O_5	N = 14	V 51	Nb 94	—	Ta 182	—
VI.	RO_3	O = 16	Cr 52	Mo 96	—	W 184	Ur 240
VII.	R_2O_7	F = 19	Mn 55	—	—	—	—
			Fe 56	Ru 103	—	Os 191	—
VIII.			Co 58.5	Rh 104	—	Ir 193	—
			Ni 59	Pd 106	—	Pt 196	—
I.	R_2O H = 1.	Na = 23	Cu 63	Ag 108	—	Au 198	—
II.	RO	Mg= 24	Zn 65	Cd 112	—	Hg 200	—
III.	R_2O_3	Al = 27	Ga 70	In 113	—	Tl 104	—
IV.	RO_2	Si = 28	Ge 72	Sn 118	—	Pb 206	—
V.	R_2O_5	P = 31	As 75	Sb 120	—	Bi 208	—
VI.	RO_3	S = 32	Se 79	Te 125	—	—	—
VII.	R_2O_7	Cl = 35.5	Br 80	I 127	—	—	—

Divisions of the Periodic Table

Because of the arrangements of the elements, those having similar properties will generally occur at fixed intervals. These properties include the elements' physical states (for example, gas versus solid) and the behavior of their outermost electrons. The groups or families were originally given Roman numeral and letter names. Based on a 1984 agreement of the International Union of Pure and Applied Chemistry (IUPAC) that system was replaced by a numbering system of 1 to 18 going from left to right.

Periods of the Table

The first three periods are the short periods, containing elements with only s and p level electrons (the lowest energy levels) and having only up to 2 and 8 electrons, respectively. Period 1 consists of hydrogen (H) and helium (He) only, the two most abundant elements in the universe. Period 2 elements begin filling the second energy level, and the period ends with neon (Ne, atomic number 10) in which the first two levels are filled. In Period 3, the third level is filled, ending with argon (Ar, atomic number 18).

Periods 4 and 5 are longer, each with 18 elements. Period 4 begins with potassium (K) followed by calcium (Ca). But after that, higher energy electrons (the d orbitals) begin to fill, giving the next elements in the center of the table characteristics unlike any of the previous elements. These elements, with their incomplete d subshell, are known as *transition* elements. This pattern repeats for Period 5 elements. Periods 6 and 7 contain 32 elements each. The Period 6 elements that follow lanthanum (La; atomic number 57) are called the *lanthanoids*. This is also called the *rare earth series* and includes cerium (Ce) through lutetium (Lu). Period 7's transitional elements follow actinium (Ac; atomic number 89) and are called *actinoids*. This

The Periodic Table of Elements

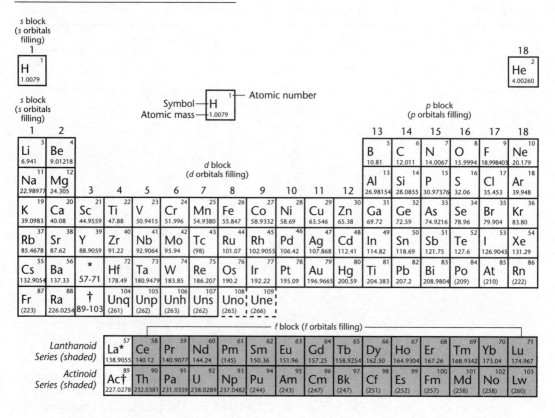

group includes thorium (Th) through atomic number 103 (unofficially called lawrencium; Lw). Both of these groups are filling the *f* sublevel orbitals.

Groups of Elements

The Periodic Table can be divided into three basic groups: metals, nonmetals, and semimetals. In general, when viewing the table, the metals are on the left, the nonmetals are on the extreme right, and the semimetals are in the center.

Metals

Metals make up the majority of the groups of elements. Most metals such as sodium (Na) are solid at room temperature, with mercury (Hg) being the only liquid metal. Metals have high melting and boiling points because the atoms in the crystals are tightly packed together. In addition, their densities are high because the heavy nuclei are also tightly packed together. Metals have only a few (usually no more than four) valence electrons in the outermost shells. These are the electrons that are often given up in a reaction, forming metallic, positive ions.

Metals (e.g., gold and copper) are generally good conductors of electricity. Elements of Group 1, including lithium, sodium, and potassium (but excluding hydrogen), are known as alkali metals; Group 2 metals, including magnesium and calcium, are the alkaline earth metals.

Nonmetals

Nonmetals are usually dull in appearance, brittle, and not good electrical conductors. Many of the chemically active nonmetals are the halogens (Group 17), the group of elements that includes chlorine, bromine, and iodine. This group is highly reactive and electronegative and contains fluorine, the most highly electronegative element.

Properties of Metals and Nonmetals

Property	Metals	Nonmetals
Ionization energy	Low	High
Ion formation	Lose electrons to form positive ions	Gain electrons to form negative ions
Electronegativity	Low	High
Luster	High	Low
Deformability	Ductile; malleable	Brittle
Heat and electrical conduction	Good	Poor
Phase at normal conditions	Solid (except mercury)	Gas or solid (except bromine, a liquid)

Activity of Some Elements

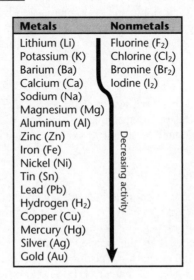

Metals	Nonmetals
Lithium (Li)	Fluorine (F_2)
Potassium (K)	Chlorine (Cl_2)
Barium (Ba)	Bromine (Br_2)
Calcium (Ca)	Iodine (I_2)
Sodium (Na)	
Magnesium (Mg)	
Aluminum (Al)	
Zinc (Zn)	
Iron (Fe)	
Nickel (Ni)	
Tin (Sn)	
Lead (Pb)	
Hydrogen (H_2)	
Copper (Cu)	
Mercury (Hg)	
Silver (Ag)	
Gold (Au)	

Decreasing activity

Semimetals

The elements that are intermediate between metals and nonmetals are often referred to as *semimetals* or *semiconductors*. Semiconductors include the elements located on the border between metals and nonmetals: boron, silicon, germanium, arsenic, and tellurium. Because of their particular properties they have become important to technology.

SEMICONDUCTOR TECHNOLOGY

Semiconductors carry electricity better than insulators but not as well as conductors. So why has silicon, a semiconductor, become the most important element in computer chip technology? It is because semiconductors can become very good conductors if treated chemically. In clean, sterile computer chip factories, workers carefully etch tiny, thin wafers of silicon with chemicals, drawing onto their surface an electric circuit in much the same way you might trace letters with a stencil. But these lines are made in miniature and with incredible precision, usually under a special microscope that allows the scientist to see tiny details. Another semiconductor, germanium is a semiconductor often used in modern electronic and industrial technologies. This element, just below silicon on the Periodic Table, was one of the elements discovered in Germany 15 years after it was predicted by Mendeléev.

Noble Gases

The *noble gases* (Group 18) are helium, neon, argon, and krypton, all gases in which the *s* and *p* subshells are completely filled with electrons and, therefore, rarely react with other elements. They were formally called the *inert* gases, but this term no longer applies because Neil Bartlett discovered noble gas compounds in 1962. Bartlett's experiment was one of the first examples of the application of the Periodic Table and periodic relationships to chemical research and was performed after he realized that the ionization energy of Xenon (Xe) was less than that of Oxygen (O_2). Many more Xe compounds were quickly synthesized.

Noble Metals

Though not included as a specific division of the Periodic Table, the noble metals are gold, silver, and mercury and the platinum group (palladium, iridium, rhodium, ruthenium, and osmium). These metals are highly resistant to oxidation and chemical reaction.

Metal Alloys

Many of the metals we come in contact with are not in their elemental state but have been combined with other elements. An *alloy* is a metallic solid produced by mixing a molten metal with one or more other substances. For example, brass is an alloy made from copper (Cu) and zinc (Zn), both metals. Steel is an alloy made from iron (Fe) and carbon (C), a metal and a nonmetal. Most alloys are developed for a specific physical characteristic, such as malleability or strength. An *amalgam* is an alloy of mercury (Hg) and another metal or metals. For example, amalgams containing mercury and silver (Ag) are often used as dental fillings.

Groups of Elements of the Periodic Table

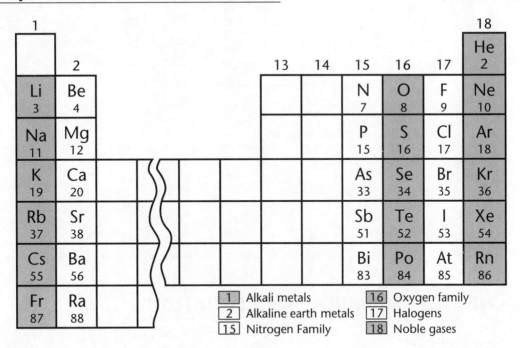

1	Alkali metals		16	Oxygen family
2	Alkaline earth metals		17	Halogens
15	Nitrogen Family		18	Noble gases

HOW DO YOU NAME A NEW ELEMENT?

Though not included as a division of the Periodic Table, the *transuranic* chemical elements are the elements that have been artificially created in the laboratory. They represent elements 93 to 109, listed after the last stable element, uranium (number 92).

When scientists discover a new transuranic element, they have the right to select a name and symbol for it to be used on the Periodic Table. The name chosen is usually the last name of the person who discovered the element or the name of the place where it was found. New names and symbols must be reviewed by an international commission. However, naming an element requires that another group of scientists confirm the discovery.

New elements are created in particle accelerators in which lighter elements have been made to collide. For example meitnerium (Mt; named for Lise Meitner, Austrian physicist and codiscoverer of nuclear fission, although the name is still debated by many), element 109, was made by colliding bismuth-209 with iron-58 to form nuclei with an atomic number of 109. Often these heavy elements last for just a fraction of a second. Element 106 has a half-life of just 0.9 second and is formed only a very few atoms at a time. Thus confirmation from another laboratory—even if it is equipped with a similar accelerator—can take years. That is why scientists have established temporary three letter names for the transuranic elements that are awaiting confirmation.

Element	Atomic Number	Symbol
Neptunium	93	Np
Plutonium	94	Pu
Americium	95	Am

Element	Atomic Number	Symbol
Curium	96	Cm
Berkelium	97	Bk
Californium	98	Cf
Einsteinium	99	Es
Fermium	100	Fm
Mendelevium	101	Md
Nobelium	102	No
Lawrencium	103	Lr
Unnilquadium* (suggested name Ruthfordium (Rf))	104	Unq
Unnilpentium* (suggested name Hahnium (Ha))	105	Unp
Unnilhexium* (suggested name Seaborghum (Sg))	106	Unh
Unnilseptium*	107	Uns
Unniloctium*	108	Uno
Unnilennium*	109	Une, (also Mt)

*The names for these elements are highly debated. There is no agreement on one name for each element.

CHEMICAL FORMULAS AND EQUATIONS

Stoichiometry

Stoichiometry is the study of the mathematical relationships that help to establish formulas. When water (H_2O) is broken down using electricity, twice as much hydrogen gas as oxygen gas will be released. This proportion reveals what is known as an *empirical formula*. However, stoichiometry is used to determine the exact molecular formulas and to show the reaction as a balanced equation.

Formulas

A *formula* is a representation of a chemical compound using symbols for the elements and subscripts for the number of atoms present. One type of formula represents two elements in combination. For example, the chemical formula for platinum oxide is PtO_2, where there is one atom of platinum (Pt) (the number 1 is understood) and two atoms of oxygen (O). By convention, a metallic element's symbol is usually placed first.

Equations

Equations represent the reactions between chemical compounds. For example, in the decomposition of water into its elements by electrolysis, the chemical equation is

$$2H_2O \Rightarrow 2H_2 + O_2$$

where two molecules of water are decomposed into two molecules of hydrogen (which consist of two atoms each) and one oxygen molecule (which consists of two atoms of oxygen). The two molecules of water are called the *reactants*; the resulting substances are called the *products*. In a chemical reaction the number of atoms and the amount of mass is conserved, i.e., there are the same number of atoms at the beginning of the reaction and at the end.

Chemical reactions are sometimes reversible. For example, if steam is passed over hot iron, the reaction proceeds to the right; if hydrogen gas is passed over heated Fe_3O_4, the reaction goes to the left:

$$3Fe + 4H_2O \Leftrightarrow Fe_3O_4 + 4H_2$$

CHEMICAL KINETICS

The branch of chemistry that studies the rates of chemical reactions is known as chemical kinetics. Kinetic theory states that molecules are always in motion. For elements or compounds to undergo chemical change and react to produce new compounds or elements, they must possess enough energy to break existing chemical bonds and form new ones. The amount of energy needed for a chemical reaction is known as *activation energy*.

Chemical equilibrium occurs when there is a fixed number of molecules of all the reactants and products present. Equilibrium is a dynamic not a static process in which forward and reverse changes are occurring at equal rates. It depends on the physical characteristics of the reactants and products, including the temperature and pressure.

Chemical Kinetics and the Gas Laws

Chemical kinetics is especially important in the study of gases and is based on the principle that all gases respond similarly to a specific volume, temperature, and pressure. All the laws about the behavior of gases are consequences of the kinetic molecular theory, which explains the physical properties of gases in terms of the motion of molecules. It assumes that all gases are composed of discrete molecules that are relatively far apart and are in continuous random motion, exerting pressure on the walls of its containing vessel. It also assumes the molecules collide with the walls of their container and with each other with perfect elasticity. The composition of the gas is not of concern in chemical kinetics.

When the temperature is raised, the speed of the molecules increases, and so does the pressure against the container. If more particles are introduced or if the volume is reduced, there are more particles bombarding per unit area of the walls and the pressure also increases. When a particle collides with the wall, it experiences a rate of change of momentum, which is proportional to the force exerted. When there are a large number of particles, this provides a steady force per unit area (or pressure) on the wall.

Vapor Pressure of Water

Temp. °C	Pressure kPa	Temp. °C	Pressure kPa	Temp. °C	Pressure kPa
0	0.61	22	2.64	50	12.33
5	0.87	23	2.81	60	19.91
10	1.23	24	2.99	70	31.15
15	1.71	25	3.17	80	47.33
16	1.81	26	3.36	90	70.08
17	1.93	27	3.56	100	101.30
18	2.07	28	3.77	105	120.80
19	2.20	29	4.00	110	143.20
20	2.33	30	4.24		
21	2.49	40	7.37		

CHEMICAL BONDING AND REACTIONS

Bonding

Elements that combine to form molecules or compounds are held together by forces, (primarily electrostatic forces), called *chemical bonds*. In a chemical reaction, substances undergo various changes, forming or breaking these bonds.

Ionic and Covalent Bonding

There are two major types of chemical bonds. In *covalent bonds*, atoms share a pair of electrons. Each atom contributes one electron to form the bond. In *ionic bonds* (also called electrovalent bonds) atoms are joined by an electrostatic charge, i.e., the natural attraction between positive and negative charges. In both covalent and ionic bonding, the atoms in the compound gain, lose, or share electrons such that their outer electron configurations become the same as the nearest noble gas on the Periodic Table.

Ionic and Covalent Bonds

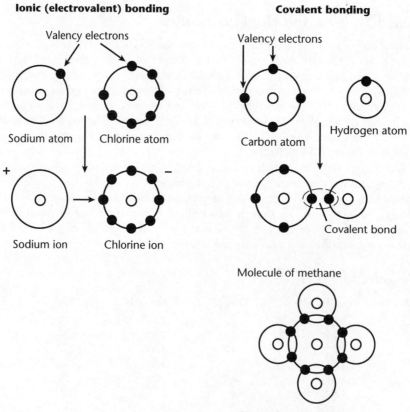

Other Intermolecular Forces

There are several other types of bonding that are generally weaker than either an ionic or a covalent bond. *Multiple bonding*, such as a double or triple bond, occurs between two atoms that share more than one pair of electrons, owing to the overlapping of electron orbitals. *Metallic bonding*, found in metals as the name implies, is similar to covalent bonding except that the attraction is between mobile electrons and the positive central ions in a lattice.

Another type of force between molecules is the *Van de Waals force*. It is an intermolecular force of attraction that is considerably weaker than a chemical bond and that arises from the constant motion of electron clouds and their attraction to nearby molecules. Still another kind of force, *hydrogen bonding*, is the intermolecular force most often associated with water. It is a weak type of bond that occurs when a hydrogen atom bonds with a highly electronegative atom like oxygen.

Diatomic Molecules

Some elements are generally found as pairs of atoms bound together and are known as *diatomic elements*. Common diatomic molecules include gases under normal conditions, such as oxygen (O_2), hydrogen (H_2), nitrogen (N_2), and chlorine (Cl_2); liquids, such as bromine (Br_2); and solids, such as iodine (I_2).

Types of Chemical Reactions

Combination

Combination is the direct joining of two or more simple substances, either elements or simple compounds. These substances form a more complex compound. In this example, copper and oxygen form copper oxide:

$$2Cu + O_2 \Rightarrow 2CuO$$

As mentioned earlier, the metallic reactant (copper, in this example) is shown first, followed by the nonmetal (oxygen). Another way to think of the reaction is that the electron donor comes first followed by the electron receiver.

Decomposition

Decomposition is the breakdown of a compound into simpler elements or compounds. Water is decomposed during electrolysis, resulting in the separation of water into its constituent elements, hydrogen and oxygen. This example of decomposition is represented by the following equation:

$$2H_2O \Rightarrow 2H_2 + O_2$$

Replacement

Replacement is the substitution of one element for another in a compound. The reaction that occurs in car batteries can be shown as the element iron and the compound sulfuric acid react to form iron sulfate and hydrogen. The iron replaces the hydrogen that was bonded to the sulfate. In this case, the SO_4, which is actually made of five atoms, acts as one unit known as a *radical*. Here's the equation for this example of replacement:

$$Fe + (H_2SO_4) \Rightarrow FeSO_4 + H_2$$

Double replacement is the process in which two compounds react to form two new compounds as they exchange parts. An example of the double replacement process is represented by the equation:

$$AgNO_3 + NaCl \Rightarrow AgCl \downarrow + NaNO_3$$

In this equation, silver nitrate and sodium chloride (table salt) react to form silver chloride, which precipitates out of solution (indicated by the down arrow), and sodium nitrate.

Oxidation-Reduction Reactions

Oxidation is a process in which electrons are lost; *reduction* is a process in which electrons are gained. For the most part, oxidation describes the way in which an element or compound reacts with oxygen. Oxygen is highly electronegative, i.e., it takes electrons from other elements to fill its electron subshell. Thus when pure iron is exposed to moist air, it *oxidizes*, forming rust. The iron atoms lose electrons to the oxygen in the air. The oxygen gains these electrons, thereby filling its outer shell. This process is called an *oxidation-reduction* reaction, or a *redox reaction*.

Corrosion

The single most destructive chemical reaction is *corrosion*. It is caused by chemical processes such as oxidation or through the action of a chemical agent(s). For example, despite the strong electronegativity of oxygen, iron will not rust in dry air: the presence of oxygen and water (H_2O) causes the corrosion (although the actual mechanics of rust formation is still debated). Generally, iron ions react with the OH⁻ ions in the water and then with oxygen to form rust; the equations for the redox reaction described above are as follows:

$$Fe^{2+} + 2OH^- \Rightarrow Fe(OH)_2$$
$$4Fe(OH)_2 + O_2 \Rightarrow 2(Fe_2O_3 + 2H_2O) \text{ (iron rust)}$$

Another type of corrosion occurs when the industrial pollutant sulfur dioxide (SO_2) combines with water to form dilute hydrogen sulfide (H_2SO_3). Because it readily supplies H^+ ions, this compound is corrosive to structural materials. In fact, saltwater oil rigs are kept from rusting by using batteries that essentially forces electricity into the iron, arresting the corrosion from minerals in ocean water.

Catalysts

Catalysts are substances that control the rates of chemical reactions. Initially, catalysts were thought to change the rates of reaction but not to interact in the reaction. It is now known that some catalysts do interact with some reactants in a reaction. Examples of catalysts in biochemistry are the enzymes that aid in the breakdown of large food molecules, such as proteins, into smaller molecules of amino acids. Catalysts are also used in catalytic converters, the pollution-control devices in automobiles.

Terms and Common Chemical Substances

Selected Terms Used to Describe Everyday Materials

Caustic materials burn or destroy tissue and include bases or alkaline substances
Corrosive materials irritate, burn, or destroy tissue and include acids
Flammable materials catch fire easily
Irritants make the skin, eyes, or nose sore
Toxic materials are poisonous

Common Substances

Common Name	Formula	Chemical Substance
Asbestos	$CaMg_3(SiO_3)_4$	Silicate of calcium and magnesium
Aspirin	$CH_3CO_2C_6H_4COOH$	Acetyl-salicylic acid
Beet and sugar cane sugars	$C_{12}H_{22}O_{11}$	Sucrose
Bleaching powder	$CaOCl_2$	Calcium oxychloride
Charcoal	$Ca_3(PO_4)_2 + C$	Calcium phosphate plus carbon
Clay	$H_2Al_2(SiO_4)_2 \cdot H_2O$	Hydrated ferric oxide
Common glass	$CaSiO_3 + Na_2SiO_3$	Calcium and other silicates
Diamond, graphite, fullerene (C_{60})	C	Carbon
Dry ice	CO_2	Frozen carbon dioxide
Fool's gold, pyrite	FeS_2	Iron disulfide
Grain alcohol	C_2H_5OH	Ethyl alcohol
Laughing gas	N_2O	Nitrous oxide
Limestone	$CaCO_3$	Calcium carbonate
Moth balls	$C_{10}H_8$	Naphthalene
Natural gas	CH_4^+	Impure methane
Nitroglycerin	$C_3H_5(NO_3)_3$	Glyceryl trinitrate
Quartz, agate, flint, chert	SiO_2	Silicon dioxide
Quicksilver	Hg	Mercury
Ruby, sapphire	Al_2O_3	Aluminum oxide
Rust	$(Fe_2O_3)_3 \cdot H_2O$	Hydrated ferric oxide
Soap lye	NaOH	Sodium hydroxide
Table and rock salts	NaCl	Sodium chloride
TNT	$C_6H_2(CH_3)(NO_2)_3$	Trinitrotoluene

ORGANIC CHEMISTRY

Organic chemistry is the branch of chemistry that specializes in the composition, properties, and reactions of hydrocarbon compounds.

Hydrocarbons

Compounds that contain only the elements carbon and hydrogen are called *hydrocarbons*. The principal source of hydrocarbons is crude oil, which is distilled to produce its many components.

Hydrocarbons are classified into several series, depending on the types of bonds. The *alkanes* have open chains (known as aliphatic chains) in which hydrogen attaches to carbon atoms in all of the available bonding sites. The *alkenes* are also aliphatic but contain one pair of carbon atoms connected by a double bond. The *alkynes* are also aliphatic but contain one pair of carbon atoms connected with a triple bond. The *alkadienes* are aliphatic and contain two pairs of carbon atoms connected with a double bond. The fifth series is called the *aromatics* because they each have a strong characteristic odor. Aromatics have six carbons arranged in a closed ring. Benzene is a typical aromatic hydrocarbon; its carbon ring is usually referred to as a benzene ring.

Structural Formula of Benzene

Single bonds are represented by single lines between elements; double bonds are represented by double lines between elements.

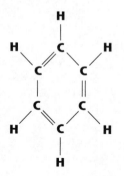

Functional Groups

The properties of many organic compounds are related to that portion of a molecule involved in a chemical reaction. That portion is referred to as a functional group.

Name of Group	Structure	Examples of the Group in a Compound	
Hydroxyl, or alcohol group (occurs in organic compounds called alcohols)	— OH	H │ H — C — O — H │ H Methanol (methyl alcohol)	H H │ │ H — C — C — O — H │ │ H H Ethanol (ethyl alcohol)
Aldehyde group (occurs in aldehydes)	O ╱╱ — C ╲ H	O ╱╱ H — C ╲ H Methanal (formaldehyde)	H O │ ╱╱ H — C — C │ ╲ H H Ethanal (acetaldehyde)
Carbonyl group (occurs in ketones)	O ‖ — C —	H O H │ ‖ │ H — C — C — C — H │ │ H H Propanone (methyl ketone)	H H O H H │ │ ‖ │ │ H — C — C — C — C — C — H │ │ │ │ H H H H 3-pentanone (ethyl ketone)
Ether group (occurs in ethers)	│ │ — C — O — C — │ │	H H │ │ H — C — O — C — H │ │ H H Dimethyl ether (methyl ether)	H H H H │ │ │ │ H — C — C — O — C — C — H │ │ │ │ H H H H Diethyl ether (ethyl ether)
Carboxyl group (occurs in carboxylic acids)	OH ╱ — C ╲╲ O	OH ╱ H — C ╲╲ O Methanoic acid (formic acid)	H OH │ ╱ H — C — C │ ╲╲ H O Ethanoic acid (acetic acid)

Polymers

Polymers are compounds with very large molecules made up of repeating molecular units. *Monomers* are small molecules from which polymer molecules are made. They may be natural substances, such as proteins, starch, cellulose, and rubber, or synthetic substances such as nylon and plastic. The flexibility and toughness of polymers make them versatile for use in many different types of products. Some polymers are made of many connecting chains, such as the coiled chains of thousands of isoprene monomers that make up natural rubber polymers. Other polymers, such as those of plastics, are made of polyethylene monomers, which are tangled and intertwined with one another.

DISCOVERING BUCKYBALLS

"Buckyballs" (or fullerenes or buckminsterfullerenes) are microscopic spheres of 60 atoms of pure carbon in a spherelike structure that resembles a geodesic dome. They were named after R. Buckminster Fuller, who invented the geodesic dome. Before buckyballs, the only pure carbon came in two naturally occurring forms: either graphite or diamonds. Buckyballs have a strange characteristic that makes them of interest to almost every scientific field. The molecules harbor a cavity large enough to hold other elements, even whole molecules. Once inside the cavity, an element cannot emerge unless it is heated to a high temperature. In addition, buckyballs accept and give electrons quite easily. Such characteristics may one day lead to their being used in medicine (to deliver medication within the body) as well as for new lubricants in miniature motors, in rechargeable batteries, and in high-strength materials.

ACIDS AND BASES

What Is an Acid?

There are three modern definitions of an *acid:*
- An acid can be a solution of a compound that contains hydrogen ions as the only positive ions.
- An acid can be a substance that acts as a proton donor.
- An acid is a molecular substance that releases positive hydrogen ions in aqueous solution.

There are many types of acids. For example, acetic or ethanoic acid is vinegar and ascorbic acid is vitamin C. Acid is also responsible for the sour taste of wine that has aged by exposure to the air; oxygen in the air reacts with the ethanol in the wine to form the acid.

What Is a Base?

A *base* can also be defined in three ways:
- A base is a substance that reacts with an acid to produce only water and a salt. When a base reacts with an acid, the process is called *neutralization.* (A salt consists of the positive and negative ions left over after all the H^+ ions have combined with the OH^- ions.)

- A base is a substance that acts as a proton acceptor, rather than donor.
- A base is the hydroxide of a metal, i.e., a metal combined with the hydroxide (OH-) ion. A soluble base is called an alkali. Strong alkalis include sodium and potassium hydroxides, which are good solvents for oil and grease, but they can burn the skin.

Common Acids and Bases

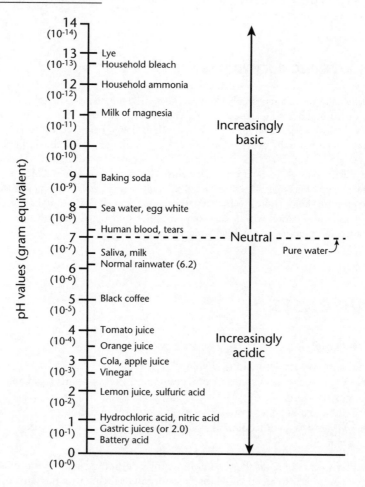

Measures of pH Values

The measure *pH* indicates the acidity or alkalinity of a substance and describes the concentration of free hydrogen ions in a solution. Because an acid is by definition a solution in which there are hydrogen ions, an acidic solution has a high concentration of free ions. However, pH is not a count of ions but is a measure of gram equivalent, or mass in grams per liter of solution. The concentration of hydrogen ions in a liter of solution ranges from 1 gram equivalent to 10 to

14 gram equivalents. Rather than use the actual number, the pH scale uses the negative exponent of the concentration. For example, if a solution's concentration is 10^{-7}, its pH is 7.

In 1909, Danish chemist Søren Sørensen devised the pH scale to represent pH. The scale ranges from 0 to 14, with 0 to 6.9 indicating more acidic solutions (i.e., those with higher concentrations of hydrogen ions). Measurements of 7.5 to 14 indicate more alkaline solutions (those with lower concentrations of hydrogen ions). The number 7.1 (pure water) represents a neutral solution. The *p* of pH is from the Danish word *potenz,* which means "strength"; the *H* is the symbol for hydrogen. Thus, pH means the strength of the hydrogen ions.

Neutralization

When an acid such as common household vinegar is added to a base such as ammonia, a chemical reaction occurs to form a neutral salt in water as indicated by the following equation:

$$HC_2H_3O_2 + NH_4OH \Rightarrow NH_4C_2H_3O_2 + H_2O$$

This can be read as "vinegar plus ammonia yields ammonium acetate plus water."

Chemical Indicators

A compound that changes color in the presence of an acid or base is known as an *indicator*. In many chemical tests, indicators such as bromthymol blue and phenolphthalein are added to solutions and undergo color changes when the pH reaches a certain level. Specially coated paper, such as litmus paper, can be used to test for pH.

ELECTROCHEMISTRY OF BATTERIES

A *battery* is an electrochemical cell in which terminals are connected to electrodes immersed in a solution of electrolytes. In solution, the electrolytes are dissociated into their ions. The battery "pulls" electrons out of one of the metal electrodes and "pushes" them into the other. When this occurs, the first electrode, with a deficiency of electrons, becomes positively charged; the other electrode has an excess of electrons and becomes negatively charged. Such movement of electrons creates an electric current.

A lead storage cell has a set of lead grids in a dilute sulfuric acid (H_2SO_4) solution. One grid is made of lead (Pb) and acts as an anode. The other grid contains lead dioxide (PbO_2) and acts as a cathode. The condition of lead storage batteries may be obtained by determining the density (or specific gravity) of the sulfuric acid solution. The higher the density, the greater the battery's charge. Lead cells are usually rechargeable if an external electrical potential is applied to a discharged battery; the reactions during recharging are the reverse of those occurring while the battery is discharging.

A *dry cell battery,* or irreversible cell battery (so-called because it cannot be recharged), has a carbon rod that acts as a cathode imbedded in a paste of ammonium chloride (NH_4Cl) surrounded by a zinc can, which acts as an anode. A porous separator is inserted between the zinc can and the ammonium chloride, with additional magnesium oxide (MnO_2) surrounding the carbon rod. When the cell is in use, electrons flow externally from the zinc can to the carbon rod. The extent of the chemical reactions depends on the amount of current required.

Basic Batteries

Dry cell battery

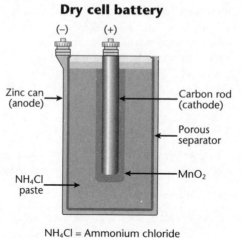

(−)   (+)

Zinc can (anode)

Carbon rod (cathode)

Porous separator

MnO_2

NH_4Cl paste

NH_4Cl = Ammonium chloride
MnO_2 = Manganese dioxide

Lead storage battery

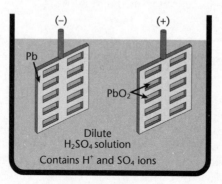

(−)   (+)

Pb

PbO_2

Dilute H_2SO_4 solution
Contains H^+ and SO_4 ions

H^+ = Hydrogen ion
SO_4^{2-} = Sulfide ion
PbO_2 = Lead dioxide
H_2SO_4 = Sulfuric acid

BETTER WITH BATTERIES

Emissions from cars have long been of concern to environmentalists, especially in cities with heavy automobile traffic, such as Los Angeles. To answer such environmental concerns, California and several other states will soon require that 2 percent of vehicles sold in the state must not produce any emissions. One idea is to power these vehicles with batteries. Accordingly, some of the large auto makers have formed consortiums to develop batteries and produce parts for electrical vehicles.

Today, the most efficient electric cars can travel about 120 miles on one 25-minute charge. Goals are to reduce the charge time to 15 minutes and to make the charging procedure mobile enough to allow roadside emergency assistance. Eventually, public recharging stations will be located throughout a city and will charge at 500 volts, more than a home's wiring can handle. Plans call for recharging stations to be located at convenience stores—so you can shop while you recharge.

RADIOCHEMISTRY

What Is Radioactivity?

Radioactivity was first discovered in 1896 by Antoine Henri Becquerel, a French physicist who exposed photographic film to uranium. Although wrapped in opaque black paper, the film showed that it had been exposed to rays similar to x-rays, which had been discovered the previous year by Wilhelm Roentgen. Fascinated by Becquerel's inexplicable rays, Marie and Pierre Curie began experimenting with uranium ore, isolating from it two new elements: radium and polonium. They found that the breakdown or transmutation of uranium into other elements was accompanied by a release of energy. More than 30 years later, their daughter, Irene Joliot-Curie and her husband Frederic Joliot-Curie discovered a way to artificially induce radioactivity by bombarding atoms with helium nuclei, also known as alpha-particles. Since that time many more radioactive elements have been discovered.

Isotopes

All atoms of a particular element have the same number of protons in their nuclei. However, not all the atoms of some elements contain the same number of neutrons, and in nature, a given element will have various forms each with a different number of neutrons. Additional neutrons do not add any charge to the nucleus of an atom, but rather increase its atomic mass, leaving the atom with the same atomic number. Such forms of the same elements are known as *isotopes*.

Sometimes an isotope of an element has a further characteristic. It is unstable and "decays" into another isotope. In the case of the heavier elements especially, an isotope of one element decays into another element altogether. For example, an atom of the radioactive element uranium-238 decays first into an atom of thorium-234 with the release of an alpha-particle (2 protons and 2 neutrons is generally called an alpha-particle), which has a mass of 4. The decay of one isotope into another takes a constant amount of time for each element. The time it takes for half of the isotope to break down is called its *half-life*. One element's half-life may be a few seconds, while another's may be millions of years.

Types of Radioactive Particles

Characteristic	*Alpha-Rays or Particles*	*Beta-Rays or Particles*	*Gamma-Rays*
Nature	Sometimes behave like particles; sometimes like waves	Sometimes behave like particles; sometimes like waves	Electromagnetic waves of extremely short wavelength

Types of Radioactive Particles (cont'd)

Characteristic	Alpha-Rays or Particles	Beta-Rays or Particles	Gamma-Rays
Speed	About $1/10$ the speed of light	Approaching the speed of light	Speed of light
Mass	4 atomic mass units	0.00055 atomic mass units	0 atomic mass units
Penetrating power	Relatively weak (can be stopped by a single sheet of paper)	Greater than alpha (can be stopped by a thin sheet of aluminum)	Very penetrating (can be stopped by several centimeters of lead)
Ionizing ability	Will ionize gas molecules	Will ionize gas molecules	Will ionize atoms in flesh, causing severe damage to the cells

Decay of Radioactive Uranium

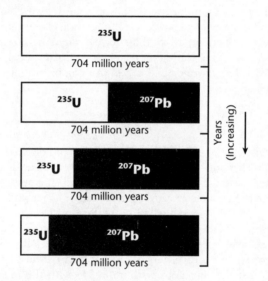

The radioactive decay of uranium-235 (^{235}U) into lead-207 (^{207}Pb).

Half-life of Some Radioactive Nuclei

Note that the associated number (e.g., the "222" in radon-222) refers to the mass number of the isotype.

Isotope	Daughter Nucleus	Half-life
Carbon-14 (^{14}C)	Nitrogen-14	5,730 years
Potassium-40 (^{40}K)	Argon-40	50 billion years
Radon-222 (^{222}Rn)	Polonium-218	3.82 days
Rubidium-87 (^{87}Rb)	Strontium-87	50 billion years
Thorium-232 (^{232}Th)	Lead-208	14.1 billion years
Uranium-235 (^{235}U)	Lead-207	713 million years
Uranium-238 (^{238}U)	Lead-206	4.5 billion years

PRESERVING FOOD

New developments in food preservation technology include irradiating some foods with gamma radiation to keep it fresh. The procedure is relatively simple: Food travels by conveyer belt through an irradiation chamber containing pellets of gamma-emitting radioisotopes (usually cobalt-60). As the food passes, the gamma radiation destroys bacteria, molds, and yeasts that cause spoilage. The radiation is also used to sterilize vacuum-packed meat, which then can be stored for years at room temperature.

Irradiation has been approved in the United States for use with spices and bacon and in the state of Florida for use with strawberries. Although food irradiation has been approved in more than 30 nations and for greater than 40 different foods, it is not widely accepted by the public in the United States. One concern is that the energetic radiation might break down and rearrange chemical bonds in foods, possibly creating harmful by-products. Many researchers believe that given the low radiation levels such concerns are not justified, and they point instead to the benefits of prolonging foods' shelf life—thus increasing world food supplies.

Radioactive Dating

Radioactive dating is the most important method of determining the age of rocks and fossils found on the surface of the Earth. When rocks or fossils are formed, the minerals in them contain certain radioactive atoms that decay at a known rate. After measuring the amount of a radioactive element that is present in an object, scientists can calculate how long ago the rock or fossil was formed.

Depending on the actual age of the rocks, several different radioactive elements are used for dating. For example, the uranium-thorium dating method is used to determine the age of the oldest rocks on the Earth. Uranium-238, with half-life of 4.5 billion years, decays into thorium. The potassium-argon dating method is used to date early human fossil remains. Potassium-40 has a half-life of 1.3 billion years and decays into argon. Tritium, with a half-life of 12.5 years, is an isotope of hydrogen; it is often used to determine how long it takes for rainwater to travel through cracks in rocks and to check the age of wine.

Carbon Dating

Carbon dating uses radioactive carbon to date organic remains such as wood, parchment, and bones. Carbon-14, which decays to nitrogen-14, has a half-life of approximately 5,730 years. Carbon-14 is constantly being created in the Earth's atmosphere, as the sun's rays strike nitrogen gas. The carbon-14 then combines with oxygen to form carbon dioxide (CO_2), which enters all living organisms. As long as the organism is alive, the supply of carbon-14 remains constant. However, when the organism dies, carbon-14 ceases to enter the organism and the carbon-14 already present begins to decay. The amount of C-14 that remains allows scientists to determine the age of the organism's remains.

CHEMICAL LAWS AND RULES

Avogadro's law   Avogadro's law (also called a principle or hypothesis) states that equal volumes of all gases at the same temperature and pressure contain equal numbers of molecules. It is true only for ideal gases. It was first proposed in the early 1800s by Italian chemist Amedeo Avogadro.

Bernoulli's principle   Bernoulli's principle states when a fluid flows through a pipe of varying diameter, the amount of energy per kilogram of liquid does not change. For example, pressure is lowest when velocity of the flow is greatest; also, flow is slowest through the widest parts and fastest through the thinnest parts of a tube. The principle was discovered by Swiss scientist Daniel Bernoulli.

Bohr's theory   Introduced by Niels Bohr in 1911, Bohr's theory explains the spectrum of atomic hydrogen, the ultimate source of quantum mechanical chemistry; the theory is used to identify atomic shells.

Boyle's law   Boyle's law is called Mariotte's law in Europe. It was discovered by Robert Boyle in the 1600s and states that at a given temperature the volume occupied by a gas is inversely proportional to the pressure, or at a constant temperature the pressure (p) of a fixed mass of gas is inversely proportional to its volume (V): $pV = K$, where K is a constant. It applies only to ideal gases; real gases follow Boyle's law only at low pressures and high temperatures.

Bragg equation   The Bragg equation, proposed by British physicist Sir William Lawrence Bragg, is used to deduce the crystal structure of a material using data obtained from x-rays directed at its surface. The formula measures the conditions under which a crystal will reflect a beam of x-rays with maximum intensity.

Charles's law of pressures   Charles's law of pressures is called Gay-Lussac's law in France. It states that the volume occupied by a given mass of gas at a constant pressure is directly proportional to the absolute temperature; in other words, the volume increases by a constant fraction of the volume for each degree rise in temperature. French chemists (and hot-air ballooning enthusiasts) Jacques Charles and Joseph Gay-Lussac developed the theory in the 1780s, but it was difficult to prove until Baron Kelvin (English scientist William Thomson) developed a new temperature scale.

Dalton's atomic theory   Dalton's atomic theory explains the formation of compounds by elements; it was first published in 1803 by John Dalton. The theory was used to explain the law of conservation of mass and the laws of chemical combination. The first modern attempt to describe chemical behavior in terms of atoms, it is based on the premises that all elements are composed of atoms, that all atoms of the same element are identical, that atoms can be neither created nor destroyed, and that atoms combine to form "compound atoms" (or molecules) in simple ratios. (See also *Law of multiple proportions*.)

Dalton's law (of partial pressures)   Dalton's law states that the pressure of a mixture of gases is the sum of the partial pressures of all the constituent gases. It applies only to ideal gases.

Faraday's laws (of electrolysis)   Faraday's laws state that (1) the amount of chemical change produced is proportional to the electric charge passed and (2) the amount of chemical change produced by a given charge depends on the ion concerned. It was proposed by Michael Faraday (see also Chapter 7, "Physics").

Graham's law (of diffusion)   Graham's law was proposed by Thomas Graham in the 1800s. It states that gases diffuse at a rate that is inversely proportional to the square root of their density, i.e., light molecules diffuse faster than heavy molecules.

Heisenberg's uncertainty principle   Heisenberg's uncertainty principle, proposed by physicist Werner Heisenberg, stipulates the impossibility of making simultaneous measurements of both the position and the momentum of a subatomic particle (e.g., an electron) with absolute accuracy. The uncertainty arises because to detect the particle, radiation must be "bounced" off it; the process itself disrupts the particle's position. This phenomenon is not a consequence of experimental error but represents a fundamental limit to objective scientific observation and arises from the wave-particle duality of particles and radiation.

Hess's law   Hess's law states that the amount of heat needed to change one substance to another depends on the substances and not on the reactions involved. The law was determined in 1840 by chemist Germain Hess.

Law of conservation of energy   The law of conservation of energy was formulated by physicist Hermann Helmholtz in 1847. It states that in all processes occurring in an isolated system, the energy of the system will remain constant.

Law of conservation of mass   The law of conservation of mass was formulated by chemist Antoine Lavoisier in 1774. It states that matter cannot be created or destroyed. Thus in a chemical reaction, the total mass of the products equals the total mass of the reactants.

Law of constant proportions (or composition)   The law of constant proportions was formulated by chemist Joseph Proust in 1779. It is the principle that the proportion of each element in a compound is fixed, or constant. The composition of a pure chemical compound is independent of the method of preparation. For example, chalk, or calcium carbonate, is always 40 percent calcium, 12 percent carbon, and 48 percent oxygen, by weight. This is also called the law of definite proportions.

Law of multiple proportions   The law of multiple proportions was proposed by chemist John Dalton in 1804. It is the principle that when two elements A and B combine to form more than one compound, the weights of B that combine with a fixed weight of A are in small whole-number ratios. For example, carbon and oxygen can form two compounds—carbon monoxide (CO) and carbon dioxide (CO_2). The former has a carbon to oxygen ratio of 1 to 1; while the latter has a ratio of 1 to 2.

Le Chatelier's principle   Le Chatelier's principle was determined by chemist Henri Le Chatelier and states that if a system is at equilibrium and a change is made in the conditions, the equilibrium adjusts in a manner to oppose the change. The principle is often applied to the effect of temperature and pressure on chemical reactions.

Newlands's law (law of octaves)   Newlands's law is based on the observation that when the elements are arranged in order of increasing atomic weight there is a similarity between members that are eight elements apart. Chemist John Newlands discovered this relationship in 1863, before the publication of Dmitri Mendeléev's periodic law (1869).

Perfect (or ideal) gas law   The perfect gas law states that for a given amount of gas the product of the volume, absolute temperature, and pressure are the same. A gas is called perfect, or ideal, when it follows this law.

MAJOR CHEMISTS

Arrhenius, Svante August (1859–1927)   Swedish physical chemist whose work established the basis for modern electrochemistry. He also developed the theory of panspermia, in which bacterial spores were thought to travel from space to Earth. He won the Nobel Prize in 1903.

Avogadro, Lorenzo Romano Amedeo Carlo, count of Quaregna and Cerreto (1776–1856) Italian physicist and chemist who expanded on Gay-Lussac's law of combining volumes and determined the formula for water. He differentiated molecules from atoms and was the first to use the word *molecule*. He developed Avogadro's constant and is considered one of the founders of modern physical chemistry.

Bernoulli, Daniel (1700–1782)   Swiss mathematician who introduced many ideas in hydrodynamics and made important contributions to the kinetic theory of gases.

Berzelius, Jöns Jacob (1779–1848)   Swedish chemist who was the first to establish accurate measurements of the atomic weights of elements and developed the symbols for many of them.

Boyle, Robert (1627–1691)   Irish chemist and physicist who explored the characteristics of gases and developed the law that bears his name.

Bunsen, Robert Wilhelm (1811–1899)   German chemist who worked on methods to identify, separate, and measure quantities of inorganic substances. He also invented many pieces of laboratory equipment, including the spectroscope and an electrochemical battery. Though the Bunsen burner is named after him, his technician, C. Desaga, is thought to have developed it; Michael Faraday had invented a similar burner much earlier.

Cannizzaro, Stanislao (1826–1910)   Italian chemist who established the use of atomic weights in chemical formulas and calculations.

Castner, Hamilton Young (1858–1898)   American chemist who developed, along with Karl Kellner in 1894, the process used in the manufacture of caustic soda—an important industrial process in petroleum refining and the plastics industries. It is still used today, but not as often as the Down's process.

Cavendish, Henry (1731–1810)   English chemist and physicist who discovered hydrogen and determined the mass of the Earth.

Charles, Jacques Alexandre César (1746–1823)   French physicist and physical chemist who investigated, along with Gay-Lussac, changes in gas volume caused by temperature changes at constant pressure. The resulting law is commonly referred to as Charles's law of pressures.

Crookes, Sir William (1832–1919)   British chemist and physicist who contributed to many fields of physics and chemistry in the nineteenth century. He also discovered the element thallium (using the then-new method of spectroscopy), invented the radiometer, and investigated radioactivity.

Curie, Marie Sklodowska (1867–1934)   Polish-born French chemist, wife of Pierre Curie. She isolated the radioactive elements radium (with Pierre Curie and Gustav Bémont) and polonium (with Pierre Curie)and was the first person to win two Nobel Prizes (1903 and 1911). The element curium is named after her.

Curie, Pierre (1859–1906)   French physicist, husband of Marie Curie. He was a codiscoverer of radium and polonium and shared the Nobel Prize in 1903. He also discovered the piezo-electric effect, in which certain substances produce a current as the result of pressure.

Dalton, John (1766–1844)   British chemist and physicist who, as a student of weather and the nature of gases, determined Dalton's law of partial pressures and an atomic theory of matter.

Davy, Sir Humphry (1778–1829)   British chemist who established the important connection between electrochemistry and the elements.

de Broglie, Prince Louis Victor Pierre Raymond (1892–1987)   French physicist who discovered the wave nature of electrons and other particles. He won the Nobel Prize in 1929.

Erlenmeyer, Richard August Carl Emil (1825–1909)   German chemist who developed the Erlenmeyer flask. He also synthesized important organic compounds.

Flory, Paul John (1910–1986)   American polymer chemist who investigated steps in polymerization reactions, including how they occur; polymers' structures; and properties of plastics, rubbers, and fibers. He won the Nobel Prize in 1974.

Galvani, Luigi (1737–1798)   Italian anatomist and physiologist who experimented with animal tissues and muscles, which lead to the discovery of current electricity by Volta. Galvani believed that animals had an electrical fluid; Volta proved that current resulted from different metals coming in moist contact with each other. The galvanic cell and galvanometer are named after Galvani.

Gay-Lussac, Joseph-Louis (1778–1850) French chemist and physicist who studied, along with Jacques Charles, the changes in gas volume caused by temperature changes at constant pressure. The resulting law, developed in 1802, is commonly referred to as Charles's law of pressures.

Gibbs, Josiah Willard (1839–1903) American mathematician and theoretical physicist and chemist who applied the principles of thermodynamics to chemistry. He was also the founder of chemical thermodynamics, the core of modern physical chemistry.

Glauber, Johann Rudolf (1604–1668) German chemist who discovered Glauber's salt, the traditional name for hydrated sodium sulfate. He also improved laboratory apparatus that contributed to the development of many industrial, agricultural, and medical products.

Graham, Thomas (1805–1869) Scottish chemist, who developed Graham's law of diffusion, explaining the movement of gases. He is also the founder of colloidal chemistry and is considered one of the founders of physical chemistry.

Haber, Fritz (1868–1934) German physical chemist who discovered a method of synthesizing ammonia by combining hydrogen and nitrogen under high pressure. His discovery made it possible for Germany to continue developing explosives during World War I, after the Allied blockade halted the importation of nitrate. He won the Nobel Prize in 1918.

Hahn, Otto (1879–1968) German chemist and discoverer of element 105, unnilpentium (one of the proposed, but disputed, names for the element was hahnium). He also discovered the process of fission of heavy nuclei, which lead to the development of the atomic bomb.

Hess, Germain Henri (1802–1850) Swiss-born Russian chemist who developed Hess's law, involving the amount of heat involved in a reaction.

Higgins, William (1763–1825) Irish chemist who was the first to propose the laws of simple and multiple proportions of chemical compounds (later formulated by John Dalton), though he had no experimental support.

Hodgkin, Dorothy Crowfoot (1910–) British chemist who determined the structure of vitamin B_{12}, the most complex vitamin. She also analyzed the structure of penicillin. She won the Nobel Prize in 1964.

Kolbe, Adolph Wilhelm Hermann (1818–1884) German chemist who synthesized acetic acid from nonorganic compounds. He also discovered the Kolbe reaction, involving the large-scale synthesis of acetyl-salicylic acid (aspirin).

Langmuir, Irving (1881–1957) American chemist who studied chemical reactions at high temperatures and low pressures, leading to the development of the gas-filled tungsten lamp. He also worked on thermal effects on gases, which led to using atomic hydrogen in welding torches. He won the Nobel Prize in 1932.

Lavoisier, Antoine Laurent (1743–1794) French chemist who was one of the first to quantify methods in chemistry. He determined the nature of combustion, noted the composition of the atmosphere, articulated the law of conservation of matter, and wrote the first modern chemistry book.

Le Chatelier, Henri Louis (1850–1936) French chemist who developed the thermodynamic principle that every change in a system in stable chemical equilibrium results in a rearrangement of the system so that the original change is minimized (also known as Le Chatelier's principle).

Lewis, Gilbert Newton (1875–1946)   American physical chemist who developed numerous theories on chemical thermodynamics, atomic structure, and bonding. He also discovered the distinction between ionic and covalent bonds.

Mendeléev, Dmitri Ivanovich (1834–1907)   Russian chemist who published the first Periodic Table of the Elements in 1869, leaving gaps in the table for elements then unknown. Element 101, mendelevium, is named after him.

Nernst, Walther Hermann (1864–1941)   German physical chemist who discovered the Third Law of Thermodynamics. He also worked on electrical insulators, and the specific heat of solids at low temperature. He won the Nobel Prize in 1920.

Newlands, John Alexander Reina (1836–1898)   British chemist who was one of the first to determine periodicity in the properties of chemical elements. He also developed the law of octaves, in which he positioned the 62 known elements in order of increasing atomic weight and determined that these could be further broken down into groups of eight based on similar properties.

Nobel, Alfred Bernhard (1833–1896)   Swedish chemist, engineer, and inventor who discovered the element nobelium; he is credited as the inventor of dynamite and several other explosives. He also instituted the Nobel Prize.

Ostwald, Friedrich Wilhelm (1853–1932)   German chemist who was the founder of modern physical chemistry. He also is responsible for the modern understanding of how catalysts work. He won the Nobel Prize in 1909.

Pauling, Linus Carl (1901–1994)   American chemist who applied quantum theory to molecular structures, establishing modern theoretical organic chemistry. He also determined the role of electrons in the formation of molecules and developed theories on ionic and covalent bonding. He proposed the idea that vitamin C could help prevent cancer. He won the Nobel Prize in chemistry in 1954; he was awarded the Nobel Peace Prize in 1962 for his efforts to stop atomic bomb research.

Perkin, Sir William Henry (1838–1907)   British chemist who was one of the first to initiate the synthesis of organic compounds, including coumarin, and thus founding the synthetic perfume industry (called the Perkin synthesis).

Priestley, Joseph (1733–1804)   British chemist and Presbyterian minister who first reported the discovery of oxygen. (Though Scheele discovered the element earlier, he published his results after Priestley).

Proust, Joseph Louis (1754–1826)   French chemist who worked to measure the mass of each component of a compound. He formulated the law of definite proportions, which states that compounds always contain certain elements in the same proportion, regardless of the method of preparation.

Rutherford, Daniel (1749–1819)   Scottish chemist who was one of the discoverers of nitrogen gas.

Scheele, Karl Wilhelm (1742–1786)   Swedish chemist who discovered oxygen, chlorine, manganese, and other chemical substances and compounds through extensive experimentation.

Soddy, Frederick (1877–1966)   English chemist who proposed the isotope theory of the elements. He also determined how radioactive elements break down. He won the Nobel Prize in 1921.

Sørensen, Søren Peter Lauritz (1868–1939) Danish chemist who developed the standard pH scale to measure the acidity of a solution. He also examined amino acids, enzymes, and proteins. He and his wife were the first to crystallize the egg protein albumin.

Takamine, Jokichi (1854–1922) Japanese-born American chemist who in 1901 was the first to synthesize adrenaline. (Thomas Bell simultaneously made the same discovery).

van't Hoff, Jacobus Henricus (1852–1911) Dutch theoretical chemist who advanced the field of chemical thermodynamics and was one of the first to describe molecular structures in three dimensions.

Winkler, Clemens Alexander (1838–1904) German chemist who discovered germanium, the third element predicted by Mendeléev on the basis of the Periodic Table.

Wittig, Georg Friedrich Karl (1897-1987) German organic chemist who developed reagents to simplify the synthesis of organic materials. He concentrated on organic compounds that contained phosphorus. He won the Nobel Prize in 1979.

Wöhler, Friedrich (1800–1882) German chemist who was the first to form an organic compound from an inorganic precursor. He is called the founder of modern organic chemistry.

Ziegler, Karl (1898–1973) German chemist who experimented with the polymerization of hydrocarbons and the organometallic catalysts for these reactions. He shared the Nobel Prize in 1963 with Guilio Natta, for their work on the synthesis of polymers for plastics.

SIGNIFICANT SCIENTIFIC DISCOVERIES IN CHEMISTRY

B.C.	600	Thales of Miletus (Turkey), founder of the Ionion school of natural philosophy, asserted that matter exists in three forms: mist, water and earth
	530	Greek natural philosopher Anaximenes suggested that air is the primary substance
	450	Leucippus of Miletus introduced the idea of atoms as indivisible units of matter
		Empedocles of Akraga (Sicily) introduced fire, air, earth and water as the primary elements
	430	Democritus of Abdera (Greece), student of Leucippus, expanded the concept of atoms, asserting that they explain the nature of all matter
	340	Aristotle taught that space is always filled with matter and the four elements undergo change when combined
	270	Zou Yan outlined the Chinese theory of five elements: water, metal, wood, fire, and earth
A.D.	100	Hero of Alexandria (Egypt) showed that air expands when heated
	180	The first alchemy writings appeared in Egypt
	400	The term *chemistry* used for the first time by Alexandrian scholars to describe the activity of changing matter
	750	Arabic alchemist known as Geber described how to prepare several acids and salts
	880	Arab chemists made alcohol by distilling wine
		Arrazi (or Rhazes) was the first to classify chemical substances into mineral, vegetable, animal, and derivative
	1300	Alum discovered in Rocca, Spain
		Arab alchemist known as the "False Geber" described sulfuric acid
	1473	Atomic theory of Democritus became known to European scholars when Lucretius's *On the Nature of Things* was translated into Latin

1597   Andreas Libavius (Saxony, Germany) wrote one of the first important chemistry textbooks, *Alchemia*

1610   Jean Beguin (Lorraine, France) wrote the first chemistry textbook that did not concentrate on alchemy

1620   Flemish scientist Johannes van Helmont used the word *gas* to describe substances like air

1625   Johann Glauber (Karlstadt, Germany), discovered hydrated sodium sulfate, which was named Glauber's salt

1661   Robert Boyle (Ireland) refuted Aristotle's ideas on the chemical composition of matter in *The Sceptical Chymist,* introducing the concepts of elements, alkalis, and acids

1662   Boyle formulated his law to explain the relationship of pressure, temperature, and volume in gases

1669   Johann Becher, German alchemist, wrote that *terra pingus* (oily earth) causes fire, which is later the basis of the erroneous phlogiston theory

1675   French chemist Nicolas Lemery wrote a chemistry text that is later published 31 times

1697   Georg Stahl (Germany) introduced the idea that phlogiston is the cause of burning and rusting

1755   Scottish chemist Joseph Black named carbon dioxide "fixed air"

1766   English chemist Henry Cavendish discovered hydrogen, which he called "inflammable air"

1767   Joseph Priestley, an English minister and chemist, described rings formed by electrical discharge on metals (called Priestley rings); he also described the characteristics of electricity and the experiments of Benjamin Franklin, whom he met in London

1772   Nitrogen independently discovered by Daniel Rutherford (a Scotsman who is usually credited), Karl Wilhelm Scheele (Swedish), Cavendish, and Priestley; Scheele discovered oxygen and called it "fire air" (he did not publish his results until 1777 after Priestley's publication in 1774)
       French chemist Antoine Lavoisier begins experiments on burning

1775   Priestley discovered hydrochloric and sulfuric acids

1778   Lavoisier suggested that air is made of two different gases (oxygen and nitrogen)
       Alessandro Volta (Italy) discovered methane gas in marshes

1779   Lavoisier proposed the name *oxygen* for the component of air that is breathable by living organisms and responsible for combustion

1781   Priestley ignited hydrogen in oxygen, producing water

1783   Cavendish observed that the combustion of hydrogen produces water, but he explained it in terms of phlogiston theory
       Lavoisier asserted that hydrogen is a new gas
       Scheele discovered citric acid and later glycerin

1785   Cavendish determined the composition of air

1791   German chemist Jeremias Richter observed that acids and bases always neutralize in the same proportions, establishing the idea of stoichiometry

1793   World's first chemical society founded in Philadelphia

1799   Joseph-Louis Proust (French chemist) asserted that elements in a compound always combine in definite proportions; he later identified three plant sugars: glucose, fructose, and sucrose

1801   John Dalton formulated the law of partial pressure for gases

1803   Dalton formulated his atomic theory of matter

1807   English chemist Humphrey Davy discovered sodium and potassium and later barium, strontium, and calcium

1811	Amedeo Avogadro developed his law
	Jöns Jakob Berzelius (Swedish chemist) introduced his system of chemical symbols, most of which are still used today
1812	Berzelius determined that atoms have electrical charges and later discovered lithium, silicon, and zirconium
1825	Richard Erlenmeyer (German chemist) synthesized many important organic compounds, develops ideas about types of bonding, and invents the flask that bears his name
1826	Henri Dutrochet discovered osmosis
1829	Precursor to the Periodic Table developed by German chemist Wolfgang Döbereiner
1833	French chemist Anselme Payen discovered the first enzyme, diastase
1840	Ozone discovered by Christian Schönbein, a German chemist
1850	Thomas Graham determined the differences between crystalloids and colloids, founding colloidal chemistry
1852	Concept of valence introduced by English chemist Edward Frankland
1859	Aspirin widely synthesized after reaction process determined by German chemist Adolph Kolbe
1860	Gustav Kirchhoff and Robert Bunsen used a spectroscope to identify an element for the first time and name it cesium
1863	John Newlands (English chemist) developed the law of octaves, an early version of the Periodic Table
1868	Helium named by Sir Joseph Norman Lockyer after he examined spectra from the Sun; it was discovered on Earth in 1895 by William Ramsey
1869	Russian chemist Dmitri Mendeléev publishes the first version of the Periodic Table of the Elements
1879	Saccharin discovered by Constantin Fahlbert
1900	Radon discovered by German physicist Friedrich Dorn
1907	Emil Fischer, Prussian chemist, synthesized a polypeptide (small protein) from amino acids
1909	Russian-American chemist Phoebus Levene discovered ribose sugars of ribonucleic acid (RNA)
1913	German chemist Friedrich Bergius introduced the hydrogenation of coal at high pressures to produce gasoline
	Isotopes of lead discovered by American chemist Theodore Richard
1918	Czech chemist Jaroslav Heyrovsk developed polarography to measure the concentration of ions in a solution
1929	Levene discovered deoxyribose sugars of DNA
1930	Electrophoresis introduced by Swedish chemist Arne Tiselius as a way to separate proteins in suspension using electric currents
1934	Vitamin C synthesized by English chemist Walter Haworth
1939	Du Pont marketed nylon; British firm ICI made polythene (polyethylene); Otto Bayer and the Germany industrial giants developed plastics
1940	First element created with an atomic number higher than uranium (element 93, neptunium) by Americans Philip Abelson and Edwin McMillan
	Carbon-14 discovered by Canadian-American biochemist Martin Kamen
1941	American Glenn Seaborg and co-workers created plutonium (number 94) and later will create atomic numbers 95, 96, and 99
1944	Paper chromatography developed by British biochemists Archer Martin and Richard Synge to identify organic compounds
1949	English biochemist Dorothy Hodgkin first to use a computer to work out the structure of an organic chemical, penicillin
1956	Choh Hao Li determined amino acid sequence of a hormone (ACTH) and isolated human growth hormone, which will be synthesized in 1970

1982   A single atom of element 109 produced in a German laboratory

1987   A form of polyacetylene with iodine developed by Herbert Naarmann and N. Theophilou that is a better conductor of electricity than copper

1988   Chemists estimated that 10 million specific compounds are recorded, with 400,000 more described each year

COMMON TERMS IN CHEMISTRY

absorption   The process or act of absorbing; when a solid substance takes up and holds a gas, liquid, or solid interspersed within its structure (see also *adsorption*).

activation energy   The amount of energy needed to start a chemical reaction.

adhesion   The attraction force between molecules of different materials. For example, there is adhesion between molecules of water and molecules of a glass.

adsorption   The surface attraction between atoms or molecules on the surface of particles of colloidal size that tend to attract substances with which they come into contact. Adsorption is an important part of dying cloth and other industrial processes.

alcohol   A compound that contains a hydrocarbon group and one or more -OH groups; also the common name for ethyl alcohol.

alkali metal   An element in Group 1 of the Periodic Table; lithium, sodium, potassium, rubidium, cesium, and francium are alkali metals.

alkali   A compound having basic (as opposed to acidic) properties.

alkaline earth   An oxide of an element in Group 2 of the Periodic Table; also called alkaline-earth oxide.

amorphous   Describing a state of matter where there is no orderly arrangement of atoms, as in glass, for example.

anion   An ion possessing a negative electrical charge; also an ion that migrates to an anode.

anode   The positive plate in an electrolytic system (such as a lead battery) where electrons are lost and oxidation occurs.

association   The combining of molecules in a substance with those of another substance to form a more complex species, such as a mixture of water and ethanol where the molecules combine by hydrogen bonding.

atomic mass unit   A unit of mass that is exactly $1/12$ of a carbon-12 atom.

atomic mass   The exact mass of an atom's protons and neutrons in atomic mass units.

atomic number   The number of protons in the nucleus of an atom.

binary compound   A chemical compound formed by two elements, such as sodium chloride ($NaCl$), table salt, which is composed of sodium (Na) and chlorine (Cl).

binding energy   The amount of energy necessary to separate protons and neutrons found in the nucleus of an atom.

boil   The phase change in a material from a liquid to a gas as a result of the application of heat or when pressure is lowered.

buffer   A solution in which the pH remains somewhat constant when acids or bases are added.

catalyst   A substance that changes the speed of a chemical reaction without itself being permanently changed.

cathode   The negative plate in an electrolytic system (e.g., a lead battery) where the electrons are taken up and reduction takes place.

cation   An ion possessing a positive electrical charge. Also, an ion that migrates to a cathode.

cell   A system in which two plates (electrodes) are submerged into a liquid (electrolytes), allowing the electrons to be transferred from one plate to another.

chain   Two or more atoms forming bonds with each other in a molecule. Chains can be straight or branched.

coagulation   The collection of particles into clusters, such as colloids.

cohesion   The attraction between molecules of the same solid or liquid such as the cohesion between molecules of water.

colloid   Intermediate-size solute particles that are small enough to remain suspended in solution, such as small butterfat particles dispersed in milk.

combustion   The emission of heat and light through rapid oxidation.

compound   A chemical combination of atoms of different elements to form a substance in which the ratio of combining atoms is unvarying and is specific to that substance. The constituent atoms cannot be separated by physical means, but only by a chemical reaction.

concentration   The amount of substance per unit volume or unit mass in a solution. Molar concentration is the amount of substance (in moles) per cubic liter, mass concentration is the mass of solute per unit volume, and molar concentration is the amount of substance (in moles) per kilogram of solute.

condensation   The conversion of a gas or vapor into a liquid by cooling.

configuration   The arrangement of electrons about the nucleus of an atom.

corrosion   Reaction of a metal with an acid, oxygen, or other compound with destruction of the surface of the metal; rusting is an example.

coupling   A chemical reaction in which two groups of molecules join together.

critical point   The specific conditions of temperature and pressure under which a liquid being heated in a closed vessel becomes indistinguishable from the gas or vapor phase. At temperatures below the critical point, the substance can be liquefied by applying pressure.

crystal   A solid in which the particles, either molecules or atoms, are arranged in a distinctive, repeating pattern.

crystalloid   Having the characteristics of a crystal.

degassing   The removal of dissolved or absorbed gases from liquids or solids.

degradation   A chemical reaction involving the decomposition of a molecule into simpler molecules, usually in stages.

density   The mass per unit volume of a substance.

diffusion   The spreading of a material's molecules through a solid, liquid, or gas caused by the kinetic motion of molecules.

dilute   Describing a solution in which the amount of solute is low relative to that of the solvent.

dissociation   The separation of ions in an ionic compound often brought on by dissolving an ionic compound in water.

distillation   The process of boiling a liquid and condensing the vapor often used to purify liquids or to separate components of a liquid mixture.

electric charge   The property of matter, either positive or negative, that gives rise to electrical forces.

electricity   The effect produced by moving charges.

electrolysis   The decomposition of a substance by passing an electric current through a liquid.

electrolyte   A substance that will conduct a current when melted or in solution, or a substance decomposable by an electric current. All ionic compounds are electrolytes.

electron pair   A pair of valence electrons that forms a nonpolar bond between two neighboring atoms.

electronegativity   Attraction of an atom for electrons in a covalent bond as measured by the electronegativity scale.

endothermic   Describing a process in which heat is absorbed, such as the dissolving of a salt in water.

evaporation   A change of state from a liquid to a gas.

excited state   Condition in which an atom's electrons are at higher energy levels than the ones they would normally occupy.

exothermic   Denoting a chemical reaction in which heat is released such as in combustion.

fermentation   A chemical reaction in which microorganisms such as molds, bacteria, and yeast metabolize sugar and release ethanol as a by-product.

filtration   The process of removing suspended particles from a fluid by passing or forcing the fluid through a porous material called the filter.

fluorescence   The absorption of energy by atoms, molecules, and other particles, followed by immediate emission of visible electromagnetic radiation as the particles make transitions to lower energy states.

formula mass   The sum of the atomic masses in a compound's formula.

formula   A representation of a chemical compound using symbols for the atoms and subscript numbers to show the numbers of atoms present; in some formulas, superscripts are also used, i.e. charge.

gamma-rays   High-frequency electromagnetic waves similar to x-rays but of higher frequency.

ground state   The state in which an atom's electrons are in the lowest energy levels possible.

halogens   Active nonmetals in Group 17 of the Periodic Table including fluorine, chlorine, and bromine, all of which are highly electronegative.

heat   Energy produced by molecular motion.

heterogeneous   Relating to matter that is of nonuniform composition.

homogeneous   Relating to matter that is of uniform composition throughout.

hydrocarbon   A compound composed solely of carbon and hydrogen, such as methane.

hydrolysis   A reaction in which water is one of the reactants.

inert   Matter that does not enter chemical reactions.

inhibitor   A substance that slows down the rate of a chemical reaction.

ion   An atom (or a group of atoms) that is electrically charged as a result of a gain or loss of electrons.

ionic compounds   Compounds that are formed by the process of electron transfer, such as the product of a metal and nonmetal.

ionization   The process of producing ions.

isomer   Any one of the possible compounds arising from the different ways of grouping the atoms in a given molecular formula. Isomers have the same molecular formula but slightly different physical properties.

isotopes   Atoms that have the same atomic number but different atomic mass due to the different number of neutrons in their nuclei.

lattice   A regular, three-dimensional arrangement of points, used to describe the position of particles (atoms, ions, or molecules) in a crystalline solid.

lipids   Organic compounds, including fats, waxes, and steroids.

matter   Anything that occupies space and has mass when at rest.

mechanism   A step-by-step description of the events taking place in a chemical reaction.

melt   To change from a solid to a liquid as a result of heating.

meniscus   The curved surface of liquid in a column.

metal   An element that tends to lose its valence electrons.

molecule   The smallest particle of an element or compound that contains the chemical properties of that material.

nonmetal   An element that tends to gain electrons to complete its outer electron shell.

orbital   Part of an atom in which electrons are most likely to be found.

oxidation   The process in which an atom, ion, or molecule loses electrons.

partial pressure   The pressure a gas in a mixture would exert if it alone were present in a container.

polymerization   The bonding or the chemical reaction that produces a polymer from two or more monomers.

precipitate   A solid that forms in and settles out of solution. Also, a suspension of small particles of a solid in a liquid formed by a chemical reaction.

quantum   A definite amount of energy released or absorbed in a process. For example, the quantum of electromagnetic radiation is the photon.

radioactivity   The breakdown of atomic nuclei accompanied by the release of radiation such as alpha-, beta-, or gamma-rays.

radioelement   The radioactive isotope of an element.

rare earth elements   Chemical elements with atomic numbers 58 to 71.

reactant   A substance taking part in a chemical reaction.

reagent   A substance, chemical, or solution used in the laboratory to detect or measure other chemicals, substances, or solutions. It is also a compound that supplies the molecule, ion, or free radical in a chemical reaction.

reduction   The process by which a substance gains electrons, decreases in valence number, or combines with hydrogen. It often involves the loss of oxygen from a compound or the addition of hydrogen.

saturated solution   A solution that contains the maximum equilibrium amount of solute at a given temperature. A solution is saturated if it is in equilibrium with its solute.

solidify   The change in a substance from a liquid to a solid as a result of cooling.

sublimation   The conversion of a solid into a vapor without first melting, such as solid carbon dioxide (dry ice) becoming gaseous carbon dioxide.

superconductivity   A property of many metals, chemical compounds, and alloys at temperatures near absolute zero, when their electrical resistivity vanishes and they become strongly repelled by magnets, positioning themselves at right angles to the magnetic lines of force.

supersaturated solution   A solution that contains more than the equilibrium amount of solute.

surface tension   The tendency of the surface of a liquid to behave as if it were covered by a skin, due to cohesive forces on the surface.

suspension   A system in which particles of a solid or liquid are dispersed in a liquid or gas.

thermodynamics   The study of energy changes in chemical reactions and the influence of energy on those changes.

transmutation   The conversion of one element into another by means of nuclear change.

valence electrons   The electrons of the outermost shell of an atom.

vaporization   The process by which a liquid or solid is converted into a gas or vapor by heat. Although vaporization can occur at any temperature, its rate increases as the temperature rises.

water of hydration   Water that is held in chemical combination in a hydrate.

ADDITIONAL SOURCES OF INFORMATION

American Chemical Society. *ChemCom: Chemistry in the Community.* Kendall/Hunt, 1993.

Boorse, Henry, A., et al. *The Atomic Scientists, A Biographical History.* Wiley, 1989.

Corrick, James A. *Recent Revolutions in Chemistry.* Franklin Watts, 1986.

Daintith, John, ed. *The Facts On File Dictionary of Chemistry.* Facts On File, 1988.

Dorin, Henry, et al. *Chemistry: The Study of Matter, 4th ed.* Prentice-Hall, 1992.

Heiserman, David L. *Exploring Chemical Elements and Their Compounds.* TAB, 1992.

Hess, Fred C. *Chemistry Made Simple.* Doubleday, 1984.

VanCleave, Janice. *A+ Projects in Chemistry.* Wiley, 1993.

Chapter 7

Physics

What Is Physics?   272

Branches of Physics   272

Mass and Gravitation   272

Motion   273

Work and Energy   276

Newton's Universal Law of Gravitation   277

Einstein and Relativity   279

Basic Forces in Nature   281

Grand Unified Theories   281

Heat and Temperature   282

Waves   284

Reflection and Refraction   288

Sound Waves   290

Electricity   291

Magnetism   293

Electromagnetism   294

Particles of the Universe   295

Nuclear Physics   299

Quantum Physics   300

Major Physicists   302

Significant Scientific Discoveries
in Physics   307

Common Terms in Physics   309

Additional Sources of Information   312

WHAT IS PHYSICS?

The study of *physics* began in ancient Greece, as philosophers attempted to understand the physical world. With the adoption of the scientific method, "physics" at first included all the natural sciences. Today, physics seeks to discover the laws of the universe that govern the behavior of matter and energy. Accordingly, other sciences and technology owe a debt to physics. For example, chemistry studies how atoms and molecules join and separate; physics studies the laws that govern the joining and separation. Astronomy studies the movements of celestial bodies; physics deals with the laws that govern those movements.

BRANCHES OF PHYSICS

Traditionally, physics is broken down into classical and modern, though many subdivisions of the two overlap. *Classical physics* includes Newtonian mechanics, thermodynamics, statistical mechanics, acoustics, optics, electricity, and magnetism. *Modern physics* includes relativistic mechanics, atomic, nuclear and particle physics, and quantum physics.

Physics may also be divided into experimental and theoretical. *Theoretical physicists* use mathematics to describe the physical world and predict how it will behave. *Experimental physicists* test those predictions with practical experiments. Theorists depend on experimental results to check, understand, amend, or discard their theories.

In science, a *theory* is usually not just a guess but rather a mathematical construction that predicts something about the physical world. For example, Albert Einstein's theory of relativity is a set of equations that describes the behavior of bodies moving at high velocities and in strong gravitational fields.

MASS AND GRAVITATION

Much of physics deals with the behavior of *matter* (matter is anything that has mass and occupies space). A fundamental property of matter is *mass*, which is not the same thing as weight. Mass is the tendency of an object to resist being moved, or if it is moving, to resist a change in speed or direction. This property is also called *inertia* or *inertial mass*.

Objects are attracted to one another by a force called *gravitation*, which is proportional to the mass of the objects and decreases with their distance. The force that results from the gravitational attraction of the Earth on bodies at its surface is what we call *weight*. Science has chosen to measure the mass of objects in units that are roughly equivalent to the weight of those objects on Earth. For example, if an object weighs 150 pounds on Earth, it would have a mass of 150 pounds in an orbiting spaceship. The object would be "weightless" because it does not feel the gravitational attraction of the Earth, but, even in outer space, to push the object from one place to another, someone or something would have to exert a force sufficient to overcome the inertial mass of 150 pounds.

MOTION

Everything in the universe exhibits some form of *motion*. For example, objects on Earth that appear to be stationary really are moving with the rotation of the Earth (for more information on motion, see "Newton's Laws of Motion," later in this chapter).

Speed and Velocity

Speed and velocity are often erroneously used as synonyms. *Speed* is the rate at which something moves; *velocity* is speed in a particular direction. Speed is called a scalar quantity, represented by the following formula.

$$\text{speed} = \frac{\text{distance}}{\text{time}}$$

For example, if you drive 100 miles in 2 hours, your average speed is 100 divided by 2, or 50 miles per hour (for information on speed conversions, such as miles per hour to kilometers per hour, see Chapter 1, "Scientific Measurements").

Velocity is called a vector quantity, often shown as an arrow, which specifies both the magnitude and the direction of the speed. (A *vector* is any quantity that states both magnitude and direction; force, velocity, acceleration, angular momentum, and torque are all examples of quantities that are vectors.) Velocity may change with time, as an object changes either its speed or its direction.

Acceleration

Acceleration is the rate of change in velocity, or the change in velocity divided by the time it takes for the change to occur. It is also a vector quantity—when a force is applied, it causes an object to move in a particular direction. It is often represented by the following equation:

$$a = \frac{\Delta v}{\Delta t} = \frac{\Delta x}{\Delta t^2} \ \left(\text{since } \Delta v = \frac{\Delta x}{\Delta t}\right)$$

where a is the acceleration, Δv ("delta vee") is the change in velocity of the object, Δt is the change in time required to produce the change in velocity, and x is the change in the object's position, i.e., the distance it has travelled.

Acceleration due to gravity was explored by Galileo Galilei. He demonstrated that a falling body will increase its distance as the square of time, if the effects of the surrounding air are ignored. The *constant acceleration due to gravity* is denoted as g and has a value of 32 feet (9.8 meters) per second-per second near the Earth's surface. To determine the distance of an object falling in a vacuum (this means with no air resistance), we use the equation:

$$d = 1/2 \ gt^2$$

where d is the distance fallen over a period of time t. For example, after 1/2 second, a falling object would travel a distance of 4 feet and have a velocity of 8 feet/second; at 2 seconds it would have fallen 64 feet and its velocity would have reached 32 feet/second.

Force

Force is anything that tends to change the state of rest or motion of an object. It is represented not only by the magnitude of force (such as tons or pounds) but also by its direction in space. Thus force is a vector. When a number of forces act simultaneously on an object, the object moves as if acted on by a single force with a magnitude and direction that are the *vector sum* of all the forces, called a *resultant*. If the resultant of forces is zero, the object is said to be in equilibrium.

Torque

The ability of a force to cause rotation or twisting around an axle or pivot point is called *torque*. It consists of a linear force applied perpendicular to the radius of the object being turned (torque arm). In equation form, it is often written as:

$$T = Fh$$

where T is the torque, F is the amount of force, and h is the perpendicular distance from the pivot to the line of force.

Momentum

Momentum is related to the amount of energy possessed by a moving object. It is often explained as the force necessary to stop an object from moving and depends on the mass of the object and its velocity. A baseball thrown at 50 miles per hour can be caught by a human hand; the same baseball fired out of a cannon at 500 miles per hour could not be caught by hand. Conversely, a person cannot stop a 20-ton locomotive moving only 1 mile per hour. In physics, momentum (M) is defined as mass (m) times velocity (v), or:

$$M = mv$$

If a body's linear momentum has no external, unbalanced forces acting on it, it is conserved and does not change with time (for more information on conservation of energy, see "Newton's First Law of Motion," later in this chapter).

Inertia

The law of inertia states that a body at rest remains at rest until acted on by outside forces (see "Newton's Third Law of Motion," later in this chapter).

Centripetal and Centrifugal Forces

The force required to hold a moving object in a circular path is called *centripetal force*. For example, a satellite is held in Earth's orbit by the centripetal force from the planet's gravity. A rock swinging on a string is held in a circular path by the centripetal force applied by the string.

Centrifugal force refers to the force that causes an object to fly off on a tangent to its circular movement, for example, if the string on the swinging rock was cut. It is not a true force but rather an expression of a spinning object's momentum: When the string is cut, the rock simply continues moving in a straight line as if centripetal force had not continued along the string. When mud flies off the spinning wheel of a moving car, it is thrown by centrifugal force. In reality, the wheel is spinning fast enough for the momentum of the mud to overcome the friction that held it to the tire.

Angular Momentum

Angular momentum exists when an object follows a path around a fixed point, such as a comet traveling around the Sun or a wheel spinning on a shaft.

Angular momentum equals mvr, where m is the mass, v is the velocity, and r is the object's distance from the center of motion. It is conserved if the angular momentum remains steady and no external, unbalanced torque (or twisting effect) is exerted on the object. However, if one of the elements of the formula is changed, the others must adjust. For example, when a comet swings closer to the Sun, its velocity increases because its distance from the center of motion decreases, thus conserving the angular momentum. Similarly, if an ice skater spins with his or her arms extended, then pulls the arms inward, the skater will spin faster because part of his or her mass has moved closer to the center of rotation.

Newton's Laws of Motion

Sir Isaac Newton founded the study of mechanics by setting down simple laws by which the planets—and all other objects—move when acted on by gravity or any other force. The laws were later modified by Albert Einstein for special situations, such as a subatomic particle moving at very high velocity; but Newton's original laws still remain valid.

Newton's First Law (Law of Inertia)

Newton's first law states that in the absence of outside forces, the momentum of a system remains constant: An object that is sitting still will stay in place until it is pushed, and something that is moving will keep moving in a straight line until it is pushed to change its speed or direction. The reason why moving objects on Earth eventually slow down and stop is because they are acted on by the force called *friction*. For example, a rolling skateboard experiences friction in its wheel bearings and its rider experiences friction from the air.

Newton's Second Law (Law of Constant Acceleration)

Newton's second law states that if force acts on a body, the body accelerates in the direction of the force. The greater the force, the greater the acceleration. The greater the mass of the body, the less the acceleration. This law agrees with everyday experience: The more an object is pushed, the more it moves; and the more massive an object is, the more push it takes to move it.

The second law is expressed in the following equation:

$$F = ma$$

where F is the force required to impart an acceleration a to a mass m. Newton actually expressed this in calculus, a form of mathematics he created for the purpose of explaining these physical laws. Since instantaneous acceleration is the instantaneous change in velocity in an instant of time (or change in time):

$$F = m\frac{\Delta v}{\Delta t} \text{ or } F = ma$$

Newton's Third Law (Law of Conservation of Momentum)

Newton's third law states that forces are always mutual. This means if a force is exerted on a body, that body reacts with an equal and opposite force on the body that exerted the force. This is also stated this way: For every action there is an equal and opposite reaction.

This is seen in everyday experience. For example, two people of equal mass face one another on skateboards. If they push on each other, both will roll backward; if just one skateboarder pushes on the other, both will still roll backward. If a skateboarder throws a bowling ball forward, he will roll backward. This is how spaceships move through the vacuum of space even though there is nothing to push on—the rocket engine pushes hot gases out of its thrusters and the spaceship is pushed in the opposite direction.

WORK AND ENERGY

Work

In physics, *work* is used to express the forces applied to an object to set it in motion. Work is expressed as:

$$W = Fd$$

where W is the work, F is the magnitude of the force, and d is the distance moved in the direction of the force.

Power

Power is the rate of doing work. Power is often expressed as:

$$P = \frac{W}{t}$$

where P is power, W is the amount of work done, and t is the time it takes to do the work. This is commonly expressed as:

$$P = \frac{Fd}{t}$$

where, as above, $W = Fd$.

Kinetic and Potential Energies

Energy is defined as the capacity to do work or as stored work. Physical objects may possess *kinetic energy* (the energy of motion) or *potential energy* (the object's stored energy because of its position or configuration). For example, a crane hoisting a weight uses kinetic energy to lift the weight against the force of gravity. Once poised above the ground, the weight possesses potential (stored) energy, because if it is released, the Earth's gravitational attraction will put it into motion. If the dropped weight is attached to a bungee cord, energy will be stored in the stretched cord because of its changed configuration. When the cord pulls back, it will again give kinetic energy to the weight.

Kinetic energy depends on both the mass of the object and its velocity. It is related to momentum, but it is defined as the mass times the square of the velocity divided by 2:

$$E_k = \tfrac{1}{2}\, mv^2 \text{ or also written as } \tfrac{1}{2}\, Mv$$

where M is momentum.

An object's potential energy is defined as the amount of work required to put the object into its original position or configuration. For example, an object's potential energy in a gravitational field can be calculated by multiplying the acceleration due to gravity (which is related to the force needed to lift the object against gravitational attraction) by the height and the mass:

$$E_p = mhg$$

where g is the acceleration of a body freely falling in a vacuum close to the Earth's surface, or about 32 feet (9.8 meters) per second-per second.

Mechanical energy of an object or body is measured by the amount of work it can do. Other forms of energy, such as thermal, electrical, and chemical, are really expressions of the kinetic or potential energy of atoms and subatomic particles. *Thermal energy* is the kinetic energy of a substance's atoms; the faster the atoms are moving, the hotter the object. *Electrical energy* is the motion of electrons in an object that conducts electricity, such as copper. *Chemical energy* is energy stored in the configuration of atoms in molecules.

Conservation of Energy

One of the fundamental principles of physics is the Law of Conservation of Energy, which states that energy may not be created or destroyed, only changed in form. For example, when fuel is burned, stored chemical energy is turned into thermal energy. The resulting thermal energy can be used to impart kinetic energy to the moving parts of a generator and produce electrical energy.

NEWTON'S UNIVERSAL LAW OF GRAVITATION

Though gravity was known about many years before Sir Isaac Newton conducted his experiments, he is popularly thought of as the discoverer of gravity. Astronomer Johannes Kepler did not know why the planets moved in ellipses, but he sensed that planetary bodies and the Sun probably had a natural affinity for each other and that magnetism was involved (for information on Kepler's laws of planetary motion, see Chapter 8, "Astronomy"). By studying Kepler's observations, Newton derived laws that described how the force of gravity acted. He was the first to declare that the pull of the Earth extended to infinity, and he determined that the attraction diminished with the square of the distance.

Newton's law of gravitation states that objects attract each other with a force that varies directly as the product of their masses and also inversely as the square of the distances between them. The law is universal and applies to planets revolving around the Sun as well as to an apple falling toward the Earth.

Newton's law is written as:

$$F = G\left(\frac{m_1 m_2}{r^2}\right)$$

where F is the force of gravity between masses m_1 and m_2, G is a universal constant, and r is the distance between the centers of both masses.

BLACK HOLES AND GRAVITY WAVES

Do black holes really exist? Or are they just the dream of science fiction writers and readers? So far, we have one possible black hole to help prove the theory—but more black holes must be found and verified to solidify their existence.

Black holes are points in space where matter has collapsed under its own gravitational attraction and has become incredibly dense. The gravitational field of a black hole is so strong that nothing can escape from it, not even photon particles (light). Initially, black holes may be formed when stars greater than or equal to two solar masses collide. The cores of the stars are crushed into a singularity—a place in which the known laws of physics fail. The presence of black holes are usually inferred by the gravitational effects on material falling into a hole. Astrophysicist Stephen Hawking described, by combining general relativity theory and quantum mechanics, what may happen to a black hole: He predicts that a black hole will convert its mass into radiation (called Hawking radiation), then disappear after a long period.

There is other research in progress to prove the existence of black holes. For example, scientists are now trying to find the gravitational wave signatures of black holes, and the Laser Interferometric Gravitational Wave Observatories (LIGOs) are now searching for the waves that were predicted by Einstein's theory of general relativity. The scientists at the LIGOs hope that when a major cataclysmic event occurs in the universe, such as a supernova explosion, the sensitive instruments—which measure variations in the Earth's gravitational field on the order of one–one-millionth of a nuclear radius over 3 feet—will detect gravity waves. Scientists are also searching for gravitons, the theoretical particles that are thought to carry gravity waves around the universe.

Orbits

Only certain *orbits* are possible under the law of gravitation: circles, ellipses, parabolas, and hyperbolas. These curves can all be formed from the intersection, at various angles, of a plane with a cone (for an illustration of conic sections, see Chapter 1, "Scientific Measurements").

Few, if any, objects in space have a truly circular orbit. The orbits of the planets around the Sun and of moons around planets are ellipses, although in many cases they are very close to circular. In a parabolic or hyperbolic orbit, a body will pass by the attractive central force only once and retreat into infinity never to return (objects coming from outside the solar system often fall into one of these two paths). However, if an object entering the solar system from outside is gravitationally attracted by a planet or satellite, the object may be forced into an elliptical orbit around the Sun.

An object in an elliptical orbit around the Earth is in balance: If its velocity were lower, it would fall toward the Earth; if its velocity were higher, it would pull away from the Earth. Usually, a change in velocity results in a change in orbit. A spaceship moving up or down does not fire its rockets toward or away from the Earth but fires forward or backward along the direction of its orbit. If a ship has enough velocity to achieve a parabolic or hyperbolic orbit, it will escape completely from the Earth's attraction, or achieve *escape velocity* (about 7 miles [11 kilometers] per second).

INTO ORBIT

Imagine a shell fired from a cannon traveling parallel to the Earth's surface. If there were no air resistance, the shell would continue indefinitely in a straight line with a constant velocity, in accordance with Newton's first law of motion. But the Earth's gravity pulls the shell down, causing it to travel in a curved path and eventually strike the ground.

If the shell is accelerated to such a high velocity that its arched path as it fell exactly matched the curvature of the Earth, the shell would continue to fall, but the Earth would continue to fall away beneath it. It would be in orbit around the Earth. This is the principle that enables spaceships and satellites to orbit our planet. It is not the satellite's height that places it in orbit, but its velocity.

Once a spaceship is in orbit, it is constantly falling toward the Earth. As a result, a space traveler does not feel the acceleration of gravity but instead experiences "weightlessness," a feeling similar to a drop in a roller-coaster ride. Objects (including astronauts) in an orbiting spaceship are not "weightless" because they are outside the Earth's gravitational field; the gravitational attraction is still present but is not felt because the ship is in freefall. Technically, the condition on most spaceships is not true weightlessness because objects in the ship are gravitationally attracted to one another, experiencing what is commonly called *microgravity*.

EINSTEIN AND RELATIVITY

Newton's laws of motion apply in most familiar situations. But in the world of subatomic particles (especially those moving at high velocities) or more distant or exotic parts of the universe (especially areas of strong gravitational fields), some of the physical laws seem to break down. It was not until the early twentieth century that Albert Einstein proposed new versions of the laws to explain these inconsistencies.

CAN IT BE WARP SPEED?

Einstein and others have shown that objects cannot travel faster than the speed of light—186,291 miles (299,792,458 meters) per second. As an object goes faster, its mass increases. And if the object were to travel as fast as the speed of light, its mass would become infinite. Since it would take an infinite force to accelerate an infinite mass, it seems we should forget about anything traveling faster than the speed of light.

But scientists suggest that a particle called a tachyon (from the Greek for "swift") may travel faster than the speed of light and cannot be slowed down. Some scientists believe that if tachyons could be detected—and harnessed—they would help us communicate anywhere in the universe instantaneously. But so far, the particle has not been found.

Einstein's Theories

The theory of special relativity, announced by Albert Einstein in 1905, deals with conditions in which gravitational forces are not present. It is called "special" because it holds only for systems that move at a constant velocity with respect to one another. Relativity refers to the idea that velocity of an object can be determined only relative to the observer. For example, a fly flying along the aisle of a supersonic aircraft (traveling 700 miles [1,126 kilometers] per hour) appears to be traveling about 1 mile (1.6 kilometers) per hour in the "frame of reference" of the aircraft. But to an observer on the ground, the fly seems to be moving at 701 miles (1,128 kilometers) per hour.

This concept was understood before Einstein. What Einstein did was to assume—based on earlier experiments—that the speed of light traveling between two frames of reference remains the same for observers in both places: 186,291 miles (299,792,458 meters) per second. Since light is what an observer in one frame uses to determine the position and velocity of objects in another frame, this changes the way an observer in one frame sees the position and velocity of objects in another frame. Einstein used this fact to derive several formulas that describe how objects in one frame of reference appear when viewed from another that is in uniform motion relative to the first. This led to several strange conclusions—although the effects only become noticeable when relative velocity approaches the speed of light (therefore, they have been seen only in the behavior of fast-moving subatomic particles).

- As the velocity of an object relative to an observer increases, its length decreases.
- Time intervals in a moving frame are shorter, e.g., a space traveler moving at or near the speed of light could be away for many Earth years but return having experienced a time lapse of only a few months.
- The mass of a moving object increases with its velocity. As the velocity approaches the speed of light, the mass approaches infinity; this is the reason most scientists state that it is impossible to travel faster than the speed of light: infinite energy would be required to accelerate an infinite mass.

The Energy Equivalent of Mass

Einstein showed mathematically that there is a connection between mass and energy: Energy has mass, and mass represents energy. The relationship is expressed in the now-famous equation:

$$E = mc^2$$

where c is the speed of light. Since c is a very large number, even a very small amount of mass represents a very large amount of energy.

For example, in nuclear bombs and power plants, mass is converted to energy by either fission or fusion reactions. In nuclear fission, an atom of a heavy element, such as uranium, is split into two or more small atoms. The mass of the smaller atoms adds up to less than the mass of the original atom, and the difference is released as energy. In fusion, two atoms of a very light element, such as hydrogen, join to form an atom of a heavier element, usually helium. Again, the mass of the resulting atom is less than the total mass of the original atoms, and energy is released (the Sun's energy comes from fusion reactions).

General Relativity

There is no way to tell the difference between the force of gravity and a force caused by some other acceleration. For example, if a person stands in an elevator and feels a pull toward the floor, it is not known whether the elevator is standing still or is accelerating through space at a rate that pushes the person against the floor with a force equal to Earth's gravity. In his general theory of relativity, Einstein proposed that there is no difference and that the acceleration due to gravity results from the fact that space and time are curved in the vicinity of any mass. He treated time as a fourth dimension perpendicular to the three spatial dimensions of length, width, and height.

When a baseball is thrown, it arcs toward the ground. In the frame of reference of the baseball, Einstein said, the baseball is moving in a straight line, but following the curvature of space-time created by the presence of the Earth. The more massive the object, the more space-time is deformed. His general theory of relativity (1915) actually consists of a set of 10 equations from which the degree of curvature of space-time can be predicted based on the amount and distribution of mass present.

Einstein proposed several tests of the theory. One was that a beam of light would be bent by a certain amount as it passed through a gravitational field. This was confirmed by observations of starlight passing near the Sun during a solar eclipse. He also calculated the amount by which the orbit of the planet Mercury would be perturbed by the curvature of space-time due to the Sun's gravitational field. Radar measurements of Mercury's position agreed with his calculations within about 0.5 percent. The theory also contends that cataclysmic astrophysical events, such as colliding black holes and exploding supernovas, send gravitational waves through the curved geometry of space-time (for more information on space-time and gravity waves, see "Black Holes and Gravity Waves," earlier in this chapter), although there has never been any evidence sighted.

Scientists have also found gravitational lenses in space that support general relativity: Large galaxies often act similarly to a lens, bending the light of stars beyond them and distorting the actual location of the stars.

BASIC FORCES IN NATURE

There are four basic forces in nature: gravity, strong nuclear, weak interaction, and electromagnetic forces. All are now thought of as distortions in space-time.

Gravity is the weakest force but has an infinite range. It cannot be canceled by a "negative" force, the way electromagnetism can, or be negated after a short distance, like nuclear forces. Gravitational pull is proportional to the mass of the object exerting it. For example, gravity is stronger on Earth than the Moon because space-time is less curved around the Moon than around the Earth (the Moon has less mass than the Earth). Because of the lesser curvature, objects do not accelerate as fast when they fall on the Moon, which means the objects weigh less.

The *strong nuclear forces* hold particles in atoms' nuclei together. They are also thought to hold quarks—believed to be the basic building blocks of all atomic particles—together in a unit within a particle. However, the nuclear force falls to zero after a distance of only a few atomic diameters.

The *weak interaction* also applies at the subatomic level and is responsible for certain radioactive decay processes, such as beta-decay of the neutron.

Electromagnetic force is responsible for the interaction between electrical charges and magnets. Electromagnetic force holds electrons in orbit and can be positive or negative.

GRAND UNIFIED THEORIES

Electrostatic and magnetic attraction and repulsion were once thought to be separate forces. British scientist James Clerk Maxwell determined that they were really different aspects of one force, which he called electromagnetism. In the latter part of his career, Albert Einstein searched unsuccessfully for what he called a unified field theory that would extend the general theory of relativity to encompass electromagnetism along with gravitation. The strong nuclear and weak interactive forces were unknown at that time. In 1979 the Nobel Prize for physics was awarded to Sheldon Glashow, Steven Weinberg, and Aldus Salam for what they called the "electroweak theory," a set of equations linking electromagnetism and the weak interactive force. The theory has been confirmed by experiment.

FINDING GUT

Theoretical physicists continue to search for a theory that would link all four fundamental forces—gravity, strong nuclear, weak interaction, and electromagnetic forces—which would be called the grand unified theory (GUT) or the "theory of everything."

The most promising candidates are "string theories," which propose that subatomic particles are not pointlike but are strings so tiny that they appear to us as points. It is thought that these strings vibrate at different frequencies, like a violin string playing different notes, and each different vibration is seen in our world as a different particle.

Recent versions of "superstring theories" propose that the strings vibrate in at least 10 dimensions—9 of space and 1 of time—and perhaps as many as 25 dimensions. It is thought that these dimensions existed in the first few moments after the creation of the universe (the Big Bang), but that as the universe cooled, they collapsed and became virtually invisible. They exist at the atomic scale, but disappear when viewed from far away.

None of these theories has yet been confirmed by experiment, and some of them offer no predictions that can easily be tested. Many of them propose that the proton—previously thought to be stable—will decay with a half-life many orders of magnitude longer than the lifetime of the universe. Experiments have been conducted to detect proton decay, but so far it has not been seen. Other theories predict the existence of new particles, which no one knows how to detect.

HEAT AND TEMPERATURE

Perceived heat is the kinetic energy of molecules. For example, when a fuel is burned, chemical energy is released, as combustion sets the molecules of gas into more vigorous motion. When an iron bar is heated, the moving molecules in the flame bump into molecules in the bar, setting them in motion and making the bar "hot." If you touch the bar, its moving molecules cause the molecules in your skin to move, activating nerves that send a signal to your brain. The signals are interpreted as heat, while the breakdown they cause in the chemical structure of your skin proteins causes a burn.

Heat is a measure of the total kinetic energy of all the molecules in a system. A common measure of heat is the calorie, defined as the amount of energy required to raise the temperature of 1 gram of water by 1°C. This should not be confused with the "calorie" used to measure the energy content of food, in which 1 calorie of food contains enough energy to generate 1,000 calories of heat.

Temperature is the measure of the average kinetic energy of the molecules of a system. There are many different temperature scales. Most are based on the temperatures at which water boils and freezes.

Common Temperature Scales

Two temperature scales are commonly used in everyday life; another, Kelvin or absolute temperature, is used mainly in science (for more information on temperature scales, see Chapter 1, "Scientific Measurements").

Celsius (formerly called centigrade) temperatures are measured on a scale in which the melting point of ice is designated as 0°C and the boiling point of water as 100°C. Between the boiling and freezing points, the scale is divided into 100 parts. It is named after Anders Celsius.

Fahrenheit temperatures are measured on a scale where water boils at 212°F and freezes at 32°F. The Fahrenheit scale was developed by Gabriel Daniel Fahrenheit.

Kelvin temperatures are sometimes called absolute temperatures. A Kelvin degree is equivalent to a Celsius degree, but the scale is adjusted so that zero represents absolute zero, the temperature at which all molecular motion ceases. On this scale, water freezes at about 273°K and boils at about 373°K. The scale is named after the nineteenth-century British scientist Lord Kelvin (born William Thomson).

Absolute Zero

Absolute zero is the theoretical temperature where all molecular motion stops, or approximately −459.67°F (−273.16°C). This temperature has never been reached in the laboratory. It is thought that it can never be reached because the methods of measuring such temperatures change the temperature of the system; in addition, even if molecular motion ceases, the atomic particles still vibrate, thus changing the temperature. However, scientists have achieved temperatures within about a millionth of a degree of absolute zero.

Thermodynamics

Thermodynamics studies the dynamics of heat, or the flow, production, and conversion of heat energy into work. It arose from the study of steam engines, cannons, and other "heat engines" that convert heat into mechanical work. The results of that work had far-reaching implications in other branches of science and even in philosophy.

Four Laws of Thermodynamics

The four laws of thermodynamics were developed during the nineteenth and early twentieth centuries (the most recent law is called the "zero law," since it was formulated after the first law had been well established).

0. No heat flows between any two bodies that are at the same temperature.

1. When heat is converted to work, the process is never totally efficient, e.g., when steam drives a piston, most of the heat energy in the steam is converted to mechanical energy but some is wasted heating up the sides of the cylinder. In narrow terms, the first law of thermodynamics states that the energy used in doing work will be equal to the amount of work done, plus the heat lost in the process. The broader law of conservation of energy—that energy cannot be created or destroyed—was derived from this idea. This law was independently discovered by three or four people around the same time, although James Joule was probably first.

2. Heat will always flow "downhill," i.e., from an object having a higher temperature to one having a lower temperature; thus it is impossible for heat to flow spontaneously from an object with a lower temperature to one with a higher temperature, and work must be done to transfer heat energy from a lower temperature to a higher temperature. The law was discovered by Rudolf J. E. Clausius (1850), although many others came close to proposing the law as early as 1824.

3. A temperature of absolute zero—believed to be the lowest possible temperature in the universe—is the point at which all molecular motion ceases. This law was discovered by Lord Kelvin in 1851.

Entropy

Since heat always flows "downhill," within a closed system everything will eventually reach the same temperature. For example, a warm mug of tea set on a cold table will pass heat to the table. Once the mug and table are the same temperature, no more work can be extracted from the mug. The molecules of the system (mug and table) are more disordered than initially and cannot be made more orderly without an injection of energy from the outside.

In mathematical and physical terms, a system in which everything is at the same temperature is considered "orderly," and higher temperatures introduce "disorder." The term *entropy* is the quantitative measure of the relative disorder of a system. When work is done, the total entropy of the system increases. This principle applies to all kinds of energy. Some scientists believe that the energy in the universe will eventually be distributed evenly and irrevocably, creating a condition of universal entropy—or the "heat death" of the universe.

GETTING TO KNOW SUPERCONDUCTIVITY

When certain metals such as lead or mercury are cooled to temperatures very near absolute zero, they exhibit a phenomenon known as superconductivity, where they lose almost all resistance to the flow of electric current. If a current is set moving in a closed loop of superconducting wire, the current will continue to flow indefinitely.

Superconductors are used to make very powerful electromagnets for particle accelerators. Someday, they may be used to build trains that float above their tracks on magnetic fields, allowing them to travel at very high speed because of the reduced friction. Superconductors also may be used to build superfast computers.

Until recently, the highest temperature at which any known superconductor would operate was around 22°K, or 22 degrees above absolute zero. Such superconductors must be cooled by immersing them in liquid helium, which boils at about 4°K. Unfortunately, liquid helium is expensive and in fairly short supply. Recently, new ceramic materials have been found that become superconducting at temperatures up to around 70°K. These can be cooled with liquid nitrogen, which is much cheaper and more abundant.

So far these new materials have not been able to carry as much current as metal superconductors, and because they are ceramics, they have been difficult to form into wires. Eventually, superconductors may be cooled with conventional refrigeration equipment. But the real dream is to find superconductors that function at room temperature.

WAVES

Parts of a Wave

Besides electromagnetic and sound waves, there are also physical waves, such as seismic waves and ocean waves (for more information on seismic and ocean waves, see Chapter 9, "Earth Science"). Sound and electromagnetic waves are usually rhythmic, meaning they have a repeating pattern. A common pattern is a "sine wave," where the amplitude can be depicted as a rolling up-and-down pattern like a side view of ripples in a pond. A sound wave that fits a sine wave pattern would sound like a continuous musical tone. On the other hand, a "square wave," in which the amplitude jumps suddenly up and down, would sound like an annoying buzz. Waves may also be brief, nonrepeating bursts, such as the shock wave from an explosion or the sonic boom created by a supersonic aircraft.

Certain terms are used to describe all waves; these are defined below.

Frequency is the number of complete waves (or oscillations) that occur over a given time period. Frequency is usually measured in cycles per second. For example, if 10 wave crests pass a point in 1 second, the frequency would be 10 cycles per second. The term *Hertz* (Hz, named for physicist Heinrich Hertz, who first generated electromagnetic radiation) also defines the cycles; a frequency of 100 cycles per second is stated as 100 Hertz. A kilohertz (kHz) is 1,000 cycles per second; a megahertz (mHz) is 1 million cycles per second.

The *wave crest* is the highest point of a wave. The *wave trough* is the lowest point of a wave.

A *period* is the time it takes for one complete wave oscillation to occur. If 10 wave crests pass a point in 1 second, the period would be 0.1 second.

Wavelength is the distance from any point on a wave to an identical point on the next wave. The lower the frequency, the longer the wavelength. Very low frequency radio waves can measure more than 6 miles (9.7 kilometers) from crest to crest. FM and television broadcasting waves can measure from 1 to 10 yards (0.91 to 9.1 meters). Light waves measure less than 1 millionth of a meter.

Amplitude is the maximum displacement of any part of the wave from its balanced (or equilibrium) condition. It is also the height of the crests and troughs of a wave: The taller the crests and troughs, the higher the amplitude; the shorter the crests and troughs, the lower the amplitude. Amplitude does not affect wave velocity. The energy transmitted by the wave is proportional to the amplitude squared.

Diagram of a Wave

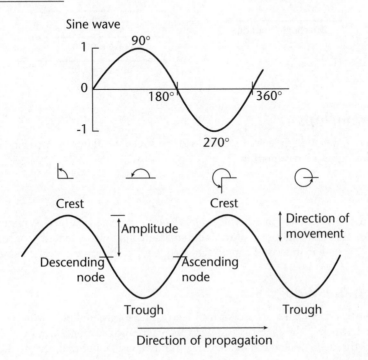

Wave Properties

A wave is a disturbance that moves through a medium without causing the medium itself to move significantly. No particle carrying the wave ever moves far from its original position. For example, when a stone is dropped in a pond, a piece of wood in the direct path of the ripples radiating from the disturbance will simply bob up and down. Different types of waves cause particles in the medium to move in different ways.

Longitudinal waves cause particles to oscillate, or move back and forth around a center, along a line in the direction the waves are moving. Sound waves are longitudinal waves.

In *transverse waves*, individual particles move perpendicular to the direction of the advancing waves. Water waves are transverse, as is all electromagnetic radiation. Transverse waves are said to be polarized when the particle disturbance occurs in only one direction, perpendicular to the direction the wave is traveling. Some waves are combinations of longitudinal and transverse waves.

Transverse and Longitudinal Wave Motions

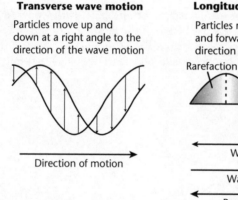

Transverse wave motion

Particles move up and down at a right angle to the direction of the wave motion

Direction of motion

Longitudinal wave motion

Particles move backwards and forwards in the same direction as the wave motion

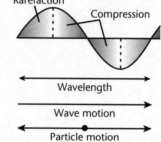

Rarefaction

Compression

Wavelength

Wave motion

Particle motion

Wave Relationships

The frequency, wavelength, velocity, and period of waves are all interrelated, and these relationships can be expressed by equations.

$$v = \frac{\lambda}{T} \quad \text{or} \quad v = \lambda f$$

where v (the Greek letter nu) is the wave velocity measured in feet or meters per second, λ (the Greek letter lambda) is the wavelength measured in units of length, T is the period of the wave usually measured in seconds, and f is the frequency of the wave in cycles per second (Hertz).

Electromagnetic Waves

Electromagnetic waves consist of oscillating electric and magnetic fields, which radiate outward at the speed of light. The spectrum of electromagnetic waves ranges from very low frequency radio waves through AM and FM radio, radar, infrared, visible light, ultraviolet light, x-rays and gamma-rays. All these types of radiation are produced when energy is given off by subatomic particles.

The Electromagnetic Spectrum

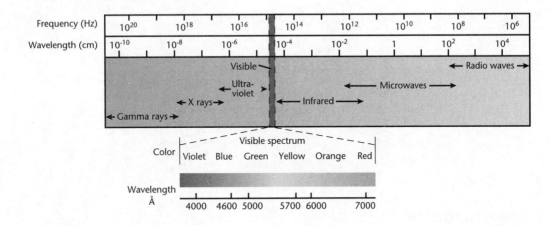

Interference

When two waves overlap, a phenomenon called *interference* results. If the crests and troughs of the two waves coincide, they will reinforce each other and produce a wave with a larger amplitude (in the case of light, manifest as increased brightness). If the crest of one wave coincides with the trough of the other, the two waves may cancel each other.

ON THE RADIO

The numbers on your radio dial represent frequencies. AM radio operates between about 525 and 1,700 kiloHertz (525,000 and 1,700,000 cycles per second); the FM band extends from 88 to 108 megaHertz (88,000,000 to 108,000,000 cycles per second). VHF television channels extend above and below the FM band. UHF channels are higher, at about 470 to 890 megaHertz; cable television adds channels at about 174 to 216 megaHertz, and others above the VHF TV bands. One CB radio band is between 460 and 470 megaHertz, which explains why we sometimes get CB interference on our television sets.

What Is Light?

Light is a form of electromagnetic radiation released by various sources, such as the Sun and other stars, flames, and light bulbs. The light that we see with the human eye spans only a small part of the whole electromagnetic spectrum; visible light has wavelengths from 0.75 to 0.40 micrometer (1 micrometer is equal to 0.001 millimeter). Radiation above 0.75 millimeter, the infrared part of the spectrum, is perceived only as heat by humans. Wavelengths shorter than 0.40 millimeter are called ultraviolet radiation. (Ultraviolet is not perceived by human eyes, though some insects can see it. Excessive amounts of ultraviolet radiation can cause tanning, sunburning, and cell damage to the human skin.)

Humans perceive different wavelengths of the visible spectrum as different colors. From the long wavelength end of the spectrum to the smaller wavelengths, the colors we see are red, orange, yellow, green, blue, indigo, and violet. The combination of all colors gives white light; the absence of all color is seen as black.

Dispersion of Color: White Light Through a Prism

Prism Spectrum

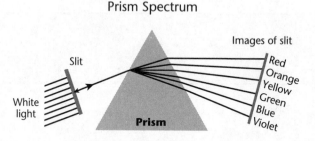

LIGHTEN UP!

Objects may emit light in two ways. Thermal radiation (or incandescence) is associated with an object's temperature; "cold light" (or luminescence) is produced by chemical action. When a living organism generates light it is called *bioluminescence*.

Bioluminescence is common among organisms in the ocean. Certain types of plankton often light up the upper levels of the ocean with a blue glow and some fish found deep in the oceans also exhibit bioluminescence. On land, fireflies "shine" on and off during breeding season and certain mushrooms glow in the dark. This bioluminescence is usually used for defense, to attract a mate, or in the case of the mushroom, to spread seeds.

In nonliving matter, luminescence can result when a substance is exposed to electron bombardment, electromagnetic radiation, or electric fields. Energy from any of these sources may be absorbed by certain atoms, then released as light. Fluorescence, common in many rocks, is the emission of light when atoms are excited by certain types of radiation, especially ultraviolet (commonly called "black light"). Phosphorescence is a similar process, resulting either from absorption of light or from chemical action. Fluorescence takes longer to start and continues for some time after the excitation stops. A familiar example is a glow-in-the-dark clock face that lights up only after the face paint has been exposed to light.

REFLECTION AND REFRACTION

Electromagnetic waves travel though space in a straight line, unless forced to deviate from that line. Not all waves deviate to the same degree by the same forces. For example, visible light changes direction when it strikes certain surfaces (a mirror) or the boundary between media of different densities (air and water), but gamma radiation will pass through these surfaces.

Reflection is the rebounding of light from a surface. Most objects are visible because of light reflected off them. Smooth surfaces such as clean glass, reflect light back to the observer in parallel rays, which is called regular reflection. Surfaces that are not smooth reflect light to the observer in many different directions, which is called diffuse reflection. For example, the uneven surface of paper (compared with glass or polished silver) exhibits diffuse reflection.

Refraction is the bending of light waves when they pass from one medium to another. If the velocity of light is different in the two media, the wave deviates from its original path. The amount of bending depends on the media involved and the frequency of the light. A pencil sticking partly in and partly out of a glass of water looks bent at the water's surface; this is because the light rays traveling from the pencil to the eye are refracted where they emerge from the water. Air and water have different densities, and the velocity of light is thus different in each.

The ratio of the velocity change is called the *index of refraction*. The index is defined as equal to 1 in a vacuum. For any other medium it is defined as the velocity of light in a vacuum divided by the velocity of light in the medium. The index of refraction in air is close to 1 (since the velocity of light traveling in a vacuum and in air are very similar); in water, it is 1.33 (in other words, light travels faster in a vacuum than through water).

The *angle of refraction* also depends on the light's frequency. Different frequencies diffract at slightly different angles. This phenomenon is called *dispersion*. The most familiar example is the dispersion of white light into a spectrum of colors when it is passed through a prism. Sometimes after a rainstorm, sunlight is refracted, reflected, and refracted again in droplets of water, and the resulting dispersion causes a rainbow (for more information on rainbows, see Chapter 10, "Meteorology").

Reflection and Refraction of Light

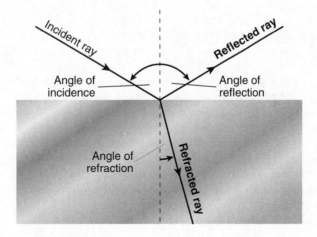

DIAMONDS AND FIBER OPTICS

When light strikes the boundary between a medium with a very high index of refraction and another with a very low index, the light is often totally reflected and none refracted—in other words, it remains inside the medium in which it is traveling. This phenomena is called total internal reflection. For example, a diamond exhibits internal reflection, which gives the gem its brilliance. A light source at the bottom of a fountain exploits the same effect—the light is trapped inside the streams of water, giving the fountain a sparkling glow.

Perhaps the most interesting example of internal reflection can be found in fiber optic cables. Light travels long distances inside these strands of plastic or glass, bouncing off the outer boundary even when the cables bend. Fiber optics are replacing copper wire in telephone lines and are being used to construct new types of computers in which circuits carry pulses of light instead of electrons.

SOUND WAVES

Sound waves move through air, water, or solids as a series of compressions and rarefactions. For example, a loudspeaker rapidly vibrates forward and backward in response to the electrical signals it receives. When it moves forward it compresses the air; when it moves backward it expands the air. These alternating compressions and expansions travel through the air to the eardrum. The eardrum translates the varying pressures of the sound waves into signals that are interpreted by the brain as sounds.

Several terms are used to measure sound (for details about decibel and pitch ranges, see Chapter 1, "Scientific Measurements").

The *amplitude* is the distance between the height of a crest and the depth of a trough of a sound wave.

A *decibel* (dB) is a unit of measurement of sound intensity. The faintest sound is 0 decibel; a sound of about 130 decibels produces pain in humans. The measurements are not linear but are logarithmic, meaning that a sound of 11 decibels has a sound wave with an amplitude 10 times as large as that for a sound of 10 decibels, although an increase of 1 decibel is heard by the human ear as approximately a doubling of volume.

Intensity is the rate of energy transfer per unit area of a wave front or the loudness of a sound. The greater the amplitude, the louder the sound.

Pitch is the frequency, or number of cycles per second, of a sound. The ear interprets this as the highness or lowness of the sound.

Resonance is a phenomenon that occurs when two objects naturally vibrate at the same frequency; the sound produced by one object causes the other to vibrate. For example, if two tuning forks tuned to the same frequency are held close together and one is struck, the other will begin to vibrate. Solid objects or columns of air tuned to vibrate at certain frequencies form the basis of most musical instruments. Acoustic resonances are also found in the human body, in which the structures of the head and throat give the voice its tone. Resonance can also produce problems. For example, wind can cause vibrations to build up in a steel bridge. As parts of it begin to resonate, it produces a mechanical resonance that can eventually rupture the structural integrity of the bridge.

Speed of Sound

Although electromagnetic waves can travel through a vacuum, sound waves cannot and need some type of matter as a carrier. Their speed is affected by the density of the substance through which they pass, as well as by its temperature: At higher temperatures, the velocity of sound waves increases. The speed of sound in different media and at room temperature (about 72°F [20°C]) is listed below.

Carbon dioxide	877 feet (267 meters) per second
Air	1,126 feet (343 meters) per second
Hydrogen	4,315 feet (1,315 meters) per second
Water	4,820 feet (1,469 meters) per second

Brass	11,500 feet (3,505 meters) per second
Granite	12,960 feet (3,950 meters) per second
Iron or steel	16,800 feet (5,121 meters) per second

Whenever the speed of a source exceeds the speed of the sound wave, a shock wave is formed. For example, a jet plane that exceeds the speed of sound creates a sonic boom, which is a shock wave of compressed air ahead of the plane (for more information on sonic booms, see Chapter 1, "Scientific Measurements").

The Doppler Effect

A change in sound wave frequency results when the source and the observer are in relative motion. For example, when an ambulance approaches a stationary observer with its siren blasting, the sound waves compress as the vehicle comes closer, and the pitch of the siren rises; as the ambulance passes, the waves begin to spread out, and the pitch of the siren lowers. This change in pitch due to the movement of the sound source relative to the observer is called the *Doppler effect*, named after Austrian physicist Christian Doppler.

The Doppler effect is applicable to all types of waves, including water, sound, and light waves. The Doppler effect is used in astronomy to determine whether a stellar object is moving toward or away from the Earth. A shift in the color of light to red indicates that the light source is moving away; a blue shift means the light source is approaching. The amount of red or blue shift reveals the velocity of the light source. Radar systems use the Doppler effect to measure the speed of an aircraft, the movement of clouds, and the speed of a car on the freeway.

ELECTRICITY

Electrostatics

All matter is composed of atoms, which in turn are composed of subatomic particles. Many of those particles possess a property called "charge," which may be positive or negative. The most familiar charged particles are electrons, which possess a negative charge, and protons, which possess a positive charge. Particles with the same charge repel one another, while particles with the opposite charge attract one another. Ordinarily, the electrons and protons in an atom are in balance, and the atom has no net charge. Sometimes electrons are pulled free from atoms, creating an excess of negative charge in one place and an excess of positive charge in another. This often happens when two materials are rubbed together, transferring electrons from one to another. The result is "static electricity," which results, for example, when you walk across a wool rug wearing leather shoes.

In the eighteenth century, Charles Coulomb determined that positive and negative electric charges attract one another and that like charges repel one another with a force that is proportional to the amount of charge and diminishes with the square of the distance. This is called Coulomb's law in honor of Coulomb, and electric charge is now measured in units called *coulombs*.

If negative and positive charges are separated, an electrical potential energy is created. This potential is also called *voltage*, representing the amount of work it would take to move the charge between two points. When separated electric charges are allowed to move, they create an *electric current*; the current is the rate of flow of the electric charge.

Electric Current

An *electric current* consists of charged particles—most often electrons—moving through a conductor. The electrons in some atoms, such as copper and aluminum, are free to move and to jump from one atom to another. Such materials are called *conductors*; other materials, such as wood, do not contain as many moving electrons, and are called *insulators*. When a material is neither completely a conductor nor an insulator, it is called a *semiconductor*.

When an electric current moves continuously in one direction, it is called a *direct current*. When the current fluctuates rapidly back and forth it is called an *alternating current*. Alternating current is used in almost all worldwide household wiring today. Direct current is commonly seen in battery-operated devices. It is a convention to say that direct current flows from the positive terminal of a battery to the negative—however we know that the current actually consists of electrons flowing from the negative terminal to the positive (the convention of negative and positive was set up long before the discovery of electrons).

Several units of measure are used in connection with electricity (for more information on electrical units, see Chapter 1, "Scientific Measurements"); some of these are listed below.

amp The amp, short for ampere, is the amount of electric current flowing in a wire. The electric current is measured in electrons per second.

ohm The ohm is a measure of resistance to current. The higher the resistance at a given voltage, the less current flows. Higher resistance can be obtained by using thinner wires or by using materials that are poorer conductors.

volt The volt is a measure of the potential energy of the source or the "pressure" pushing electrons through the wire.

watt A watt is a unit of electric power or the speed at which an electric current can do work. Wattage multiplied by time gives the amount of work an appliance is capable of producing (and, therefore, the amount of energy it uses to do work). This energy is expressed in units called watt-hours, which is what we usually refer to in everyday speech when we say "watts." A 100-watt light bulb, operating for 1 hour, uses 100 watt-hours. Electricity used in the home is usually metered in kilowatt-hours, or thousands of watt-hours.

Turning on a Light

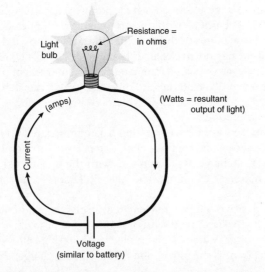

Ohm's Law—Formulas

Electric Symbols and Units of Measure

Electric Quantity	Letter in Formula	Unit of Measure	Unit Symbol
Voltage	V	Volts	V
Current	I	Amps	A
Resistance	R	Ohms	Ω
Power	P	Watts	W

Ohm's Law

Formula with letter symbols	$V = I \times R$
Formula with electrical quantities	voltage = current × resistance
Formula with units of measure	volts = amps × ohms
Formula with unit symbols	$V = A \times \Omega$

Kilowatts Used by Common Appliances

Appliance	Kilowatt Per Hour
Light bulb	0.001 (per watt)
Stereo	0.10
Color television	0.23
Washer	0.25
Coffee maker	0.60
Vacuum cleaner	0.75
Iron	1.00
Dishwasher	1.00
Toaster	1.20
Oven	1.30
Air-conditioner (1,500 watts)	1.50
Hair dryer	1.50
Microwave oven	1.50
Clothes dryer	4.00
Refrigerator/freezer (16 cubic feet)	5.00
Frostless freezer	5.10
Refrigerator/freezer (22 cubic feet)	7.00

MAGNETISM

A *magnetic field* is a field of attractive or repulsive forces generated by moving or spinning electric charges. A magnetic field can be described as a set of imaginary lines that indicate the direction a compass needle would point to at a particular spot. These are called *lines of force*. Magnets have a south and north pole. The north pole attracts the south pole, while like poles repel. The strength of the attraction or repulsion depends on the strength of the magnetic field, and is inversely proportional to the distance between the magnetic poles.

In some atoms, the moving electric charges generate a tiny magnetic field (a field with a north and south pole); in some materials, most notably iron, nickel, and cobalt (known as ferromagnetic materials), atoms can be aligned to the north and south poles to produce a large magnetic field. For example, if a known magnet is moved along a piece of soft iron, the iron atoms will be drawn into alignment and the iron will also become magnetized. Magnetism was first observed in naturally occurring materials such as the ore magnetite, which contains a great deal of iron that sometimes becomes magnetized by the Earth's magnetic field.

A magnetic field can also be generated by an electric current. When a current flows through a coil of wire wrapped around a piece of soft iron, the iron is magnetized. When the current is turned off, the magnetism ceases. This is called an *electromagnet*. Electromagnets were commonly used in telephone ringers and are still used in such devices as doorbells (for more information, see "Electromagnetism," below).

Magnetic Lines of Force

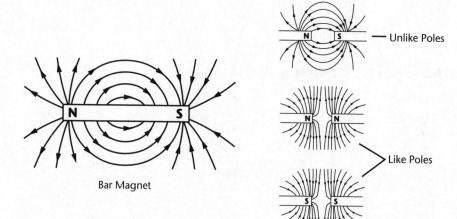

Bar Magnet

Unlike Poles

Like Poles

ELECTROMAGNETISM

Moving and spinning electric charges create magnetic fields; conversely, a moving magnetic field sets charges in motion, generating an electric current. This principle makes electric motors, generators, and transformers possible. For example, in an electric motor, magnetic fields generated by electric currents push against one another, causing a shaft to rotate. In a generator, a rotating shaft moves a magnetic field, causing electrons to move in a wire and generate electric current (an electric motor and a generator are really just the same device in reverse). In a transformer, a fluctuating electric current in a coil of wire (say 220 volts) creates a moving magnetic field, which in turn generates another fluctuating current (110 volts, for example) in another coil of wire. The difference in voltage is caused by using different-size coils.

Maxwell's Equations

In the 1870s, Scottish physicist James Clerk Maxwell wrote four equations that summarize the relationship between electricity and magnetism (Maxwell did not discover the underlying principles). The equations showed the following.

1. Unlike charges attract each other; like charges repel (also called Coulomb's Law).

2. There are no single, isolated magnetic poles (if there is a north, there will be an equivalent south pole).

3. Electrical currents can cause magnetic fields.

4. Changing magnetic fields can cause electrical currents.

Maxwell showed mathematically that an oscillating electric and magnetic field would propagate through space at the speed of light, demonstrating that light was, in fact, a form of electromagnetic radiation. Like other scientists of his time, Maxwell still believed that light moved as waves in a mysterious substance called the ether, but ultimately his equations led to the conclusion that there was no ether.

PARTICLES OF THE UNIVERSE

Physics of the Atom

The atom's name comes from the Greek word *atomos*, meaning "indivisible." As early as 5 B.C. it was proposed that all matter was composed of tiny particles called atoms, which could not be further broken down (for more information on atoms and molecules, see Chapter 6, "Chemistry").

Ernest Rutherford was the first to show that the atom is not the smallest unit of matter. In the early twentieth century, Rutherford observed alpha-particles—one result of radioactive decay—with the use of a simple particle detector. When a sheet of metal was placed in the path of a stream of particles, they were deflected. Rutherford correctly concluded that the atoms of the metal had a positively charged nucleus that would repel the positively charged alpha-particles (like charges repel). He also determined that the nucleus was surrounded by negatively charged electrons.

Models of Atoms

Atoms are held together by the attraction of negative and positive charges. The simplest atom is hydrogen (the lightest and most prevalent atom in the universe), whose nucleus is a single positively charged proton; a single negatively charged electron orbits the nucleus. The nuclei of heavier atoms also contain particles called neutrons, which have the mass of a proton but no electrical charge. The heaviest atom that naturally occurs on the Earth is uranium, which has 92 protons and 92 electrons, along with a varying number of neutrons, most often 146.

For years, the proton, neutron, and electron were thought to be fundamental particles. Electrons are still considered fundamental particles, but protons and neutrons are now known to be triplets of more basic particles called quarks (see "Subatomic Particles," later in this chapter).

Many models of the atom have been suggested. Niels Bohr's and Erwin Schrödinger's models are the two most important. In *Bohr's model* of the atom developed in 1913, electrons circle the nucleus in fixed orbits, arranged in successive shells around the nucleus. The farther the orbit from the nucleus, the greater the energy of the electrons. If an electron moves to a different orbit, it either absorbs or emits radiation in definite amounts (or quanta) equal to the energy difference between the orbits. The energy released is inversely related to the wavelength of the radiation; thus blue light, which has a short wavelength, has a higher energy than red light (which has a longer wavelength). (For more information on atomic models, see Chapter 6, "Chemistry".)

Schrödinger's model of the atom, developed in 1926, replaced Bohr's model, mainly because of Einstein's explanation of light as streams of particles (or photons, also called "wavicles") and waves, which led to the ideas of quantum mechanics and the uncertainty principle (see "The Uncertainty Principle," later in this chapter). Because the uncertainty principle precludes our knowing the precise location of any given electron, the new model uses indistinct and overlapping "probability clouds" to define the position of the electrons. Where a cloud is dense, the probability of finding an electron is high. Several other researchers developed a similar model around the same time; it is often called the *charge-cloud* model.

Isotopes

The chemical properties of an atom are determined by the number and arrangement of its electrons, which is determined by the number of positively charged protons in its nucleus. Atoms of some elements exist in several forms, each having the same number of protons in its nucleus but different numbers of neutrons.

These different forms of an atom are called *isotopes*. All isotopes of the same element will have similar chemical properties, but they may behave differently physically: Some, for example, may be radioactive while others are not. The number of protons in a nucleus is called the atomic number of the element. The total number of protons and neutrons is called the atomic mass. Thus uranium has an atomic number of 92, but is found in several isotopes, the two most important having atomic masses of 238 (isotope ^{238}U, 92 protons and 146 neutrons) and 235 (isotope ^{235}U, 92 protons and 143 neutrons).

Radioactivity

The nuclei of some heavy atoms are unstable. Occasionally, they convert some of their mass into energy, ejecting it in the form of a particle or a photon of radiation. Such atoms are called *radioactive*. All elements with atomic numbers above 82 are naturally radioactive; additional radioactive isotopes have been artificially created. A radioactive atom may emit an *alpha-particle*, which consists of two protons and two neutrons (making it identical to the nucleus of a helium atom); a *beta-particle*, which is an electron; or a *gamma-ray*, which is a highly energetic photon (for more information on radioactivity, see Chapter 6, "Chemistry").

The loss of mass turns the atom into a different element. For example, an atom of uranium may emit an alpha-particle and decay into an atom of thorium (other decays are possible for uranium). Thorium is also radioactive and can decay into palladium. The decay will continue through many steps (and generally over a period of years) until an atom of nonradioactive lead results.

There is no way to know when any particular atom will decay, but by observing a large number of atoms of a particular element, the decay rate over a certain period can be statistically predicted. The rate of decay of an element is stated as its *half-life*, which is the time it will take for half the atoms to decay. Each element has a unique half-life. For example, uranium-238 has a half-life of about 4.5 billion years; thorium-234 has a half-life of about 24 days; and tellurium-206 has a half-life of 4.2 minutes.

ANTIPARTICLES IN THE UNIVERSE

Every particle is known to have an antiparticle with properties opposite those of the particle (except when the particle and antiparticle are identical—an antineutron is still neutral in charge). For example, the antiparticle of the negatively charged electron is the positron, which has the mass of an electron but a positive charge; an antiproton has the mass of a proton but a negative charge.

It is theoretically possible that somewhere in the universe there might be stars and planets composed entirely of "antimatter," in which atoms would have a negatively charged nucleus surrounded by positrons. If a particle collides with its antiparticle, the two will annihilate each other, producing a burst of energy—and this would also be true if antimatter, i.e., antiatoms or antimolecules, came in contact with normal matter.

Subatomic Particles

In the early view of the atom, only three *subatomic particles* existed: protons, neutrons and electrons. In the last half of the twentieth century, dozens of new particles have been discovered. Machines called particle accelerators (popularly known as "atom smashers") use powerful magnetic and electric fields to push atoms and subatomic particles to tremendous speeds—sometimes approaching the speed of light. This imparts enormous energy to the particles, and when they are allowed to smash into atoms or other particles, the energy is converted to mass, creating a variety of particles.

Each particle has a certain function in the subatomic world. For example, some help to hold the nucleus of the atom together; others are carried by particles, such as electromagnetism (which is carried by photons) and the strong force (which is carried by pions). Each particle can be described in terms of its mass, charge, and a property called "spin." Whether a "spinning" subatomic particle actually resembles a spinning ball in the macroscopic world is currently impossible to say, but the spin of a charged particle does produce a small magnetic field, known as the *magnetic moment of the particle*.

Current theory suggests that most of the different particles are made out of a few basic particles called *quarks*. Quarks possess various masses and have charges that are either one-third or two-thirds of a single positive or negative charge. They combine in twos or threes to form other particles, making it feasible to combine them in ways that produce a positive, negative, or neutral charge. For example, three one-third positive charges combine to produce one positive charge, as in a proton; while two one-third positive charges plus one two-thirds negative charge could combine to form a net charge of zero, as in a neutron. Some particles possess properties that have no counterpart in the everyday world, so physicists have assigned arbitrary names such as "color," "charm," "strangeness," and "beauty" to these properties.

Subatomic particles, although all of these have not been observed, are often divided into the following groups.

Fermions

Electrons, muons, tauons, neutrinos, quarks (called leptons or elementary particles)
Baryons: protons, neutrons, two hyperons, three sigmas, two xis, and an omega

Bosons

Bosons made from quarks: mesons (π meson, k meson, others)
Bosons not made from quarks: gluons, photons, positive and negative W particles, neutral Z particles, Higgs particle, graviton

The following is a partial list of subatomic particles.

alpha-particle   An alpha-particle is the nucleus of a helium-4 atom.

baryon   Any hadron that contains one proton in its final set of decay products is a baryon.

beta-particle   An electron is a beta-particle.

electron   An electron is the negatively charged particle surrounding an atomic nucleus.

hadron   A hadron is any particle that participates in strong interactions.

heavy leptons   Heavy leptons have properties similar to the electron or neutrino but are more massive.

Higgs particle   A Higgs particle helps give mass to W and Z particles.

lepton   A lepton, like the electron, muon, and neutrino, participates in the weak interactions but not in the strong forces.

meson   Originally, a meson was any particle with a mass between that of the electron and proton; in modern terms, it is a particle formed from two quarks.

mu-neutrino   The mu-neutrino is given off in the decay of the muon.

muon   A muon has a negative charge like an electron.

neutrino   A neutrino is a zero-mass (though many scientists question whether it has a low mass that is yet undetectable), uncharged particle emitted in the process of beta decay.

neutron   A neutron has approximately the same mass as a proton but is uncharged.

photon   A photon is a particle associated with light.

pion   A pion holds the nucleus of an atom together, producing the strong force.

positron   The positron is the antiparticle of the electron.

proton   The proton is the massive, positively charged particle in an atomic nucleus; it is the nucleus of the hydrogen atom.

quarks   Quarks are believed to be the basic constituent of the elementary particles. All quarks combine to equal charges that are zero or whole number multiples of the electron's charge. The six quarks (along with their previous whimsical names) are strange quark, top quark (truth), up quark, bottom quark (beauty), charm quark (C quark), and down quark. It is not thought that quarks can exist as separate entities.

tachyons   Tachyons are hypothetical particles that move faster than the speed of light.

W boson   The W boson (or positive and negative W particles) is exchanged in beta decay and other weak interactions (it was observed in the early 1980s).

NEUTRINO DETECTORS

Neutrinos are passing through you even as you read this text. These particles carry no electrical charge, have either no mass or a very small mass, and travel at the speed of light. Neutrinos seldom interact with any other matter, and they are very difficult to detect.

When neutrinos collide with the nuclei of some atoms, however, a reaction may occur that results in the release of a photon of radiation, which may be detectable. In one experiment designed to detect neutrinos from the Sun, huge vats filled with an organic solvent (essentially cleaning fluid) have been placed in deep underground salt mines where interference from other particles will be minimal. Scientists have detected neutrinos; when a neutrino strikes atoms of the cleaning fluid head on, light can be seen and recorded by radiation detectors.

Another type of detector to find stellar-induced neutrinos is located in the ocean off Hawaii. The Deep Underwater Muon and Neutrino Detector (DUMAND) project uses long lines of special detectors spread over the ocean floor. The arrays of detectors—with a diameter of 340 feet (104 meters) and sensor strings rising to a height of about 1,100 feet (335 meters)—are used to catch the spark of a neutrino as it runs vertically through the oceans. The Earth acts as a gigantic filter, blocking the noise of cosmic rays and other unwanted forms of radiation from space, down to a level where neutrinos are detectable. But even under these nearly ideal conditions, finding the elusive neutrino will be like looking for the proverbial needle in a haystack.

NUCLEAR PHYSICS

Fission—Nuclear Power and Chain Reactions

Certain heavy, unstable atoms can be split by *fission*. For example, uranium-235 will split when it absorbs a neutron. The result is two or more lighter atoms whose mass totals less than that of the original atom; the missing mass is converted to heat and kinetic energy. The reaction also liberates more neutrons. Thus, if other U-235 atoms are nearby, these new neutrons can cause more fission, resulting in a "chain reaction."

In a nuclear bomb, the chain reaction rapidly proceeds, creating an explosion. In a nuclear power plant the speed of the reaction is carefully controlled to produce a steady supply of heat that can be used to produce steam to drive electric generators. Some of the radioactive fission products produced in these reactors are also used for medical applications and scientific research.

Some reactors contain heavy water, which slows down fast neutrons and controls the chain reactions. Normally, hydrogen atoms in regular water have one proton each in their nuclei, but 1 in 5,000 hydrogen atoms has a neutron in its nucleus as well, making it twice as heavy. This heavy hydrogen is called deuterium (the nucleus of a heavy hydrogen atom is called a deuteron) and is used to make heavy water, or deuterium oxide, which is about 10 times denser than regular water.

HOW BIG IS THE ATOM?

Everything in the universe is composed of atoms—yet atoms are almost entirely empty space. The reason is that 99.9 percent of an atom's mass is concentrated in its nucleus: If the atom were the size of a basketball, its nucleus would still be invisible to the naked eye. If the nucleus were magnified to the size of a softball, the nearest electron (in the first shell) would be located about 0.5 mile (0.8 kilometer) away. In reality, atoms are about 1 angstrom (one-ten-billionth meter) in diameter.

Splitting the Atom

There are usually five types of nuclear reactions that may result when a particle collides with the nucleus of an atom. These are described below.

Neutron-induced reactions result in the formation of a heavier isotope of the bombarded element (which may lead to fission) or the emission of protons or alpha-particles.

Proton-induced reactions result in the formation of the next-higher element (an element with an atomic number that is one higher than the previously existing element).

Deuteron-induced reactions result in the formation of either protons, neutrons, or alpha-particles.

Alpha-particle-induced reactions result in the formation of either protons or neutrons.

Gamma-ray-induced reactions also result in the formation of either protons or neutrons.

NUCLEAR REACTIONS IN THE BACKYARD

Scientists believe that natural chain reactions occurred millions of years ago, when radioactive isotopes were relatively young. In the African country of Gabon between about 1 billion and 100,000 years ago, radioactive uranium experienced a spontaneous nuclear reaction. The evidence was found in 1972, when scientists noted that the concentration of the isotope uranium-235 in the ore from a mine was as low as 0.29 percent, whereas natural uranium contains about 0.72 percent. This suggested that the uranium's natural rate of decay had been sped up somehow; the most likely explanation is a natural nuclear chain reaction.

Such a reaction in your backyard (even if you live near radioactive rock) would be impossible today, mainly because the Earth is getting older. The ever-decreasing amounts of uranium-235 in natural ores are just too low to start a chain reaction.

Fusion—Thermonuclear Reactions

Nuclear *fusion* is the combining of atoms. Fusion reactions are classified as thermonuclear, because they occur only in the presence of great heat. It is believed that the Sun fuses lighter elements such as hydrogen into heavier ones, releasing energy in the form of heat and visible light. Fusion is also the basis of the thermonuclear, or hydrogen, bomb.

QUANTUM PHYSICS

Quanta

In 1900 the German physicist Max Planck proposed that light, heat, and other forms of radiation come in tiny bundles, which he called *quanta*. The amount of energy in a single particle, he said, depended on the frequency and can be given by the following equation.

$E = hv$

where v is the frequency of the wave and h is a constant that came to be called *Planck's constant*. Eventually, scientists came to think of that single bundle of energy as a particle called a *photon*.

Quantum Mechanics

The study of *quantum mechanics* looks at the structure and behavior of the atom and of subatomic particles from the view that all energy comes in tiny, indivisible bundles. An important illustration is the *photoelectric effect*: Light shining on certain materials will knock electrons loose from atoms (which makes photoelectric cells and solar batteries possible). Albert

Einstein proposed that a certain precise amount of energy was required to knock an electron loose from its orbit. A photon of sufficient energy (of a certain frequency or higher) could knock an electron loose, and the electron would fly off with a kinetic energy equal to the energy of the photon minus the bundle of energy needed to detach the electron from the atom. This was confirmed by experiments.

Later theories determined that each electron sits in a certain "energy state." An electron can move to a higher energy state only by absorbing a certain precise amount, or quantum, of energy, whereupon it makes a "*quantum jump*." An electron can drop to a lower state by throwing off energy in the form of a photon, and the energy of the photon—and, therefore, its frequency—will always be the same for the same change in energy state. This is what happens in fluorescence: Atoms of a fluorescent material absorb energy from ultraviolet light, exciting electrons to higher states. Some of the electrons fall back partway, releasing photons of visible light.

This also explains why every element emits characteristic wavelengths of light when heated: Some of the kinetic energy of the molecules that results from heating raises electrons in the atoms to higher energy levels, then they fall back, emitting light. The wavelengths that are emitted depend on the structure of the atom; these wavelengths can be used by scientists to identify the element. Instruments that use this process to identify elements are called spectrographs. Similar instruments are used to analyze the light from distant stars to determine their composition.

HOW LASERS WORK

The fact that an atom will emit a photon of radiation when one of its electrons drops to a lower energy state has made possible a powerful new tool—the laser, the acronym for light amplification by stimulated emission of radiation. In its simplest form, a laser consists of a rod of transparent crystal or a tube filled with gas or liquid. A mirror is placed at one end and a half-silvered mirror at the other. The laser is "pumped" by adding energy—for example, by shining another light source into it, by adding electrical energy, or by stimulating a chemical reaction. This raises electrons in the laser to higher energy states.

Some of the electrons will spontaneously fall back to a lower state, emitting photons. The photons that travel toward the sides of the laser are quickly lost, but those traveling along the length of the rod or tube are reflected back by the mirrors. When they strike other excited atoms, they stimulate those atoms to release photons of the exact same energy level (or wavelength), which travel in the same direction as the stimulating photons. The result is an intense, highly focused beam of light escaping through the half-silvered end of the laser.

Because the photon wavelength is determined by the characteristics of the atoms in the lasing material, laser light is of a single wavelength. And because it travels in a tight beam, it can carry a great deal of energy over a great distance without loss. Newer variations include electron lasers, in which photons are emitted when electrons are wiggled back and forth by magnetic fields, and solid state lasers that can be built into microchips. In addition to visible light, lasers can be made that produce infrared and ultraviolet radiation and even x-rays.

The Uncertainty Principle

Although light can be described as consisting of tiny particles called photons, it also behaves as if it consists of waves. It has been shown that all subatomic particles sometimes behave as if they were also waves, called de Broglie waves (pronounced *de-broylee*), after the physicist who first suggested their existence.

As a wave, a given particle cannot be precisely located. A graph of the wave can be seen only as a description of the probability that the particle is in a certain place at a certain time. This idea was stated by the German physicist Werner Heisenberg as the *uncertainty principle*: It is impossible to determine at the same time exactly where a particle is and how fast it is moving.

Heisenberg showed that the product of the uncertainty in position and the uncertainty in momentum (which is mass times velocity) would equal Planck's constant. Planck's constant is a very small number, so for fast-moving particles the uncertainty in position is extremely small. The uncertainty principle has been explained in physical terms by saying that any attempt to measure the position and velocity of a particle will disturb the particle. However, in some situations the uncertainty appears to have physical reality, for example, in electronic devices called tunnel diodes, electrons on one side of a barrier may appear on the other side because the barrier is thinner than the predicted uncertainty in position of the electrons.

Exclusion Principle

The Pauli exclusion principle states that two particles of a certain class, fermions, cannot be in the same exact energy state. The fermions include electrons, neutrons, and protons. Wolfgang Pauli devised the principle in 1925.

MAJOR PHYSICISTS

Alvarez, Luis Walter (1911–1988)   American physicist who greatly advanced the field of high particle physics; he was also the developer of the proton linear accelerator in 1946. He won the Nobel Prize in 1968. Alvarez and his son Walter, along with several others, first proposed the theory that massive extinctions around the Cretaceous-Tertiary time were caused by the impact of a large space object.

Ampère, André Marie (1775–1836)   French physicist and mathematician who laid the foundation of the science of electrodynamics and determined that electric currents produce magnetic fields.

Babinet, Jacques (1794–1872)   French physicist who first suggested using wavelengths of light to standardize measurements. His idea was used between 1960 and 1983, when a meter was defined as a wavelength of light from krypton gas.

Becquerel, Antoine Henri (1852–1908)   French physicist who discovered natural radioactivity produced by uranium.

Bohr, Niels Hendrik David (1885–1962)   Danish physicist who was the first to apply quantum theory to atomic structure and to note the connection between electronic energy levels and spectral lines. The Bohr atom and Bohr radius are named after him; he won the Nobel Prize in 1922.

Boltzmann, Ludwig Edward (1844–1906)   Austrian theoretical physicist who was the founder of statistical mechanics; he also worked out the kinetic theory of gases and developed a statistical interpretation of the second law of thermodynamics.

Born, Max (1882–1970)   German-born British physicist who is known for his work on the probability interpretation of quantum mechanics.

Bose, Satyendra Nath (1894–1974)   Indian physicist who worked out the boson particle's behavior with Albert Einstein. The boson is named after Bose.

Brewster, Sir David (1781–1868)   British physicist who worked on the polarization of light and discovered the law dealing with the relationship between the index of refraction and the angle of incidence at which reflected light becomes polarized.

Celsius, Anders (1701–1744)   Swedish astronomer who was the developer, in 1742, of the temperature scale that was named after him.

Chadwick, Sir James (1891–1974)   British physicist who is known for his studies in radiation and radiation particle behavior; he was the discoverer of the neutron.

Clausius, Rudolf Julius Emmanuel (1822–1888)   German physicist who discovered the second law of thermodynamics. He also developed a mathematical explanation of the kinetic theory of heat.

Coriolis, Gustave-Gaspard (1792–1843)   French physicist who was first to coin the term *kinetic energy*. He was also the first to describe the effect that was named after him, which deals with the apparent force on a moving object when observed from a rotating system.

de Broglie, Prince Louis Victor Pierre Raymond (1892–1987)   French physicist who discovered the wave nature of electrons and of particles in general. He won the Nobel Prize in 1929.

Debye, Peter Joseph William (1884–1966)   Dutch-American physicist and physical chemist who studied molecular structures, the distances between atoms, and the distribution of electric charges in molecules.

Doppler, Christian Johann (1803–1853)   Austrian physicist who discovered that a wave's frequency changes when the source and observer are in motion relative to each other (called the Doppler effect).

Einstein, Albert (1879–1955)   German-born American theoretical physicist who revolutionized numerous theories on the physics of the universe. He established quantum theory (first put forth by Max Planck) by using it to describe photoelectric effects. He also worked out two major theories of relativity that still hold true (although they are often debated). He won the Nobel Prize in 1921.

Fahrenheit, (Gabriel) Daniel (1686–1736)   German physicist who developed, in 1717, the temperature scale that was named after him. In 1718, he developed the mercury thermometer.

Faraday, Michael (1791–1867)   British physicist and chemist who proposed the idea of magnetic "lines of force," developed the first electric generator, and pioneered the study of low temperatures.

Fermi, Enrico (1901–1954)   Italian-American physicist who investigated the neutron bombardment of uranium, which led to the development of the atomic bomb. He also developed several theoretical ideas in subatomic physics and won the Nobel Prize in 1938.

Feynman, Richard Phillips (1918–1988)   American theoretical physicist, one of the century's greatest, who is known for his work on the basic principles of quantum electrodynamics. He shared the Nobel Prize in physics in 1965.

Fleming, Sir John Ambrose (1849–1945)   British physicist and electrical engineer who invented the first vacuum tube (which changes alternating current to direct current).

Foucault, Jean Bernard Léon (1819–1868)   French physicist, who was instrumental in measuring the velocity of light using mirrors. He also developed mirrors and lenses for telescopes and the gyroscope. He worked out a way to deduce the rotation of the Earth using a pendulum, which was then named after him.

Franklin, Benjamin (1706–1790)   American general scientist and philosopher (among other talents) who experimented with electricity. He defined negative and positive charges.

Fraunhofer, Josef von (1787–1826)   German physicist and optician who was the first to realize that the dark lines in the solar spectrum are important in determining the composition of celestial bodies.

Fresnel, Augustin Jean (1788–1827)   French physicist who demonstrated the wave nature of light and gave an explanation of polarization.

Geiger, Hans Wilhelm (1882–1945)   German physicist who, along with Ernest Rutherford, invented a radiation detector. It was named after Geiger.

Glaser, Donald Arthur (1926–)   American physicist who invented the bubble chamber, which is used to detect the characteristics of elementary atomic particles.

Grimaldi, Francesco Maria (1618–1663)   Italian physicist who discovered optical diffraction and accepted the idea of waves of light. He also made one of the first lunar maps and started the tradition of naming the Moon's features after famous scientists.

Heisenberg, Werner Karl (1901–1976)   German physicist who developed the Uncertainty Principle, which advanced modern physics. He also realized that the atomic nucleus consisted of protons and neutrons. He won the Nobel Prize in 1932.

Helmholtz, Hermann Ludwig Ferdinand von (1821–1894)   German physiologist and theoretical physicist who developed theories on color vision and hearing. He was one of the first to determine the law of conservation of energy, and he studied nerve impulses.

Henry, Joseph (1797–1878)   American physicist who invented the large-scale electromagnet, electric relay (used in the telegraph), and electric motor.

Hertz, Heinrich Rudolf (1857–1894)   German physicist who discovered radio waves. He also determined the velocity of radio waves (called Hertzian waves).

Hofstadter, Robert (1915–1990)   American physicist who discovered the structures of protons and neutrons.

Hooke, Robert (1635–1703)   British physicist who, among other scientific finds, determined that the amount a spring stretches varies directly with its tension.

Joliot-Curie, Frédéric (1900–1958)   French physicist who, along with his wife, Irène, developed the first artificial radioactive element, a form of phosphorus.

Joliot-Curie, Irène (1897–1956)   French physicist and daughter of chemists Marie and Pierre Curie. She, along with her husband, Frédéric, developed the first artificial radioactive element, a form of phosphorus.

Joule, James Prescott (1818–1889)   British physicist who determined the amount of heat produced by an electric current (it is named Joule in his honor). He also determined that if a gas expands without performing work, its temperature falls.

Kelvin, first baron of Largs (né William Thomson) (1824–1907)   British theoretical and experimental physicist who proposed the absolute scale of temperature (1848) and developed the idea of entropy. He also developed an idea that led to syntony in 1894—or a receiver tuned to the wavelength of a transmitter to receive a signal. He received his title of nobility from the British government in 1892.

Kerr, Roy Patrick (1934–)   New Zealand mathematician who solved Albert Einstein's field equations of general relativity to describe rotating black holes.

Kirchhoff, Gustav Robert (1824–1887)   German physicist who founded modern spectroscopy by using spectral lines to identify chemical elements. He also studied black-body radiation, which eventually led to quantum theory.

Land, Edwin Herbert (1909–1991)   American physicist who developed the polarizing filter. He is also known for his work in photography.

Larmor, Sir Joseph (1857–1942)   Irish physicist who was one of the first to develop a theory explaining the magnetic fields of the Earth and the Sun.

Lawrence, Ernest Orlando (1901–1958)   American physicist who invented the cyclotron, which is used to induce large-scale nuclear reactions. He won the Nobel Prize in 1939.

Lederman, Leon M. (1922–)   American physicist who discovered the upsilon particle, which confirmed the quark theory of baryons.

Mach, Ernst (1838–1916)   Austrian physicist who discovered that airflow becomes disturbed at the speed of sound. Mach numbers (which represent how fast a craft is traveling beyond the speed of sound) were named after him.

Maxwell, James Clerk (1831–1879)   British physicist who developed equations that served as a basis for the understanding of electromagnetism. He also determined that light is electromagnetic radiation; predicted other types of radiation beyond visible light; and developed the kinetic theory of gases, a foundation of modern physical chemistry.

Michelson, Albert Abraham (1852–1931)   American physicist who accurately determined the speed of light. (It is measured at 186,291 miles [299,792,458 meters] per second. Michelson was accurate within several thousandths of a percent.) He also invented, along with Morley, the interferometer to show that light travels at a constant velocity (regardless of the movement of the Earth), an idea that eventually led to Einstein's theory of relativity (called the Michelson-Morley experiment).

Morley, Edward William (1838–1923)   American chemist and physicist who, along with Michelson, developed the interferometer to show that the velocity of light is a constant (called the Michelson-Morley experiment).

Moseley, Henry Gwyn Jeffreys (1887–1915)   British physicist who worked on x-ray emissions of elements; he determined that each element had a different number of electrons.

Newton, Sir Isaac (1642–1727)   English physicist and mathematician who was one of the greatest scientists of all time. He invented calculus, determined the nature of white light, constructed the first reflecting telescope, and formulated the laws of motion and the theory of universal gravitation.

Ohm, Georg Simon (1787–1854)   German physicist who determined the law that states that electrical current is equal to the ratio of the voltage to the resistance; the law is known as Ohm's law.

Oliphant, Sir Mark (Marcus) Laurence Elwin (1901–)   Australian physicist who discovered the radioactive isotope of hydrogen, called tritium.

Oppenheimer, Julius Robert (1904–1967)   American physicist who, besides his work in astrophysics, was the director of the Manhattan project to build the first atomic bomb.

Paschen, Louis Carl Heinrich (1865–1947)   German physicist who determined that helium found on Earth is the same as helium on the Sun. He also discovered a series of lines in the hydrogen spectrum (named after him).

Pauli, Wolfgang (1900–1958)   Austrian-born Swiss physicist who was the discover of the exclusion principle (i.e., that two electrons with the same quantum number cannot occupy the same atom). He also worked on theories in the quantum field and predicted the neutrino (but Enrico Fermi named the neutrino).

Planck, Max Karl Ernst Ludwig (1858–1947)   German physicist who used the quantum theory to explain the nature of black-body radiation, where energy is discontinuous. The terms classical and modern physics are often distinguished as "before Planck" and "after Planck," respectively. He won the Nobel Prize in 1918.

Poisson, Siméon Denis (1781–1840)   French mathematician and mathematical physicist who advanced ideas that defined integrals, electromagnetic theory, and probability.

Prandtl, Ludwig (1875–1953)   German physicist who discovered that a flowing liquid in a tube has a thin boundary layer along the sides of the tube, which does not move as fast as the rest of the liquid.

Rayleigh, John William Strutt, Lord (1842–1919)   British physicist who discovered the gas argon. (He also noticed a specific type of earthquake wave, now called Rayleigh waves.)

Richardson, Sir Owen Willans (1879–1959)   British physicist who explained the Edison effect (first discovered by Thomas Alva Edison), in which heated metals emit electrons.

Roentgen, Wilhelm Conrad (1845–1923)   German physicist who discovered x-rays. He won the Nobel Prize in 1901.

Rumford, Benjamin Thompson, Count (1753–1814)   American-born British physicist who was the first to determine that heat is a kind of motion (he disproved the caloric theory of heat).

Ruska, Ernst August Friedrich (1906–1988)   German physicist who determined that a magnetic coil can focus a beam of light. He developed the first electron microscope (which was independently developed by Rheinhold Ruedenberg at about the same time).

Rutherford, Ernest, Lord (1871–1937)   New Zealand-born British physicist who suggested the theory of the nuclear atom, thus helping to found subatomic physics (he is often called the father of nuclear physics). He was also the first to change one element to another by an artificial nuclear reaction. He won the Nobel Prize in 1908.

Rydberg, Johannes Robert (1854–1919)   Swedish physicist and spectroscopist who derived the quantitative relationships for spectroscopic data. He also proposed that the periodic table be listed by atomic number, not by atomic weight. A hypothetical atom of infinite mass is called a Rydberg in his honor.

Schrödinger, Erwin (1887–1961)   Austrian physicist who developed a model of the atom that was different from Niels Bohr's model.

Stokes, Sir George Gabriel (1819–1903)   British mathematician and physicist who described how a small body falls through a fluid and thus the mathematical behavior of viscous fluid flow. His calculations were included in a formula called Stokes's law.

Sturgeon, William (1783–1850)   British physicist who invented the first electromagnet.

Thomson, Sir Joseph John (1856–1940)   British physicist who determined that cathode rays consisted of particles smaller than the atom, thus discovering the electrons. His work helped to found the study of subatomic physics. He won the Nobel Prize in 1906.

Thomson, William   See *Kelvin*.

Torricelli, Evangelista (1608–1647)   Italian physicist who used Galileo Galilei's ideas on the laws of motion to describe the motion of fluids. He is called the father of hydrodynamics.

van de Graaff, Robert Jemison (1901–1967)   American physicist who developed the first static electricity generator.

van de Waals, Johannes Diderik (1837–1923)   Dutch physicist who developed an improved set of gas laws.

Volta, Count Alessandro Giuseppe Antonio Anastasio (1745–1827)   Italian physicist who built the first chemical battery; he was also the first to produce and work with electric currents.

Weiss, Pierre Ernst (1865–1940)   French physicist who developed the idea of ferromagnetism (that iron and other ferromagnetic materials form domains of polarity that create a strong magnetic force when aligned).

Wheatstone, Sir Charles (1802–1875)   British physicist who created the first commercial electric telegraph. He also developed a device for measuring electrical resistance.

Wigner, Eugene Paul (1902–)   Hungarian-born American physicist who was an early researcher of nuclear power. He also worked on the Manhattan project (to develop the atomic bomb), and shared the Nobel Prize in 1963.

Wilson, Charles Thomson Rees (1869–1959)   British physicist who invented the Wilson Cloud Chamber, which revolutionized the study of particle physics by allowing subatomic particle activity to be easily viewed.

Wilson, Kenneth G. (1937–)   American theoretical physicist who is noted for his work on the theory of phase transition. He won the Nobel Prize in 1982.

Young, Robert (1773–1829)   British physicist who is called the founder of the wave theory of light because of his demonstration of the interference of light.

SIGNIFICANT SCIENTIFIC DISCOVERIES IN PHYSICS

B.C.	~450	Leucippus of Miletus introduced the idea of the atom
	~340	Greek physicist Strato suggested incorrectly that heavier bodies fall faster than lighter bodies
	~260	Writings in China suggested the first law of motion later formulated by Newton
A.D.	1010	Arabian physicist Abu 'Ali Al-Hasan ibn Al-Haytham explained how lenses work and developed the parabolic mirror
	~1050	First "perpetual motion machine" developed
	1492	Christopher Columbus noticed that a magnetic compass points in different directions at different longitudes
	1581	Galileo Galilei studied swinging hanging lamps, which eventually led to the pendulum and accurate clocks
	1586	Simon Stevinus showed that objects of two different weights dropped at the same time from the same height in a vacuum will reach the ground at the same time
	1612	Galileo Galilei developed elementary hydrostatics
	1665	Robert Hooke compared light to waves in water
	1666	Isaac Newton developed his law of universal gravitation and invented calculus
	1668	John Wallis suggested the law of conservation of momentum (eventually Newton's third law)

1675	Ole Rømer measured the speed of light (lower than the actual number); it was later refined by Armand Fizeau, Jean Foucault, and then Albert Michelson
1676	Robert Hooke discovered that the stretch of a spring varies directly with its tension (Hooke's Law)
1683	Terms *conductor* and *insulator* are introduced in electricity by John Desagulier, French physicist
1687	Newton established his three laws of motion and theory of gravity
1705	Experiments by Francis Hauksbee proved that sound needs a medium to travel
1737	The term *physics* is introduced to replace natural or experimental philosophy
1747	Benjamin Franklin discovered that a conductor can draw an electric charge from a charged body; it became the basis for the development of the lightning rod (he installed a lightning rod in his house in 1749)
1749	First artificial magnet developed by John Canton
1751	Benjamin Franklin distinguished between positive and negative electricity and showed it can magnetize forces of attraction and repulsion between two charged bodies and between magnetic poles
1791	Luigi Galvani determined that when two metals touch in a frog's muscle, an electric current is produced
1798	Henry Cavendish measured the mass of the Earth and determined the gravitational constant
1800	Alessandro Volta announced a method for storing electricity
1801	Johann W. Ritter discovered ultraviolet light
1807	Thomas Young used the term *energy* in the modern sense of the word
1815	Circular polarization discovered by Jean-Baptiste Biot
1819	Discovery of electromagnetism by Hans Christian Oersted (his finding would not be published until 1920)
1820	André Marie Ampère formulated the first laws of electromagnetism
1823	First electromagnet developed by William Sturgeon
1848	Baron Kelvin (William Thomson) proposed the idea of absolute zero
1873	James Clerk Maxwell explained electromagnetism, and determined that radio waves must exist
1888	Heinrich Hertz detected and produced radio waves
1895	Wilhelm Roentgen discovered x-rays
1896	Henri Becquerel discovered natural radioactivity
1897	Sir Joseph Thomson discovered the electron
1905	Albert Einstein developed his special theory of relativity
1911	Ernest Rutherford discovered the proton
1913	Neils Bohr determined the basic structure of the atom
1915	Albert Einstein developed his general theory of relativity
1924	Louis-Victor de Broglie theorized that particles have a wave nature
1926	Erwin Schrödinger developed the wave version of quantum mechanics
1932	First particle accelerator made by Sir John Cockcorft and Ernest Walton
1934	Irène and Frédéric Joliot-Curie discovered artificial radioactivity by bombarding aluminum with alpha-particles to obtain radioactive phosphorus
1938	Nuclear fission discovered by Otto Hahn, the first to split an atom of uranium
1942	Enrico Fermi built the first nuclear reactor as part of the Manhattan project, the U.S. program to build an atomic bomb
1945	First nuclear explosion at Alamogordo, New Mexico
1946	Felix Bloch and Edward Mills Purcell discover nuclear magnetic resonance (NMR)
1951	First electricity generated from a nuclear breeder reactor in Idaho
1952	First hydrogen bomb detonated at the Eniwetok atoll, Marshall Islands
1955	Neutrinos observed by Clyde Cowan and Frederick Reines

1964	The concept of quarks introduced by Murray Gell-Mann
1979	Three Mile Island, Pennsylvania, is the site of the first major nuclear power plant accident
1980	Scanning-tunneling microscope invented by Heinrich Rohrer and Gerd Binning
1986	A major nuclear power plant accident occurred at the Chernobyl plant in Ukraine
1994	Top quark reportedly observed for the first time

COMMON TERMS IN PHYSICS

acoustics   The science of the production, transmission, and effect of sound waves.

action   The effect produced by a force, e.g., the force of a hammer hits a nail: The action of the force is its effect, and the nail is driven into the wood.

adhesion   The tendency for matter to cling to other types of matter, due to intermolecular forces.

antimatter   Matter composed of antiparticles; if an elementary particle and antiparticle met, they would annihilate one another and their combined mass would be converted into electromagnetic radiation.

antiparticle   A particle having mass, lifetime, and spin identical to a particle of matter but opposite to it in charge and magnetic moment.

black body   An ideal object that absorbs all incident radiation and radiates according to Planck's law.

bubble chamber   A tank that detects elementary atomic particles. It photographs the vapor bubbles left by the electrically charged particles passing though the tank of heavy liquid. It is used to determine the electric charge, momentum, and mass of the particles.

buoyancy   The resulting vertical force on an object by a static fluid in which the object is floating or submerged.

conduction   The transfer of heat by molecular motion from a region of high temperature to a region of lower temperature, tending toward equalizing temperatures.

constant   A quantity or measurement that never changes in magnitude.

convection   The mechanical transfer of heated molecules of a gas or liquid from a source to another area, as when a room is warmed by the mass movement of air molecules heated by a radiator.

deceleration   The decrease in velocity per unit time. It is also called negative acceleration.

density   The mass per unit volume of a material. Every material has a characteristic density.

diffraction   The spreading out of any type of wave (such as sound or light waves) when they pass through an opening that is smaller than or equal to this wavelength.

echo   The reflection of sound from a surface.

electromotive force   The force that causes the movement of electrons through an electrical circuit.

elementary particles   Also called fundamental particles, they are the constituents of all matter. Today, six quarks and six leptons (12 total particles) are considered elementary particles; all others are derived particles.

energy   The ability or capacity to do work. There are numerous types of energy, including potential (stored), kinetic (from motion), heat, light, electrical, chemical, and nuclear energy. One form of energy can be transformed into another form, but energy normally is not created or destroyed.

entropy   A physical quantity that is the measurement of the amount of disorder in a system.

equilibrium   A state of balance between opposing forces or effects.

friction   The resistance to motion between two surfaces moving over each other. It is usually measured in terms of force and velocity.

gravitational collapse   The collapse of a massive body. It occurs when the body is so massive that the gravitational forces of attraction are stronger than the forces of repulsion. For example, this type of collapse would cause a star to contract to a point where it would be so dense that even light could not escape. Such conditions are thought to exist around black holes.

gyroscope   An instrument with a rapidly spinning, heavy mass that maintains a fixed reference direction by conserving angular momentum. A massive, rapidly spinning body rigidly resists being disturbed and tends to react to a disturbing torque by precessing (rotating slowly) in a direction at right angles to the direction of torque.

interferometer   An instrument that precisely measures light, sound, and radio waves through interference patterns. For example, acoustical interferometers can measure the velocity of sound in a gas or in water.

kinematics   The study of motion that neglects the forces producing the motion.

laser   A device that converts power into a very narrow, intense monochromatic beam of visible or infrared light. The light is amplified by the stimulated emission of radiation.

medium   The matter through which a wave travels. Sound waves need a medium; light waves do not need a medium and can travel through a vacuum.

Minkowski space   Space-time in the absence of a gravitational field.

opaque   Not permitting light to pass through.

particle   Anything small and discrete, such as a proton, neutron, atom, molecules, etc.

phase   The state of matter of a material—either solid, liquid, gas, or plasma.

physical law   A description of a certain behavior in nature, e.g., the idea that an object does not change its position until it is acted on by an outside force is a physical law.

piezoelectric effect   The ability of an object to generate a voltage when mechanical force is applied, as in crystal oscillators and microphones.

Planck's law   Relates temperature to wavelength, stating that hotter objects radiate most at shorter wavelengths.

plasma   A hot, ionized (electrically charged) gas.

polarization   The limitation of electromagnetic waves' oscillation to a certain plane. For example, when light is transmitted through variously oriented crystals or other suitable media, such as polarized sunglasses, it "filters out" light traveling perpendicular to the plane of polarization.

pressure   The force acting on a per unit area of a surface.

radiation   The emission and propagation of radiant energy—either atomic, by radioactive substances, or spectral, as in light.

reaction   The effect opposite of an action. A reaction is equal to an action but is in the opposite direction. For example, when a stone strikes a wall, the wall does not move or change shape—it pushes back with a reaction that is equal to the action.

reflectance   The ratio of the radiant flux reflected from a given surface to the total light that falls on the surface. Other types of waves also have reflectance, including sound and heat waves.

relative density   The density of a material divided by the density of water. It is also referred to as specific gravity.

resistance   A force that opposes a change in motion or shape.

Seebeck effect   The production of an electric current by joining two wires of different metals (e.g., copper and iron) at the ends to form a closed circuit with two junctions. If the junctions are different temperatures, an electric current flows through the circuit.

space-time   A four-dimensional space that specifies the location and time coordinates of a certain event.

specific gravity   See *relative density*

spectroscope   An instrument used to determine the spectrum or wavelength of a ray of light emanating from an object. It is often used in astronomy.

spectrum   A band of varying color observed when a beam of white light is passed through a prism or diffraction grating that separates each component of the light into its respective wavelengths. The colors, from longest to shortest wavelength, are red, orange, yellow, green, blue, indigo, and violet.

speed   The distance traveled divided by the time it takes to travel the distance.

statics   The branch of mechanics that deals with objects at rest and with the interaction of forces in equilibrium. It also applies to stationary electric charges or nonactive chemical elements.

strain   The change in a shape or size of a body caused by pressure and movement.

stress   Tension forces exerted on a body that tend to produce a deformation of that body.

supercooling   The cooling of a liquid at a given pressure to a temperature below its freezing point at that pressure, without changing its phase state.

superheating   The raising of a liquid's temperature above its boiling point, by increasing the pressure, without changing its phase state.

surface tension   The property of a liquid in which the surface molecules show a strong inward attraction. This forms an apparent membrane across the surface of the liquid.

thermodynamics   The study of the movement of heat from one body to another and the relations between heat and other forms of energy.

transition point   The point where the constants of a circuit change and cause reflection of a wave being propagated along the circuit.

translucent   Pertaining to a solid or liquid medium through which light will travel but no clear image is formed. Frosted glass is translucent, not transparent.

transparent   Pertaining to a solid or liquid medium through which light will travel and form a clear image. Window glass is transparent.

vacuum   In theory, it is the absence of matter; in space, a vacuum is where air or other gases are almost exhausted.

vector   A quantity that has magnitude and direction. Velocity and weight are vector quantities (speed and mass are scalar quantities). Vectors can be multiplied by scalars, but addition with a scalar has no meaning. Two vectors can be added; e.g., two forces acting on an object can be added to determine the overall force on the object.

velocity   The speed and direction that an object travels over a specified distance during a measured amount of time.

vibration   The regular oscillation, backward and forward, of a material. For example, elastic vibrates, as do most fluids.

viscosity   The property of a liquid that makes it resist flow or any change in the arrangement of its molecules. The higher the viscosity, the "thicker" a liquid seems.

ADDITIONAL SOURCES OF INFORMATION

Asimov, Isaac. *Understanding Physics*. Dorset, 1988.

Bartusiak, Marcia. *Through a Universe Darkly: A Cosmic Tale of Ancient Ethers, Dark Matter, and the Fate of the Universe*. HarperCollins, 1993.

Davies, Paul, ed. *The New Physics*. Cambridge Univ. Press, 1989.

Ferris, Timothy. *The World Treasury of Physics, Astronomy, and Mathematics*. Little, Brown, 1993.

Freeman, Ira M. (rev. by Durden, William). *Physics Made Simple*. Doubleday, 1990.

Gonick, Larry, and Huffman, Art. *The Cartoon Guide to Physics*. Harper, 1990.

Hawking, Stephen. *A Brief History of Time: From the Big Bang to Black Holes*. Bantam, 1988.

Krauss, Lawrence. *Fear of Physics: A Guide for the Perplexed*. HarperCollins, 1993.

Nahin, Paul J. *Time Machines: Time Travel in Physics, Metaphysics, and Science Fiction*. American Institute of Physics, 1993.

Shroyer, Jo Ann. *Quarks, Critters, and Chaos: What Science Terms Really Mean*. Prentice-Hall, 1993.

Chapter

8

Astronomy

What Is Astronomy?   314

The Universe   314

The Solar System   317

The Earth's Moon   330

Constellations   336

The Stars   337

Galaxies   340

Other Astronomical Objects   342

Common Telescopes   342

The Space Age   347

Major Astronomers and Space Scientists   354

Significant Scientific Discoveries in
Astronomy   360

Common Terms in Astronomy   362

Additional Sources of Information   365

WHAT IS ASTRONOMY?

Astronomy is the study of the universe. It entails the observation of objects in space, such as planets, satellites, stars, and galaxies as well as the interpretation of radiation received from the various objects in the universe. Astronomy is mostly an observational science. In most cases, astronomers use known physical laws to determine how objects in the universe respond and react.

THE UNIVERSE

The *universe* is the total amount of matter and radiation that exists and the space occupied by the same and in between. The interactions within the universe are often explained using four basic physical forces—gravity, electromagnetism, strong nuclear, and weak interactions.

The First Moments of the Universe

Astronomers infer that conditions before the birth of the universe were unimaginably chaotic and superdense, with temperatures greater than 1,500 billion°K (for more information on temperature, see Chapter 1, "Scientific Measurements"). The commonly accepted model of the universe suggests that it began in an infinitely compact and singular state, enclosing a space even smaller than an atomic particle.

The beginning of our universe, often referred to as the Big Bang, occurred when the compact ball grew—not in a violent explosion but through rapid expansion. Several events occurred after the Big Bang. The first three events separated the basic physical forces of the universe

10^{-43} seconds	Gravity separated from the three other forces (before 10^{-43} seconds is called Planck time): electromagnetic, strong nuclear, and weak interaction
10^{-33} seconds	Three forces were operating: electromagnetic, strong nuclear, and gravitational
10^{-10} seconds	Weak interaction and electromagnetic force separated
10 microseconds	Quarks combined to form particles
3 minutes	The nuclei of light atoms formed
500,000 years	The first true, complex atoms formed
Several hundred million to a billion years	Gaseous clouds of hydrogen and helium began to condense into protogalaxies and stars.

EVIDENCE FOR THE BIG BANG

Cosmologists believe that cosmic microwave background radiation is compelling evidence for the Big Bang. Cosmic microwave radiation—or very high frequency radio waves with wavelengths between 1 millimeter to 1 meter on the electromagnetic spectrum—were discovered coming from space in 1964. Arno Penzias and Robert Wilson, two scientists at Bell Laboratories, were measuring microwave radiation to aid communications and discovered microwaves coming from all directions of the sky. The staticlike hiss Penzias and Wilson heard in their receivers was believed to be the "echo" of the Big Bang—the radiation released from the initial expansion of the universe.

The microwave radiation measurements seemed to indicate an expanding, cooling universe, though the idea that radiation spread out evenly in all directions in the early universe was difficult to reconcile with this theory (the Big Bang was evenly distributed, but matter is not—for instance, there is more matter in a galaxy than the space in between). Many scientists believe that distortions in the universe's background radiation would explain huge stellar explosions, decaying subatomic particles, or methods of galaxy formation. In the late 1980s, data from the Cosmic Background Explorer (COBE) spacecraft continued to show smooth background microwave radiation. But more recent data from the COBE's instruments do show subtle variations across the sky—possible evidence of the distortions scientists have predicted.

Cosmology and the Universe

Cosmology is the study of the origin, properties, processes, and evolution of the universe. The problem of determining the actual evolution of the universe stems from obtaining reliable data on the furthermost galaxies and quasars. There are also assumptions made in describing the universe: (1) that all earthly physical laws are valid everywhere in the cosmos, (2) that the universe is homogeneous, and (3) that the observed red shift of galaxies—which indicates that galaxies are moving away from the observer—are really due to the expansion of the universe and not to some other cause.

Based on these assumptions, cosmologists have developed numerous models of the universe. Each model is based on certain premises; in addition, many of the theories overlap one another. There is no one theory that is agreed on by all astronomers.

In the *open universe* model, the universe expands toward infinity, and the galaxies, stars, and planets spread out uniformly in all directions. In this model, the universe continues to expand forever, and density throughout the universe gets lower over time.

In the *closed universe* model, the universe expands, but gravity takes over at some point, causing the universe to collapse.

In the *balanced universe* model, the force of gravity exactly equals the force of expansion, and the universe just eventually stops expanding.

In the *oscillating universe* model, the universe collapses and then rebounds rhythmically over a period of billions of years. Because there is so much matter in the universe, gravity eventually pulls the matter back toward the center; the matter contracts to the point of origin, and eventually expands again as another Big Bang, starting the cycle again.

In the *inflationary universe* model, the universe will keep expanding or stop, all based on the presence of dark matter: If scientists find that dark matter does not exist (or is a low percent of the universe), then the universe will expand forever; if dark matter is present, then expansion will eventually stop.

In the *steady state* model, the universe has no beginning or end. As the universe expands, the distribution of galaxies and other objects (i.e., the density of the universe) remains constant, with old galaxies being replaced by new galaxies, making the universe appear to remain unchanged. This requires that new hydrogen protons be created spontaneously to keep the density of matter constant, but just how, no one knows.

Age of the Universe

To determine the age of the universe, it is necessary to calculate how fast galaxies are moving away from one another. The ratio of a galaxy's recessional speed to its distance is called the Hubble constant (H), named after astronomer Edwin Hubble, where H is often expressed in kilometers per second per million light-years. If the resulting number is high, the universe was born only a short time ago; if the number is low, the universe is much more ancient.

Currently, the exact value for the Hubble constant is poorly known. It will continue to change as more accurate measurements of galactic distances are made. Estimates range between 15 and 30 kilometers per second per million light-years, making the universe 10 to 20 billion years old. In general, accepted values are between 15 and 18 billion years old (although some astronomers have set the date back to 12 billion years based on recent satellite data).

ASTRONOMICAL THEORIES AND DISCOVERIES

There are plenty of unproved astronomical theories in the universe. What are some of the most popular?

dark matter   One problem in determining the expansion or contraction of the universe is the possible existence of dark matter, or "missing" mass, which may constitute 90 percent of all mass in the universe (made up of dead stars, black holes, and unknown exotic particles). Astronomers believe there is more mass than has been observed, based on unexplained gravitational tugging on visible matter. If this is true, there may be enough mass to reverse the universe's apparent expansion and lead to its eventual collapse, as the closed universe theory predicts.

antiuniverse   One of the most intriguing theories concerns the possibility of an antiuniverse, i.e., a universe just the opposite from our own. Scientists know that antiprotons and antielectrons exist, because such particles have been produced in particle accelerators. Could there be a mirror of our own universe? Presently, this is only a theory.

white holes; wormholes   White holes and wormholes have been topics of numerous science fiction stories. The theory states that a black hole would lead to a matching white hole in another universe. A spaceship crossing over the event horizon—the boundary between the edge of the black hole effect and normal space—would pop out from the white hole. Wormholes—often referred to as gateways, portholes, or tunnels to another universe—are thought to be the connection through the event horizon to the other universe. In reality, the excessive gravitational pull of the black hole would rip the spacecraft apart long before it passed through either a wormhole or a white hole. In other words, we could never really discover directly whether either phenomenon exists.

New discoveries about the universe are constantly being made; some recent ones are discussed below.

gravitational lensing   Astronomers know that gravity bends light, as predicted by Einstein's theories of relativity; therefore, a massive body can also act as a gravitational lens, bending the light from a nearby object. For example, light from a quasar lying almost directly behind a nearer massive body can be deflected by gravity, creating a distortion in space-time. From Earth, the image appears shifted or broken into several images; or as the distortion often spreads into an Einstein ring, a circular ring of light.

microlensing   Microlensing occurs when a massive object comes between two celestial bodies, i.e., the Earth and a star, bending and magnifying the light from one of the bodies (here, the star), thus brightening the light for a short period. Microlensing is closely related to the search for dark matter: One study indicated that the existence of a form of dark matter called massive compact halo objects (MACHOs) at the periphery of the Milky Way galaxy could act as microlenses. The scientists detected the brightening of several stars near the Large Magellanic Cloud in the Southern Hemisphere, speculating that the MACHOs (probably about the size of small stars) bent and enhanced the stars' light.

black holes   Black holes, or regions of space where the gravitational field is so strong that photon particles (light) cannot escape, have long been proposed. In 1994, in a region of elliptical galaxy M87, the best evidence yet for a black hole was discovered. Scientists using the Hubble Space Telescope noticed the alleged black hole based on its effects on its surroundings. The gravitational pull of the black hole should densely pack the stars, increasing the intensity of the starlight and tugging the gases and stars in a spiral toward the center.

THE SOLAR SYSTEM

A solar system includes planets, their satellites, comets, minor planets (asteroids), and other interplanetary materials. Our solar system consists of a central star, the Sun, nine planets (possibly more in the past), more than 60 satellites (or moons), more than 5,000 minor planets (asteroids), numerous comets, and smaller interplanetary dust and debris. It is a compact unit, with most of the planets and satellites traveling along the same plane (called the plane of the ecliptic). Gravity holds the entire system together.

Astronomers believe there are other solar systems around stars similar to our own Sun. No one has visually recorded the presence of another solar system because it is difficult to locate planet- and satellite-size objects at great distances using current telescope technology. Astronomers have inferred solar systems by measuring the minute changes in a star's velocity caused by the gravitational pull of planets and satellites. For example, it is thought that two extrasolar planets, a few times more massive than the Earth, are orbiting radio pulsar (neutron star) PSR 1257+12 with orbital periods of two and three months, respectively. Scientists also suspect that pancake-shaped clouds of orbiting debris around certain stars may be forming solar systems.

Birth of Our Solar System

A variety of theories have been proposed to explain the origin of our solar system.

The *nebular (centrifugal-force) hypothesis* was first proposed in 1796 by Simon de Laplace. According to the theory, a rapidly rotating disk of hot gas extended beyond the present orbit of Pluto. Centrifugal force acted on the outer regions of the cloud, causing a ring of material to develop, which eventually condensed into the planets.

The *tidal theory* (also called the Chamberlin-Moulton theory) suggests that a passing star pulled dust and gas from the forming Sun. The star was ejected from the solar system, leaving behind a ribbon of debris that eventually formed the planets.

The *collision theory* assumes that the Sun collided with another star, spewing gases that eventually formed the planets. Another collision theory proposes that the Sun was a double star, and that collision between the Sun's companion and another star created the material to produce the planets.

Currently, scientists believe the *protoplanet hypothesis* best describes the actual formation of our solar system. About 10 to 12 billion years ago, an aggregation of gas and dust with a high-density central core formed. About 5 to 6 billion years ago, the center collapsed as a protostar (or protosun, the precursor to the Sun). Approximately 5 percent of the material remained as a dust cloud around the center, which flattened as it spun. Turbulence within the cloud caused the outer particles to clump together (or accrete), forming large protoplanets (the precursors to the modern planets and satellites).

Thermonuclear reactions began in the center of the cloud. Most of the light gases around the smaller protoplanets in the inner solar system (such as hydrogen and helium) were blown away by the protosun's intense solar wind. Because of their greater distances from the solar wind, planets in the outer solar system kept most of their gaseous atmospheres.

About 4.56 billion years ago, the Earth, and probably most of the other inner solar system planets, began to form their outer crusts (for more information on the formation of the Earth, see Chapter 9, "Earth Science"). Between 3.8 to 4 billion years ago, the inner (and probably the outer) planets were bombarded by smaller bodies leftover from planetary formation. The "Late Heavy Bombardment" may explain the breakup of many larger asteroids, and the tilt of Uranus (its rotational axis is almost parallel with the plane of the ecliptic). It may also explain the origin of the Moon, which may have formed when a planet-size body struck the Earth, sending a large chunk of material into space. Intense heating from the Late Heavy Bombardment probably contributed to the atmospheres of the inner planets (Venus, Earth, and Mars), as the striking bodies caused the release of primitive gases from under the newly formed crusts. The outer planets may have also experienced a heavy bombardment, but the start, extent, and duration are unknown.

Distribution of Mass in the Solar System

Object	Percent of Mass
Sun	99.86
Planets	0.135
Satellites	0.00004
Comets	0.00003 (estimated)
Asteroids (minor planets)	0.0000003 (estimated)
Interplanetary medium (dust and gases)	> 0.0000001 (estimated)

The Sun

The Sun is located at the center of the solar system. Its sphere of hot gases comprises 99.86 percent of the entire solar system's mass.

Star type: Typical G2-class star

Diameter: 864,000 miles (1,390,180 kilometers); 109 times the diameter of the Earth

Mass: 2.2×10^{27} tons (2×10^{30} kilograms); 333,400 times the weight of the Earth

Tilt: 7° to the ecliptic

Rotation: 36 days at the poles, 28 days at 30° latitude, and 25 days at the equator; it is unknown if the Sun's underlying layers rotate faster or slower than its surface layers

Temperature: Center of the Sun is about 14 million°K; a pleasant day on Earth is about 300°K

Composition: Hydrogen (about 78 percent by weight) and helium account for 95 percent of the total elements; more than 60 elements have been detected on the Sun via spectrographic analysis (there are 88 naturally occurring elements on Earth, or 89, if technetium—thought to be naturally occuring, but so far only created in the laboratory—is counted)

Surface gravity: 38 times that at the Earth's surface

Density: Average 1.4 grams per cubic centimeter (water on Earth is equal to 1 gram per cubic centimeter)

Because the Sun is compressible, the density increases sharply as distance increases downward from its "surface." A total of 1 cubic foot of its matter from the "surface" would weigh 87.4 pounds (39.3 kilograms) on Earth; 1 cubic inch of the Sun's dense core material would weigh as much as forty 100,000-ton aircraft carriers concentrated in an area the size of a thumbnail.

Thermonuclear fusion reactions are the Sun's basic source of energy, as hydrogen is converted into helium. The lighter nuclei fuse to create more complex nuclei, releasing heat and light—close to 5×10^{23} horsepower in all directions at one time. The light from the Sun reaches the Earth in just over 8 minutes (the time varies by seconds, depending on the Earth's distance from the Sun).

Astronomers believe that the Sun reached its present brightness and temperature about 800 million years ago. Its brightness should not change for another 1.5 billion years. It has a potential life span of about 13 billion years, but it has already existed for about 6 billion years, meaning it should burn for another 7 billion years. At that time, most of the Sun's hydrogen will fuse to helium, and it will contract. Its heat and surrounding hydrogen shell will expand, encompassing Mercury, Venus, and the Earth.

Layers of the Sun

The Sun's atmosphere is divided into several layers—from the central core to the surrounding corona—though there are no distinct boundaries between them.

The Sun's core is about 248,560 miles (400,000 kilometers) in diameter and is about 60 percent of the Sun's mass. The core reaches temperatures close to 27,000,000°F (15,000,000°C). Pressures at the center of the Sun are estimated to be 7 trillion pounds per inch square (0.5 million million kilograms per centimeter square).

The *convective zone* is an envelope of gases surrounding the Sun's core. This layer is responsible for transferring heat and light energy from the core to the outer layers.

The *photosphere* ("sphere of light") is the visible surface of the Sun, where the Sun's heat and light are emitted. This mottled layer (the mottling is called granulation) is about 500 miles (805 kilometers) thick. The photosphere is composed of noncharged gas atoms at temperatures averaging about 9,750°F (5,400°C), which constantly move by convection, as warmer gases are transferred upward from below.

Cooler regions called *sunspots* are depressions that appear as dark patches (some large enough to be seen from Earth with the naked eye) in the photosphere. Sunspots have a typical lifespan of a few days and temperatures of about 6,700°F (3,700°C) at their dark centers. The Sun has a sunspot cycle, which was first recorded in 1843 by German astronomer Heinrich Schwabe, who noted that sunspot activity reached a maximum every 11 years.

Plages (faculae)—bright patches that have a higher temperature than the surrounding area—occur in the photosphere and are usually found in association with sunspots (though some are found far from sunspots). Other sunspot-related phenomena include *solar flares*, which are tremendous outbursts of energy that quickly hurl particles and radiation into space (particles from giant flares are associated with Earth's auroral displays), and loops and fountains of gas called *prominences (filaments)*.

The low-density *chromosphere* is about 2,000 miles (3,212 kilometers) thick. Its temperature ranges from 7,200 to 90,000°F (4,000 to 50,000°C). The upper regions are broken into jetlike spikes of gas (*spicules*) and other irregular forms. Prominences and flares that originate in the photosphere also shoot through the chromosphere to the corona.

The Sun's outermost layer is the *corona*, a changing zone of ionized gases, visible only to Earth observers during a solar eclipse (or by simulating an eclipse with a solar telescope). The temperatures increase with height in the corona, with the rarefied gases reaching 3,600,000°F (2,000,000°C) at about 45,600 miles (75,000 kilometers) above the surface. The coronal halo is about 1 million miles thick. Changes in its shape are closely associated with the 11-year sunspot cycle.

Layers and Features of the Sun

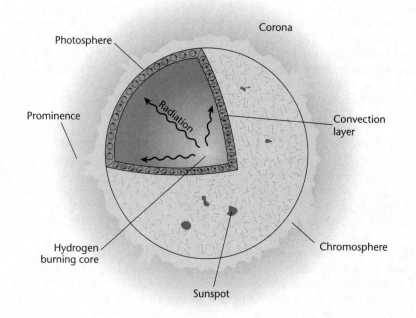

The Planets and Satellites

The solar system has nine known planets. From the Sun outward, they are Mercury, Venus, Earth, Mars, Jupiter, Saturn, Uranus, Neptune, and Pluto (although from about 1978 to 1999 Pluto is closer to the Sun than Neptune, because of Pluto's irregular orbit). The solar system also has an asteroid belt—a somewhat orderly collection of small to miles-wide rocky objects, most of which lie between the orbits of Mars and Jupiter.

The *inner*, or *terrestrial*, planets are Mercury, Venus, Earth, and Mars (Pluto is often classified as a terrestrial planet, but it is located in the outer solar system). The inner planets are relatively small and, with the exception of Mercury, have thinner atmospheres than the outer planets.

The *outer* (also called *gaseous* or *nonterrestrial*) planets are Jupiter, Saturn, Uranus, and Neptune. Pluto is an outer planet by location, but its physical nature is similar to the terrestrial planets.

There are more than 60 known moons around the planets of the solar system. Mercury and Venus are the only planets without moons. Saturn has the most moons, with at least 20 (and probably more hidden in the planet's rings); the Earth and Pluto each have one moon.

Planetary Statistics

| Planet | MEAN DISTANCE FROM THE SUN | | PERIOD OF REVOLUTION | | | Inclination of Equator to Plane of Orbit (Degrees) | EQUATORIAL DIAMETER | | Mass (Earth = 1) |
	Miles (millions)	Kilometers (millions)	Sidereal	Synodic	Rotational Period		Miles	Kilometers	
Mercury	36.0	57.9	88.0 days	116 days	58.64 days	2	3,031	4,878	0.0553
Venus	67.2	108.1	224.7 days	584 days	243 days (retrograde)	178	7,521	12,104	0.8150
Earth	92.9	149.5	365.26 days	—	23 hrs, 56 min, 4.1 sec	23.4	7,926	12,756	1.0
Mars	141.5	227.9	687.0 days	780 days	24 hrs, 37 min, 22.3 sec	25.2	4,217	6,787	0.1074
Jupiter	483.3	778.3	11.86 years	339 days	9 hrs, 50 min (equatorial) 9 hrs, 55 min (polar)	3.1	88,730	142,800	317.83
Saturn	886.2	1,427.0	29.46 years	378 days	10 hrs, 39 min	26.7	74,900	120,540	95.18
Uranus	1,783.1	2,869.6	84.01 years	370 days	17 hrs, 54 min	97.9	31,763	51,118	14.53
Neptune	2,794.0	4,496.6	168.79 years	367 days	19 hrs, 12 min	29.6	30,775	49,528	17.13
Pluto	3,666.0	5,900.0	247.69 years	367 days	6 days, 9 hrs	122.5	1,430	2,300	0.002

Planetary Distances

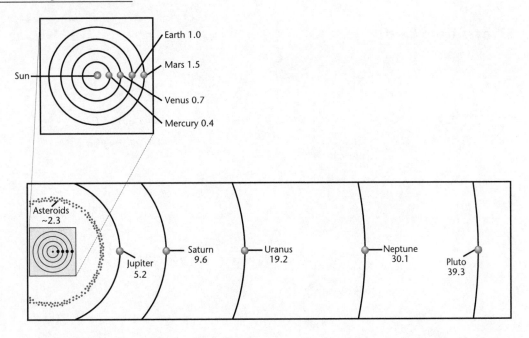

The average distances of the planets from the Sun. The numbers in the diagram are astronomical units (AU), i.e., based on the average distance between the Earth and the Sun: 1 AU = 9.30×10^7 miles (1.50×10^6 kilometers). (Not to scale.)

Size Comparisons of the Planets

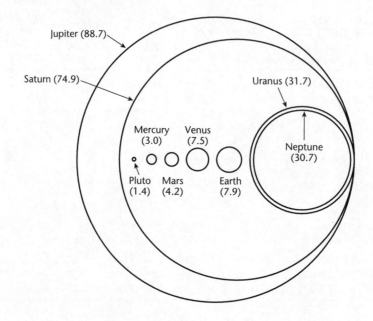

The diameters of the planets, in thousands of miles. (Not to scale.)

Planets from Earth

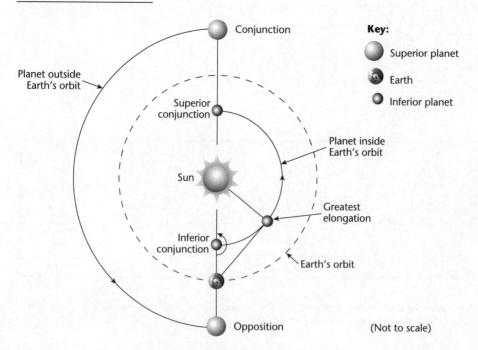

Satellites of Our Solar System

Planet	Satellite	Discoverer and Year of Discovery	DIAMETER* Miles	DIAMETER* Kilometers	PERIOD OF REVOLUTION D	PERIOD OF REVOLUTION Hr	PERIOD OF REVOLUTION Min
Earth	Moon	—	2,160	3,476	27	07	44
Mars	Phobos	A. Hall (1877)	17 × 12	27 × 19	00	07	39
	Deimos	A. Hall (1877)	9 × 7	15 × 11	01	06	18
Jupiter	Metis	*Voyager 2* (1980)	(25)	(40)	00	07	05
	Adrastea	*Voyager 2* (1979)	15 × 10	24 × 16	00	07	09
	Amalthea	E. Barnard (1892)	168 × 93	270 × 150	00	11	57
	Thebe	*Voyager 2* (1979)	(62)	(100)	00	16	12
	Io	Galileo (1610)	2,256	3,630	01	18	27
	Europa	Galileo (1610)	1,950	3,138	03	13	13
	Ganymede	Galileo (1610)	3,270	5,262	07	03	43
	Callisto	Galileo (1610)	2,983	4,800	16	16	32
	Leda	C. Kowal (1974)	(10)	(16)	238	17	17
	Himalia	C. Perrine (1904)	(112)	(180)	250	13	41
	Lysithea	S. Nicholson (1938)	(25)	(40)	259	05	17
	Elara	C. Perrine (1905)	(50)	(80)	259	15	36
	Ananke	S. Nicholson (1951)	(19)	(30)	631	00	00 (retrograde)
	Carme	S. Nicholson (1938)	(28)	(45)	692	00	00 (retrograde)
	Pasiphae	P. Melotte (1908)	(43)	(70)	735	00	00 (retrograde)
	Sinope	S. Nicholson (1914)	(25)	(40)	758	00	00 (retrograde)
Saturn	Pan	*Voyager 2* (1990)	(6)	(10)	00	11	48
	Atlas	*Voyager 1* (1980)	25 × 19	40 × 30	00	14	27
	Prometheus	*Voyager 1* (1980)	87 × 50	140 × 80	00	14	43
	Pandora	*Voyager 1* (1980)	68 × 43	110 × 70	00	15	06
	Janus	A. Dollfus (1966)	137 × 99	220 × 160	00	16	41
	Epimetheus	J. Fountain and S. Larson (1978)	87 × 62	140 × 100	00	16	39
	Mimas	W. Herschel (1789)	242	390	00	22	36
	Enceladus	W. Herschel (1789)	311	500	01	08	53
	Tethys	G. Cassini (1684)	652	1,050	01	21	19
	Telesto	*Voyager 1* (1980)	(16)	(25)	01	21	19
	Calypso	*Voyager 1* (1980)	19 × 12	30 × 20	01	21	19
	Dione	G. Cassini (1684)	696	1,120	02	17	41
	Helene	P. Lacques and J. Lecacheux (1980)	22 × 19	36 × 30	02	17	41
	Rhea	G. Cassini (1672)	951	1,530	04	12	26
	Titan	C. Huygens (1655)	3,200	5,150	15	22	41
	Hyperion	G. Bond (1848)	217 × 124	350 × 200	21	06	39
	Iapetus	G. Cassini (1671)	895	1,440	79	07	57
	Phoebe	W. Pickering (1898)	137	220	550	11	31 (retrograde)
Uranus	Cordelia	*Voyager 2* (1986)	(19)	(30)	00	08	02
	Ophelia	*Voyager 2* (1986)	(19)	(30)	00	09	01
	Bianca	*Voyager 2* (1986)	(25)	(40)	00	10	26
	Cressida	*Voyager 2* (1986)	(43)	(70)	00	11	08
	Desdemona	*Voyager 2* (1986)	(37)	(60)	00	11	23
	Juliet	*Voyager 2* (1986)	(50)	(80)	00	11	50
	Portia	*Voyager 2* (1986)	(68)	(110)	00	12	19
	Rosalind	*Voyager 2* (1986)	(37)	(60)	00	13	24
	Belinda	*Voyager 2* (1986)	(43)	(70)	00	14	59
	Puck	Voyager 2 (1985)	(93)	(150)	00	18	17
	Miranda	G. Kuiper (1948)	292	470	01	09	56
	Ariel	W. Lassell (1851)	721	1,160	02	12	29

Satellites of Our Solar System (cont'd)

Planet	Satellite	Discoverer and Year of Discovery	DIAMETER* Miles	Kilometers	PERIOD OF REVOLUTION D	Hr	Min
	Umbriel	W. Lassell (1851)	727	1,170	04	09	52
	Titania	W. Herschel (1787)	982	1,580	08	16	57
	Oberon	W. Herschel (1787)	945	1,520	13	11	07
Neptune	Naiad	Voyager 2 (1989)	(31)	(50)	00	07	06
	Thalassa	Voyager 2 (1989)	(50)	(80)	00	07	29
	Despoina	Voyager 2 (1989)	(112)	(180)	00	07	60
	Galatea	Voyager 2 (1989)	(93)	(150)	00	10	18
	Larissa	Voyager 2 (1989)	(118)	(190)	00	13	18
	Proteus	Voyager 2 (1989)	(249)	(400)	01	02	54
	Triton	W. Lassell (1846)	1,678	2,700	05	21	03 (retrograde)
	Nereid	G. Kuiper (1949)	(211)	(340)	360	03	50
Pluto	Charon	J. Christy (1978)	739	1,190	06	09	17

Numbers in parentheses are approximations.

KEPLER'S LAWS OF PLANETARY MOTION

Johannes Kepler, the German astronomer who was the assistant and successor to astronomer Tycho Brahe, used Brahe's detailed records to devise several major laws of planetary motion. After 17 years of observation, Kepler determined that the orbits of the planets are ellipses, not circles, and that the planets' orbital sizes are due to their varying distances from the Sun. Kepler's laws are universal and apply to any two bodies gravitationally bound to each other.

Kepler's first law (law of elliptic orbits): Each planet moves about the Sun in an orbit that is an ellipse, with the Sun at one of the two foci of the ellipse.

Kepler's second law (law of areas): An imaginary straight line joining a planet to the Sun sweeps out equal areas of the ellipse in space in equal intervals of time.

Kepler's third law (harmonic law): The square of the period of revolution of a planet is in direct proportion to the cube of the semimajor axis of its orbit.

Comets

Comets are small objects made of rock, ice, and gases that orbit the Sun. Short-term comets complete their elliptical orbits in 6 to 200 years (although some orbits are parabolic and the comet is never seen again); long-term comets take thousands of years to complete their orbit or may never return at all.

Most comets are composed of frozen water, carbon dioxide, methane, ammonia, and nonicy materials such as silicates and organic compounds. They were once described as "dirty snowballs" mixed with small amounts of rock, debris, dust, and organics. But more recent studies suggest that comets are more like "mud balls," with rocky debris accounting for more than half the volume.

Comets have three main parts:

Nucleus: The center, which is made up of rock and ice
Coma: Consists of gases and dust around the nucleus
Tail: Made up of gases and dust that spread out from the nucleus and coma

The sizes of these features vary from comet to comet.

As a comet approaches the Sun, solar radiation vaporizes the gases within the nucleus. This increases the size of the coma, which may reach millions of miles across. Dust and gases that leave the coma stream away from the comet, forming a long tail (or many tails) as much as a hundred million miles long. The solar wind usually causes the comet's tail to point away from the Sun at the comet's closest approach. Though a comet's tail may appear large when observed from Earth, only $1/500$ of the nucleus's mass vaporizes during its passage around the Sun.

Comets are thought to have originated from the *Oort Cloud,* a hypothetical reservoir of comets that lies outside our planetary system, about 100,000 astronomical units beyond the orbit of the planet Pluto. According to the theory, when the surrounding cloud of comets is perturbed—by passing stars, nebula, or even by the up-and-down movement of the solar system through the plane of the galaxy—gravity diverts some comets into the solar system. Some comets are thrown out of the solar system by the gravity of the planets; other comets eventually develop orbits around the Sun.

FARTHEST OUT?

Numerous small objects were recently found traveling near or just outside Neptune's orbit. The asteroid-size objects—including 1992 QB1, 1993 FW, and 1992 RO—are considered the most distant bodies ever imaged in our solar system. In 1995, about 30 more were found by researchers using the Hubble Space Telescope.

Astronomers believe that these distant objects may be from the Kuiper Belt—a hypothetical ring-shaped reservoir of icy bodies surrounding the solar system that is thought to contain primitive bodies left over from the formation of the planets. It is unknown whether these objects are definitely from a thin belt of icy comet-like bodies surrounding the solar system, but if they are, the objects would have circular orbits around the Sun. Scientists certainly hope that these objects are indeed from the Kuiper Belt, as this, along with the Oort Cloud, would explain the seemingly endless supply of short-period comets that frequently enter our inner solar system.

Short-Period Comet Returns

Comet	Perihelion Passage	Perihelion Distance (AU)	Period (Years)
Giacobini-Zinner	September 1985	1.0282	6.59
Halley	February 1986	0.5871	76.0
Whipple	June 1986	3.0775	8.49
Encke	July 1987	0.3317	3.29
Borelly	December 1987	1.3567	6.86
Tempel 2	September 1988	1.3834	5.29
Tempel 1	January 1989	1.4967	5.50
d'Arrest	February 1989	1.2921	6.39
Perrine-Mrkos	March 1989	1.2977	6.78
Tempel-Swift	April 1989	1.5884	6.40

Short-Period Comet Returns (cont'd)

Comet	Perihelion Passage	Perihelion Distance (AU)	Period (Years)
Schwassman-Wachmann 1	October 1989	5.7718	14.9
Tuttle-Giacobini-Kresak	February 1990	1.0680	5.46
Honda-Mrkos-Pajdusakova	September 1990	0.5412	5.30
Wild 2	December 1990	1.5779	6.37
Faye	November 1991	1.5934	7.34

Asteroids

Asteroids, or minor planets, are small, rocky objects in the solar system. Astronomers believe that asteroids formed from the collision of larger bodies and that some may be extinct comets. More than 5,000 asteroids have been discovered, and astronomers estimate there may be more than 10,000 in the solar system.

The majority of asteroids are found in the *asteroid belt*, located between 2.0 and 3.3 astronomical units from the Sun, between the orbits of Mars and Jupiter; although several asteroids have eccentric orbits. For example, Hidalgo, discovered in 1920, has a strange orbit that takes the asteroid from just beyond Mars's orbit to near Saturn. Chiron, detected in 1977, was first thought to be an asteroid. Though some scientists often use Chiron as an example of the largest comet known, other astronomers still believe that Chiron is an asteroid with an eccentric orbit that takes it from inside Saturn's orbit to near the orbit of Uranus.

Composition of asteroids is inferred from meteorites that fall to Earth (many of which are thought to originate from the asteroid belt) and by spectral measurements. The majority of asteroids fall into three classes, depending on their spectra from reflected sunlight.

C-types: About 72 percent of asteroids are these dark, carbonaceous rocks
S-types: About 13 percent are these grayish, stony asteroids
M-types: About 10 percent of asteroids are of this metallic type

Sampling of Asteroids

Number	Name	Discoverer (Year)	Closest Distance to the Sun (AU)	Diameter (miles)[kilometers]
1	Ceres	Piazzi (1801)	2.55	584 [940]
2	Pallas	Olbers (1802)	2.11	334 [538]
3	Juno	Harding (1804)	1.98	177 [285]
4	Vesta	Olbers (1807)	2.15	345 [555]
5	Astraea	Hencke (1845)	2.10	73 [117]
6	Hebe	Hencke (1847)	1.93	121 [195]
7	Iris	Hind (1847)	1.84	130 [209]
8	Flora	Hind (1847)	1.86	94 [151]
9	Metis	Graham (1848)	2.09	94 [151]
10	Hygeia	De Gasparis (1849)	2.84	280 [450]
13	Egeria	De Gasparis (1850)	2.36	139 [224]
15	Eunomia	De Gasparis (1851)	2.15	169 [272]
16	Psyche	De Gasparis (1851)	2.53	155 [250]
24	Themis	De Gasparis (1853)	2.76	145 [234]
31	Euphrosyne	Ferguson (1854)	2.45	230 [370]
48	Doris	Goldschmidt (1857)	2.93	155 [250]
52	Europa	Goldschmidt (1858)	2.75	180 [289]

Sampling of Asteroids (cont'd)

Number	Name	Discoverer (Year)	Closest Distance to the Sun (AU)	Diameter (miles)[kilometers]
65	Cybele	Tempe (1861)	3.01	192 [309]
92	Undina	Peters (1867)	2.97	155 [250]
95	Arethusa	Luther (1867)	2.61	143 [230]
324	Bamberga	Palisa (1892)	1.78	153 [246]
349	Dembowska	Charlois (1892)	2.66	89 [144]
451	Patienta	Charlois (1899)	2.82	172 [276]
511	Davida	Dugan (1903)	2.66	201 [323]
617	Patrocius	Kopff (1906)	4.48	91 [147]
624	Hector	Kopff (1907)	4.99	111 [179]
704	Interamnia	Cerulli (1910)	2.58	217 [350]
944	Hildago	Baade (1920)	2.00	9 [15]
1172	Aeneas	Reinmuth (1930)	4.64	81 [130]
1566	Icarus	Baade (1949)	0.19	?
1862	Apollo	Reinmuth (1932)	0.65	?
2060	Chiron	Kowal (1977)	8.50	68 [110]

Impacts on the Earth

All members of the solar system, including the Earth, have been struck by asteroids and comets in the past. On the planet Mercury and on our Moon, where there is no thick atmosphere and crustal activity, we can see thousands of craters caused by ancient impacts. Many of the moons in the outer solar system are also covered with impact craters.

On Earth, scientists have found about 140 impact features scattered over the surface of the planet, caused by comet and asteroid impacts. But not all bodies form an impact crater; for instance, a stony meteorite about 100 feet (30 meters) in diameter vaporized above the northern Siberian region called Tunguska in 1908, knocking down trees within a 20-mile (32-kilometer) radius (the object was originally thought to be a comet).

It is theorized that impacts of asteroids caused major extinctions of flora and fauna on Earth in the past. For example, some scientists believe that the extinction of about 50 percent of all species (including the dinosaurs) 65 million years ago was caused by such an impact or many impacts (for more information on extinctions, see Chapter 9, "Earth Science").

Occasionally, a small asteroid will stray from the asteroid belt, because of either a collision with another asteroid or the gravitational pull of Jupiter. A number of these asteroids have unusual orbits around the Sun, and some eventually reach the inner solar system. The asteroids that come close to the Earth are called *Earth-approaching* or *near-Earth* asteroids. These asteroids are categorized into several groups.

Aten asteroids have orbits that lie inside the Earth's orbit

Amor asteroids have orbits that cross the orbit of Mars and approach the Earth's orbit

Apollo asteroids have orbits that cross the Earth's orbit

Arjuna asteroids, which measure no more than 328 feet (100 meters) across, orbit the Sun in a nearly circular path (the existence of this category is still debated).

Though bodies come close to Earth, they often pass by with no effect. For example, the asteroid 1989 FC came within 430,000 miles (691,870 kilometers) of Earth on March 22, 1989, and asteroid 4179 Toutatis flew by the Earth on December 9, 1992, at a distance of 1.5 million miles (2.5 million kilometers).

AN IMPACT TODAY

What would happen if a large object struck the Earth today? Because the Earth is covered mostly by water, there is a 70 percent chance that the strike would occur in the ocean. A larger asteroid or comet could cause temporary, localized climate changes by splashing a circular wall of water into the air, and generating steam. If the impact were close to land, sea waves, resembling the seismic sea waves called *tsunamis*, could inundate coastal cities.

A land strike would be even more destructive. If an object as large as the one that formed Meteor Crater in Arizona (an object 150 feet [46 meters] wide created the 4,000-foot [1,219 meters] diameter crater) were to strike, heat from the friction as the object entered the atmosphere would sear everything for miles around. The rock would hit the Earth with 75 percent of its original velocity, throwing black dust high into the atmosphere and filtering the sunlight for weeks or months—and possibly cooling the planet. Acid rain and wildfires would also follow the collision. Larger strikes would cause even more damage.

Terrestrial Impact Craters

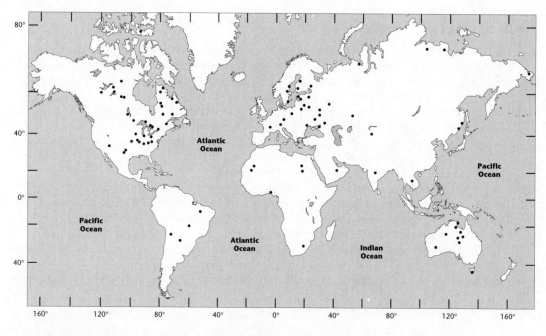

Distribution of most of the known terrestrial impacts.

Meteors

Meteoroids are small (up to several feet in diameter) solid objects that travel through space often along the same orbits as comets. Collections of particles, called *streams*, are naturally released from comets and eventually extend along their orbits; when a comet eventually breaks apart, the material travels in a pack called a *swarm*.

When a meteoroid enters the Earth's upper atmosphere, it is called a *meteor* (commonly referred to as a shooting or falling star). Meteors are seen as a bright trail of light, which is caused as the atmosphere's friction vaporizes the object. Larger meteors are called *bolides* and are sometimes heard hissing and crackling as they enter the atmosphere. A *fireball* is an exceptionally bright meteor. If a meteor survives its flight through the atmosphere and strikes the surface, it is called a *meteorite*. It is estimated that 50 tons of meteoric mass enter the Earth's atmosphere every day. Only about one-tenth of the meteoric material reaches land or oceans. The rest burns up in the atmosphere.

Meteor showers occur periodically when the Earth travels through a meteoroid swarm or stream. The material is usually associated with the orbits of comets. Most meteors during a shower seem to be observed in a particular constellation (called the *radiant*).

Major Meteor Showers

Dates	Name	Constellation (Radiant)	Number per Hour at Maximum
January 1–6	Quadrantids	Boötes	110
March 9–12	Zeta Boötids	Boötes	10
April 19–24	April Lyrids	Hercules	12
May 1–8	Eta Aquarids (associated with Comet Halley)	Aquarius	20
June 10–21	June Lyrids	Lyra	12
June 17–26	Ophiuchids	Ophiuchus	15
July 15–August 15	Delta Aquarids	Aquarius	35
July 15–August 25	Alpha Capricornids	Capricornus	8
July 15–August 25	Iota Aquarids	Aquarius	6
July 25–August 18	Perseids	Cassiopeia	68
July 26–August 15	Capricornids	Capricornus	6
August 19–22	Kappa Cygnids	Cygnus	4
September 7–15	Beta Cassiopeids	Cassiopeia	10
October 10	Draconids	Draco	Variable
October 16–26	Orionids (associated with Comet Halley)	Orion	30
October 20–November 30	Taurids (associated with Comet Encke)	Taurus	12
November 7–11	Cepheids	Cassiopeia	8
November 15–19	Leonids	Leo	10–100
November 15–December 6	Andromedids	Cassiopeia	Variable
December 7–15	Geminids	Gemini	58
December 17–24	Ursids (associated with Comet Tuttle)	Ursa Minor	6

SAMPLES FROM SPACE?

Meteorites fall on the Earth quite frequently, but because the Earth is 70 percent ocean, most of them are never found. Meteorites are usually divided into *siderites*, or iron meteorites; the more common *aerolites*, or stony meteorites composed mostly of silicates; and *siderolites*, or stony iron meteorites. Most of the meteorites found on the Earth are thought to have originated in the asteroid belt—though some may have come from the Moon or Mars.

Tektites are glassy objects found in certain areas of the world, including parts of Australia and Thailand. Some astronomers believe that tektites came from the Moon when a large object struck our satellite, sending tons of debris into space toward the Earth. But most evidence suggests that tektites are terrestrial in origin—material thrown to great heights by large impact events on the Earth. As the material fell back to the Earth's surface, it was melted and deformed by the frictional heat of the atmosphere, creating the glassy tektites we find today.

Several meteorites may have originated on Mars. Eight of these meteorites, called Shergotty-Nakhla-Chassigny (SNCs; named after their places of origin) meteorites have been found—all differing in composition when compared with other meteorites. Scientists believe the rocks may have been ejected from the Martian surface when a large object struck the red planet. One problem: No known craters on Mars are large or deep enough to support this theory.

Between the Planets

Though interplanetary space is mostly a vacuum, it is not empty. In the spaces between the planets are found three major types of particles: the solar wind, interplanetary dust, and cosmic rays.

The *solar wind*, also called interplanetary gas, is composed of thin, invisible streams of charged subatomic particles, mostly protons and electrons. The particles vary in density, depending on the position in the solar system. Near the Sun, the solar wind travels close to the speed of sound in air, or about 1,116 feet (340 meters) per second; it travels from 186 to 373 miles (300 to 600 kilometers) per second—about a thousand times faster—near the Earth.

The solar wind increases during eruptive bursts of solar flares—which is why the Sun is carefully observed during a space shuttle mission, as humans and the spacecraft can be adversely affected by excessive solar wind particles. Particles from periodic solar flares penetrate the Earth's upper atmosphere around the magnetic poles. Often these particles react with and excite the upper atmosphere's oxygen and nitrogen, causing the colorful, shimmering *aurora borealis* (northern lights) and *aurora australis* (southern lights) at their respective poles.

Cosmic rays are high-speed subatomic particles, consisting mostly of protons with a few heavier atomic nuclei. Most cosmic rays originate outside the solar system, though the Sun emits some cosmic rays. The rays are faster and more destructive to humans than are the solar wind particles. The Earth is protected from the rays by its thick atmosphere, but on long space voyages, special protection will have to be built into the spacecraft to protect the astronauts from the constant bombardment of cosmic rays.

Interplanetary dust is composed of micrometeoric debris scattered by comets, and granular powder from asteroid and meteoroid collisions. The interplanetary dust is best observed in the Northern Hemisphere in the form of *zodiacal light*—seen in the west after sundown in the early spring, and in the east just before sunrise in the late fall. The faint, triangular band of light is caused by the reflection from dust and small particles along the plane of the planets' orbits (or the plane of the ecliptic).

THE EARTH'S MOON

The Moon is the Earth's only natural satellite. Here are some of its characteristics:

Diameter: 2,160 miles (3,476 kilometers)
Mean distance from the Earth: 238,866 miles (384,400 kilometers)
Perigee distance from the Earth: 222,756 miles (356,410 kilometers)
Apogee distance from the Earth: 254,186 miles (406,697 kilometers)

Rotation and revolution: 27.32 days (because of its equal rotation and revolution, the same side of the Moon is always facing the Earth)

Movement in Earth's sky: When viewed from the Earth, the Moon crosses the local meridian each day (on the average) about 50 minutes later than the previous day

Temperatures: 273°F (134°C) on the sunlit side at noon; –243°F (–153°C) during the darkness of the 2-week-long lunar night

The Earth's Moon is fifth in size of all the moons in the solar system. It has no real atmosphere, though there is some evidence that the solar wind particles form a thin layer around the Moon. The lunar surface is covered with craters, mare (the so-called seas of the Moon), mountains, domes, and rays (streaks around craters from ejected material). Most of the lunar rocks are similar to Earth's volcanic rocks, but with lower percentages of iron and higher percentages of titanium. The Moon is thought to have a thick crust, a thin, partially molten mantle, and possibly a core. It is also more active than once thought—seismic instruments left on the Moon by the *Apollo* missions recorded slight tremors, or moonquakes.

ORIGIN OF THE MOON?

There are numerous theories about the origin of the Moon. George Darwin, son of Charles Darwin, proposed the fission theory, in which part of the rapidly spinning Earth was flung off to create the Moon; another version of the fission theory stated that the Moon originated from the Pacific Ocean. The capture theory stated that the Moon was an independent body—captured as it traveled past the Earth. In a third theory, the Moon and Earth formed side-by-side from solar nebula material.

One of the most interesting theories was developed in the 1980s: As the early Earth formed, a Mars-size object struck the Earth. This cataclysmic impact threw a large part of the Earth into space—enough rock to eventually accrete and form the Moon. Such a scenario would explain the closeness and "double-planet" (two bodies locked in synchronous orbit) appearance of the Earth and Moon.

The Moon Around the Earth

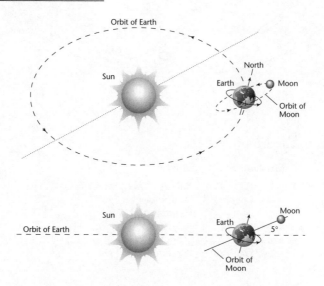

Faces of the Moon

N

Pythagoras
J. Herschel
W. Bond
Babbage
Mare Frigoris
Mare Humboldtianum
Plato
Aristoteles
Cassini
Zeno
Aristillus
Franklin
Gauss
Geminus
Autolycus
Mare Imbrium
A15
Mare Serenitatis
Cleomedes
Archimedes
Prinz
Euler
Montes Apenninus
A17
Mare Crisium
Mare Marginis
Aristarchus
Montes Carpatus
Oceanus Procellarum
Eratosthenes
Mare Vaporum
Julius Caesar
Mare Undarum
Olbers
Kepler
Copernicus
Bode
Mare Tranquillitatis
Mare Spumans
Encke
Pallas
Agrippa
Mare Fecunditatis
Riccioli
Reinhold
Godin
Messier
Mare Smythii
Lansberg
A12   A14
Delambre
A11
Flamsteed
Fra Mauro
Herschel
Mare Nectaris
Grimaldi   Hansteen
Mare Cognitum
Ptolemaeus
A16
Kant
Albategnius
Alphonsus
Almanon
Gassendi
Mare Nibium
Arzachet
Playfair   Geber
Mare Humorum
Kies
Apianus
Borda
Petavius
Vieta
Purbach
Snellius
Fourier
Hell
Adams
Walter
Stevinus
Furnerius
Schickard
Wilhelm
Buch
Metius
Fabricius
Tycho
Schiller
Longomontanus
Cuvier   Baco
Mare Australe
Jacobi
Mutus

S

Apollo Missions to the Moon

Map Listing	Mission	Date
*A11	Apollo 11	July 20, 1969
*A12	Apollo 12	November 19, 1969
*A14	Apollo 14	February 5, 1971
*A15	Apollo 15	July 30, 1971
*A16	Apollo 16	April 21, 1972
*A17	Apollo 17	December 11, 1972

Probes to the Moon

Probe	Date of Reaching the Moon	Probe	Date of Reaching the Moon
Luna 2	September 13, 1959	Surveyor 5	September 11, 1967
Ranger 7	July 31 , 1964	Surveyor 6	November 10, 1967
Ranger 8	February 20, 1965	Surveyor 7	January 19, 1968
Ranger 9	March 24, 1965	Luna 16	September 21, 1970
Luna 9	February 3, 1966	Luna 17	November 17, 1970
Surveyor 1	June 2, 1966	Luna 20	February 21, 1972
Luna 13	December 24, 1966	Luna 21	January 15, 1973
Surveyor 3	April 10, 1967	Luna 24	August 18, 1976

Phases of the Moon

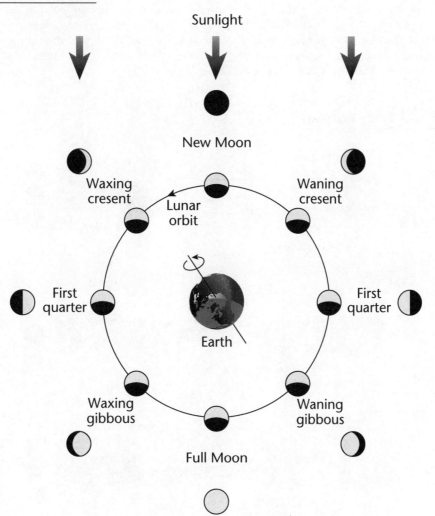

Eclipses of the Sun and Moon

Lunar and solar eclipses occur because of the relative alignments of the Sun, Earth, and Moon along the same plane. Lunar eclipses occur only at full moon; solar eclipses occur only at new moon. Lunar eclipses can be seen from anywhere on the hemisphere facing the Moon at eclipse time; solar eclipses are seen only from areas within or near the path of totality. A maximum of three lunar eclipses is possible per year; a maximum of five solar eclipses is possible per year.

Lunar eclipses occur when the Moon passes into the Earth's shadow. There are three types of lunar eclipses: A *total eclipse* occurs when the Moon passes through the umbra of the Earth's shadow, *a partial eclipse* occurs when the Moon passes through a part of the umbra, and a *penumbral eclipse* occurs when the Moon passes through the penumbra of the Earth's shadow. The Moon rarely becomes completely blackened; in most cases, the Earth's atmosphere refracts the sunlight onto the lunar surface, giving the Moon a deep coppery or red color.

Solar eclipses occur when the Moon passes between the Earth and the Sun; during these eclipses, the shadow of the Moon follows along a narrow path on the Earth. During an *annular eclipse*, the apparent size of the Moon is insufficient to cover the Sun completely; from the surface, a ring of Sun is seen around the Moon. In a *partial solar eclipse*, the Moon covers only a part of the Sun as seen from the Earth, and from the Earth's surface, the Sun is seen as a crescent, the size dependent on how much of the Sun is blocked by the Moon. And in a *total eclipse* of the Sun, the Moon blocks out the Sun's entire disk.

Lunar and Solar Eclipses

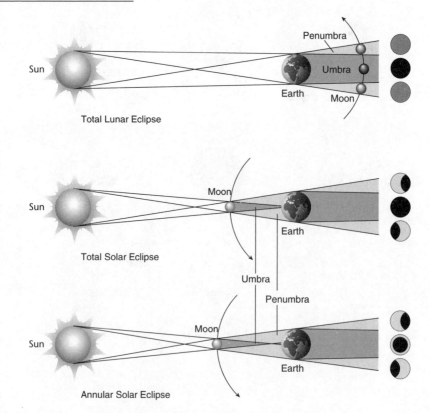

Total Lunar Eclipse

Total Solar Eclipse

Annular Solar Eclipse

Lunar and Solar Eclipses (1995–2010)

SOLAR ECLIPSES

Year	Date	Type	Area of Visibility
1995	April 29	Annular	C and S America, Caribbean
	October 24	Total	Arabia, Asia, Japan, Australia, Pacific
1996	April 17	Partial	New Zealand, Pacific
	October 12	Partial	NE Canada, Greenland, Europe, N Africa
1997	March 8	Total	E Asia, Japan, NW N America
	September 1	Partial	S Australia, New Zealand, S Pacific
1998	February 26	Total	S and E N America, C America
	August 21	Annular	S and SE Asia, Indonesia, Australia
1999	February 16	Annular	Indian Ocean, Antarctica, Indonesia
	August 11	Total	NE N America, Arctic, Europe, Arabia
2000	February 5	Partial	Antarctica
	July 1	Partial	S South America, SE Pacific Ocean
	July 31	Partial	NW North America
2001	June 21	Total	S Atlantic Ocean, S Africa
	December 14	Annular	Pacific Ocean, Costa Rica
2002	June 10	Annular	Celebes Sea to Mexico
	December 4	Total	S Africa to S Australia
2003	May 31	Annular	Iceland, Greenland
	November 23	Total	Antarctica
2004	April 19	Partial	S Africa, S Atlantic Ocean
	October 14	Partial	Japan, NE Asia, N Pacific Ocean
2005	April 8	Annular/Total	SW Pacific Ocean, N South America
	October 3	Annular	Spain, N Africa, Kenya
2006	March 29	Total	W and N Africa, Central Asia
	September 22	Annular	Guyana, S Atlantic Ocean
2007	March 19	Partial	Asia
	September 11	Partial	S S America
2008	August 1	Total	Siberia, N China
2009	January 26	Annular	Indonesia, Borneo
	July 22	Total	India, S China, S Pacific Ocean
2010	July 11	Total	S Pacific Ocean

LUNAR ECLIPSES

Year	Date	Type	Year	Date	Type
1995	April 15	Partial	2004	May 4	Total
1996	April 3	Total		October 28	Total
	September 26	Total	2007	March 3	Total
1997	March 23	Partial		August 28	Total
	September 6	Total	2008	February 21	Total
1999	July 28	Partial		August 16	Partial
2000	January 21	Total	2010	June 25	Partial
	July 16	Total			
2003	May 16	Total			
	November 7	Total			

CONSTELLATIONS

Constellations are patterns of stars in the sky. Each civilization gave names to conspicuous patterns of bright stars, with most constellations having no real boundaries. Today, the generally accepted constellations in Northern and Southern Hemisphere skies are divided into 88 constellations. The origin of most of these constellation names descended from Arabic and Greek legends; patterns of Southern Hemisphere constellations date from the eighteenth and nineteenth centuries.

The boundaries of constellations do not just include the familiar six to eight stars that form a figure; constellations are divided into large regions—like tiles—that cover the sky to aid astronomers in mapping the stars. In 1801, Johann Bode drew the first boundaries of constellations; by 1930, the International Astronomical Union standardized the boundaries. Because of the Earth's precession, and thus changes in stellar coordinates, a new constellation atlas is released about every 50 years.

The Constellations (Northern and Southern Hemispheres)

Name	Abbreviation	Name	Abbreviation	Name	Abbreviation
Andromeda	And	Crux	Cru	Orion	Ori
Antlia	Ant	Cygnus	Cyg	Pavo	Pav
Apus	Aps	Delphinus	Del	Pegasus	Peg
Aquarius	Aqr	Dorado	Dor	Perseus	Per
Aquila	Aql	Draco	Dra	Phoenix	Phe
Ara	Ara	Equuleus	Equ	Pictor	Pic
Aries	Ari	Eridanus	Eri	Pisces	Psc
Auriga	Aur	Fornax	For	Piscis Austrinus	PsA
Boötes	Boo	Gemini	Gem	Puppis	Pup
Cælum	Cae	Grus	Gru	Pyxis	Pyx
Camelopardalis	Cam	Hercules	Her	Reticulum	Ret
Cancer	Cnc	Horologium	Hor	Sagitta	Sge
Canes Venatici	CVn	Hydra	Hya	Sagittarius	Sgr
Canis Major	CMa	Hydrus	Hyi	Scorpius	Sco
Canis Minor	CMi	Indus	Ind	Sculptor	Scl
Capricornus	Cap	Lacerta	Lac	Scutum	Sct
Carina	Car	Leo	Leo	Serpens	Ser
Cassiopeia	Cas	Leo Minor	LMi	Sextans	Sex
Centaurus	Cen	Lepus	Lep	Taurus	Tau
Cepheus	Cep	Libra	Lib	Telescopium	Tel
Cetus	Cet	Lupus	Lup	Triangulum	Tri
Chamæleon	Cha	Lynx	Lyn	Triangulum Australe	TrA
Circinus	Cir	Lyra	Lyr		
Columba	Col	Mensa	Men	Tucana	Tuc
Coma Berenices	Com	Microscopium	Mic	Ursa Major	UMa
Corona Austrinus	CrA	Monoceros	Mon	Ursa Minor	UMi
		Musca	Mus	Vela	Vel
Corona Borealis	CrB	Norma	Nor	Virgo	Vir
Corvus	Crv	Octans	Oct	Volans	Vol
Crater	Crt	Ophiuchus	Oph	Vulpecula	Vul

THE STARS

Scientists believe that stars originate as a collection of interstellar gases and dust. The cloud begins to shrink and rotate, eventually developing into a protostar and accretion disk. Protostars of sufficient mass begin to convert hydrogen to helium by nuclear reactions (fusion) and become full-fledged stars. Some that are too small to accomplish this become brown dwarfs and are often referred to as "failed stars."

Star Classification

Spectral Class	Example Stars	Color	Approximate Temperature (°K)
O	10 Lacertae	Blue	>30,000–60,000
B	Rigel	Blue	10,000–30,000
A	Sirius, Vega	Blue	7,500–10,000
F	Canopus, Polaris	Blue to white	6,000–7,500
G	Sun, Capella	White to yellow	5,000–6,000
K	Aldebaran, Arcturus	Orange to red	3,500–5,000
M	Betelgeuse	Red	<3,500

Lives of the Stars

Stars change over time. After a star's birth and infancy, (i.e., from a collection of gases and dust to a protostar), the star enters the mature stage, when stable nuclear reactions begin. The typical star spends most of its life at this stage. The star eventually ages and enters the late evolution state, often swelling to a red giant. Instability follows, causing stars to become variables, novas, planetary nebulas, or supernovas. At the end of a star's life, it becomes a white dwarf, neutron star, or black dwarf, depending on the original stellar mass. The Hertzsprung-Russell Diagram, which is a chart of stellar luminosity (absolute magnitude) versus temperature, depicts the characteristics of stars and the stages of stars' life cycles.

Hertzsprung-Russell Diagram

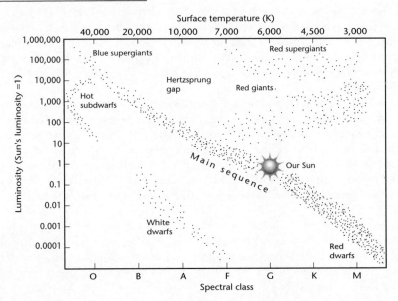

Types of Stars

Not all stars are like our Sun. The differences are usually related to the age, size, formation, and structure of each star.

A *black dwarf* is the final stage of a star after it has used its energy supplies as a white dwarf. Such a star is no longer luminous. Theoretically, the universe is not old enough to have formed any black dwarfs.

Black holes are theoretical regions of space (although a possible black hole has been observed) where the gravitational field is so strong that even photons of light cannot escape. Black holes are formed when massive stars collapse. Black holes are inferred to exist by their gravitational effects on material falling into them. They are thought to be associated with certain x-ray sources, such as the binary star system Cygnus X-1, and are thought to exist at the center of some spiral galaxies.

The bluest, hottest, and most luminous stars are *blue supergiants*. They have large masses, low densities, and are very rare. Rigel in the constellation of Orion is a blue supergiant.

Hot subdwarfs are hot blue stars with very high densities and are usually the central stars of planetary nebulas. The central star in Lyra's Ring Nebula is a hot subdwarf.

A *neutron star* is the remnant of a star with a mass between 1.4 and 3 solar masses that collapses under gravity (or implodes), with the protons and electrons smashing together to form neutrons.

As seen from the Earth, a *nova* is a star that suddenly increases in brightness, then declines gradually over a short period. Novas are usually associated with binary star systems in which one member is a white dwarf, with material from the companion star interacting with the white dwarf, creating a flare reaction.

A stellar object that often emits regular bursts of radio waves in specific directions is a *pulsar*. The average time between pulses ranges from milliseconds for pulsars in binary systems up to 4 seconds for the slower pulsars. Discovered in 1967, pulsars are thought to be rotating neutron stars.

Red giant stars are considerably larger and brighter than our Sun, with low densities. Arcturus, in the constellation Boötes, is a red giant.

Red supergiants are the largest class of stars and among the brightest. They have large masses and low densities. Betelgeuse, in the constellation of Orion, is a red supergiant.

A gigantic explosion in which a massive star undergoes gravitational collapse and ejects its outer layers into space is a *supernova*. This is accompanied by an immense outburst of light and charged particles, with the core collapsing to form a neutron star (or possibly a black hole). The Crab Nebula in Taurus is the result of a supernova explosion that was recorded in 1054, by Chinese astronomers. More recently, supernova 1987A exploded in the Southern Hemisphere's Large Magellanic Cloud.

Variable stars are any stars that exhibit a change in magnitude over time. Variable stars change in brightness as a result of two stars eclipsing each other, from explosions in the star, or because of a natural pulsation caused by an imbalance between the star's outer layer and core. Variable stars include Cepheid variables (vary in a regular fashion, such as the star Delta Cephei), RR Lyrae variables (vary in the course of about a day, such as the star RR in the constellation Lyra), long-period variables (vary for periods of over a year, such as the star Mira), and eclipsing binaries (such as the star Epsilon Aurigae, with a period of 27 years, one of the longest periods known).

White dwarf stars are in the last stage of stellar evolution, formed when a star finally exhausts its sources of fuel for thermonuclear fusion and becomes very dense. The star collapses under its own gravity, and the gravitational energy is converted to heat, allowing the star to continue to shine. There are many white dwarf stars, including the companion star of Sirius in the constellation of Canis Major.

White holes are hypothetical objects, never observed, that have properties opposite to those of a black hole. Scientists believe that white holes occur where matter spontaneously appears.

Brightest Stars

Star	Proper Name	Distance (light-years)	Absolute Magnitude*	Apparent Magnitude*
α Cma	Sirius	8.7	+1.41	−1.47
α Car	Canopus	180	−4.7	−0.71
α Cen	Rigil Kent	4.3	+4.3	−0.1
α Boo	Arcturus	36	−0.2	−0.06
α Lyr	Vega	26	+0.5	+0.03
β Ori	Rigel	815	−7.0	0.08
α Aur	Capella (binary)	45	+0.12, +0.37	0.09
α Cmi	Procyon	11	+2.65	0.34
α Eri	Achernar	142	−2.2	0.49
β Cen	Hadar	400	−5.0	0.61
α Aql	Altair	16	+2.3	0.75
α Tau	Aldebaran	68	−0.7	0.78
α Cru	Acrux	270	−3.5	0.80
α Ori	Betelgeuse (variable)	650	−6.0	0.85 (mean)
α Sco	Antares	400	−4.7	0.92
α Vir	Spica	270	−3.4	0.98
β Gem	Pollux	35	+0.95	1.15
α PsA	Fomalhaut	23	+1.9	1.16
α Cyg	Deneb	1600	−7.3	1.26
β Cru	Mimosa	460	−4.7	1.28
α Leo	Regulus	85	−0.6	1.33
ε CMa	Adhara	650	−5.0	1.42
γ Ori	Bellatrix	300	−3.3	1.61
λ Sco	Shaula	300	−3.4	1.61
β Tau	El Nath	180	−2.0	1.64

Note: Absolute magnitude is the brightness of a star if it were 10 parsecs from the observer. Apparent magnitude is the brightness of a star as seen by an observer without regard to distance.

Closest Stars

Star	Distance (light-years)	Spectral Type	Apparent Magnitude*	Absolute Magnitude*
Sun	—	G2	−26.73	+4.84
Proxima Cen	4.3	M5e	+10.75	+15.1
α Cen A	4.3	G2	0.0	4.4
α Cen B	4.3	K1	1.4	5.8
Barnard's star	6.0	M5	9.5	13.2
Wolf 359	8.1	M8	13.5	16.5
Lal 21185	8.2	M2	7.5	10.5
Sirius A	8.7	A1	−1.5	1.4
Sirius B	8.7	wA5	+8.5	11.4
UV Cet A	9.0	M6e	12.5	15.3

Closest Stars

Star	Distance (light-years)	Spectral Type	Apparent Magnitude*	Absolute Magnitude*
UV Cet B	9.0	M6e	13.0	15.8
Ross 154	9.3	M6	10.6	13.3
Ross 248	10.3	M6	12.2	14.7
ε Eri	10.8	K2	3.7	6.1
L 789-6	11.1	M7	12.2	14.6
Ross 128	11.1	M5	11.1	13.5
61 Cyg A	11.2	K5	5.2	7.5
61 Cyg B	11.2	K7	6.0	8.4
Procyon A	11.3	F5	0.3	2.6
Procyon B	11.3	wF	10.8	13.1
ε Ind	11.4	K3	4.7	7.0
Σ 2398 A	11.6	M4	8.9	11.1
Σ2398 B	11.6	M5	9.7	11.9
Grb 34 A	11.7	M1	8.1	10.3
Grb 34 B	11.7	M6	11.0	13.3
Lac 9352	11.9	M2	7.4	9.6

Note: Absolute magnitude is the brightness of a star if it were 10 parsecs from the observer. Apparent magnitude is the brightness of a star as seen by an observer without regard to distance.

THE CLOSEST STAR SYSTEM

The closest star system to Earth is Alpha Centauri. Although it is often said that Alpha Centauri is our closest star, Proxima Centauri (or Centauri C) actually is closer.

The Centauri system is composed of three stars: Centauri A and B are medium-size stars and are type G2 (similar to our own Sun) and KO, respectively. Centauri A and B revolve around each other every 80 years. Smaller Centauri C, a type M5 (red dwarf) star, revolves around A and B every 500,000 years.

Scientists believe that the Centauri system may have planets orbiting around Centauri A and/or B. If that is true, it would be the closest planetary system to our own solar system. But because of the distance, it would take thousands of years for one of today's spacecraft to reach it. The Centauri system is 4.4 light-years away from Earth, or about 270,000 astronomical units (1 astronomical unit is the mean distance between the Earth and the Sun)—or equal to just over 1 billion trips around the Earth.

GALAXIES

What Is a Galaxy?

A *galaxy* is a family of between 1 million and 1 trillion stars, plus dust and gases, that are held together by their mutual gravitational attraction. Galaxies come in various sizes and are classified by their shapes, including spiral, elliptical, or irregular. The *Milky Way galaxy*, where our solar system is located, is a spiral galaxy. The solar system is located in the Orion arm of the galaxy.

Shapes of Galaxies

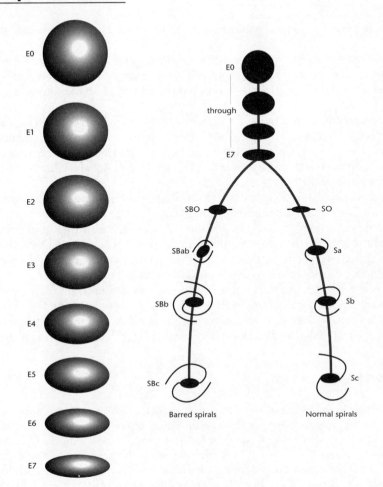

Galaxies are classified by how tightly or loosely wound they are and whether they are normal or "barred" at their centers. E = elliptical; S = spiral.

MEMBERS OF THE LOCAL GROUP

The Milky Way galaxy is surrounded by other galaxies called the Local Group. There are more than 27 identified objects in the Local Group, with the possibility of up to 10 other members, such as dwarf galaxies hidden by the heavy interstellar absorption of radiation by the Milky Way dust clouds. The Local Group covers an area about 3 million light-years in diameter.

The two largest galaxies in the Local Group are the Milky Way (our own) and the Andromeda. The Milky Way is surrounded by about 13 other galaxies and the Andromeda by about 9 galaxies; and there are about 5 other galaxies outside both groups. The total mass of the Local Group is about 700 billion solar masses. The reason for the Local Group's existence is not known. It is thought that either the gravitational attraction of the larger galaxies pulled the group together or that the galaxies all formed at the same time around the same material and have traveled together in space ever since.

OTHER ASTRONOMICAL OBJECTS

Stars and galaxies are not the only large objects found in the universe. The most common are *clusters* and *nebulas*.

Clusters are either open or globular. *Open* clusters are often found within the spiral arms of the Milky Way galaxy. They are irregular in shape and measure no more than a few tens of light-years in diameter. One of the best known open clusters is the Pleiades, in the constellation Taurus.

Globular clusters are spherical collections of stars tightly packed together. Many are located around the Milky Way in what is called the galactic halo. There are around 200 globular clusters known to exist in our galaxy. The two brightest in the Southern Hemisphere are Omega Centauri and NGC 104. In the Northern Hemisphere, M13, the Great Globular Cluster in the constellation Hercules, is one of the brightest.

There are four types of nebulas. *Reflective* nebulas are collections of dust and gas that reflect the light of nearby stars. The Pleiades star cluster in Taurus contains reflective nebulas.

Emission nebulas are collections of dust, gas, and ionized gases that emit their own light. They are often sites of stellar birth; the Great Nebula in Orion (M42) is an emission nebula.

Dark nebulas are collections of opaque dust and gas that often obscure or dim the view of stars behind them. The Horsehead Nebula in Orion includes a dark nebula.

Planetary nebulas are mostly circular, expanding envelopes of gas surrounding a central star; they are the results of an exploding star, usually at the end of its stellar life. The Ring Nebula in Lyra (M57) is a planetary nebula. A very massive star at the end of its life also throws off most of its material, scattering the material in all directions; the Crab Nebula in Taurus is such a nebula.

CATALOGING SPACE

Astronomers have long known the necessity of cataloging celestial objects, not only to track new phenomena but to allow other astronomers to locate astronomical objects. One of the earliest star catalogs was developed by Johann Kepler, based on his and Tycho Brahe's observations. In 1712, the first volume of John Flamsteed's star catalog was published (without his permission). It listed the positions of close to 3,000 stars and replaced the star catalog that was developed by Johann Kepler. The *General Catalogue of Double Stars* by Sherburne Wesley Burnham listed data on 1,274 double stars; *The New General Catalogue of Double Stars Within 120 Degrees of the North Pole* by Robert Grant Aitken and Joseph Hussey listed 17,180 double stars.

Other catalogs listed objects other than stars. *The Messier Catalogue*, compiled by French astronomer Charles Messier, was published in 1774 and contained 45 celestial objects, such as globular clusters and nebulas. More objects were eventually added, totaling about 103. The current *Messier Catalogue* lists 109 objects—though three really do not exist, as they were mistakes made by Messier.

Expanding the early works of William and John Herschel, a more extensive listing was the *New General Catalogue of Nebulae and Star Clusters* (NGC), a catalog of nonstellar objects published in 1888, by J. L. E. Dreyer. It eventually listed 7,840 objects—1,529 objects were added seven years later—and was called the *Index Catalogue* (IC). By 1908, another list expanded the IC.

COMMON TELESCOPES

Telescopes are instruments that collect light from a celestial object, bring the light into focus, and produce a magnified image. There are two major types of optical telescopes: refracting (uses lenses) and reflecting (uses mirrors); a third telescope, the catadioptric, uses a combination of lenses and mirrors (for more information on refraction and reflection, see Chapter 7, "Physics").

The largest telescopes are reflecting telescopes, which use two or more mirrors. The primary mirror is used to gather the light from the object; the secondary mirror is used to focus the image to the objective (eyepiece). Refracting telescopes use lenses to magnify the image from distant objects. They are limited in size because of problems finding defect-free glass for lenses, long focal lengths, and distortion caused by the sagging of a lens under its own weight.

Reflecting and Refracting Telescopes

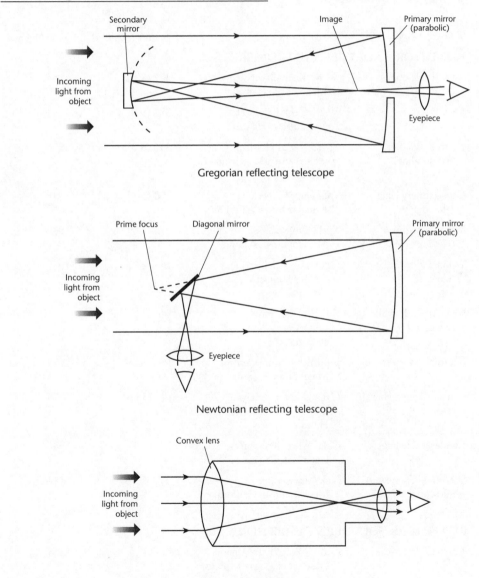

Gregorian reflecting telescope

Newtonian reflecting telescope

Refracting telescope

USING CCDS

The newest devices for larger telescopes are now reaching into the amateur astronomy world. One such device is the charge-coupled device (CCD), a light-sensitive semiconductor that responds to incoming light from a celestial object. As the light hits the CCD, it builds up an electrical charge on picture elements, or pixels. These pixels are transferred to a computer screen and are pieced together to form an image. In this way, the user can manipulate the data to improve the detail in the image.

World's Largest Telescopes

Telescope Name	Observatory	Diameter Inches (Meters)	Year Opened
REFLECTORS: NORTHERN HEMISPHERE			
Keck II telescope	W. M. Keck Observatory, Mauna Kea, Hawaii	387 (9.82) (segmented)	1994
Keck I	W. M. Keck Observatory, Mauna Kea, Hawaii	387 (9.82)	1991
Bol'shoi Teleskop Azimutal'nyi	Special Astrophysical Observatory, Mt. Pastukhov, Russia	236 (6.0)	1975
George Ellery Hale telescope	Palomar Observatory, Palomar Mt., California	200 (5.1)	1948
Multiple Mirror telescope (MMT)	MMT Observatory, Mt. Hopkins, Arizona	176 (4.5)	1979
William Herschel telescope	Observatory del Roque de los Muchachos, Canary Islands	165 (4.2)	1987
Nicholas U. Mayall reflector	Kitt Peak National Observatory, Kitt Peak, Arizona	146 (3.81)	1973
UK infrared telescope	Joint Astronomy Centre, Mauna Kea, Hawaii	150 (3.8)	1978
Canada-France-Hawaii telescope	Canada-France-Hawaii Telescope Corp., Mauna Kea, Hawaii	141 (3.58)	1979
3.5-meter telescope	Calar Alto Observatory, Calar Alto, Spain	138 (3.5)	1984
C. Donald Shane telescope	Lick Observatory, Mt. Hamilton, California	120 (3.05)	1959
REFLECTORS: SOUTHERN HEMISPHERE			
4-meter telescope	Cerro Tololo Inter-American Observatory, Cerro Tololo, Chile	158 (4.0)	1976

Telescope Name	Observatory	Diameter Inches (Meters)	Year Opened
Anglo-Australian telescope	Anglo-Australian Observatory, Siding Spring, Coonabarabran, New South Wales, Australia	153 (3.893)	1975
ESO 3.6-meter telescope	European Southern Observatory, La Silla, Chile	141 (3.57)	1977
New Technology telescope	European Southern Observatory, La Silla, Chile	138 (3.5)	1989
Irénée du Pont telescope	Las Campanas Observatory, Las Campanas, Chile	100 (2.54)	1976

REFRACTORS

Yerkes 40-inch refractor	Yerkes Observatory, Williams Bay, Wisconsin	40 (1.016)	1897
36-inch refractor	Lick Observatory, Mt. Hamilton, California	36 (0.895)	1888
Meudon refractor	Observatoire de Paris, Meudon, France	33 (0.83)	1889
Potsdam refractor	Zentralinstitut für Astrophysik Telegrafenberg, Potsdam, Germany	31 (0.8)	1899
Thaw refractor	Allegheny Observatory, Pittsburgh, Pennsylvania	30 (0.76)	1895
Lunette Bischoffscheim	Observatoire de Nice, Mont Gros, France	29 (0.74)	1886
28-inch visual refractor	Old Royal Observatory, Greenwich, United Kingdom	28 (0.711)	1894
Grosser refraktor	Archenhold-Sternwarte, Alt Treptow, Berlin, Germany	27 (0.68)	1896
Grosser refraktor	Astronomisches Institut, University Observatory, Vienna, Austria	26 (0.67)	1880
McCormick refractor	Leander McCormick Observatory, Charlottesville, Virginia	26 (0.667)	1883

PLANNED REFLECTORS

Very large telescope (VLT)	European Southern Observatory, Cerro Paranal, Chile	four 316 (8) (equivalent to one 632 [16] telescope)	[2000]
Large binocular telescope	Columbus Project, Mt. Graham, Arizona	465 (11.8) (equivalent)	[1997]

World's Largest Telescopes (cont'd)

Telescope Name	Observatory	Diameter Inches (Meters)	Year Opened
Spectroscopic survey telescope	McDonald Observatory, Mt. Locke, Texas	433 (11.0) (segmented)	[1996]
Subaru telescope	National Astronomy Observatory (of Japan), Mauna Kea, Hawaii	327 (8.3)	[1999]
Gemini telescope north	Joint Astronomical Centre, Mauna Kea, Hawaii	319 (8.1)	[1999]
Gemini telescope south	Cerro Tololo Inter-American Observatory, Cerro Pachon, Chile	319 (8.1)	[2001]

Radio Astronomy

Radio telescopes gather radio waves from space that have wavelengths longer than about 100 microns, or just above the infrared waves on the electromagnetic spectrum. Stand-alone, parabolic, radio telescope disks catch radio signals from space objects. Collections, or arrays, of radio telescopes linked together with computers expand the coverage of the telescope and act as an *interferometer*. Radio telescopes from numerous locations can also be used to simulate a telescope that is thousands of miles in diameter.

Radio telescopes are used to examine some of the most active objects in the universe. For example, radio waves from radio galaxies, quasars, novas, supernovas, pulsars, and emission nebulas are often studied. Radio telescopes also observe the planets. For example, Jupiter has three types of radio emissions that can be detected by radio telescopes—thermal from the planet's body, decimeter from the planet's magnetic field, and decameter bursts—depending on the position of the satellite Io.

Radio Telescope Highlights

The *first report of radio waves from outside the solar system* was made in 1931 by Karl Jansky, at Bell Labs, New Jersey.

The *first parabolic radio telescope* was built between 1935 and 1941, by Grote Reber in Wheaton, Illinois; he was the first to survey the radio sky with the radio telescope.

The *first large modern radio telescope* was the 250-foot (76.2-meter) Jodrell Bank radio telescope in Jodrell Bank, United Kingdom, built in 1957.

The *largest in-ground radio telescope* is in Arecibo, Puerto Rico and is 1,000 feet (304.8 meters) in diameter, built in 1963.

The *largest steerable radio telescope* is in Greenbank, West Virginia and has a 328 by 367-foot (100 by 111.9-meter) disk; in 1995, it replaced the 300-foot (91.4-meter) radio telescope that was built in 1962 and collapsed in 1988.

The *largest collection of radio telescopes* is the Very Large Array (VLA) in Socorro, New Mexico, which has 27 telescopes linked together and was built in 1980.

The *largest dedicated telescope* on Earth is the Very Long Baseline Interferometer, a collection of telescopes around the world that are often linked by computer and the Very Long Baseline Array (headquartered in Socorro, New Mexico). It is a collection of 10 disks that act as one large radio telescope 5,000 miles (8,000 kilometers) in diameter.

In the future, astronomers hope to have an orbiting array of satellite radio telescopes. Other plans call for a collection of radio telescopes on the Earth and the Moon that would simulate a telescope about 238,866 miles (384,400 kilometers) wide—the approximate mean distance between the Earth and the Moon.

THE OTHER TELESCOPES

Optical and radio telescopes are not the only types of telescopes. Others include those that study other wavelengths—ultraviolet, infrared, x-rays, and gamma-rays. Most of these telescopes are located in space to eliminate background noise from the Earth and its atmosphere. Here are some examples of spacecraft that have collected these types of data.

ultraviolet   Copernicus, launched in 1972, and the Extreme Ultraviolet Explorer, launched in 1991, conducted sky surveys in the ultraviolet range.

infrared   The Infrared Astronomical Satellite was launched in 1983 and has since measured the infrared emissions of many objects, including dust, gas, stars, and galaxies. Data from the mission are still being analyzed.

x-rays   The Einstein Observatory, launched in 1978, was one of the most productive satellite telescopes, collecting x-ray data from space.

gamma-rays   The Gamma-Ray Observatory was launched in 1990 and had a wider range than any previous satellite telescopes.

THE SPACE AGE

Space Firsts

Year	Event
1926	First launch of a liquid fuel rocket: Robert Goddard (United States)
1957	First satellite orbits Earth: Sputnik 1 (U.S.S.R.); first animal in space: Sputnik 2 (U.S.S.R.)
1958	First U.S. satellite launched and first scientific discovery in space (Van Allen radiation belt): Explorer 1; first satellite to use solar power: Vanguard (United States)
1959	First craft to leave gravity of Earth: Luna 1 probe to the Moon (U.S.S.R.); first craft to impact another world: Luna 2 probe to the Moon (U.S.S.R.); first craft to photograph the Moon's far side: Luna 3 (U.S.S.R.); first television images from space: Explorer 6 (United States)
1960	First U.S. weather satellite: Tiros 1
1961	First human in space and to orbit Earth: Yuri A. Gagarin (U.S.S.R.), in the *Vostok 1*; first U.S. astronaut into space (suborbital) Alan B. Shepard Jr. in *Mercury-Redstone 3*; first interplanetary probe: Venera 1 to Venus (U.S.S.R.)
1962	First U.S. astronaut to orbit Earth: John Herschel Glenn Jr. in *Mercury-Atlas 6*; first successful scientific planetary mission, the fly-by of Venus: Mariner 2 (United States); first observatory in space: Orbiting Solar Observatory 1 (United States)
1963	First woman in space: Valentina Vladimirovna Tereshkova in *Vostok 6* (U.S.S.R.)
1964	First successful fly-by of Mars: Mariner 4 (United States); first multiperson space mission: *Voskhod 1* (U.S.S.R.)

1965	First spacewalk: Alexei Leonov in *Voskhod 2* (U.S.S.R.); first U.S. spacewalk: Edward H. White II in *Gemini 4*
1966	First craft to enter the atmosphere of another planet (Venus): Venera 2 (U.S.S.R.); first unmanned spacecraft to soft land on the Moon: Luna 9 (U.S.S.R.); first unmanned spacecraft to orbit another world (Moon): Luna 10 (U.S.S.R.); first U.S. unmanned soft landing on the Moon: Surveyor 1
1968	First humans to orbit another world (Moon), Frank Borman, James Lovell, and William Anders in *Apollo 8* (United States)
1969	First humans on another world (Moon), July 20, Neil Alden Armstrong and Edwin E. "Buzz" Aldrin Jr. in *Apollo 11* and first samples of the Moon returned to Earth (United States) (Mike Collins orbited the Moon in the Command Module)
1970	First unmanned spacecraft to return samples of another world to Earth (Moon): Luna 16 (U.S.S.R.); first roving vehicle on the Moon: Luna 17 (U.S.S.R.)
1971	First manned space station: *Salyut* (U.S.S.R.); first human-operated roving vehicle on another world (Moon): *Apollo 15* (United States); first soft-landing on another planet (Mars): Mars 3 (U.S.S.R.)
1973	First fly-by of Jupiter: Pioneer 10 (United States); first U.S. space station: *Skylab 1*
1974	First fly-by of Mercury: Mariner 10 (United States); first duel-planet mission (Venus and Mercury): Mariner 10 (United States)
1975	First photos from the surface of Venus: Venera 9 (U.S.S.R.); first international space flight: *Apollo-Soyuz* (United States and U.S.S.R.)
1976	First unmanned Mars landing: Viking 1 (United States); first craft to search for life on another planet: Viking 1 (United States)
1979	First fly-by of Saturn: Pioneer 11 (United States)
1980–1984	First satellite to be retrieved, repaired, and redeployed in space: Solar Maximum Mission (United States); launch (1980), repair mission (1984), ceased functioning (1989)
1981	Flight of the first space shuttle: John Watts Young and Robert L. Crippen, of the United States (and first reusable spacecraft with human crew) aboard the *Columbia* (the *Enterprise,* the prototype space shuttle, was never flown in space)
1983	First U.S. woman astronaut: Sally Kirsten Ride; first orbital radar mapping of another world: Venera 15 (U.S.S.R.)
1984	First U.S. untethered spacewalk: Bruce McCandless
1985	First spacecraft pictures of comet nucleus (Halley), by Giotto (Europe), though numerous other probes, such as the Vega 1 (U.S.S.R.) and Suisei (Japan), also took pictures; the Vega 1 was the first to reach the comet
1986	First fly-by of Uranus: Voyager 2 (United States); first permanently inhabited space station: *Mir* (U.S.S.R.)
1989	First fly-by of Neptune: Voyager 2 (United States)
1991	First fly-by of an asteroid (Gaspra): Galileo (United States)
1994–1995	Longest duration spaceflight: 438 days, Valery Polyakov on the *Mir* space station (Russia)
1995	First U.S. astronaut to board the Russian *Mir* space station: Norman Thagard; First woman U.S. space shuttle pilot: Eileen M. Collins

Human Missions to the Moon

Mission	Launch Date	Crew	Comments
Apollo 8	December 21, 1968	Frank Borman, James A. Lovell Jr., William A. Anders	First manned mission to orbit the Moon
Apollo 10	May 18, 1969	Thomas P. Stafford, John W. Young, Eugene A. Cernan	Rehearsal for first landing; lunar module to within 2.2 miles (3.5 kilometers) of the Moon's surface

Mission	Launch Date	Crew	Comments
Apollo 11	July 16, 1969	Neil A. Armstrong,* Michael Collins,† Edwin E. "Buzz" Aldrin Jr.*	First manned landing in Mare Tranquillitatis; Armstrong, first human to walk on the Moon (July 20, 1969)
Apollo 12	November 14, 1969	Charles Conrad Jr.,* Richard F. Gordon,† Alan L. Bean*	Landed in Oceanus Procellarum
Apollo 13	April 11, 1970	James A. Lovell Jr., John L. Swigert Jr., Fred W. Haise Jr.	Never landed on the Moon; an accident en route required the craft to return after swinging around the far side of the Moon
Apollo 14	January 31, 1971	Alan B. Shepard Jr.,* Stuart A. Roosa,† Edgar D. Mitchell*	Landed in Fra Mauro
Apollo 15	July 26, 1971	David R. Scott,* Alfred M. Worden,† James B. Irwin*	Landed adjacent to the Imbrium Basin near Apennine Mountains
Apollo 16	April 16, 1972	John W. Young,* Thomas K. Mattingley II,† Charles M. Duke Jr.*	Landed in highlands near Crater Descartes
Apollo 17	December 7, 1972	Eugene A. Cernan,* Ronald E. Evans,† Harrison H. Schmitt*	Landed in Taurus Littrow Valley

*Walked on Moon.
†Remained in command module, orbiting the Moon.

Special Spacecraft

Manned Spacecraft (Alphabetically listed)

Apollo was the manned U.S. space program that eventually put 12 men on the Moon. The Apollo spacecraft included a command module for orbiting and lunar module for landing on the Moon. The first Apollo mission to circle the Moon was Apollo 8; the first to land on the Moon was Apollo 11; the last to land was Apollo 17.

Gemini was the second series of U.S. manned missions, after the Mercury launches. The Gemini spacecraft held two astronauts and was used to test docking maneuvers, human responses to weightlessness, and landing techniques.

Mercury was the first series of U.S. manned missions, including the first suborbital and orbital flights. These one-person crafts were to test the feasibility of flight, monitor a human's reaction to space, and test techniques for their successor in the series—the Gemini spacecraft.

The Mir space station, built by the U.S.S.R. (now maintained by Russia) is the largest permanent working space station. First launched in 1986, the third-generation Mir station has been expanded with the use of modules. It has been used to determine the effects of the space environment on humans—with some cosmonauts staying in the station for more than 400 days straight.

The U.S.S.R. *Salyut* spacecraft were the first nonpermanent space stations and laid the ground-work for the *Mir* space station. The first docking with a *Salyut* was in April 1971.

Skylab, the only U.S. space station, was launched in 1973. It was not permanently staffed but was visited by alternating crews of three astronauts. In 1979, due to technical problems and lack of funding to keep the craft in orbit (NASA was then concentrating on building a reusable shuttle), *Skylab* fell from orbit and burned up in the atmosphere.

The *Soyuz* spacecraft is the most recent of the Russian space capsules. Russia uses them to carry space travelers to the *Mir* space station. The first was launched April 23, 1967 (by the former U.S.S.R.); there have been more than 60 *Soyuz* flights.

The space shuttle is a reusable Earth-orbiting, manned vehicle for the U.S. space program; the first (*Columbia*) was flown on April 12, 1981. The shuttles are *Columbia, Atlantis, Endeavor,* and *Discovery.* (The *Challenger* space shuttle did not survive a flight in 1986; seven astronauts died in the explosion.) Each shuttle can comfortably carry a crew of five to eight astronauts. Most of the work done by the space shuttles consists of testing the reaction of humans in space, performing space lab experiments, monitoring the Earth, and launching satellites from orbit. There have been more than 30 space shuttle flights.

Voskhod, developed by the U.S.S.R., were actually *Vostok* craft converted to three-person capsules; they were the first craft to carry more than two people. The first flight was October 12, 1964. Because of space restrictions, cosmonauts often did not have ejection equipment and individual parachutes. One large parachute was designed to allow the capsule to float to a soft landing.

Vostok capsules, used by the U.S.S.R. in its first man-in-space program, were two-person vehicles. They had two sections: an instrument module and a reentry vehicle. Flight was controlled from the ground. Yuri A. Gagarin, the first human in space, rode in a *Vostok* capsule on April 12, 1961.

THE FIRST SPACE SHUTTLE

The first U.S. space shuttle was named *Enterprise,* chosen by President Gerald Ford and suggested by thousands of fans of the television series *Star Trek.* NASA wanted to call the shuttle the *Constitution.*

The Enterprise had no engines; it was a glider meant to test the shuttle's aerodynamics (the first shuttle built with engines was the *Challenger*). Its first tests, in 1977, were unmanned: the shuttle was bolted to a Boeing 747 jumbo jet. On subsequent flights, the shuttle was dropped from the jet and piloted to a landing. It was also used for fit tests, so scientists could build the correct size launch pad for future shuttles.

Eventually, the *Enterprise* was flown around the country on the back of an airplane for publicity. It was later stripped of instruments and gear and flown to Washington, D.C., where it is hoped that a structure will be built to house the glider. Until then, it remains on a Washington-Dulles International airport back lot.

Recent and Future Unmanned Spacecraft

- The Cosmic Background Explorer (COBE), launched in 1989, has revealed new findings of the universe that supports the Big Bang theory.
- The Great Observatories (HST, GRO, SIRTF, AXAF) are combinations of instru-ments placed on several satellites by a number of countries, including the United

States, Germany, the Netherlands, the United Kingdom, and the European Space Agency.

- The Hubble Space Telescope is the first of the Great Observatories, which has obtained better images and readings of the universe than Earth-based telescopes by being above the Earth's atmosphere. The HST, run by the Space Telescope Science Institute (STScI) in Baltimore, Maryland, was launched in 1990. The telescope has five major scientific instruments: a widefield planetary camera, faint object camera, faint object spectrograph, high-resolution spectrograph, and high-speed photometer. Several HST instruments were replaced during a space shuttle mission in December, 1993, because of telescope resolution problems.
- The second observatory will be the Gamma-Ray Observatory. The Space Infrared Telescope Facility and Advanced X-ray Astrophysics Facility will follow.
- Launched in 1990, Ulysses is a joint U.S.-European project. It is being used to explore the solar wind and effects of the Sun in detail; it traveled toward Jupiter and then swung back toward the Sun, reaching the Sun's south pole in 1994.

Unmanned Spacecraft to the Planets

Spacecraft	Launch	Arrival	Remarks
MERCURY			
Mariner 10	November 3, 1973	March 29, 1974 September 21, 1974 March 16, 1975	Trajectory allowed 3 working flybys
VENUS			
Mariner 2	August 26, 1962	December 14, 1962	Fly-by
Venera 4*	June 12, 1967	October 18, 1967	Atmosphere probe
Mariner 5	June 14, 1967	October 19, 1967	Fly-by
Venera 5*	January 5, 1969	May 16, 1969	Atmosphere probe
Venera 6*	January 10, 1969	May 17, 1969	Atmosphere probe
Venera 7*	August 17, 1970	December 15, 1970	Lander (functioned 23 minutes)
Venera 8*	March 27, 1972	July 22, 1972	Lander (functioned 50 minutes)
Mariner 10	November 3, 1973	February 5, 1974	Fly-by
Venera 9*	June 8, 1975	October 22, 1975	Orbiter and lander
Venera 10*	June 14, 1975	October 25, 1975	Orbiter and lander
Pioneer/Venus:			
Orbiter	May 20, 1978	December 4, 1978	Orbiter (ceased functioning October 1992)
Multiprobe	August 8, 1978	December 9, 1978	Five atmospheric probes
Venera 11*	September 9, 1978	December 21, 1978	Fly-by and lander
Venera 12*	September 14, 1978	December 25, 1978	Fly-by and lander
Venera 13*	October 30, 1981	March 1, 1982	Lander
Venera 14*	November 4, 1981	March 5, 1982	Lander
Venera 15*	June 2, 1983	October 10, 1983	Orbiter with imaging radar
Venera 16*	June 7, 1983	October 14, 1983	Orbiter with imaging radar
VEGA 1*	December 15, 1984	June 11, 1985	Lander and atmospheric probe
VEGA 2*	December 21, 1984	June 15, 1985	Lander and atmospheric probe
Magellan	May 4, 1989	August 1990	High-resolution radar (ceased functioning October 1994)
Galileo	October 18, 1989	February 1990	Fly-by on way to Jupiter

Unmanned Spacecraft to the Planets (cont'd)

Spacecraft	Launch	Arrival	Remarks
MARS			
Mariner 4	November 28, 1964	July 14, 1965	Fly-by
Mariner 6	February 25, 1969	July 31, 1969	Fly-by
Mariner 7	March 27, 1969	August 5, 1969	Fly-by
Mariner 9	May 30, 1971	November 13, 1971	Orbiter (ceased functioning on October 27, 1972)
Mars 2*	May 19, 1971	November 27, 1971	Orbiter and lander (no data returned)
Mars 3*	May 28, 1971	December 2, 1971	Orbiter and lander (no data returned)
Mars 5*	July 25, 1973	February 12, 1974	Orbiter and lander (landing failed)
Mars 6*	August 5, 1973	March 12, 1974	Orbiter (landing failed)
Mars 7*	August 9, 1973	March 9, 1974	Orbiter (missed planet)
Viking 1	August 20, 1975	June 19, 1976	Orbiter (ceased operating on August 17, 1980)
		July 20, 1976	Lander (ceased operating in November 1982)
Viking 2	September 9, 1975	August 7, 1976	Orbiter (ceased operating on July 24, 1978)
		September 3, 1976	Lander (ceased operating on April 12, 1980)
Phobos 2*	July 1988	June 1989	Lost contact with Earth on March 27, 1989 after 2 months
Mars Observer	September 1992	August 1993	Orbiter (lost contact with Earth as it reached Mars)
JUPITER			
Pioneer 10	March 3, 1972	December 3, 1973	Fly-by
Pioneer 11	April 5, 1973	December 2, 1974	Fly-by
Voyager 1	September 5, 1977	March 5, 1979	Fly-by
Voyager 2	August 20, 1977	July 9, 1979	Fly-by
Galileo	October 18, 1989	December 1995	Orbiter and atmospheric probe
Ulysses	October 2, 1990	February 1992	Fly-by on way to study polar regions of the Sun (1995)
SATURN			
Pioneer 11	April 5, 1973	September 1, 1979	Fly-by
Voyager 1	September 5, 1977	November 12, 1980	Fly-by
Voyager 2	August 20, 1977	August 25, 1981	Fly-by
URANUS			
Voyager 2	August 20, 1977	January 24, 1986	Fly-by

Spacecraft	Launch	Arrival	Remarks
NEPTUNE			
Voyager 2	August 20, 1977	August 24, 1989	Fly-by
COMET HALLEY			
ISEE-3/ICE	August 12, 1978	March 25, 1986	ISEE-3 renamed ICE on September 11, 1985 and redirected to Comet Halley December 23, 1983; flew by at 17 million miles (28 million kilometers)
VEGA 1*	December 15, 1984	March 6, 1986	Penetrated coma
Suisei (Japan)	August 18, 1985	March 8, 1986	Flew by at a distance of 93,210 miles (150,000 kilometers) from nucleus
VEGA 2*	December 21, 1984	March 9, 1986	Penetrated coma
Sakigake (Japan)	January 8, 1985	August 11, 1986	Flew by at a distance of 4 million miles (6 million kilometers) from nucleus
Giotto (Europe)	July 2, 1985	August 14, 1986	Penetrated densest part of coma
COMET GRIGG-SKJELLERUP			
Giotto (Europe)	July 2, 1985	July 1992	Fly-by within 124 miles (200 kilometers) of the comet's core; the closest to date
ASTERIODS			
Galileo	October 18, 1989	1992 (at asteroid)	Fly-by of asteroid Gaspra, on way to Jupiter
Galileo	October 18, 1989	1993 (at asteroid)	Fly-by of asteroid, Ida, on way to Jupiter; found first moon around an asteroid (Dactyl)

Soviet (Russian) spacecraft

WHERE ARE THEY NOW?

Planetary spacecraft launched by the United States have had a varied history. Some of the craft never made it off the launch pad; some, such as the Mars Observer, lost contact with the Earth and were never heard from again. Other craft have had long and productive lives—especially Pioneers 10 and 11 and Voyagers 1 and 2.

Pioneer 10 is moving in the opposite direction from the solar system and will probably continue to send data to the Earth until 1998; Pioneer 11 is almost out of power, and may stop sending signals by the mid-1990s. Voyager 1 is now following a trajectory that takes it above the plane of the solar system, while Voyager 2 is traveling in a trajectory below the plane of the solar system.

In late 1993, the Voyagers' instruments detected what may be the first indications of the solar system's edge: the heliopause, where the pressures of the Sun's solar wind (particles put out by the Sun) are balanced with the pressures from other star particles—or the boundary that separates our solar system from interstellar space. But before the craft reach the boundary, they will pass through the terminal shock, where the solar wind first plows into the interstellar matter, at about 70 to 130 astronomical units (AU). (The hiss of radio noise from the Voyagers are a signal that particles are more active.) The heliopause is thought to be between 130 and 170 AU from the Sun; some scientists believe that it will be detected by around the turn of the century.

Both Voyager craft will probably lose their power source by the year 2015. But by then, scientists hope that at least Voyager 1, at about 130 AU, will have crossed the heliopause. Voyager 2 will probably die away when it is at 112 AU—not far enough to detect the heliopause.

THE SEARCH FOR OTHERS

The search for other beings in the universe has been a common theme for the past century. Science fiction writers, including Jules Verne, Ray Bradbury, Arthur Clark, and Isaac Asimov, have been fascinated by the possible existence of extraterrestrials. Aliens are also prevalent in science fiction motion pictures and television shows, such as *Star Trek*.

But scientists are also searching the skies for extraterrestrials. In 1960, Frank Drake sent signals to Epsilon Eridani and Tau Ceti from the Greenbank National Radio Astronomy Observatory, in Project Ozma, the first real attempt to contact other life. A search for extraterrestrial intelligence (SETI) program that included a two-prong attempt at communication was initiated by NASA in 1992, but canceled in 1993. Since then, the SETI Institute in Mountain View, California, has their own project similar to a part of NASA's old program—a privately funded program called Project Phoenix. Among other sites, the program has used the Southern Hemisphere's largest radio telescope, the 210-foot (63-meter) Parkes Radio Astronomy Observatory in New South Wales, Australia.

Another SETI program is the privately funded Megachannel Extraterrestrial Assay (META) sponsored by the Planetary Society: META I uses a radio telescope near Harvard University to scan the entire northern sky; META II uses a radio telescope at the Argentine Institute of Radio Astronomy near Buenos Aires. There are also programs called communication with extraterrestrial intelligence (CETI), which implies a two-way conversation with extraterrestrial beings, not just listening. The major problems with CETIs are the distances involved to receive a signal and figuring out what language to use.

What are the chances of hearing from another intelligence? No one really knows. Some scientists believe the chances are low that beings would have developed the same as humans, with the ability to analyze and interpret radio signals. On the other hand, we may be receiving signals from other beings right now, but are not yet able to interpret their way of communication.

MAJOR ASTRONOMERS AND SPACE SCIENTISTS

Adams, John Couch (1819–1892) British astronomer whose records helped Johann Galle find the planet Neptune in 1846.

Aristotle (384–322 B.C.) Greek philosopher and scientist who determined many of the astronomical beliefs of his time, including the idea that the Earth was the center of the universe, a theory that dominated astronomy for close to 1,800 years.

Baade, Wilhelm Heinrich Walter (1893–1960) German-born American astronomer who studied stars, including the Cepheid variable stars, to estimate the size of the universe.

Babcock, Harold Delos (1882–1968) American astronomer who conducted numerous studies of the Sun using special spectroscopic techniques.

Baily, Francis (1774–1844) British astronomer who studied the Sun and discovered the bright spots along the Moon's edge seen during a total solar eclipse; these are now called Baily's beads.

Balmer, Johann Jakob (1825–1898) Swiss astronomer who devised a formula important to the development of the atomic theory. His idea was based on the wavelength of hydrogen spectral lines.

Barnard, Edward Emerson (1857–1923) American astronomer who discovered a ninth-magnitude star in the constellation of Ophiuchus. The star, called Barnard's Star, has the largest proper motion of any star yet discovered.

Barringer, Daniel Moreau (1860–1929) American mining engineer and geologist who was the first to suggest that the large crater in Arizona (now called Meteor Crater) was not volcanic in origin, but was caused by the impact of a meteorite.

Bayer, Johann (1572–1625) German astronomer who, in 1603, wrote a star atlas distinguishing the brightness of stars by a designated Greek letter—a system still used today.

Bell, Jocelyn (1948–) American astronomer who discovered the first pulsar in 1967. She was an assistant to Anthony Hewish at Cambridge University at that time.

Bessel, Friedrich Wilhelm (1784–1846) German astronomer and mathematician who was the first to measure a star directly using trigonometric parallax. The terms *Bessel functions* and *Bessel year* are named after him.

Bethe, Hans Albrecht (1906–) German-born American physicist who determined that the fusion of hydrogen atoms into helium creates nuclear reactions inside stars.

Bode, Johann Elert (1747–1826) German astronomer who was the first to publish a mathematical formula for the distances of the planets, now called the Titius-Bode Law (Johann Titius discovered the law a few years before but it was published only as a footnote in a book).

Bok, Bart Jan (1906–1983) Dutch-born American astronomer who discovered clumps of matter in bright nebulas (now called Bok globules), possibly the birthplaces of stars.

Brahe, Tycho (1546–1601) Danish astronomer and one of the greatest astronomical observers before the advent of the telescope. He made the most accurate measurements of stellar and planetary positions before telescopes and astrophotography.

Brahmagupta (c. 598–c. 665) Indian mathematician and astronomer who was the most accomplished of the ancient Indian astronomers. He set forth the Hindu astronomical system in verse form, including events such as lunar and solar eclipses, planetary conjunctions, and the positions of the planets.

Brown, Robert Hanbury (1916–) British radio astronomer who also designed, developed, and used the intensity interferometer, which measures the angular size of bright visual stars.

Burbidge, (Eleanor) Margaret (1922–) British astronomer who developed theories of quasars (or "quasi-stellar" objects), calculated how elements formed in stars through nuclear fusion, and was the first woman director of the Royal Greenwich Observatory.

Cannon, Annie Jump (1863–1941) American astronomer who worked on stellar spectra and was a major contributor to the *Draper Catalogue*.

Cassini, Giovanni Domenico (1625–1712)   Italian-born French astronomer who discovered several moons around Saturn and the dark division in Saturn's rings. He was the first of four generations of Italian astronomers.

Chandler, Seth Carlo (1846–1913)   American astronomer who discovered the 14-month period of oscillation of the Earth's polar axis, which was named the Chandler wobble or period.

Chandrasekhar, Subrahmanyan (1910–)   Indian-born American astrophysicist who discovered white dwarf stars and successfully predicted that they can only exist if their mass is 1.4 times that of the Sun (now known as the Chandrasekhar limit).

Clark, Alvan Graham (1832–1897)   American astronomer and instrument maker who directed the making of the Yerkes 40-inch (102-centimeter) diameter refracting telescope in Wisconsin. He made several other lenses for other refracting telescopes around the United States. He also discovered that the star Sirius has a companion star and noted other double stars.

Copernicus, Nicolaus (1473–1543)   Polish scientist who revolutionized astronomy by proposing that the Sun, not the Earth, is the center of the solar system. This idea is called the Copernican system.

Dawes, William Rutter (1799–1868)   British astronomer who measured double stars and made detailed planetary observations.

de Sitter, Willem (1872–1934)   Dutch astronomer and mathematician who developed several relativity theories. The Einstein-de Sitter law bears his name.

Draper, Henry (1837–1882)   American physician and amateur astronomer who made the first photograph of the Orion Nebula and spectrum of the star Vega (1872). His father, John William Draper, made the first photographs of the Moon in 1840. The *Henry Draper Catalogue* of stellar spectra is named in his honor.

Dreyer, Johann Louis Emil (1852–1926)   Danish astronomer who assembled the *New General Catalogue of Nebulae and Clusters of Stars* (NGC) in 1888, and in 1895, the *Index Catalogue of Nebulae*, the NGC's supplement.

Eddington, Sir Arthur Stanley (1882–1944)   British astrophysicist and mathematician who studied the evolution of stars and cosmology.

Encke, Johann Franz (1791–1865)   German astronomer whose name graces the Encke division (a division in Saturn's A ring, which he found) and the Encke comet.

Eratosthenes of Cyrene (c. 276–c. 194 B.C.)   Hellenic librarian and astronomer and one of the first to estimate correctly the circumference of the Earth.

Flamsteed, John (1646–1719)   British astronomer whose observations led to many star catalogs and lunar tables.

Galileo Galilei (1564–1642)   Italian astronomer and physicist who was the first to use scientific experimental investigations. He was the first to use a telescope for astronomical observations, discovering the moons around Jupiter and the phases of Venus.

Galle, Johann Gottfried (1812–1910)   German astronomer and believed to be the true discoverer of the planet Neptune in 1846 (see also *John Adams*). He found the planet, using observations made by other astronomers who were trying to explain planetary perturbations in the outer solar system.

Gamow, George (1904–1968)   Soviet physicist who worked in nuclear physics, including the Manhattan Project (on the development of the atomic bomb). His astronomical studies were concerned mainly with the origin of the universe and evolution of the stars. He also was a great early supporter of the Big Bang theory.

Gill, Sir David (1843–1914)   British astronomer who measured solar and stellar parallax, and one of the first to use photography to map the heavens.

Goddard, Robert Hutchings (1882–1945)   American physicist and inventor of rocket propulsion technology, and often called the father of American rocketry.

Gold, Thomas (1920–)   Austrian-born American astronomer who proved that the first pulsar signal detected was caused by a rapidly rotating neutron star.

Gould, Benjamin Apthorp (1824–1896)   American astronomer who developed star catalogs that fixed the list of Southern Hemisphere constellations. He also was the first to use the telegraph to determine longitude.

Greenstein, Jesse Leonard (1909–)   American astronomer who was the first (along with Maarten Schmidt) to discover quasars.

Gregory, James (1638–1675)   Scottish mathematician and astronomer who developed the Gregorian reflecting telescope.

Hale, George Ellery (1868–1938)   American astrophysicist who built the 200-inch Hale telescope in California. He also did extensive studies of the Sun.

Hall, Asaph (1829–1907)   American astronomer who discovered Phobos and Deimos, the two moons of Mars.

Halley, Edmund (1656–1742)   British astronomer and physicist who determined the periodicity of the comet that bears his name.

Hawking, Stephen William (1942–)   British theoretical physicist and astronomer who discovered numerous fundamental concepts in cosmology. He is considered to be the greatest theoretical theorist of the latter twentieth century. He is especially known for his theories on black holes and the origin and evolution of the universe (especially in association with the nature of space-time).

Herschel, Caroline Lucretia (1750–1848)   German-born British astronomer who was the sister of William Herschel. She discovered more comets than anyone else of her time (eight), along with star clusters and nebulas.

Herschel, Sir (Frederick) William (1738–1822)   German-born British astronomer who was the father of John Herschel and the brother of Caroline Herschel. He discovered the planet Uranus. He also founded modern stellar astronomy, determined the general shape and size of the Milky Way, wrote numerous catalogs of celestial objects, and developed an improved telescope (the Herschelian telescope).

Herschel, Sir John Frederick William (1792–1871)   British Astronomer, son of William Herschel, who investigated deep-sky objects and double stars in both celestial hemispheres.

Hertzsprung, Ejnar (1873–1967)   Danish astronomer who developed, along with Henry Russell, the diagram of the stellar life cycle based on temperature and absolute magnitude.

Hevelius, Johannes (1611–1687)   German astronomer who was one of the first to draw accurate maps of the Moon's surface.

Hewish, Anthony (1924–)   British radio astronomer and physicist whose work in radio scintillation helped to lead to the discovery of pulsars (Jocelyn Bell discovered the first pulsar in 1967). His work with radio telescopes also included the study of the solar atmosphere.

Hipparchus (c. 170– c. 120 B.C.)   Greek astronomer and geographer who worked out the epicycle theory of the solar system, with the Earth at the center. He also discovered the precession of the equinox, calculated the length of a year within 6.5 minutes, and devised the first known star map.

Hooke, Robert (1635–1703)   English physicist and astronomer who discovered numerous features of the planets with telescope, including Jupiter's Great Red Spot.

Horrocks, Jeremiah (c. 1617–1641)   English astronomer and clergyman who first predicted and observed a transit of Venus across the face of the Sun.

Hoyle, Sir Fred (1915–)   British astrophysicist who has developed numerous cosmological theories, including the steady-state hypothesis of the universe.

Hubble, Edwin Powell (1889–1953)   American astronomer and cosmologist whose work demonstrated that the universe was expanding. He also formulated the Hubble constant, which measures the rate of expansion of the universe, and is used to determine the age of the universe. The Hubble Space Telescope is named after Edwin Hubble.

Huygens, Christiaan (1629–1695)   Dutch physicist and astronomer who discovered Titan, a moon of Saturn, and determined that Saturn has rings. He was also an expert in optics and lenses.

Jansky, Karl Guthe (1905–1950)   American radio engineer who, by discovering radio emissions from the Milky Way galaxy, founded the field of radio astronomy.

Janssen, Pierre Jules César (1824–1907)   French astronomer who discovered, with the use of a spectroscope, the elements in the Sun.

Jastrow, Robert (1925–)   American astronomer and physicist who founded the Goddard Institute for Space Studies and is known for his work on the Earth's climate, planetary physics, and his publications on space.

Jeans, Sir James Hopwood (1877–1946)   British mathematician, astronomer, and physicist who was the first to propose that matter is continuously created throughout the universe. He also investigated spiral galaxies, and binary and multiple star systems, and was a writer of popular astronomy books.

Jeffreys, Sir Harold (1891–1989)   British astronomer and geophysicist who developed early models of the outer planets' structures. He also detailed the thermal history of the Earth, discovered the origins of monsoons and sea breezes, and first hypothesized that the Earth's core was liquid.

Kepler, Johannes (1571–1630)   German astronomer who formulated the three principal laws governing the motion and orbits of planetary bodies—thus eliminating the epicycle models that had governed astronomy for close to 2,000 years. He also assisted astronomer Tycho Brahe.

Kirkwood, Daniel (1814–1895)   American astronomer and discoverer of the gaps in the asteroid belt, caused by the gravitational pull of nearby Jupiter.

Kuiper, Gerard Peter (1905–1973)   Dutch-born American astronomer and a lunar and planetary scientist who founded the Lunar and Planetary Laboratory in Arizona. The Kuiper Airborne Observatory is named after him.

Lagrange, Comte Joseph Louis (1736–1813)   Italian-born French mathematician and theoretical physicist, who developed the theory of numbers and excelled in analytic and celestial mechanics.

Laplace, Marquis Pierre Simon de (1749–1827)   French mathematician, astronomer, and physicist who worked out the gravitational mechanics of the solar system. He also suggested that the planets formed from the same primitive mass of material, a theory that is known as Laplace's nebular hypothesis.

Leavitt, Henrietta Swan (1868–1921)   American astronomer who discovered how to use Cepheid variables as stellar yardsticks to measure distances to other galaxies.

Leverrier, Urbain Jean Joseph (1811–1877)   French astronomer who, by using mathematical calculations, was able to determine the orbit of Neptune. He did not locate Neptune, but his work led others to find the planet.

Lovell, Sir (Alfred Charles) Bernard (1913–)   British radio astronomer who besides his work in radio astronomy, obtained funds to build the Jodrell Bank radio telescope in the United Kingdom.

Lowell, Percival (1855–1916)   American astronomer who founded the Lowell Observatory in Flagstaff, Arizona. He was also influential in the development of theories of life on Mars and predicted a ninth planet (Pluto, which would not be discovered until 1930).

Messier, Charles (1730–1817)   French astronomer who developed the *Messier Catalogue*, the first listing of nebulous objects to aid observers.

Oort, Jan Hendrik (1900–1992)   Dutch astronomer who developed the idea that a collection of comets surrounds the solar system far outside the orbit of Pluto, now called the Oort Cloud.

Payne-Gaposchkin, Cecilia Helena (1900–1979)   British-born American astronomer and author whose work in stellar evolution and galactic structure led to important discoveries in variable, binary, and eclipsing stars.

Piazzi, Giuseppe (1746–1826)   Italian astronomer who discovered the first asteroid (minor planet), Ceres.

Pickering, Edward Charles (1846–1919)   American astronomer and brother of William Pickering. He contributed numerous discoveries in stellar spectroscopy.

Pickering, William Henry (1858–1938)   American astronomer and brother of Edward Pickering. He was the first to find a satellite of other planets using photographic techniques (Saturn's moon Phoebe). He also produced a photographic atlas of the Moon.

Pons, Jean Louis (1761–1831)   French astronomer who found 36 comets. He holds the record for comets found visually.

Ptolemy (Claudius Ptolemaeus) (c. A.D. 2)   Egyptian astronomer and encyclopedist who held that the Earth was the center of the universe, an idea that continued to dominate astronomy for over a thousand years after.

Roche, Édouard Albert (1820–1883)   French mathematician who first calculated the minimum distance to which a large satellite can approach its primary body without being torn apart, known as Roche's Limit.

Rømer, Ole Christensen (1644–1710)   Dutch astronomer who was first to determine the speed of light. He also developed the transit instrument.

Russell, Henry Norris (1877–1957)   American astronomer who, along with Ejnar Hertzsprung, developed a diagram of stellar life cycles based on temperature and absolute magnitude.

Sagan, Carl Edward (1934–)   American astronomer and exobiologist who worked on several planetary missions and is known for advancing public awareness and support of science through his popular writings and television presentations.

Schiaparelli, Giovanni Viginio (1835–1910)   Italian astronomer who studied the planets and is known mostly for his report of "canals" on the planet Mars.

Schmidt, Bernhard Voldemar (1879–1935)   Estonian-born German telescope maker who developed the Schmidt telescope (also called the Schmidt camera).

Schmidt, Maarten (1929–)   Dutch-born American astronomer who codiscovered, along with Jesse Greenstein, quasars.

Seyfert, Carl Keenan (1911–1960)   American astronomer who was instrumental in advancing galactic studies. Seyfert galaxies are named after him.

Shapley, Harlow (1885–1972)   American astronomer who first determined the true size of our universe.

Shoemaker, Carolyn (1929–)   American astronomer and wife of Eugene Shoemaker. She has discovered the most comets of any astronomer (by 1994, she had found 30), many of which were found while working on Eugene Shoemaker's program to search for planet-crossing asteroids.

Shoemaker, Eugene (1928–)   American astrogeologist and husband of Carolyn Shoemaker. He is known for his work in mapping the Moon for the *Apollo* missions. He is also an expert in planet-crossing asteroids, including near-Earth asteroids, and a proponent of the asteroid/comet-extinction theory (asteroid/comet strikes on Earth are responsible for massive extinctions).

Titius, Johann Daniel (1729–1796)   German astronomer who developed a mathematical explanation for the distances of the planets, now called the Titius-Bode Law but published it in an obscure journal. Johann Bode brought Titius' idea to the forefront several years later.

Tombaugh, Clyde William (1906–)   American astronomer who discovered the planet Pluto in 1930.

Tsiolkovsky, Konstantin Eduardovich (1857–1935)   Russian rocket pioneer and research scientist in aeronautics and astronautics who was one of the first to publish scientific papers about space flight. In Russia, he is often referred to as the father of space flight.

Urey, Harold Clayton (1893–1981)   American astronomer who was one of the founders of modern planetary science. He was a major proponent of solar system exploration, experimental solar system cosmogony, and the search for extraterrestrial life.

Whipple, Fred Lawrence (1906–)   American astronomer who developed a model of comet composition, in which the nucleus resembles a "dirty snowball."

Zwicky, Fritz (1898–1974)   Swiss-born American astronomer and physicist who determined the differences between supernovas and novas. He discovered unusual galaxies, clusters of galaxies, and about 18 supernovas; determined that neutron stars were the leftovers of supernova explosions; and developed some of the earliest jet engines.

SIGNIFICANT SCIENTIFIC DISCOVERIES IN ASTRONOMY

B.C.	2296	Chinese recorded earliest comet sighting
	2000	Sumerians made the first records of constellations
	1000	Egyptians based a calendar on movement of the star Sirius
	600–350	Greeks developed ideas in astronomy, such as the Earth is the center of the universe, and predicted events based on astrology
	352	Chinese recorded earliest supernova sighting
	240	Eratosthenes first to calculate the Earth's circumference
		Chinese recorded earliest sighting of Halley's comet

A.D. 140   Ptolemy defined the universe
1270   First known astronomical device to use an equatorial mounting called a torquetum, around Arabia
1543   Nicolaus Copernicus published *Concerning Revolutions*, which stated that the Earth and other planets revolve around the Sun
1608   Dutchman Hans Lippershey applied for the first patent of a telescope
1609   Galileo Galilei built the first astronomical telescope
1611   Sunspots first discovered by Galileo, Thomas Harriot, Johannes Fabricius, and Father Scheiner around the same time
       Orion nebula discovered
1639   First transit observed by Jeremiah Horrocks, of Venus across the Sun's face
1659   Christiaan Huygens first to observe surface features on Mars
1664   Robert Hooke discovered Jupiter's rotation and the Great Red Spot
1668   Isaac Newton invented the Newtonian reflecting telescope, the first telescope to use mirrors rather than lenses
1682   Edmond Halley discovered the comet that will bear his name
1687   Isaac Newton published *The Principia*, describing how planetary objects are governed by gravity
1755   German philosopher Immanuel Kant observed that nebulas are large star systems like the Milky Way; postulated that the solar system originated from a dust cloud
1766   Johann Titius proposed that the distances from the Sun to the planets are proportional (publicized by Bode in 1772)
1781   Uranus discovered by William Herschel
1790   William Hershel discovered planetary nebulas
1801   Giuseppe Piazzi discovered the first asteroid, Ceres
1839   First official observatory in the United States built, the Harvard College Observatory
1846   Neptune discovered by Johann Galle
1877   Asaph Hall discovered the two moons of Mars
1891   First discovery of an asteroid using photography by Maximilian Wolf
1905   Percival Lowell predicted the existence of a ninth planet beyond Neptune
       Einstein published his special theory of relativity
1915   Einstein published his general theory of relativity
1930   Pluto discovered by Clyde Tombaugh
1931   Radio waves detected from stars by Karl Jansky
1937   First actual radio telescope built by Grote Reber
1942   First radio maps of the universe made by Grote Reber
1948   The Hale Telescope was opened on Mt. Palomar, California, the largest telescope on Earth until 1975; it was 200 inches in diameter
1949   Rocket testing ground established at Cape Canaveral, Florida
       Fred Whipple developed the "dirty snowball" theory of comets
1950   Jan Oort proposed that a great cloud of comets orbits the Sun far beyond Pluto, now called the Oort Cloud
1957   The first spacecraft, Sputnik 1 (U.S.S.R.) began the Space Age
1963   Maarten Schmidt and Jesse Greenstein discovered the first quasars
1965   Radio wave remnants of the Big Bang found by Arno Penzias and Robert Wilson
1967   Pulsars discovered by Jocelyn Bell
1969   Humans landed on the Moon, Neil Armstrong and Buzz Aldrin
1977   Rings of Uranus discovered from Kuiper Airborne Observatory
1978   First known satellite of an asteroid found, orbiting Herculina (although this was disputed; an actual photo of the moon Dactyl around the asteroid, Ida, was taken in 1994)
       Charon, Pluto's only moon, discovered by James Christy and Robert Harrington

1979	*Skylab* fell to Earth after being abandoned
1980	Very Large Array radio telescope began operation in New Mexico
1981	Joseph Cassinelli and coworkers discovered the most massive star known, R136a, at 2,500 times the mass of our Sun
1987	The nearest observable supernova to Earth since 1604 occurred in the Large Magellanic Cloud, called 1987A; 19 neutrinos were detected from 1987A
1990	Hubble Space Telescope placed in orbit around the Earth; it was the first optical telescope in space
	The Cosmic Background Explorer (COBE) detected background radiation in the universe thought to have come from the Big Bang
1991	Astronomers reported that Comet Yanaka may have once orbited a star other than the Sun
1992	First high-energy gamma-rays from an object outside of the Milky Way galaxy detected
	Hubble Space Telescope detected possible evidence of a black hole
1993	Astronomers detected possible evidence of dark matter around the Large Magellanic Cloud galaxy
1994	Astronomers were able to predict and watch the outcome of comet Shoemaker-Levy 9 fragments striking the planet Jupiter; it was the first time impacts (and results) on another planetary body were observed
1995	The Hubble Space Telescope detects possible evidence of the Kuiper Belt

COMMON TERMS IN ASTRONOMY

absolute magnitude   The magnitude of a star as it would appear at a standard distance of 10 parsecs. Absolute magnitude is a way of comparing the intrinsic brightness of stars.

absorption nebula   A nebula seen in silhouette because it is absorbing or blocking light from behind. It is also called a dark nebula.

accretion   The process where small particles coalesce by collisions or mutual gravitational pull, creating larger bodies. Accretion is suspected as a major process in the formation of the planets and satellites in any solar system.

altitude   Number of degrees above the horizon of an object on the celestial sphere.

analemma   The Sun's apparent figure-eight path in the sky during the course of a year.

aphelion   Usually in reference to the Earth, aphelion is the point in an object's orbit that is farthest from the Sun. Earth's aphelion occurs in early July (see *perihelion*).

apogee   The point in the Moon's orbit (or any other orbiting body, such as an artificial satellite) when it is farthest from the Earth.

apparent magnitude   The brightness (magnitude) of a star as seen by an observer on Earth. Apparent magnitude depends on the star's emitted light and distance. The smallest numbers refer to the brightest bodies. The full moon has an apparent magnitude of −12.6.

asterism   A pattern of stars that does not constitute one of the 88 official constellations. For example, the Big Dipper in the constellation of Ursa Major is an asterism.

astrometry   The measure of the positions and apparent motions of celestial objects and attempt to understand the factors that influence such movements.

astronomical unit   An astronomical distance, equal to the average distance from the Earth to the Sun, or about 93,000,000 miles (149,598,770 kilometers).

Barnard's Star   A ninth magnitude star in the constellation Ophiuchus that has the largest known stellar proper motion. Discovered by Edward E. Barnard in 1916, it is the third-nearest star to the Sun and has an apparent wobble—a possible indication of unseen planets.

Bayer designations   The Greek letters assigned to the stars in the constellations to identify the brighter stars. It was developed in 1603, by German astronomer Johann Bayer.

binary star   Stars that are gravitationally attracted to each other, forming a double star system. Often binary stars include more than two stars and are referred to as multiple star systems (see also *double star*).

celestial sphere   An imaginary sphere used to locate the positions and track the motions of all astronomical objects.

cosmic maser   Region in a cloud of interstellar gas that is stimulated to produce radiation by starlight; the radiation produced is similar to light from a laser.

cosmogony   The study of how the universe was formed.

cosmology   The study of the properties, processes, and evolution of the universe.

dark matter   Matter that is thought to exist in the universe but has not yet been observed. It is based on measurements of unexplained gravitational effects on visible matter.

declination   On the celestial sphere, the coordinate analogous to latitude on the Earth. Declination is measured in degrees, minutes, and seconds of arc north (positive above the celestial equator) or south (negative below the celestial equator).

Doppler effect   The phenomenon in which, as a source of waves (i.e., sound or light) and the observer move relative to each other, the emitted wavelength appears to change. In astronomy, Doppler shifts are used to determine the velocity and direction of distant objects. For example, light from a galaxy shifts to the red on the electromagnetic spectrum if the galaxy is moving away from the observer (red shift) and to the blue if it is moving toward the observer (blue shift).

double star   A stellar system containing pairs of stars. Double stars may be an optical double, which are stars that just appear to be close as seen from Earth; or double stars may be true binaries, stars that are gravitationally bound to one another.

ecliptic   The apparent path of the Sun, planets, and Moon in the sky as seen from the Earth.

fireball   A bright meteor, with an apparent magnitude ranging from about –5 to –20 (to compare, the Sun has an apparent magnitude of –26.7). Fireballs are sometimes seen during the day.

globular cluster   A nearly spherical, dense cluster of hundreds of thousands to millions of stars.

gravitational collapse   A sudden collapse at the end of a star's life, when the central temperature falls and the internal, outward pressure is no longer powerful enough to counteract the inward gravitational force. Depending on the original mass, such a collapse can form a white dwarf star, a neutron star, a black hole or can trigger a supernova explosion.

Hubble flow   The uniform and mutual recession of celestial objects because of the expansion of the universe.

inferior conjunction   The passage of Mercury or Venus between the Earth and the Sun.

libration   The effect that allows an observer on Earth to see about 59 percent of the Moon's surface, slightly more than would otherwise be visible. Because the Moon's rotation and orbital period are equal (on average), the Moon always keeps the same face to the Earth. Libration occurs because the Moon's elliptical orbit speed is not constant and its orbit is slightly tilted.

light-year   The distance light travels in a year, equal to 5.88 trillion miles (9.46 trillion kilometers).

magnitude   The measure of a celestial object's brightness, usually based on a logarithmic scale (see also *absolute magnitude* and *apparent magnitude*).

nadir   The point directly below the observer, or 90 degrees below the horizon (see also *zenith*).

nebula   A concentration of gas and dust in the galaxy.

oblate   The shape of a planet or natural satellite that is not completely spherical but bulges in the center and is flattened at the poles. The shape is usually caused by rapid spinning or the gravitational pull from an accompanying moon. For example, rapidly rotating Jupiter is an oblate spheroid.

occultation   The crossing of one body in front of another, such as the Moon in front of a star, relative to an observer.

opposition   The point in a planet's orbit when it is 180 degrees from the Sun, usually as observed from Earth.

orbit   The path of an object around a central body; gravitational attraction keeps the bodies in orbit.

parallax   The change in the relative position of an object when viewed from different places; in astronomy, the closer the object, the greater the parallax.

penumbra   The lighter area between the umbra and the edge of a shadow. For example, a penumbra can be seen during a total lunar eclipse as the lighter, fuzzier edge of the shadow as the eclipse progresses.

perigee   The point where the Moon (or any other orbiting body, such as an artificial satellite) is closest in its orbit to the Earth.

perihelion   Usually in reference to the Earth, it is the point in the orbit of an object when it is closest to the Sun. Earth's perihelion occurs in early January (see also *aphelion*).

perturbation   A local gravitational disturbance in the uniform motion of a body because of the gravitational influence of another object. For example, a comet orbiting the Sun can be perturbed by a close encounter with Jupiter, the solar system's largest planet, which influences the orbit of the comet.

planetoid   A mostly obsolete term, usually used to describe the larger remnants of rocks left over from the formation of the solar system.

plasma   Matter in the form of electrically charged particles; the state in which most of the universe exists.

proper motion   The apparent angular motion of an object across the sky, determined as change in position with respect to the background star; caused by the star's true motion and the relative motion of the solar system.

quasar   Quasars, an acronym for quasi-stellar radio sources, are thought to be the most distant objects in the universe. They are small, extremely luminous for their size, and have high red shifts, indicating that they are receding at great speed from Earth. Yet unexplained x-ray measurements reveal that some of these objects can turn the energy output of 10 billion suns on and off—all within a span of 1 or 2 hours.

revolution   The movement of an object around a central body.

right ascension   The angle of an object eastward from the vernal equinox, along the celestial equator; right ascension is measured in hours, minutes, and seconds.

rotation   The movement of a body as it turns on its axis.

solar wind   A stream of particles, primarily protons and electrons, that constantly flow outward from the Sun.

space-time   A four-dimensional way of describing events and locations with three units of distance and one of time. Under the influence of gravity, space-time can actually warp and bend.

spectrum   Radiation (usually visible light) broken into its component wavelengths.

star   A spherical celestial body consisting of a large mass of hot gas held together by its own gravity. It is self-luminating because of extensive internal nuclear reactions. Our Sun is a typical star.

superior conjunction   For a planet inside the Earth's orbit, the condition when the planet is behind the Sun, relative to the Earth.

syzygy   The condition when three celestial bodies are arranged in a straight line. It occurs during solar and lunar eclipses, when the Sun, Moon, and Earth are aligned.

terminator   The line separating sunlight and darkness on a planet or moon.

transit   The movement of a smaller object across the lighted face of a larger object, i.e., the movement of Mercury across the face of the Sun or the moon Io across the face of the planet Jupiter.

umbra   The area in shadow from which light is completely cut off, i.e., during a total lunar eclipse, the umbra completely covers the Moon at totality.

universe   The entirety of all that is known to exist. The size of the observable universe is limited to the distance light has traveled since the Big Bang.

zenith   The point directly overhead from the observer, or 90 degrees above the horizon (see also *nadir*).

zodiacal light   A faint cone of light seen along the ecliptic at sunset, usually around the time of the equinox. It is caused by sunlight scattering small dust particles, which are possibly of interplanetary origin.

ADDITIONAL SOURCES OF INFORMATION

Abell, George O., Morrison, David, and Wolff, Sidney C. *Exploration of the Universe*. Saunders College, 1991.

Asimov, Isaac. *Isaac Asimov's Guide to Earth and Space*. Random House, 1991.

Beatty, J. Kelly, and Chaikin, Andrew. *The New Solar System*. Cambridge Univ. Press, 1990.

Gibson, Bob. *The Astronomer's Sourcebook*. Woodbine, 1992.

Goldsmith, Donald. *The Astronomers*. St. Martin's, 1991.

Hamburg, Michael. *Astronomy Made Simple*. Doubleday, 1993.

Moore, Patrick, Hunt, Garry, Nicolson, Iain, and Cattermole, Peter. *The Atlas of the Solar System*. Crescent, 1990.

Ridpath, Ian, ed.. *Norton's 2000.0: Star Atlas and Reference Handbook*. Longman, 1989.

———. *Astronomy*. Gallery, 1991.

Ronan, Colin A. *The Natural History of the Universe*. Macmillan, 1991.

Chapter 9 Earth Science

The Earth   368

Earth in Space   368

Lists of the Earth   372

Geology   376

Earthquakes and Volcanoes   389

Marine Science   395

Past Life   401

Major Earth Scientists   407

Significant Scientific Discoveries in
Earth Science   411

Common Terms in Earth Science   412

Additional Sources of Information   417

THE EARTH

The Earth is the third planet from the Sun. Other bodies in the solar system possess oceans (although probably not of water) and/or an atmosphere, but Earth is the only planet known to be inhabited by carbon-based life forms.

The Early Earth

The most widely accepted explanation of the formation of the solar system (and thus of the Earth) is the protoplanet hypothesis. About 10 to 15 billion years ago, according to this theory, a gas cloud (nebula) began to form. About 5 to 6 billion years ago, shock waves (possibly from a nearby stellar explosion, called a supernova) caused the large aggregation of spinning gases and dust to collapse and spin. The spinning cloud flattened, and material began to fall toward the cloud's center, creating the protosun (the precursor of today's Sun).

Turbulence within the outer cloud caused particles to clump together (accrete) and form planetoids, which broke apart and reformed numerous times. These forming planetoids acted like gravitational collectors, sweeping through space and gathering more mass—eventually accreting into a small number of protoplanets. As pressures and temperatures increased at the center of the collapsing cloud, thermonuclear reactions eventually ignited the Sun. A short time later, the protoplanets evolved into true planets (for more information on the formation of the solar system, see Chapter 8, "Astronomy").

As planetoids accreted to form the Earth, they melted and began to stratify by density. About 4.56 billion years ago, high density materials, such as iron, had sunk to the planet's center, while lighter materials, such as silica, had risen toward the surface. This stratification formed the Earth's central iron core, multilayered mantle, and hardened outer crust. The planet's surface was extremely active, with volcanoes emitting water vapor and gases into space. This created a primitive atmosphere and contributed water and gases to the oceans and atmosphere. Another hypothesis proposes that comets bombarding the Earth at this time may have contributed additional water and gases to the primitive atmosphere and oceans.

Between about 3.8 and 4 billion years ago, the inner solar system planets experienced a developmental stage called the Late Heavy Bombardment, in which larger planetoids (chunks of rock leftover from the formation of the planets) impacted the planets and satellites of the inner solar system. On Earth, such a bombardment may have opened cracks in the crust, contributing more gases to the atmosphere. On the Moon, the bombardment created many of the mares (or dark "seas") seen today.

Life apparently appeared in the Earth's oceans about 3.8 billion years ago. About 600 million years ago, Earth experienced an explosion of life in its oceans, starting during the part of geologic time known as the Late Precambrian. It is unknown why this explosion of life occurred (for more information on early life, see Chapter 4, "Biology").

EARTH IN SPACE

Rotation

The Earth rotates around a central axis, approximately identified by the North and South Poles. The Earth's axis tilts 23° 27' (23.5°) away from a line perpendicular to the plane of its orbit. One complete rotation of the Earth on its axis results in a day. A mean solar day lasts 24 hours, which is the average of all apparent solar days in the orbital year; the mean sidereal day is 23 hours, 56 minutes, and 4.091 seconds; this is the time required for a star to go from one spot to the same spot in the sky (for more information on days, months, and years, see Chapter 3, "Time").

There are variations in the Earth's rotation. *Secular variations*, caused by friction from the Earth's tidal bulge, can increase the length of the day by about 1 millisecond per century. *Periodic variations* occur during seasonal changes and regular events. For example, tidal forces from the Sun can cause minute distortions in the Earth's shape, which result in a slight increase or decrease in the planet's rotational speed. *Irregular variations*, resulting from turbulent core-mantle interactions, cause the Earth to rotate more or less rapidly every 5 to 10 years. Because of this, the Earth has accumulated a difference in rotational speed of about 40 seconds over the past century.

WHY SLOW DOWN?

By precisely measuring the movement of the stars and planets, scientists can determine the speed of the Earth's rotation. Rotation measurements often differ by fractions of a second—differences caused by climatic conditions across wide areas. For example, El Niño is a periodic upwelling of warmer waters around the equatorial Pacific Ocean, which changes ocean water temperatures and air pressures, contributing to large-scale weather variations around the world. Between 1982 and 1983, one of the most severe El Niños in 100 years was blamed for the slowing down of the Earth's rotation by $1/5,000$ second.

Another example of the slowing of the Earth's rotation occurred during January 1990, when the Earth's day lengthened by $1/2,000$ second. This change was again due to the weather—westerly wind bursts from Asia and across the Pacific Ocean.

Revolution

The Earth revolves around the Sun along an elliptical orbit, producing an apparent annual motion of the Sun in the sky. It takes 365 days, 5 hours, 48 minutes, and 46 seconds (365.2422 days) for the Earth to revolve around the Sun (a tropical year). The Earth travels along this path at an average velocity of 66,672 miles (107,275 kilometers) per hour, which varies depending on the Earth's distance from the Sun. Because of natural variations in the Earth's orbit, the time required to complete one revolution is decreasing at a rate of 0.53 seconds per century.

The Sun is not at the center of the Earth's elliptical orbit, which means that the distance from the Earth to the Sun varies.

The *perihelion*, the closest point to the Sun, occurs between January 1 and 4; the Earth is then 406,076 miles (147,072,376 kilometers) from the Sun.

The *aphelion*, the farthest point from the Sun, occurs between July 2 and 6; the Earth is then 94,506,240 miles (152,060,540 kilometers) from the Sun.

The *mean distance* between the Sun and Earth is 92,960,117 miles (149,573,881 kilometers, or 1 astronomical unit); for simplicity, 1 astronomical unit is often rounded off to be 93,000,000 miles (149,637,000 kilometers).

Earth's Seasons

The Earth experiences seasonal changes during its revolution around the Sun because the plane in which the planet revolves does not coincide with the plane of its equator (in other words, the Earth is tilted). The relation of the two planes, inclined to each other by 23.5°, is known as the *obliquity of the ecliptic*. A *solstice* occurs in the Northern Hemisphere when the Earth is maximally inclined toward the Sun in June and away from it in December; in the Southern Hemisphere, a solstice occurs when the Earth is maximally inclined toward the Sun in December and away from it in June. An *equinox* (a day with equal hours of daylight and dark) occurs in both hemispheres when the Sun's light is most directly on the equator, in March and September (for more information on the seasons, see Chapter 3, "Time").

Earth Around the Sun

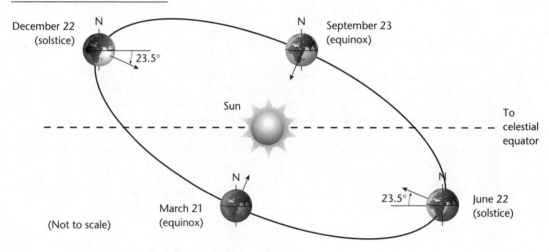

Precession of the Equinoxes

As the Earth moves, it experiences *precession*—a wobbling on its axis like a top. Rotation causes the Earth to bulge around its center, and the gravitation of the Sun and the Moon pulls the bulge toward the ecliptic plane. As the Earth tries to resist the pull, its rotational axis moves slowly westward around the pole of the ecliptic. Thus the Earth's axis describes a cone about the perpendicular to the plane of the ecliptic, moving at a rate of about 50 arc seconds per year and completing a precessional cycle in about 26,000 years.

The Earth's axis of rotation retains its tilt of 23.5° during this cycle, but the north celestial pole changes. The north celestial pole is currently pointing in the direction of Polaris (the North Star) in the constellation of the Ursa Minor. In about 11,000 years, the north celestial pole will point in the direction of the star Vega in the constellation Lyra. The vernal and autumnal equinoxes—and, therefore, the position of the Sun at the equinoxes—will also change; thus the term *precession of the equinoxes*. Approximately 2,000 ago, at the time of the vernal equinox, the Sun was in the constellation Aries; today it is in the constellation Pisces; in 1,000 years, it will be in the constellation Aquarius.

Earth's Precession

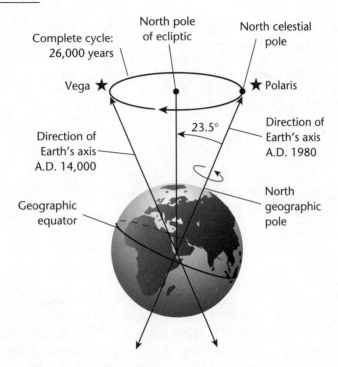

Complete cycle:
26,000 years

North pole
of ecliptic

North celestial
pole

Vega ★

★ Polaris

23.5°

Direction of
Earth's axis—
A.D. 14,000

Direction of
Earth's axis
A.D. 1980

Geographic
equator

North
geographic
pole

THE EARTH'S MAGNETIC FIELD

The Earth's magnetosphere is a teardrop-shaped magnetic field that protects the Earth from the lethal bombardment of high-energy particles from the Sun. Scientists theorize that eddy currents, created by the heat released by radioactive elements in the Earth's conductive outer core, generate the magnetic field.

The parts of the magnetosphere include the *bow shock*, where the solar wind particles slow down after the first contact with the magnetic field; the *magnetopause*, the boundary between the Sun's influence and the Earth's magnetosphere; the *magnetic force lines*, lines that flow downward at the magnetic North Pole and upward at the magnetic South Pole; and the doughnut-shaped *Van Allen radiation belts*, (discovered by James Van Allen in 1958), which consist of highly energetic, charged particles trapped in the Earth's magnetic field. It is thought that there are additional, thinner belts within the Van Allen radiation belts, but their existence has only tentatively been verified.

Earth's Movement Through the Galaxy

As the Earth moves around the Sun, the Sun is moving around the spiral arm of the Milky Way galaxy at speeds of about 150 miles (250 kilometers) per second. The apparent direction of movement of the solar system is toward the constellation Lyra. The Sun and its solar system will complete one revolution around the galaxy's center in about 200 to 250 million years.

LISTS OF THE EARTH

The numbers in the following lists are approximations for several reasons. Numbers are often represented by miles and kilometers, and the conversion between the systems causes the numbers to be rounded and thus slightly modified. In addition, because we live on a dynamic planet, the Earth's physical features change all the time. For example, after a major flood, a river often alters its course, which can change its length.

Earth Facts and Figures

Size

Mean radius	3,958.7 miles (6,370.95 kilometers)
Polar radius	3,950 miles (6,332 kilometers)
Equatorial radius	3,964 miles (6,378 kilometers)
Polar circumference	24,857 miles (39,995 kilometers)
Equatorial circumference	24,900 miles (40,064 kilometers)

Volumes

Mass	6 sextillion, 588 quintillion short tons (5.9763×10^{27} grams)
Total Earth volume	259.8 billion cubic miles (1083.1579×10^9 cubic kilometers)
Total water volume	330 million cubic miles ($1,370 \times 10^6$ cubic kilometers)
Total crust volume	2 billion cubic miles ($6,210 \times 10^6$ cubic kilometers)
Total mantle volume	216 billion cubic miles ($898,000 \times 10^6$ cubic kilometers)
Total core volume	41 billion cubic miles ($175,500 \times 10^6$ cubic kilometers)

Surface Areas

Surface area	196,950,711 square miles (510.0501×10^6 square kilometers)
Land area	57.5 million square miles (149×10^6 square kilometers); 29.22 percent of total
Water area	139.4 million square miles (361×10^6 square kilometers); 70.78 percent of total

Average Densities

Water	1.00 grams per cubic centimeter
Entire Earth	5.52 grams per cubic centimeter
Crust	2.85 grams per cubic centimeter
Mantle	4.53 grams per cubic centimeter
Core	10.70 grams per cubic centimeter

Distances and Heights

Distance from Sun (mean)	92,960,117 miles (149,573,881 kilometers)
Distance from Moon (mean)	238,866 miles (384,400 kilometers)
Greatest height above mean sea level, Mt. Everest	29,022 feet, 7 inches (8,846 meters); established 1993

Greatest depth below mean sea level, Marianas Trench	36,198 feet (11,033 meters)
Average land height	2,757 feet (840 meters)
Average ocean depth	12,460 feet (3,798 meters)

Velocities

Escape velocity	6.96 miles per second (11.2 kilometers per second)
Orbital velocity	66,672 miles per hour (107,280 kilometers per hour)

Geomagnetic Poles

Magnetic North Pole (1990)	78.0° North, 104° W
Magnetic South Pole (1990)	65.0° S, 139 ° E

The exact location of the geomagnetic poles is constantly changing, often moving several miles a day due to magnetic disturbances. Because of this irregularity, the geomagnetic poles are not symmetrically opposite to one another. Generally, the geomagnetic pole best approximating the Earth's observed magnetic field is one inclined 11.5° from the axis of rotation.

Largest Lakes

Name	Location	Average Area (Square Miles) [Kilometers]		Average Depth (Feet) [Meters]	
Caspian Sea	Asia	143,630	[372,002]	3,264	[995]
Lake Superior	North America	31,700	[82,103]	1,330	[405]
Lake Victoria	Africa	26,828	[69,485]	270	[82]
Lake Huron	North America	23,000	[59,570]	750	[229]
Lake Michigan	North America	22,300	[57,757]	923	[281]
Aral Sea	Asia	15,500	[40,145]	177	[54]
Tanganyika	Africa	12,700	[32,893]	4,708	[1,435]
Baykal (Baikal)	Asia	12,162	[31,500]	5,315	[1,620]
Great Bear	North America	12,096	[31,329]	1,299	[396]
Nyasa (Malawi)	Africa	11,150	[28,879]	2,280	[695]
Great Slave	North America	11,031	[28,570]	2,015	[614]
Lake Erie	North America	9,910	[25,667]	210	[64]
Winnipeg	North America	9,417	[24,390]	60	[18]
Ontario	North America	7,550	[19,555]	802	[244]
Balkhash	Asia	7,115	[18,428]	85	[26]
Ladoga	Europe	6,835	[17,703]	738	[225]
Chad	Africa	6,300	[16,317]	24	[7]
Maracaibo	South America	5,217	[13,512]	115	[35]
Onega	Europe	3,710	[9,609]	328	[100]
Eyre	Australia	3,600	[9,324]	52	[16]
Volta	Africa	3,276	[8,485]	Unknown	
Titicaca	South America	3,200	[8,288]	922	[281]
Nicaragua	North America	3,100	[8,029]	230	[70]
Athabasca	North America	3,064	[7,936]	407	[124]

Principal Waterfalls

Name	Location	Total Height (Feet) [Meters]
Angel	Venezuela	3,212 [979]
Yosemite	United States	2,425 [739]
Southern Mardalsfossen	Norway	2,149 [655]
Tugela	South Africa	2,014 [614]
Cuquenán	Venezuela	2,000 [610]
Sutherland	New Zealand	1,904 [580]
Ribbon	United States	1,612 [491]
Great Kamarang	Guyana	1,600 [488]
Northern Mardalsfossen	Norway	1,535 [468]
Della	Canada	1,443 [440]
Gavarnie	France	1,385 [422]
Skjeggedal	Norway	1,378 [420]
Glass	Brazil	1,325 [404]

Principal Rivers

Name	Location	Approximate Length (Miles) [Kilometers]
Nile	Africa	4,160 [6,693]
Amazon	South America	4,000 [6,436]
Chang Jiang (Yangtze)	Asia	3,964 [6,378]
Mississippi/Missouri	North America	3,740 [6,017]
Huang (Yellow)	Asia	3,395 [5,463]
Ob-Irtysh	Asia	3,362 [5,409]
Amur	Asia	2,744 [4,415]
Lena	Asia	2,734 [4,399]
Congo	Africa	2,718 [4,373]
Mackenzie	North America	2,635 [4,240]
Mekong	Asia	2,600 [4,183]
Niger	Africa	2,590 [4,167]
Yenisey	Asia	2,543 [4,092]
Paraná	South America	2,485 [3,998]
Mississippi	North America	2,340 [3,765]
Missouri	North America	2,315 [3,725]
Murray-Darling	Australia	2,310 [3,717]
Volga	Asia	2,290 [3,685]
Purus	South America	2,100 [3,379]
Madeira	South America	2,013 [3,239]
São Francisco	South America	1,988 [3,199]
Yukon	North America	1,979 [3,184]
Rio Grande	North America	1,900 [3,057]
Brahmaputra	Asia	1,800 [2,896]
Indus	Asia	1,800 [2,896]
Danube	Europe	1,776 [2,858]
Japura	South America	1,750 [2,816]
Zambezi	Africa	1,700 [2,735]
Euphrates	Asia	1,700 [2,735]

Principal Mountain Peaks

Name	Mountain Range	Location	Height Above Sea Level (Feet) [Meters]
Everest	Himalayas	Asia	29,022 [8,846]
K2* (Godwin Austen)	Himalayas	Asia	28,250 [8,611]
Kanchenjunga	Himalayas	Asia	28,208 [8,598]
Lhotse I	Himalayas	Asia	27,923 [8,511]
Makalu	Himalayas	Asia	27,824 [8,481]
Lhotse II	Himalayas	Asia	27,560 [8,400]
Dhaulagiri	Himalayas	Asia	26,810 [8,172]
Manaslu I	Himalayas	Asia	26,760 [8,156]
Cho Oyu	Himalayas	Asia	26,750 [8,153]
Nanga Parbat	Himalayas	Asia	26,660 [8,126]

Although not confirmed, satellite measurement of K2 recorded a height of 29,064 feet (8,859 meters)

Highest and Lowest Continental Points

Name	Continent	Height or Depth (Feet) [Meters]
HIGHEST POINTS ABOVE SEA LEVEL		
Mount Everest	Asia	29,022 [8,846]
Mount Aconcagua	South America	22,834 [6,960]
Mount McKinley	North America	20,320 [6,194]
Mount Kibo (Kilimanjaro)	Africa	19,340 [5,895]
Mount El'Brus	Europe	18,510 [5,642]
Vinson Massif	Antarctica	16,860 [5,139]
Mount Kosciusko	Australia	7,310 [2,228]
LOWEST POINTS BELOW SEA LEVEL		
Lake Eyre	Australia	52 [16]
Caspian Sea	Europe	92 [28]
Salinas Grandes	South America	131 [40]
Death Valley	North America	282 [86]
Lake Assal	Africa	512 [156]
Dead Sea	Asia	1,299 [396]

Principal Deserts

Name	Location	Approximate Length (Miles) [Kilometers]
Sahara	North Africa	3,500,000 [9,065,000]
Gobi	Asia	500,000 [1,295,000]
Libyan	Africa	450,000 [1,165,500]
Rub al-Khali	Africa	250,000 [647,500]
Kalahari	Africa	225,000 [582,800]
Great Sandy	Australia	150,000 [338,500]
Great Victoria	Australia	150,000 [338,500]

NATURAL WONDERS

Not everyone agrees on the most spectacular natural wonders of the world—or of the United States. The following lists of the natural wonders of the world and of the United States represent the most commonly cited locations, along with alternates that are frequently noted.

Natural Wonders of the World

- Grand Canyon, United States
- Rio de Janeiro Harbor, Brazil
- Iguazu Falls, Argentina (alternates: Yellowstone Falls in the United States, Niagara Falls in the United States and Canada, or Victoria Falls in Zimbabwe)
- Yosemite Valley and the Giant Sequoias (oldest known living organisms), United States
- Natural Bridge, United States
- Mt. Everest, Tibet and Nepal (alternates: Matterhorn in Switzerland and Italy and/or the towering wall of the Peruvian Andes)
- The Nile River, Egypt (alternate: the northern lights, or aurora borealis)

Natural Wonders of the United States

- Grand Canyon, Arizona
- Yosemite Valley and Giant Sequoias, California
- Carslbad Caverns, New Mexico (alternate: Mammoth Cave, Kentucky)
- Yellowstone Falls, Wyoming (alternate: Niagara Falls, New York)
- Petrified Forest, Arizona (alternate: Badlands, North Dakota)
- Crater Lake and Wizard Island, Oregon
- Rainbow Natural Bridge, Utah

GEOLOGY

What Is Geology?

Geology is the study of the Earth's composition, structure, processes, and history. In 1830, Sir Charles Lyell defined geology. Since that time, the study of geology has been extended to planets and their satellites (planetary geology).

There are many branches of geology. The major ones include *geochemistry*, the study of the chemistry of the Earth; *mineralogy*, the examination of minerals; *paleontology*, the study of fossils; *crystallography*, the description of atomic and molecular structure of minerals to understand their material properties; *marine geology* (a branch of oceanography), the study of the geology of the oceans; *geomorphology*, the field of landform development; *geophysics*, the study of the physics of the Earth; *structural geology*, the examination of rock deformation and resulting configurations; *planetary geology* (or planetology), the study of planet and satellite morphology in the solar system; and *stratigraphy*, the description of sedimentary rock sequences and ages (closely related to sedimentology). There are other discipline combinations, such as petroleum geology (the study of petroleum resources), which combines geophysics, stratigraphy, and geochemistry.

Layers of the Earth

Because the Earth's interior is inaccessible to observation, geologists have discerned its many layers by indirect methods. Earthquakes reveal the Earth's interior structure because certain seismic waves travel at varying speeds through materials of different densities (see also "Earthquakes," later in this chapter). Other properties of the planet's interior can be inferred from magnetic, thermal, and gravitational characteristics.

Crust

The Earth's outer solid *crust* surrounds the mantle. The crust makes up about 0.6 percent of the Earth's volume and 0.4 percent of its mass. Its overall thickness varies widely: Beneath the oceans, the crust (mainly composed of basalt) ranges between 3 and 6.8 miles (5 to 11 kilometers) thick; beneath the continents, the crust (mostly light rocks such as granite) ranges between 12 and 40 miles (19 and 64 kilometers) thick.

The upper layer of the Earth is called the *lithosphere*. It includes the oceanic and continental crusts and part of the cooler, solid upper mantle.

Mantle

The *mantle* makes up 84 percent of the Earth by volume and 67 percent by mass. It is about 1,802 miles (2,900 kilometers) thick and consists of silica, plus iron-, magnesium-, and other metal-rich minerals. The *Gutenberg discontinuity* separates the Earth's mantle from the outer core; the *Mohorovičić discontinuity* separates the uppermost portion of the mantle from the crust.

The hot plastic *asthenosphere*, part upper mantle and lower crust, separates the more brittle crust-mantle lithosphere above from the mesosphere below. Thought to be responsible for the movement of the lithospheric plates (crustal plates) that slowly "carry" the continents around the planet, the asthenosphere is about 186 miles (300 kilometers) thick (see also "Plate Tectonics," later in this chapter). The more solid *mesosphere*, located below the asthenosphere, includes part of the upper and all of the lower mantle.

Core

The inner and outer *core* make up about 15 percent of the Earth by volume and 32 percent by mass. The *inner core* is about 800 miles (1,287 kilometers) thick; the *outer core* is about 1,400 miles (2,253 kilometers) thick. The inner core, thought to be solid, extends from the center of the Earth to the lower border of the outer core. The outer core, which appears to have characteristics of a liquid, extends to the Gutenberg discontinuity, the border between the mantle and outer core. Because of its extreme density, the entire core seems to be composed of mostly iron, with smaller amounts of other dense elements such as nickel. The pressures within the solid inner core reach about 3 million atmospheres (1 atmosphere equals the atmosphere pressure at sea level); temperatures measure between 7,200 and 9,000°F (4,000 to 5,000°C)—nearly as hot as the Sun's surface. The heat is from the natural radioactive decay of uranium; it is also from dissipated heat from the Earth as it cooled after formation.

Earth's Layers

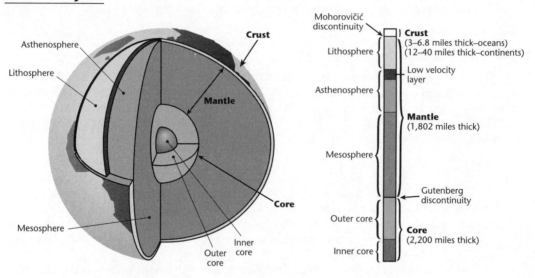

DEEPEST IN THE EARTH

The deepest mines reach into the Earth only about 2 miles (3.2 kilometers)—or about one-tenth of the crust's average thickness. Still, the mines are proof that the pressures and temperatures in the Earth's crust rise with depth. For example, in deep gold mines, temperatures can reach 120°F (49°C).

The following list compares several depths.

Earth's average radius	3,958.7 miles (6,370 kilometers)
Crust's average thickness	20 miles (32 kilometers)
Deepest geologic borehole (Zapolyarnyy, Russia)	9 miles (14.5 kilometers)
Deepest mine (Carletonville, South Africa)	2.3 miles (3.7 kilometers)
Deepest ocean dive (Bathyscaphe in Marianas Trench)	6 miles (9.7 kilometers)
Deepest ocean trench (Marianas Trench)	7 miles (11.3 kilometers)

Composition of the Earth's Crust

Nine elements constitute nearly 99%, by mass, of the Earth's crust. The following list notes the various elements in the Earth's crust and their approximate percentages (the numbers add up to more than 100 percent because of rounding).

Name	Percent by Mass
Oxygen	45.0
Silicon	27.0
Aluminum	8.0
Iron	5.8
Calcium	5.1
Magnesium	2.8
Sodium	2.3

Name	Percent by Mass
Potassium	1.7
Hydrogen	1.5
Titanium	0.86
Phosphorus	0.1
Manganese	0.1
Fluorine	0.046
Strontium	0.045
Barium	0.038
Sulfur	0.030
Chlorine	0.019
Vanadium	0.017
Zirconium	0.014

Plate Tectonics

About six large and more than a dozen small crustal (lithospheric or tectonic) plates make up the Earth's crust, all moving around the planet in different directions and at various speeds (fractions of an inch per year). Most plates lie beneath a combination of ocean and continent; several lie only beneath oceans.

The theory of *plate tectonics* states that the lithosphere is divided into plates, or tabular blocks, that interact with each other over time. The crust and part of the solid upper mantle comprise each crustal plate. The true mechanism for the movement of the crustal plates is still unknown. Scientists theorize that convection in the upper mantle-lower crust, or asthenosphere, slowly "carries" the lithospheric plates around the planet; another theory states that convection at a depth of about 375 to 435 miles (603 to 700 kilometers) in the part of the mantle (mesosphere) is transferred to the asthenosphere and moves the plates.

Crustal plates are created, destroyed, or move past each other in a variety of ways.

Plate movement in ocean basins includes *sea-floor spreading,* or diverging plates. A rift in the ocean floor constantly forms new crustal material—usually from volcanic action—and the ocean floor literally spreads apart. For example, the Mid-Atlantic Ridge is an area of sea-floor spreading that splits the Atlantic Ocean; the plates move laterally about 1 inch (2.54 centimeters) per year. Shallow, substantial earthquakes are associated with diverging plates (see "Earthquakes," later in this chapter).

When one plate sinks under another, it is called *subduction,* with the subducting plate gradually breaking apart. For example, the Japan Trench off the island of Honshu is the line where the Pacific plate subducts under the Eurasian plate. Some of the largest and deepest earthquakes are associated with subducting plates.

When two plates ram into one another, it is called *colliding plate boundaries,* causing the crust to buckle from intense pressure. For example, the Himalayas were formed by the collision of the Indo-Australian plate and the Eurasian plate. Deep, substantial earthquakes are associated with colliding plates. Even today, the Himalayas are still rising because of this collision—about 1/5 inches (5 millimeters) per year.

When plates slide by each other, and no plate is created or destroyed, it is called a *transform boundary plate*. For example, along the San Andreas Fault in California, the Pacific plate slides northwest past the North American plate. (Contrary to popular belief, part of California will not "fall" into the ocean; rather part of the state is simply a section of the Pacific plate moving northwest at about 0.5 inch [1.3 centimeters] per year.) Shallow, substantial earthquakes are associated with transform boundary plates.

Crustal Plates Around the World

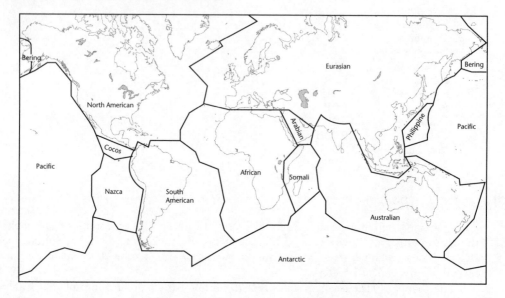

Note: Locations of crustal plates are approximate.

Movement of Crustal Plates Over Time

Crustal plates have moved across the planet for at least the past 600 million years—and probably for billions of years before. Presently, each plate moves at a different rate. For example, measurements of the North American and Eurasian plates at the Mid-Atlantic Ridge show that the plates separate about 1 inch (2.54 centimeters) per year.

Scientists believe that a supercontinent called *Pangaea* existed about 250 million years ago (Pangaea was first proposed by Alfred Wegener in 1915). By 180 million years ago, the supercontinent had broken up into *Gondwanaland,* or Gondwana (a hypothetical continent formed by the union of South America, Africa, Australia, India, and Antarctica), and *Laurasia* (composed of North America and Eurasia). About 65 million years ago—at approximately the time of the extinction of the dinosaurs—the two continents began to separate, slowly forming the familiar outlines of today's continents. Scientists estimate that in 50 million years, the west coast of North America will tear itself free from the mainland, Australia will move northward and collide with Indonesia, and Africa and Asia will split apart at the Red Sea.

SWITCHING NORTH AND SOUTH

In 1963, researchers at Cambridge University discovered why strips of rocks that hold a magnetic record (for example, in the magnetic mineral, magnetite) around sea-floor spreading regions alternate in polarity. They reasoned that iron-rich lava emerging from a sea-floor spreading region acquired and preserved the Earth's magnetic record when it formed. Each strip represents a different polarity, because it corresponds to when the Earth's magnetic field changed from north to south, or south to north.

The Earth Through Time

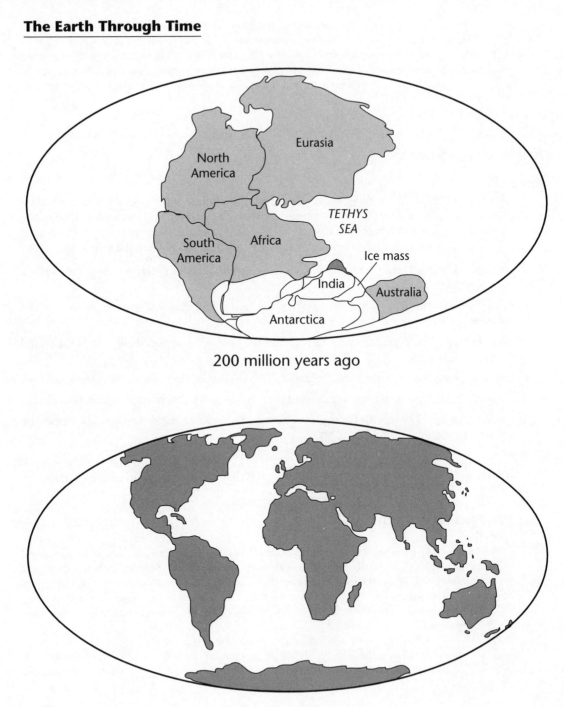

200 million years ago

Today

In the past 85 million years, the magnetic poles have switched at least 177 times—and have even changed within the last 2 million years. Scientists know that the Earth experiences magnetic reversals, but they do not know how or why. One theory is that electric currents flowing in the molten iron-nickel core of the Earth generate changes in magnetism. And without knowing why the reversals occur, it is impossible to predict the changes—or even what happens when the poles are reversed.

Rocks and Minerals

Minerals

Minerals are naturally forming, usually inorganic, crystalline substances with characteristic physical and chemical properties determined by their composition and internal structure. The atomic arrangement of component elements is identical in all specimens of a particular mineral.

The major physical properties that help to identify minerals include the following.

cleavage   Cleavage is the tendency of a mineral to break in certain preferred directions along a smooth surface.

color   Certain minerals have a characteristic color that distinguishes them from other minerals.

crystal shape   The crystal shape is the natural configuration the mineral takes on as the crystal forms.

fracture   Fracture is the way a mineral naturally breaks other than along a flat, cleavage plane.

hardness   Hardness is the measure of resistance that a mineral's surface has to abrasion.

specific gravity   The specific gravity is the weight of a mineral per unit volume. The higher the specific gravity, the heavier the mineral.

streak   The streak is the color of a mineral in finely powdered form.

striations   Striations are the narrow lines or bands that run across certain mineral surfaces.

FALSE DIAMONDS

For many decades, scientists have tried to create diamonds—the hardest naturally occurring mineral known on Earth—in the laboratory. One early failed attempt involved melting carbon at the center of an iron ball. When the ball was heated then rapidly cooled, scientists hoped that the carbon would be pressurized into diamonds. Another experiment used explosives to generate high temperatures and pressures—but the lack of sustained pressure caused the carbon to turn to graphite instead of a diamond.

Small, industrial diamonds called "grit" have been made in the past by heating certain carbon compounds to 4,900°F (2,704°C) at pressures of 1.5 million pounds per square inch (105,000 kilograms per square centimeter). But the best and largest diamonds are still those made by nature.

Crystals

Under the right conditions, most minerals form crystals. Crystals develop when the atomic structure of any material is arranged in an orderly manner. Each crystal can be described by a three-dimensional shape, formed from atoms that occur in one of seven possible crystal systems (though some systems classify hexagonal and trigonal together). Each of these shapes is a polyhedron—a solid whose faces are polygons. The following list includes the common crystals systems.

hexagonal system   Hexagonal crystals are composed of two axes aligned to each other, at 120° angles to each other. The third axis is at right angles to the two others and is a different length. Calcite, graphite, tourmaline, beryl, and apatite crystals are hexagonal.

isometric (or cubic) system   Isometric crystals have three axes of equal length at right angles to each other. Diamond, galena, fluorite, halite, pyrite, and garnet crystals are isometric.

monoclinic system   Monoclinic crystals have two of the three axes not at right angles, but a third axis at right angles to both, and none equivalent. Muscovite, azurite, gypsum, malachite, and borax crystals are monoclinic.

orthorhombic system   Orthorhombic crystals have three axes at right angles to each other, with none equivalent. Topaz, chalcocite (chalcosine), marcasite, sulfur, and stibnite crystals are orthorhombic.

tetragonal system   Tetragonal crystals are composed of rectangles, with three axes at right angles to each other and two or three of the axes equivalent. Rutile, zircon, and cassiterite crystals are tetragonal.

triclinic system   Triclinic crystals have no axes at right angles, and none equivalent. Such crystals are rare. Sanidine and turquoise crystals are triclinic.

trigonal system   Trigonal crystals are composed of one vertical threefold axis that develops similar to the hexagonal system. Corundum, dolomite, cinnabar, and arsenic crystals are trigonal.

Some crystals are combinations of shapes, such as pyramid-shaped crystals (a prismatic hornblende crystal), and other crystals may belong to the same system, but have different shapes. Satin spar, selenite, and granular gypsum are all examples of this type. In addition, some minerals form as aggregates of crystals that rarely show a perfect crystal shape—for example, fibrous serpentine and botryoidal hematite.

Common Crystal Shapes

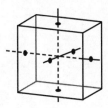

Cubic

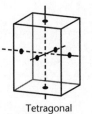

Tetragonal

Orthorhombic

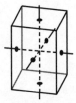

Monoclinic

Triclinic

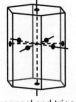

Hexagonal and trigonal

CURIOUS CRYSTALS

The arrangement of atoms in a crystal determines the material's characteristics. For example, diamond (the hardest natural mineral known) and graphite (used in lubricants) are both made entirely of carbon atoms. The diamond is one huge isometric carbon molecule; the carbon atoms in graphite are arranged in layers of flat hexagons that slide relative to each other. Recently, scientists discovered another curious carbon chemical called C-60 in which each molecule consists of 60 carbon atoms. Nicknamed a buckyball (or buckminsterfullerene, after Buckminster Fuller, the American architect), it resembles a soccer ball and has unusual chemical, magnetic, and electric properties.

Just as curious are quasicrystals—also called impossible crystals—somewhere between glassy and crystalline. The atoms are arranged in a regular pattern repeated over and over, something crystallographers considered impossible because there is no way that this molecular arrangement should work. But x-ray diffraction studies show that these crystals do indeed have 5- to 12-fold external symmetry.

Mineral Hardness Scale

Hardness is one of many physical characteristics used to identify minerals. The mineral hardness scale, also called *Mohs Scale of Hardness* after Friedrich Mohs, was developed in 1812. Scratching the smooth surface of a mineral with the edge of another mineral (or an object of known hardness) identifies the relative hardness of the scratched mineral. A mineral with a high Mohs number will scratch a mineral with a lower number. The scale is not linear: minerals of a hardness of 7 measure seven times as hard as a mineral with a hardness of 1, but a hardness of 10 measures about forty times as hard as a hardness of 1.

The following list orders 10 minerals from softest to hardest on the Mohs scale and includes some familiar objects (in parentheses) for comparison.

Mineral (Object)	Hardness
(Graphite)	0.7
Talc	1
(Asphalt)	1.3
Gypsum	2
(Fingernail)	2.5
Calcite	3
(Copper coin)	3
(Brass)	3.5
Fluorite	4
Apatite	5
(Knife blade)	5.5–6
(Plate glass)	5.5–6
Orthoclase	6
(Steel file)	6.5–7
Quartz	7
Topaz	8
Corundum	9
Diamond	10

Rocks

Rocks are aggregates of minerals. The Earth's crust has three families, or classes, of rock based on their origin: igneous, sedimentary, and metamorphic.

Igneous rocks make up 95 percent of the Earth's crust. They form from molten or partially molten material (called *magma*) during such events as volcanic eruptions (magma that reaches the surface is called *lava*). Igneous rocks are classified on the basis of texture (e.g., coarse grained, fine grained, or glassy) and mineral composition.

Sedimentary rocks cover about 75 percent of the world's land surface, but just less than 5 percent of the volume of the crust's outer 10 miles (16 kilometers). Sedimentary rocks are hardened layers of sediment that form when preexisting igneous, sedimentary, and metamorphic rocks are physically, chemically, or biochemically weathered or eroded. This sediment is redeposited by natural elements such as water, wind, and ice. Sedimentary rocks are classified as detrital (having particles of differing size and shape that are naturally cemented together) and chemical (usually formed by the precipitation of mineral matter from solution).

Metamorphic rocks are any preexisting rocks that have undergone change (deformation or recrystallization) by heat and pressure, as the formation of mountain ranges and volcanic action. Metamorphic textures include foliated (with cleavage) and nonfoliated (with no cleavage).

The oldest known rocks found to date on the Earth's surface are igneous granites from northwest Canada, estimated to be about 3.96 billion years old; some zircons have been dated at 4.3 billion years old, the oldest objects known on Earth.

Rock Cycle

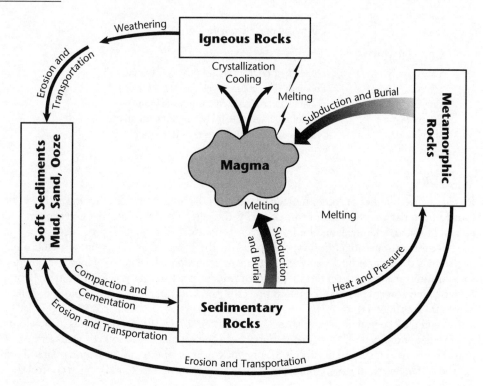

Common Igneous, Sedimentary, and Metamorphic Rocks

Name	Description (texture and mineral composition)
IGNEOUS	
Granite	Coarse grained; quartz and feldspar
Granodiorite	Coarse grained; quartz and feldspar
Diorite	Coarse grained; feldspar abundant
Gabbro	Coarse grained; dark colored minerals abundant
Peridotite	Coarse grained; dark colored minerals and olivine
Diabase	Medium grained; dark gray minerals
Rhyolite	Fine grained; light colored minerals
Andesite	Fine grained; dark colored minerals
Basalt	Fine grained; dark colored minerals
Obsidian	Glassy; dense and dark colored minerals
Pumice	Glassy; light colored and lightweight minerals
SEDIMENTARY	
Conglomerate	Detrital; rounded, cemented paticles
Breccia	Detrital; angular, cemented particles
Sandstone	Detrital; rounded, sand size particles
Siltstone	Detrital; silt-size particles
Shale, claystone	Detrital; clay-size particles
Limestone	Chemical; organic origin, calcite
Gypsum	Chemical; saline origin
Chert, flint	Chemical; siliceous origin
Coal	Chemical; organic origin
METAMORPHIC	
Slate	Foliated; often from shale, cleaves into plates
Schist	Foliated; elongated
Gneiss	Foliated; coarse grained, often from granites
Quartzite	Nonfoliated; quartz sand cemented with quartz
Marble	Nonfoliated; from limestone or dolostone

What Is Soil?

Regolith is the blanket of loose, noncemented, disintegrated rock particles and mineral grains formed from the weathering of bedrock. *Soil* is the part of the regolith that can support rooted plants. Physical, chemical, and biological factors control soil formation processes.

Not all soils are alike. Soil types depend on the parent material, climate (which mainly determines the soil texture, i.e., the size of its unconsolidated particles), length of time in the soil-forming processes, vegetation (which provides organic matter, usually in the form of humus), and topography (which determines soil thickness, ranging from about 1 to 6 feet, or 30 to 200 centimeters).

A soil may be immature or mature. An immature soil is still in the process of developing a soil profile, or defined O, A, B, and C horizons in the soil; a mature soil has well-defined A, B, and C horizons. The O soil horizon is the organic top layer; the A and B horizons of a soil profile are the active layers, in which living plant roots and organisms are found, which control the soil conditions. The C horizon is below the root activity. It is lowest level and contains the parent material (or mineral matter suitable for transformation into soil), which is subjected to inorganic (chemical or physical) processes.

Typical Soil Profiles

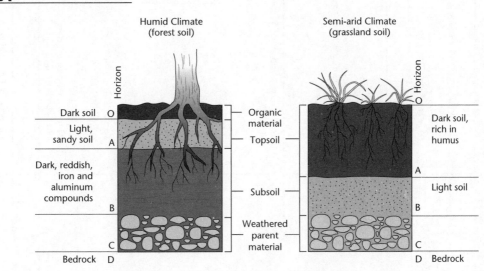

Soil Taxonomy

The soil taxonomy, or classification, devised in 1975 is probably the most widely used system in the world. The soils are classed based on their observable soil profile characteristics. Each order is broken down into suborders, great groups, subgroups, families, and series (not listed here). In total, there are about 10,000 different kinds of soil at the series level.

Soil Order	Description
Alfisols	Gray-brown surface horizons; subsurface clays
Aridisols	Dry for more than 6 months per year; low organic matter
Mollisols	Black, organic surface horizons
Spodosols	Amorphous materials in subsurface horizons
Ultisols	Moist soils with clays
Histosols	Organic soils
Inceptisol	Moist soils, greatly influenced by parent matter
Entisols	No pedogenic horizons

Geologic Time Scale

The *geologic time scale* is the standard method used to divide the Earth's long natural history into manageable parts. The units used in the geologic time scale are extremely long compared with everyday standards. An organism's geologic age or the age of a major geologic event is determined by information from fossil finds as well as the radioactive dating of rocks and fossils (for more information on radioactive elements, see Chapter 6, "Chemistry").

Geologic Time Scale

Eon	Era	Period	Epoch	Millions of Years Ago (approximate)	Life Forms
Phanerozoic	Cenozoic (recent life)	Quaternary	Holocene	(~10,000 years ago)	Rise of mammals and appearance of modern marine animals; rise of herbaceous plants; large carnivores (Tertiary); extinction of many species (65 mya)
			Pleistocene	2	
		Tertiary	Pliocene	5	
			Miocene	24	
			Oligocene	37	
			Eocene	58	
			Paleocene	65	
	Mesozoic (middle life)	Cretaceous	Late / Early	144	Abundant reptiles (including dinosaurs); more advanced marine invertebrates; first modern birds (Jurassic)
		Jurassic	Late / Middle / Early	208	
		Triassic	Late / Middle / Early	245	Conifers evolve and modern insects appear
	Paleozoic (ancient life)	Permian	Late / Early	286	First reptiles
		Pennsylvanian (Carboniferous)	Middle / Early		Terrestrial (land) plants established; first terrestrial vertebrates—amphibians; "Age of Fish"
		Mississippian (Carboniferous)	Late / Early	360	
		Devonian	Late / Middle / Early	408	Algae dominant
		Silurian	Late / Middle / Early	438	Terrestrial (land) plants first appear (Devonian); First vertebrates—fish
		Ordovician	Late / Middle / Early	505	
		Cambrian	Late / Middle / Early	570	Primitive invertebrate fossils; algae dominant
Precambrian	Archeozoic and Protozoic Eras			3800+	Meager evidence of life
	Azoic			4.56B	Formation of Earth and crust

Note that scientists disagree about the exact dates on the geologic time scale.

ICE IN THE EARTH'S PAST AND TODAY

During various times in Earth's history, global temperatures dropped between 7 and 21°F (4 and 12°C), plunging about 40 percent of the world into a 100,000-year winter. These occasional drops in temperature resulted in ice ages, with the Earth experiencing as many as 20 such climatic events in the past 2.5 million years. The last glacial ice covered close to 16 million square miles (42 million square kilometers) at its peak; the ice sheet fully retreated from the United States about 11,000 years ago. Today, ice (in the form of ice sheets and caps, and glaciers) covers about 6 million square miles (15 million square kilometers), including less than 5 million square miles (12 million square kilometers) in Antarctica and about 2 million square miles (6 million square kilometers) in Greenland and the northern polar region.

What caused thick ice to cover a major portion of the Earth? Theories include long-term variations in the Earth's orbit (called the Milankovich theory, after Yugoslav scientist Miluti Milankovich who formulated the idea in the 1920s), an increase in volcanic activity that blocked out the Sun's energy to the Earth, fluctuations in the Earth's own radiant energy (the heat from the radioactive decay of elements in the planet's interior), and changes in the direction of oceanic currents.

EARTHQUAKES AND VOLCANOES

Earthquakes

Earthquakes are considered one of the most deadly natural catastrophes that can affect human life. Most often, a quake occurs in earthquake-prone zones where two tectonic plates meet, split, or slip by one another (see "Plate Tectonics," earlier in this chapter); the type of plate contact determines whether the earthquake will be shallow or deep. During the movement of these plates, intense forces overcome the friction between the plates. If the plates become "locked together," forces build up and eventually must give away—with the plates lurching into new positions and creating an earthquake. Other earthquakes form in association with volcanic regions, where the buildup of heat and pressure often triggers smaller tremors and localized quakes.

The *focus* is the point under the Earth's surface where the earthquake energy is released. The point on the surface just above the focus is called the *epicenter*. Most earthquake foci occur no more than 62 miles (100 kilometers) below the surface.

Earthquake waves, or *seismic waves*, travel out from the focus of an earthquake in all directions. Primary waves (*P-waves*) move in a back-and-forth direction; they are the fastest seismic waves, reaching the far side of the globe in 20 minutes. The waves travel though the Earth's molten core. Secondary waves (*S-waves*) move in a side-to-side direction; they are slower than P-waves and can move only through solids, stopping at the Earth's central molten core. Love and Raleigh waves (both called *L-waves*) travel along the Earth's surface, moving up, down, and sideways and creating much of the structural damage associated with earthquakes.

THE THREAT OF TSUNAMIS

A tsunami (or seismic sea wave), from the Japanese words *tsu* ("harbor") and *nami* ("wave"), is a very large wave caused by underwater earthquakes or volcanic eruptions. Often incorrectly called "tidal waves," tsunamis are not caused or influenced by the tides, though at high tide, the size of a tsunami may be significantly increased.

About 80 percent of these great waves occur in the Pacific Ocean, about 10 percent in the Atlantic Ocean, and 10 percent in other oceans. Tsunami wavelengths, or crest-to-crest measurements, often reach up to 600 miles (965 kilometers), but their amplitudes, or heights, range only from 1 to 2 feet, making them undetectable at sea. The destructive power of a tsunami occurs as the wave approaches a coastline, when the shallower bottom causes the wavelength to become shorter and the amplitude greater. A tsunami may be up to 200 feet (61 meters) high when it reaches shore. It can reach speeds of 150 miles (241 kilometers) per hour, destroying any structures in its path.

Modified Mercalli Scale

The *Mercalli earthquake intensity scale*, developed by Italian seismologist Giuseppe Mercalli in 1902, is a measure of an earthquake's destructiveness. The scale was modified by American seismologists in the 1930s (called the modified Mercalli scale). Modern technology has made the Mercalli scale obsolete, though the method is often used to fill in "seismic blanks" when there is an insufficient number of seismographs.

Level	Characteristic Effects in Populated Areas
I	Generally not felt; detectable by seismographs
II	Felt by few people; objects may swing if suspended
III	Felt by few people, mostly indoors; vibrations like a passing truck
IV	Felt by many people indoors but few outdoors; windows, dishes and doors rattle
V	Felt by nearly everyone; sleepers awaken; small unstable objects may fall and break; doors move
VI	Felt by everyone; some heavy furniture moves; people walk unsteadily; windows and dishes break; books fall from shelf; bushes and trees visibly shake
VII	Difficult to stand; moderate to heavy damage to poorly constructed buildings; plaster, loose bricks, tiles, and stones fall; small landslides along slopes; water becomes turbid
VIII	Difficult to steer cars; damage to good unbraced masonry; chimneys, monuments, towers, and elevated tanks fall; tree branches break; steep slopes crack
IX	Extensive building damage; good masonry damaged seriously; foundations crack; serious damage to reservoirs; underground pipes break
X	Most masonry, frame structures, and foundations destroyed; numerous large landslides; water thrown on banks of rivers and lakes; railroad tracks bend slightly
XI	Few masonry buildings stand; railroad tracks bend severely; many bridges destroyed; underground pipelines completely inoperative
XII	Nearly total destruction; large rock masses displaced; objects thrown into the air

Richter Scale

The *Richter scale*, used to measure earthquake intensity, was developed in 1935, by Charles Richter. It measures an earthquake's magnitude (intensity) on a scale of 1 to 8.8 (some scales range up to 9). The scale is logarithmic, which means that each successive whole number represents a 10-fold increase in power.

Each magnitude number represents the maximum amplitude of a seismic wave at a distance of 100 miles (161 kilometers). The difference in time between the first and second (primary and secondary) waves is measured, and an empirical factor is added (which takes into account the fact that the waves become weaker as they travel away from the focus) to determine the magnitude of the quake.

Richter Number	Increase in Magnitude
1	1
2	10
3	100
4	1,000
5	10,000
6	100,000
7	1,000,000
8	10,000,000

Comparison of Richter Magnitude and Energy Released

Richter Number	Approximate Energy Released (Amount of TNT)
1	170 grams
2	6 kilograms
3	179 kilograms
4	5 metric tons
5	179 metric tons
6	5,643 metric tons
7	179,100 metric tons
8	5,643,000 metric tons

FAMOUS EARTHQUAKES

Famous earthquakes are usually arranged by their magnitude on the Richter scale. To compare, the average tornado can rumble with a Richter scale magnitude of 4.8, and a 1-megaton nuclear bomb can measure 7.5 on the Richter scale. The highest magnitude earthquake recorded to date—at about 9.6 (although the magnitude is debated)—was the 1960 Chilean earthquake, in which a fault 621 miles (1,000 kilometers) long slipped 33 feet (10 meters); the largest deep quake on record was on June 9, 1994, beneath a remote area in the Amazon rain forest of northern Bolivia, with a Richter scale magnitude of 8.3. Below are some of the more famous quakes of the last two centuries.

Year	Location	Richter Number
1811–1812	New Madrid earthquake, Missouri (a series of quakes from December 1811 to March 1812)	8.0–8.3
1899	Yakutat Bay earthquake, Alaska	8.3–8.6 (estimate)
1906	San Francisco earthquake, California	7.7–8.25 (estimate)
1960	Chilean earthquake, Chile	9.6 (disagreement on magnitude)
1964	Alaskan earthquake, Alaska	8.5
1971	San Fernando earthquake, California	6.5
1976	Tangshan earthquake, China	8.2
1985	Mexico City earthquake, Mexico	8.1
1988	Armenian earthquake, Armenia	6.9
1989	Loma Prieta earthquake, California	7.1
1990	Northwest Iran earthquake, Iran	7.7
1994	Bolivian earthquake, South America	8.3 (largest deep quake on record)
1994	Northridge earthquake, California	6.8
1995	Kobe earthquake, Japan	6.8

Major Earthquake and Volcanic Zones

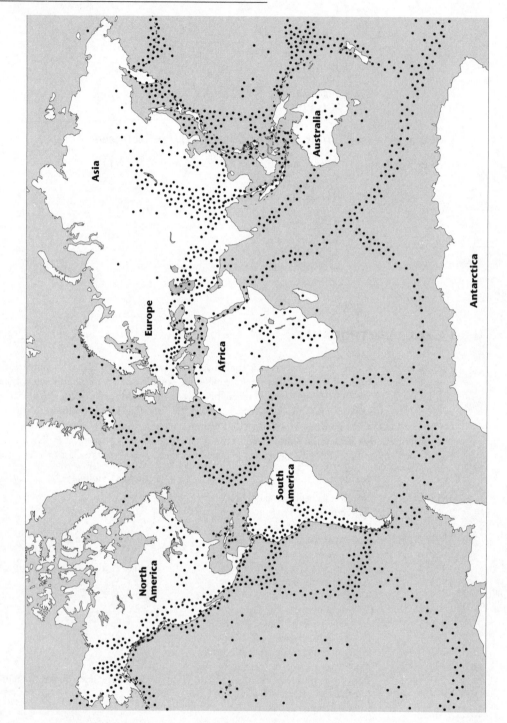

Volcanoes

Volcanoes form when magma, the hot, molten rock under the Earth's surface, upwells between tectonic plate boundaries (Iceland formed in this way) or at hot spots (Yellowstone National Park). A magma chamber holds the hot material, and weaker areas of solid rock above the magma chamber allow the magma to rise. When the surface can no longer hold back the pressure of the magma and the dissolved gases associated with it, an eruption occurs at the surface. Volcanoes can remain dormant for hundreds to thousands of years, then erupt violently.

Most of the world's active volcanoes (and earthquakes) occur in specific zones. The volcanoes of the Pacific Ocean form the *Ring of Fire* (Circle of Fire), in which many tectonic plates undergo subduction (see "Plate Tectonics," earlier in this chapter). Hot spots also produce volcanoes but are not associated with plate boundaries. They form from the upwelling of magma though weak spots in the crust; the Hawaiian Islands resulted from hot spot activity.

There are four types of volcanoes:

Shield volcanoes form by layers of lava flows. The Hawaiian Islands are shield volcanoes.

Composite volcanoes form by alternating layers of ash and lava. Mount St. Helens in Washington State is a composite volcano.

Cinder volcanoes are composed of small lava fragments and form slopes of 30 to 40°. Sunset Crater in Arizona is a cinder volcano.

Lava domes are thick, pasty layers of lava. Lassen Peak, California is a lava dome.

Recent Active Volcanoes

Volcano Name	Location	Date of Last Activity
AFRICA AND THE INDIAN OCEAN		
Lengai Ol Doinyo	Tanzania	1993
Nyamuragira	Zaire	1992
Piton de la Fournaise	Zaire	1992
ANTARCTICA		
Mount Erebus	Ross Island	1990
Big Ben	Heard Island	1986
Deception Island	South Shetland Island	1970
ASIA		
Aso	Japan	1993
Krakatau (Anak Krakatau)	Indonesia	1993
Mayon	Philippines	1993
Sakura-jima	Japan	1993
Sheveluch	Russia	1993
CENTRAL AMERICA AND THE CARIBBEAN		
Arenal	Costa Rica	1994
Pacaya	Guatemala	1994
Santiaguito (Santa Maria) Dome	Guatemala	1993
Rincon de la Vieja	Costa Rica	1992
Poas	Costa Rica	1991

EUROPE AND THE ATLANTIC OCEAN

Stromboli	Italy	1994
Etna	Italy	1993
Hekla	Iceland	1991

NORTH AMERICA

Cleveland	Alaska	1994
Kanaga	Alaska	1994
Kilauea	Hawaii	1993
Seguam	Alaska	1993
Akutan	Alaska	1992
Spurr	Alaska	1992
Westdahl	Alaska	1992
Colima	Mexico	1991
Mount St. Helens	Washington	1991

AUSTRALIA, NEW ZEALAND, AND THE PACIFIC ISLANDS

Mount Semeru	Indonesia	1994
Langila	Papua New Guinea	1993
Ulawun	Papua New Guinea	1993
Manam	Papua New Guinea	1992
Ruapehu	New Zealand	1992
White Island	New Zealand	1992

SOUTH AMERICA

Galeras	Columbia	1993
Guagua Pichincha	Ecuador	1993
Copahue	Argentina and Chile	1992
Lascar	Chile	1992

AFTERMATH OF A MODERN VOLCANO

From June 14 to 16, 1991, on the Philippine island of Luzon, Mount Pinatubo erupted, resulting in a stratospheric cloud that contained roughly twice as much sulfur dioxide as the one produced by Mexico's El Chichón in 1982. But even more amazing was the fact that the cloud circled the Earth within the short span of 3 weeks. The potential effect was evident for months after the eruption: Mount Pinatubo's release of sulfur dioxide resulted in unusually brilliant sunsets in different parts of the world.

Scientists predicted even greater effects from this eruption—that the volcanic particles in the air would reflect radiation from the Sun and cause a reduction in surface temperatures. As a result, the Northern Hemisphere would have colder than normal weather. The decrease in solar energy would decrease the wind strength along the equatorial belt. If the winds died down, the surface temperature of the Pacific Ocean would rise—contributing to the development of El Niño, the anomalous current of warm water that flows north along the west coast of South America.

Did the volcano create such problems? Scientists do not totally agree. But in the years following the eruption of Mount Pinatubo, El Niño conditions persisted longer than usual; there was a major blizzard in March 1993—one of the worst of the century—along the East Coast of the United States, and other weather oddities occurred.

MARINE SCIENCE

Marine science, or oceanography, is the study of the Earth's oceans, including the geological, chemical, and physical elements that interact to create the ocean environment.

The Earth's Oceans and Seas

The Earth's oceans cover more than 70 percent of the planet's surface. Scientists theorize that when the Earth's crust formed about 4.56 billion years ago, low areas began collecting liquids from the release of liquids and gases from the Earth's interior, until this degassing eventually created the oceans and atmosphere. Another theory states that the impacts of water-bearing comets contributed to the development of the oceans in the early stages of the Earth's formation.

The ocean and seas are not evenly distributed over the globe. Approximately 61 percent of the Northern Hemisphere is covered by oceans; about 81 percent of the Southern Hemisphere is covered by oceans. The five major oceans are the Atlantic, Pacific, Indian, Arctic, and Antarctic (although on some lists, the Antarctic is considered an extension of the Atlantic, Pacific, and Indian Oceans, and the Arctic Ocean is called a marginal sea). Subdivisions or extensions of the larger oceans as well as landlocked bodies of water, are called "seas" or "gulfs." Adjacent bodies include the South China Sea, Caribbean Sea, Mediterranean Sea, Bering Sea, Gulf of Mexico, Hudson Bay, Gulf of California, Sea of Japan, and the Persian Gulf. Inland seas (though often referred to as lakes) include the Caspian Sea, Sea of Galilee, and the Dead Sea.

Circulation in the upper oceans is caused by wind-driven surface currents, tidal currents, and the warmth of the Sun. The upper ocean comprises 2 percent of the oceans' volume and contains most marine life. The *thermocline*, a zone in which the water temperature suddenly changes, separates the warmer upper layer from the cooler deeper layer. The deeper layer's heavier cold water takes about 1,000 years to recirculate with the upper layer; movement of seawater usually occurs by the movement of deep-water density currents.

WHY DO WE NEED THE OCEANS?

The oceans are the reason why life has flourished on Earth for millions of years. If ocean life were to suddenly disappear, the carbon dioxide content of the Earth's atmosphere would almost triple (marine plants use carbon for cellular functions), causing most oxygen-breathing organisms to die. The ocean itself is a major repository of atmospheric carbon dioxide and contains 45 times more of this gas than does the atmosphere.

In addition, if the oceans evaporated, life as we know it would cease, as every life form needs water to survive. It is thought that in about 7 billion years, the oceans will evaporate—when our Sun, in its natural life cycle, grows larger and boils away the atmosphere and oceans (for more information on the life of the Sun, see Chapter 8, "Astronomy").

Ocean Facts and Figures

Volume	350 million cubic miles (1.5×10^9 cubic kilometers)
Salinity	34.482 parts per thousand (3.5%)
Dissolved material	1.1×10^{20} pounds (5×10^{22} grams)
Average seawater density	0.037 pounds per cubic inch (1.025 grams per cubic centimeter)

Area: Oceans and Adjacent Seas

All oceans	145,000,000 square miles (375,550,000 square kilometers)
Pacific	64,170,000 square miles (166,242,500 square kilometers)
Atlantic	33,420,000 square miles (86,557,800 square kilometers)
Indian	28,350,500 square miles (73,427,795 square kilometers)

Average Depth

All oceans and seas	2.5 miles (4 kilometers)
Pacific	13,740 feet (4,188 meters)
Atlantic	12,254 feet (3,735 meters)
Indian	12,704 feet (3,872 meters)
Arctic	3,407 feet (1,038 meters)

Deepest Points

Pacific	Marianas Trench	36,200 feet (11,034 meters)
Atlantic	Puerto Rico Trench	28,374 feet (8,648 meters)
Indian	Java Trench	25,344 feet (7,725 meters)
Arctic	Eurasia Basin	17,880 feet (5,450 meters)
Mediterranean Sea	Ionian Basin	16,896 feet (5,150 meters)

Tide Heights

Average highest tide height	Bay of Fundy, Canada	45 feet (14 meters)
Average world tide height	2.5 feet (0.8 meters)	

HOT VENTS AND OCEAN LIFE

Just over two decades ago, scientists began diving into the oceans with deep-sea submersibles, examining the areas around recently erupted undersea volcanoes. More recently, scientists detected and monitored the eruption of a deep-sea volcano—the first time ever along the 31,070-mile (50,000-kilometer) chain of volcanoes that wend through the Earth's oceans.

Scientists have found that the areas surrounding the Atlantic and Pacific vents, where temperatures hit 750°F (399°C) and pressures can reach almost 300 times that on the Earth's surface, are filled with hyperthermophilic organisms. Pacific deep-sea volcanic rifts include such creatures as high-temperature bacteria called *Pyrococcus furiosus*, dense beds of large mussels, thick patches of 3.3-foot-long (1-meter-long) tube worms, and red-fleshed clams. Rifts along the Mid-Atlantic Ridge are home to vent shrimps and to creatures that resemble those around Pacific vents. Undersea vent eruptions in both oceans also produce dense clouds of precipitated minerals (called smokers). Such black and white smokers are often surrounded by bulbous pillow lava.

Composition of Sea Water

There are about 70 chemical elements in seawater. The major constituents, which add up to about 99.89 percent of all solutes in seawater by mass, are as follows.

Constituent	Percent of all Dissolved Material
Chlorine	55.50
Sodium	30.61
Sulfate	7.68
Magnesium	3.69
Calcium	1.16
Potassium	1.10
Bicarbonate	0.41
Bromine	0.19

Taking the water itself into account, here are the major constituents of seawater, in order of decreasing percentage.

Constituent	Percent of Substances by Mass
Oxygen	85.4
Hydrogen	10.7
Chlorine	1.85
Sodium	1.03
Magnesium	0.127
Sulfur	0.087
Calcium	0.040
Potassium	0.038
Bromine	0.0065
Carbon	0.0027
Nitrogen	0.0016
Strontium	0.00079
Boron	0.00043
Silicon	0.00028
Fluorine	0.00013

Ocean Shoreline

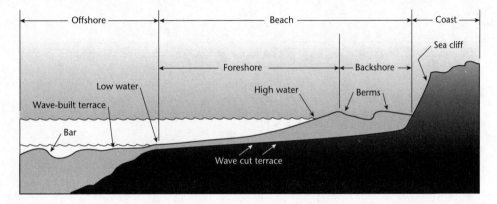

Ocean Surface Current

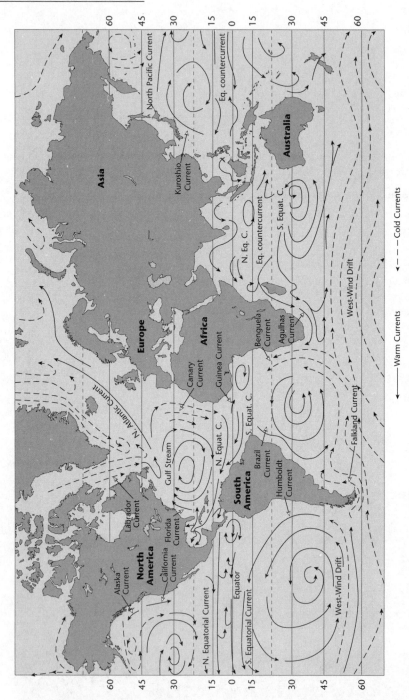

Ocean Zones

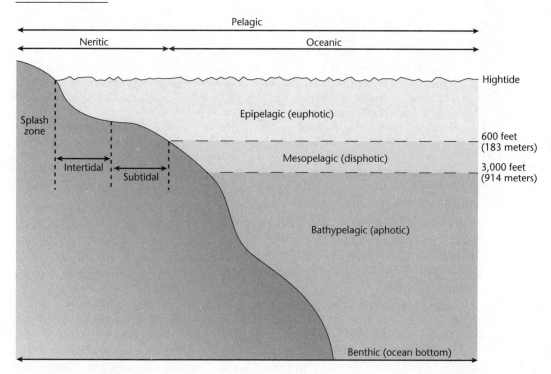

Ocean Features

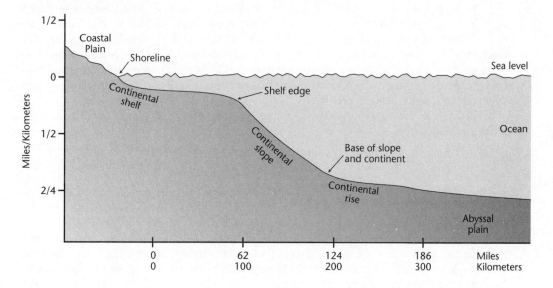

ARE THERE OTHER OCEANS?

Is Earth the only planetary body with oceans? Scientists have speculated for many years that there are liquid oceans on the other planets and satellites in our solar system—including Titan, the largest moon around Saturn; Europa, one of Jupiter's larger moons; and possibly Pluto.

Titan, one of the few solar system satellites with an atmosphere, may be covered with oceans filled with ethane and methane. Because of the moon's thick atmosphere, it is impossible, so far, to see Titan's surface. But recent radar images of Titan show the possibility of small pockets of liquid on it similar to Earth ponds, although there appear to be no large oceans.

It is thought that Jupiter's moon, Europa, is covered by a frozen ocean of ice. Because the moon has virtually no craters, it must be relatively young. To be that smooth, it is thought the surface would have to be similar to frozen slush—which would swallow any striking object.

Pluto may be another planetary body that has frozen oceans, of methane or nitrogen. But Pluto is so far from Earth that we may never know until we send a spacecraft to visit the solar system's smallest planet.

Ocean Tides

Tides are the periodic rise and fall of the Earth's oceans, especially noticeable along the shoreline as high and low tides. Tides are caused primarily by the gravitational attraction of the Moon; the Sun also influences the tides, though its effects are secondary compared with tides caused by the Moon. Because the moon's distance from the Earth varies, the attractive forces differ, as do the size and times of the tides.

The times and heights of high and low tides change each day. Generally, when the tide is at its highest on a certain day, it is called *high tide*; when the tide is at its lowest, it is called *low tide*. As the Moon's gravity pulls on the oceans, the Earth's solid body pulls away from the oceans on the opposite side, creating high tides on both sides of the Earth. Low tides occur as ocean water flows toward the high-tide areas.

The average interval between successive high tides is 12 hours, 25.5 minutes, but tidal highs can vary by intervals of less than 12 hours to more than 14 hours. In places such as Vietnam and the Caribbean, there is one high and one low tide (or diurnal tides) each day; in places such as the North Sea, there are two high and two low tides (or semidiurnal tides) each day, though the two high or two low tides during the day are not necessarily equal in height. Some Pacific and Indian Ocean coasts experience a mixture of these two types of tides, with a diurnal tide on some days and semidiurnal tides on others.

Though the Sun's gravitational pull on Earth is less than half that of the Moon, it still influences major tides during the year. When the Moon aligns with the Sun at times of full or new moons, the combined gravitational pull produces a maximum tide range known as a *spring tide*; the highest spring tides are at the equinoxes, when the Sun is over the equator, and smallest at the solstices, when the Sun is over the Tropic of Cancer or Tropic of Capricorn. During a waning or waxing half Moon, when the Sun and Moon exert perpendicular forces, the generally lower ranges are called *neap tides*. Barely 15 days (14.765 days) separates spring and neap tides (for more information on the tides, see Chapter 3, "Time").

The Earth's landmasses also experience tides caused by the Moon and Sun. The solid sphere of the Earth distorts about 4.5 to 14 inches (11.4 to 35.6 centimeters) from the pull of the Moon and Sun. Most lakes and ponds do not experience tides because the water and the surrounding land both "rise" simultaneously.

How Neap and Spring Tides Are Produced

Spring   Neap   Spring   Neap

PAST LIFE

Paleontology

Paleontology is the study of ancient life. Clues to the Earth's past environment, climate, and living organisms are based on the preserved remains of plants and animals, or *fossils*. Fossils are buried deep in the Earth and the great majority of animals and plants decay before becoming fossilized. Therefore, fossil finds represent only a fraction of all the billions of organisms that have lived on Earth.

EXTINCTIONS OF THE PAST

Over the past 600 million years on Earth, there have been numerous extinctions of plant and animal species. Records of fossils in rock layers reveal at least six major extinctions over time. A major extinction occurred about 250 million years ago during the Permian period, when about 96 percent of marine species died—an extinction that exceeded all other known die-offs. One of the most famous extinctions occurred 65 million years ago, when about 50 percent of all species died off—including the well-known dinosaurs, the largest creatures that ever roamed the land.

Many scientists speculate that most major extinctions may have been caused by a large space object (or objects) striking the Earth, causing dust and debris to enter the atmosphere. The blanket of particles could have blocked the Sun, changing the climate and thus disrupting the food chain. Recently, dinosaur extinction research has centered on the Chicxulub Crater, on the coast of the Yucatan Peninsula. It is estimated that this crater could be the remnant of an impact crater that formed 65 million years ago—possibly created by an object about the size of Comet Halley that triggered tsunamis, major earthquakes, and the eventual extinction of dinosaurs and their contemporaries. But there is still no physical evidence of a major impact 250 million years old.

Common Fossils

The term *fossil,* from the Latin *fossilis,* means "something dug up." Fossils are the remains of ancient organisms preserved close to their original shape. It is unusual to find a completely preserved organism. Usually, the hard parts survive, such as bones, teeth, and shells of animals, and woody parts or seeds of plants. These are also often replaced by mineralization, such as when the shell of a nautilus is replaced by the mineral calcite. Other fossils include the *molds, casts,* or *imprints* of an animal or plant, such as the shell of a brachiopod or the leaf of a ginkgo; *petrified organisms,* such as wood; *coprolites,* or petrified excrement; or indirect evidence of an organism (called *trace fossils*), such as the footprint of a dinosaur or the feeding trail of a trilobite.

The chances for an organism to leave fossil evidence on the Earth depends on the natural conditions. For example, it estimated that of the 3,000 plant and animal species living in today's coral reefs, only around 75 are recognizable after they die, because most dead organisms decay quickly in the ocean.

The largest fossils are not the oldest. Microscopic, single-celled organisms lived about 3.75 billion years ago. Larger organisms, such as trilobites, lived in the oceans about 600 million years ago. The first amphibians emerged about 380 million years ago, reptiles appeared about 320 million years ago, and dinosaurs emerged about 225 million years ago.

KEEPING UP WITH THE DINOSAURS

Paleontologists believe that the first true dinosaurs evolved on Earth about 225 million years ago and became extinct about 65 million years ago. There are many disagreements about these early reptiles. What are some of the facts about these creatures?

- Dinosaurs are members of a group of reptiles known as archosaurs ("ruling reptiles"). They are divided into two main orders: the Saurischia ("reptile hipped") and Ornithischia ("bird-hipped").
- All dinosaurs were land-living creatures. Thus the gigantic sea monsters of the Mesozoic, such as the ichthyosaurs, mosasaurs, and plesiosaurs, were not dinosaurs.
- Pterosaurs were not dinosaurs either. They were flying reptiles that looked like lizards with wings.
- The Brontosaurus's correct name is Apatosaurus. The animal fossils identified at the turn of the century as Brontosaurus sported the wrong head for its body. The creature never really existed.
- Today's birds are thought to be the closest relatives to the dinosaurs; crocodiles are also thought to be more distant relatives of the dinosaurs. All organisms living on the Earth today are the descendants of creatures that lived when the dinosaurs roamed the Earth.

How Fossils Are Preserved

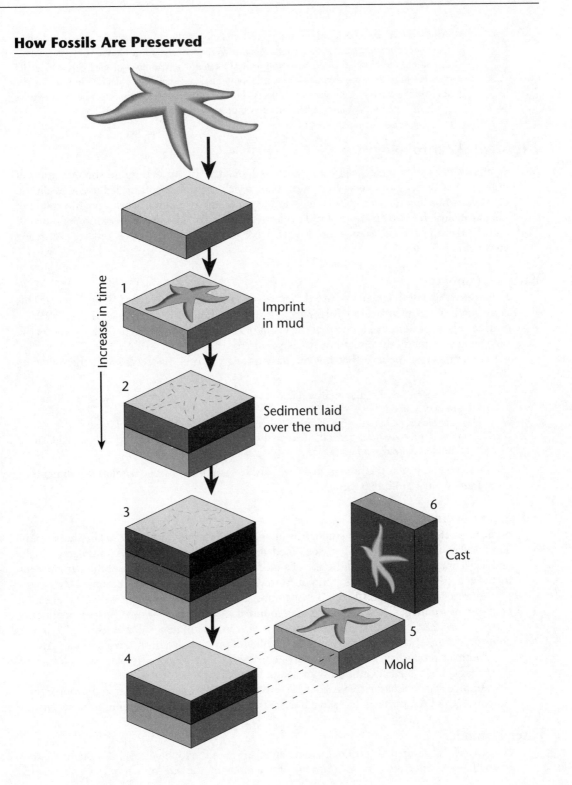

Increase in time

1 Imprint in mud

2 Sediment laid over the mud

3

4

5 Mold

6 Cast

- Although we have been able to tell a great deal about the dinosaurs from fossils and other evidence, many fundamental questions remain: Were there any warm-blooded dinosaurs? Were dinosaurs cold blooded when born and warm blooded when adults—or vice versa? How did the dinosaurs become extinct—from a climate change, increased volcanic activity, or the impact of a large space object (or objects) on the Earth? Did the dinosaurs become extinct gradually or abruptly? These questions continue to be studied and debated.

Physical Anthropology

A branch of *physical anthropology* uses ancient human fossils to determine the evolution of humans over time. Controversy continues about which ancient organisms led to the evolution of modern humans (*Homo sapiens*). The following is one of many theories on the stages of human evolution based on known fossil evidence. (Note: Theories on the evolution of humans, and the dates of their existence, are highly debated. The following list is only one of many viewpoints.)

Early Hominoids

It was once thought that humans were direct descendants of *Ramaphithecus* ("Rama's ape"). This early hominoid roamed areas of Africa about 8 to 14 million years ago. But in the early 1980s, molecular biological studies found that the fossils of *Ramaphithecus* were actually ancestors of the orangutan and not on the direct line to *Homo sapiens*.

Some scientists believe that human early ancestry can be traced through the following lineage.

Catopithecus browni, a higher primate related to monkeys, apes, and humans, lived about 40 million years ago around Egypt.

Aegyptopithecus, perhaps the first hominoid, lived 30 million years ago around Egypt.

Proconsul (three species), generally accepted to be part of the ancestry of all hominoids, lived 20 million years ago in East Africa.

Because of a gap in the human fossil records, humankind's lineage is relatively difficult to chart from about 10 million years ago.

Australopithecines

Some researchers believe the Australopithecines ("southern apes") gave rise to later hominoids: They walked fully erect on two legs, measured about 4 to 5 feet (120 to 150 centimeters) high, and had a brain about one-third the size of a modern human's. Descendants of these hominoids included a specialized, vegetarian form of *Australopithecus*, who eventually became extinct.

Australopithecus afarensis is the oldest known fossil hominoid thought to be the ultimate ancestor of humans. This hominoid was found in 4-million-year-old African sediments (Ethiopia and East Africa). The ancestors of *A. afarensis* are unknown. Other fossils of a similar group are *Australopithecus africanus*, who lived 2.5 million years ago in the area of South Africa.

Australopithecus boisei is a controversial species, thought to be an African relation to *A. afarensis*. They lived 2.5 million years ago in East Africa.

Australopithecus robustus lived about 1.5 million years ago and were larger and stronger than *A. afarensis* and *A. africanus*. They lived in South Africa, about the same time as *Homo habilis*.

Later Hominids

Homo habilis (translated as "skillful human being" or "man the toolmaker") had a slightly larger brain than *A. afarensis* and *A. africanus* and was about the size of a modern 12-year-old.

One Possible Lineage to *Homo sapiens*

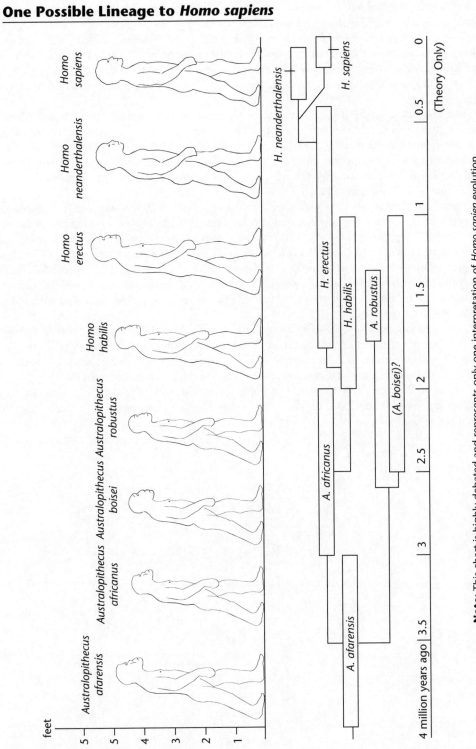

Note: This chart is highly debated and represents only one interpretation of *Homo sapien* evolution.

H. habilis, who lived about 2.2 million years ago in East Africa, was also the first to develop significant "technology," making and using stone tools.

The even larger-brained *Homo erectus* ("man the erect"; formally called Java Man and Peking Man, among others) developed about 1.8 million years ago. *H. erectus* made stone hand axes, knew how to control fire, may have been the first hominid to leave Africa, migrating to Asia and Europe, and lived until approximately 100,000 years ago (although this information is highly debated).

Homo erectus resembled today's human beings from the neck down, but they had a lower forehead and larger jaw. One major anthropological debate is how to interpret *H. erectus* fossils: One group maintains that *H. erectus* is a single species. Another group believes that *H. erectus* is actually two species, only one of which evolved into modern humans. A third group seeks to abolish the species completely, placing it with a diverse group of *Homo sapiens* that split with *Homo habilis* 2 million years ago.

Homo neanderthalensis ("Neanderthal man") lived about 100,000 years ago in Europe and Asia and may have closely resembled modern humans. It is not known whether the Neanderthals were a subspecies of *Homo sapiens* (*Homo sapiens neanderthalensis*) or a separate species. Their brains (based on the size of fossil skulls) were larger than modern humans. They had complex religious beliefs, and before they became extinct 35,000 years ago, they had developed ways of making ornaments. Some reasearchers believe that the *Homo neanderthalensis* did not become extinct. Many believe that they are also in our direct line, interbreeding with *Homo sapiens* of 40,000 years ago.

Archaic *Homo sapiens* probably emerged about 90,000 years ago and are thought to have evolved from *H. erectus*. Their physical characteristics included an increased brain size compared with their body size (for example, the brain measured almost twice the size of a gorilla's, as in modern humans), an increase in average height, and long and straight limbs.

About 90,000 years ago, *H. sapiens* probably resembled modern humans but were not fully evolved. Between about 40,000 to 35,000 years ago, *Homo sapiens sapiens*, or modern humans spread across the world.

Comparing the Skull

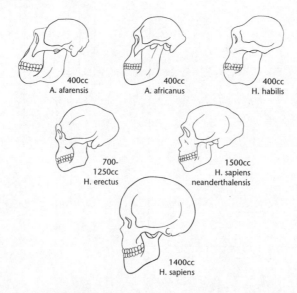

400cc
A. afarensis

400cc
A. africanus

400cc
H. habilis

700-
1250cc
H. erectus

1500cc
H. sapiens
neanderthalensis

1400cc
H. sapiens

EVIDENCE OF ANCIENT HUMANS

Hominoid fossils are our only touch with our very ancient past. Here are some important fossil finds.

- The first hominoid fossil found was a fragmentary skull unearthed in the Neander Tal (*Tal* means "valley"), near Düsseldorf, Germany, in 1856.
- One of the oldest and most complete hominoid fossils found to date, was uncovered in 1974 by Don Johanson—the *Australopithecus afarensis* skeleton known as "Lucy." It was recovered in Hadar, in a region of Ethiopia known as the Afar Depression, nearby the Great Rift Valley of Africa. The small bones are thought to be from a female around 3.5 feet high. Her teeth and bone growth suggests that she was in her mid-20s when she died; she lived between 3–3.5 million years ago (the oldest fossils of *Australopithecus afarensis* are about 3.9 million years old). The fossil was nicknamed from the Beatles's song "Lucy in the Sky with Diamonds." Her Ethiopian name is Dinquinesh, or "thou art wonderful."
- In 1994, "Lucy's Grandson" was found not far from where Lucy was discovered in Ethiopia. The nearly intact skull from a male A. *afarensis* who lived about 3 million years ago, was found along with several arm bones from other males. Because the fossils are about a million years younger than the oldest A. *afarensis* bones, it may prove that Lucy and her relatives were very successful as a species. Many researchers also believe that Lucy is in our direct evolutionary line, making her species very long-lived indeed.
- Some of the oldest footprints of a walking humanoid were discovered by Mary Leakey in 1976 and are dated at 3.75 million years old. The footprints of A. *afarensis* were made in soft volcanic ash near the Olduvai Gorge in Tanzania.

MAJOR EARTH SCIENTISTS

Agassiz, Jean Louis Rodolphe (1807–1873)   Swiss-born American geologist and biologist who introduced the idea of the Ice Age, a period when ice sheets covered most of the Northern Hemisphere.

Agricola, Georgius (Georg Bauer) (1494–1555)   German mineralogist who coined the word *fossil* but did not differentiate fossils from other types of rock.

Alvarez, Luis Walter (1911–1988)   American physicist who proposed, along with his son, geologist Walter Alvarez, Frank Asaro, and Helen Michel, the theory that the extinctions at the Cretaceous-Tertiary (K-T) boundary were caused by the impact of a large space object. Their evidence included the discovery of a layer of iridium at the K-T boundary, which is associated with extraterrestrial impacts.

Boltwood, Bertram Borden (1870–1927)   American chemist and physicist who first discovered how to apply uranium decay to obtain the age of a rock.

Brongniart, Alexandre (1770–1847)   French geologist and paleontologist who pioneered the idea of using fossils to identify ages and layers of sedimentary rock.

Chamberlin, Thomas Chrowder (1843–1928)   American geologist who established the origin of loess (windblown deposits); discovered fossil forms beneath the Greenland ice sheet; and first proposed dating the ice sheets of the Pleistocene Epoch on the geologic time scale.

Conybeare, William Daniel (1787–1857)   British geologist and minister who developed the ideas of catastrophism (that geologic changes occur in brief bursts separated by long quiet periods) and progressivism (the biological theory that a series of creations yields organisms that are increasingly more complex).

Cope, Edward Drinker (1840–1897)   American paleontologist and comparative anatomist who searched in the western United States for fossils, especially of dinosaurs. His competition with Othniel Charles Marsh increased the number of dinosaur finds in the 1800s.

Cousteau, Jacques-Yves (1910–)   French oceanographer who developed numerous innovative underwater techniques: the aqualung, underwater photography techniques, and the bathyscaph. He is also an author and filmmaker who increased public awareness of the diversity of ocean life and environmental problems of the oceans and the Earth.

Cuvier, Georges Léopold Chrétien Frédéric Dagobert, Baron (1769–1832)   French paleontologist who was the first to propose that catastrophes were responsible for the extinctions of species.

Dana, James Dwight (1813–1895)   American geologist and mineralogist who wrote the first standard reference books in geology and mineralogy, many of which are still used today.

Davis, William Morris (1850–1934)   American geographer and geologist who wrote detailed descriptions of landforms and advanced the field of geomorphology.

Desmarest, Nicholas (1725–1815)   French physician, geologist, and mineralogist who was one of the first scientists to recognize igneous rocks as products of volcanic eruptions.

Dokuchaiev, Vasilii Vasiliievich (1846–1903)   Russian geographer who is regarded as the founder of modern soil science.

Drake, Edwin Laurentine (1819–1880)   American investor who drilled the world's first oil well in Titusville, Pennsylvania, in 1859. His work greatly advanced geological studies in the search for more oil.

Dutton, Clarence Edward (1841–1912)   American geologist who correctly explained isostasy (or how lighter mountains "float" in denser rock) and surveyed the structure of the Rocky Mountain region. His studies of volcanoes and earthquakes led him to conclude correctly that continental rocks are lighter than oceanic rock.

Ekman, Vagn Walfrid (1874–1954)   Swedish oceanographer who determined the dynamics of ocean currents and the effect of the Earth's rotation on wind-driven currents. Ekman was one of the founders of modern oceanography and invented many instruments to measure various ocean parameters.

Ewing, William Maurice (1913–1974)   American oceanographer who made detailed maps of the sea bottom using refraction of waves caused by explosions (similar to sonar). He helped describe the Mid-Atlantic Ridge, an area of sea-floor spreading that cuts through the Atlantic Ocean.

Gilbert, Grove Karl (1843–1918)   American geologist and geomorphologist who developed the foundations of twentieth-century earth science. He contributed detailed descriptions of river and other geologic processes that became standards for his time.

Gilbert, William (1544–1603)   English physicist and physician who suggested that the Earth is a great spherical magnet, establishing the scientific study of magnetism. He was also the first to write a physical science treatise based entirely on experimentation.

Gutenberg, Beno (1889–1960)   German-American geologist who determined the boundary between the Earth's mantle and core, based on the behavior of earthquake waves.

Hall, James (1811–1898)   American geologist who developed a theory of mountain building based on his geologic work in the Appalachian Mountains. He also founded the study of American stratigraphy and was the first president of the Geological Society of America.

Hall, James Sir (1761–1832) British chemist and geologist who was one of the first scientists to use laboratory experiments to test geologic theories. He also showed that crystals form from melted rock.

Hess, Harry Hammond (1906–1969) American geologist who developed the theory of sea-floor spreading (the development of new crust created at midocean ridges), which is a basic premise of plate tectonics.

Holmes, Arthur (1890–1965) English geologist who used radioactivity to date various rock formations; he was the first to recognize that the Earth's crust is about 4.56 billion years old.

Horton, Robert Elmer (1875–1945) American engineer, hydrologist, and geomorphologist who detailed what happens to water after a rainfall (infiltration or runoff). His studies formed the foundation of modern theories on river basin hydrology.

Humboldt, (Friedrich Wilhelm Heinrich) Alexander, Baron von (1769–1859) Prussian scientific explorer who made detailed investigations of the Earth's magnetism. He also identified the Jurassic Period of geologic time and explored the cold current running north along the Pacific coast of South America (the Peru current was once called the Humboldt current).

Hutton, James (1726–1797) Scottish natural philosopher who was the founder of modern geology and geomorphology. He also was the first to propose the idea of uniformitarianism (i.e., that all geologic features can be explained by rocks from the past).

Lartet, Édouard Armand Isidore Hippolyte (1801–1871) French paleontologist who was one of the pioneers of that science. He was the first to find evidence of humanlike fossils and extinct animals in one place; and helped excavate numerous prehistoric sites in France.

Leakey, Louis Seymour Bazett (1903–1972) British anthropologist and archaeologist, husband of Mary Leakey and father of Richard Leakey; along with Mary, he found some of the oldest humanoid fossils in the Olduvai Gorge, Africa, including members of the Australopithecines.

Leakey, Mary Nichol (1913–) British paleoanthropologist, wife of Louis Leakey and mother of Richard Leakey; along with Louis, she found some of the oldest humanoid fossils in the Olduvai Gorge, Africa. She later found a 3.75 million-year-old humanoid fossil at Laetoli, Africa.

Leakey, Richard Erskine Frere (1944–) Kenyan paleontologist, son of Louis and Mary Leakey; he found some of the oldest known humanoid fossils in Kenya, including a nearly complete fossil of a large *Homo erectus* (found with colleagues) in Kenya. In 1989, he was appointed director of the Wildlife Service in Kenya.

Lyell, Sir Charles (1797–1875) Scottish geologist who produced one of the most influential works on geology, *Principles of Geology*; his work also influenced Charles Darwin's views. Lyell shared James Hutton's belief that the present is the key to the past and held that fossils were the best guides to describing geologic rock layers. He was also one of the first to postulate that the Earth was millions of years old.

Mantell, Gideon A. (1790–1852) English geologist, who, with his wife, Mary Ann, was the first to recognize dinosaur bones as the remains of ancient, giant reptiles.

Marbut, Curtis Fletcher (1863–1935) American pedologist who applied Vasilii Dokuchaiev's soil formation ideas to the United States and developed the first soil classification system in the country.

Marsh, Othniel Charles (1831–1899) American paleontologist who searched for fossils, especially of dinosaurs, in the western United States, in competition with Edward Drinker Cope.

Maury, Matthew Fontaine (1806–1873)   American hydrologist and oceanographer who wrote the first text of modern oceanography, detailing the trade winds and ocean currents.

Mercalli, Giuseppe (1850–1914)   Italian seismologist who developed a scale to measure the intensity of earthquakes based on the resulting damage; the Mercalli scale is not commonly used today.

Miller, William Hallowes (1801–1880)   English mineralogist who classified crystals based on their coordinate (crystal) systems and wrote one of the first treatises on crystallography.

Milne, John (1850–1913)   British seismologist and geologist who, in 1880, invented the modern seismograph for measuring earthquake waves.

Mohorovičić, Andrija (1857–1936)   Yugoslavian (Croatian) seismologist who discovered that characteristics of earthquake waves change as they travel just below the earth's crust. The change in waves follows an uneven boundary between the crust and mantle and is called the Mohorovičić discontinuity (often shortened to "the Moho").

Mohs, Friedrich (1773–1839)   German mineralogist who was the first to classify minerals based on hardness. This scale is often referred to as Mohs Scale of Hardness, or the Mohs Scale.

Murchison, Sir Roderick Impey (1792–1871)   Scottish geologist who first described several layers of ancient rock, including rocks of Devonian Period, with Adam Sedgwick.

Owen, Sir Richard (1804–1892)   British comparative anatomist and paleontologist who coined the term *dinosaur* (in 1842).

Penck, Albrecht (1858–1945)   German geologist and geomorphologist (father of Walther) who pioneered work on the most recent glaciations in the European Alps, showing evidence of four glacial advances and retreats.

Penck, Walther (1888–1923)   German geologist and geomorphologist (son of Albrecht) who worked on theories of landscape development, including the relationship of the uplift of land and how a river cuts into a valley.

Playfair, John (1748–1819)   Scottish mathematician, geologist, and philosopher, who expanded on the work of his friend James Hutton. Playfair's law states that river tributaries are as deep as the surrounding major valley; he used this information to distinguish river valleys from glacial hanging valleys.

Pliny the Younger (Gaius Plinius Caecilius Secundus) (c. 61–112)   Roman senator who wrote the first detailed account of a volcanic eruption—Mount Vesuvius that destroyed Pompeii in A.D. 79.

Powell, John Wesley (1834–1902)   American soldier and geologist who led the first successful expedition through the Grand Canyon. Later, as head of the U.S. Geological Survey, he advised on the best way to develop western U.S. resources and warned of problems with soil erosion.

Pytheas (c. 350 B.C.)   Greek geographer and explorer who observed the strong Atlantic tides, and correctly theorized that they were caused by the Moon.

Richter, Charles Francis (1900–1985)   American seismologist who developed a scale for measuring the intensity, or magnitude, of earthquakes, called the Richter scale.

Sedgwick, Adam (1785–1873)   British geologist and mathematician who determined the time sequence of various rock layers, identified Cambrian Period rocks in Wales, and discovered Devonian Period rocks in southwest England with Roderick Murchinson.

Smith, William (1769–1839)   British surveyor and geologist who wrote the first book used to identified rock layers based on fossils within the rocks.

Steno, Nicolaus (Niels Stensen) (1638–1686)   Danish anatomist and geologist who identified the origin of many common fossils.

Van Allen, James Alfred (1914–)   American physicist who developed the rockoon, a rocket launched from a balloon, to study the physics of the upper atmosphere. He later discovered radiation belts circling the Earth (now called Van Allen belts), based on satellite data.

Wegener, Alfred Lothar (1880–1930)   German geologist and meteorologist who suggested the idea of continental drift in 1912, noting that the coastlines of several continents fit roughly together into a supercontinent he named Pangaea. His ideas were not accepted until the 1960s, when measurements proved that the continents move, which helped pave the way for the theory of plate tectonics.

Werner, Abraham Gottlob (1750–1817)   German mineralogist and geologist who developed the first systematic classification of minerals.

Xenophanes (c. 570–475 B.C.)   Greek philosopher who speculated that because fossil seashells were found in the mountains the Earth's surface must have risen and fallen in the past.

SIGNIFICANT SCIENTIFIC DISCOVERIES IN EARTH SCIENCE

	Year	Discovery or Achievement
B.C.	c. 1000	Industrial use of iron in Egypt and Mesopotamia
	c. 900	Natural gas from wells used in China
	c. 390	Plato proposed there must be another continent directly opposite Europe
	c. 330	Pytheas proposed tides are caused by the Moon
A.D.	c. 20	Stabo's *Geography* collected all known geographical information
	132	Zhang Heng invented the world's first crude seismograph
	1086	Shen Kua's *Dream Pool Essays* described the principles of erosion, uplift, and sedimentation—the foundations of earth science
	1298	Marco Polo described coal and asbestos in Europe
	1517	Girolamo Fracastoro described the remains of ancient organisms (now called fossils)
	1546	Georgius Agricola introduced the word *fossil*
	1565	First drawings of fossils by Konrad von Gesner
	1743	First geologic map produced by Christopher Packe
	1774	Abraham Werner introduced a classification of minerals
	1780	First known fossil found that would eventually be interpreted as dinosaur bones found in England
	1811	Mary Anning, 12 years old, found the first known fossil of an ichthyosaur in England
	1821	Mary Anning, 21 years old, discovered the first known fossil of a plesiosaur in England
	1822	Scale of hardness for minerals developed by F. Mohs
	1828	First measurement of the Earth's magnetic field by Paul Erman
	1837	Louis Agassiz proposed the idea of Ice Ages
	1842	Richard Owen introduced term *dinosaur*
	1850	First chart drawn of the Atlantic Ocean by Matthew Fontaine Maury
	1859	World's first oil well drilled by Edwin Drake
	1860	Fossil of earliest known bird found by Hermon von Meyer

1906	Earthquake waves first used to determine the Earth's layers by R. Oldham
1907	Bertram Boltwood used uranium to date rocks
1909	Moho discontinuity discovered by Andrija Mohorovičić
1912	Alfred Wegener first proposed the theory of continental drift
1914	Gutenberg discontinuity discovered by Beno Gutenberg
1925	Mid-Atlantic Ridge discovered by a German expedition
1935	Charles Richter develops a scale to determine earthquake intensity
1958	Radiation belts found by James Van Allen, based on satellite data
1960	First geothermal power used in the United States
	Sea-floor spreading first proposed by Harry Hess
1968	*Glomar Challenger* went into service to study the ocean depths
1977	Deep-sea vents discovered around Galapagos Islands by John Corliss and Robert Ballard
1980	Luis Alvarez and others proposed the idea of a large space object striking the Earth and causing the extinction of the dinosaurs
1985	Peter Rona finds the first deep-sea vents discovered in the Atlantic Ocean
1987	Oldest known embryo from fossil dinosaur egg found by Wade Miller
1990	The oldest portion of the Pacific plate was found
1991	Researchers found the first earthquake fault rupturing the surface in the eastern United States in northern North America
1992	Scientists found evidence of a crater beneath the Yucatan Peninsula that may have formed coincident with dinosaur extinctions
	Ice drilled in Greenland indicated that climatic changes over the last Ice Age changed dramatically, even over spans as short as a year
	A belt of interstellar matter is confirmed inside the Van Allen belts

COMMON TERMS IN EARTH SCIENCE

abrasion   The process by which solid particles moved by ice, water, wind, or gravity erode rock.

absolute time   Geologic time measured in years, from information gathered by direct means, such as radioactive dating.

abyssal plains   Flat or very gently sloping areas of the ocean floor, at the foot of a continental rise.

aeolian deposits   Deposits from windblown sediments.

aftershock   Tremor that occurs after a major earthquake. Many times an aftershock's magnitude measures close to the original shock.

alkaline   Usually referring to igneous rocks high in alkali metals and sodium and potassium, e.g., alkali feldspar is an alkaline rock.

aphotic   The ocean zone that is entirely devoid of light.

aquifer   A rock layer that can store a large amount of groundwater.

artesian well   A well in which hydraulic pressure forces the water naturally upward. The water lies within impermeable rock layers and the outlet to the well is above the water table.

ash   The finest rock material ejected from a volcanic explosion.

atoll   A coral reef that encloses an area of water. Many Pacific Ocean archipelagos are collections of atolls.

avalanche   A mass of earth, rock, ice, or snow that is suddenly and swiftly dislodged from a mountainside. For example, snow on a slope of more than 22° is often poised for an avalanche.

basic   Usually referring to igneous rocks with a relatively low silica and high iron, calcium, or magnesia content. For example, basalt is a basic rock.

basin   An area where rock dips toward a central spot or depression. Basins can cover hundreds of miles and are often filled with ancient sediments.

bathymetry   The study of measuring the ocean depths to determine sea floor topography.

bed   A rock layer laid down parallel to the surface. Movement of the Earth's crust can eventually fold or fault a rock bed.

bedrock   Solid rock that makes up the Earth's crust. It also refers to the exposed, solid mass of rock after soil is removed.

benthic   Of or pertaining to the ocean bottom, or the deepest parts of a large body of water.

breccia   A sedimentary rock that contains angular rock fragments held together by natural cement.

brine   Salty water, usually extracted from the ground. It is often found around rocks with a high salt content.

butte   A small, flat-topped hill with steep sides formed from the erosion of a mesa. The top rock is usually more resistant to erosion than the underlying rock.

caldera   The deep, roughly round depression at the mouth of a volcano. Extinct volcanoes usually contain lakes or secondary cones within the caldera.

canyon   A long, steep-sided valley formed in dry regions by running water. Submarine, or ocean, canyons are found along the continental slopes and are thought to be carved by the movement of turbidity currents.

carbonaceous   Pertaining to materials such as rocks, meteorites, or asteroids that contain carbon.

channel   The bed and sides of a watercourse, such as a river or stream channel.

cleavage   The property of a mineral that allows it to break along a smooth plane surface.

coal   A solid, black or brownish-black combustible material that was formed through the partial decomposition of vegetation. Types of coal include bituminous, lignite, and anthracite.

conglomerate   A sedimentary rock that contains smooth rock fragments held together by natural cement.

continental rise   The lower portion of the ocean's continental shelf that leads to the abyssal plain.

continental shelf   The gentle sloping ocean floor that is closest to the shore.

continental slope   The higher section of the continental shelf; it is the steep section between the continental shelf and rise.

coral reef   A mound or ridge of rock produced by the accumulation of skeletons from living coral. Most coral polyps deposit calcium around themselves; when a polyp dies, the calcium structure is left behind. Another polyp builds its "shell" on top of the calcium skeleton—thus the coral reef grows.

crater   A circular, steep-sided basin associated with a volcano or meteorite impact. A crater, especially of volcanic origin, is often defined as a basin with a diameter less than three times its depth.

crystal   A solid material with an orderly atomic arrangement.

delta   A large collection of sediments deposited at the mouth of a river. When sediment suspended in a river reaches slower-moving waters, it settles and forms a delta.

density current   Deep ocean current usually caused by differences in water temperature, salinity, or turbidity.

deposition   A process in which sediment is deposited on the Earth, usually carried by wind, water, or ice.

detritus   Rock worn down or broken by physical means.

dinosaur   From the Greek *deinos* ("terrible") and *sauros* ("reptile"); they were represented by two reptile orders that lived from about 225 to 65 million years ago.

disphotic   The ocean zone where small amounts of light penetrate the water.

drift   All rock material deposited by glacial ice and streams.

drumlin   A smooth, streamlined hill formed by a glacier and composed of till.

dune   A sand mound or ridge deposited and moved by wind action.

erosion   The process whereby rock is worn away by wind, water, or ice or the wearing away of rock by reactive natural chemicals.

erratic   Usually refers to large stones and boulders that were carried by a glacier and then deposited in regions where the rock is not naturally found.

estuary   The wide tidal part of a coastal river, close to the mouth, where freshwater mixes with ocean water.

euphotic   The ocean zone that allows enough light to penetrate the water to support photosynthesis.

fault   A crack or fracture in the Earth, usually precipitated by the movement of the crust during an earthquake.

flood plain   The flat land that is periodically inundated during flooding along river or stream banks. The flooding drops nutrient-rich sediment (alluvium) along the flood plain.

flood   The overflow of water along river or stream banks. It usually occurs in the spring and summer months, as the result of winter snow melt, heavy seasonal rains, and/or changes in a river's normal channel. Humans build earthen dikes and other flood-prevention controls to protect housing and other structures along a river from flood damage, though such structures are not always effective.

fluvial   Referring to water processes (such as deposition and erosion) along streams and rivers.

formation   A locally widespread type of rock bearing a specific set of fossils or characteristics. A formation is usually named after the place where it is initially found.

fossil   The remains of a plant or animal buried in sediment. Fossils are the surviving hard parts of the organism or impressions of the organism in the sediment.

fracture   To break a mineral other than along a cleavage plane. For example, glass exhibits conchoidal (shell-shaped) fracturing.

geysers (or gushers) Natural thermal springs that intermittently eject hot water and steam from cracks in the Earth. Geysers are usually associated with volcanically active areas.

glaciers Flowing bodies of land ice that develop in the colder regions and higher latitudes of the Earth. They originate on land by the accumulation and compression of snow.

gravel Loose particles—larger than sand grains—resulting from natural erosion.

groundwater Subsurface water that lies in a rock zone completely saturated with water. Groundwater is recharged by the infiltration (percolation) of precipitation and surface water into the soil, and on to the water table.

hardness A mineral's resistance to scratching by another object or mineral.

hiatus A rock layer that displays a break or gap in the geologic record.

hominoid Any animal resembling humans.

Ice Age (or ice age) A period in the Earth's history when temperatures were much colder than today and glacial ice sheets covered large sections of the Earth. Past glacial advances and retreats lasted from thousands to millions of years. The last ice age glacier in North America retreated north to its present ice cap position about 11,000 years ago.

intermittent stream A stream, usually in desert areas, that carries water only part of the time, usually during a flash flood.

lake A natural or artificial body of inland water. Natural lakes are often fed by underground springs; artificial lakes are often created by blocking a river or stream.

landslide Landslides are the rapid movement of land down a slope, such as a rock slide, mud flow, or debris slide. Landslides are usually precipitated by excessive rain on weakened or weathered slopes.

living fossil A living organism whose characteristics are closely akin to those of fossilized organisms. Many deep-sea organisms are called living fossils.

loess Windblown deposits of silt that contain a high percentage of calcium carbonate.

longshore drift The movement of material along a beach caused by waves breaking at an angle on the shore.

magma Hot, molten material from deep underground, usually associated with volcanic eruptions. Magma that reaches the surface is called lava.

magnitude A measure of the total energy released by an earthquake. The Richter scale uses magnitudes to define earthquake intensity.

mass movement The movement of material on the Earth's surface induced by gravity. For example, landslides are considered mass movements.

mesa A flat-topped plateau with steep sides. The mesa's top rock is usually more resistant to erosion than the underlying rock. Mesas eventually erode into buttes.

mid-ocean ridge A ridge of volcanic mountains on the ocean floor, usually associated with sea-floor spreading of crustal plates.

mountain An elevated part of the landscape that is conspicuous above its surroundings. Various mountain elevations are associated with characteristic physical, chemical, and biological features.

natural gas Gaseous hydrocarbons, mostly methane, that occur in certain sedimentary rocks.

neritic   The ocean zone (within the pelagic zone) that extends from high tide to a water depth of 600 feet (183 meters).

nutation   The wobbling of the Earth as it turns on its axis (from the Latin word for "nodding"). Each "nod" completes a cycle (from crest to crest) every 19 years and is caused by the gravitational pull of the Moon as it orbits the Earth.

ocean trench   Deep, narrow depressions in the Earth's oceans, usually formed by the subduction of one crustal plate under another.

ore   A naturally occurring deposit with a high metallic content.

organic   Pertaining to or derived from life, usually in reference to organisms. Chemically, an organic compound has hydrogen or nitrogen directly linked with carbon.

outcrop   An exposed body of rock.

permafrost   Permanently frozen ground.

permeability   The ability of a material, usually a rock layer, to allow water to pass through by joints, cracks, and other spaces within it. For example, sandstones are more permeable than shale because of their larger grain size.

porosity   A measure of the amount of space between grains of a rock; not all porous rocks are permeable.

sediment   Material from the erosion of rock. It is usually deposited by wind, water, or ice.

seismograph   An instrument that measures the intensity and direction of seismic waves from an earthquake, aftershock, or tremor.

sinkhole   A depression formed by the natural collapse of the surface, usually in association with karst (limestone) topography.

spring   A place where the water table intersects the Earth's surface. Water under such conditions is usually freeflowing and continuous.

subsidence   The natural or artificial sinking of a large area of the Earth's crust. For example, subsidence can occur in a limestone region from the natural sinking of the ground; it can also occur when oil is extracted from under a region.

tide   The alternate rising and falling of water surfaces caused by the pull of the Moon, and to a lesser degree, by the pull of the Sun.

till   Unsorted drift deposited by a glacier.

tsunami   From the Japanese words *tsu* ("harbor") and *nami* ("wave"), a seismic sea wave caused by underwater earthquakes or volcanic eruptions.

turbidity currents   The fast movement of a water and sediment mix down steep slopes in the oceans. They are often triggered by earthquakes and are associated with the formation of submarine canyons.

upwelling   The upward movement of cold bottom water in the ocean that occurs when winds or currents displace the lighter surface water.

vein   A long, thin deposit of foreign minerals that follows a rock fracture or joint.

viscosity   The property of a material that offers a resistance to flow. For example, oil is more viscous than water (also said oil has a higher viscosity than water).

volatiles   Gases that rapidly evaporate at ordinary temperatures on exposure to the air.

water table　The irregular upper surface of underground water. It is usually highest beneath hills (though still farther below the surface) and about the same level as river channels in valleys.

weathering　The decaying effect of the atmosphere on the Earth's crust. It can be physical or chemical and depends especially on the surrounding climate.

ADDITIONAL SOURCES OF INFORMATION

Baker, James D. *Planet Earth: The View from Space*. Harvard Univ. Press, 1990.

Brown, Bruce. *The Miracle Planet*. Gallery, 1990.

Calder, Nigel. *Spaceship Earth*. Viking, London, 1991.

Cattermole, Peter, and Moore, Patrick. *The Story of the Earth*. Cambridge Univ. Press, 1985.

Elsom, D. *Earth: The Making, Shaping and Workings of a Planet*. Macmillan, 1992.

Emiliani, Cesare. *Planet Earth: Cosmology, Geology, and the Evolution of Life and the Environment*. Cambridge Univ. Press, 1992.

Fuchs, Sir Vivian. *Oxford Illustrated Encyclopedia, Volume 1: The Physical World*. Oxford Univ. Press, 1985.

Johanson, D. C., and O'Farrell, K., *Journey from the Dawn: Life with the World's First Family*. Villard, 1990.

Lambert, David, L. *The Field Guide to Prehistoric Life*. Facts on File, 1985.

Leakey, Richard, and Lewin, Roger. *Origins Reconsidered: In Search of What Makes Us Human*. Doubleday, 1992.

Raup, David M. *Extinction: Bad Genes or Bad Luck?* Norton, 1992.

Strahler, Arthur N., and Strahler, Alan H. *Modern Physical Geography*. Wiley, 1992.

Tattersall, Ian. *The Human Odyssey: Four Million Years of Human Evolution*. Prentice-Hall, 1993.

World Almanac and Book of Facts. Funk & Wagnalls, 1995.

Chapter 10

Meteorology

What Is Meteorology?   420

The Earth's Atmosphere   420

The Earth's Winds   423

The Earth's Weather   428

Definitions of Major Storms   441

Weather Forecasting   450

Major Meteorologists   451

Significant Scientific Discoveries
in Meteorology   453

Common Terms in Meteorology   454

Additional Sources of Information   456

WHAT IS METEOROLOGY?

Meteorology is the study of the complex motions and interactions of the atmosphere, including the observation of phenomena such as temperature, density, winds, clouds, and precipitation. *Meteorology* applies mainly to the Earth's atmosphere. *Atmospheric science* usually refers to the study of atmospheres on the planets and satellites of the solar system. *Aeronomy* is the study of the physics and chemistry of the upper atmospheres of planetary bodies, including the Earth.

An atmosphere on any planet or satellite is composed of gases that are held by the planet's gravitation. All planetary atmospheres differ in composition; it is clear that most planets' primitive atmospheres were unlike their modern ones. Atmospheric differences within the solar system often reflect the planet's or satellite's distance from the Sun, the initial evolution of the planet, and the chemical reactions between the planet's air and its rocks.

THE EARTH'S ATMOSPHERE

Over the Earth's long history, natural changes have taken place in the atmosphere. For example, it is believed that several major volcanic eruptions in the past have released ash and dust into the atmosphere, causing periodic cooling of the climate. Several theories propose that human pollution has affected the natural responses of the atmosphere in the last century, changing the Earth's climate and weather. These theories are still being debated (for more information on climate change, see Chapter 11, "Environmental Science").

Though the Earth's atmosphere extends 1,500 miles (2,414 kilometers) above the surface, the greatest bulk of the gases (about 75 percent) reside within 10 miles (16 kilometers) of the Earth's surface.

Atmospheric Layers

The atmosphere is divided into the *heterosphere*, the upper portion approximating the region of the thermosphere and ionosphere, and the lower portion called the *homosphere*. The atmosphere is further divided into several layers.

The lower part of the atmosphere is called the *troposphere*. It is where living organisms spend most of their time and where weather takes place. The troposphere averages about 7 miles (11 kilometers) in height. It is about 5 miles (8 kilometers) thick at the poles and about 10 miles (16 kilometers) thick at the equator.

Atmospheric gases become much thinner at the next layer, the *stratosphere*, which is located between about 7 to 30 miles (11 to 48 kilometers) above the Earth's surface. The *ozonosphere* (ozone layer), which protects all organisms from the harmful ultraviolet rays of the Sun, is located within the stratosphere, between 10 to 30 miles (16 to 48 kilometers) in altitude.

The temperature drops dramatically in the next layer, called the *mesosphere*. It is located between about 30 to 55 miles (48 to 88 kilometers) from the Earth's surface.

The temperature rises again in the next layer, called the *thermosphere*. The thermosphere is located between about 55 to 435 miles (85 to 700 kilometers) above the Earth.

The final layer is the *exosphere*, the atmospheric fringe beginning at 435 miles (700 kilometers) above sea level.

Divisions of the Earth's Atmosphere

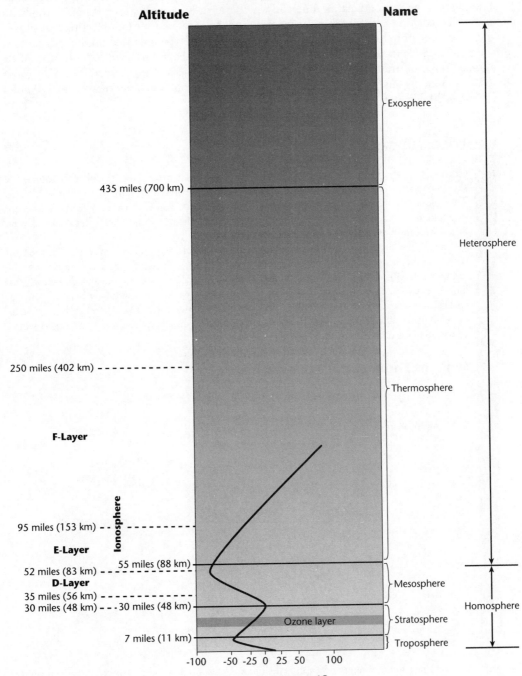

Note: not to scale.

A layer that overlaps many of the other layers is the *ionosphere*, from 30 to 250 miles (48 to 402 kilometers), as part of the upper mesosphere and lower thermosphere. The ionosphere is the part of the atmosphere in which the air is ionized by such factors as the Sun's ultraviolet radiation. Layers within the ionosphere are also responsible for reflecting radio waves and are important to long-distance communication. These layers are based on the transmission and reflection characteristics of radio waves: the *D layer*, between 35 to 52 miles (56 to 83 kilometers) in altitude; the *E layer* (Heaviside-Kennelly layer), between 52 to 95 miles (83 to 153 kilometers) in altitude; and the *F layer* (Appleton layer), between 95 to 250 miles (153 to 402 kilometers) in altitude.

COLORFUL SKIES

One of the major characteristics of the Earth's atmosphere is its color. From the planet's surface, the sky appears to be blue. About 20 miles (32 kilometers) above the surface, the sky is relatively black. The color of the sky on other planets depends on the composition of the atmosphere; on Mars, for example, the sky is pinkish because of the iron particles in its thin atmosphere. But apparently, no other place in the solar system has a blue sky like Earth's.

Our sky is blue because the short blue wavelengths of sunlight scatter in all directions as the light strikes air molecules, other particles, and water and ice from clouds. Sunsets are red because the sunlight is traveling through more of the atmosphere to reach us (see the illustration below); this longer passage scatters all other colors away from the observer except the longer red wavelengths. Reddish sunsets are occasionally enhanced by excessive dust in the atmosphere, such as particles from a recent volcanic eruption. Clouds, haze, and fog are white because the water droplets scatter all wavelengths of the spectrum equally.

Sunlight Through the Atmosphere

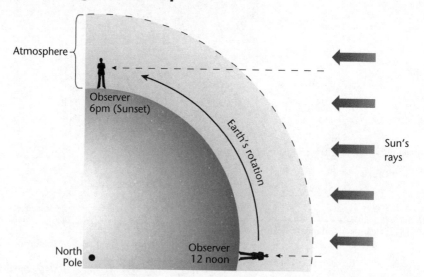

The Sun's rays to an observer on Earth at 12 noon pass through a shorter length of the atmosphere than rays travelling to the same observer at 6 PM. Since there is more atmosphere to travel through, there are more particles to scatter the light. As more scattering occurs, the shorter wavelengths (the blue end of the spectrum) are filtered out and only the longer wavelengths (oranges and reds) are left—thus the characteristic colors of sunset.

Composition of Dry Air at Sea Level (in percent)

Components	Percent of Dry Air
Nitrogen	76.08
Oxygen	20.95
Argon	0.93
Carbon dioxide	0.032
Neon	0.001
Helium	0.0005
Methane	0.00015
Krypton	0.00011
Hydrogen	0.00005
Nitrous oxide	0.00003
Carbon monoxide	0.00001
Ozone (average)*	0.00004
Xenon	0.000009
Water (average)*	up to 1
Other trace gases	< 0.000001

Ozone and water concentrations vary widely depending on temperature, sunshine, and environmental factors.

THE EARTH'S WINDS

Earth's winds are divided into three groups: planetary winds (i.e. trade winds and westerlies), secondary winds (i.e. cyclonic, monsoons, sea breezes), and regional winds (i.e. mostly anabatic and katabatic winds).

Planetary Winds

Major Circulation Cells

The Earth's global winds are the result of contrasting pressure and temperature belts that exist on a semipermanent or permanent basis. Earth's major wind circulation patterns occur because warm air at the equator rises and migrates to the poles, and cold air at the poles sinks and moves toward the equator. The circulation slowly changes with the seasons, as the Sun's rays differentially heat the Earth.

There are three major cells that carry air currents in both hemispheres.

Named after English meteorologist George Hadley, the *Hadley cells* (tropical cells) are caused by the rising and sinking of heated and cooled air, respectively. The heated air rises near the equator, travels toward the poles, and sinks again at 30° north and south latitudes.

With the *Polar cells*, heated air rises about 30° north and south latitudes and sinks at the respective pole.

Named after American meteorologist William Ferrel, the *Ferrel cells* exist between the two tropical (Hadley) and Polar cells. The Ferrel cells circulate in the reverse direction from the Hadley and Polar cells: cold air rises at 60° north and south latitudes, and warm air descends at 30° north and south latitudes. These cells act as slight brakes on the general circulation. They cause heavy precipitation between latitudes 40 and 60° (ascending circulation), and arid conditions in the subtropics (descending circulation).

Prevailing Winds

The *prevailing winds* are produced by the global patterns of barometric pressure, both at the surface and aloft. The prevailing winds are influenced by the Earth's rotation (Coriolis effect), with the northern winds curving to the east, and the southern winds to the west. The prevailing winds are the polar high, polar easterlies, subpolar lows, westerlies, subtropical high horse latitudes, and trade winds in both the Northern and Southern Hemispheres. These northern and southern prevailing wind bands are mirror images of each other. The equatorial low doldrums are found along a belt at the equator.

The Earth's General Circulation

Secondary Winds

Land and Sea Breezes

When sailors a century ago said, "In by day, out by night," they were referring to the *land* and *sea breezes*. Land and sea breezes are common at the seashore and on the shores of large lakes. They are confined to within 12.5 miles (20 kilometers) of a coast and extend only a few miles vertically.

On a warm day, the land heats to a higher temperature than the nearby water, causing a pressure difference. As the heated air rises, the cooler air rushes in to take its place, creating a sea breeze from water to the land (also called an onshore breeze). At night, the opposite occurs: As the land cools and the water retains the heat it gathered during the warm day, the winds flow from the land to the water (also called an offshore breeze).

Monsoons

Monsoons are the often predictable winds that bring the rainy (summer monsoon) and dry (winter monsoon) weather to India and Southeast Asia. Monsoons were once defined as the reversal of wind directions that occur in and around the Indian Ocean and Arabian Sea, blowing from the southwest for half the year (summer) and northeast for the other half of the year (winter). It is now known that the monsoons are not local, but worldwide winds, but with less remarkable extremes than is experienced in Southeast Asia. Monsoon winds occur because of the differential heating of oceans and land.

Regional Winds

Most regional winds are influenced by the local topography. For example, as air is forced up and over a mountain, it cools adiabatically. The cool, rising air produces clouds, rain, or snow that falls on the windward side of a mountain. As the air descends on the leeward side, the adiabatic heating and heat from condensation on the windward side causes a very warm wind. The ascending winds are called anabatic; the descending winds are called katabatic. For example, Chinook winds are katabatic.

Here are some reoccurring regional winds that have been given their own names; some are caused by local topography and others are less directly related to local terrain.

The *bora* are winds that sweep down from the coastal mountains in the Balkans, along the Adriatic coast between Trieste and the Albanian border. Some squalls can travel at 100 miles (161 kilometers) per hour.

The *buran* is the often violent and bitterly cold wind associated with blizzard conditions, particularly in Siberia and southern Russia.

The *Chinook* winds occur on the eastern slopes of the Rocky Mountains, as winds from the Pacific blow up the sides of the Rockies, mostly in the spring. The winds drop most of their moisture on the western side; then dry, cool winds flow down the eastern slopes, warm as they descend, and often melt winter snow quickly. In the Alps, such winds are called *foehn*.

The *haboob* is a dust storm or sandstorm that occurs in northern and central Sudan, in which walls of dust can reach several thousand feet in height.

The *mistral* is a cold, violent wind, often reaching 125 miles (200 kilometers) per hour, that travels from a north or northwest direction down the lower Rhône valley in France. It is caused by a depression in the Gulf of Genoa, which attracts cold air from the north. In the summer, the winds spread forest fires; in the spring, they often bring a killing frost to early season fruits and vegetables.

The *nor'easter* of New England is part of the wind circulation around intense cyclones that are centered off the mid-Atlantic coast. They usually are violent, windy storms that travel quickly along the coast.

Santa Ana winds are hot, dry winds that descend from the mountains into southern California. They form when the outward flow of dry air from a strong high pressure system combines with the local effects of mountainous terrain.

The *sirocco* (or *scirocco*) are the strong, gusty winds that occur when the leading edge of eastward-moving storms draws air northward from the hot interior of the Sahara Desert. Sirocco is called *chili* in Tunisia, the *ghibli* in Libya, and *khamsin* in Egypt.

The *sukhovey* is a hot, dry, dusty wind that blows to the south or southeast in southern Russia. If it blows for a few days at a time, it can be harmful to crops in the region; it may last long enough to cause a drought.

The *williwaws* are characteristic of the fjords of the Aleutian Islands and Alaskan coast, and are caused by the local topography.

WIND SHEAR AND MICROBURSTS

Wind shear, or the sudden change in horizontal or vertical wind speed or direction over a short distance, is one of the most unusual winds. It is caused by differences in wind speeds that stir up swirling eddies (turbulence). Wind shear is present everywhere in the atmosphere but it is usually small in scale. The bumps you feel in a high-flying airliner are usually caused by small-scale wind shear in the jet stream. Larger wind shears are usually restricted to various types of fronts, such as thunderstorms or gusty wind conditions.

Microbursts are forms of wind shear usually associated with localized storms; they were not really understood until the 1980s. One reason for the intense study of microbursts was the danger to planes close to the ground—either taking off or landing. Low-level wind shear—below 1,500 feet (457 meters)—often causes the wind to switch from a head to a tail wind, dropping the speed of the wind over the tail, and causing the plane to loose its lift. Most planes operate at airspeeds well above the stall value, but a decrease in air speed could make the plane susceptible to microbursts. (Advanced Doppler radar is now being used to detect shifting wind patterns that will help anticipate possible microbursts at airports.) Planes aren't the only things affected—microbursts have been known to capsize boats and to fan forest fires.

Beaufort Wind Scale: Land and Sea

The *Beaufort wind scale* was developed by Admiral Sir Francis Beaufort (1774–1857) in 1806 as a way of measuring wind force at sea. Beaufort developed the force scale based on the effects of wind on a canvas of a full-rigged frigate. The actual wind speeds were not measured initially; by 1946, the speeds were determined with an anemometer (an instrument that measures wind speed). The land scale is measured in miles (kilometers) per hour, whereas the sea scale is measured in knots.

Land Scale

Force	Miles [Kilometers] per Hour	Conditions
0	1 [1.61]	Light winds; smoke rises vertically
1	1–3 [1.61–4.8]	Light winds; smoke drifts slowly
2	4–7 [6.4–11.2]	Light winds; wind is felt on face and rustles leaves
3	8–12 [12.9–19.3]	Gentle winds; leaves and small twigs in constant motion
4	13–18 [20.9–29]	Moderate winds; dust blows and small branches move
5	19–24 [30.6–38.6]	Moderate winds; small trees sway; small crests on inland waters
6	25–31 [40.2–49.9]	Strong winds; large branches in motion; telephone wires whistle
7	32–38 [51.5–61.1]	Strong winds; whole trees in motion; walking in wind becomes slightly difficult

Force	Miles [Kilometers] per Hour	Conditions
8	39–46 [62.8–74]	Gale winds; twigs break off trees
9	47–54 [75.6–86.9]	Gale winds; slight structural damage; tiles or slate pulled from roofs
10	55–63 [88.5–101.4]	Storm winds; smaller trees uprooted; roofs damaged
11	64–74 [103–119.1]	Violent storm winds; widespread damage
12	> 74 [> 119.1]	Hurricane winds

Sea Scale

Force	Knots	Conditions
0	< 1	Sea flat, like a mirror; calm wind
1	1–3	Ripples form but no crests; light breeze; average wave height 0.25 foot (0.08 meter)
2	4–6	Small wavelets with slight crests; light breeze; average wave height 0.5 foot (0.15 meter)
3	7–10	Large wavelets, some crests break; gentle breeze; average wave height 2 feet (0.61 meter)
4	11–16	Small waves; moderate breeze; average wave height 3.5 feet (1.07 meters)
5	17–21	Moderate waves, chance of some spray; brisk breeze; average wave height 6 feet (1.83 meters)
6	22–27	Large waves form, and white foam crests; some spray; strong breeze; average wave height 13.5 feet (4.11 meters)
7	28–33	White foam from breaking waves; near gale-force winds; average wave height 18 feet (5.49 meters)
8	34–40	Moderately high waves, and much foam; gale winds; average wave height 23 feet (7.01 meters)
9	41–47	High waves; streaks of foam follow direction of wind; strong gale winds; average wave height 25 feet (7.62 meters)
10	48–55	Extremely high waves with crests; visibility affected; storm winds; average wave height 29 feet (8.84 meters)
11	56–65	Exceptionally high waves with crests; violent storm winds; visibility greatly affected; average wave height 37 feet (11.28 meters)
12	68+	Hurricane winds; average wave height 45 feet (13.72 meters)

WIND CHILL CHART

Wind can make it seem much colder outside, especially during the cooler seasons. In the winter, when temperatures are already in the teens or twenties, a strong wind can make it feel like temperatures are in the single digits—an effect known as wind chill (the term was coined by Antarctic explorer Paul A. Siple in 1939).

Wind chill is the rate of heat loss, or how many calories of heat are carried away, from a person's exposed skin caused by air motion. For example, at a temperature of 0°F and a wind speed of 30 miles per hour, the heat loss is equivalent to –49°F. In other words, if you were standing outside, the temperature would seem like –49 °F, which could be a dangerous situation if you were not wearing enough warm clothing.

Wind Chill Factors*

Wind Speed (mph)	THERMOMETER READING (°F)												
	50	40	30	20	10	0	–10	–20	–25	–30	–35	–40	–45
Calm	50	40	30	20	10	0	–10	–20	–31	–36	–42	–47	–52
5	48	37	27	16	6	–5	–15	–26	–52	–58	–64	–71	–77
10	40	28	16	4	–9	–24	–33	–46	–65	–72	–78	–85	–92
15	36	22	9	–5	–18	–32	–45	–58	–74	–81	–88	–95	–103
20	32	18	4	–10	–25	–39	–53	–67	–81	–88	–96	–103	–110
25	30	16	0	–15	–29	–44	–59	–74	–86	–93	–101	–109	–116
30	28	13	–2	–18	–33	–48	–63	–79	–89	–97	–105	–113	–120
35	27	11	–4	–20	–35	–51	–67	–82	–92	–100	–107	–115	–123
40	26	10	–6	–21	–37	–53	–69	–86	–93	–102	–109	–117	–125

**The numbers are the equivalent calm-air temperature (°F).*

THE EARTH'S WEATHER

Air Masses

The movement of air is dominated by low and high pressure systems, or air masses. Air will flow from high pressure to a low pressure area. Daily weather patterns are controlled by the movements of these pressure systems.

Major Air Masses in the United States

The property of an air mass is derived partly from the regions over which it passes; or in terms of the type of ocean (maritime) or landmass (continental) over which it travels.

Air Mass Type	Season	Temperature	Humidity
Arctic	Winter	Very cold	Very dry
Continental polar	Winter	Cold	Dry
	Summer	Cool	Variable
Maritime polar	Winter	Mild	Moist
	Summer	Cool	Moist
Continental tropical	Summer	Hot	Dry
Maritime tropical	Winter	Warm	Moist
	Summer	Very warm	Moist
Equatorial	Summer	Very warm	Moist

OLD WEATHER WAYS

Before weather forecasting adopted sophisticated computer models, prediction was the domain of farmers, almanacs, and weather watchers. The forecasting methods were not precise, but many people swore by some of the following ways to predict weather.

- A breastbone from a goose was often used to tell whether there would be a harsh winter. As the breastbone dried on the shelf, it would change color. If the dried bone was white, it would be a mild winter; if the tips turned purple, a cold spring. If the bone turned mostly black, purple, or blue, it would be a cold winter. Weather watchers believed that the darker colors meant that the goose had conserved oil in its wings as a natural protection against the cold.

- Groundhog day (February 2) was started in Pennsylvania by German immigrants. In Germany, farmers would watch a badger emerge from hibernation: If the badger emerged on a sunny day, it would be scared by its shadow, and there would be 6 more weeks of winter. If the badger emerged on a cloudy day, it would see no shadow, thus heralding the beginning of spring. When German immigrants found fewer badgers on arriving in Pennsylvania, they substituted the more plentiful groundhog. Unfortunately the method of forecasting has not proved all that accurate—groundhog "predictions" have been wrong about 70 percent of the time.
- The saying, "A ring around the Moon is a sure sign of rain," refers to the appearance of the Moon when it is viewed through high cirrostratus clouds. The Moon appears with a diffuse halo as its light refracts through ice crystals in the clouds. Cirrostratus clouds normally precede an approaching warm front, which is accompanied by turbulent weather—usually in the form of rain.
- The saying, "It smells like rain," may be true: Precipitation is accompanied by low pressure and rising air. These conditions often cause air and gases in the ground to diffuse out just before it starts to rain, causing an earthy or musty odor.
- It is thought that the bands on woolybear caterpillars can be used to predict the severity of the coming winter. In the fall, the black and reddish brown caterpillar's thick stripes mean a hard winter; thinner bands mean a mild winter. But there is no proof that such characteristics can predict winter weather trends.
- Buys Ballot was a professor at Utrecht in 1857, who stated, "Standing with back to wind, low pressure is to left and high pressure to right in Northern Hemisphere; with the reverse being true in the Southern Hemisphere." He was right (the effect is due to the Coriolis force)—and this law is still accepted today as one of meteorology's major principles.

Weather Fronts

Fronts are the sharp, well-defined boundaries between air masses. There are four major types of fronts: *cold*, *warm*, *stationary*, and *occluded*. A cold front occurs when a cold air mass is followed by a warm air mass. A warm front occurs when a warm air mass is followed by a cold air mass. A front that does not advance is stationary; an occluded front occurs when cold, warm, and cool air run into each other, which forms warm or cold occlusions.

The Jet Streams

The *jet streams* are flattened tubes of high-speed winds that separate the warm flow of air (usually from the midlatitudes) from the cold (usually from the poles). There are two jet streams each in the Northern and Southern Hemispheres. They range between 25,000 to 45,000 feet (7,620 to 13,716 meters) in altitude. The jet streams travel in a general west-to-east direction in both hemispheres, though they can temporarily swoop northward and southward. The jet stream was discovered during World War II, when military aircraft, even when at full throttle, would sometimes remain stationary with respect to the ground—as the plane tried to fly "upstream" against a jet stream current.

Air Temperature

Air temperatures are measurements of atmospheric warmth, which is influenced primarily by radiation from the Sun as the Earth rotates on its axis (for more information on temperature, see Chapter 1, "Scientific Measurements").

Air temperatures recorded at weather stations are taken in the shade. These daily ground-level temperatures vary with location, time of the day, and season. Temperature

Weather Fronts

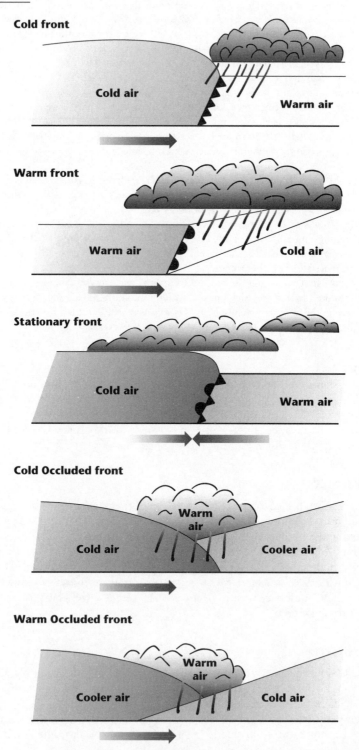

Cold front

Cold air

Warm air

Warm front

Warm air

Cold air

Stationary front

Cold air

Warm air

Cold Occluded front

Cold air

Warm air

Cooler air

Warm Occluded front

Cooler air

Warm air

Cold air

measurements may also be affected by winds, with warmer temperatures in calm weather and cooler temperatures under windy conditions. Average annual temperatures are the differences between the highest mean monthly temperatures and the lowest mean monthly temperatures.

Average Monthly High Temperature, Precipitation, and Snowfall for Selected U.S. Cities*†

City	Jan.	Feb.	Mar.	Apr.	May	June	July	Aug.	Sept.	Oct.	Nov.	Dec.
Atlanta, GA	51	55	63	73	80	86	88	88	82	73	63	54
	4.9	4.4	5.9	4.4	4.0	3.4	4.7	3.4	3.2	2.5	3.4	4.2
	0.9	0.5	0.4	T	—	—	—	—	—	—	—	0.2
Baltimore, MD	41	44	53	65	74	83	87	86	79	68	56	45
	3.0	3.0	3.7	3.4	3.4	3.8	3.9	4.6	3.5	3.1	3.1	3.4
	6.1	6.5	3.6	0.1	T	—	T	—	—	—	1.1	3.5
Boston, MA	36	38	45	57	67	77	82	80	72	62	52	40
	4.0	3.7	4.1	3.7	3.5	2.9	2.7	3.7	3.4	3.4	4.2	4.5
	12.2	11.3	7.3	0.9	—	—	—	—	—	—	1.4	7.3
Charlotte, NC	50	54	62	72	79	85	88	88	82	72	62	53
	3.8	3.8	4.8	3.3	3.6	3.6	3.9	3.8	3.6	2.7	2.9	3.4
	2.1	1.8	1.3	—	—	—	—	—	—	—	0.1	0.5
Chicago, IL	29	34	44	59	70	79	83	82	76	64	48	35
	1.6	1.3	2.6	3.7	3.2	4.1	3.6	3.5	3.4	2.3	2.1	2.1
	10.7	8.3	6.6	1.7	0.1	—	—	T	T	0.5	2.0	8.6
Cleveland, OH	32	35	45	58	68	78	82	80	74	63	49	38
	2.5	2.2	3.0	3.3	3.3	3.5	3.4	3.4	2.9	2.4	2.8	2.8
	12.4	11.9	10.2	2.3	0.1	—	—	—	T	0.6	5.0	11.9
Columbus, OH	35	38	49	62	73	81	84	83	77	65	51	39
	2.8	2.2	3.2	3.4	3.8	4.0	4.0	3.7	2.8	1.9	2.6	2.6
	8.2	6.2	4.5	0.9	—	T	—	—	T	—	2.3	5.6
Dallas–Fort Worth, TX	54	59	67	77	84	93	98	97	90	80	66	58
	1.6	1.9	2.4	3.6	4.3	2.6	2.0	1.8	3.3	2.5	1.8	1.7
	1.3	1.0	0.2	T	T	—	—	—	—	—	0.1	0.3
Denver, CO	43	47	51	61	71	82	88	86	78	67	52	46
	0.5	0.7	1.2	1.8	2.5	1.6	1.9	1.5	1.2	1.0	0.8	0.6
	8.0	7.4	12.6	9.1	1.7	—	T	T	1.6	3.8	8.6	7.3
Detroit, MI	31	34	43	58	69	79	83	82	74	62	48	35
	1.9	1.7	2.5	3.2	2.8	3.4	3.1	3.2	2.2	2.1	2.3	2.5
	9.9	9.1	6.6	1.6	T	—	—	—	T	0.2	3.1	10.6
El Paso, TX	58	63	60	79	87	96	95	93	88	78	66	58
	0.4	0.4	0.3	0.2	0.2	0.6	1.6	1.2	1.4	0.7	0.3	0.4
	1.3	0.9	0.4	0.4	T	—	T	—	—	—	1.0	1.7
Honolulu, HI	80	80	81	83	85	86	87	88	88	87	84	81
	3.8	2.7	3.5	1.5	1.2	0.5	0.5	0.6	0.6	1.9	3.2	3.4
	—	—	—	—	—	—	—	—	—	—	—	—
Houston, TX	62	66	72	79	85	91	94	93	89	82	72	65
	3.2	3.2	2.7	4.2	4.7	4.1	3.3	3.7	4.9	3.7	3.4	3.7
	0.2	0.2	—	—	—	T	—	—	—	—	T	—
Indianapolis, IN	34	38	49	63	73	82	85	84	78	66	51	39
	2.6	2.5	3.6	3.7	3.7	4.0	4.3	3.5	2.7	2.5	3.0	3.0
	6.1	5.7	3.4	0.5	—	—	—	T	—	0.2	1.8	4.9
Jacksonville, FL	65	67	73	80	85	89	91	90	87	80	72	66
	3.1	3.5	3.7	3.3	4.9	5.4	6.5	7.2	7.3	3.4	1.9	2.6
	T	—	—	—	—	—	T	—	—	—	—	—

(continued)

Average Monthly High Temperature, Precipitation, and Snowfall for Selected U.S. Cities*† (cont'd)

City	Jan.	Feb.	Mar.	Apr.	May	June	July	Aug.	Sept.	Oct.	Nov.	Dec.
Kansas City, MO	34	41	51	65	75	83	89	87	79	68	52	40
	1.1	1.2	2.4	3.2	4.4	4.7	4.4	3.6	4.1	3.1	1.6	1.4
	5.8	4.3	3.7	0.7	T	T	—	—	—	—	1.1	4.5
Las Vegas, NV	56	62	68	77	87	99	104	102	95	82	66	57
	0.5	0.5	0.4	0.2	0.2	0.1	0.4	0.5	0.3	0.2	0.4	0.3
	1.0	0.1	—	T	—	—	—	T	—	T	0.1	0.1
Los Angeles, CA	67	68	69	71	73	78	84	84	83	78	73	68
	3.7	3.0	2.4	1.2	0.2	—	—	0.1	0.3	0.2	1.8	2.0
	—	T	—	—	—	—	—	—	—	—	—	T
Memphis, TN	48	53	61	73	81	88	92	90	84	74	61	52
	4.6	4.3	5.4	5.8	5.1	3.6	4.0	3.7	3.6	2.4	4.2	4.8
	2.4	1.4	0.9	T	T	—	—	—	—	T	0.1	0.7
Miami, FL	75	76	79	82	85	87	89	89	88	84	80	76
	2.1	2.0	1.9	3.1	6.5	9.2	6.0	7.0	8.1	7.1	2.7	1.9
	—	—	—	—	—	—	—	—	—	—	—	—
Milwaukee, WI	26	30	39	54	65	75	80	78	71	60	45	32
	1.6	1.3	2.6	3.4	2.7	3.6	3.5	3.1	2.9	2.2	2.0	2.0
	13.0	9.7	8.6	1.7	0.1	—	T	T	T	0.2	3.0	10.6
Minneapolis– St. Paul, MN	20	26	38	56	69	78	83	81	71	60	41	27
	0.8	0.8	1.7	2.0	3.2	4.1	3.5	3.6	2.5	1.8	1.3	0.9
	9.8	8.5	10.8	2.9	0.1	T	—	T	—	0.5	7.8	9.4
New Orleans, LA	62	65	71	79	84	90	91	90	87	79	70	64
	5.0	5.2	4.7	4.5	5.1	4.6	6.7	6.0	5.9	2.7	4.1	5.3
	—	0.1	T	T	T	—	—	—	—	—	T	0.1
New York, NY	38	40	49	61	72	80	85	84	76	66	54	42
	3.2	3.1	4.2	3.8	3.8	3.2	3.8	4.0	3.7	3.4	4.1	3.8
	7.6	8.5	4.9	0.9	T	—	T	—	—	—	0.9	5.4
Oklahoma City, OK	47	52	61	72	79	88	94	93	85	74	60	51
	1.0	1.3	2.1	2.9	5.5	3.9	3.0	2.4	3.4	2.7	1.5	1.2
	3.0	2.5	1.4	—	T	—	—	—	—	T	0.5	1.8
Philadelphia, PA	39	41	50	63	73	82	86	85	78	66	54	43
	3.2	2.8	3.9	3.5	3.2	3.9	3.9	4.1	3.4	2.8	3.3	3.4
	6.6	6.4	3.6	0.3	T	—	—	—	—	—	0.7	3.5
Phoenix, AZ	65	70	74	83	92	102	105	102	98	88	74	66
	0.7	0.6	0.8	0.3	0.1	0.2	0.7	1.0	0.6	0.6	0.5	0.8
	T	—	T	T	—	—	—	—	—	—	—	—
Pittsburgh, PA	34	37	48	61	71	79	83	81	75	63	50	38
	2.9	2.4	3.6	3.3	3.5	3.3	3.8	3.3	2.8	2.5	2.3	2.6
	11.5	9.2	8.0	1.7	0.1	T	T	—	T	0.2	3.4	8.1
St. Louis, MO	38	43	53	67	76	85	89	87	81	69	54	43
	1.7	2.1	3.3	3.6	3.5	3.7	3.6	2.6	2.7	2.3	2.5	2.2
	5.3	4.4	4.3	0.4	T	T	—	—	—	T	1.4	3.9
San Antonio, TX	62	66	74	80	86	92	95	95	89	82	71	65
	1.6	1.9	1.3	2.7	3.7	3.0	1.9	2.7	3.8	2.9	2.3	1.4
	0.5	0.2	T	T	T	T	—	—	—	—	—	—
San Diego, CA	65	66	66	68	69	71	76	78	77	75	70	66
	2.1	1.4	1.6	0.8	0.2	0.1	—	0.1	0.2	0.3	1.1	1.4
	T	—	T	—	—	—	—	—	—	—	T	T
San Francisco, CA	57	61	62	63	65	68	69	70	72	70	63	57
	4.5	2.8	2.6	1.5	0.4	0.2	—	0.1	0.2	1.1	2.5	3.5
	T	T	T	—	—	—	—	—	—	—	T	T

Average Monthly High Temperature, Precipitation, and Snowfall for Selected U.S. Cities†(cont'd)

City	Jan.	Feb.	Mar.	Apr.	May	June	July	Aug.	Sept.	Oct.	Nov.	Dec.
Seattle, WA	45	50	53	58	65	69	75	74	69	60	51	47
	5.9	4.2	3.7	2.5	1.7	1.5	0.9	1.4	2.0	3.4	5.4	6.3
	3.2	0.9	0.7	—	T	—	—	—	—	T	0.7	1.9
Washington, DC	43	46	55	67	76	84	88	86	80	69	57	47
	2.8	2.6	3.5	2.9	3.5	3.4	3.9	4.4	3.2	2.9	2.8	3.2
	5.5	5.3	2.0	—	T	—	T	—	—	—	0.9	3.1

* *The first line following each city lists the average daily high temperatures (°F); the second line lists the normal precipitation—rain, snow, and melted ice (inches); the third line lists average snowfall (inches).*

† *T = trace, — = no precipitation.*

Source: U.S. Department of Commerce, National Oceanic and Atmospheric Administration, Comparative Climatic Data for the United States through 1991 (1992).

World's Highest and Lowest Temperatures

Temperature	Place	Year
Highest Temperatures on Record (in the shade)		
136°F (58°C)	el-Azizia(Al Aziziah), Libya	1922
134°F (56°C)	Death Valley, California	1913
Highest Average Temperature per Year		
95°F (35°C)	Dalol Danakil Depression, Ethiopia	—
Lowest Temperatures on Record		
–128.6°F (–89°C)	Vostok Station, Antarctica	1983
–79.8°F (–62°C)	Prospect Creek, Alaska	1971
–70°F (–57°C)	Rogers Pass, Montana	1954
Lowest Average Temperature per Year		
–71.7°F (–56.7°C)	Plateau Station, Antarctica	—

Humidity and Relative Humidity

Humidity is the amount of moisture in the air. It can be measured in various ways, but the most common is as *relative humidity*—the amount of water vapor actually present in the air, expressed as the percent of the maximum amount of water vapor that the air can hold at that temperature. Because temperature greatly affects water vapor, air that has only 30 percent relative humidity at 85°F has 100 percent relative humidity at 50°F, which means that at 50°F, dew would form on the ground or fog would form in the air.

Similar to a wind chill chart, a *heat index chart* (or comfort index) is used to determine apparent temperature—or how the temperature feels to an observer—for a certain temperature and relative humidity. For example, at 85°F and a relative humidity of 100 percent, the apparent temperature is 108°F.

Apparent Temperature Chart*

Air Temp (°F)	0	5	10	15	20	25	30	35	40	45	50	55	60	65	70	75	80	85	90	95	100
								RELATIVE HUMIDITY (%)													
140	125																				
135	120	128																			
130	117	122	131																		
125	111	116	123	131	141																
120	107	111	116	123	130	139	148														
115	103	107	111	115	120	127	135	143	151												
110	99	102	105	108	112	117	123	130	137	143	150										
105	95	97	100	102	105	109	113	118	123	129	135	142	149								
100	91	93	95	97	99	101	104	107	110	115	120	126	132	138	144						
95	87	88	90	91	93	94	96	98	101	104	107	110	114	119	124	130	136				
90	83	84	85	86	87	88	90	91	93	95	96	98	100	102	106	109	113	117	122		
85	78	79	80	81	82	83	84	85	86	87	88	89	90	91	93	95	97	99	102	105	108
80	73	74	75	76	77	77	78	79	79	80	81	81	82	83	85	86	86	87	88	89	91
75	69	69	70	71	72	72	73	73	74	74	75	75	76	76	77	77	78	78	79	79	80
70	64	64	65	65	66	66	67	67	68	68	69	69	70	70	70	70	71	71	71	71	72

*The numbers are the apparent temperature.

Barometric (Air) Pressure

The atmosphere exerts a force on everything it touches. This is called *barometric* or *air pressure* and is caused by the weight of the air around the object. As the altitude above sea level increases, the average air pressure decreases. The barometric pressure close to the Earth's surface is high because the air's molecules are being compressed by the weight of the air above; the barometric pressure is lower in the upper atmosphere because there is less air pressing on the molecules.

At sea level, the average air pressure is equal to about 14.7 pounds per square inch (1 kilogram per square centimeter), which is equal to a reading of 29.92 inches of mercury, approximately 1 atmosphere, or 1,013 millibars.

Altitude (Feet) [Meters]	Average Air Pressure (Inches of Mercury)
sea level	29.92
5,000 [1,524]	24.90
10,000 [3,048]	20.58
20,000 [6,096]	13.76
30,000 [9,144]	8.90
40,000 [12,192]	5.56
50,000 [15,240]	3.44
60,000 [18,288]	2.14

Altitude (Feet) [Meters]	Average Air Pressure (Inches of Mercury)
70,000 [21,336]	1.32
80,000 [24,384]	0.82
90,000 [27,432]	0.51
100,000 [30,480]	0.33

Weather Predictions Using the Barometer

Changes in barometric pressure create wind, and the movement of air in low- and high-pressure areas cause changing skies. Change in air pressure alone is not an infallible indicator of current weather or weather change, but along with wind direction, it can be a good short-term weather indicator. Here are several wind direction and barometer cases and possible weather indications.

Wind Direction	Barometer Reading	Weather Indications
SE to NE	30.1–30.2, falling slowly	Rain within 12–18 hours
	30.1–30.2, falling rapidly	Winds increasing; rain within 12 hours
S to SE	30.1–30.2, falling slowly	Rain within 24 hours
	30.1–30.2, falling rapidly	Winds increasing; rain within 12–24 hours
SW to NW	30.1–30.2, steady	Fair weather for 1–2 days
	30.1–30.2, rising rapidly	Fair weather; rain within 2 days
	30.2+, steady	Fair weather
	30.2+, falling slowly	Fair weather for 2 days; slowly rising temperatures

Clouds

Clouds are accumulations of water droplets or ice crystals in the atmosphere. They usually form in the troposphere, though a few, such as noctilucent clouds, are found at higher altitudes.

Clouds form when atmospheric cooling causes some of the water vapor in the air to condense into water droplets or ice crystals. If the cloud is thick and long lasting, it can produce raindrops or snowflakes large enough to overcome rising air currents; these then fall to the ground as rain or snow. Rain and clouds are usually associated with low pressure systems, in which air cools as it rises. Air sinks and warms in high pressure systems, and water droplets evaporate.

Types of clouds were named by English scientist Luke Howard in 1803. The clouds were classified by shape. For example, stratus (Latin for "layer") are horizontal clouds in layers; cirrus (Latin for "curled") are wispy, curled clouds; and cumulus (Latin for "to heap up") are lumpy clouds. There are 10 main types of clouds: cirrus, cirrostratus, altostratus, stratocumulus, cumulus, cirrocumulus, altocumulus, nimbostratus, stratus, and cumulonimbus.

High-Altitude Clouds

Noctilucent clouds are rare; they are thin, wavy, low-density clouds of unknown composition. Theories suggest that they are formed by ice on meteoric dust or fine ice crystals. These clouds occur between 45 to 54 miles (75 to 90 kilometers) in altitude. They are usually seen at dusk or dawn and are silver, blue, or orange.

High Clouds

Generally, *cirrus* (Ci) clouds are the highest clouds, forming "mares' tails" at altitudes between 20,000 to 40,000 feet (6,000 to 12,000 meters). The clouds are often seen as delicate white filaments, featherlike tufts, or fibrous bands of ice crystals.

Cirrostratus (Cs) clouds are translucent veils of white fibrous clouds that occur at about 20,000 feet (6,000 meters) or more. They often cover the entire sky and cause the appearance of halos around the Sun and Moon. They usually are indications of a storm approaching within 24 hours.

Cirrocumulus (Cc) clouds are small white cloud segments of ice crystals or water droplets at about 18,000 to 20,000 feet (5,500 to 6,000 meters). They often are referred to as "mackerel skies" because of their resemblance to fish scales. Vertical air currents cause the patchy patterns and may indicate the approach of a storm within 24 hours.

Middle Clouds

Altostratus (As) clouds are drab gray or blue, opaque clouds that give a "ground glass" view of the Moon and Sun. Altostratus clouds are generally found between 15,000 to 20,000 feet (4,500 to 6,000 meters) and usually contain water droplets; they may be a source of virga, filaments of ice crystals or water droplets that fall toward the Earth but never reach the ground.

Altocumulus (Ac) clouds resemble cirrocumulus clouds' mackerel sky, but are lower, at about 10,000 feet (3,000 meters). Small patches of the clouds are often separated by thin breaks. These clouds may form directly overhead (depending on the atmospheric temperature) and produce a shower.

Low Clouds

Stratus (St) clouds are wispy, foglike clouds that hover a few hundred feet above the ground. These clouds can obscure hills or tall buildings and may begin as ground fog. They are often a source of drizzle.

Stratocumulus (Sc) clouds are dark gray clouds that usually cover the entire sky at about 1,500 to 6,500 feet (450 to 2,000 meters). They may be rounded or wavelike, and there are often blue sky breaks between them. Stratocumulus clouds contain moisture but usually do not produce rain.

Nimbostratus (Ns) clouds are low dark rain clouds with ragged tops. The bottom of the clouds are only a few hundred feet above the ground to about 3,000 feet (900 meters) high. They are associated with continuous rain, sleet, or snow but are rarely accompanied by thunder and lightning.

Vertically Developing Clouds

Cumulus (Cu) clouds are the low-level, billowy clouds that are often dark on the bottom, with the tops resembling a giant white cotton ball. They may rise from 2,000 to 10,000 feet (600 to 3,000 meters) high. They may be a source of moisture but generally produce no more than a brief shower.

Cumulonimbus (Cb) clouds are called thunderheads. They vary in altitude, from dark lower portions below 5,000 feet (1,500 meters) to white, anvil-shaped tops that can reach up to 50,000 feet (15,250 meters). They contain large amounts of moisture and often include hail. Cumulonimbus clouds may appear as single clouds or as part of a wall of an advancing storm cloud.

Common Clouds

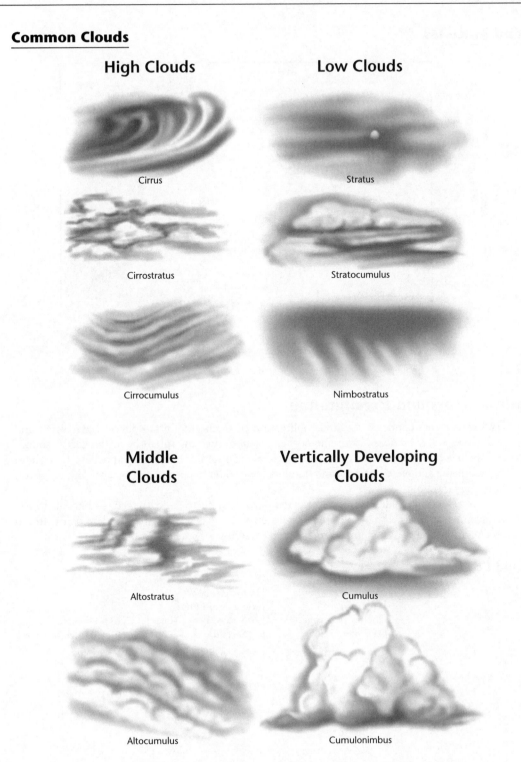

High Clouds

Cirrus

Cirrostratus

Cirrocumulus

Low Clouds

Stratus

Stratocumulus

Nimbostratus

Middle Clouds

Altostratus

Altocumulus

Vertically Developing Clouds

Cumulus

Cumulonimbus

Cloud Altitudes

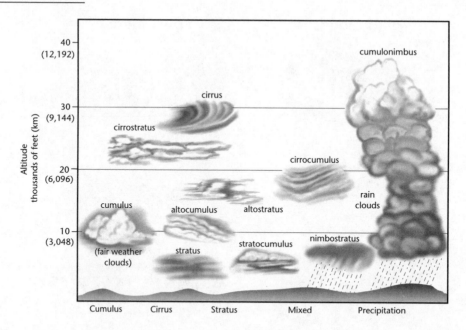

Hydrometeors and Precipitation

Hydrometeors are condensation and sublimation products from atmospheric water vapor and windblown water particles. Hydrometeors can form in the atmosphere or at the Earth's surface and include haze, fog, drizzle, rain, freezing drizzle and rain, ice crystals and pellets, hail, snow, virga, drifting and blowing snow, and liquid or solid water deposited on objects (dew, hoarfrost, rime, or glaze).

Precipitation includes all forms of water—from liquid to solid (frozen)—that fall to the surface of the Earth. Precipitation forms when water vapor cools to the dew point; frozen precipitation occurs if the temperature is below freezing, or at the frost point.

Liquid Precipitation

Type	Intensity (Inches [Centimeters] per Hour)	Drop Density (Number of Drops per Square Foot [Meter] per Second)		Drop Diameter (Inches) [Millimeters]
Fog	0.005 [0.013]	6,264,000	[581,925]	0.00039 [0.01]
Mist	0.002 [0.005]	2,510	[233]	0.0039 [0.10]
Drizzle*	0.01 [0.03]	14	[1.30]	0.0378 [0.96]
Light rain	0.04 [0.10]	26	[2.41]	0.0488 [1.24]

Type	Intensity (Inches [Centimeters] per Hour)	Drop Density (Number of Drops per Square Foot [Meter] per Second)	Drop Diameter (Inches) [Millimeters]
Moderate rain	0.15 [0.38]	46 [4.27]	0.0630 [1.60]
Heavy rain	0.60 [1.52]	46 [4.27]	0.0807 [2.05]
Excessive rain	1.60 [4.06]	76 [7.06]	0.0945 [2.40]
Cloudburst	4.00 [10.16]	113 [10.5]	0.1122 [2.85]

Drizzle is further broken down into light drizzle (visibility more than 5/8 mile), moderate drizzle (visibility from 5/16 to 5/8 mile), and heavy drizzle (visibility less than 5/16 mile).

High and Low Precipitation Records

Place	Precipitation (Inches) [Centimeters]	Remarks
GREATEST PRECIPITATION		
Tutunendo, Colombia	463.4 [1,177]	Average per year, wettest spot known on Earth
Mount Waialeale, Hawaii	460 [1,168]	Average per year, rainiest spot known on Earth (about 350 rain days per year)
Barst, Guadeloupe	1.5 [3.8]	Most rain in 1 minute, November 26, 1970
Unionville, Maryland	1.23 [3.12]	Most rain in 1 minute in the United States, July 4, 1956
Réunion Island	74 [188]	Most rain in 24 hours, March 15 to 16, 1952
Alvin, Texas	19 [48.3]	Most rain in 24 hours in the United States, July 25 to 26, 1979
Cherrapunji, India	1,042 [2,647]	Most rain in 1 year, August 1860 to August 1861
Kukui, Hawaii	739 [1,877]	Most rain in 1 year in the United States, December 1981 to December 1982
LEAST PRECIPITATION		
Arica, Chili	0 [0]	No rain for 14 years, October 1903 to January 1918
Bagdad, California	0 [0]	No rain for 767 days, October 3, 1912 to November 8, 1914
Death Valley, California	1.2 [3]	Average per year, driest spot in the United States
Atacama Desert, Chile	—	Average per year is too small to measure, driest spot in the world

Highest Normal Annual Precipitation in the United States

Place	Precipitation per Year (Inches) [Centimeters]
Mount Waialeale, Hawaii	460.00 [1,168]
Yakutat, Alaska	134.96 [342.8]
Hilo, Hawaii	128.15 [325.5]
Annette, Alaska	115.47 [293.3]
Quillayute, Washington	104.50 [265.4]
Kodiak, Alaska	74.24 [188.6]
Astoria, Oregon	69.60 [176.8]
Blue Canyon, California	67.87 [172.4]
Mobile, Alabama	64.64 [164.2]
Tallahassee, Florida	64.59 [164.1]
Pensacola, Florida	61.16 [155.3]

HOW HAIL FORMS

Hail, most often associated with violent thunderstorms during warm weather, is thought to form as a frozen raindrop high in the thundercloud. As it gets heavier, it drops through the cloud, but strong updrafts carry it back to the cooler upper regions of the cloud. As the ice moves up and down in the upper cloud, it gathers supercooled drops, growing in size—often by layers, or by a glaze formed by the supercooled drops. When the chunk of ice is too large to be held by the updraft or when the updraft weakens, the ice falls in the form of a hailstone. Another theory is that a frozen pellet forms at the top of the cloud; as it descends for some 20 minutes, it gathers layer upon layer of ice and eventually falls as hail.

Either way, some of the smallest hailstones measure no more than 0.2 inch (approximately 0.5 centimeter); the largest are about the size of a grapefruit. They can fall as round balls or as cones, disks, stars, or even as doughnut shapes. One place in the United States, called Hail Alley, around the borders of Nebraska, Wyoming, and Colorado, has an average of 10 hail storms per year—more than anyplace else in North America.

Freezing Water

Frozen water comes in many forms.

Frost is the result of sublimation of water vapor in saturated air. It exists when the temperature at the Earth's surface is below freezing. A "killing frost" refers to a heavy frost that ends the region's growing season. (The white frost seen on indoor surfaces of window panes is caused by low relative humidity of the indoor air; otherwise the water droplets would condense first, then freeze into clear ice.)

Glaze is a clear, smooth coating of ice, similar to rime ice, but much harder and denser. It may be what coats ice particles to form hail. Glaze (and rime ice) are often reported in aircraft icing. Glaze forms when supercooled water strikes an object at temperatures below freezing.

Hail is precipitation in the form of balls or lumps of ice. It is nearly always produced in cumulonimbus clouds and is mainly associated with thunderstorms (see also "How Hail Forms," above).

Hoarfrost (or "white frost") is a deposit of ice crystals that form directly on objects by sublimation. It forms much like dew, except the object that becomes frosted has a temperature below freezing. Hoarfrost frequently forms on exposed objects and inside unheated structures.

Rime is a white, milky granular deposit of ice, similar to hoarfrost, but much harder. Rime ice (and glaze) is often reported in aircraft icing. Rime forms when supercooled water strikes an object at temperatures below freezing.

Sleet (ice pellet) is a type of precipitation made up of transparent or translucent ice pellets. The ice pellets have a diameter of about 0.2 inches (5 millimeters) or less and create a coating of ice on surfaces during a sleet storm.

DEFINITIONS OF MAJOR STORMS

Comparisons of Storms

Type	Wind Speeds	Width	Duration	Energy*
Cyclone	0–50 miles/hour	500–1,000 miles	Week or more	10^{14}
Hurricane	74–200 miles/hour	300–600 miles	Week	10^{15}
Tornado	200–250 miles/hour	$1/8$ mile	Few minutes	10^{10}
Thunderstorm	20–30 miles/hour	1–2 miles	Hour or less	10^{9}

Energy is based on wind velocity, in joules, e.g., a cyclone has a wind velocity of 10^{14} joules, about the same energy as that released from an atomic bomb.

Rainstorms

Rainstorms are local storms resulting from atmospheric disturbances associated with vertical air motion. If an air mass rises rapidly, it may cause condensation in the form of water droplets. As the updraft suspends the water droplets, they coalesce into larger drops. If there is enough water vapor available, the drops will become heavy enough to fall, and a rainstorm will result. A heavy, fast rain is often called a *cloudburst*; such rains often result in a flash flood, as the ground is not able to absorb such a great amount of water in a short time.

RAINBOWS AND HALOS

Rainbows are formed from the refraction of light by raindrops, mainly when the Sun comes out immediately after a rainstorm. Rainbows are brightest when light is refracted by small drops that measure between $1/50$ and $1/25$ inch in diameter. The rainbow is seen either as a bow or as segments of arcs. In the latter case, no rain is falling in the blank areas or there are obstructions, such as hills or clouds, to the sunlight.

In reality, a rainbow is a perfect circle (since it is only the refraction of the Sun's rays), but we only see the top of the circle because of the position of the Sun or because of where we are standing (the horizon cuts the other half from our sight). In an airplane, it is possible to see a complete, circular rainbow (called a glory) if the Sun is high behind the aircraft.

There are other visual phenomena caused by moisture in the air, most of which are caused by reflection or refraction by ice crystals high in the sky. These include the following.

A *lunar or solar halo* is a 22° circle (halo) (a 22° angular radius from the Moon or Sun) that forms around the Moon and Sun, respectively, from the refraction of the body's light on ice crystals in high cirrostratus clouds. The larger and rarer 46° halo can occur in conjunction with the smaller halo.

Parhelia (sundogs or mock suns) are partial halos or bright spots that form about 22° on either side of the Sun from the light reflecting off ice crystals in cirrostratus clouds.

Sun pillars are tall streaks of light rising from the Sun—usually at sunrise or sunset—from the reflection of sunlight off ice crystals in high clouds. A double sun may really be an incomplete sun pillar.

How a Rainbow Forms

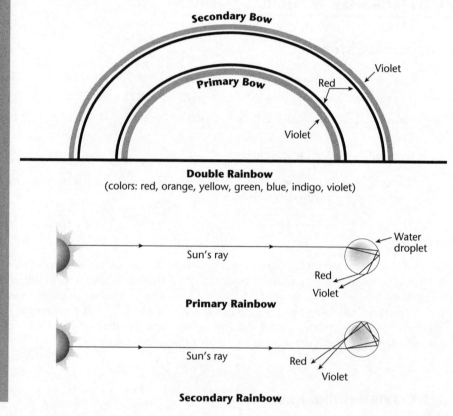

Double Rainbow
(colors: red, orange, yellow, green, blue, indigo, violet)

Primary Rainbow

Secondary Rainbow

Snowstorms

Snowstorms are localized storms and, like rainstorms, result from atmospheric disturbances associated with vertical air motion. Snow consists of clear or cloudy ice particles in the form of ice plates, needles, or columns. Snow particles can cluster until they reach several inches in diameter.

Temperature and Ice Crystal Shapes

32°F to 25°F
Thin Plates

25°F to 21°F
Needles

21°F to 14°F
Hollow columns

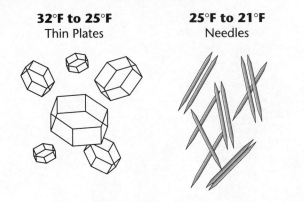
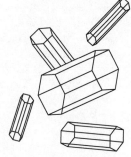

14°F to 10°F
Sector plates

10°F to 3°F
Dendrites

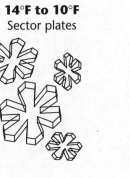

3°F to -8°F
Sector plates

Below -8°F
Hollow columns

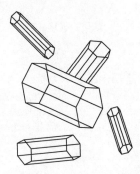

U.S. Greatest Annual Snowfalls

Location	Amount per Year (Inches) [Centimeters]
Blue Canyon, California	240.8 [611.6]
Marquette, Michigan	126.0 [320.0]
Sault St. Marie, Michigan	116.4 [295.7]
Caribou, Maine	111.5 [283.2]
Syracuse, New York	110.5 [280.7]
Mount Shasta, California	104.9 [266.4]
Lander, Wyoming	103.9 [263.9]
Muskegon, Michigan	98.4 [249.9]
Sexton Summit, Oregon	97.8 [248.4]
Flagstaff, Arizona	96.4 [244.9]

Thunderstorms

Thunderstorms are localized rainstorms characterized by thunder and lightning and, occasionally, hail. Thunderstorm cells form along strong frontal cyclonic disturbances usually in the spring and summer months (though rare, they can occur in winter). They also form from convection over heated land, usually in the hot summer months. One mature thunderstorm cell can cover a 5- to 10-square mile (8- to 16-square kilometer) area.

First, warm humid air (called an updraft) rises from the ground. Air cools to its dew point, and a cloud begins to form from condensation. As water vapor in the upper portions of the cloud becomes supercooled, raindrops begin to form and fall (if it is below freezing, the raindrops can develop into hail), dragging down the air and producing downdrafts. Updrafts continue to feed warm humid air into the maturing storm cloud, while downdrafts also continue—all adding to the storm. Soon, downdrafts choke off the updrafts and spread out over the ground, which are felt as cool winds just before the rain begins to fall. With the warm air of the updrafts cut off, the storm begins to dissipate.

More intense downward blasts of wind from thunderstorms are called downbursts or microbursts (also see "Wind Shear and Microbursts," earlier in this chapter). A microburst forms when the air below a thunderstorm is dry; as the falling rain evaporates in the dry air, the air cools and plunges toward the ground. Wet downbursts form when dry air entering an upper thunderstorm cloud causes the rain to evaporate, cooling the air and causing it to plunge to the surface. Both may or may not be noticed on the ground. Winds on the Fujita scale up to F-3 are often found in downbursts (for more information on the Fujita scale, see "Tornadoes," later in this chapter).

Lightning and Thunder

The explosive release of electrical energy in a thunderstorm cloud causes a *lightning* bolt and a resulting *thunder* clap. Initially, a cloud builds up an electrical potential (or charge) of about 300,000 volts per foot (1 million volts per meter) by the rise and fall of air currents. The electrical charge is transferred through the cloud as raindrops, hailstones, and ice pellets collide with smaller water droplets and ice. A falling stream of electrons create a negative charge, which accumulates in the lower part of the cloud; the rising electrons create a positive charge, which accumulates in the upper part of the cloud. Lightning is the reaction that neutralizes these charges.

The positive and negative charges in the clouds seek the best conducting route to the ground, such as tall buildings, trees, and lightning rods (cloud-to-ground lightning), or opposite-charged clouds (cloud-to-cloud lightning). A typical lightning bolt travels along an air channel that is only 0.5 to 2 inches (1 to 5 centimeters) in diameter. It can generate as much as a few hundred megawatts of power, or as much energy as a medium-size nuclear reactor.

Thunder is caused by the heating of air around a lightning bolt to around 54,000°F (30,000°C). This sudden expansion of the air (moving at supersonic speeds under a force 10 to 100 times the normal atmospheric pressure) forms compression (shock) waves that travel out from different parts of the lightning bolt at speeds close to 1,080 feet (330 meters) per second. Thunder appears to rumble because of the varying distances between the observer and portions of the lightning bolt (though a lightning bolt appears to be a single flash, it is actually a combination of bolts strung together). To determine the approximate distance to a lightning strike, multiply the number of seconds between the flash and thunder by 360 (the result is in yards) or divide the number of seconds by 5 (the result is in miles).

At any one time, it is estimated that there are between 1,500 and 2,000 thunderstorms occurring on the Earth, which trigger 6,000 or more lightning flashes per minute. Lightning also occurs around atmospheric storms on other members of our solar system, including Jupiter and perhaps Venus.

Hurricanes

Most storms in the tropics die out before they can develop into the large swirling storms called *hurricanes*. A hurricane starts as a tropical storm (or tropical cyclone), a low-pressure weather system, in which the central core of the storm is warmer than the surrounding atmosphere. *Tropical depressions* sustain winds near the surface of less than 39 miles (63 kilometers) per hour. A *tropical storm* has more intense winds, reaching from 39 to 74 miles (63 to 119 kilometers) per hour. A tropical storm becomes a hurricane when its wind speed exceeds 74 miles (119 kilometers) per hour in any part of the weather system.

These major storms are called hurricanes in the Atlantic Ocean and the eastern Pacific Ocean, *typhoons* in Southeast Asia (the Pacific Ocean west of the International Date Line), *cyclones* in the Indian Ocean, and *willy-willys* off the coast of Australia. All hurricanes have high-speed, rotating winds, range in size from 300 to 600 miles (483 to 965 kilometers) in diameter, have wind speeds of 74 to 200 miles (119 to 322 kilometers) per hour, and move at an average rate between 5 and 15 miles (8 and 24 kilometers) per hour.

Hurricanes form over tropical ocean regions—usually between 5 and 20° northern latitudes in the hemisphere's late summer—when the Sun heats up huge masses of moist air. An ascending spiral motion results and when the moisture of the rising air condenses, the latent heat (when water changes phase, it emits or absorbs heat) provides more energy. As the air rises in the column, it gains more strength and energy. The winds and clouds increase, creating a low pressure area called the eye, which may be 20 to 30 miles (32 to 48 kilometers) wide. The air pressure in the eye may be 6 to 7 percent lower than the rest of the system.

As the hurricane system forms, it travels in the direction of prevailing trade winds. As the system moves, it is eventually affected by the Coriolis effect: Thus many of the hurricanes that hit the United States follow a northwest path—from the Caribbean to the Gulf of Mexico or to the southeastern coastline. A hurricane rarely affects the inland United States for very long periods, because the storm must be over water to sustain its energy and moisture.

A hurricane's destructiveness is caused mainly by its winds, which tear apart structures and produce huge waves along the coasts; slow- or fast-moving hurricane rains can also cause major flooding. Tornadoes are often spawned by hurricanes as well.

Forming Tropical Storms Around the World

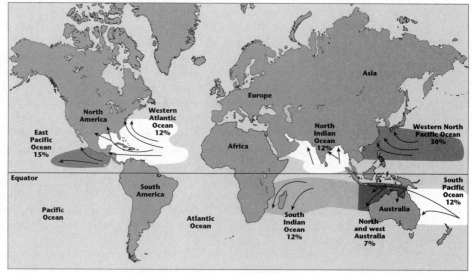

Average percentage of storms by region

Major Hurricanes Since 1950

Name	Date	Location
Carol	August 30, 1954	Northeast United States
Hazel	October 5–18, 1954	Haiti, east United States
Connie	August 12–13, 1955	Carolinas, Virginia, Maryland
Diane	August 7–21, 1955	East United States
Hilda	September 19, 1955	Mexico
Janet	September 22–28, 1955	Caribbean
Audrey	June 25–30, 1957	Texas to Alabama
Donna	September 4–12, 1960	Caribbean, east United States
Carla	September 11–14, 1961	Texas
Hattie	October 31, 1961	Honduras
Flora	October 4–8, 1963	Caribbean
Hilda	October 4–7, 1964	Georgia, Mississippi, Louisiana
Betsy	September 7–12, 1965	Florida, Mississippi, Georgia
Alma	June 4–10, 1966	Honduras, southeast United States
Inez	September 24–30, 1966	Caribbean, Florida, Mexico
Beulah	September 5–23, 1967	Caribbean, Texas, Mexico
Camille	August 17–18, 1969	Mississippi, Louisiana
Celia	July 30–August 5, 1970	Cuba, Florida, Texas
Dorothy	August 20–21, 1970	Martinique
Agnes	June 19–29, 1972	Florida to New York
Fifi	September 19–20, 1974	Honduras
Eloise	September 13–27, 1975	Caribbean, northeast United States
David	August 30–September 7, 1979	Caribbean, eastern United States
Allen	August 4–11, 1980	Caribbean, Texas
Alicia	August 18, 1983	South Texas

Name	Date	Location
Juan	October 26–November 6, 1985	Southeast United States
Gilbert	September 10–17, 1988	Caribbean, Gulf of Mexico
Hugo	September 16–22, 1989	Caribbean, southeast United States
Andrew	August 24–26, 1992	South Florida, Louisiana

HOW ARE HURRICANES NAMED?

For hundreds of years, hurricanes in the West Indies were named after the particular saint's day on which the hurricane occurred. (The term *hurricane* is from Huracán, the West Indian god of storms.) The first person to record names of Australian hurricanes was Clement L. Wragge, a nineteenth-century Australian weatherman, who used biblical names such as Sacar and Talmon. Hurricanes were named after women by the Army Meteorological Service during World War II (after their wives and girlfriends back home); and by 1953, the National Weather Service began the same practice of naming hurricanes after women, using names that began with successive letters of the alphabet as the storms formed.

In 1978 to 1979, the method of naming hurricanes changed so that alternating female and male names are now used; lists are available each year for the Atlantic and Pacific Oceans. The lists are recycled—usually every five years; names are retired if the storm causes a great deal of devastation and damage. Names beginning with the letters Q, U, X, Y, and Z are not used, because there so few names available.

Six-Year Cycle for Names of Atlantic Ocean, Caribbean Sea, or Gulf of Mexico Hurricanes

1992	1993	1994	1995	1996	1997
Andrew	Arlene	Alberto	Allison	Arthur	Ana
Bonnie	Bret	Beryl	Barry	Bertha	Not decided
Charley	Cindy	Chris	Chantal	Cesar	Claudette
Danielle	Dennis	Debby	Dean	Diana	Danny
Earl	Emily	Ernesto	Erin	Edouard	Erika
Frances	Floyd	Florence	Felix	Fran	Fabian
Georges	Gert	Gordon	Gabrielle	Gustav	Grace
Hermine	Harvey	Helene	Humberto	Hortense	Henri
Ivan	Irene	Isaac	Iris	Isidore	Isabel
Jeanne	Jose	Joyce	Jerry	Josephine	Juan
Karl	Katrina	Keith	Karen	Klaus	Kata
Lisa	Lenny	Leslie	Luis	Lili	Larry
Mitch	Maria	Michael	Marilyn	Marco	Mindy
Nicole	Nate	Nadine	Noel	Nana	Nicholas
Otto	Ophelia	Oscar	Opal	Omar	Odette
Paula	Philippe	Patty	Pablo	Paloma	Peter
Richard	Rita	Rafael	Roxanne	Rene	Rose
Shary	Stan	Sandy	Sebastien	Sally	Sam
Thomas	Tammy	Tony	Tanya	Teddy	Teresa
Virginie	Vince	Valerie	Van	Vicky	Victor
Walter	Wilma	William	Wendy	Wilfred	Wanda

Saffir-Simpson Hurricane Damage Potential Scale

Scale Number	Central Pressure (Inches) [Millibars of Mercury]	Winds (Miles) [Kilometers per Hour]	Damage
1 (minimal)	>28.94 [>980]	74–95 [119–153]	Shrubs, trees, mobile homes damaged; low-lying roads inundated
2 (moderate)	28.5–28.91 [965–979]	96–110 [154–177]	Some roofs damaged; some trees blown down; evacuation of shorelines required
3 (extensive)	27.91–28.47 [945–964]	111–130 [178–209]	Mobile homes destroyed; large trees blown down; flooding on coast
4 (extreme)	27.17–27.88 [920–944]	131–155 [210–249]	Complete destruction of mobile homes; trees blown down; major erosion of shore; evacuation within 2 miles of shore required
5 (catastrophic)	<27.17 [<920]	>155 [>249]	Severe and extensive damage to all buildings; major evacuation from all areas many miles from shore required

Tornadoes

Though a *tornado* has less energy than most storms, the concentration of its energy makes it the most violent of storms. Tornadoes, commonly called twisters, are swirling, funnel-shaped clouds that hang from a dark cloud mass, usually in the presence of a severe thunderstorm's mature cumulonimbus cloud. Tornadoes usually darken after striking the ground, as the funnel cloud picks up dust and other debris. Tornadoes usually travel from southwest to northeast and average 5 to 10 minutes on the ground. They generally cut a path of about 1/8 to 1 mile (.2 to 1.6 km) wide and 2 to 5 miles (3.2 to 8 km) long. Smaller tornadoes often bounce across an area and cause damage only where they contact the ground.

Most tornadoes occur in the United States and Australia and peak at certain seasons. In the United States, tornadoes peak in the southern states in winter and spring and in the northern states in spring and summer. In the United States, the area from the Texas panhandle to the Dakotas is referred to as Tornado Alley. The fastest winds ever recorded occurred during a tornado: 440 feet (134 meters) per second.

Tornadoes that occur over the water are called *waterspouts*. The cloud of the waterspout forms from the condensation of water vapor when winds of differing temperatures meet in the upper atmosphere.

Approximately 25 percent of all tornadoes occur between 4 and 6 P.M., and about 80 percent occur between noon and midnight. When a tornado strikes, it can cause the air pressure to drop as much as 10 percent in a few seconds. It is this sudden drop in pressure that causes houses and other structures literally to explode.

The reason why tornadoes form is not fully understood. In the United States, many tornadoes form when the humid air moving north from the Gulf of Mexico meets cold, dry air streaming westward from the Rocky Mountains. The spin of a tornado is thought to be from the Coriolis effect caused by the Earth's rotation.

Fujita and Pearson Wind Damage Scale

The Fujita and Pearson wind damage scale (or Fujita and Pearson tornado scale) was developed by T. Theodore Fujita and Allen Pearson to determine the damage caused by wind—especially tornado winds.

Scale Number (Tornado Ranking)	Wind Speed (Miles) [Kilometers per Hour]	Damage
F-0	up to 72 [116]	Light
F-1	73 to 112 [117 to 180]	Moderate
F-2	113 to 157 [182 to 253]	Considerable
F-3	158 to 206 [254 to 331]	Severe
F-4	207 to 260 [333 to 418]	Devastating
F-5	261 to 318 [420 to 512]	Incredible
F-6	319 to 380 [513 to 611]	Not expected

When and Where? Tornadoes in the United States

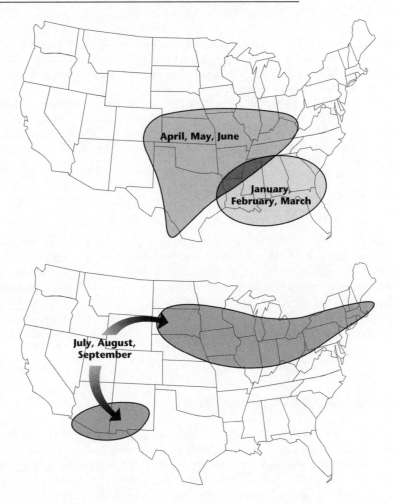

WEATHER FORECASTING

Weather forecasting today is based on a combination of data (especially images) from radar and satellite, up-to-the-minute reports from observation points around the country, and computer projections. Predictions are based on computer models that use data from previous storm systems to predict events.

WEATHER FROM SPACE

Ways of predicting the weather, though primitive, have been around for centuries. By the late 1800s, the United States formed the Weather Bureau, which changed its name to the National Weather Service in the 1970s. Today, most weather information is gathered from space via satellites. Cloud images seen on television and in the newspaper are taken by satellites and transmitted to weather bureau stations.

The United States has two geostationary satellites (meaning that the satellite's speed matches the Earth's rotation, so the craft is always over the same point on the Earth's surface) that travel in an east-west orbit. The satellites image clouds and measure cloud heights for use in three-dimensional weather models. In 1989, one of the weather satellites—Geostationary Operational Environmental Satellite (GOES)—failed, leaving only one satellite above the United States. The replacement satellite, GOES-8, was launched in April 1994 and is now providing the additional detailed weather images of the entire United States.

Lower-orbiting polar satellites, especially the U.S. National Oceanographic and Atmospheric Association (NOAA) satellites, are sun-synchronous (always passing over the same spot at the same time every day). They are used to detect small differences in the Earth's radiation, thus giving meteorologists information on upper air temperatures for computer forecasting models—a definite advantage over using less reliable weather balloons.

Storm Watches and Warnings

Storm watches and warnings are issued for long- and short-term weather-related events, including hurricanes, floods, blizzards, and tornadoes. For example, a hurricane "watch" means that there is a possibility that a hurricane could threaten an area within 24 to 36 hours; a hurricane "warning" means that hurricane conditions are expected within 24 hours or less and appropriate precautionary actions should be taken.

For sudden weather phenomena such as tornadoes, a tornado "watch" means that conditions are right for a tornado to form; a tornado "warning" means that a tornado has been sighted or has appeared on radar in the area.

RADAR WATCHES THE WEATHER

Radar has been used since World War II to locate and track storms all over the world. Radar (an acronym for radio detection and ranging) antennas send out radio wave pulses toward the clouds. All types of precipitation and even boundaries created by air temperature differences reflect some of the waves back to the antennas. The received radio wave data are plotted on maps, which are used to create many of the weather maps we see on television and in newspapers.

The latest weather radar techniques use the Doppler effect—a phenomenon discovered by Austrian scientist Christian Doppler in 1842, who noted that the frequency of sound waves from an approaching source is shifted to a higher frequency and that those from a receding source shifted to a lower frequency. The same principle is applied to Doppler radar—radar that gathers radio wave frequency to "read" weather events.

Doppler radar can determine precipitation moving toward a weather station, from the increase in the radio wave frequency reflected from the clouds. The radar detects any frequency changes in the speed of the clouds and uses the data to show wind patterns. For example, if the precipitation is being blown away from the antenna, the frequency of the radio waves decreases. Doppler radar is also used to predict tornadoes: The changeable winds around a storm could indicate the internal circulation in a storm that could lead to a twister.

MAJOR METEOROLOGISTS

Abbe, Cleveland (1838–1916)   American meteorologist who was the first to send out weather bulletins from the Cincinnati observatory in 1869. He later became scientific assistant in the first U.S. weather bureau (which was part of the U.S. Army) and eventually head of the bureau after it separated from the army.

Anaximander (c. 610–546 B.C.)   Greek philosopher and astronomer who believed that the wind was a natural phenomena, not a divine one, and that air is the basic principle of the universe.

Appleton, Sir Edward Victor (1892–1965)   British physicist who discovered the layer of the atmosphere, called the ionosphere, that is responsible for reflecting radio waves. The Appleton layer, or F-layer, of the atmosphere is named after him.

Aratus (c 270 B.C.)   Greek poet, who, around 270 B.C., wrote down (in verse) thoughts on weather prediction, including a version of "Red sky in the morning, sailor take warning; red sky at night, sailor's delight."

Aristotle (384 –322 B.C.)   Greek philosopher and scientist who began the science of meteorology. Around 340 B.C., he published *Meteorologica*. The book was mostly wrong, but it summarized early ideas on meteorology and astronomy. He believed that everything in the universe was composed of four "basic elements"—earth, water, air, and fire.

Bergeron, Tor Harold Percival (1891–1977)   Swedish meteorologist and cloud physicist who demonstrated that raindrops can form in the upper parts of clouds where there is little water, through the growth of ice crystals. This is called the Bergeron process.

Bjerknes, Jakob Aall Bonnevie (1897–1975)   Norwegian meteorologist and son of Vilhelm who discovered that depressions form, develop, and decay along polar fronts. He also found large-scale atmospheric waves in the high westerly flow of the middle latitudes.

Bjerknes, Vilhelm Friman Koren (1862–1951)   Norwegian meteorologist who explored the science of dynamical meteorology, worked on the origin and characteristics of depressions, and developed methods of weather forecasting.

Brückner, Edouard (1862–1927)   German geographer and climatologist who studied the Alps' Pleistocene glaciation, and climatic fluctuations. He postulated that there was a 35-year period when the weather turned from damp and cold to dry and warm.

Buys Ballot, Christoph Hendrik Diederik (1817–1890)   Dutch meteorologist who formulated the law for determining areas of low pressure based on observing the wind's direction.

Coriolis, Gustave-Gaspard (1792–1843)   French physicist who, in 1835, first described the curving deflection of winds caused by the Earth's rotation, now called the Coriolis effect.

Dampier, William (1652–1715)   English explorer and buccaneer, who first described the inner workings of a tropical storm in a treatise titled *Discourse of Trade-Winds*. He also was an expert in hydrology, pilotage, and winds, producing numerous navigator maps and charts.

Descartes, René du Perron (1596–1650)   French philosopher, scientist, and mathematician who, along with important discoveries in other fields of science, explained the phenomenon of rainbow formation.

Espy, James Pollard (1785–1860)   American meteorologist who put together the first annual weather reports in 1843 and was a pioneer in weather forecasting.

Ferrel, William (1817–1891)   American meteorologist who determined the law of atmospheric circulation, where winds are deflected to the right in the Northern Hemisphere and to the left in the Southern Hemisphere.

Fitzroy, Robert (1805–1865)   British naval officer, hydrographer, and meteorologist, who commanded the HMS *Beagle* (the same ship that carried Charles Darwin). Fitzroy specialized in weather forecasting.

Galton, Francis Sir (1822–1911)   British anthropologist and explorer who introduced the modern symbols for mapping the weather.

Hadley, George (1685–1768)   English lawyer and climatologist who discovered that the additional heat from the Sun in the equatorial regions was responsible for global wind patterns.

Howard, Luke (1772–1864)   English amateur meteorologist who was the first to publish a classification system for clouds. His three primary classifications are still used, though 10 major cloud types are described in modern meteorology.

Köppen, Wladimir Peter (1846–1940)   Russian-born German climatologist and biologist who classified climatic types by annual temperature and precipitation and by relating them to the Earth's vegetation regions.

Piccard, Auguste (1884–1962)   Swiss-born Belgian physicist who explored the upper stratosphere in an air balloon of his own design. In 1932, he launched a new cabin design for balloons to protect himself from the thin, cold upper atmosphere; he was the first human to enter the stratosphere, reaching an altitude of about 53,153 feet (16,201 meters). He also developed the deep decent bathyscaphe in 1948.

Pliny the Elder (Gaius Plinius Secundus) (23–79)   Roman naturalist who believed that steady winds fall from the stars, or are created by the impact of the stars and the Earth as they travel in opposite directions.

Redfield, William C. (1789–1857)   American amateur meteorologist who studied hurricanes and was first to discover that the winds within the storms moved in a counterclockwise direction.

Rossby, Carl-Gustaf Arvid (1898–1957)   Swedish-born American meteorologist who discovered upper level air waves (called Rossby waves) and characteristics of air masses.

Teisserenc De Bort, Léon Philippe (1855–1913)   French meteorologist who was the first to use unmanned balloons with instruments to measure the atmosphere; through his balloon experiments, he discovered the stratosphere.

Thornthwaite, Charles Warren (1889–1963)   American climatologist who classified climatic types by the moisture they contain. He developed the idea of the global water balance.

Torricelli, Evangelista (1608–1647)   Italian mathematician and physicist who is considered the father of hydrodynamics. He proposed an experiment (which was later performed by his colleague Vincenzo Viviani) that demonstrated that atmospheric pressure determines the height a fluid will rise in a tube when it is inverted over a saucer of the same liquid. This idea led to the development of the barometer. (He was also secretary to Galileo Galilei.)

SIGNIFICANT SCIENTIFIC DISCOVERIES IN METEOROLOGY

B.C.	570	Greek philosopher Anaximenes of Miletus, suggested that air was primary substance, and that it changed to create wind, clouds, and rain
	140	Han Ying text contained the first known reference to the hexagonal nature of snowflakes
A.D.	100	Hero of Alexandria described experiments with air, including expanding air by heating it
	1304	Theodoric of Freibourg, investigated the rainbow, correctly concluding that water is responsible
	1586	Simon Stevinus demonstrated that the pressure of a liquid on a given surface depends on the height of the liquid and the area of the surface
	1644	Evangelista Torricelli and Vincenzo Viviani constructed the first barometer using mercury
	1654	The grand duke of Tuscany, Ferdinand II, invented the first sealed thermometer
	1662	Robert Boyle showed that air pressure was not constant but changed with elevation
	1663	Robert Hooke determined that the height in a column of mercury would change before a storm, thus pointing the way toward using the barometer in meteorology
	1709	Gabriel Daniel Fahrenheit constructed the first alcohol thermometer
	1714	Fahrenheit built a mercury thermometer with a scale that now bears his name
	1735	George Hadley described what is now called the Hadley cell, which models part of the Earth's wind circulation
	1823	John Frederic Daniell presented the first comprehensive study of the atmosphere and trade winds
	1853	James Coffin discovered three distinct wind zones in the Northern Hemisphere
	1863	Francis Galton coined the term *anticyclone* and founded modern methods of mapping the weather
	1869	Cleveland Abbe sent out the first weather bulletins from the Cincinnati observatory where he worked
	1902	Teisserenc de Bort was the first to discover that the Earth's atmosphere has at least two layers—the troposphere and stratosphere
	1904	Vilhelm Bjerknes wrote the first scientific studies of weather forecasting
	1913	Charles Fabry discovered the ozonosphere
	1921	Vilhelm Bjerknes discovered that the atmosphere was made up of sharply different air masses
	1927	Rudolf Geiger founded the study of microclimatology

1931	Auguste and Jean Felix Piccard were the first to ride a balloon to an altitude of 11 miles, with a sealed gondola to protect themselves from the cold and thinness of the upper atmosphere
1932	Carl-Gustav Rossby first to diagram air mass properties
1946	Vincent Schaefer discovered that carbon dioxide caused supercooled water to turn to snow; he also seeded clouds with dry ice, causing the first artificial snowstorm
1959	The U.S. Weather Bureau began the temperature-humidity index as a way of determining the comfort or discomfort of a hot day to humans
1960	The United States launched the first weather satellite, the Television Infrared Observing Satellite 1 (TIROS 1)
1976	The first Geostationary Operational Environmental Satellite (GOES) was launched
1984	Satellites launched by the National Oceanic and Atmospheric Administration (NOAA) started to measure new parameters in the atmosphere to determine weather and climate phenomena for meteorological models
1989	Doppler radar used for weather forecasting
1992	Ice cores from Greenland showed that during the last Ice Age, the climate changed dramatically over short periods—as short as 1 or 2 years

COMMON TERMS IN METEOROLOGY

absolute humidity   The mass of water vapor in a given amount of the air.

adiabatic process   The process by which the temperature of the air changes without adding or taking away heat.

advection fog   Fog that forms when warmer humid air flows over cooler ground or water.

air mass   A body of air in the lower atmosphere, which is more or less at a constant temperature and moisture content, and is often bounded by cold and warm fronts.

air pressure   Measured with a barometer, the force per unit area that the air exerts on any surface; it results from the collision of air molecules.

air   The general term for the gases that make up the atmosphere.

anabatic wind   A localized wind that is warmed by sunshine, rises, and blows up a slope (see *katabatic wind*).

anticyclone   A high-pressure area with closed circulation, which rotates clockwise in the Northern Hemisphere and counterclockwise in the Southern Hemisphere.

atmospheric pressure   The pressure created by the effect of gravity on the air above the Earth; atmospheric pressure decreases with altitude.

barometer   A device used to measure atmospheric pressure.

blizzard   A snow storm that is accompanied by high winds. The wind and snow often cause snowdrifts that can measure several feet in height and "whiteouts," in which visibility is zero.

climate   The long-term weather conditions prevalent in a region over time. Weather conditions include temperature, rainfall, and other atmospheric factors.

climatology   A branch of meteorology that studies the atmosphere by comparing statistical variations in both space and time, as seen in weather behavior over the course of many years.

cloud seeding The use of substances to increase precipitation; silver iodide and dry ice are often used. The process has never been very successful.

cloud Collection of water droplets or ice crystals suspended in the air, which forms when the air is cooled to its dew point and condensation occurs.

cold front The boundary of a cold-air system, usually from the polar regions, that surges into the warmer air masses of the temperate latitudes.

condensation The process that turns water vapor to liquid water.

convection The transfer of heat caused by the movement of heated material. In clouds, convection is the up-and-down movement of air caused by heat gradients (areas of different temperatures).

Coriolis force (Coriolis effect) The force that causes winds to deviate to the right in the Northern Hemisphere and left in the Southern Hemisphere, as a result of the Earth's rotation.

dew Droplets that form when water vapor condenses.

dew point The temperature at which air becomes saturated, or it can hold no more water vapor, creating dew.

diamond dust Tiny, airborne ice crystals that reflect sunlight, often creating pillars of light.

evaporation The process in which a liquid (e.g., water) converts to a gas.

flash flood A sudden flood usually associated with a sudden heavy rainfall.

fog The base of a cloud that reaches the ground (see also *advection fog* and *ground fog*).

front The boundary between two air masses of varying temperature and humidity, usually warm and cold air masses; certain weather phenomena, such as rain, are associated with fronts.

frost A layer of ice formed when the temperature of the Earth's surface (and objects) falls below freezing.

fulgurite A glasslike piece of rock formed when lightning strikes dry sand. Some fulgurites measure up to 10 feet (3 meters) in length.

funnel cloud A rotating extension of a cloud that does or does not touch the ground; usually associated with clouds that have the potential to form tornadoes or waterspouts.

gale A wind with a velocity that ranges from 32 to 63 miles (51 to 101 kilometers) per hour.

glory The colorful, circular halo seen when looking down at an object's shadow; it is caused by diffraction of sunlight. It is often observed when the shadow of a flying airplane is seen on a cloud.

ground fog Fog that forms when the ground cools; it rises less than about 200 feet (61 meters).

gust A sudden, brief increase in wind speed; usually associated with fast-moving high pressure systems, squalls, and thunderstorms.

hail Pellets of ice that range in size from less than a half inch to several inches (or more) in diameter, usually formed in the tops of cumulonimbus clouds when water droplets freeze.

heat lightning Cloud-to-cloud lightning, common in the summer, which occurs behind a cloud or below the horizon but lights up the surrounding clouds. Usually no thunder is heard because of the distance from the observer.

humidity Water vapor content of the air, usually expressed as relative humidity.

inversion   The condition when the air on the ground is cooler than the air at a higher latitude. Inversions are usually associated with stable (but stagnant) air conditions.

isobars   Lines connecting areas of equal pressure on weather maps.

katabatic wind   Winds that occur in a valley as the air cools, usually after sunset, and flow down the slope (see *anabatic wind*).

lightning   An electrical discharge in the atmosphere.

precipitation   Water vapor that condenses from the atmosphere, forms droplets or ice crystals, and eventually reaches the surface. It can fall as rain, snow, ice, frost, dew, and other forms of atmospheric water.

relative humidity   The amount of water vapor in the air, as a percentage of what the air could hold at that temperature.

rime   Ice that forms when small drops of water freeze on an object on contact. They form small balls of ice with space between them.

saturation   The condition when the air holds the maximum water vapor it can at that temperature and pressure.

sea smoke (or steam fog)   Fog that forms when cooler air flows over a warmer body of water.

shower   Intermittent precipitation that can be heavy or light and can fall as snow or rain.

storm surge   An abnormal and rapid rise in ocean levels along a coast, caused by strong winds.

storm tracks   The path that a storm takes. The term is usually used with hurricanes, tornadoes, blizzards, and other major storms.

sublimation   Phase changes from water vapor to ice or ice to water vapor, without going through the liquid phase.

temperature lapse rate   The rate at which temperatures decrease with height.

temperature   A measurement of average kinetic energy, or heat.

trough   A narrow, elongated area of low atmospheric pressure that usually runs north to south.

virga   Particles of water that fall from clouds but evaporate before reaching the ground.

warm front   Warm air systems, usually from the temperate regions, that press into colder air masses.

weather   Short-term changes in temperature, humidity, rainfall, and barometric pressure in the atmosphere. It is usually in reference to local atmospheric changes.

wind   The movement of air with respect to the Earth's surface, caused locally by the Sun's heating of the ground; and globally, by the Sun's radiation and the spin of the Earth.

ADDITIONAL SOURCES OF INFORMATION

Dennis, Jerry, and Wolff, Glenn. *It's Raining Frogs and Fishes: Four Seasons of Natural Phenomena and Oddities of the Sky.* HarperCollins, 1992.

Ludlum, David M. *The Weather Factor.* Houghton Mifflin, 1984.

Sanders, Ti. *Weather: A User's Guide to the Atmosphere.* Icarus, 1985.

Williams, Jack. *The Weather Book.* Vintage, 1992.

11

Environmental Science

What Is Environmental Science?   458

Natural Cycles of the Earth   458

The Earth's Climate Zones   461

The Earth's Environments   461

Environmental Pollution   469

Current Environmental Concerns   476

Global Environmental Concerns   480

Recycling   484

Our Energy Sources   486

Preserving Nature   487

Major Environmentalists   489

Significant Scientific Discoveries in
Environmental Science   490

Common Terms in Environmental Science   491

Additional Sources of Information   494

WHAT IS ENVIRONMENTAL SCIENCE?

Environmental science is the study of the surrounding air, water, and land in relation to an individual organism or a community of organisms, ranging from a small area to the Earth's entire biosphere; more recently, it includes the study of the impact of humans on the environment.

What Is Ecology?

The terms ecology and environment are often erroneously used as synonyms. The term *ecology* (from the Greek *oikos* or "house" and *logos* "study of") was coined in 1869 by Ernst Haeckel. It is a branch of biology that deals with the observation and analysis of systems of living organisms, concerning how they interact with their environment. Ecological studies look at communities of organisms, patterns of life, natural cycles, population changes, and biogeography.

The definition of *environment* is not as clear: Some define environment as all natural systems in the world; others say the environment represents the various ecosystems—but most ecosystems overlap, thus the confusion.

NATURAL CYCLES OF THE EARTH

There are numerous environmental *cycles*—environmental phenomena that change a system and complete themselves in a definite order—on the Earth. The major cycles include the water, carbon, nitrogen, and oxygen cycles. These cycles are the Earth's natural way to recycle resources; our recent attempts at recycling are a direct extension of trying to help maintain balance within these cycles.

The Water Cycle

The water, or hydrologic cycle, represents the balance between the water in the oceans, atmosphere, and on land, and water's continuous interchanges, both geographically and physically, around the world.

The Carbon Cycle

There are two major carbon cycles: the short-term, organic carbon cycle and the long-term, geochemical carbon cycle. (For more information on carbon dioxide in the environment, see "Is There Global Warming?" in this chapter.)

Nitrogen Cycle

The nitrogen cycle is made up of chemical processes on land and in the atmosphere, as well as metabolic processes in organisms, that contribute to atmospheric nitrogen (N_2).

Oxygen Cycle

The Earth's atmosphere is about 21 percent oxygen by volume, an amount that is unusually high compared with the atmospheres of other planets and satellites in the solar system. About

2 billion years ago, plant photosynthesis began in the Earth's oceans and resulted in the release of oxygen. Oxygen levels reached their present levels about 400 million years ago and have remained balanced mainly by the production of oxygen from plant photosynthesis and consumption of oxygen by animal respiration.

Global Water Cycle

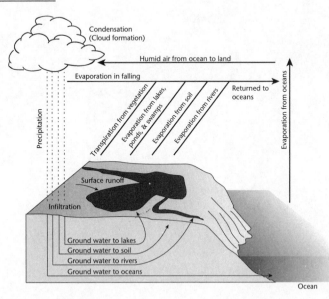

Organic Carbon Cycle

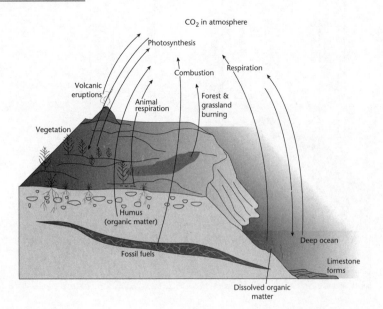

The Nitrogen Cycle

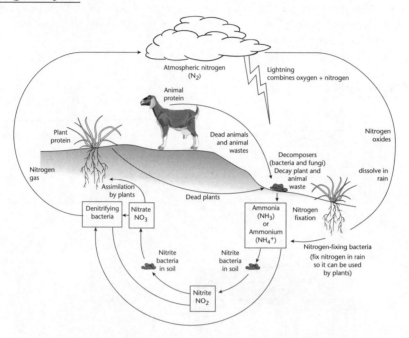

The Oxygen Cycle

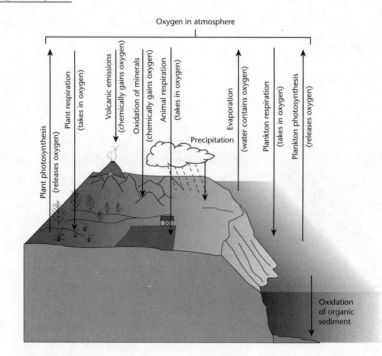

THE EARTH'S CLIMATE ZONES

Earth's climate zones are among the most important characteristics of the planet, and distinguish areas of differing plant and animal ecosystems, landscapes, agriculture, and human comfort zones. When the global climate changes, the climate zones respond by shifting their borders. (For more information on plant and animal ecosystems, see "What Is Environmental Science?" in this chapter.)

Earth's Climate Zone Classification

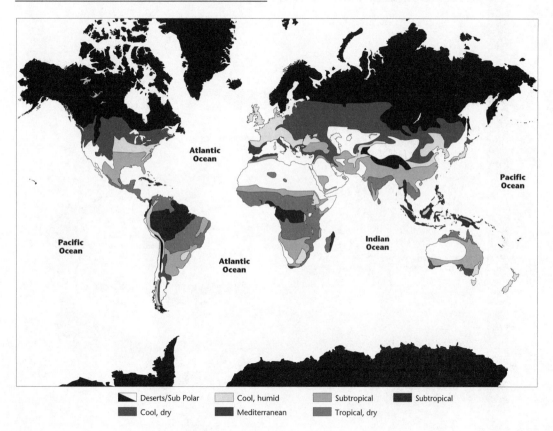

Deserts/Sub Polar	Cool, humid	Subtropical	Subtropical
Cool, dry	Mediterranean	Tropical, dry	

THE EARTH'S ENVIRONMENTS

The Earth is often broken down into regions with distinct types of climate, topographic features, water, soil, plants, and animals. Within these ecosystems, organisms live in groups called *communities*; the most extensive communities are called *biomes*. Ecological studies include the interaction of the chemical, physical, and biotic factors of the environment with the organisms in the region. Ecology is commonly divided into terrestrial, fresh water, and marine.

WHAT DO THEY EAT?

Over hundreds of millions of years, terrestrial and marine organisms have evolved systems that allow them to either manufacture their own food (i.e. through photosynthesis) or to obtain energy from other organisms (i.e. by eating them). A *food chain* is when a larger creature eats a smaller one, which has likewise eaten an even smaller one, and so on; a *food pyramid* is a representation of how energy extends into a system—from the originators (plants), to the animals that eat the plants, to the creatures who eat the animals who ate the plants. *Food webs* are the weaving together of food chains.

Idealized Aquatic Food Pyramid (upper ocean layers)

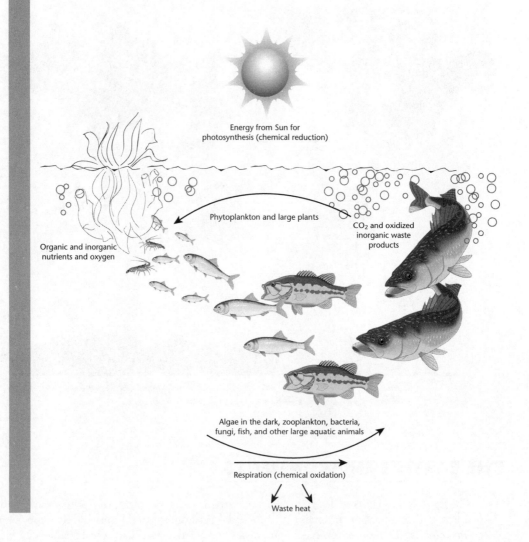

Energy from Sun for photosynthesis (chemical reduction)

Phytoplankton and large plants

CO_2 and oxidized inorganic waste products

Organic and inorganic nutrients and oxygen

Algae in the dark, zooplankton, bacteria, fungi, fish, and other large aquatic animals

Respiration (chemical oxidation)

Waste heat

Idealized Terrestrial Food Pyramid (temperate deciduous forest)

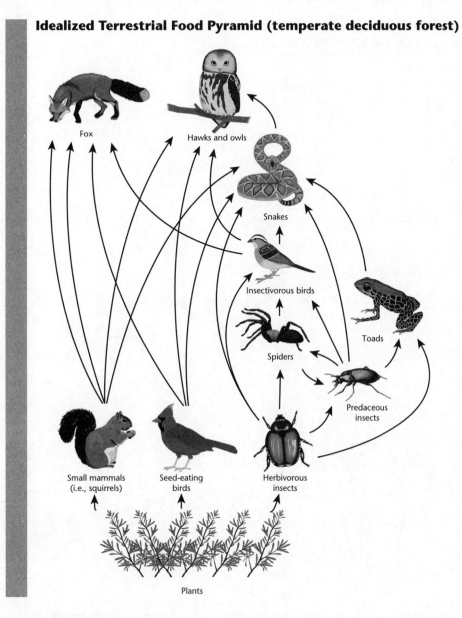

Fox

Hawks and owls

Snakes

Insectivorous birds

Toads

Spiders

Predaceous insects

Small mammals (i.e., squirrels)

Seed-eating birds

Herbivorous insects

Plants

Terrestrial Ecology

Terrestrial ecosystems include tundra, taiga, grasslands, savanna, forests (including coniferous forests, temperate woodlands, and tropical forests), deserts, and ice caps (glaciers). In addition, mountain and inland water environments are scattered all over the world. Chaparrals (shrubby forests) and coniferous rain forests are also often considered biomes.

Altitudinal and Latitudinal Life Zones (Eastern North America)

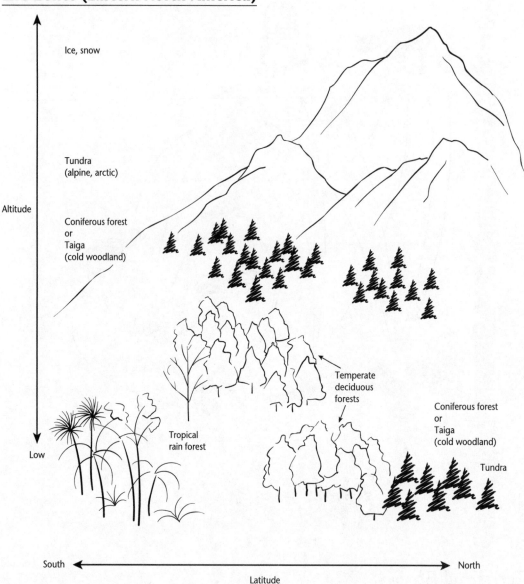

Altitude

Ice, snow

Tundra
(alpine, arctic)

Coniferous forest
or
Taiga
(cold woodland)

Temperate
deciduous
forests

Coniferous forest
or
Taiga
(cold woodland)

Tropical
rain forest

Tundra

Low

South ← Latitude → North

Tundra and Taiga

The cold lands north of the Arctic Circle—surrounding the Arctic Ocean and stretching across northern North America, adjacent to the ice cap in Greenland, and northern Scandinavia and Asia—are called tundra. A tundra habitat is dry (about eight or more consecutive months of no water) and cold, and the air cannot hold much moisture. The Sun is only seen six months of the year. Many of the plants are dwarves, and because the area is snowbound for most of the year, no trees grow on the tundra. Few animals, mostly birds and smaller animals, live in the frigid temperatures all year round. The musk ox is one of the largest animals found here; others include the snowy owl, caribou (known as reindeer in Europe), Arctic hare, Arctic lemming, Arctic fox, and the stoat (ermine); and polar bears are often found on the edge of the tundra, but more often on ice. In the summer months, many birds and animals take advantage of the warmer, short season to breed.

The taiga, or cold woodlands, are located along the southern fringes of the tundra. The trees are low and spaced far apart. A thin shrub layer is often found around the trees, and the ground cover is mostly lichens and mosses. (For more information on taiga, see "Forests," below.)

World's Tundra and Taiga

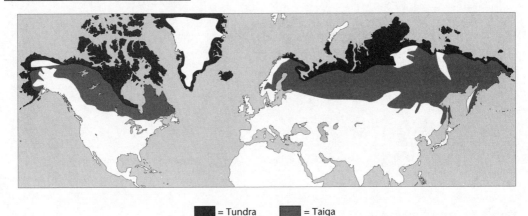

■ = Tundra   ■ = Taiga

Forests

The world's major forest divisions are coniferous, temperate, and tropical. There are other types of forests, but they are not as extensive.

Coniferous forests are often referred to as taiga, boreal forests, or northern evergreen forests. Coniferous forests grow where there are long, cold winters and brief summers. Coniferous trees, including the cone-bearing evergreens, provide food for many insects (such as moth and pine sawfly) and a few birds (such as grouse and crossbill). Sables and martens hunt for smaller animals, such as red squirrels, chipmunks, and flying squirrels. Larger animals are mostly herbaceous, such as moose and elk. These forests are a prime source of timber. In recent decades, they have also been sites for the extraction of oil, gas, and mineral resources.

Temperate, or *deciduous, forests* are common in areas where temperatures are less extreme. Here, trees go dormant, dropping their leaves in autumn, but they still provide enough food (in the form of bark or seeds) for certain animals in the winter. The largest temperate forests are found in the regions of the Northern Hemisphere that have a mild climate, frequent rainfall, and rich soil that supports a variety of vegetation. Temperate forests also contain extensive animal life, including deer, gray squirrels, badgers, rabbits, hawks, owls, and hundreds of others.

Tropical forests grow where rainfall is highest and temperatures are consistently warm. Trees, flowers, and fruit grow throughout the year. There is little underbrush, and most of the vegetation grows fast and to great heights. Plant and animal species in the tropical forests, including the tropical rain forests of South America, are some of the most prolific and abundant in the world.

Tropical rain forests are important to the world's climate, as they help cleanse the atmosphere. Rapid recycling of vegetation allows the constant recirculation of water vapor, carbon dioxide, and oxygen associated with photosynthesis (for more information on photosynthesis, see Chapter 4, "Biology").

World's Rainforests

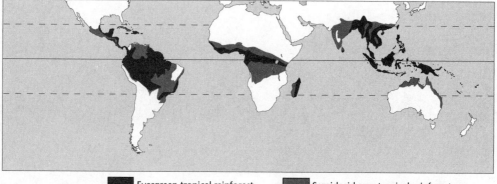

■ Evergreen tropical rainforest   ■ Semideciduous tropical rainforest

Grasslands and Savannas

Grasslands and savannas are considered some of the most valuable places on Earth, ecologically and economically, as they are used for animal grazing and agriculture. *Grasslands*—including prairies and steppes—are found in the temperate areas of the world, on wide plains in the dry continental interiors. Trees do not grow on grasslands because the rainfall is so low. Animals have learned to survive in the open grasslands, which have little or no cover. For example, in the United States, some animals, such as the prairie dog and the burrowing owl, live underground where they are hidden from view. Other animals rely on speed to survive, such as the pronghorn antelopes, or congregate in packs, such as some species of wolf.

Savannas are hot, tropical grasslands in the interiors of the continents, usually bordered by forest on one side and desert on the other. Many savannas support sparse tree and shrub life. Animals of Africa's savanna are mostly browsers and grazers that compete minimally for food. The browsers, such as the giraffe and the gazelle, feed at different heights in the trees; the grazers, such as the wildebeest and the zebra, eat different grasses at different times of the year.

World's Grasslands and Savannas

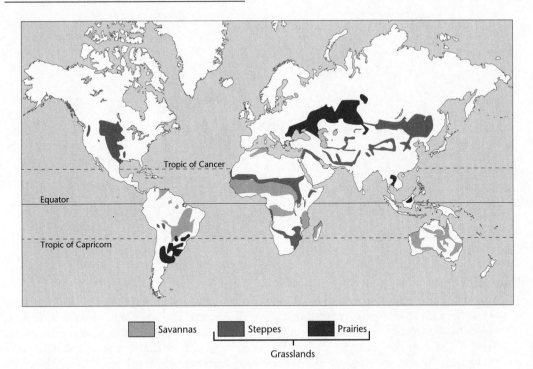

Savannas   Steppes   Prairies

Grasslands

Deserts

Like the tundra, the desert has little water. The animals and plants of the desert must survive under harsh conditions; they have evolved the ability to go for long periods without water. Desert animals include numerous reptiles (such as the rattlesnake and Gila monster), amphibians (such as spadefoot toads), and mammals (such as camels and fennec foxes). All desert animals have adapted to their environment by reducing their need for water, by developing physical characteristics that conserve water, and by maintaining certain habits to survive, such as remaining inactive during the hottest time of the day.

Many desert plants survive times of drought by sprouting only when rain falls, then quickly maturing and dropping seeds that will be activated during the next rainfall. Some plants store water in leaves or in underground tubers and bulbs. Trees found in the deserts usually have long tap roots that seek water far underground.

World's Deserts

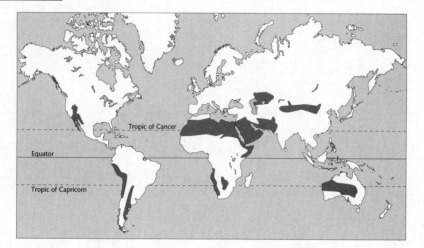

Mountains

Mountains are found scattered all over the world and cover one fifth of the dry land area (the ocean floor also has expansive mountain ranges). Animals and plants that live in mountain ranges have adapted to environments of rough terrain, thin air, extreme cold, and little water. Most of the mountain animals are excellent climbers, such as the ibex and mountain goat. Moving up the mountainside, one finds deciduous trees on the lower slopes, followed by conifers, and higher up, shrubs and flowers in sheltered areas. Next are lichens and mosses, while the top of the mountain is usually only barren rock or snow.

Mountain Belts

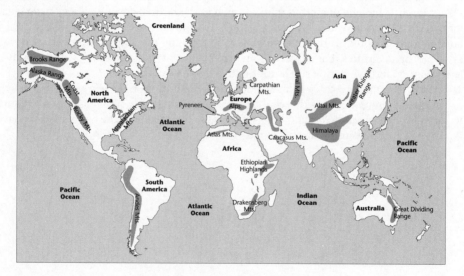

Freshwater Ecology

The inland fresh waters of the Earth represent less than one percent of the world's water, and include lakes, ponds, streams, rivers, and wetlands. Estuaries, where fresh water meets salt water, are also considered freshwater environments. The extent and types of animal and plant life found in fresh water are dependent on the size of the body, the depth, velocity, and temperature of the water; the climate of the area; and often the surrounding human activities. Animals in freshwater habitats include beaver and otters, along with a wide variety of fish. Freshwater plants include those that grow in shallow water (often called wetlands) and along the water's edge.

Marine Ecology

More than 70 percent of the Earth is covered by oceans, which are rich with animals and plants. The majority of life exists above a depth of 660 feet (200 meters), and most of it is sustained by animal and plant life-forms called plankton. Plankton thrive on the recycled nutrients locked in the bodies of dead animals, which are released by bacterial action. Upwelling currents, wind-driven waves, and storms bring the nutrients to the surface.

The marine environment includes the tidal zone, shallow water, and the deep ocean. (For more information on ocean zones, see Chapter 9, "Earth Science.")

In the *tidal zone* (or shoreline) community, various animals and plants have adapted to the daily ebb and flow of the tides. They have also adapted to different types of shorelines, such as sandy or rocky. Among the various plant communities found in the tidal zone are mangroves and salt marshes.

Shallow water marine environments may often be the sites of coral reefs, which are communities of simple colonial organisms called polyps. A polyp secretes limestone, and after it dies, another polyp grows on the remains, secreting more limestone, and so on—continually adding to the coral reef (although some species of coral do not build reefs). It is believed that the first coral reefs originated in the Earth's oceans about 500 million years ago.

It is estimated that coral reefs support one-third of all the world's fish species, and possibly close to one million animal species in total. But there are also many organisms that keep the reef going. From the smallest diatoms and algae to the sharks, the coral reef is able to support such a diversity of life because of plentiful food, hiding places, and shelter. All the creatures in the reef are members of the reef's extensive food chain—a self-sustaining, natural recycling system. The variety of species is not the same at all coral reefs and certain species are only found in specific locations, such as the remote reefs around the Hawaiian Islands, which harbor a number of unique species. The greatest variety of species is found in tropical reefs in waters north of Australia, including the Celebes and South China Sea.

In *deep ocean*, beyond the continental slope and rise, the little or no sunlight means that organisms must have special adaptations to survive. A recent discovery off Madagascar was of a coelacanth—a species of lungfish. Thought to have gone extinct 60 million years ago, the creature may not be the only "living fossil" surviving deep in the oceans.

ENVIRONMENTAL POLLUTION

Environmental pollution is caused by contaminants in air, water, or land. It is caused by both natural phenomena and human activity.

Air Pollution

Natural processes, such as volcanic eruptions, may release substances that are considered *pollutants*. These pollutants can be dispersed over a wide area and may or may not have an effect on the environment. Human activity also produces pollutants. The greatest source of air pollution is the burning of fossil fuels by power plants and other coal-, oil-, and gas-burning industrial facilities, as well as by motor vehicles. Primary air pollutants enter the atmosphere directly; secondary air pollutants form in the atmosphere by chemical reaction with primary air pollutants and/or natural components in the air.

Man-made air pollution often impacts the growth of forests. Industrial chemicals in the atmosphere exacerbate the erosion of natural and man-made structures. It is estimated that pollutants in the atmosphere have changed the composition of the global air less than 0.01 percent. But some scientists believe that even such a small change can have an adverse effect on the climate, ecosystems, and species on the planet.

World's Primary Air Pollutants

Pollutant	Natural Source	Human Source
Carbon dioxide	Decay, release from oceans, and animal respiration	Wood and fossil-fuel combustion
Nitrogen oxides	Lightning, bacterial activity in soils	High-temperature combustion
Nonmethane hydrocarbons	Biological processes	Incomplete combustion
Sulfur dioxide	Decay, volcanic eruptions	Coal and oil combustion, smelting of ores
Ammonia	Anaerobic decay	Sewage treatment plants
Methane	Termites, anaerobic decay, and ruminants (cud-chewing animals such as cows, deer, and sheep)	Combustion and natural-gas leaks
Ozone	Produced in the troposphere	Smog from auto and industrial emissions
*Particulates	Forest fires, volcanic eruptions, and wind erosion	Waste burning, road building, and mining

*Not a specific chemical substance, but still classified as a pollutant

Known and Suspected Effects of Common Air Pollutants on Human Health

Pollutant	Source and Known or Suspected Effects
Carbon monoxide	Mainly from motor vehicles; carbon monoxide reduces the oxygen-carrying capacity of the blood by combining with hemoglobin, and deprives the tissues of oxygen; low concentrations can impair mental abilities and especially affect those with heart and respiratory conditions; high concentrations can cause death
Lead	Mainly from smelting and manufacturing processes; also little from gasoline emissions; excessive amounts cause lead poisoning, which can impair mental ability, especially in younger children
Nitrogen oxides	Nitrogen oxides, such as nitrogen oxide, are pollutants that cause smog and acid rain; they are produced mainly from burning fuel in utilities, industrial boilers, and motor vehicles; they can cause eye, throat, and lung irritation, especially in children and people with respiratory problems

Ozone	As a secondary pollutant, ozone is not emitted by any vehicle or factory; it is produced mainly from photochemical reactions of certain air pollutants; ozone can cause irritation of the nose and throat; it can impair lung function, especially in people susceptible to chronic lung disease or asthma
Particulate matter	This is solid matter or droplets found in smoke, dust, car emissions, and at the sites of unsheltered agricultural fields, industrial processes, and construction; particulate matter can cause breathing difficulties, especially in those suffering from heart or lung disease
Sulfur Oxides	Sulfur oxides, such as sulfur dioxide, are mainly from industrial, institutional, utility, and apartment furnace and boiler emissions, as well as petroleum refineries, smelters, paper mills, and chemical plants; sulfur oxides are one of the major pollutants that cause smog, and can aggravate upper-respiratory disease and cause eye and throat irritation; they can also affect people with heart conditions
Toxic air pollutants	These are particles that are toxic to organisms, such as asbestos, arsenic, and benzene; these pollutants are often emitted by chemical plants, industrial processes, and motor vehicles and are often found in building materials; health problems depend on the type of particle; for example, inhaled asbestos remains permanently in the lungs, irritating lung tissue; it has also been associated with lung disease and cancer (although this has recently been debated); some particles, if released in large amounts, can cause serious injury or death

United States Air-Quality Index Values

Air Pollutant Levels (micrograms per cubic meter)

Air Quality Index Value	Air Quality Description	Total Suspended Particulate Matter (24 Hours)	Sulfur Dioxide (24 Hours)	Carbon Monoxide (8 Hours)	Ozone (1 Hour)	Nitrogen Dioxide (1 Hour)	Effects and Suggested Actions
500	Hazardous	1,000	2,620	57,000	1,200	3,750	Normal activity impossible. All should remain indoors with windows and doors closed. Risk especially to elderly and those with heart and lung ailments.
400	Hazardous	875	2,100	46,000	1,000	3,000	High-risk group should stay quietly indoors. Others should avoid outdoor activity.

(continued)

Air Pollutant Levels (micrograms per cubic meter)(cont'd)

Air Quality Index Value	Air Quality Description	Total Suspended Particulate Matter (24 Hours)	Sulfur Dioxide (24 Hours)	Carbon Monoxide (8 Hours)	Ozone (1 Hour)	Nitrogen Dioxide (1 Hour)	Effects and Suggested Actions
300	Very unhealthful	625	1,600	34,000	800	2,260	High-risk group has more symptoms and should stay indoors and reduce physical activity. All persons notice lung irritation.
200	Unhealthful	375	800	17,000	400	1,130	Those with lung or heart disease should reduce physical exertion. Healthy persons notice irritations.
100	Moderate	260	365	10,000	235	?	Some damage to materials and plants. Human health not affected unless levels continue for many days.
50	Good	75	80	5,000	118	?	No significant effects.

Water Pollution

Water pollution affects oceans, streams, rivers, lakes, ponds, and groundwater, and can be caused by natural impurities or human activities that pollute the nearby water or water supplies.

Natural impurities in water are sometimes, but not always, pollutants. They are divided into three categories of particles: *suspended particles* that absorb light and make water cloudy, such as beach sand, coal dust, and bacteria; *colloidal particles*, such as soot and some viruses, which cannot be removed from water by ordinary filtration and cause the water to look cloudy when observed at right angles to a beam of light; and *dissolved matter*, which are the smallest impurities in water, including molecules and ions of various substances, such as chloride or sodium ions or carbon dioxide molecules.

Human activities are often the cause of localized water pollution, as water becomes contaminated with heavy metals, toxic chemicals, and bacteria. Rivers may experience oil and chemical spills, untreated sewage runoff from homes and industry, and nonpoint source pollution, such as contaminated runoff from highways, parking lots, and agricultural fields. Groundwater (or subsurface water) may be contaminated by the infiltration of pollutants from landfills and septic tanks, or by percolation of water containing contaminated runoff. Parts of the ocean are sometimes polluted by oil tanker spills and garbage dumping.

A SHRINKING SEA

One of the world's worst man-made environmental disasters is the shrinking of the Aral Sea in south-central Asia. Today, the sea covers only three-fifths of the area it did 30 years ago. It was once the fourth largest sea in the world. It is now sixth, and still dwindling.

The problems began in the 1950s, when the then Soviet Union planned to turn much of the area over to growing cotton. The water was directed to the plantations by damming the rivers that once flowed into the sea. Heavy use of chemical fertilizer exacerbated the problem, by polluting the water with salt and chemicals, including nitrates. The draining of the water also dried out the area's top-soil, producing dust filled with poisonous chemicals and causing respiratory problems in nearby residents. The contamination resulted in an increase in birth abnormalities, liver cancer, and blood disease in some areas. Fish were once caught in hundreds of tons per year in the Aral Sea, but fishing became confined to contaminated ponds around the sea.

Today, the ex-Soviet republics in the region are trying to restore the area by studying the extent of contamination and the depth of environmental damage. And the Aral Sea is not the only such disaster in the world: Mono Lake in California is also shrinking due to changes in water use in that region.

The Earth's Water

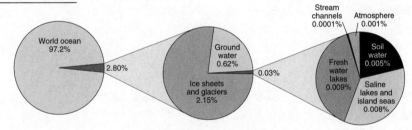

Percent of Water Used in the United States

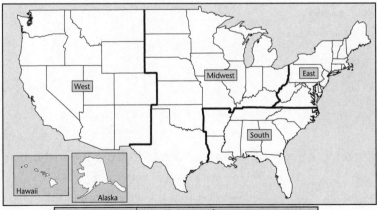

Purpose	Area					
	East	South	Midwest	West	Alaska	Hawaii
Irrigation	6%	53%	75%	90%	1%	79%
Other agricultural	2%	3%	4%	1%	—	—
Homes, offices	32%	14%	6%	5%	13%	11%
Manufacturing	40%	17%	8%	2%	19%	10%
Steam-electric generating	13%	10%	4%	1%	1%	—
Mining	7%	3%	3%	1%	66%	—

*Approximate percents

How Is Water Used?

Item	Water Used gallons (liters)
Bathing (per bath)	34.3 (130)
Showering (per minute)	
Regular showerhead	5.0 (19)
Water-saving showerhead	2.4 (9)
Flushing toilet	
Conventional	5.0 (19)
Water saving	3.4 (13)
Low flow	1.6 (6)
Washing clothes (per load)	
Low setting	19.0 (72)
High setting	44.9 (170)
Washing dishes (per load)	
By hand (with water running)	30.1 (114)
By hand (rinsing in dishpans)	5.0 (19)
Machine—low setting	6.9 (26)
Machine—high setting	16.1 (61)
Production of a tankful of gasoline	401.6 (1,520)
Production of an automobile	50,198.0 (190,000)
Production of a ton of synthetic rubber	602,376.0 (2,280,000)

Common Water Pollutants

Point sources	Bacteria	Nutrients	Ammonia	Total dissolved solids	Acids	Toxics
Municipal sewage treatment plants	x	x	x			x
Industrial facilities						x
Combined sewer overflows	x	x	x	x		x
Nonpoint sources						
Agricultural runoff	x	x		x		x
Urban runoff	x	x		x		x
Construction runoff		x				x
Mining runoff				x	x	x
Septic systems	x	x				x
Landfills spills						x
Forestry runoff		x				x

Known or Suspected Effects of Common Water Pollutants on Human Health

Pollutant	Sources and Known or Suspected Effects
Heavy metals	Heavy metals include lead, cadmium, nickel, and mercury; many are poisonous in excessive amounts; most, such as mercury, can build up to toxic levels in the tissues of animals; heavy metals enter the water

Pollutant	Sources and Known or Suspected Effects
	from a variety of sources, including leachate from landfills or chemically treated agricultural fields (both of which contain heavy metals and enter nearby water wells); high levels of heavy metals in animal tissue can result from eating excessive amounts of mercury-contaminated fish from certain lakes and rivers
Human waste	Can carry diseases such as dysentery, typhoid, cholera, salmonellosis, and hepatitis
Lead	Intake through water, mainly from older lead piping in homes; it is thought to impair mental ability, especially in younger children, when ingested in larger quantities
Nitrates	Nitrates usually enter the water supply by runoff from agricultural areas; nitrates are converted to nitrites in the digestive tract, which interfere with the absorption of oxygen by hemoglobin, and may lead to anemia in children and older adults
Oil and hydrocarbons	Oils and hydrocarbons enter water systems from a variety of sources, including oil spills, natural oil leaks, and oil-field runoff; in the oceans, the most direct effect is on marine organisms, which are part of the food chain; the death of certain organisms from oil and hydrocarbon pollution can disrupt the chain, which often has a direct effect on fishing along the affected coastline; in rivers, oils and hydrocarbons can enter and contaminate drinkable (potable) water supplies; ingestion of hydrocarbons can lead to possible damage of the nervous system or liver

THE "OTHER" POLLUTIONS

Three of the more ignored, but prevalent, pollution problems are soil, light, and noise.

Soil pollution is a by-product of water pollution, as the soil can become polluted by chemically contaminated water percolating down or up through it. Soil can also become contaminated when pollutants, such as lead from auto emissions, settle into the soil from the air. One of the common solutions for soil pollution is expensive—digging it up and carting it to a sealed area or landfill.

Light pollution is the excessive amount of light in the nighttime sky caused by streetlights and industrial and commercial lighting. It produces numerous problems for nocturnal animals and plants: Birds that migrate at night are often confused by lights, especially in big cities; hatching sea turtles that depend on the natural ocean glow to find their way to the sea often move away from the sea and toward streetlights; and some plants can bloom prematurely if exposed to too much artificial light. Light pollution is also a serious problem for astronomers, when details of the nighttime sky are lost in the artificial glow.

Noise pollution is often a problem in cities, and can be caused by traffic, airplanes, industry, commercial enterprises—and even people's voices. It is thought that excessive noise can cause behavioral and chemical changes in the human body. Not much has been done to curtail noise pollution, but small steps are being made: Aircraft designers are trying to make quieter engines; automobile manufacturers are designing more quiet cars (for those inside and outside the vehicle); and computer, air-conditioning, and heating-unit designers are working on developing quieter motors.

CURRENT ENVIRONMENTAL CONCERNS

Wetland Loss

Wetlands, found in every corner of the world, hold some of the most diverse flora and fauna on the planet. Swamps, freshwater and saltwater marshes, and mangrove forests are considered wetlands. Innumerable animal species, ranging from amphibians and fish to large mammals, depend on wetlands for food and water. Birds are some of the most prevalent creatures in wetland environments, using them for nesting, layovers during migration, and permanent homes.

Wetlands act as natural filters. They trap nutrients and purify the water by filtering out pesticides and heavy metals. Wetlands also act as retaining pools for floodwaters and as anchors to stabilize shorelines.

A few short decades ago, wetlands were considered bug-infested wastelands. It is estimated that between 1950 and 1970, the United States lost an average of 457,000 acres (185,000 hectares) of its remaining wetlands each year. Many wetlands were filled in for development, while others were turned to agriculture. This loss of wetlands decreased available habitats for wildlife, increased the likelihood of flooding, and decreased water quality of certain regions. Today, special zoning laws are used to slow wetland loss, and many such areas are being set aside for conservation.

Acid Rain

Acid rain forms when water vapor and certain elements chemically combine with natural and man-made pollutants—such as sulfur dioxide or nitrogen oxides—in the stratosphere, forming sulfuric and nitric acids. Acids have a pH of 6 or less; acid rain includes precipitation with a pH lower than 5 to 5.6, though it has been recorded as low as pH 2.4 to 2.8 (for more information on pH, see Chapter 6, "Chemistry"). Acid rain can fall as "wet" deposits in the form of rain, fog, or snow, or as "dry" deposits, in the form of gases and particles.

Currently, it is thought that natural pollutants from volcanoes, forest fires, and decaying organic matter are responsible for about 10 percent of acid rain. The other 90 percent is caused by industrial activity, vehicle exhaust, coal and other fossil-fuel emissions from electrical power plants, and residential and commercial heating units (although acid rain has apparently leveled off after increasing steadily for the past several decades).

Acid rain increased around the start of the Industrial Revolution, in the late eighteenth century. Industrial smoke stacks were shorter than those of today and polluted the immediate environment, with the ground-hugging pollutants causing upper respiratory and other health problems. In an effort to decrease health problems and pollution, smoke stack heights were increased, allowing the pollutants to reach higher into the atmosphere. The pollutants—carried extreme distances by the prevailing winds—reacted with certain elements higher in the atmosphere, creating acid rains.

Widespread acid rain has caused an increase in the acidity of lakes, streams, and wetlands, especially in the northeastern United States, Scandinavia, Germany, and Canada, causing damage to many local (especially aquatic) ecosystems. Acid rain may also heighten the incidence of soil acidification, increasing the amount of leached minerals from rock, which eventually enter the surrounding soil and water regime. There is still disagreement as to the extent of the ecological effects of acid rain. Certain acid-sensitive plants and animals are now being studied as indicators of acid precipitation effects.

Waste Disposal

Landfills

Dumps (now called *landfills*) originated as places to put waste material. The first dumps were open pits. In sanitary landfills, developed in the 1950s, refuse was deposited in a trench, then covered over by a layer of earth.

Numerous materials are taken to a landfill, including solid wastes, garbage, and trash. *Solid wastes* are defined by the U.S. Congress, in the 1976 Resource Conservation and Recovery Act, as "any garbage, refuse, sludge from a waste treatment plant, or air pollution control facility and other discarded material, including solid, liquid, semisolid or contained gaseous material resulting from industrial, commercial, mining, and agricultural operations and community activities."

The terms *refuse* and solid waste are usually considered to be synonymous, and include discarded appliances and junk autos. *Garbage* is food waste. *Trash* refers to grass and shrubbery clippings, paper, glass, cans, and other household materials. *Rubbish* is synonymous with trash, but also includes demolition materials such as brick, broken concrete, and discarded roofing and lumber.

THE PROBLEMS WITH LANDFILLS

There are several major concerns with landfills. The material placed in landfills is subject to decomposition by microorganisms, initially aerobic. As the oxygen is depleted, it cannot be replenished because of compaction and cover. The microbial action soon becomes anaerobic, slowing the rate of decomposition. In addition, water, sunlight, and air that would normally accelerate degradation do not reach the buried materials. Particularly because of this lack of degradation, many landfills are filled (or almost filled) to capacity.

Another concern about landfills is their potential to leak toxic chemicals and pollutants into the nearby potable surface water and groundwater, especially if the landfill containment is breached (many sanitary landfills have a clay lining, which is not supposed to leak but often does) or the landfill is older. Of special concern is the leaking of hazardous wastes, including pesticide residues, asbestos, acids and bases, and polychlorobiphenyls (PCBs)—all hazardous to living organisms.

Recycling programs have been implemented in many areas to conserve space in the landfills. Some consumers are also trying to "precycle," or to buy goods that have recyclable packaging or no packaging at all. New methods of building landfills, including stronger linings to curtail the leaching of chemicals into the groundwater, and new laws about what is to be accepted into the landfill are also being implemented.

Landfill Loads

Material Sources	Percent of Material Found in Average Landfill
Household wastes	72
Commercial wastes	19
Construction and demolition wastes	6
Sewage sludge and industrial wastes	3

DIGGING GARBAGE

Landfills have been in use for several decades, making them perfect places to study the decay of materials. But scientists recently found that instead of decaying, much of our garbage remains intact—thanks to the inability of light, water, and air to reach deep underground.

Extensive excavation of landfills all around the country by The Garbage Project, at the University of Arizona, has unearthed several interesting findings, such as the following, based on a study of more than 9,000 loads of garbage examined around the country.

- Food and yard debris degrade slowly—by around 25 to 50 percent every 10 or 15 years. Uneaten food was recognizable as long as a quarter of a century after it was thrown away.
- 30 percent of the trash, by volume, was nondegradable plastics.
- Paper products constitute over half of the trash in landfills. Much of the paper was "mummified," and newspapers buried deep in some landfills were still legible decades later. Some scientists note that this slow decay may be somewhat positive: At least the ink toxins are not released quickly into the surrounding groundwater and soil.

Nuclear Wastes

Nuclear wastes are unusable radioactive materials. The wastes are created by all aspects of nuclear technology, including nuclear power plants, nuclear weapons programs, and medical, industrial, and research applications. They include *low-level nuclear wastes*, which are slightly contaminated materials, *high-level nuclear wastes*, which are usually spent fuel from nuclear power reactors, and *transuranic wastes*, which include materials contaminated with man-made radioisotopes formed by the transmutation of uranium in nuclear reactions (the most common is plutonium). A single, large nuclear power plant produces 1,300 cubic yards (1,000 cubic meters) of low-level waste per year; a large nuclear reactor can discharge about 33 tons (30 metric tons) of spent fuel per year.

From 1957 (the start of nuclear power generation) to 1983, it is estimated that 17 million pounds of radioactive wastes were generated. Direct exposure to all nuclear wastes is harmful to humans. Thus, it is difficult to decide where to store radioactive wastes, as the materials remain radioactive for thousands to millions of years. Most low-level wastes need only a small amount of shielding—about 3.3 feet (1 meter) of soil is sufficient to protect humans. The problem is that water could seep into the soil, causing the radioactive materials to migrate.

NOT IN MY BACKYARD

Where do we put all the nuclear waste? One of the main problems with finding sites is the "not in my backyard"—NIMBY—syndrome. Although people want the benefits of nuclear power, they generally do not want the wastes stored in their town. Reports of seeping radioactive elements contaminating groundwater supplies, and problems with radioactive leaks from earthquake activity, have scared citizens into action—and have left very few sites across the country in which to store the wastes.

There have been plenty of suggestions: The Nuclear Waste Policy Act of 1982 proposed a permanent storage in metal canisters kept at 2,000 to 4,000 feet (610 to 1,219 meters) underground in solid rock caverns, which theoretically should keep the radioactive waste safe and dry for at least 10,000 years. Several natural sites have been suggested to hold the wastes, including salt domes, which are relatively free of water and would naturally seal after any ground movement. The tuff (ancient volcanic ash deposits) of Nevada's Yucca Mountain has also been suggested, but previously unknown faults have been found around the site, hampering the decision to build the repository.

Many people suggest that the only way to solve the radioactive waste problems is to find alternatives to nuclear power. In the meantime, we still have thousands of years (and longer) before already-existing radioactive wastes become harmless to humans.

Radon

Radon is a naturally occurring, invisible, odorless gas that is produced as a result of radioactive decay of uranium in rock and soil. There has always been radon in the air and soil (the average outdoor level is 0.2 picocuries per liter); and there are naturally occurring underground patches of radon-emitting rock below certain regions. Recently, it was discovered that radon can reach high levels in homes and other buildings; the contamination is often worse in well-insulated homes and offices that exist near radon sites.

Radon is radioactive and has been linked to lung cancer, but it is generally not known what amounts are carcinogenic. Miners who were exposed to high levels of radon gas on the job have been found to have a higher than normal risk of lung cancer.

The first step in detecting radon in the home is to call your state health department or the Environmental Protection Agency for information. Methods of lowering radon levels in buildings include installing ventilation fans in basements, sealing cracks and leaks in basement floors and walls, and having periodic radon tests.

Indoor Air Levels for Radon

Level*	Comments on Radon Test Results
Below 4 pCi/L (below 0.02 WL)	Exposure at this level is considered average for residential structures; some research states that there is a degree of risk for lung cancer at this level, but it has not been proven; at this range, a reduction in radon level is difficult
4 to 20 pCi/L (0.02 to 0.1 WL)	Exposure at this level is above average for residential structures; at this range, reductions in radon levels can be achieved by sealing cracks and providing some ventilation, and should be effected within a few years (sooner if the levels are at the high end of the scale)
20 to 200 pCi/L (0.1 to 1.0 WL)	Exposure at this level is greatly above average for residential structures; at this range, reductions in radon levels should be effected within a few months
Greater than 200 pCi/L (greater than 1.0 WL)	Exposure at this level is among the highest recorded in residential structures; at this range, reductions in radon levels should be effected within several weeks

pCi/L, picocuries per liter, from devices that measure concentrations of radon gas; WL, working levels, from devices that measure radon decay products.

Lead Contamination

Years ago, most *lead contamination* was caused by certain types of ceramic cookware, lead-based paints, old lead water pipes, and leaded gasoline. Today, most lead exposure results from industrial releases and paint on some older homes. Young children are most susceptible to health problems from lead, including possible brain and nervous system damage. Older people can also suffer from lead poisoning, exhibiting signs of decreased mental abilities.

One way to reduce the risk of lead poisoning is to eliminate old lead paint from homes and other structures and to replace it with leadless paints. Lead testing for soil is also available.

THE DEBATE OVER EMFS

During the twentieth century, the use of electric devices has grown dramatically. As a result, our exposure to electromagnetic fields (EMFs) has increased. Accordingly, the concern has been raised: Are these electric and electronic systems harmful to our health?

Despite many epidemiological and other scientific studies conducted by federal authorities and independent laboratories, no evidence has been found that EMFs pose any health risk. Yet some studies claim that the risk of contracting certain cancers, especially leukemia and brain cancer, might be raised by exposure to EMFs; in addition, a recent study indicated that women who worked in the electrical trades had a greater risk of contracting breast cancer.

Questions to be answered include how to measure a person's exposure to electricity (it is all around us, and even our body produces its own electricity), how EMFs affect tissues at the cellular level—and why our increase in power consumption over time has not triggered a cancer epidemic.

Soil Erosion

Soil erosion occurs when vegetation is removed or land use is changed in an area, causing the topsoil to be carried away by water, wind, or ice action. Soil erosion decreases the fertility of cultivated land, with topsoil around the world being washed or blown into the sea at a rate of about 75 billion tons a year—much greater than the amount being naturally replenished.

Soil erosion is caused by many natural and man-made factors: the loss of vegetation after a major forest fire; deforestation, such as for cattle grazing or development; uncontrolled land use; and poor agricultural and forestry practices.

GLOBAL ENVIRONMENTAL CONCERNS

The Earth's Natural Warming Cycle

The Earth is blanketed by an atmosphere of nitrogen, oxygen, and argon, with smaller amounts of trace gases, such as carbon dioxide, water vapor, methane, and others. These trace gases, or *"greenhouse gases,"* capture some of the heat that is reflected back from the Sun-warmed Earth (about 30 percent of the Sun's energy is reflected back into space).

The Earth as a Greenhouse

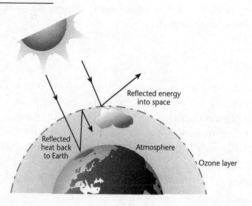

Major Greenhouse Gases and Sources

Greenhouse Gas	*Sources/Causes*
Carbon dioxide (CO_2)	Fossil fuels, deforestation, animal respiration
Methane (CH_4)	Cattle, rice paddies, gas leaks, termites, mining
Nitrous oxide (N_2O)	Burning of fossil fuels, deforestation
Chlorofluorocarbons (CFC 11, 12)	Air-conditioning, some solvents, some chemicals used in refrigeration
Ozone and other trace gases	Cars' exhaust, power plants, photochemical reactions with other elements, solvents

Is There Global Warming?

Increase in Greenhouse Gases

Geologic evidence shows that levels of carbon dioxide and other naturally occurring greenhouse gases have remained relatively stable on Earth for the past several thousand years. But ever since the Industrial Revolution started in England about 1750 (and about 100 years later in the United States), levels of greenhouse gases have been increasing. Greenhouse gases include mainly carbon dioxide (from the burning of fossil fuels), methane (from the increase in rice paddies and cow pastures to feed the world's growing population), nitrous oxides (from fertilizers and fossil-fuel burning), chlorofluorocarbons (CFCs), and low-level ozone (O_3, from photochemical processes and motor vehicles).

There is no real consensus concerning the increase in global temperatures. Some studies have shown that the world's average temperature has risen by 0.9° F (0.5° C) since 1600. Other studies have noted a 0.5° F (0.3° C) to 1° F (0.6° C) rise in mean surface air temperatures in the past 100 years. It is unknown whether the rise is part of the Earth's natural climate cycle or a result of the increase in greenhouse gases from human activity.

According to many researchers, an unnatural increase in the greenhouse gases could theoretically cause a warming of the global climate. The effect of warming is still a matter of speculation. For example, one theory states that runaway greenhouse gases will cause a rise in temperature of 9° over the next 100 years. Some scientists believe that such a major increase could melt glacial ice sheets, raising sea levels from anywhere between 4 inches and 6 feet (10 centimeters and 2 meters), inundating coastal cities; in addition, cloud cover would increase, greatly affecting flora and fauna because of weather changes around habitats. Another study states that the global average temperature will be at least 1° warmer by the year 2030; and some scientists contend that if global temperatures rise even by 1°, weather and agricultural patterns, and flora and fauna habitats could change around the world.

Solid evidence for greenhouse warming has not yet been found, though there is agreement that atmospheric concentration of carbon dioxide is increasing. But warming is difficult to determine: Natural fluctuations in local climate, and even the world climate, is common, and climate conditions have been recorded only for a short period when compared to the millions of years the world's climate has existed. Though researchers are using supercomputers to examine the global climate, the number of variables needed to determine a general circulation model of the Earth's atmosphere is enormous.

Deforestation

Trees have always been important to the survival of life on Earth. Forests and trees clean the air, stop soil from eroding, store water, and help to regulate and balance Earth's water, air, and climate cycles. Forests provide habitat for wildlife and are a source of food and fuel for humans.

In the past half century, both the temperate and tropical forests of the world have been declining in area. For example, in many industrialized nations, air pollutants weaken trees and make them more susceptible to disease. The intentional destruction of the rain forests by cutting and burning takes place to make room for agriculture and livestock grazing. Such practices, especially in such areas as South America's Amazon Basin, are also a major concern. It is estimated that almost half the world's tropical rain forests have been destroyed in the past half century. Such a decline may cause an increase in erosion of the soil (and thus, increased flooding) and a loss of biological diversity. In particular, some researchers believe that a decline in the rain forests has the potential to change the world climate. Both the increase in forest burning and the lack of trees to absorb and maintain the balance of carbon dioxide in the atmosphere are cited as factors in global warming.

Recently, deforestation has been declining or holding steady in several industrialized and third world countries. But as these latter countries develop their economies, that growth will certainly come, at least in part, at the expense of the forest system.

READING THE ICE

The Earth's past climate—including temperature and elements in the atmosphere—has recently been studied by analyzing ice samples from Greenland and Antarctica. The air bubbles in the ice have shown that, over the past 160,000 years, there has been a close correlation between temperature changes and level of natural greenhouse gases carbon dioxide and methane. One recent analysis from Greenland showed that at the end of the last glacial period (when the great ice sheets began to retreat to their present positions), temperatures in southern Greenland rose by 5° to 7° in about 100 years.

Air bubbles are not the only method of determining characteristics of the Earth's ancient climate history: Analysis of dust layers from ancient volcanic activity is another such method; as is the study of ice cores with beryllium-10 dating methods, which interpret past solar activity that may have affected our climate.

The Disappearing Ozone?

Ozone is produced by a photochemical reaction involving oxygen and ultraviolet radiation from the Sun: The radiation splits two-atom oxygen molecules into two separate atoms; the single atoms seek out other two-atom molecules and create ozone (O_3)—a three-atom oxygen molecule.

Ozone occurs in small quantities in the Earth's lower troposphere, around areas where certain pollutants are prevalent, especially in city smog. Surface ozone forms when certain volatile organic compounds, oxygen, and nitrogen oxides chemically react in the presence of sunlight, especially during hot weather. The sources of such pollutants include motor vehicle and power-plant emissions, landfills, and solvents, and, less importantly, from such sources as farm and lawn equipment and gas stations. Surface ozone can reduce the yield of agricultural crops and damage forests and other vegetation. Ozone, in combination with sulfur dioxide, can have a more severe effect on human health than either pollutant can separately.

The stratosphere, extending from about 7 to 30 miles (11 to 48 kilometers), also contains a diffuse ozone layer concentrated at a height of about 15 miles (25 kilometers). This layer, called the ozonosphere, extends around the Earth and protects living organisms from harmful ultraviolet radiation from the Sun. In the first half of Earth's history, only trace amounts of oxygen existed in the atmosphere, and early marine plants were protected from the Sun's ultraviolet radiation by the oceans. About two billion years ago, plants began to produce abundant free oxygen as waste gas, forming a thin layer of ozone close to the surface. By about one billion years ago, the formation of a thicker protective ozone layer may have allowed plants, and eventually animals, to move from the oceans to live on the land.

WHAT IS OZONE?

Ozone gas was found in the atmosphere in 1913 by French physicist Charles Fabry. At room temperature, ozone is a colorless gas; it condenses to a dark blue liquid at -170° F (-112° C); and above the boiling point of water (212° F; 100° C) it decomposes into diatomic oxygen.

Ozone is all around us. After a thunderstorm (especially around a lightning strike), or around electrical equipment, ozone is often detected as a sharp odor. Ozone is used as a strong oxidizing agent, a bleaching agent, and to sterilize drinking water. The gas is also highly reactive. For example, rubber insulation around a car's spark plug wires will need to be replaced eventually, due to the small amounts of ozone produced when electricity flows from the engine to the plug.

The Ozone "Hole"

The ozone layer (ozonosphere) above Antarctica has a "hole" that naturally expands and contracts each year in response to the seasons, with the minimum ozone concentrations (thus, maximum opening of the "hole") occurring between September and November. It was discovered over Halley Bay during the International Geophysical Year, between 1957 and 1958, and confirmed by ground-based and satellite data taken since the early 1960s.

Measurements taken every October since 1979 indicate that the ozone hole over the Antarctic has grown. Many scientists believe that the changes in the ozone hole size are a naturally occurring phenomenon, and that many natural and human activities have amplified the event. For example, volcanic eruptions, such as the 1991 eruption of Mount Pinatubo in the Philippines, throw volcanic sulfuric acid high in the atmosphere, which can enhance the destructiveness of the chlorine chemicals that attack the ozone layer.

Other scientists believe that the hole increases each year because of human activities, especially the introduction of chlorofluorocarbons (CFCs)—substances used in coolants in refrigerators and air conditioners, and in cleaning solvents—into the atmosphere. As the CFCs rise into the stratosphere, ultraviolet radiation is intense enough to split the CFC molecules and liberate chlorine atoms. The chlorine then attacks the ozone, stealing an oxygen atom from an ozone molecule to form chlorine monoxide (ClO) and leaving behind an ordinary molecule of oxygen (O_2). When the ClO collides with a free oxygen atom, the oxygens combine into an ordinary molecule of oxygen and frees the chlorine to steal another oxygen atom from another ozone molecule, and so on.

The solution to ozone-hole expansion has been to ban or reduce the use of ozone-depleting chemicals, including CFCs, halons, and methyl bromide. By the mid-1990s, many countries slowed production of methyl bromide and HCFCs. As of 1994, there was a ban on halons. Under the 1987 international agreement known as the Montreal Protocol, and a later amendment in 1990, 56 nations have banned CFC production by the year 2000; the accord also provides funds to developing nations to build industries that do not rely on ozone-depleting chemicals. But past emissions will remain in the atmosphere for decades, with the potential to continue to harm the ozone layer.

The effects of the ozone hole's expansion and contraction are unknown. It is believed that a thinning of the ozone layer could cause a higher incidence of human skin cancer and cataracts.

In addition, the loss of delicate single-celled plankton, killed by increased radiation from the Sun, could cause an imbalance in the ocean food chain and decrease worldwide levels of oxygen.

EL NIÑO AND THE WORLD CLIMATE

El Niño is a seasonal ocean current flowing south along the coast of northern Peru; it peaks between January and March. The current is warm, nutrient-poor, and has low salinity. It travels a few degrees south of the equator before converging with the north-flowing Peru current. But some years, a weakening of normally strong southeast trade winds allows the current to extend farther south.

As the water temperature rises, it kills the plankton (single-celled organisms), forcing larger organisms to starve or leave the area. The warmer water also causes an increase in evaporation, which results in more rainfall in some areas. And if the ocean current patterns change, the Western Hemisphere, Europe, Asia, and the south Pacific Ocean can experience either floods or droughts.

Because of the changes in weather patterns brought on by El Niño, the current can precipitate several environmental disasters. One of the worst El Niños occurred between 1982 and 1983: Kelp forests in the upper levels of the ocean were killed and there was a major loss of sea birds—all of which had a major effect on the local Pacific food chain. Two minor El Niños occurred between 1987 and 1988, and in 1993.

Urbanization and Overpopulation

Urbanization and *overpopulation* create several environmental concerns. Rapid growth of cities can cause polluted air, inadequate sewage system and water supplies, and inadequate health care, food, and water. Around cities, deforestation and soil erosion—from increased developments and agriculture—can create air and water pollution. At the end of 1994, approximately 6 billion people shared the Earth and its resources. United Nations' studies estimate that the world population will reach 7.5 billion by 2100; other studies suggest that it will reach 11 to 14 billion people by that year.

RECYCLING

What Is Recycling?

Recycling reduces the amount of materials entering the environment. There is a definite need to recycle: Without recycling, many of our renewable and nonrenewable resources will eventually become severely depleted.

The major points of recycling include reducing waste, reusing materials, recycling materials that can be converted to other products, and conserving energy. Recycling helps keep large amounts of solid waste out of the landfills, thus saving the cost of waste disposal. It conserves resources, saves money, and generally uses less energy and creates less pollution than primary manufacturing. Recycling includes backyard composting of lawn and food wastes and community collection of recyclables. In the past decade, mandatory recycling has decreased the amount of wastes reaching landfills in some areas by more than 50 percent.

There are some drawbacks to recycling. Some materials that are reformed into other products cause pollution problems of their own as they are manufactured. Probably the worst problem is the market for the recyclables: Though many communities are enthusiastic about recycling, it is difficult to find potential buyers of the materials. For example, the American Paper Institute reported an 86 percent rise in newsprint recycling between 1989 and 1990, but due to a glut of newsprint on the market, recycling facilities lost money and closed. However, companies continue to find new uses for newsprint and develop new methods of processing recycled newsprint. In addition, people are demanding recycled paper, thus creating a market (though it can initially be expensive to produce it).

What Our Garbage Contains

Material	Amounts Generated in United States (millions of tons) per year	Recovered (%)
Nonfood products		
Paper and paperboard	72	26
Glass	13	12
Aluminum	3	38
Ferrous (iron) metals	12	6
Other metals	1	65
Plastics	14	1
Rubber and leather	5	2
Textiles	4	0.6
Wood	7	0
Other	3	22
Other wastes		
Food	13	0
Yard	32	2
Miscellaneous inorganic	3	0
Approximate total municipal solid wastes	180	13

What Is Recycling Worth?

Recycled Material	Worth (average price per ton in dollars)
Paper	
White ledger	45
Cardboard boxes	35
Newspapers	10
Metals	
Aluminum cans	1,050
Steel	55
Other	
Plastic (clear soda bottles)	120
Glass	40

OUR ENERGY SOURCES

Energy Sources

In many cases, energy sources are dependent on nonrenewable resources.

Fossil fuels, usually in the form of coal, oil, and natural gas, are burned to produce power. Use of fossil fuels has grown tenfold in the twentieth century, providing about 90 percent of the world's commercial energy supplies. The traditional fossil-fuel power plant produces electricity by burning the fuel to create the heat necessary to produce steam. The steam is then used to turn turbogenerators to produce electricity. The major concern with fossil fuels is the amount of carbon dioxide (and other greenhouse gases) released, which some scientists believe contributes to global warming. In addition, all fossil fuels are nonrenewable resources.

Hydropower, or hydroelectric power, harnesses the kinetic energy of falling water and is derived from water sources. Only about four percent of the energy used in the United States is derived from hydropower, owing to the scarcity of good locations for building large dams.

Nuclear power is generated with radioactive fuel. It uses the thermal energy released by nuclear fission to generate steam, which turns turbogenerators to produce electricity. There are two major concerns with nuclear energy: the safety of the plant itself and the disposal of radioactive waste.

Other energy sources are based on renewable resources.

Geothermal energy is derived from the natural heat below the surface of the Earth. The hot springs and geysers of Yellowstone National Park, Wyoming, are examples of geothermal sites. The potential for geothermal power is low for many reasons, including the facts that there are not enough hot springs at the Earth's surface, many of the wells run dry in a short period, and the steam or hot water is often contaminated with sulfur compounds. So far, the development of geothermal power has also been hampered by the high costs involved in developing these energy sources.

Incineration is one of the more controversial methods of generating electrical power. In this system, solid waste is burned to produce steam for generators. Incinerators, which have been used for more than a half century in various countries around the world, also help solve waste disposal problems. However, the drawbacks include the disposal of the ash and concern over the impact on air quality.

Nuclear fusion (as opposed to nuclear fission, the process currently used in nuclear power plants) is the same process that produces the Sun's energy—converting hydrogen to helium. On Earth, the fuel for fusion is heavy water, that is, water formed with deuterium (a hydrogen atom with a neutron in the nucleus). To produce fusion power, two forms of hydrogen must fuse and form helium and neutrons. As the energetic neutrons slow and cool down, they give up energy as heat. The heat is transferred to water where it creates steam, which is used to drive turbine generators to produce electricity. But this method of producing power is expensive and time-consuming (it takes enormous amounts of energy to get the reaction started), and a simple method has not been discovered. A simpler, but still theoretical (and controversial), method is called "cold fusion," which would not require heat to start the reaction. The advantages of fusion over fission are increased safety and fewer radioactive wastes.

With *solar power*, the Sun's energy is converted into usable forms of electricity. Solar power is relatively low cost and is essentially free from pollution. Passive solar energy systems have been installed in homes, factories, and offices in the past decade; but other sources of power continue to dominate, and solar collection devices are most likely to be used for communications and on satellites. Three major concerns with solar power include the means of storing the energy on cloudy days (and in areas with less sunlight), the amount of space required for a solar power facility, and ways of generating adequate power for larger facilities at a reasonable price.

Tidal power, capturing the force of ocean tides, has long been intriguing as a potential source of power. Small turbine generators would produce energy, as the tides turn the blades, but the amount of electricity produced would be low. A more practical alternative is to build a tidal dam across a bay or estuary; in fact, a tidal dam in France generates about as much power as a small fossil fuel–burning electric plant. Unfortunately, there are few bays and estuaries that are appropriate for this type of power plant. In addition, such plants would potentially interfere with the ecological balance of the region.

Wind power has been used for centuries to pump water and grind grain. Today, wind power turns propeller-shaped windmills—such as on the large-scale electric-generating stations (or "wind farms") found in central California. Problems with wind power include the need to site windmills where winds are consistent, the amount of space they require, and the difficulty in storing large amounts of energy during calm periods.

GASOLINE ALTERNATIVES

Because of gasoline's high cost to consumers and to the environment, researchers are exploring alternative fuels for automobiles and motor vehicles. Although all are being used on an experimental basis, the alternatives are years away from availability to the consumer—until they are cost competitive with gasoline.

Compressed natural gas (CNG) held in high-pressure tanks in a car's trunk could power a car for 250 miles, and be refilled at special stations.

Electric cars—which run on batteries or solar cells—have been around for decades. Most electric cars run fewer miles per charge than gasoline-driven cars do on a tankful of gas, but they are definitely less polluting. The biggest need is for a faster way to recharge the batteries.

A way to *reformulate gasoline* to reduce toxic emissions would be a boon for the environment. The problem with cleaner gas is it would cost more to produce and would still pollute the air, although to a lesser degree.

Alcohol alternatives include *gasohol*, a 90 percent gasoline and 10 percent alcohol blend, made from natural gas, corn, coal, or wood, that can be used without adjustments to most gasoline-driven engines; *methanol* (wood alcohol), which is clean and in relatively abundant supply but is not a renewable resource and yields lower mileage than gasoline; and *ethanol* (grain alcohol), which is made from renewable resources but emits toxic aldehydes, is twice the cost of gasoline, and requires abundant amounts of agricultural land for production.

Hydrogen emits no pollutants and is up to 45 percent more efficient than gasoline (it is burned as gas by a specially designed engine). The source of electricity to separate the hydrogen is the main environmental impact; another problem is how to store the hydrogen, which is highly explosive.

PRESERVING NATURE

In order to preserve nature, national parks, wildlife refuges, and caves and caverns have been set aside in the United States. National parks not only preserve nature but also commemorate certain events or historic figures. Wildlife refuges preserve habitats, for the protection of animals and plants. Caves are preserved for their unique environment, for the habitat they provide for specialized wildlife, and for their role in early human history. (For a listing of United States National Parks, United States National Wildlife Refuges, and caves, see Chapter 14.)

There are about 367 sites in the national park system; these are located in 48 states and the District of Columbia, and include historic sites, battlefields, parks, memorials, military parks, parkways, preserves, rivers, scenic trails, seashores, and other types of sites. The largest site is Alaska's Wrangell–St. Elias National Park and Preserve, covering 13,200,000 acres; the smallest site is Philadelphia's Thaddeus Kosciuszko National Memorial, covering only 0.02 acre and commemorating the Polish-born Revolutionary War hero.

National wildlife refuges, also called wildlife preserves, total more than 450 and include more than 90 million acres. Every state has at least one national wildlife refuge. They are home to more than 800 species of animals and birds. The first refuge, founded in 1903, was the three-acre Pelican Island, Florida, a pelican and heron rookery. This rookery was the impetus that eventually led to the National Wildlife Refuge (NWR) system, which was established to ensure the acquisition, establishment, and maintenance of wildlife habitats. The largest is Alaska's Yukon Delta, measuring about 20 million acres; the smallest is Minnesota's Mille Lacs, which is less than an acre. The refuges are managed by the U.S. Fish and Wildlife Service.

Compared to more obvious habitats such as oceans, rivers, and forests, caves are often ignored in terms of preservation. But caves are fragile, with unique wildlife numbering about 1,200 species, including troglophiles (animals that can live nowhere else but in caves) such as certain bats and blindfish. Most caves are found on land in areas with karst topography, characterized by limestone rock that is worn away by underground water; they are more rarely found carved out along a rocky sea coast. Caves supply water from springs; raw materials, such as guano, a fertilizer derived from the excrement of bats and other animals; organic molds used for antibiotics; animal and human fossils; and, often, contain evidence of ancient human activity. They are divided into show caves, which are usually open to the public, and wild caves, which are not. It is estimated that there are 30,000 caves in the United States, and additional ones are discovered every year. Most caves are run by private groups or under the auspices of the National Park Service.

HOLDING ON TO THE LAST WILDERNESS

Antarctica accounts for 10 percent of the Earth's land surface. Covered with ice and rock, the continent is nonetheless home to a vast number of organisms. But Antarctica has been a center of controversy for the past decade: How do we protect this unique habitat yet open it to access by everyone?

Most of the continent is covered with ice, in places almost 3 miles (5 kilometers) deep. If the ice were to melt, it would raise ocean levels by more than 160 feet (50 meters). The seas around the continent are some of the richest, in terms of life, in the world. They are filled with krill, or small shrimp, which are the staple of many animals, including whales, penguins, seals, and dolphins. But there are now fears that commercial harvesting of krill will disrupt Antarctica's food chain.

Despite several treaties, there are still arguments about the future of the continent. Should countries be allowed to mine Antarctica's oil and mineral resources and proceed with other economic development? Or should it be protected from commercial exploitation, with strict controls on tourism and scientific research? It is a decision that has to be agreed upon by everyone who has laid claim to some part of Antarctica—which now includes over 39 countries.

MAJOR ENVIRONMENTALISTS

Carson, Rachel Louise (1907–1964)   American ecologist and author of several scientific and popular publications concerning ecology and the environment, many of which inspired environmental protection policies.

Commoner, Barry (1917–)   American biologist and educator who, since the early 1950s, has warned the public about the dangerous effects of modern technology on the environment.

Ehrlich, Paul Ralph (1932–)   American biologist and educator who first proposed the theory that human survival depends on the realization that the earth's natural resources are nonrenewable and too limited to support the growing population. He wrote *The Population Bomb* (1968).

Elton, Charles Sutherland (1900–1991)   British ecologist who developed, in the 1920s, the idea that organisms form a pyramid of food levels that keep the energy flow within the ecosystem in balance. At the base are the producers and at the top are herbivores and a small number of carnivores.

Leopold, Aldo (1886–1948)   American naturalist who was one of the first scientists to arouse public interest in wilderness conservation. He wrote *A Sand County Almanac* (1949).

MacArthur, Robert Helmer (1930–1972)   American ecologist who, along with Edward O. Wilson, wrote *The Theory of Island Biogeography*, which marked the beginning of biogeography, a branch of ecology that focuses on stable ecological systems.

Malthus, Thomas Robert (1766–1834)   British economist who wrote some of the earliest accounts of the problems encountered by an expanding human population.

Marsh, George Perkins (1801–1882)   American statesman, diplomat, and scholar who is noted for his pioneering work in the field of conservation.

Muir, John (1838–1914)   British-born American naturalist who is noted for his work to gain popular and federal support of forest conservation.

Müller, Paul Hermann (1899–1965)   Swiss chemist who discovered the effect of the insecticide DDT. He won the Nobel Prize in 1948.

Pinchot, Gifford (1865–1946)   American public official who made several great conservation contributions during Theodore Roosevelt's presidency (1901–1909).

Powell, John Wesley (1834–1902)   American geologist, ethnologist, and anthropologist whose explorations of the United States, especially in the West, laid the groundwork for numerous federal conservation projects.

White, Gilbert (1720–1793)   British naturalist who wrote *The Natural History and Antiquities of Selborne*, one of the first known works on ecology.

Wilson, Edward Osborne (1929–)   American entomologist, ecologist, and sociobiologist who, along with Robert H. MacArthur, wrote *The Theory of Island Biogeography*, which marked the beginning of biogeography, a branch of ecology that focuses on stable ecological systems.

SIGNIFICANT SCIENTIFIC DISCOVERIES IN ENVIRONMENTAL SCIENCE

B.C.	20	Strabo's *Geography* was the first collection of all geographic knowledge
A.D.	100	Chinese invented the first insecticide using a powder of dried chrysanthemum flowers
	304	Chinese recorded the first example of a biological control of pests, in which selected ants were used to protect mandarin oranges from other insects
	1789	Gilbert White wrote the first book on ecology, *The Natural History and Antiquities of Selborne*
	1804	Nicholas de Saussure discovered that plants need carbon dioxide from the air and nitrogen from the soil
	1849	U.S. Department of the Interior established
	1857	First great city park, Central Park in New York City, established
	1869	John W. Powell led the first party to navigate the Colorado River through the Grand Canyon
	1879	U.S. Geological Survey established
	1882	First hydroelectric plant opened in Wisconsin
	1891	Yosemite National Park opened in California
	1892	John Muir established the Sierra Club
	1897	The establishment of progressive environmentalism, a movement that supports government intervention to modify the exploitation of natural resources by private developers
	1898	Rivers and Harbors Act banned pollution of navigable waters in the United States
	1908	The Grand Canyon was set aside as a national monument
	1908	Chlorination was first used to treat water, making the water 10 times purer than when filtered
	1916	U.S. National Park Service established
	1930	Chlorofluorocarbons (CFCs) determined to be safe refrigerants because of their nontoxic and noncombustible properties
	1933	Tennessee Valley Authority formed to determine the impact of hydropower projects before building on the Tennessee River
		Development of the Civilian Conservation Corps, which employed over 2 million Americans to help in forestry, flood control, and beautification projects around the United States
	1934	Worst drought recorded in the United States
		Russian ecologist G. F. Gause determined that two similar species cannot occupy the same ecological niches for long periods of time, called Gause's principle
	1935	U.S. Soil Conservation Service established
	1946	U.S. Atomic Energy Commission established for the development of peaceful use of nuclear power
	1956	Water Pollution Control Act made federal money available for water treatment plants
	1962	Rachel Carson published *Silent Spring*, a look at the dangers of the unchecked use of pesticides in nature
	1963	The Nuclear Test Ban Treaty stopped the aboveground testing of nuclear weapons
	1970	First Earth Day celebrated in the United States
		National Environmental Policy Act established, which calls for federal agencies to issue an environmental impact statement for all construction projects thus undertaken
		An amended Clean Air Act was toughened but failed to address acid rain and airborne toxic chemicals

1972	DDT, a pesticide that caused a decline in several bird species, was phased out in the United States
	Oregon passed the first bottle recycling law
1973	Congress approved licensing of a 789-mile pipeline in Alaska, from the North Slope oil fields to the Port of Valdez
	Arab oil embargo created an energy crisis in the United States, with gasoline and heating oil shortages
1976	Studies showed that chlorofluorocarbons from spray cans contributed to the decrease in ozone
1978	People were evacuated from Love Canal, New York, which was discovered to have been a major chemical waste dump
1979	Three Mile Island nuclear power plant in Pennsylvania experienced a near meltdown
1980	The U.S. Supreme Court ruled that a microbe developed by General Electric could be patented for oil cleanup
1986	Chernobyl nuclear power plant in the Soviet Union experienced a massive failure, contaminating large areas of the surrounding region and northern Europe
1987	The Montreal Protocol was signed by 24 countries, reducing, and eventually phasing out, the use of chlorofluorocarbons by the end of the century
1988	Radon contamination found to be more prevalent in United States homes than previously thought
1990	Scientists determined that 1990 was the warmest year on record.
1991	The United States agreed to protect Antarctica from mineral excavation, and to preserve the region's native flora and fauna
	Weed scientists reveal the "smother plant," the first intentionally developed biological herbicide
1992	Small amounts of ozone depletion were reported for the first time in the Northern Hemisphere
1993	The ozone hole over Antarctica reached record size, thought to be the continuing result of the volcanic eruption of Mount Pinatubo

COMMON TERMS IN ENVIRONMENTAL SCIENCE

adaptation   Any feature of an organism that increases its chances of survival.

aerobic organism   An organism that can live only in the presence of oxygen.

aerosols   Particles so small that they tend to remain suspended in the atmosphere for years.

anaerobic organism   An organism that does not need oxygen to survive.

aquaculture   The growing of marine and freshwater organisms—mainly fish—in a controlled environment. The organisms are used either for food or to stock lakes, streams, and rivers.

biodegradable   Able to degrade into components that are easily accepted into the local environment.

biological oxygen demand (BOD)   The measure of the amount of organic material in waste water. Municipal and industrial waste waters must be treated physically and chemically to lower the BOD before the water is returned to the natural environment.

biome   A climax community that is characteristic of a certain region.

biosphere   The entire zone of the Earth that is able to sustain life. It includes the atmosphere, hydrosphere (water regions), and parts of the lithosphere.

carbon dioxide A gas that constitutes less than one percent of the Earth's atmosphere. In general, it is released by animal respiration and is taken in by plants during photosynthesis.

carcinogen A substance that is shown to cause cancer.

carnivore An animal whose diet consists mainly of flesh. Lions and wolves are carnivorous.

chlorinated hydrocarbons A group of persistent chemicals that are used in the manufacture of certain pesticides.

climax The final, stable stage of development that a community or species obtains in a given environment. Climax communities are often called biomes.

competition The contest between living organisms for limited space, food, and/or light.

contaminant A foreign or unwanted material that enters the environment.

dichloro-diphenyl-trichloro-ethane (DDT) An odorless, colorless, water-insoluble crystal-line insecticide. It was eventually banned in the United States, after it was shown to cause the decline of certain birdlife.

decomposition The more or less permanent structural breakdown of a molecule into its components (atoms or molecules). It is also used in reference to the decay of organic material in the environment.

ecological succession The natural progression of plant and animal species within an area following the disturbance of the plant cover.

ecotone The border between two major ecosystems, such as the region between the tundra and the northern forests.

eutrophication The process by which water becomes better nourished, either by natural processes of maturation or artificial processes.

fire ecology Also known as prescribed burning, the natural burning of the land that allows for new growth of forests and flatland areas.

forest management The management of a forest that ensures continued production of its resources and services.

fossil fuels Coal, oil, and natural gas, which were formed from the remains of decaying plants and animals. Fossil fuels are nonrenewable. They also contain sulfur and nitrogen; when burned for energy, they release these elements into the atmosphere as gases, which often contribute to air pollution.

Gaia hypothesis Named for the Greek goddess of the Earth, Gaea, the Gaia hypothesis (an idea put forth by James Lovelock) proposes that the Earth should be regarded as a living organism. It suggests that the biosphere influences Earth processes in order to sustain and advance life.

Gause's principle Developed by Russian ecologist G. F. Gause and American naturalist J. Grinnell, this principle, also known as the principle of competitive exclusion, states that two similar species cannot occupy the same ecological niche for long periods.

habitat Characteristic surroundings of an area, determined chiefly by the vegetation.

habitat degradation The destruction of a habitat by physical means, by either natural or human activity. The degradation of a barrier island habitat by a hurricane is an example of a natural means; the degradation of wetland habitats by development is an example of human activity.

hazardous wastes   Materials that are considered dangerous to human, animal, or plant life, including pesticide residues, asbestos, acids and bases, and polychlorobiphenyls (PCBs).

heavy metals   See *trace metals*

herbivore   An animal whose diet consists mainly of plants. Deer and rabbit are herbivores.

insectivore   An animal whose diet consists mainly of insects. The bat is an insectivore.

land use   Classifications of land areas according to their present or potential economic use.

marsh gas   A combustible gas, mostly methane, that is produced from the decay of vegetation in stagnant water.

methane   A combustible, colorless, odorless, and tasteless gas, usually found in association with natural gas. Methane is a greenhouse gas and reacts with chlorine and bromine in sunlight.

niche   The dominate role of a species in nature, determined by what it eats, what eats it, where it lives, how it survives, and so on.

nutrient cycle   The movement of a chemical between the living and nonliving worlds, such as carbon migrating from the atmosphere into the human body, then into the atmosphere again.

omnivore   An animal whose diet consists of a combination of plants and flesh. Bears are omnivorous.

pesticide   A chemical agent that destroys pests. It is also called a biocide.

photosynthesis   The manufacture of food by green plants, using the energy from the Sun, soil nutrients, water, and carbon dioxide gas from the atmosphere.

pollutant   A chemical, particulate, or refuse material that impairs the purity of the water, air, or soil.

pollution   The destruction or impairment of a natural environment's purity by contaminants.

potable water   Water that is used for human consumption.

prescribed burning   See *fire ecology*

renewable resource   Resources, such as trees, that can be replaced into the environment. Most resources are nonrenewable, such as minerals and metal ores.

silviculture   The theory and practice of controlling the establishment and growth of stands of trees for goods or other benefits.

smog   A term coined that used to represent "smoke and fog," e.g., smoke and fog in London (1952, from industrial and residential releases) caused a major air pollution problem. Today, smog is often used to represent photochemical "smog," but it is not really smoke and fog. Photochemical smogs—common in many metropolitan areas—are the result of air changed into more harmful chemicals by the action of sunlight.

species diversity   The number of different species within a community.

temperature inversion   A layer of warm air overlying a layer of cooler surface air. The inversion layer often acts as a cap on the cooler air, preventing air pollutants from mixing with the upper layers of air and causing an excessive concentration of pollutants to remain in the surrounding air for long periods of time.

toxic substance   A substance that has a poisonous effect on humans or other organisms by physical contact, ingestion, and/or inhalation.

trace metals   Metals found in chemical products and nature that often find their way into the water and soil. Some trace metals, or heavy metals, are essential to health; others, especially in large amounts, may be toxic, including mercury, cadmium, and lead.

ADDITIONAL SOURCES OF INFORMATION

Anderson, B. N.,ed. *Ecologue: The Environmental Catalogue and Consumer's Guide for a Safe Earth.* Prentice-Hall, 1990.

Freudenthal, R. I., and S. L. Freudenthal. *What You Need to Know to Live with Chemicals.* Hill & Garnett, 1989.

Langone, J. *Our Endangered Earth: What We Can Do to Save It.* Little, Brown & Co., 1992.

Marchok, J. *Oh, No, Not My Electric Blanket, Too?* Jetmarc Group, 1991.

National Park Foundation. *The Complete Guide to America's National Parks.* National Park Foundation, 1993.

Rathje, William, and Cullen Murphy. *Rubbish! The Archaeology of Garbage: What Our Garbage Tells Us About Ourselves.* Harper Perennial, 1993.

Wight, Nebel. *Environmental Science.* Prentice-Hall, 1993.

12

Computer Science

What Is Computer Science?   496

Personal Computers   498

High-Performance Computers   505

Computer Languages   506

Computer Uses in Science and Technology   510

Computer Information and
Retrieval Services   511

Major Computer Scientists   513

Significant Discoveries in
Computer Science   514

Common Terms in Computer Science   516

Additional Sources of Information   522

WHAT IS COMPUTER SCIENCE?

Computer science is the study of computers, especially the interaction of their hardware and software. *Computer hardware specialists* concentrate on parts of the computer such as the disk drives or memory circuits; *computer programmers* develop the programs that run the computer.

The term *computer* is difficult to define: It was once defined as any machine that handled data—even manual calculators. Now computers are generally defined as devices that accept digital or analog data and process it into numerical or graphical results. To compare, a user obtains results on a calculator by manually entering each number and mathematical function in a step-by-step process; whereas computers process all data using internal, resident programs (or mathematical functions that are "built into" the program)—thus eliminating manual steps to obtain results.

Computers are used as tools for various purposes. For example, there are commercial, general-purpose, data-acquisition (hooked to instruments to obtain data), and process-control computers (computers that control processes such as those used in the robotics industry). Some computers are no larger than a thumbnail (called computer chips) and are single-purpose, programmed models that work inside another machine (for example, those inside a microwave oven or an automobile engine). The largest computers (which are not necessarily the most powerful) are often called supercomputers, though there is disagreement as to the real definition of the term.

Modern computers evolved due to several major advances in technology: Foremost is the harnessing of electricity, which powers the computer; integrated circuits, mostly arrays of transistors (and, previously, vacuum tubes), which improve the memory and speed of computers; and video technology, which makes computer monitors possible. In addition, computers use technically advanced materials, including metallic materials that act as conductors, and silicon and simple magnetic materials that act as memory elements.

BINARY COMPUTING

Strange as it may seem, digital computers come down to one basic premise: They operate with a series of on and off switches, using two digits in the binary (base 2) number system—0 (for off) and 1 (for on). This simple concept allows computers to work, our phone lines to ring, and even helps banks keep track of our money.

The binary system is much different than the decimal system. The decimal system is based on powers of ten. For example, in base 10, the number "111" means one 100, plus one 10, plus one 1. Since the binary system is based on powers of two, the binary number "111" means one 4, plus one 2, plus one 1.

Decimal and Binary Equivalents

Decimal	Binary	Decimal	Binary
1	1	7	111
2	10	8	1000
3	11	9	1001
4	100	10	1010
5	101	100	1100100
6	110	1000	1111101000

Early Computing

Aside from fingers and toes, one of the earliest counting devices was the *abacus*, which was known in Egypt by at least 500 B.C. (it may have been invented by the Babylonians about 3000 B.C.). It later became popular in China and in ancient Greece and Rome. The portable, manually controlled device featured pebbles (or other objects, such as bamboo, ivory, or wood) that were moved along levels (usually wooden slats; wires for each level were used later); when properly aligned, the objects were in rows and columns. Each movement of a pebble represented a certain number, and the arrangement of the pebbles in the rows and columns would supply the user with a numeric result. Abaci were first used extensively by merchants and later by mathematicians. Experienced users could add, subtract, multiply, and divide—often as fast as today's manual, nonelectronic calculators.

Later calculating devices included a set of rods called Napier's bones, invented by Scottish mathematician John Napier in the seventeenth century (Napier also developed logarithms). In 1642, at the age of eighteen, French mathematician Blaise Pascal built the first automatic mechanical calculator that could add and subtract, called the Pascaline. It did not become commercially popular, as it was less expensive to hire a person to do the calculations by hand. In 1671, German mathematician Gottfried Wilhelm von Leibnitz invented a calculator that could also do multiplication and division. In 1745, Jacques de Vaucanson used holes punched in metal drums (and later in cards) to control textile looms, a step toward automation and computers. By 1801, Joseph-Marie Jacquard also used punched cards to program patterns in his textile looms.

The next major step toward computing took place in 1889 when the U.S. Census Department announced a contest to invent a machine that would make the 1890 census count easier. American inventor Herman Hollerith entered a machine that used punched cards and electromagnetic relays. The machine only took a month to process the data, but it was not capable of storing or acting on the information.

Early Abacus

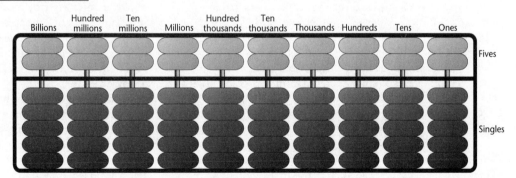

WHEN A COMPUTER CATCHES A VIRUS

A computer with a virus is a bit like a human with a cold: A foreign "body" (in the form of a hidden code attached to a program) "infects" the computer. But this virus can do more than cause sniffles and sneezing—it can cause the loss of irreplaceable data.

Computer viruses are a relatively new phenomenon, first appearing in the early 1980s. They are found in software (a virus is similar to a program within a program) and enter the computers unsuspectingly, either on an infected diskette or downloaded from another computer, usually over phone lines. Once in the computer, the virus can multiply, infecting other programs on the computer's hard disk. Some viruses perform seemingly "innocent" actions, such as flashing "Happy Birthday, Columbus," on Columbus Day. Other viruses are more insidious, and after being triggered by a certain key stroke, a date, or time, can wipe out whole files of data.

There are ways to cope with computer viruses. Some specialists suggest you never interact over phone lines with other computers and don't trade or buy software from a private party if at all possible. But if you do find it necessary to transfer data, try using antivirus software, which either works in the background at all times (as a Terminate-and-Stay-Resident program [TSR]) or searches files on command. The software cannot detect and kill every deadly virus (perpetrators are unfortunately creating more viruses even as you read this), but good anti-virus software programs are frequently updated as new viruses are found, greatly increasing your chances of keeping your computer healthy.

PERSONAL COMPUTERS

Personal computers (also called *microcomputers* or *PCs*) are small, single-user computers. The first PCs were often thought of as electronic toys; today, they are used as tools in most businesses and many homes and have become an integral part of society. The Altair 8800 is often referred to as the first successful PC (1975); faster and more efficient models are produced every year.

Generally, personal computers have a screen for displaying information entered into the computer and information output from the computer, a keyboard to enter data, and a central storage device that allows the user to save data and run software. The main parts of a personal computer include the following.

The *monitor* is a type of output device. It is similar to a television screen in appearance and is often referred to as a cathode ray tube (CRT) or video display terminal (VDT). Liquid crystal displays (LCDs) are used for monitors in small laptops or notebook computers (for more information on smaller computers, see "Other Personal Computers," later in this chapter). Monitors allow the user to see the information entered, monitor the progress of the computer's compilation of the data or execution of commands, and view the final output of the computer's work. Monitors can be monochrome (including black on white, white on black, amber on black, or green on black) or color (ranging from four colors to hundreds of colors).

The *system unit* is the central part of the computer and houses the main components of the PC. The system unit includes the microprocessor (central processing unit, or CPU), memory, ports, drives, and wires—all the components that help pass data from one point to another.

The *keyboard* is an input device used to enter the data into the personal computer. There is no standard keyboard, but most follow the layout of letters on a typewriter (known as the QWERTY keyboard, named after the first five letters on the top left row). Depending on the type of computer, a keyboard has 84 (standard keyboard) to 101 keys (enhanced keyboard). In addition to the typewriter-style keyboard, most PC keyboards also contain a numeric keypad, function keys (sometimes called the "F keys"), and other special keys.

The *mouse* is a device that controls the movement of the cursor or pointer on the screen, usually acting in place of a keyboard. A mouse can be attached to a serial port of a personal computer by a long wire; some newer mice are wireless and send messages to the computer by infrared or radio signals.

The three types of mice are *mechanical, optical,* and *optomechanical.* The mechanical mouse (the most common) comes in a variety of shapes and sizes. Most mechanical mice fit into the hand and are equipped with two or three buttons at the top that control certain programmed functions. A rubber or metal ball on the bottom of the mouse rolls on a surface (for example, a mouse pad), directing the movement of the cursor or pointer. A mechanical mouse controlled by a finger is called a *trackball*—or simply an upside-down mouse—and is mainly found on notebook computers.

An optical mouse uses a laser that detects the mouse's movement over a special grid mat. An optomechanical mouse uses a combination of the mechanical and optical mouse techniques, but without the grid mat. More recently, *graphics tablets,* computers in which much of the input can be made by writing on a screen, use a stylus—a penlike device—instead of a mouse, but with the same types of buttons to control certain programmed functions.

A Typical Computer Keyboard

Computer Necessities

Each computer component and program has particular functions. In most cases, each is also dependent on other components and programs to function properly.

The *central processing unit* (CPU) is responsible for executing the instructions that a user enters into the personal computer.

Data from personal computers can be stored on computer *disks.* Disks are categorized as either magnetic or optical.

- *Magnetic disks* include floppy diskettes, hard disks, and tape and removable cartridges. Standard-size floppy disks are either 5.25 inches wide, holding 360K or 1.2MB of data (though 160K, 180K, and 320K disks still exist) or 3.5 inches wide (a microfloppy), holding 720K, 1.44MB, or 2.88MB of data. (Bernoulli disks, which resemble a cross between a floppy and a hard drive, can hold more than 20MB of data.) Hard drives are magnetic disks that run 2 to 20 times faster than a floppy drive and can store from 5MB to more than 3GB (gigabytes) of data. *Magnetic tapes* are often used for hard-drive backup; they resemble audio cassette tapes. *Removable cartridges* are magnetic and resemble a removable hard drive. They are slower than a hard drive and store about 40MB of data.

- Lasers are used to write information on *optical disks*, which usually hold more data than magnetic disks—up to 1,000 megabytes. Each requires a specific drive in which to run. CD-ROMs can be read many times, but the data is permanent and cannot be modified. WORMs (write-once, read-many) are optical disks that can be written on once but then behave as a CD, on which the data is permanent and cannot be changed. The data on EO disks (erasable optical or floptical disks) can be erased and replaced with new data.

- A computer *disk drive* can hold a diskette (floppy drive), a hard disk (hard drive), tape (tape drive), or CD (CD drive). Disk drives read data from, and generally write data to, a disk. Floppy and hard drives resemble the turntable of a record player, but they are much smaller and the disk rotates more rapidly; a tape drive resembles a small, compact cassette player; CD drives resemble an audio CD player.

  – *Floppy disk drives* are usually built into a computer's system unit. Floppy diskettes (often shortened to "floppy disks" or "floppies") are small, moveable diskettes that fit into a floppy drive. Data is accessed from, and saved to, a removable floppy diskette that is placed in the drive.

  – *Hard disk drives* are permanently installed disks inside the computer's system unit. Data is accessed and saved on the internal hard drive. There are also external hard drives.

  – *Tape drives* can be located either inside or outside a computer's system unit and are usually used to save or backup data from the hard drive; they are comparatively slower than a hard drive.

  – *CD drives* (compact disk) read CD-ROM (compact disk-read only memory) disks, which are becoming more popular because massive amounts of data can be stored on the disk. CD-ROM drives are usually external, though they are now becoming increasingly common as part of the computer's system unit. In most cases, data are accessed only from a CD drive.

The computer's *memory* is where the currently operating computer program and its data reside while the computer is in use. The term memory sometimes also refers to the amount of data stored in the computer and on tapes or disks (see also "Memory," later in this chapter).

The *motherboard* is the heart of the computer. It is the main circuit board and holds the memory chips, CPU, and serial and parallel ports. The motherboard contains the controllers that run the monitor, keyboard, and disk drives. It also has expansion slots that allow other boards or cards (called add-ons or expansion boards) to be attached.

The *operating system* is the most important program on the computer. It is necessary to run all the other programs, control peripheral devices, recognize the input from the keyboard, send output to the monitor, and keep track of files entered into the computer.

Computer *ports*, or interfaces, are used to attach peripherals (add-on devices) to the computer. Most computers have a parallel, serial, and game port. A *serial port* is used for transmitting one bit of data to the computer at a time. For example, a mouse and modem are often attached to a serial port. A *parallel port* allows more than one bit at a time to be transferred from the computer to a peripheral. For example, printers are usually attached to a parallel port (though some printers use a serial port). A *game port* is where peripherals such as joysticks are attached to the computer in order to play games.

Another type of port, the *small computer system interface* (SCSI, pronounced "scuzzy"), supports higher transmission speeds than conventional ports. SCSI ports allow the computer user to attach up to seven devices to the same port and are often used to connect such things as an external hard drive.

COMPUTER TALK

Computers have a language of their own. Here are some of the acronyms, abbreviations, and numbers to remember.

bit   The smallest unit of memory in a computer. A bit is a switch with a value of 0 (off) or 1 (on). Eight bits make up one byte, or character.

byte   A unit of memory used to represent one character, such as "R" or "5."

FAT   File allocation table; a table at the start of a disk that contains information on the location of each file on the disk.

GB   Gigabyte; is equal to 1024 megabytes.

K   Kilobytes; is equal to 1024 bytes.

MB   Megabytes; equal to 1024 kilobytes.

RAM   Random access memory; the "memory" used to run the programs, as well as data that can be written over and changed.

ROM   Read only memory; data that can only be read, not written over.

Adding On

There are several peripheral (usually outside) devices that can be added to a personal computer system.

The *modem* (an acronym for modulator-demodulator) is a device that allows a computer to contact another computer and transfer data over phone lines. Though computer data is stored digitally, it is transferred across phone lines in the form of analog waves, with the modem converting the waves back and forth. The first modems held the telephone's receiver in a cradle, with wire connections from the cradle to the computer; most of today's modems are internal or external solid-state devices. A number of modem interfaces are standard, but some computers need a certain protocol (a special way of formatting the data) in order to communicate with other computers over the modem.

In order for one computer to contact another computer, their modems must have similar settings. These settings include *baud rate* (in bits per second, or bps—the rate at which the data is sent and received, usually ranging from 300 baud to 28,800 baud, although higher bauds are becoming common); *parity*, which ensures the validity of the data and is set as either odd or even; and *data bits*, usually seven or eight, which tells the receiving computer the size of each character it should expect to receive.

Optical scanners, either handheld or stand-alone units, are devices that translate text and/or graphics from a piece of paper into a digital (graphic) image. There are two types of scanners: one that distinguishes graphics only; and one that distinguishes text only, by optical character recognition (OCR) that translates the text image into ASCII characters (see "Programming Codes," later in this chapter). There are also combination graphics/text scanners.

Optical scanners have various characteristics, including resolution (a higher number of dots per inch gives a clearer image), size and shape (ranging from handheld models to larger page scanners), and gray scaling (the number of shades of gray that a scanner can duplicate from an image, ranging from 16 to 256). Color scanners are also available, with many capable of translating hundreds of colors from the image to the computer screen (special printers can print the color images from the scanner).

The *printer* is a device that prints words or graphics on paper (see "Printers," below). Printers can range in sophistication from dot matrix (simple) to laser (more complicated).

MORE AND MORE FROM YOUR PC

How many times have you heard someone lament, "I just bought my computer last month, and it's already obsolete!" To an extent, this is true—what's new today in computers will be old by next month. Computer companies are constantly trying to make computers faster, more efficient, smaller, and more powerful—and all at a reduced cost to the computer user.

For example, one feature to hit the commercial market is the Bernoulli disk—a cross between a hard disk and a floppy disk, but slower than a hard drive. It is based on the principle of aerodynamic lift, where the disks float between the read/write heads, so there is never any contact. And because the disk is flexible, there are fewer hard disk crashes. The Bernoulli disk has been successfully introduced into the commercial market—at a low cost to the consumer.

But don't try to keep up with the latest and greatest in computers. The best way to approach your computer purchase is to examine what you really need to use a computer for, then determine the memory, peripherals, and style you want based on your analysis. Even if the computer you purchase is out-of-date in a few short months, it should still be close to what you really need. And remember—many computer parts are becoming more and more compatible with each other, so you may be able to upgrade parts of your computer to fit your changing needs.

The Personal Computer

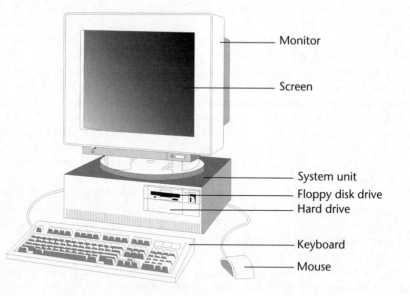

Monitor

Screen

System unit
Floppy disk drive
Hard drive

Keyboard
Mouse

Printers

Printers are devices that print text or illustrations onto paper. They are often classified by the quality of the type (draft, near-letter quality, or letter quality), impacting or nonimpacting, speed, font capability, and whether they can print graphics. Most printers fall into the following categories.

Dot-matrix printers create characters by striking an inked ribbon with pins. If the printer can also print graphics, it is called a dot matrix graphics printer.

Daisy-wheel printers create characters using a wheel with imprinted letters that strikes a ribbon, much like the ballhead of an electric typewriter. Daisy-wheels produce letter-quality print but do not print graphics.

Ink jet printers spray the ink on the paper through tiny nozzles moving rapidly across the page, producing letter-quality type and sharp graphics. A variation of the ink-jet printer is the bubble-jet printer.

Laser printers use a form of technology similar to photocopy machines, using heat to apply toner to paper. Laser printers produce sharper images than do ink-jet printers, and higher quality graphics. They are second only to line printers in speed.

Liquid crystal shutter printers are similar to laser printers but use liquid crystals to produce an image on the drum instead of lasers. Like lasers, they produce high-quality print and graphics.

Line printers use pins that print an entire line at a time. They are fast but produce lower-quality prints and graphics than laser and thermal printers.

Thermal printers push heated pins into heat-sensitive papers to produce print and graphics. They produce somewhat lower-quality print and graphics than laser printers. (Thermal printer technology is also used in most facsimile machines.)

Memory

Every computer comes with a certain amount of internal main memory, usually referred to as random-access memory (RAM); this is what is usually meant when someone speaks of computer "memory." There are other types of memory, depending on the type of computer.

An *electrically erasable programmable read-only memory* (EEPROM) is a memory chip capable of storing a computer program. Unlike PROM or EPROM, it can be erased and used over by exposing it to an electrical charge.

The *erasable programmable read-only memory* (EPROM) is a memory chip capable of storing a computer program. Unlike a PROM, it can be erased by exposing it to ultraviolet light, and used over.

A *programmable read-only memory* (PROM) is a memory chip capable of storing a computer program. As with ROM, once a PROM is used, no other information can replace the data.

The *random-access memory* (RAM) of a computer represents the amount of data the memory chips can hold at one time. For example, a computer with 640 kilobytes of memory can hold nearly 655,360 characters. Larger computers can hold megabytes of RAM. For example, a computer with four megabytes of RAM can hold over 4 million bytes of information.

RAM is also called "read and write" memory, in which a user can read data from, or write data to, memory. RAM can be thought of as the computer's work space and is considered to be volatile, or needing electricity to keep its contents; therefore, when the electricity to the computer is turned off, information in RAM is lost (unless it was previously saved to a disk drive or floppy).

The *read-only memory* (ROM) of a computer represents memory that cannot be changed or written to; ROM data can only be read. The ROM of a computer usually contains the set of instructions that allows the computer to work when it is turned on; ROM is not lost when the electricity to the computer is turned off.

The *video random-access memory* (VRAM) is a special type of memory used by video adapters.

Other Personal Computers

Today's personal computers are more compact and easier to use than the original personal computers. The following are a few new styles of personal computers.

Laptop computers are small, portable computers that often have the same disk capacity, amount of memory, and speed as larger, desktop personal computers. They have smaller keyboards and, with the use of flat-panel (monochrome or active matrix [color]) technology, the screens are lightweight and small. They range from about 4 pounds to 20 pounds. Because they are portable, laptop computers use rechargeable batteries.

Notebook computers are often classified as laptop computers, but more recently they have developed into a class of their own. A notebook computer folds up into a flat, notebooklike box and has a small keyboard and flat screen. Notebooks often have the same disk capacity, amount of memory, and speed as larger, desktop personal computers. The major differences between laptops and notebooks are weight—with most notebooks weighing under six pounds—and thinness. Because they are portable, notebook computers use rechargeable batteries.

Palmtop computers fit into the palm of the hand. They are portable computers but have fewer capabilities than desktop, laptop, or notebook computers. They are practical for certain specific uses, such as keeping a calendar and a list of addresses and telephone numbers.

Pad computers (or *graphics tablets*) resemble a writing pad, but the pen (sometimes attached by a cord, sometimes cordless) is really a mouse. The pen allows the user to write information instead of using a keyboard, or to draw without using a large mouse.

More Powerful Computing

Besides personal computers, there are other relatively small computers that are classified by power, size, and memory: For example, workstations, single-user computers considered to be in a class between personal computers and minicomputers, have extensive graphics capability and power. Minicomputers are considered to be medium-size computers, between microcomputers and mainframes in power (see also "High Performance Computers," later in this chapter), though this division has blurred in recent years. Generally, a minicomputer is a multiprocessing system that can support 10 to 200 users simultaneously, or run 10 to 200 programs at the same time.

Programs and the Personal Computer

There are several major uses for personal computers—all needing specific software in order to run.

Communication programs are used for communication between computers. They allow a user to connect with other users via modem and telephone lines. Once hooked to another computer, the user can send and receive messages and retrieve information (such as magazine and newspaper articles) over communication services.

Database programs replace address books, directories, and a filing cabinet of folders. Databases store lists of various items; for example, they are often used to make mailing lists.

Game programs allow the user to play interactive or single-user computer games.

Graphics programs allow a user to draw images on the computer; graphics can also be in the form of clip art or premade drawings. Some graphics programs may be used for laying out newsletters, brochures, flyers, and similar materials.

Spreadsheet programs are used to manipulate and store numbers. Spreadsheets replace the calculator and can reproduce columnar pads.

In most situations, *word-processing* programs have replaced the typewriter. Word-processing software allows a user to create and store letters, manuscripts, and memos. Many word processors also check spelling and grammar and can do specialized tasks, such as checking a word in a thesaurus, zooming in on a page, or creating an outline of a manuscript.

GETTING WITH THE PROGRAM

Many computer scientists break program types into two categories: applications and systems programs. Applications are just what the word implies—a way of applying the computer to a problem that needs to be solved. For example, a chemist may use an applications program to determine how protein folding takes place in the human body; an individual might use an applications program to keep track of monthly expenses and balance the checkbook.

Systems programs control the operation of the computer, independent of the application. For example, the computer's operating system is a system program.

HIGH-PERFORMANCE COMPUTERS

Numerous fields—especially the sciences, mathematics, and business—often require the use of high-performance computers to do complex tasks. The major advantage of high-performance computing is its ability to analyze extremely large groups of data at rapid speeds.

High-performance computers use computer languages that are more complex than languages for personal computers. Most high-performance computing output is conducive to scientific visualization (visual simulations of complex physical and biological systems based on the manipulation of data in the computer). These visualizations, many of which resemble movies or animations of a physical or biological event, allow the scientists to "see" certain scientific events or structures—such as the formation of a galaxy over millions of years (in only five minutes), or how DNA coils and knots during its fundamental biological processes.

Mainframe

Mainframe computers are large, high-performance computers that rank between minicomputers and supercomputers in power and memory. They can support hundreds of users and thus run hundreds of programs at the same time. To compare, mainframes are often considered more powerful than supercomputers; but supercomputers are faster when executing a single program (or a few programs).

Supercomputers

Supercomputers are stand-alone systems that currently have the highest level of computing power for a single unit. They are extremely expensive and are used for applications that need extensive amounts of memory and speed to perform complex mathematical calculations.

Supercomputers are ideal for scientific applications because of their ability to quickly analyze and manipulate large data sets with numerous variables. They are used in fluid dynamics calculations, weather prediction models, the study of environmental pollutants in the air or water, and in seismology, to name a few areas.

FINDING FRACTALS

The idea of fractal geometry began at the end of the nineteenth century, as mathematicians began to look more deeply into traditional Euclidean geometry. Fractals use a combination of the techniques from Euclidean geometry and calculus; the resulting data represent selected members of purely geometric shapes. The results are self-similar patterns, and when magnified their parts bear an exact resemblance to the whole; and fractals depart from the normally smooth curves of Euclidean geometry, with rough, jagged edges at all scales.

The word *fractal* is from the Latin *frangere* ("to break") and the related adjective *fractus* ("irregular and fragmented"). Fractals in nature include a goose down feather, a galaxy of stars, or the holes in a sponge. Scientists are using supercomputers to make "fake" fractal generations and explain how fractals appear in and affect the natural world. Their fractal studies generally include the mechanics behind the formation of certain physical phenomena—the meandering of a river, the way weather makes its way across the Earth, the chaotic convolutions of the brain, or even the aerodynamics of the air around a space shuttle wing.

Massive Parallel Processing

Massive parallel processing links more than one central processing unit (CPU) together and runs them simultaneously. The speed of the processing results from the way a problem is analyzed. Massive parallel processing involves either hooking several computers together or using a computer that has multiple CPUs.

COMPUTER LANGUAGES

Computer languages are currently broken down into four types.

Fourth-generation languages (4GL) are currently the highest level of computer language and are closest to human language.

Computer programming languages (or *high-level languages* or *third-generation languages*) are instructions for a computer to perform specific tasks. They are based on a specific vocabulary and set of grammatical rules. Each language, including BASIC, COBOL, FORTRAN, and C, contains specific words that mean something to the computer. For example, in some versions of BASIC, the word *run* at the end of a program tells the computer to start the program with all the directions that appeared before that command.

Assembly languages (or *second-generation language*) are a crossover between computer programming languages and machine languages, as they use both numbers and words.

Machine language (or *first-generation language*) refers to the language that computers understand. Unlike computer programming languages that use words, machine language uses numbers. Each type of computer processing unit (CPU) has its own machine language based on that hardware.

CREATING CHAOS

Scientists have always wrestled with this major problem: How to formulate theories based on patterns found in nature. Some events are predictable; complex systems, however, such as weather, are chaotic.

Because chaotic systems are nonlinear (in a linear system, one change is directly proportional to the other) and thus very difficult to solve, computers have been instrumental in the science of chaos. In the study of a chaotic system, a large number of variables need to be entered into the computer, which must be fast enough to get through all the numerous interacting calculations and have extensive memory to hold all the data.

Some scientists are using the theory of chaos to describe all natural systems in the universe, while others believe that chaos is not significant enough to change the way we think about the physical world. But there is no doubt that it can yield some insights into more complex phenomena, such as turbulence (for instance, as the turbulent movement of air over the wing of a space shuttle) or the growth of living systems.

High-Level Programming Languages

High-level programming languages are complex computer languages that enable a programmer to write programs that are independent of the type of computer they are developed on. They are called high-level because they are closer to human languages than any machine language. High-level languages must eventually be translated into machine language, usually by a compiler.

Ada was developed in 1979 for the U.S. Defense Department and was designed to do all types of applications, most in real time—from running missile guidance systems to performing business applications. It is still in use, mostly by the military.

BASIC, beginner's all-purpose symbolic instruction code, is a programming language that is used as a standard in most personal computers. It was developed by John Kemeny and Thomas Kurtz in 1965 at Dartmouth College. BASIC is a language that is "conversational" (mostly written words run the program) and is considered one of the simplest and easiest languages to learn and run. It is often one of the first computer languages studied by computer science students and is used in a variety of business applications.

C is a programming language that was developed in 1972 by Dennis Ritchie and Brian Kernighan at Bell Laboratories (now AT&T Bell Laboratories). It is used for all types of applications (including science and engineering), and its coding is similar to assembly language. It is popular because it uses relatively little memory. The first program written in C was for the UNIX operating system. It later became a popular programming language separate from UNIX.

C++ (pronounced *C-plus-plus*) is a programming language designed as a superset of C. It was developed by Bjarne Stroustrup at Bell Laboratories (now AT&T Bell Laboratories). C++ combines the C programming language and object-oriented features.

COBOL, common business-oriented language, was developed in 1959 by Grace Hopper for business applications that must be run on larger computers. Programs written in COBOL tend to be longer than most programs. COBOL is the most widely used programming language in the world.

FORTRAN, formula translator, was developed in 1956 at International Business Machines (IBM) and is the oldest high-level programming language. It is used mainly for scientific and mathematical applications, as it can easily handle complex and extensive computations. New forms of FORTRAN have evolved since the language was developed, such as FORTRAN IV and FORTRAN 77.

LISP, list processor, was conceived in 1958 by John McCarthy at the Massachusetts Institute of Technology. It is used extensively for artificial intelligence applications.

Pascal (named after Blaise Pascal, who, in the seventeenth century, built one of the first mechanical adding machines) is a programming language designed to allow programmers to write a program carefully and methodically. It was developed in 1971 by Niklaus Wirth. It is not used as extensively as the other programming languages because it is not as flexible and lacks certain tools needed to write some programs. (Wirth eventually addressed some of these problems by designing a second Pascal-type programming language, Modula-2.)

STICKING TOGETHER

What happens when you take a few smaller computers and hook them together? You get one of the best ways to stay in touch—a local-access network, or LAN.

Each computer (or node) has its own central processing unit (CPU) but can access data from other computers on the LAN. LANs are especially convenient for multiple users who need to work on the same information or use a single program simultaneously. And not only does the LAN connect like computers, it is also possible to attach unlike computers, allowing Macintosh and IBM-compatible computers to run on the same LAN.

Hookup of the LAN computers

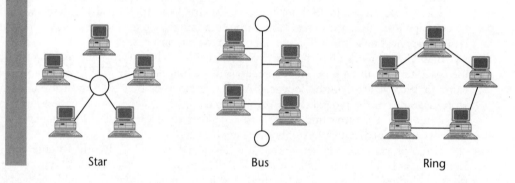

Star   Bus   Ring

Programming Codes

Programming codes are used to translate a program from one computer to another, by using a set of symbols or numbers that represent certain other symbols or text.

ASCII (pronounced *ask-ee*), the best-known programming code, stands for American standard code for information interchange. The numbers in ASCII, from 0 to 127, represent certain characters (letters and numbers) in a program; extended ASCII, which includes 128 additional characters, represents numbers, letters (standard letters and non-English characters), graphic representations, and mathematical symbols in a program. Each character in ASCII requires a full byte.

The ASCII code is used by many computer systems so that data can be easily exchanged between various programs. For example, in order to read the text output from one word-processing program in another word processor, the text file is translated into ASCII.

EBCDIC (pronounced *ebsi-dick*), standing for extended binary-coded decimal interchange code, is used by IBM-compatible computers and represents characters as numbers. It is used mainly to code larger computers, not personal computers.

Partial List of ASCII Codes

Binary	Octal			Binary	Octal	
0000000	000	NUL	(Blank)	0110001	061	1
0000001	001	SOH	(Start of Header)	0110010	062	2
0000010	002	STX	(Start of Text)	0110011	063	3
0000011	003	ETX	(End of Text)	0110100	064	4
0000100	004	EOT	(End of Transmission)	0110101	065	5
0000101	005	ENQ	(Enquiry)	0110110	066	6
0000110	006	ACK	(Acknowledge [Positive])	0110111	067	7
0000111	007	BEL	(Bell)	0111000	070	8
0001000	010	BS	(Backspace)	0111001	071	9
0001001	011	HT	(Horizontal Tabulation)	0111010	072	:
0001010	012	LF	(Line Feed)	0111011	073	.;
0001011	013	VT	(Vertical Tabulation)	0111100	074	< (Less Than)
0001100	014	FF	(Form Feed)	0111101	075	=
0001101	015	CR	(Carriage Return)	0111110	076	> (Greater Than)
0001110	016	SO	(Shift Out)	0111111	077	?
0001111	017	SI	(Shift In)	1000000	100	@
0010000	020	DLE	(Data Link Escape)	1000001	101	A
0010001	021	DC1	(Device Control 1)	1000010	102	B
0010010	022	DC2	(Device Control 2)	1000011	103	C
0010011	023	DC3	(Device Control 3)	1000100	104	D
0010100	024	DC4	(Device Control 4-Stop)	1000101	105	E
0010101	025	NAK	(Negative Acknowledge)	1000110	106	F
0010110	026	SYN	(Synchronization)	1000111	107	G
0010111	027	ETB	(End of Text Block)	1001000	110	H
0011000	030	CAN	(Cancel)	1001001	111	I
0011001	031	EM	(End of Medium)	1001010	112	J
0011010	032	SUB	(Substitute)	1001011	113	K
0011011	033	ESC	(Escape)	1001100	114	L
0011100	034	FS	(File Separator)	1001101	115	M
0011101	035	GS	(Group Separator)	1001110	116	N
0011110	036	RS	(Record Separator)	1001111	117	O
0011111	037	US	(Unit Separator)	1010000	120	P
0100000	040	SP	(Space)	1010001	121	Q
0100001	041	!		1010010	122	R
0100010	042	"		1010011	123	S
0100011	043	#		1010100	124	T
0100100	044	$		1010101	125	U
0100101	045	%		1010110	126	V
0100110	046	&		1010111	127	W
0100111	047	'	(Closing Single Quote)	1011000	130	X
0101000	050	(		1011001	131	Y
0101001	051	)		1011010	132	Z
0101010	052	*		1011011	133	[(Opening bracket)
0101011	053	+		1011100	134	\ (Reverse slant)
0101100	054	,	(Comma)	1011101	135	] (Closing bracket)
0101101	055	-	(Hyphen)	1011110	136	^ (Circumflex)
0101110	056	.	(Period)	1011111	137	_ (Underline)
0101111	057	/		1100000	140	' (Opening single quote)
0110000	060	0		1100001	141	a

Binary	Octal			Binary	Octal		
1100010	142	b		1110001	161	q	
1100011	143	c		1110010	162	r	
1100100	144	d		1110011	163	s	
1100101	145	e		1110100	164	t	
1100110	146	f		1110101	165	u	
1100111	147	g		1110110	166	v	
1101000	150	h		1110111	167	w	
1101001	151	i		1111000	170	x	
1101010	152	j		1111001	171	y	
1101011	153	k		1111010	172	z	
1101100	154	l		1111011	173	{	(Opening brace)
1101101	155	m		1111100	174	|	(Vertical line)
1101110	156	n		1111101	175	}	(Closing brace)
1101111	157	o		1111110	176	~	(Overline [tilde])
1110000	160	p		1111111	177	DEL	(Delete/rubout)

COMPUTER USES IN SCIENCE AND TECHNOLOGY

Artificial Intelligence

Artificial intelligence (AI)—the development of computers that think and respond like a human—is one of the fastest growing branches of computer science. The term was coined in the mid-1950s by John McCarthy at the Massachusetts Institute of Technology. AI languages include list processor (LISP).

One of the greatest results of artificial intelligence thus far is the ability for a computer to understand human speech. So far, however, programming a computer to comprehend anything but the most rudimentary commands has been difficult. Scientists believe that artificial intelligence will have a multitude of other applications, including the following.

expert systems Artificial intelligence can be used to decide real-life situations, such as the diagnoses of disease based on symptoms or the scheduling of a project that has hundreds of variables. Expert systems can replace certain tasks or add to the knowledge of the user.

fuzzy logic Fuzzy logic is the process of solving problems that are filled with ambiguous data, such as if the room temperature is too hot, too cold, or just right. It uses a multivalued logic to produce an answer that is a "best guess" and, thus, a more precise and weighted answer.

interpreting languages Artificial intelligence incorporated into certain types of computers could interpret languages in real time.

neural networks Artificial intelligence may eventually allow a computer to work and act like a human brain. The parts of some computers that come close to simulating the human brain are called neural networks, which do not use the traditional digital model (manipulating 0s and 1s) but create connections between processing elements, the computer's equivalent of the brain's neurons. So far neural networks and AI have been used to some extent in voice-recognition applications and in translating languages.

precision decisions Computers that have artificial intelligence can make precision decisions as to the best interpretation of scientific data.

robotics Robots can be developed that will see and hear for humans. For example, an unmanned mission to Mars could include a "smart" robot, which would be intelligent enough to "know" that it had to stop at the edge of a cliff—without any input from humans. Other such robots can eventually be used in assembly plants to manipulate objects and make certain decisions.

game playing Computer games that deal with decision-making skills, such as chess, often use a low-end type of artificial intelligence to make decisions.

CAD/CAM Animation

Computer-aided design/computer-aided manufacturing (CAD/CAM) use computer systems to design and manufacture products, respectively. The CAD system allows the designer to represent an object graphically on a computer, and to move or rotate the object in any direction. When the designer changes one part of the design, the CAD system compensates and redraws the object to the designer's new specifications. Computer-aided design and drafting (CADD) is a version of CAD that adds drafting features. This allows the engineer to insert size annotations and other specifications into the design of the product.

The CAM system allows the manufacturer to make the product. Generally, the information from the CAD controls the manufacturing process under CAM, often with robotics directing the actual manufacturing.

Desktop Publishing and Multimedia

Desktop publishing involves using a personal computer or workstation to develop high-quality printed documents. *Multimedia* presentations combine video and audio capabilities with computer applications.

THE VIRTUAL WORLD

Some scientists believe that virtual reality—or the use of computers to allow a person to "see" an artificial, three-dimensional world—will have many uses in science. For example, what better way to visit the planet Mars without even leaving Earth? Virtual reality allows a person to interact with an environment (produced by a computer) as if it were real. The user wears a large headset that covers his eyes (called a head-mounted display) and special glove or body suit, all attached to a computer. When the user turns his head, or moves his hand or body, the visual display moves accordingly. The displayed images are cartoonlike, but scientists continue to perfect the graphics.

The uses of virtual reality are many: A person can virtually "walk" around an office, "moving" furniture, doors, or any other object to find the desired decor. Space scientists can virtually "visit" a planet, roving around objects on the surface, exploring a canyon, and checking the soil. On a more down-to-earth scale, virtual reality can be used for training the physically disabled—to simulate wheelchairs, for instance.

Could there one day be a "holodeck," as on the television program "Star Trek: Voyager"? Will we be able to walk around a blank room filled will holographic images that seem real to our eyes? It seems more and more possible every day.

COMPUTER INFORMATION AND RETRIEVAL SERVICES

Computers are used not only in science, mathematics, and business, but also to store and communicate information. One of the best ways to communicate around the country or the world is by computer information and retrieval services, also called *on-line data services* or *database services.*

In order to contact a data service, a computer must use a modem, a device that can transmit and receive data across telephone lines. There are thousands of on-line services. Some are for general use and offer a wide variety of services, including bulletin boards (special-interest messages sent among computer service users), encyclopedias, and weather information; other services are more specific, including, for example, communication services that provide information from a specific government agency.

Some of the better-known communication (or on-line) services include the following.

AOL   America Online provides information to the general public. It includes a magazine database, forums, bulletin boards, personal message exchange, and much more.

BRS   The Bibliographic Retrieval Service provides general information and has one of the largest collections of medical databases.

CompuServe   CompuServe is one of the largest general information services, and a gateway to numerous other services. Its offerings include forums, magazine databases, personal message exchange, bulletin boards, and much more.

Dialog   The largest public database service, Dialog was developed by Lockheed originally as a tool for NASA researchers. The service includes hundreds of databases and full-text journals, magazines, newspapers, and newsletters. It also offers the Knowledge Index, providing access to Dialog's most popular databases (including *Magazine Index, Books in Print,* and ERIC [Educational Resources Information Center]).

GEnie   The General Electric Network for Information Exchange offers a news service, a custom clipping service, and medical, law, and educational roundtables.

Internet   Internet was a project put together in the late 1960s by the United States' Defense Advanced Research Projects Agency (DARPA), linking together seven university computer science departments and allowing the users to exchange messages and research with each other. It has now grown to possibly 2 million host computers all over the world—and continues to grow. Internet is a complex system, giving access to massive amounts of information and allowing communication between users. Messages can be sent via various communication services to other users on Internet by using special computer addresses.

Lexis/Nexis   Nexis has an extensive database for publications and has information on news events; Lexis offers a legal database.

NewsNet   NewsNet provides information on hundreds of newsletters and information services in more than 45 subject areas, and scans numerous domestic and international newswires.

Prodigy   Prodigy is a general computer communications service that offers easy access and user-friendly methods of communication (mainly menu-driven). It is intended for the general public, offering such features as numerous bulletin boards for roundtable discussions, an encyclopedia, the exchange of personal messages between users, and much more.

MAKING COMPUTERS WORK

There are many things we take for granted when we turn on our computers. In addition to something as basic as electricity, there are standard components that our computers need to do tasks for us.

Computers perform logical calculations based on interpretation of input and output. This is accomplished using a series of *gates*—or circuitry that uses two input wires and one output wire in order to interpret electrical impulse patterns (the output wire receives a pulse only when a certain pattern of pulses is received by the input wires). The following are four types of gates.

OR   If either input gate receives a pulse, an OR gate produces an output.

NOR   If either input gate receives no pulse, a NOR gate produces an output.

AND   If both input gates receive a pulse at the same time, an AND gate produces an output.

NOT (or inverters)   NOT gates have only one input, with the output always opposite the input.

The invention of the *silicon chip* revolutionized computers. Pure silicon is an insulator (it does not allow an electric current to flow through). But when silicon is impure, it becomes a semiconductor, allowing a minute amount of current to pass. The average chip is relatively easy to make: Cylindrical bars about four inches long are sliced into 0.02-inch disks, with each disk supplying about 250 chips. Principles of physics and chemistry allow electronic circuitry (transistors, capacitors, and resistors) to be added to the disks—either deposited or etched onto the disk using special processes.

MAJOR COMPUTER SCIENTISTS

Aiken, Howard Hathaway (1900–1973)   American mathematician and computer engineer who, along with a team of IBM engineers in 1944, developed the Mark I, the second electronic digital computer.

Babbage, Charles (1792–1871)   British mathematician and inventor who developed one of the first early computers in 1832, called the difference machine.

Boole, George S. (1815–1864)   British mathematician who formulated a method for representing logic with mathematical formulas (modern symbolic logic). Boolean algebra was named after Boole, which is basic to the design of digital computer circuits: His work eventually led to the discovery (in 1946) that transistors could electronically translate and execute Boolean logic.

Eckert, John Presper (1919–)   American electronics engineer who, with J. W. Mauchly, developed the first electronic computer, the ENIAC (electronic numerical integrator and calculator), in 1946, which used vacuum tubes instead of transistors.

Gates, William Henry (1955–)   American computer scientist who was instrumental in developing the Microsoft Disk Operating System (MS-DOS) used in IBM-compatible computers.

Hollerith, Herman (1860–1929)   American inventor who developed the first electrically driven computer; it used punch cards to count the census.

Hopper, Grace Murray (1906–1992)   American computer programmer who, in 1959, invented COBOL, the computer language for business use.

Jacquard, Joseph Marie (1752–1834)   French inventor who created the Jacquard loom; his simple "yes" and "no" mechanism was the basis for future digital computers.

Jobs, Steven Paul (1955–)   American computer scientist who, along with Stephen Wozniak, was the co-founder of Apple Computer Company in 1976. Jobs also helped to develop the NeXT Personal Computer, which used an operating system with a graphical user interface, high-resolution graphics, and digital sound processing.

Pascal, Blaise (1623–1662)   French mathematician, physicist, and religious philosopher who invented the first mechanical calculating machine.

Turing, Allan (1912–1954)   American mathematician who developed the idea of a universal computer called the Turing Machine, which could solve any type of mathematical problem by reducing it to coding in a given set of commands. (Bell Laboratories put his ideas into practice in 1939, by developing the first relay computer.)

von Leibnitz, Gottfried Wilhelm (1646–1716)   German mathematician who, in 1673, invented a calculator that could also do multiplication and division.

Von Neumann, John (1903–1957)   Hungarian-born American mathematician who developed principles of design for digital computers. His ideas were followed during the next several decades as computer technology grew.

Wilkes, Maurice Vincent (1913–)   British computer engineer who developed an early version of assembly, a computer language.

Wozniak, Stephen (1951–)   American computer scientist, who, along with Steven Jobs, co-founded Apple Computer Company in 1976.

SIGNIFICANT DISCOVERIES IN COMPUTER SCIENCE

B.C.	500	Abacus known in Egypt (it is possible that it was invented by the Babylonians much earlier)
A.D.	1642	Blaise Pascal invented the first mechanical calculating machine that could add and subtract
	1671	Gottfried Wilhelm von Leibnitz invented a calculator that could do multiplication and division
	1745	Jacques de Vaucanson used holes punched in metal drums (and later in cards) to control textile looms
	1804	Joseph-Marie Jaquard also used holes to control textile looms, similar to de Vaucanson's system
	1832	Charles Babbage developed the difference machine, which was able to calculate trigonometric and logarithmic tables
	1876	William Thomson (Lord Kelvin) showed that machines can be programmed to perform mathematical calculations
	c. 1887	Herman Hollerith invented a punch card to count and sort information for the 1890 census; his revised punch card became the so-called "IBM card" still used today for punch-card machines
	1936	Konrad Zuse built a primitive form of digital computer using electromagnetic relays
	1939	Konrad Zuse built a binary calculating machine
		Bell Laboratories (now AT&T Bell Laboratories) announced the first relay computer, called a complex number calculator and based on the Turing Machine
	1941	Konrad Zuse developed the Z3 machine in Germany, which had a mechanical storage base but was constructed with telephone relays and punched tape; it was destroyed during World War II
	1943	The first electronic digital computer (using vacuum tubes) was put into operation, called the ABC (Atanasoff Berry Computer) after its developers, John Vincent Atanasoff and Clifford Berry (the first operational prototype was completed in 1939)
		The first all-electronic calculation device (using vacuum tubes and named the Colossus) was developed in England to crack German codes

1944   Howard Aiken, of IBM, invented the second significant relay computer, which is also referred to as the first general-purpose digital machine; it was a huge electromechanical calculator called Mark I

1946   The first electronic computer was developed by John P. Eckert and J. W. Mauchly, to calculate ballistic tables for the U.S. Army; the computer, called ENIAC (electronic numerical integrator and calculator), used about 18,000 vacuum tubes for switching elements and weighed over 30 tons

John Von Neumann, a mathematician, wrote a paper suggesting the principles of designing a digital computer, and his suggestion was the foundation for building digital computers for the next several decades

1948   The first transistor was invented by William Shockley, John Bardeen, and Walter Brattain

IBM developed the SSEC (selective sequence electronic calculator)

1949   The EDSAC (electronic delay storage automatic computer) went into operation at Cambridge University

BINAC (binary automatic computer), the first electronic stored program, went into operation in the United States

1950   The U.S. National Bureau of Standards developed the SEAC (Standards Eastern Automatic Computer), which used an ultrasonic memory

1951   UNIVAC I (Universal Automatic Computer) was the first commercially available electronic computer and the first to store data on a magnetic tape; it was based on John Von Neumann's ideas and was built by Remington-Rand, a company that was the largest computer manufacturer until IBM started its 700 line of computers

1952   IBM built the 701 mainframe computer

1953   IBM began the first large-scale manufacture of the 650 mainframe computer

The first magnetic core memory was developed

1954   The first completely transistorized computer was developed

1956   John Backus and a team at IBM invented the high-level computer programming language FORTRAN, previous programs having been written in machine language

The MANIAC I was the first software to beat a human at a game (chess)

1958   The integrated circuit was developed by Jack St. Clair Kilby

1959   Grace Murray Hopper invented the high-level computer programming language, COBOL, for business use

1960   Keyboards were first used to enter data into a computer

1965   John Kemeny and Thomas Kurtz developed the BASIC computer programming language

1967   The idea of parallel processing (using many computers together to work as one) was proposed by Gene Amdahl

The first personal computer game was developed, the Mac Hack

1968   Douglas Engelbart (Stanford Research Center) invented the computer mouse

1969   Bubble memory (or the ability of a computer to remember commands even when the computer is turned off) was developed

1970   The first floppy disk was introduced to store data; it was originally invented by Yoshiro Nakamata about 1950

1971   The first microprocessor (now called a chip) was introduced by the U.S. company Intel

The first pocket calculator was introduced by Texas Instruments (it could do only simple calculations)

Niklaus Wirth developed the high-level computer programming language Pascal

1972	C computer language was created by Dennis Ritchie and Brian Kernighan at Bell Laboratories
1974	Hewlett Packard introduced the first programmable pocket calculator
1975	The first personal computer, the Altair 8800, was introduced as a kit in the United States and had 256 bytes of memory
1977	The first assembled personal computer, the Apple II, was introduced
1979	Jean Ichbiah and team developed the high-level computer programming language Ada, which was used by the U.S. military
1981	The first DOS operating system was introduced by IBM
1982	The first IBM "clone" computer was introduced by Compaq
	3.5 inch diskettes were introduced
	The first notebook personal computer was developed
	The first laser printer was introduced by IBM
1983	IBM introduced the first personal computer with a built-in hard drive
1984	IBM introduced a new chip in its AT (advanced technology) personal computers that expanded speed and memory
	The first CD-ROMs were introduced by Hitachi
1985	Postscript first used in Apple's Laserwriter printer (Postscript was developed by Adobe Systems, U.S.)
1988	One of the first major steps toward parallel processing was made by John Gustafson, Gary Montry, and Robert Benner, whose computer system decreased calculation time by a factor of 1,000
	The first magneto-optical diskettes were introduced
1990	A rudimentary optical computer (one that uses light instead of the traditional electricity) was demonstrated
	Pen-based personal computers were introduced
	The optical microprocessor was presented by AT&T Bell Labs
1991	IBM invented the single-atom switch
1992	The world's tiniest transistor was introduced by IBM
	The microchip diskette, which is a dedicated processor with no magnetic disk, was introduced by a subsidiary of the Innovatron group

COMMON TERMS IN COMPUTER SCIENCE

address   A location in the memory where a particular unit of data is stored. The address may be in the form of an identifying label, name, or number.

algorithm   A defined set of instructions or procedural steps that leads to a logical conclusion to a problem. In computer science, algorithms are generally the programmed steps that manipulate data and produce the desired result.

analog   Describing a computer that processes data represented by a continuous physical variable, such as electric current (see *digital*).

application   A computer program that performs a particular task, such as a word-processing or spreadsheet software.

architecture   In computers, hardware and/or software design. In hardware, open architecture means that the hardware consists of components purchased off the shelf; closed architecture means that the computer is designed first, and all parts are made to order.

archive   Backup of files on a long-term storage medium; files that are important should be archived.

assembler   A computer program that translates from assembly to machine language.

autosave   A feature of a computer program (usually a word-processing program) to save input data automatically at short, regular intervals.

backup   To copy files or programs onto a disk or tape. File backups are used as insurance in case a computer hard drive crashes or a floppy disk is destroyed. The backups can then be used to replace the lost data.

batch file   A file that has a sequence (or batch) of commands. It is used to store a set of commands that are frequently found together; in particular, it avoids repetitive typing.

binary   Referring to the two numbers 0 and 1. Binary codes are translated into instructions to run the computer.

BIOS   An acronym for basic input/output system. Built into certain software (often placed on the read-only memory [ROM] chip), it determines what a computer can do without accessing programs from a disk. For example, the BIOS often controls the code required for working the keyboard, monitor, and disk drives.

boot   To turn on a computer. At this point, certain software automatically starts a sequence of actions that make it possible for the computer to run. The operating system is the first piece of software loaded during the boot process. A user can also reboot (or warm boot) an already-running computer by pressing a series of keys, usually Control-Alternate-Delete (Ctrl-Alt-Del).

bps   Bits per second; refers to the speed at which a modem transmits data through telephone lines. Standard telephone lines can transmit about 9,600 bps; fiber optic cables can transmit more than 500,000 bps.

buffer   The area in random-access memory (RAM) in which data is temporarily stored.

bug   An error or defect in software or hardware that causes a computer to malfunction. The process of finding such problems is termed debugging.

bulletin board (BBS)   A computer information and retrieval service that has an electronic message center. When connected to a BBS via a modem, messages can be received or sent.

bus   Wire by which data is transferred from one place to another in a computer. The width of the bus determines the amount of data transferred. For example, a 16-bit bus can transfer 16 bits worth of data.

byte   A unit that holds a single character and is composed of eight bits. Memory is often measured in bytes. For example, a disk that holds 512K (512 kilobytes) stores approximately 512,000 characters.

cache   High-speed storage mechanism that can be a stand-alone unit (disk cache) or part of the computer's internal memory (memory cache).

card   A printed circuit board. Cards can have any of several functions, such as holding memory or permitting the use of graphics. Each card can be added to a computer's mother board to increase the computer's capabilities.

cathode-ray tube (CRT)   A vacuum tube in which a beam of electrons are passed along a fluorescent screen, causing phosphor dots in the tube to light up. CRTs are used in television sets as well as in desktop monitors. A typical monitor redraws the screen 60 times per second.

character   A symbol or letter that requires a byte of storage; one byte equals eight bits.

chip   A small piece, usually no larger than one-quarter inch (0.62 centimeters) square, of semiconducting material that holds an integrated circuit in a computer. The circuit board holds many chips, which come in a variety of forms.

color graphics adapter (CGA)   A graphics display system that supports 16 colors and has a resolution of 640 by 200 picture elements (pixels) on the computer monitor. It is used by IBM-compatible personal computers. It is of lesser quality than an enhanced graphics adapter (EGA) or a video graphics adapter (VGA).

command   A statement in a program that gives specific instructions to the computer. For example, in DOS the command DIR gives the user a directory of stored files.

compiler   A program that transforms a high-level-programming-language program from source code to object code. When a computer programmer writes a program, it is written in a source code; the source-code program is then passed through the compiler, which translates the language instructions into object code so it is better understood by a computer.

complex instruction set computer (CISC)   Conventional computers that need only one instruction to perform an operation. CISC developed after the emergence of reduced instruction set computers (RISC), which use a relatively limited number of instructions (see *reduced instruction set computer [RISC]*).

cursor   The blinking line or box that indicates where the next symbol or letter will be placed on a computer monitor. Some programs (usually graphics programs) also have an arrow or cross that acts as a cursor.

data compression   The taking of data from a disk or program and storage of it in a format that requires less space. Some programs use data compression to store more information on a disk. When the program is entered into a computer, the data are "decompressed."

debug   The process of removing errors or defects in software or hardware that cause a malfunction of the computer.

diagnostic routine   A program that allows the computer to check its systems in order to find a bug or problem in the hardware or software. A diagnostic routine is often run automatically when a computer is switched on.

direct memory access (DMA)   A technique that transfers data from the main memory to a device without passing through the central processing unit (CPU). It is faster than most data transfers and is ideal for real-time computations.

disk (diskette, disc)   The plate-shaped device that holds data and can be magnetic or optical.

disk crash (head crash)   The malfunction of a disk, either a floppy disk or a hard drive. Generally, floppy disks crash because of physical damage to the disk. Hard drives crash because of physical damage (lightning strikes or dropping) or contamination (dust or liquids), or an unaligned head.

disk operating system (DOS)   The operating systems used in IBM-compatible computers.

do loop   Continuous repetition of a command.

double-sided disk   A disk that uses both sides to record computer data. A double-sided disk only will work in a double-sided disk drive, whereas a single-sided disk will work in either a single-sided or a double-sided disk drive.

download   To copy information from one computer to another computer, mainly via disk or computer modem (see *upload*).

enhanced graphic adapter (EGA)   A graphics display system that supports 16 colors and has a resolution of 640 by 350 pixels on the user's computer monitor. It is used by IBM-compatible personal computers. It has a clearer display than a color graphics adapter (CGA) but not as clear as that of a video graphics adapter (VGA).

e-mail (electronic mail) "Mail" sent electronically over communications services or a network.

error message A message that states that computer software or hardware has malfunctioned.

execute To run a computer program or a command.

fax board A board that allows the computer, with the aid of a facsimile computer program, to transmit or receive faxes.

file A collection of data that is stored either on the computer's hard drive or on a floppy disk.

flops (or FLOPS) An acronym for floating point operations per second, which is a measure of a computer's power. Flops are usually measured in Mflops (megaflops) or Gflops (gigaflops).

format To prepare a storage medium—specifically floppy disks, hard drives, or tape drives—for reading and writing. By formatting a disk, the user erases any data that is on it. The procedure also checks the reliability of a disk. An unformatted disk will not work in a computer.

hard copy Paper printout from a computer. Soft copy is the electronic version of data.

hardware The physical structures of the computer, including the monitor, keyboard, and system unit.

icons Small pictures that some programs use to represent commands or files. They are usually found at the top of the screen or inside a window.

input Data that is added to the computer. For example, when writing a book in a word-processing program, the letters are the input data.

input/output (I/O) procedure The operation, device, or program that allows for data to enter (input) and exit (output) the computer. For example, in a word-processing program, the typing and printing text are I/O procedures, respectively.

interface A physical or electronic way to connect two separate entities. For example, the printer cable is an interface that connects the printer to the system unit.

integrated circuit See *chip*

joystick A device similar to a mouse that allows the user to rapidly move graphical characters around the screen. It is used most often in association with computer games.

landscape A printing format in which a document is printed with the lines of type running parallel to the long dimension of the paper (see *portrait*).

language A code used to communicate with a computer.

liquid crystal display (LCD) A type of display (monitor) that is used mostly for laptop and notebook computers. LCD monitors have two sheets of polarizing material with a liquid crystal solution between them. As electricity passes through the solution, it aligns the crystals in a certain way, blocking or passing light so as to form the characters and graphics on the display.

macro A key, character, or symbol that substitutes for a combination of keystrokes. Macros allow the computer user to enter commands much faster.

medium Any object on which data can be stored. For example, a floppy disk is a medium, as is a tape cartridge.

menu A list of commands in a program from which the user can choose to initiate an action.

menu driven Describing software in which the user chooses from menus to initiate actions.

microprocessor The chip (or integrated circuit) that contains a central processing unit (CPU). Microprocessor and CPU are often used interchangeably. Microprocessors in personal computers vary in the amount of bits they process in a single instruction, in speed, or how many instructions the computer can execute per second.

modem (modulator-demodulator)   An internal or external device that allows the user to send and receive data over telephone lines.

monitor   Another term for a computer display or screen.

monochrome monitor   A monitor that has only one color; for example, white or green on black.

multitasking (or multiprocessing)   The ability of a computer to execute more than one task at a time.

network   A group of two or more computers hooked together. A local-area network (LAN) is a network of computers connected together, usually within the same building; a wide-area network (WAN) is a network of computers connected together, usually over long distances by telephone lines or radio waves.

off-line   The opposite of on-line; when a computer or peripheral device is not physically or electronically connected to the computer being used. For example, a printer can be turned off-line, in which case no pages can be printed.

on-line   The opposite of off-line; when a computer or peripheral device is connected to the computer being used and is accessible to that computer.

output   The opposite of input; the data result or product received from the computer. Output data can be printed on paper or stored on a disk.

parallel port   A parallel interface that connects an external device to the computer. Most personal computers use a parallel port to connect a printer. A parallel port sends more than one bit of data simultaneously (see *serial port*).

peripheral device   A device that is added to the main computer system. For example, printers, monitors, and CD-ROM players are all peripherals.

pixel   Picture element; a single point in a graphic image. Hundreds or millions of tiny pixels produce the images displayed on a screen or printed out from a computer. The number of points determines the sharpness of the image. A pixel on a monochrome display is a single color; a pixel on a color screen is a combination of three dots—red, blue, and green.

plotter   A device that draws mostly line images from a computer. Unlike most printers, which use dots to simulate a straight line, the plotter uses pens to draw a continuous line.

portrait   A format in which the lines of text are printed parallel to the page's short dimension (see *landscape*).

real time   A computer feature or program that responds to input or sends output immediately. Most personal computers do not operate in real time but take seconds to minutes to respond to commands. The term *real time* is also used in computer graphics, where it means that the animation of an actual event moves along at the same speed as the event in nature.

reboot   To start the system from the beginning without turning off the computer. This is also called a warm boot.

reduced instruction set computer (RISC)   A computer in which the central processing unit (CPU) recognizes a limited number of instructions. The advantage is that the processing of the instructions takes less time; the disadvantage is that it often requires two or more instructions to perform an operation that can be executed on a traditional computer by a single instruction (see *complex instruction set computer [CISC]*).

resolution The degree of clarity of an image on the screen or on paper. The resolution of a computer screen or a printed image is determined by the number of dots (or pixels) of which it is made up. An example of a high-resolution screen is a 640 by 480–pixel screen, which has 640 dots on each of its 480 lines. A low-resolution printer prints about 72 dots per inch (dpi); a very-high-resolution printer prints about 1,200 dots per inch.

robotics The development of the hardware and software that produces a device that can move and react to sensory input. Most robots are used to do repetitious jobs in factories, to collect data under conditions that would be hazardous to humans, or to perform high-precision tasks.

root directory The main directory in a file system. The root directory is provided by the operating system. For example, when a floppy disk is formatted, a root directory is created on it so that the computer can send data to or receive data from the disk.

scroll To move among consecutive lines of data on a computer screen.

serial port A serial interface that connects an external device to the computer; the serial port allows for only one bit to be sent through the interface at one time. Most personal computers use a serial port to connect a mouse or modem.

shareware Copyrighted software programs that are distributed based on an honor system. Many shareware programs are free, but the author usually requests a small fee if the program is regularly used; the shareware can be copied for other computer users, but they too must pay a fee if the program is regularly used. Shareware cannot be sold by anyone but the author.

software Computer programs; sets of instructions in a form that can be used by a computer. For example, word-processing and database programs are software.

surge protector A device that protects software and hardware from sudden electrical surges. A surge protector is usually plugged into an electrical outlet; the computer is then plugged into the surge protector.

sysop Shorthand for "system operator," the individual who manages a bulletin board or a special interest group on a public communications service.

terminal Another name for the monitor (or display screen) and keyboard of a computer. Terminals can be categorized as intelligent (a stand-alone computer that has a main memory and CPU); smart (some processing power, but less than an intelligent terminal); or dumb (no processing power, relying on the processing power of the computer to which it is connected).

track A circle on a disk where the data is written. When a blank disk is formatted, the computer divides the disk into tracks; each disk has a specified number of tracks.

UNIX A major multi-user, multiprocessing operating system, which is the leading operating system for minicomputers. It was developed in the early 1970s by Bell Laboratories (now AT&T Bell Laboratories). It is written in a high-level programming language called C.

upload To transfer information from one computer to another, mainly via disk or computer modem (see *download*).

user-friendly Describing a program that is easily run by the computer user.

utilities Special programs that manage numerous "housekeeping" tasks on a personal computer, such as saving and moving files and formatting disks.

video display terminal (VDT) Another name for a desktop monitor.

video graphics adapter (VGA)   A graphics display system that supports 16 colors and has a resolution of 720 by 400 pixels, or 256 colors on a 320 by 200–pixel computer screen. It is used by IBM-compatible personal computers; because it is based on analog signals rather than digital signals, it cannot be used with many older computers. It has a clearer display than a color graphics adapter (CGA) or an enhanced graphics adapter (EGA).

virus   A code that enters a computer and can cause it to malfunction. The code often rapidly replicates by entering other computers via phone lines or diskettes.

warm boot   See *reboot*

wide-area network (WAN)   A system that connects a network of computers, usually over long distances, by telephone lines or radio waves.

windows   In many programs, the rectangular or square areas on the monitor. Windows can be individually displayed on the screen; multiple windows can be displayed side by side, overlapping (cascading), or not overlapping (tiled).

worm   A type of virus that affects the computer's memory but cannot attach itself to other programs.

WORM   An acronym for a write-only read-many magneto-optical disk.

write-protected disk   A disk that cannot be written on by the computer user. Most programs are write-protected, making it impossible to write over or erase the data on the disk. Write-protected disks are protected by a piece of tape (a "write-protect tab") over the write-protect notch (on 5.25-inch disks), or by flicking a write-protect switch (on 3.5-inch disks).

WYSIWYG   Pronounced *wizzy-wig* and short for "what you see is what you get." Many programs (especially word-processing programs) offer WYSIWYG screens, where the information on the screen is in the same format as if it were printed on the printer.

ADDITIONAL SOURCES OF INFORMATION

Bear, John. *Computer Wimp No More: The Intelligent Beginner's Guide to Computers*. Ten Speed Press, 1992.

Flynn, Jennifer. *20th Century Computers and How They Worked: The Official Starfleet History of Computers*. Alpha, 1993.

Kaufmann, William J., III, and Larry L. Smarr. *Supercomputing and the Transformation of Science*. Scientific American Library, 1993.

Kidder, Tracy. *Soul of a New Machine*. Little, Brown & Co., 1981.

Pickover, Clifford, ed. *Visions of the Future: Art, Technology, and Computing in the Twenty-first Century*. St. Martin, 1993.

Simons, Geoff. *Robots: The Quest for Living Machines*. Cassell, 1992.

Williams, Robin. *Jargon, an Informal Dictionary of Computer Terms*. Peachpit, 1993.

Chapter 13

Engineering and Technical Science

What Are Engineering and
Technical Science?   *524*

Types of Engineering   *524*

Highlights of Technology   *528*

Significant Discoveries and Inventions   *531*

Common Terms in Technical Science and
Engineering   *546*

Additional Sources of Information   *548*

WHAT ARE ENGINEERING AND TECHNICAL SCIENCE?

Engineering is the science by which the properties of matter and the sources of power in nature are made useful to humans in structures, devices, machines, and products. An engineer is an individual who specializes in one of the many branches of engineering. Until the eighteenth century, the terms *scientist*, *inventor*, or *builder* were rarely distinguished from engineer.

Though the terms *engineering* and *technical science* are commonly used interchangeably, the latter is the study of the products of engineering science. For example, an engineer may develop an idea for making a better automobile engine; the technical scientist determines the best materials with which to build the engine.

Tallest Buildings

Some of the tallest buildings in the world are as follows.

Name	Location	Height
TALLEST SELF-SUPPORTING STRUCTURE		
CN Tower	Toronto	1,805 feet (550 meters)
TEN TALLEST BUILDINGS IN THE UNITED STATES		
Sears Tower	Chicago	1,454 feet (443 meters)
World Trade Towers (north tower)	New York City	1,368 feet (417 meters)
World Trade Towers (south tower)	New York City	1,362 feet (415 meters)
Empire State Building	New York City	1,250 feet (381 meters)
Amoco	Chicago	1,136 feet (346 meters)
John Hancock	Chicago	1,127 feet (344 meters)
Chrysler Building	New York City	1,046 feet (319 meters)
Nation's Bank	Atlanta	1,027 feet (313 meters)
First Interstate World Center	Los Angeles	1,018 feet (310 meters)
Texas Commerce Plaza	Houston	1,000 feet (305 meters)
TEN TALLEST BUILDINGS IN THE WORLD		
Sears Tower	Chicago	1,454 feet (443 meters)
World Trade Towers (north tower)	New York City	1,368 feet (417 meters)
World Trade Towers (south tower)	New York City	1,362 feet (415 meters)
Empire State Building	New York City	1,250 feet (381 meters)
Central Plaza	Hong Kong	1,227 feet (374 meters)
Bank of China Tower	Hong Kong	1,209 feet (368 meters)
Amoco	Chicago	1,136 feet (346 meters)
John Hancock	Chicago	1,127 feet (344 meters)
Chrysler Building	New York City	1,046 feet (319 meters)
Nation's Bank	Atlanta	1,027 feet (313 meters)

TYPES OF ENGINEERING

Engineers apply the theories and principles of science and mathematics to practical technical problems. Most engineers specialize in one of the 25 major branches of engineering. Within these branches there are over 85 subdivisions, and engineers may further specialize in one industry, such as motor vehicles, or one field of technology, such as propulsion or guidance systems.

In general, engineers in a particular field may be involved in research, design, and development; production and operation; maintenance, time, and cost estimation; sales and technical assistance; or administration and management. Engineers usually work as part of a team and, regardless of specialty, may apply their knowledge across several fields. For example, an electrical engineer may work in the medical field, in computers, in missile guidance systems, or in electrical power distribution. An agricultural engineer may design farm equipment, manage water resources, or work in soil conservation.

The following paragraphs list the most common types of engineers.

Acoustical engineers study the production, transmission, and effects of sound. Most acoustical engineers are concerned with making a product quiet. For example, acoustical engineers working on new cars try to produce a product that will be less noisy.

Aeronautical and *aerospace engineers* design and develop tests for and produce commercial and military aircraft, missiles, and spacecraft. These engineers further specialize in an area such as structural design, instrumentation and communications, or production methods, or specialize in one type of product, such as helicopters, satellites, or rockets. Aeronautical engineers also help with the design of airports and space facilities.

An *airplane mechanic* performs scheduled maintenance, makes repairs, and completes inspections required by the Federal Aviation Administration (FAA). They specialize in repair work or scheduled maintenance. *Power plant mechanics* work on the engines; *airframe mechanics* work on wings, landing gear, and structural parts of the plane or work as *aircraft inspectors*, inspecting airplanes for possible problems.

Agricultural engineers design and develop a variety of products and services for farmers, ranchers, and the agricultural industry. They design the most effective layout for a farm, including placement of barns and irrigation systems; design specific buildings such as dairy barns; and develop electrical power systems for farms and food-processing companies. Manufacturers of farm equipment and machinery often hire agricultural engineers for design, development, and sales. Agricultural engineers often enter the fields of biotechnology or agroforestry.

Architectural engineers design buildings and other structures, from private homes and large office buildings to an entire city's redevelopment. They must solve complex technical problems while retaining artistic design.

Biomedical engineers are interdisciplinarians who use engineering, physics, and chemistry to develop instruments for the study of living organisms. They also develop methods for studying and treating organisms. Biomedical engineering has been recognized as a field of engineering only for the past two decades; it is usually practiced by engineers with medical and/or electronics backgrounds.

Biomedical engineers apply engineering principles to medical and health-related problems. Most are involved in research and work with life scientists, chemists, and members of the medical profession to design and develop medical devices such as artificial hearts, pacemakers, dialysis machines, and lasers for surgery. Those in private industry work on the development, design, and sales of medical instruments and devices; biomedical engineers with computer expertise adapt computers to medical needs and design and build systems to modernize laboratory and clinical procedures. Another biomedical specialty includes the design of life-support and medical monitoring systems for astronauts.

Biochemical engineers (or *biochemists*) study the chemical composition and behavior of living things and the effects of food, drugs, hormones, and other chemicals on various organisms. They try to solve problems in the fields of medicine, nutrition, and agriculture.

Ceramic engineers work with all nonmetallic, inorganic materials that require high temperatures in their processing; these include such diverse products as glassware, heat-resistant materials for furnaces, electronic components, and nuclear reactors. They also design and supervise construction of plants and equipment used in the manufacture of these products. Some specialize in one or more ceramic products: whiteware (porcelain and china or high-voltage electrical insulators), structural materials such as brick and tile, electronic ceramics, glass, or fuel elements for atomic energy. Others work in industries that use ceramic products, including the iron and steel, electrical equipment, aerospace, and chemical industries.

Chemical engineers must have a working knowledge of chemistry, physics, and mechanical and electrical engineering. They design chemical plants and manufacturing equipment; develop production methods and processes for such things as removing chemical contaminants from waste materials; specialize in a particular operation such as oxidation or polymerization; or work in a field such as pollution control. They are also active in manufacturing firms, chemicals, petroleum and related industries, and nuclear energy.

Civil engineers work in the oldest branch of the engineering profession. They design and supervise the construction of buildings, roads, harbors, airports, dams, tunnels, bridges, and water supply and sewage systems. Specialties include structural, hydraulic, environmental (sanitary), transportation, geotechnical engineering, and soil mechanics.

Computer programmers are also considered engineers. They write detailed instructions, called programs, that list the orderly steps a computer must follow to solve a problem. Once the program is complete, the programmer runs some sample data to make sure the program is correct and will produce the desired information (this process is called debugging). Any errors are corrected and the instruction manual for the program user is prepared. Programmers usually work from descriptions prepared by specialists called *system analysts* who have examined the problem and determined the steps necessary to solve it. *Programmer-analysts* handle both programmer- and system analyst-type jobs. *Applications programmers* write detailed instructions for programming the data and specialize in business or scientific work. *Systems programmers* maintain the software that controls the operation of the entire computer system.

Electrical and *electronics engineers* occupy the largest branch of engineering. These specialists design and develop electrical and electronic equipment and products. They work with power generation and transmission; machinery controls; lighting and wiring for buildings, automobiles, and aircraft; computers; radar; communications equipment; missile guidance systems; and consumer goods such as television sets and appliances. They may specialize in communications, computers, or power distribution equipment, or in a subdivision such as aviation electronic systems or in the research, development, and design of new products.

Genetic engineers (also called *biotechnical engineers*) combine biology and medicine with engineering to study changes in the genetic makeup of organisms. (For more information on genetics, see Chapter 5, "The Human Body and Biomedical Science.")

A *geological engineer* examines surface rocks and rock samples drilled from beneath the surface. Geologists study the structure, composition, and history of the Earth's crust; search for mineral resources and oil; study earthquakes; advise the construction of buildings, dams, and highways; study plant and animal fossils as well as minerals and rocks; study the ocean floor; and determine the composition of planetary bodies other than Earth.(For more information on geology, see Chapter 9, "Earth Science.")

Industrial engineers are concerned with people and methods while other engineers are usually concerned with a product. Industrial engineers seek to determine the most efficient and effective way for a company to use the basic components of production—people, machines, and materials—to develop management-control systems for financial planning and cost analysis; design production planning and control systems and time study and quality-control programs; and survey possible plant locations to find the best combination of raw materials, transportation, labor supply, and tax structure.

Mechanical engineers are involved in the production, transmission, and use of power. They design and develop power-producing machines such as internal-combustion and rocket engines, and power-using machines such as refrigeration systems, printing presses, and steel-rolling mills. They also create designs for motor vehicles, energy-conversion systems, heating plants, and machines for specialized industries, and are involved in research and testing, as well as production and maintenance.

Metallurgical or *materials engineers* develop methods to process and convert metals and other materials into usable forms. *Metallurgy* includes three branches: extractive (develops processes for extracting metals from ore, refining, and alloying); chemical or physical (determines the structure and physical properties of metals and alloys to develop methods for converting them into final products); and mechanical (introduces methods to work and shape metals, including casting, forging, rolling, and drawing). Most metallurgists work in the metal industries, where they are responsible for specifying, controlling, and testing the quality of the metals during manufacture. Others are responsible for the development of new, lightweight metals for use in communications equipment, computers, and spacecraft; the processing and recycling of industrial waste; and the processing of low-grade ores.

Materials engineers develop new materials for applications that require exceptionally high strength and heat resistance. They develop technology to produce ceramic substrates, new compounds, and metal alloys for use in computers, spacecraft, and industrial equipment. Materials engineers also determine how materials fail, using instruments (such as microprobes, scanning electron microscopes, and X-ray diffraction) that examine failed, broken, or contaminated materials.

SIX BASIC MACHINES

As far back as the ancient Greeks, humans have used six simple machines to perform work.

Screw

Wheel/Axle

Wedge

Lever

Inclined plane

Pulley

A *mining engineer* specializes in a specific mineral such as coal or copper. These engineers find, extract, and prepare minerals for manufacturing use. Some work with geologists and metallurgical engineers to locate and appraise new ore deposits. They may also design and supervise construction of open-pit and underground mines, including mine shafts and tunnels, or design methods for transporting minerals to processing plants; direct day-to-day operations of a mine, specializing in mine safety, ventilation, water supply, power and communication, and equipment maintenance; and direct mineral-processing operations, which require separating the usable ore from dirt, rocks, and other materials.

Petroleum engineers are responsible for exploring and drilling for oil and gas; for the efficient production of these resources; and for developing methods to increase the proportion of oil recovered from petroleum reservoirs.

Safety engineers (or *occupational safety and health specialists*) are responsible for the safe operation of their employers' facilities and for the physical safety of the employees. They make a detailed analysis of each job, identify potential hazards, investigate accidents to determine causes, design and install safety equipment, establish safety training programs, and supervise any employee safety committees.

HIGHLIGHTS OF TECHNOLOGY

Engineers, inventors, and researchers have developed numerous products over the course of human history. The following is a list of some of the better-known products.

abacus   The first abacus is difficult to trace, but it was known in Egypt by at least 500 B.C.; the use of the abacus spread quickly throughout China and Europe, mainly to use for trading goods. The abacus included beads or pebbles on a slatted wood board, and eventually strung on wires. There was no special way to indicate an untouched level on an abacus (e.g., the number 608 could easily be confused with 68), until around A.D. 500 when an Indian mathematician suggested a special symbol to replace the untouched abacus level. We call the symbol zero (0).

airplane   Although American astronomer Samuel Pierpont Langley (1834–1906) made several attempts between 1897 and 1903 to launch a glider with an internal-combustion engine, he did not succeed. Brothers Orville (1871–1948) and Wilbur (1867–1912) Wright flew the first airplane on December 13, 1903, at Kitty Hawk, North Carolina. Orville made the flight in less than a minute and covered 850 feet.

automobile   The first true automobile (steam driven) was invented in 1769, by French inventor Nicolas Joseph Cugnot (1725–1804). Karl Benz and Gottlieb Daimler are credited with inventing the first gasoline-powered automobiles (they developed the machines independently in 1885). The first automobile factory was built in 1899, by Ransom Eli Olds in Detroit, Michigan. Rudolf Diesel (1858–1913) perfected the diesel engine in 1897.

cellular telephone   The cellular phone was an offshoot of broadcasting technology, and greatly advanced during the 1980s and 1990s. It is similar to the small-scale communication linkage provided by large radio broadcasting systems: An area is broken into units (or cells) about 8 to 12 miles (13 to 19 kilometers) wide, each with its own radio transmitter. Computerized switching, made possible by advances in microprocessor technology, allows the user to switch from one cell to the next.

computers   Punch-card data processing started around 1890 in the United States, when equipment based on the pattern-weaving loom (programmed by Joseph-Marie Jacquard in France in 1801) was used in tabulating the United States census. Microprocessors, developed in 1971 by Intel (United States), allowed personal computers to become available from 1975 on; the first was the Altair 8800 in kit form, in the United States. (For more information on computers, see Chapter 12, "Computer Science.")

electric light   Thomas Alva Edison in America and Joseph Wilson Swan in England produced electric lamps in 1879, both using already known technology (an electric current run through a thin filament of carbon in a vacuum produces light) to produce incandescent lamps.

electronics   In 1907, Lee De Forest and R. Von Lieben advanced the field of electronics when they improved on the thermionic diode (vacuum tube) of Sir John Ambrose Fleming (1904) by incorporating a grid that regulated the passage of electrons from a heated filament (called an amplifier vacuum tube or triode). Later advances in electronic hardware included the magnetron (Albert W. Hull, 1921), which made modern radar possible by generating intense microwaves, and the transistor (1948), a small device that works like a vacuum tube but uses far less power.

facsimile machine (fax or telefax)   The first was introduced in 1865, by Abbe Caselli. The first commercial facsimile machine was refined in the early 1900s, when the process was used by newspapers to transmit photos over telephone lines. The fax received widespread attention only in the early 1980s.

flight simulator   The first flight simulator (an on-ground machine used to practice flight) was invented by American inventor Edwin A. Link (1904–1981). His "blue box" flight simulator, invented in 1929, was used extensively to train pilots during World War II. Since that time, flight simulators have been designed to simulate airplanes and manned spacecraft—including the United States' space shuttle.

holography   Dennis Gabor (1900–1979) invented holography, a three-dimensional image on film, in 1947. In 1961, Emmet Leith and Juris Upatnieks developed modern holography using lasers.

lasers   The laser (standing for light amplification by stimulated emission of radiation) was patented in 1957 by Gordon Gould. It is thought that the first effective, working model was built in 1960, by Theodore Maiman. Recently, the most powerful laser on Earth was built— a free-electron laser using a high-frequency linear accelerator to convert the electron energy into the laser beam. Like most lasers, it will be used for medicine, and industrial and military applications.

maps   One of the first maps we recognize was drawn by Hecataeus, a Greek traveler who lived between the sixth and fifth centuries B.C.; he drew a map of the known lands around the Mediterranean Sea, including Europe, Africa, and Asia, about 510 B.C.

microscope   The first compound microscope was probably invented between 1590 and 1610 by Hans and Zacharias Janssen (father and son). A more powerful microscope using various power lenses was developed around 1673 by Anton van Leeuwenhoek (1632–1723); and by 1676, a new world of biology opened up, as scientists using the microscope discovered previously unknown creatures.

optical fiber links   In 1977, the first fiber-optic systems were tested in telephone systems. By 1980, various countries installed hair-thin strands of ultrapure glass, coupled with light-emitting diodes or lasers as the transmitters, to develop the first fiber-optics links. Such cables are usually used for telephone lines and television, as the fibers allow for faster transmissions than do conventional metal wires. Fiber optics have other uses, such as for optical computers.

photography   In 1822, French inventor Joseph Nicephore Niepce (1765–1833) made the first permanent photograph. In 1839, work by French artist Louis Jacque Mande Daguerre

(1789–1851) led to the daguerreotype. Modern photography originated with William Henry Fox Talbot (1800–1877) in Britain in 1841. The roll film camera was developed in 1888 by George Eastman (1854–1932), using photographic negatives.

printing   Woodblock printing of written characters was known in China by A.D. 350. Ceramic movable type was in use in China about A.D. 1040. A printing press with moveable type that could produce massive quantities of printed material was made by German inventor Johannes Gutenberg about 1454 (he had been working on it since 1435). This printing process led to the dissemination of learning around the world. The rotary press, invented by William Bullock, arrived in 1865; Christopher Lathan Sholes's typewriter in 1867; and the linotype, created by German-born American inventor Ottmar Mergenthaler, in 1884.

radio   In 1901, Guglielmo Marconi (1874–1937), Italian electrical engineer, invented the transatlantic radio—transmitting a signal from southeast England to Newfoundland. The radio broadcasting boom started worldwide about 1922, when the number of stations in the United States increased from 8 to nearly 600, and broadcasting services began in the Soviet Union, France, and Britain.

records   Phonograph disks were invented in 1904 by Emile Berliner (1851–1929) in the United States, and dated not from the advent of Thomas Alva Edison's phonograph (1877) but from the modern system using spiral grooves in molded disks. Peter M. Goldmark, a Hungarian-American physicist, developed the first long-playing record in 1948 in the United States.

satellites   The first satellite, Sputnik 1, was launched in October 1957 by the Soviet Union. The United States' first full communications satellite Intelsat I (alias Early Bird), was launched into geosynchronous orbit in April 1965. Later satellites used for map making, weather forecasting, identification of land and ocean resources, and studying the universe included Landsat, Seasat, and TIROS. (For more information on satellites, see Chapter 8, "Astronomy.")

synthetic polymers   The first synthetic polymer was produced in the United States in 1909 by Leo Hendrik Baekeland (1863–1944), a Belgian-born American industrial chemist who was looking for a way to make artificial shellac. The material produced was bakelite (a thermosetting plastic), a good insulator and now used to make electrical plugs and switches. The first synthetic plastic was discovered by British chemist Alexander Parkes (1813–1890) in 1855.

telegraph   Samuel Finley Breese Morse demonstrated a public electric telegraph in 1844. The first transatlantic telegraph was completed in 1866, backed by Cyrus West Field and several others (the first was laid in 1858, but it only worked a short time).

telephone   The telephone was patented in the United States in 1876, by Alexander Graham Bell, who opened his first commercial telephone exchange in New Haven, Connecticut.

telescope   There is disagreement as to who invented the telescope. The German-Dutch spectacle maker Hans Lippershey was probably the first to build a telescope (he applied for a patent in 1608). Even Galileo Galilei has been credited with building the first telescope, probably because he was the first to use it for astronomical purposes.

television   The precursors to television, that is, devices with the ability to transmit images by scanning, were proposed in the 1880s. The first step toward the modern television was taken in 1938, when Russian-born American researcher Vladimir Kosma Zworykin (1889–1982) constructed the first practical television camera (he called it the iconoscope). In 1940, Hungarian-born American engineer Peter Carl Goldmark (1906–1977) was the first to develop a system to transmit television in full color. In the United States, the number of receiving sets increased tenfold between 1949 and 1951 (from 1 to 10 million) and then climbed to 50 million by 1959. Many countries initiated television broadcasting services during the 1950s.

transistor   The transistor, a small solid-state electronic component that can control current (and could transmit current across a resistor), was invented in 1948 by Walter H. Brattain (1902–1987), John Bardeen (1908–), and William Shockley (1910–) at Bell Laboratories. The transistor replaced the vacuum tube in such devices as television and radio.

GETTING SMALL

Many engineers believe that nanotechnology—or developing "small" technology—is the way of the future. There are computer memory chips as small as 500 nanometers (the prefix "nano" is equal to 10^{-9}, or one billionth) and they are getting even smaller. In fact, microwave transistors in some satellite dish receivers need features smaller than a quarter of a micron in order to function.

One of the best ways to miniaturize computer parts is with photolithography, a technique of reproducing patterns using light. Photolithography was developed in the 1960s to mass-produce integrated circuits. Although it is not fool-proof, it is an efficient way to produce these small, complex devices. Scanning tunneling microscope technology is also used to create small, detailed devices. For example, it was recently used to produce the world's smallest battery—100 of which would fit into a single human red blood cell.

But there are problems with getting smaller circuit elements: New optical techniques need to be developed to produce chips with 250 to 100 nanometer-sized features. In addition, engineers need to determine how these smaller circuits tolerate heat and cold and other physical properties—and just how small a circuit has to be before it is no longer useful.

SIGNIFICANT DISCOVERIES AND INVENTIONS

Note: Not all dates are agreed upon.

	Year	Invention or Achievement	Inventor and/or Origin
B.C.	12,000	Fire	Unknown
	c. 5000	Woven cloth	Mesopotamia
		Copper working	Rudna Glava, Yugoslavia
		Irrigation	Sumeria, Nile River, Egypt
	c. 3500	Wheeled vehicles	Sumeria, Syria
		Plow	Sumeria
		Possible first writing system	Sumeria
	c. 2700	Great Pyramid of Cheops	Imhotep (Egypt)
	c. 2500	Ox-drawn plow	Egypt
		Earliest simple glass objects	Egypt
	c. 1350	22-letter alphabet	Phoenicians
	c. 1300	Musical notation	Ugarit, Syria
	c. 700	Aqueducts (city)	King of Assyria, Sennacherib (about same time, one for King of Judah, Hezekiah)
	c. 510	First known map	Hecataeus (Greece)
	c. 500	Abacus	Egypt
	c. 400	Catapults	Dionysius of Syracuse, Greece
	c. 350	Star maps	Eudoxus (Greece)
	c. 300	Deductive system of mathematics	Euclid
	c. 280	First lighthouse, *Pharos*	Alexandria (280 feet [85 meters] high)

Year	Invention or Achievement	Inventor and/or Origin
c. 250	Principles of the lever and other simple machines	Archimedes
c. 140	Trigonometry	Hipparchus
c. 100	Stone bridge	Roman engineers (Tiber River, Rome)
	Wheel bearings	On a wagon found at Dejbjerg, Jutland
c. 85	Seed-planting machine	China
c. 50	Simple steam engine	Greece
A.D. c. 100	Paper making	Ts'ai Lun
c. 170	Function of the arteries (pulse)	Galen
c. 180	Rotary fan	China
c. 230	Wheelbarrow	China
c. 580	Iron-chain suspension bridge	China
c. 552	Silk production	Constantinople (Chinese record suggests 2640 B.C. as the beginning of silk production, but this date is unproven)
c. 500	Algebra	India
	Decimal system	India, Mesopotamia
	Zero	India
c. 700	Porcelain	T'ang dynasty (China)
c. 850	Gunpowder	China
c. 900	Moldboard plow	China
980	Canal locks	Ciao Wei-yo
1050	Crossbow	France
1100	Rocket	China
1150	Paper mill	Xativa, Spain
1249	Eyeglasses	China, Europe (simultaneously)
1250	Magnifying glass	Roger Bacon
1260	Gun/cannon	Konstantin Anklitzen
1280	Belt-driven spinning wheel	Hans Speyer
1285	Eyeglasses	Alessandro de Spina
1335	Public striking clock	Palace Chapel of the Visconti, Milan, Italy
1347	First evidence of a gun	Europe
1360	Mechanical clock	Henri de Vick of Wurttemburg for King Charles V of France
1410	Wire	Rodolph of Nuremberg
c. 1454	Printing press	Germany
1455	Cast-iron pipe (cast-iron is used earlier in the 1380s)	Castle of Dillenburgh, Germany
1474	Lunar nautical navigation	Regiomontanus
1489	First printed document of (+) and (-) signs, used to mean surplus and deficit	Johann Widmann
1492	Drawing of a flying machine	Leonardo da Vinci
1504	Pocket watch	Peter Henlein
1520	Spirally grooved rifle barrel	August Kotter
c. 1540	Heliocentric planetary model	Copernicus (he developed the model a few years earlier, but Georg Joachim Rheticus published the idea in 1540)

Year	Invention or Achievement	Inventor and/or Origin
1550	Screwdriver	Gunsmiths and armorers (location unknown)
	Ligature to stop bleeding during surgery	Ambroise Paré
	Wrench	Unknown
1557	Enamel	Bernard Palissy
	Platinum (reference to)	Julius Caesar Scaliger
1561	Dredger	Pieter Breughel
1565	Graphite pencil	Konrad Gesner
1569	Screw-cutting machine and ornamental turning lathe	Jacques Besson
1585	Time bomb	Dutch siege of Antwerp
1589	Hosiery-knitting machine	Rev. William Lee
	Flush toilet	Sir John Harington
c. 1590	Compound microscope	Hans and Zacharias Jansen
1592	Wind-powered sawmill	Cornelius Corneliszoon
	First crude thermometer	Galileo Galilei
1599	Silk-knitting machine	Rev. William Lee
1603	Pantograph	Christopher Scheiner
1606	Surveying chain	Edmund Gunter
1608	Telescope	Hans Lippershey
1609	Astronomical telescope	Galileo Galilei
	Laws of planetary motion	Johannes Kepler
1611	Coke	Simon Sturtevant
	Double convex microscope described	Johannes Kepler
1614	Logarithms	John Napier
1615	Solar-powered motor	Salomon de Caux
1616	Medical thermometer	Santorio Santorio
	Function of the heart and circulation of the blood	William Harvey
1620	Submarine	Cornelis Jocobzoon Drebbel
1621	Rectilinear slide rule	William Oughtred
	Medical thermometer	Santorio Santorio
1631	Multiplication (x) sign	William Oughtred
	Vernier scale	Pierre Vernier
1637	Analytic geometry	René Descartes
1638	Micrometer	William Gascoigne
1642	Calculating machine (addition and subtraction only)	Blaise Pascal
1643	Barometer (Torricellian tube)	Evangelista Torricelli and Vincenzo Viviani
1648	Air pressure concepts in barometer	Blaise Pascal
c. 1650	Air pump	Otto von Guericke
1654	Basic laws of probability	Blaise Pascal and Pierre de Fermat
1656	Pendulum clock	Christian Huygens
1658	Clock balance spring	Robert Hooke
	Red blood cells	Jan Swammerdam
1660	Barometer to forecast weather	Otto von Guericke
	Static electricity noted	Otto von Guericke
1666	Principles of integral calculus	Isaac Newton
1667	Wind gauge	Christian Forner
1668	Reflecting telescope	Isaac Newton

Year	Invention or Achievement	Inventor and/or Origin
1671	Silk spinning machine	Edmund Blood
	Calculating machine (multiplication and division added)	Gottfried Wilhelm Leibnitz
1674	Tourniquet	Morel, France
1675	Calibrated foot ruler	Unknown
1676	Artificial water filtration	William Woolcott
1679	Pressure cooker	Denis Papin
1682	Halley's comet	Edmond Halley
1683	Bacteria	Aton van Leeuwenhoek
1687	Hygrometer	Guillaume Amontons
1694	Plant male and female reproductive organs	Rudolph Jakob Camerarius
1695	Epsom salts	Nehemiah Grew
1701	Machine seed drill	Jethro Tull
1702	Tidal pump	George Sorocold
1709	Anemometer	Wolfius
	Alcohol thermometer	Daniel Gabriel Fahrenheit
1711	Tuning fork	John Shore
1712	Steam engine	Thomas Newcomen and Thomas Savery
1716	True porcelain (Meissen)	Johann Friedrich Bottger
1717	Fahrenheit temperature scale	Daniel Gabriel Fahrenheit
1718	Mercury thermometer	Daniel Gabriel Fahrenheit
1719	Color printing	Jakob Christof Le Blon
1728	Ship chronometer	John Harrison
1731	Octant (Hadley's quadrant)	John Hadley
1732	Copper-zinc alloy	Christopher Pinchbeck
	Threshing machine	Michael Menzies
1733	Flint-glass lens (achromatic)	Chester Moor Hall (not publicized, so credit often goes to John Dollond, in 1757)
	Flying shuttle (weaving)	John Kay
1735	System of classification organisms	Carolus Linnaeus
1742	Crucible steel production	Benjamin Huntsman
	Celsius (Centigrade) temperature scale	Anders Celsius
1743	Wool carding machine	David Bourne
	Compound lever	John Wyatt
1746	Leyden jar (prototype of electrical condenser)	Pieter van Musschenbroeck and Dean Ewald Georg von Kleist, independently
1748	Sea quadrant	B. Cole
1750	Dynamometer	Gaspard de Prony
1752	Lightning conductor	Benjamin Franklin
1755	Iron-girder bridge	M. Garvin
	Carbon dioxide	Joseph Black
1757	Sextant	John Campbell
1758	Achromatic lens (for eyeglasses)	John Dolland (also see 1733, Chester Moor Hall)
1760	Screw-manufacturing machine	Job and William Wyatt
	Cast-iron cog wheel	Carron Iron Works, Scotland
1761	Mass production of steel scissors	Robert Hinchliffe
	Medical percussion method (diagnostic technique)	Leopold Auenbrugger

Year	Invention or Achievement	Inventor and/or Origin
1762	Fire extinguisher	Dr. Godfrey
1764	Spinning jenny	James Hargreaves
1766	Hydrogen	Henry Cavendish
1768	Areometer	Antoine Baumé
1769	Hydraulic spinning frame	Richard Arkwright
	Steam carriage	Joseph Cugnot
1772	Nitrogen	Daniel Rutherford, Joseph Priestley, Karl Wilhelm Scheele, and Henry Cavendish, independently
1774	Barium, chlorine, manganese	Karl Wilhelm Scheele
1775	One-person submarine	David Bushnell
1777	Circular saw	Samuel Miller
	Iron boat	Yorkshire, England
	Torpedo	David Bushnell
	Torsion balance	Charles Augustin de Coulomb
1778	Mortise tumbler (lock)	Robert Barron
	Flush toilet (improved)	Joseph Bramah
1782	Hot-air balloon	Joseph-Michel and Jacques-Etienne Montgolfier
1783	Hydrogen balloon	Jacques Alexandre Charles and the Robert brothers
	Tungsten	Don Fausto d'Elhuyar and Juan José d'Elhuyar
1784	Bifocal lenses	Benjamin Franklin
	Model helicopter	Launoy (France)
	Rope-spinning machine	Robert March
1785	Automatic grist mill	Oliver Evans
	Rule of electrical forces	Charles Augustin de Coulomb
1787	Roller bearings	John Garnett
	Power loom	Edmund Cartwright
	Workable steamboat	John Fitch
1789	Uranium attained	Martin Heinrich Klaproth
1790	Cotton spinning and weaving machine (first U.S. patent)	William Pollard
	Semaphore (visual telegraph)	Claude Chappé
1793	Cotton gin	Eli Whitney
1794	Ball bearings	Philip Vaughan
1795	Hydraulic press	Joseph Bramah
1796	Lithography	Aloys Senefelder
	Smallpox vaccine	Edward Jenner
1797	First parachute jump	André Jacques Garnerin
1798	Process of mass production	Eli Whitney
	Submarine (metal clad)	Robert Fulton
1800	Experimental gas light (coal gas)	William Murdock
	Method for storing electricity	Alessandro Volta
1801	Asteroids	Giuseppe Piazzi
	Wave theory of light	Thomas Young
1803	Spray gun (aerosol medication)	Alan de Vilbiss
1804	Jacquard loom	Joseph Marie Charles Jacquard
	Food canning process	Nicolas Appert
	Steam locomotive	Richard Trevithick
1805	Mechanical silk loom	Joseph-Marie Jacquard
	Amphibious vehicle	Oliver Evans

Year	Invention or Achievement	Inventor and/or Origin
1806	Beaufort wind scale	Francis Beaufort
	Carbon paper	Ralph Wedgwood
1807	Patent for gas-driven automobile	Isaac de Rivez
	Long-distance steamboat	Robert Fulton
	Sensory-motor nerve system	Charles Bell
1809	Arc light (first electric-powered lamp)	Humphry Davy
1810	Metronome	Dietrich Nikolaus Winkel (Johann Maelzel patents it in 1816)
	Mowing machine	Peter Gaillard
1813	Gun cartridge	Samuel Pauly
	Gas meter	Samuel Clegg
	Mine safety lamp	Humphrey Davy and George Stephenson
1815	Macadamized highways	John Loudon McAdam
1816	Stethoscope	René Théophile Hyacinthe Laënnec
	Phosphorus match	François Derosne
1817	Dental plate	Anthony A. Plantston
1818	Geothermal energy experiment	F. de Larderel
1819	Dental amalgam	Charles Bell
	Dioptric system (for lighthouses; uses lens instead of mirrors)	Augustin Jean Fresnel
	Ocean-going steamship	United States
1821	Heliotrope	Carl Friedrich Gauss
	Caffeine	Pierre Joseph Pelletier
1822	Thermocouple	Thomas Johann Seebeck
1823	Electromagnet	William Sturgeon
1824	Galvanometer	André-Marie Ampère
	Portland cement	Joseph Aspdin
1825	Binocular telescope	J. P. Lemiere
1826	Gas stove	James Sharp
1827	Astigmatic lens	George Biddell Airy
	Crude microphone	Charles Wheatstone
	Trifocal lens	John Isaac Hawkins
	Water turbine	Benoit Fourneyron
	Electrical resistance	George Simon Ohm
1828	Differential gear	Onesiphore Pecqueur
	Stethoscope with earpiece	Pierre Adolphe Poirry
	Cocoa	Conrad van Houten
1830	Thermostat	André Ure
	Friction matches (or 1831)	Charles Sauria
	Lawn mower	Edwin Beard Budding
	Paraffin	Karl, Baron von Reichenbach
1831	Electric motor	Joseph Henry
	Electric generator	Michael Faraday
1832	Hydraulic-powered factory	E. Egbers and Timothy Bail
1833	Differential calculating machine	Charles Babbage
1834	Reaping machine	Cyrus McCormick
	Galvanic cells (continuous electric light)	James Bowman Lindsay
1835	Revolver (six-shooter) patented	Samuel Colt
1836	Steam shovel	William Smith Otis
	Color printing	George Baxter
	Stroboscope	Joseph Antoine Ferdinand Plateau
	Combine harvester	H. Hoare and J. Hascall

Year	Invention or Achievement	Inventor and/or Origin
1837	Braille reading system	Louis Braille
	Commercial electric telegraph	William Fothergill Cooke and Charles Wheatstone
1838	Morse code	Samuel Finley Breese Morse
	Stereoscope	Charles Wheatstone
1839	Daguerreotype	Louis Jacques Mandé Daguerre
	Vulcanization of rubber	Charles Goodyear
	First fuel cell	William Robert Grove
	Protoplasm	Jan Evangelista Purkinje
1840	Chronoscope	Charles Wheatstone
	Ozone	Christian Friedrich Schönbein
	Electroplating	John Wright
1842	Carbon electrode battery	Robert Wilhelm Bunsen
	Ether anesthesia	Crawford Williamson Long
	Doppler effect	Christian Doppler
1843	Transatlantic liner	Great Britain
1844	Nitrous oxide anesthesia	Horace Wells and Gardner Q. Colton
1845	First patent of arc light	Thomas Wright
1846	Sewing machine	Elias Howe
	Use of anesthetic gases in surgery	William Morton
1847	Rotary and web printing presses	Richard M. Hoe
	Nitroglycerine	Ascanio Sobrero (and, independently, Christian Friedrich Schönbein, although neither knew what he had developed)
	Chloroform anesthesia	Jacob Bell and James Young Simpson
1850	Teletype printer	Francis Galton
1851	Odometer	William Grayson
	Ophthalmoscope	Herman von Helmholtz
	Flash photography	Henry Fox Talbot
	Foucault's pendulum (proving Earth's rotation)	Jean Bernard Léon Foucault
1852	Steam-powered airship	Henri Giffard
	Gyroscope	Jean Bernard Léon Foucault
	Microfilm	John Benjamin Dancer
	Fluorescence	George Gabriel Stokes
	Passenger elevator	Elisha Graves Otis
1853	Piloted glider	George Cayley
	Hypodermic syringe	Charles Gabriel Pravaz and Alexander Wood
1855	Bunsen burner	Robert Wilhelm Eberhard von Bunsen (though it may have been his technician, C. Desaga, who actually invented the burner)
	Stopwatch	Edward Daniel Johnson
	Safety match	Johan Edvard Lundstrom
	Battlefield nursing care	Florence Nightingale
	Synthetic plastic	Alexander Parkes
1858	First aerial photo (from balloon)	Paris, France

Year	Invention or Achievement	Inventor and/or Origin
1859	Cathode rays	Julius Plucker
	Theory of evolution through natural selection	Charles Darwin
	First oil well	Edwin Drake
	Ironclad ship	France (*La Gloire*)
1860	Linoleum	Frederick Walton
	Snap button	John Newnham
	Internal-combustion engine (coal gas)	Jean Joseph Etienne Lenoir
1861	Pneumatic drill	Germain Sommelier
	Speech center of the brain	Pierre Paul Broca
1862	Machine gun	Richard Jordan Gatling
	Ironclad ship	Jon Ericsson
1863	Phonograph (machine that wrote down what was played on a piano)	Fenby, U.S.
1864	Pasteurization	Louis Pasteur
	Railroad sleeping car	George Pullman
1865	Electric arc welding	Henry Wilde
	Reinforced concrete	W. B. Wilkinson
	Yale cylinder lock	Linus Yale, Jr.
	Genetics	Gregor Johann Mendel
1867	Formaldehyde	August Wilhelm von Hofmann
	Barbed wire	Lucien Smith
	Typewriter (on sale 1874)	Christopher Latham Sholes
	Bicycle	Ernest Michaux
1868	Margarine	Hippolyte Megé-Mouries
	Stapler	Charles Henry Gould
	Plywood	John K. Mayo
	Air brake	George Westinghouse
1869	Color photography	Charles Cros and Louise Ducos du Hauron
	Celluloid	John Wesley Hyatt and Isaiah Smith Hyatt
1872	Hydroplane	Rev. Charles Meade Ramus
	Solar water distillation	Charles Wilson
	Direct current electric generator	Zénobe Théophile Gramme
1873	Electromagnetic radiation	James Clerk-Maxwell
1875	Mimeograph	Thomas Alva Edison
1876	Articulating telephone patented	Alexander Graham Bell
	Carburetor (surface type)	Gottlieb Daimler
	First practical refrigerator	Karl Paul Gottfried von Linde
	Four-stroke engine	Nikolaus August Otto
	Phonograph	Thomas Alva Edison
1877	Differential gear	James Starley
	Switchboard	Edwin T. Holmes
1878	Cathode-ray tube	William Crookes
	Modern microphone	David Hughes
	Milking machine	L. O. Colvin
	Electric alternator	Zénobe Théophile Gramme and Hippolyte Fontaine
	Public lighting (incandescent lights soon put him out of business)	Charles Brush

Year	Invention or Achievement	Inventor and/or Origin
1879	Carbon filament light bulb	Joseph Wilson Swan and Thomas Alva Edison, independently
	Cash register	James J. Ritty
	Saccharin	Constantine Fahlberg and Ira Remsen
1880	Hearing aid	R. G. Rhodes
	Vaccination	Louis Pasteur
1881	Interferometer	Albert A. Michelson
	Rechargeable battery	Camille Fauré
	Telephotography	Shelford Bidwell
1882	Induction coil	Lucien Gaulard and John Gibbs
	Commercial electric fan	Schuyler Skaats Wheeler
	Skyscraper	William Le Baron Jenny
	Three-wire system for transporting electrical power	Thomas Alva Edison
	Carburetor (float-feed spray)	Edward Butler
1883	Long-span suspension bridge (Brooklyn Bridge)	John Augustus Roebling
	Perfected rayon process	Louis Marie Hilaire Bernigaud de Chardonnet
	Fully automatic machine gun	Hiram Stevens Maxim
1884	Fountain pen patented	Lewis Edson Waterman
	Transformer	William Stanley
	Steam turbine	Charles Parsons
	Linotype machine	Ottmar Mergenthaler
1885	Gas-engine automobile	Gottlieb Daimler and Karl Friedrich Benz
1886	Railway car brake	George Westinghouse
	Comptometer (mechanical desk calculator)	Dorr Eugene Felt
1887	Mach supersonic scale	Ernst Mach
	Contact lens	Eugene Frick
	Electrocardiogram	Augustus Desire Walker
1888	Alternating current (AC) motor	Nikola Tesla
	Cellulose photographic film	John Carbutt
	Monorail	Charles Lartigue
	Monotype	Tolbert Lanston
	Roll film camera	George Easton
	Gas-engine farm tractor	Charter Engine Company, Chicago
	Cotton picker	Angus Campbell
c. 1888	Data-processing computer	Herman Hollerith (used for 1890 census)
1890	Electric subway train	London, England
1891	Electric motor car	William Morrison
	Silicon carbide	Eduard Goodrich Acheson
	Flashlight	Bristol Electric Lamp Company, England
	Aluminum boat	Escher Wyss & Company, Switzerland
	Zipper	Whitcombe L. Judson
1892	Vacuum flask (early thermos)	Sir James Dewar

Year	Invention or Achievement	Inventor and/or Origin
1893	Electric toaster	Crompton & Company, England
	Diesel engine described (built 1897)	Rudolf Diesel
	Photoelectric cell	Julius Elster and Hans F. Geitel
1894	Escalator	Jesse W. Reno
1895	Wireless telegraphy	Guglielmo Marconi
	Electric hand drill	Wilhelm Fein
	Photographic typesetting	William Friese-Greene
	X rays	Wilhelm Konrad von Roentgen
	Gas-engine motorcycle	Count Albert de Dion and Georges Bouton
1897	Plasticine	William Harbutt
	Worm gear	Frederick W. Lanchester
	Oscilloscope	Karl Ferdinand Braun
1898	Loudspeaker	Horace Short
1900	Paper clip	Johann Vaaler
	Alkaline battery	Thomas Alva Edison
	Tractor	Benjamin Holt
	Dirigible	Ferdinand Adolf August Heinrich von Zeppelin
1901	Electric typewriter	Thaddeus Cahill
	Vacuum cleaner	H. Cecil Booth
	Radio	Guglielmo Marconi
1902	Air-conditioning	Willis H. Carrier
	Disc brakes	Frederick W. Lanchester
	Ionosphere	Arthur Edwin Kennelly and Oliver Heaviside
1903	First successful airplane flight	Orville and Wilbur Wright
1904	Diode vacuum tube	John Ambrose Fleming
1905	Chemical foam fire extinguisher	Alexander Laurent
	Hydraulic centrifugal clutch	Hermann Fottinger
	Special theory of relativity	Albert Einstein
1906	Crystal radio apparatus	H. H. C. Dunwoody
	Animated cartoon film	James S. Blackton and Walter Booth
	Motion picture sound	Eugen Augustin Lauste
	AM radio invented	Reginald Aubrey Fessenden
1907	Detergents (household)	Henkel et Cié, Germany
	Upright vacuum cleaner	J. Murray Spangler
	Modern color photography	Louis Lumìre
	Radioactive dating	Bertram Borden Boltwood
1908	Cellophane	Jacques E. Brandenberger
	Geiger counter	Johannes Hans Wilhelm Geiger
	Assembly line	Henry Ford
1909	IUD (intrauterine device)	R. Richter
	Bakelite	Leo Henrik Baekeland
1910	Neon lighting	Georges Claude
1911	Cosmic rays	Victor Franz Hess
	Calculating machine (fully automatic multiplication and division)	Jay R. Monroe
	Binet intelligence test	Alfred Binet
	Monoplane	Léon Levasseur
	Seaplane	Glen Hammond Curtiss
1912	Diesel locomotive	North British Locomotive Company, England
	Cabin biplane (airliner forerunner)	Igor Sikorsky

Year	Invention or Achievement	Inventor and/or Origin
1913	Stainless steel	Harry Brearley
	Isotope labeling	Georg von Hevesy and Friedrich A. Paneth
1914	Brassiere	Mary Phelps Jacob
	Leica 35mm camera	Oskar Barnack
	Tear gas	Dr. von Tappen
1915	British army tank	Walter Wilson and William Tritton
	General theory of relativity	Albert Einstein
1917	VHF electromagnetic waves	Guglielmo Marconi
	SONAR detection system	Paul Langevin and Robert Boyle
1918	Electric food mixer	Universal Company, U.S.
	Domestic refrigerator	Nathaniel Wales and E. J. Copeland
1919	Mass spectrometer	Francis William Aston
1920	Commercial radio broadcasts	Station KDKA, Pittsburgh, PA
1921	Hydraulic four-wheel brakes	Duesenberg Motor Company, U.S.
	Lie detector	John Larsen
	Wirephoto	Western Union Cables, United States.
1922	Three-dimensional movies	Perfect Pictures, United States
1924	Wash/spin dry machine	Savage Arms Corporation, United States
1925	Hi-fi radio loudspeaker	C. W. Rice and E. W. Kellogg
1926	Aerosol can	Erik Rotheim
	Synthetic rubber	I. G. Farben, Germany
	Liquid-fueled rocket	Robert H. Goddard
1927	Iron lung	Philip Drinker and Louis Shaw
	Pop-up toaster	Charles Strite
	First solo, nonstop transatlantic flight	Charles Lindbergh
1928	Tomography	André Bocage
	Teletype	Edward Ernst Kleinschmidt
	PVC (polyvinylchloride)	Carbide Corporation, Carbon Chemical Corporation, and Du Pont, United States
1929	Electron microscope	Max Knoll and Ernst Ruska
	Coaxial cable	Bell Telephone Laboratories, United States
	Brain wave electroencephalograph	Hans Berger
	Frozen food	Clarence Birdseye
	First color television image transmission	Bell Telephone Laboratories, United States
1930	Cyclotron	Ernest O. Lawrence and N. E. Edlesfsen
	Polystyrene	I. G. Farben, Germany
	TV electronic scanning suitable for the home	Philo T. Pharnsworth
1931	Photographic exposure meter	J. Thomas Rhamstine
	Fiberglass	Owens Illinois Glass Company, United States
	Radio waves from space	Karl Guthe Jansky
	Blood bank	Sergei Sergeivitch
	TWX (teletypewriter exchange)	Bell Telephone & Telegraph, United States
	Electric razor	Jacob Schick

Year	Invention or Achievement	Inventor and/or Origin
1932	Defibrillator	William Bennett Kouwenhoven
	Wind tunnel	Ford Motor Company, United States
	Particle accelerator	John Douglas Cockcroft and Ernest Thomas Sinton Walton
1933	Frequency modulation (FM)	Edwin H. Armstrong
	Polyethylene	Reginald Gibson and E. W. Fawcett
1934	Nylon invented (patent 1935)	Wallace Carothers
	Bathysphere (steel)	Charles William Beebe
1935	Electronic hearing aid	Edwin A. Steven
	Richter earthquake scale	Charles Francis Richter
	Radar	Robert Alexander Watson-Watt
1936	Jet engine	Frank Whittle and Hans von Ohain
	Helicopter (contra-rotating rotors)	Henrich Focke
	Plexiglas	I. G. Farben, Germany
c. 1937	Radio telescope	Grote Reber
1938	Pressurized airplane cabin	Transcontinental Airways, Boeing 307 Stratoliner
	Teflon	Roy Plunkett
	Ballpoint pen	Lazlo J. Biro and Georg Biro
	Fluorescent lighting	Arthur H. Compton and George Inman
	Photocopy machine	Chester Floyd Carlson
	First practical television camera (iconoscope)	Vladimir Kosma Zworykin
1939	Binary calculator	Konrad Zuse
	Jet aircraft	Hans von Ohain
	DDT discovered as insecticide	Paul Hermann Müller
	Microfilm camera	Elgin G. Fassel
1940	Automatic auto transmission	General Motors, United States
1941	Microwave radar	U.S. Radiation Laboratory
	Dacron	John R. Whinfield
	First color television system	Peter Goldmark
1942	Man-made atomic reaction (Manhattan Project)	Enrico Fermi and team
1943	Aqualung	Jacques-Yves Cousteau
1944	Tupperware	Earl W. Tupper
1945	Artificial kidney (earlier, but hidden during World War II)	Willem J. Kolff
	Atomic bomb (nuclear fission)	J. R. Oppenheimer and team
	Vinyl floor covering	Du Pont, United States
1946	Electronic vacuum tube computer (ENIAC)	John W. Mauchly and J. Presper Eckert
1947	Holography	Dennis Gabor
	Supersonic aircraft	Bell X-1, United States
	First supersonic flight	Chuck Yeager
1948	Transistor	William Shockley, John Bardeen, and Walter H. Brattain
	Atomic clock	William F. Libby
	Long-playing phonograph record (microgroove record)	Peter Goldmark
	Solid electric guitar	Leo (Clarence) Fender, "Doc" Kauffman, and George Fullerton
	Velcro	Georges de Mestral

Year	Invention or Achievement	Inventor and/or Origin
1949	Jet airliner	R. E. Bishop and team
1950	Xerographic copying machine (for office)	Haloid Company, United States
1952	Artificial heart valve	Charles A. Hufnagel
	Hydrogen bomb	Edward Teller and team
	Experimental videotape	John Mullin and Wayne Johnson
	Transistor radio	Sony, Japan
1953	Heart-lung machine	John Gibbon
	Maser	Charles Hard Townes
1954	Regular broadcast of color television	National Television System Committee, United States
	Plastic contact lens	Norman Bier
1955	Felt-tip pen	Esterbrook, England
	Stereo tape recording	EMI Stereosonic Tapes
	Hovercraft	Christopher S. Cockerell
	Fiber optics	Narinder S. Kapany
	Ultrasound (to observe heart)	Leskell, United States
	Polio virus (killed virus)	Jonas Salk
	Plastic contact lens	Norman Bier
1956	FORTRAN computer language	John Backus and team for IBM, United States
1957	Sputnik (artificial satellite)	U.S.S.R.
	Intercontinental ballistic missile	U.S.S.R.
	Polio vaccine (live virus)	Albert S. Sabin
	Artificial heart pacemaker	Clarence Lillehie
	Tunnel diode	Sony, Japan, based on work by Leo Esaki
1958	Communications satellite	SCORE, United States
	Van Allen radiation belts	James A. Van Allen
1959	Ion engine	Alvin T. Forreste
	Integrated circuit	Jack S. Kilby, Texas Instruments, United States
	Microwave radio system	Pacific Great Eastern Railway between Vancouver and Dawson Creek-Fort, St. John, British Columbia, Canada
	COBOL computer language	Grace Murray Hopper and team
1960	Argon ion laser	D. R. Herriott. A. Javan, and W. R. Bennett, Bell Laboratories, United States
	Vertical takeoff and lift aircraft	Frank Taylor and team at Short Brothers & Harland, Northern Ireland
	Weather satellite, Tiros 1	NASA, United States
1961	Manned spaceflight	Vostok 1, U.S.S.R., Yuri Alekseyevich Gagarin
	Stereophonic radio broadcast	Zenith and General Electric Companies, United States
1962	Minicomputer	Digital Corp., United States
	Robotics	Rand Corporation and IBM, United States

Year	Invention or Achievement	Inventor and/or Origin
1963	Cassette tapes	Philips Company, The Netherlands
	Quarks	Murray Gell-Mann and George Zweig
	Quasars	Marten Schmidt
1964	Carbon fiber	RAF Farnborough. England
	Home-use transistor videotape recorder	Sony, Japan
	Laser eye surgery	H. Vernon Ingram
1965	Word processor	IBM, United States
	BASIC computer language	Thomas E. Kurtz and John G. Kemeny
1966	Integrated radio circuit	Sony, Japan
	Noise-reduction system for audio tapes	Ray M. Dolby
1967	Bubble memory prototype	A. H. Bobeck and team at Bell Telephone Laboratories, United States
	Pulsars	Jocelyn Bell
1968	Holographic storage technique	Bell Telephone Laboratories, United States
1969	Moon landing	NASA, United States
	PASCAL computer language	Niklaus Wirth
	Videotape cassette	Sony, Japan
	Jumbo jet airliner	Joe Sutherland and team at Boeing, United States
1970	Bar code system	Monarch Marking, United States, and Plessey Telecommunications, England
	Computer floppy disk	IBM, United States
	Remote-controlled lunar vehicle	U.S.S.R.
	Practical scanning electron microscope	Albert Victor Crewe
1971	Earth-orbiting space station	U.S.S.R.
	Liquid crystal display (LCD)	Hoffmann-LaRoche Laboratories, Switzerland
	Quartz digital watch	George Theiss and Willy Crabtree
	First pocket calculator on sale	Texas Instruments, United States
1972	Video disk	Philips Company, The Netherlands
	Video game	Noland Bushnel
1973	Computerized tomography (CAT scan)	Allan Macleod Cormack and Godfrey N. Hounsfield
	Earth-orbiting space station	NASA, United States
	Microcomputer	Trong Truong
1974	Nonimpact printing	Honeywell, United States
1975	Betamax videotaping system	Sony, Japan
	VHS video home system	Matsushita/JVC, Japan
1976	Mars space probes	NASA's Viking I and Viking II
1977	Neutron bomb	U.S. military
	Space shuttle	NASA, United States
	Alkyd paint	Winsor & Newton Ltd., England

Year	Invention or Achievement	Inventor and/or Origin
1978	Test-tube baby	Patrick C. Steptoe and Robert G. Edwards
1980	Solar-powered aircraft	Paul Macready
1981	Silicon 32-bit chip	Hewlett-Packard, United States
	Nuclear magnetic resonance (NMR) scanner	Thorn-EMI Research Laboratories and Nottingham University, England
1982	Artificial heart	Robert Jarvik
	Airborne observatory	NASA, United States
	Laser printers on market	IBM, United States
1983	Biosensors	Cambridge Life Sciences, England
	Carbon-fiber aircraft wing	Great Britain
	512 K dynamic access memory chip	IBM, United States
1984	Megabit computer chip	IBM, United States
	Gene cloning	National Institutes of Health, United States; Transgene, France; and Otago University, New Zealand
	CD-ROM (compact-disk, read-only memory)	Hitachi, Japan
	Compact disk player	Sony and Fujitsu Companies, Japan; and Philips Company, The Netherlands
1985	Image digitizer	Optronics, England
	Polymer electric conducter	Terje Skotheim and team, Brookhaven National Laboratory, United States
	Soft bifocal contact lens	Sofsite Contact Lens Laboratory, United States
	Positron emission tomography	Michael Phelps
	First baby born from frozen embryo	Australia
1986	Synthetic skin	G. Gregory Gallico, III
	DNA fingerprinting	Alex Jeffreys
	Diminished ozone shield	Susan Solomon, NOAA, United States
	High-temperature conductivity	Georg Bednorz and Karl Alex Müller
1987	Gene-altered bacteria	Advanced Genetic Sciences, United States
	Higher-temperature conductivity	C. W. Chu, M. K. Wu, and team
1988	Patented animal life	Philip Leder and Timothy Stewart
1989	Introduce foreign gene into human	Steven A. Rosenberg and team at National Institute of Health, United States
1991	Controlled nuclear fusion	Joint European Torus (Jet), Oxfordshire, England
1992	Smallest battery (with scanning tunneling microscope)	University of California, Irvine
1994	Electromagnets for micromotors introduced	Georgia Tech, United States
	Channel Tunnel completed	England-France

COMMON TERMS IN TECHNICAL SCIENCE AND ENGINEERING

aggregate A mixture of several materials. For example, an aggregate of gravel, natural sand, and crushed stone is used for making concrete.

alloy A substance that has metallic properties and consists of two or more elements, usually at least one a metal.

alternator A type of alternating-current generator.

ammeter An instrument that measures the strength of an electric current in amperes.

annealing The process of making glass, metal, or alloy less brittle by exposing it to heating then cooling.

cantilever A beam or other horizontal member supported on only one end.

cathode The negative terminal of an electric current system. In a vacuum tube, the filament serves as the cathode or source of electrons that are emitted.

cathode-ray tube A tube in which an electron beam is directed across a fluorescent tube in order to generate images. CRTs are used in oscilloscopes, radar, television sets, and computer monitors.

ceramic matrix composites Materials fabricated from ceramic fibers embedded in a ceramic matrix (for example glass ceramics). They are developed to be stronger, more pliable, and more heat- and cold-resistant than most materials.

circuit A line of conductors and other electrical devices along which an electrical current flows. A closed circuit allows the current to travel through all devices. If the circuit is broken at some point so the current cannot flow, it is called an open circuit.

coil A turned wire used to introduce inductance into an electrical circuit.

current The flow of electricity. Metals are good conductors of electric current.

diode A tube with two electrodes; the main use of diodes is to keep the electric current flowing in one direction.

dynamo A type of generator; usually a direct-current generator. It converts energy of mechanical motion into electric current (see *alternator*).

elasticity The ability of an object or material to return to its original size and shape, after being pushed or pulled by an outside force. For example, rubber is elastic.

electrode A rod, plate, or wire that is used to conduct electric current out of or into any device.

electromagnet A coil with a soft iron core that acts as a magnet when an electric current is passed through it.

electromotive force The force that moves an electric current around a circuit. For example, a generator produces an electromotive force.

engine A machine that applies power to do work. It converts various forms of energy into mechanical force and motion, such as an automobile engine, which uses internal combustion to create movement.

expansion joint A space left in structures or roads that allows for the expansion and contraction of the material, caused by heating and cooling of the surrounding environment.

filament   A metallic wire that is heated in an incandescent lamp in order to produce light.

fuse   A safety device that protects a circuit from receiving too much current. The fuse's wire melts in response to too much electric current passing through it, thus breaking the circuit.

galvanometer   An instrument that detects, measures, and determines the direction of a small electric current.

gasket   A deformable material, usually a ring of plastic or metal, that is used to make a pressure-tight joint between two (usually stationary) parts.

generator   A machine that converts mechanical energy into electrical energy.

girder   A large beam of wood, metal, or concrete, usually found in skyscrapers and other large buildings. It is used for structural support.

insulator   A device with high resistance to heat, electricity, or sound; for example, an electrical insulator prevents electricity from sending current to other objects.

lubricant   A substance applied to a surface to reduce friction.

machine   A device that helps to do work. Most machines either overcome a force or change the direction of the applied force.

microphone   A device that acts as a transformer and amplifier of sound waves into electric currents.

motor   A machine that converts electrical energy into mechanical energy.

oscilloscope   An instrument that produces an image of varying electrical voltages on a cathode-ray tube.

Peltier effect   The phenomenon in which, when an electric current is passed through a junction consisting of wires of different metals, the junction is warmed or cooled depending on the direction of current flow.

polymer   Large molecules made up of a series of molecular units, similar to beads on a string. Natural polymers include rubber, wool, and cotton; synthetic polymers include nylon and polythene. Polymers are often called giant molecules.

pulley   A wheel over which a rope, chain, or wire passes. Pulleys are used to ease the pulling of objects or lifting of heavy weights.

pulley system   An arrangement of two or more pulleys that form a machine.

radar (radio detection and ranging)   An instrument in which a cathode-ray tube receives reflected radio waves to detect distant objects.

radio   A system of transmitting sound signals (as electric impulses) through the air using electromagnetic waves.

receiver   A device that transforms radio waves and translates them mainly into sounds or pictures.

relay   A device that controls a large electrical current along another circuit by switching on or off. The relay uses a small electric current to control the larger current.

resistor   A device that resists an electric current.

rheostat (or variable resistor)   A resistor constructed so that its resistance value can be changed without affecting or interrupting the attached circuit.

stator   A stationary machine part about which a rotor turns.

switch   A device that is used to switch parts of a circuit on or off. When the switch is on, the electric current is flowing through; when the switch is off, the electric current is cut off.

television   A system for transmitting video and audio signals using electromagnetic waves. A televisions uses a cathode-ray tube to produce images built from 625 constantly changing lines, each of which contains 400 small dots of light.

thermocouple   Shortened term for thermoelectric couple.

thermoelectricity   The production of an electric current directly from heat, or the reverse.

transformer   A device that changes the voltage of an alternating current. Transformers are used to modify the high voltage received from power lines so it can be used by homes that require lower voltage for electrical devices.

tube (or valve)   An electrical device that allows electric current to flow only in one direction. They are also referred to as diodes, triodes, etc., depending on the number of electrodes present.

valve   See *tube*

variable resistor (or rheostat)   A device that variably resists an electrical current. The resistance can be changed by varying the contacts, allowing it to slide around a length of wire.

voltmeter   An instrument that measures electromotive force or potential difference between two points, usually in volts.

ADDITIONAL SOURCES OF INFORMATION

Adams, James L. *Flying Buttresses, Entropy, and O-Rings: The World of an Engineer.* Harvard University Press, 1991.

Asimov, Isaac. *Asimov's Chronology of Science & Discovery.* Harper & Row, 1989.

d'Estaing, Valerie-Anne Giscard, and Mark Young. *Inventions and Discoveries 1993: What's Happened, What's Coming, What's That?* Facts on File, 1993.

Dyson, Freeman J. *Infinite in All Directions.* Harper & Row, 1988.

Flatow, Ira. *They All Laughed . . . From Light Bulbs to Lasers: The Fascinating Stories Behind the Great Inventions That Have Changed Our Lives.* HarperCollins, 1993.

Hellemans, Alexander, and Bryan Bunch. *The Timetables of Science.* Simon & Schuster, 1988.

Levy, Matthys, and Mario Salvadori. *Why Buildings Fall Down.* Norton, 1992.

Roth, Leland M. *Understanding Architecture: Its Elements, History, and Meaning.* HarperCollins, 1993.

Chapter 14

Useful Science Resources

Museums, Planetariums,
and Observatories 550

Zoos and Aquariums 580

Botanical Gardens 589

National Parks Listing 592

National Wildlife Refuges 598

Notable Caves and Caverns 614

Useful Science Information 614

Additional Sources of Information:
General Science Books 637

Note: *Addresses and phone numbers change often. We have checked the following addresses and phone numbers to the best of our ability. We regret any inconvenience caused by information that may have changed after the printing of this book.*

MUSEUMS, PLANETARIUMS, AND OBSERVATORIES

Note: * denotes museums with planetariums.

Alabama
Museums and Planetariums

Anniston Museum of Natural History
4301 McClellan Boulevard
Anniston, Alabama 36202
205-237-6766

W. A. Gayle Planetarium
1010 Forest Avenue
Montgomery, Alabama 36106
205-241-4799, Seats 237

Robert R. Meyer Planetarium
Birmingham-Southern College
Arkadelphia Road, Box A-36
Birmingham, Alabama 35254
205-226-4700, Seats 87

The University of Alabama State Museum of Natural History
Smith Hall
University of Alabama
Tuscaloosa, Alabama 35487-0340
205-348-7550

University of North Alabama Planetarium
University of North Alabama
Box 5150
Florence, Alabama 35632
205-760-4334, Seats 70

U. S. Space and Rocket Center
Huntsville, Alabama 35807
205-837-3400
800-633-7280

Von Braun Planetarium
P. O. Box 1142
Huntsville, Alabama 35807
205-837-9359, Seats 100

Arizona
Museums and Planetariums

Flandrau Science Center and Planetarium
University of Arizona
N. Cherry Avenue
Tucson, Arizona 85721
602-621-4515, Seats 147

Meteor Crater Enterprises, Inc.
603 N. Beaver Street, Suite C
Flagstaff, Arizona 86001
602-289-2362

Observatories

Grasslands Observatory and Sabino Canyon Observatory
5100 W. Sabino Foothills Drive
Tucson, Arizona 85715
602-749-2224

Kitt Peak National Observatory
National Optical Astronomy Observatory
P. O. Box 26732
Tucson, Arizona 85726
602-620-5350

Lowell Observatory
1400 W. Mars Hill Road
Flagstaff, Arizona 86001
602-774-3358

Michigan Dartmouth MIT Observatory
HC 04, P. O. Box 7520
Tucson, Arizona 85735
602-620-5360

Multiple Mirror Telescope Observatory
University of Arizona
Tucson, Arizona 85721
602-621-1558

National Optical Astronomy
Observatories
P. O. Box 26732
Tucson, Arizona 85726-6732
602-325-9204

Northern Arizona University Campus
Observatory
Department of Physics and Astronomy
Northern Arizona University
Box 6010
Flagstaff, Arizona 86011
602-523-2661

Steward Observatory
University of Arizona
Tucson, Arizona 85721
602-621-6524

U. S. Naval Observatory
Flagstaff Station
P. O. Box 1149
Flagstaff, Arizona 86002
602-779-5132

Fred L. Whipple Observatory
P. O. Box 97
Amado, Arizona 85645
602-398-2432

Arkansas

Museums and Planetariums

University of Arkansas at Little Rock
Planetarium
2801 South University
Little Rock, Arkansas 72204
501-569-3259, Seats 150

Observatories

River Ridge Observatory
P. O. Box 5142
Little Rock, Arkansas 72225
501-569-3021

California

Museums and Planetariums

Apple Valley Science and Technology
Center
15552 Wichita Road
P. O. Box 2968
Apple Valley, California 92307
619-242-3514

George F. Beattle Planetarium
San Bernadino Valley College
701 Mount Vernon Avenue
San Bernardino, California 92410
714-885-6511, Seats 62

Chabot College Planetarium
25555 Hesperian Boulevard
Hayward, California 94545
415-786-6881, Seats 54

Chabot Science Center
4917 Mountain Boulevard
Oakland, California 94619
415-531-4560 (*), Seats 100

J. Frederick Ching Planetarium
Hartnell Community College
156 Homestead Avenue
Salinas, California 93901
408-755-6800, Seats 100

George Clever Planetarium and Earth
Science Center
San Joaquin Delta College
5151 Pacific Avenue
Stockton, California 95207
209-474-5110, Seats 60

Diablo Valley College Planetarium
Astronomy Department
321 Golf Club Road
Pleasant Hill, California 94553
415-685-1230, Seats 50

Discovery Center
1944 N. Winery Avenue
Fresno, California 93703
209-251-5533 (*), Seats 30

El Camino College Planetarium
16007 Crenshaw Boulevard
Torrance, California 90506
213-715-3373, Seats 77

Exploratorium, The Museum of Science,
Art and Human Perception
3601 Lyon Street
San Francisco, California 94123
415-561-0360

Reuben H. Fleet Space Theater
P. O. Box 33303
San Diego, California 92103
619-238-1233 (*), Seats 300

Jet Propulsion Laboratory
4800 Oak Grove Drive
Pasadena, California 91109
818-354-7006

Lawrence Hall of Science
University of California
Berkeley, California 94720
415-642-2858 (*)

Los Angeles Harbor College Planetarium
1111 S. Figueroa Place
Wilmington, California 90744
213-518-1000, Seats 52

Los Medanos College Planetarium
2700 E. Leland Road
Pittsburg, California 94565
415-439-2181, Seats 75

Daniel B. Millikan Planetarium
Chaffey College
5885 Haven Avenue
Alta Loma, California 91750
714-987-1737, Seats 76

Minolta Planetarium
21250 Stevens Creek Boulevard
Cupertino, California 95014
408-864-8814, Seats 170

Morrison Planetarium
California Academy of Sciences
Golden Gate Park
San Francisco, California 94118
415-750-7127, Seats 309

Mount San Antonio College Planetarium
1100 N. Grand Avenue
Walnut, California 91789
714-594-5611, ext. 4704, Seats 100

Orange Coast College Planetarium
2701 Fairview Road
Costa Mesa, California 92628
714-432-5611, Seats 51

Palomar College Planetarium
1140 W. Mission Road
San Marcos, California 92069
619-744-1150, ext. 2516, Seats 90

Planetarium Institute
Department of Physics and Astronomy
San Francisco State University
San Francisco, California 94132
415-338-1852, Seats 50

Riverside Community College Planetarium
4800 Magnolia
Riverside, California 92506
714-684-3240, ext. 365, Seats 50

Rosicrucian Museum, Planetarium and Science Center
1342 Naglee Avenue
San Jose, Calif. 95191-0001
408-287-9172, Seats 100

Sacramento Science Center
3615 Auburn Boulevard
Sacramento, California 95821
916-449-8256 (*), Seats 90

San Diego State University Planetarium
Astronomy Department
San Diego, California 92182
619-594-6182, Seats 50

Santa Barbara Museum of Natural History, Gladwin Planetarium, and Palmer Observatory
2559 Puesta del Sol Road
Santa Barbara, California 93105
805-682-3224, Seats 60

Santa Monica College Planetarium
1900 Pico Boulevard
Santa Monica, California 90405
213-452-9223, Seats 53

Santa Rosa Junior College Planetarium
1501 Mendocino Avenue
Santa Rosa, California 95401
707-527-4371, Seats 100

Schreder Planetarium
1644 Magnolia Avenue
Redding, California 96001
916-225-0250, Seats 64

Tessmann Planetarium
Rancho Santiago Community College
1530 W. 17th Street
Santa Ana, California 92706
714-564-6000

West Valley College Planetarium
14000 Fruitvale Avenue
Saratoga, California 95070
408-867-2200, ext. 6151, Seats 74

Observatories

Big Bear Solar Observatory
40386 N. Shore Lane
Big Bear City, California 92314
714-866-5791

Frank P. Brackett Observatory
Department of Physics and Astronomy
Pomona College
Claremont, California 91711
714-621-8000 (*)

Chabot Observatory
4917 Mountain Boulevard
Oakland, California 94619
415-531-4560 (*)

**Gordon D. Crowell Astrophysical
Observatory**
Rio Hondo Community College
3600 Workman Mill Road
Whittier, California 90608
213-692-0921, ext. 384

Fremont Peak Observatory
P. O. Box 1110
San Juan Batista, California 95045
408-623-4255

Griffith Observatory
2800 E. Observatory Road
Los Angeles, California 90027
213-664-1191

Hat Creek Radio Observatory
Radio Astronomy Laboratory
University of California
Route 2, Box 500
Cassel, California 96016
916-335-2364

Leuschner Observatory
Astronomy Department
University of California
Berkeley, California 94720
415-642-5275

Lick Observatory
(under University of California
Observatories, University of Santa Cruz)
P. O. Box 85
Mount Hamilton, California 95140
408-274-5061

Mount Laguna Observatory
Astronomy Department
San Diego State University
San Diego, California 92182
619-595-6182

Mount Wilson Observatory
Mount Wilson Institute
740 Holladay Road
Pasadena, California 91116
818-793-3100

Palomar Mountain Observatory
California Institute of Technology
San Diego, California 92060

**N. A. Richardson Astronomical
Observatory**
San Bernardino Valley College
701 S. Mt. Vernon Avenue
San Bernardino, California 92410
714-888-6511

San Fernando Observatory
14031 San Fernando Road
Sylmar, California 91342
818-367-9333

**San Francisco State University
Observatory**
Department of Physics and Astronomy
San Francisco, California 94132
415-338-1852

Sonoma State University Observatory
Department of Physics and Astronomy
Rohnert Park, California 94928
707-664-2267

Stony Ridge Observatory
P. O. Box 874
Big Bear City, California 92314
714-585-5486

Table Mount Observatory
(under the Jet Propulsion Laboratory,
California Institute of Technology)
P. O. Box 367
Wrightwood, California 92397
619-249-6610

Colorado

Museums and Planetariums

Fiske Planetarium and Science Center
University of Colorado
Campus Box 408
Boulder, Colorado 80309-0408
303-492-5002, Seats 213

Gates Planetarium
2001 Colorado Boulevard
Denver, Colorado 80205-5798
303-370-6317, Seats 232

USAF Academy Planetarium
50 ATS/DOP
Colorado Springs, Colorado 80840
719-472-2779, Seats 150

Harry Zachels Planetarium
Adams State College
Alamosa, Colorado 81102
719-589-7616, Seats 65

Observatories

Black Forest Observatory
12815 Porcupine Lane
Colorado Springs, Colorado 80908
719-495-3828

Chamberlin Observatory
Physics Department
University of Denver
Denver, Colorado 80208
303-871-2238

Sommers-Bausch Observatory
University of Colorado
Campus Box 391
Boulder, Colorado 80309
303-492-6732

Tiara Observatory
P. O. Box 1059
Colorado Springs, Colorado 80901
719-597-3603

Connecticut

Museums and Planetariums

The Connecticut State Museum of Natural History
75 N. Eagleville Road, Room 312
Storrs, Connecticut 06269-3023
203-486-4460

Copernican Space Science Center
Central Connecticut State University
1615 Stanley Street
New Britain, Connecticut 06050
203-827-7419 (*), Seats 108

The Discovery Museum
4450 Park Avenue
Bridgeport, Connecticut 06604
203-372-3521 (*), Seats 124

Lutz Children's Museum
247 S. Main Street
Manchester, Connecticut 06040
203-643-0949

Nature Center for Environmental Activities, Inc
10 Woodside Lane
Westport, Connecticut 06880
203-227-7253

New Canaan Nature Center
144 Oenoke Ridge
New Canaan, Connecticut 06840
203-966-9577

Peabody Museum of Natural History
Yale University
170 Whitney Avenue
New Haven, Connecticut 06511-8161
203-432-3750

Science Museum of Connecticut, Inc., and Gengras Planetarium
950 Trout Brook Drive
West Hartford, Connecticut 06119
203-236-2961, Seats 142

Southern Connecticut State University Planetarium
501 Crescent Street
New Haven, Connecticut 06515
203-397-4347, Seats 65

Stamford Museum and Nature Center
39 Scofieldtown Road
Stamford, Connecticut 06903
203-322-1646 (*), Seats 55

Thames Science Center, Inc.
Gallows Lane
New London, Connecticut 06320
203-442-0391

Wickware Planetarium
Eastern Connecticut State University
83 Windham Street
Willimantic, Connecticut 06226
203-456-5563, Seats 50

Observatories

Van Vleck Observatory
Wesleyan University
Middletown, Connecticut 06459
203-347-9411, ext. 2303

**Western Connecticut State University
Observatory**
181 White Street
Danbury, Connecticut 06810
203-797-2774 (*), Seats 50

Delaware
Observatories

Mount Cuba Astronomical Observatory
P. O. Box 3915
Greenville, Delaware 19807
302-654-6407 (*)

District of Columbia
Museums and Planetariums

Explorers Hall
National Geographic Society
17th and M Streets NW
Washington, D.C. 20036
202-857-7588

**National Air and Space Museum
(Einstein Planetarium)**
Smithsonian Institution
7th Street and Independence Avenue SW
Washington, D.C. 20560
202-357-2700, Seats 230

National Museum of American History
Smithsonian Institution
14th Street and Constitution Avenue NW
Washington, D.C. 20560
202-357-2700

National Museum of Natural History
Smithsonian Institution
10th Street and Constitution Avenue NW
Washington, D.C. 20560
202-357-2700

Rock Creek Nature Center/Planetarium
5200 Glover Road NW
Washington, D.C. 20007
202-426-6829, Seats 75

Smithsonian Institution
1000 Jefferson Drive
Washington, D.C. 20560
202-357-1300

**United States Department of the Interior
Museum**
18th and C Streets NW
Washington, D.C. 20240
202-343-3477

Observatories

U. S. Naval Observatory
34th Street and Massachusetts Ave. NW
Washington, D.C. 20392
202-653-1507

Florida
Museums and Planetariums

**Astronaut Memorial Space Science
Center**
Brevard Community College
1519 Clearlake Road
Cocoa, Florida 32922
407-631-7889 (*), Seats 88

**Bishop Planetarium/South Florida
Museum**
201 10th Street W.
Bradenton, Florida 34205
813-746-4132, Seats 220

Buehler Planetarium
Broward Community College
3501 S.E. Davie Road
Davie, Florida 33314
305-475-6681, Seats 101

Cedar Key State Museum
Off Highway 24 on Museum Drive
Cedar Key, Florida 32625
904-543-5350

Florida Museum of Natural History
University of Florida
Gainesville, Florida 32611
904-392-1721

Indian River Coastal Zone Museum
5600 Old Dixie Highway
Fort Pierce, Florida 34946
407-465-2400

Kennedy Space Center
Spaceport U.S.A.
Mail Code: TWRS, Kennedy
Space Center, Florida 32899
407-452-2121

Miami Space Transit Planetarium
3280 S. Miami Avenue
Miami, Florida 33129
305-854-4242, Seats 290

Museum of Arts and Sciences
1040 Museum Boulevard
Daytona Beach, Florida 32014
904-255-6475 (*), Seats 105

Museum of Science
3280 S. Miami Avenue
Miami, Florida 33129
305-854-4247

**Museum of Science and History and
Alexander Brest Planetarium**
1025 Gulf Life Drive
Jacksonville, Florida 32207
904-396-7062, Seats 215

Museum of Science and Industry
4801 Fowler Avenue
Tampa, Florida 33617-2099
813-985-5531

Nature Center and Planetarium
P. O. Box 06023
Fort Myers, Florida 33906
813-275-3183, Seats 92

**Orlando Science Center
(John Young Planetarium)**
810 E. Rollins Street
Orlando, Florida 32803
407-896-7151, Seats 124

**St. Petersburg Historical and
Flight One Museum**
335 Second Avenue NE
St. Petersburg, Florida 33733
813-894-1052

**St. Petersburg Junior College
Planetarium**
P. O. Box 13489
Fifth Avenue N. at 69th Street
St. Petersburg, Florida 33733
813-341-4320, Seats 47

Science Center of Pinellas County, Inc.
7701 22nd Avenue N.
St. Petersburg, Florida 33710
813-384-0027 (*), Seats 30

South Florida Science Museum
4801 Dreher Trail N.
West Palm Beach, Florida 33405
407-832-1988 (*), Seats 88

Space Coast Science Center
P. O. Box 36-1816
1510 Highland Avenue
Melbourne, Florida 32936
407-259-5572

Pat Thomas Planetarium
Department of Physics
Florida State University
Tallahassee, Florida 32306
904-644-2098, Seats 60

Observatories

Fox Observatory
Robert Markham Park
16000 W. State Road 84
Fort Lauderdale, Florida 33326

Gibson Observatory
4801 Dreher Trail N.
West Palm Beach, Florida 33405
407-832-1988

Georgia
Museums and Planetariums

**Fernbank Science Center
(Jim Cherry Memorial Planetarium)**
156 Heaton Park Drive NE
Atlanta, Georgia 30307
404-378-4311, Seats 500

Fulton Planetarium
2025 Jonesboro Road SE
Atlanta, Georgia 30315
404-691-8767, Seats 120

Georgia Southern College Planetarium
Physics Department
Statesboro, Georgia 30460
912-681-5292, Seats 75

Georgia State Museum of Science and Industry
Room 432
Georgia State Capitol
Atlanta, Georgia 30334
404-656-2846

Harper Planetarium
3399 Collier Drive NW
Atlanta, Georgia 30331
404-699-4566, Seats 120

Museum of Arts and Sciences
4182 Forsyth Road
Macon, Georgia 31210
912-477-3232 (*), Seats 118

Patterson Planetarium
2900 Woodruff Farm Road
Columbus, Georgia 31907
404-568-1730, Seats 90

Rollins Planetarium
Young Harris College
Young Harris, Georgia 30582
404-379-3990, Seats 111

Savannah Science Museum
4405 Paulsen Street
Savannah, Georgia 31405
912-355-6705 (*), Seats 60

University of Georgia Museum of Natural History
Biological Science Building
University of Georgia
Athens, Georgia 30602
404-542-1663

Valdosta State College Planetarium
Department of Physics, Astronomy, and Geology
Valdosta, Georgia 31698
912-333-5752, Seats 65

Walker County Science Center
P. O. Box 10, Highway 95
Rock Spring, Georgia 30739
404-764-1111 (*), Seats 32

Wetherbee Planetarium
100 Roosevelt Avenue
Albany, Georgia 31701
912-435-1572, Seats 50

Observatories

Bradley Observatory and Hard Labor Creek Observatory
Department of Physics and Astronomy
Agnes Scott College
Decatur, Georgia 30030
404-371-6265 (*)

Fernbank Science Center Observatory
156 Heaton Park Drive NE
Atlanta, Georgia 30307
404-378-4311

Valdosta State College Observatory
Department of Physics, Astronomy, and Geology
Valdosta, Georgia 31698
912-333-5752

Hawaii
Museums and Planetariums

Bernice P. Bishop Museum
P. O. Box 19000-A
Honolulu, Hawaii 96817
808-847-3511 (*), Seats 77

Observatories

Canada-France-Hawaii Telescope Corp.
P. O. Box 1597
Kamuela, Hawaii 96743
808-885-7944

Mauna Kea Observatory
Institute for Astronomy
P. O. Box 4729
Hilo, Hawaii 96721
808-935-3373

Idaho
Museums and Planetariums

Ricks College Planetarium
Math and Physics Department
Rexburg, Idaho 83460
208-356-1910, Seats 60

Orma Smith Museum of Natural History and Whittenberger Planetarium
College of Idaho
2112 Cleveland Boulevard
Caldwell, Idaho 83605
208-459-5011, Seats 50

Illinois

Museums and Planetariums

Adler Planetarium
1300 S. Lake Shore Drive
Chicago, Illinois 60605
312-322-0300, Seats 450

Burpee Museum of Natural History
813 N. Main Street
Rockford, Illinois 61103
815-965-3132

Cernan Earth and Space Center
Triton College
2000 Fifth Avenue
River Grove, Illinois 60171
708-456-0300 (*), Seats 100

Henry Crown Space Center
Museum of Science and Industry
57th Street and Lake Shore Drive
Chicago, Illinois 60637
312-684-1414

John Deere Planetarium
Augustana College
Rock Island, Illinois 61201
309-794-7327, Seats 92

Discovery Center Museum
711 N. Main Street
Rockford, Illinois 61103
815-963-6769 (*), Seats 48

Field Museum of Natural History
Lake Shore Drive at Roosevelt Avenue
Chicago, Illinois 60605
312-922-9410

Illinois State Museum
Spring and Edwards Streets
Springfield, Illinois 62706
217-782-7386

Illinois State University Planetarium
Physics Department
Normal, Illinois 61761
309-438-2496, Seats 110

Jurica Natural History Museum
Illinois Benedictine College
5700 College Road
Lisle, Illinois 60532
708-960-1500

Lakeview Museum of Arts and Sciences
1125 W. Lake Avenue
Peoria, Illinois 61614
309-686-7000 (*), Seats 80

Lizzadro Museum of Lapidary Art
220 Cottage Hill Avenue
Elmhurst, Illinois 60126
708-833-1616

Museum of Natural History, University of Illinois
1301 W. Green Street
Urbana, Illinois 61801
217-333-2517

Museum of the Chicago Academy of Sciences
2001 N. Clark Street
Chicago, Illinois 60614
312-549-0606

William M. Staerkel Planetarium
Parkland College
2400 W. Bradley Avenue
Champaign, Illinois 61821
217-351-2446, Seats 144

Strickler Planetarium
Olivet Nazarene University
P. O. Box 592
Kankakee, Illinois 60901
815-939-5267, Seats 100

Time Museum
7801 E. State Street
P. O. Box 5285
Rockford, Illinois 61125
815-398-6000

Herbert Trackman Planetarium
Joliet Junior College
1216 Houbolt Avenue
Joliet, Illinois 60436
815-729-9020, Seats 70

Observatories

Walter H. Blacke Observatory
Illinois College
Jacksonville, Illinois 62650

Dearborn Observatory/Lindheimer
Astronomical Research Center
2131 Sheridan
Northwestern University
Evanston, Illinois 60208
708-491-7650

Illinois Wesleyan University Observatory
Bloomington, Illinois 61702
309-556-3176

Northern Illinois University Observatory
Physics Department
De Kalb, Illinois 60115
815-753-1772

Sangamon State University Observatory
Astronomy-Physics
Springfield, Illinois 62708
217-786-6720

University of Illinois Observatory
Astronomy Department
103 Astronomy Building
1002 W. Green Street
Urbana, Illinois 61801
217-333-3090

Indiana
Museums and Planetariums

Ball State University Planetarium
Department of Physics and Astronomy
Muncie, Indiana 47306
317-285-8871, Seats 100

Biology Department Teaching Museum
and Nature Center
2000 University
Muncie, Indiana 47306
317-285-8820

Children's Museum and SpaceQuest
Planeterium
3000 N. Meridian Street
Indianapolis, Indiana 46208
317-924-5431, Seats 130

Indiana State Museum
202 N. Alabama Street
Indianapolis, Indiana 46204
317-232-1637

Koch Science Center and Planetarium
Evansville Museum of Arts and Science
411 S.E. Riverside Drive
Evansville, Indiana 47713
812-425-2406, Seats 48

Hannah Lindahl Children's Museum
1402 S. Main Street
Mishawaka, Indiana 46544
219-258-3056

E. C. Schouweller Planetarium
St. Francis College
2701 Sprint Street
Fort Wayne, Indiana 46808
219-434-3278, Seats 100

Turkey Run State Park Planetarium
R. R. 1, Box 164
Marshall, Indiana 47859
317-597-2654, Seats 40

Observatories

Goethe Link Observatory
Indiana University Astronomy
Department
Swain Hall
W. 319
Bloomington, Indiana 47405
812-855-6911

J. I. Holcomb Observatory and
Planetarium
4600 Sunset Avenue
Butler University
Indianapolis, Indiana 46208
317-283-9282

John C. Hook Memorial Observatory
Indiana State University
Terre Haute, Indiana 47809
812-237-3294

McKim Observatory
De Pauw University
Greencastle, Indiana 46135
317-658-4654

Charles S. Morris Observatory
Manchester College
North Manchester, Indiana 46962
219-982-6021

Iowa
Museums and Planetariums

Grout Museum of History and Science
503 South Street
Waterloo, Iowa 50701
319-234-6357 (*), Seats 55

Heitkamp Memorial Planetarium
Department of Physics
Loras College
P. O. Box 1
Dubuque, Iowa 52001
319-588-7154, Seats 90

Luther College Planetarium
Department of Physics
700 College Drive
Decorah, Iowa 52101
319-387-1117, Seats 65

Sanford Museum
117 E. Willow Street
Cherokee, Iowa 51012
715-225-3922 (*), Seats 40

Donald A. Schaefer Planetarium
Bettendort High School
3333 18th Street
Benendort, Iowa 52722
319-322-7001, Seats 85

Science Center of Iowa and Digistar Space Theater
4500 Grand Avenue
Des Moines, Iowa 50312
515-274-6868 (*), Seats 126

Observatories

Drake University Municipal Observatory
Des Moines, Iowa 50311
515-271-3033

Erwin W. Fick Observatory
Department of Physics and Astronomy
Iowa State University
Ames, Iowa 50011
515-294-3668

Grant O. Gale Observatory
Department of Physics
Grinnell College
Grinnell, Iowa 50012
515-269-3016

Hillside Observatory
Department of Earth Science
University of Northern Iowa
Cedar Falls, Iowa 50614
319-277-2692

Witte Observatory
610 Walnut
Burlington, Iowa 52601-5902

Kansas
Museums and Planetariums

Barton County Community College Planetarium
Great Bend, Kansas 67530
316-792-2701, Seats 70

Kansas Cosmosphere and Space Center
1100 N. Plum
Hutchinson, Kansas 67501
316-662-2305 (*), Seats 75

L. Russel Kelce Planetarium
Pittsburgh State University
Pittsburgh, Kansas 66762
316-231-7000, Seats 85

Peterson Planetarium
Division of Physical Sciences
Emporia State University
Emporia, Kansas 66801
316-343-1200, Seats 72

Washburn University Planetarium
Department of Physics and Astronomy
Topeka, Kansas 66621
913-295-6330, Seats 50

Wichita Omnisphere and Science Center
220 S. Main
Wichita, Kansas 67202
316-264-3174 (*), Seats 60

Observatories

Lake Afton Public Observatory
MacArthur Road
Wichita, Kansas 67208
316-794-8995 (recorded information) or
316-689-3891

Clyde W. Tombaugh Observatory
Department of Physics and Astronomy
University of Kansas
Lawrence, Kansas 66045
913-864-4626

Kentucky
Museums and Planetariums

Big Bone Orientation Center and Diorama
3380 Beaver Road
Union, Kentucky 41091
606-384-3522

Georgetown College Planetarium
Georgetown, Kentucky 40324
502-863-8436, Seats 50

Golden Pond Planetarium
4360 Stonewall Drive
Paducah, Kentucky 42001
Seats 82

Hardin Planetarium
Western Kentucky University
Bowling Green, Kentucky 42101
502-745-4044, Seats 150

Arnim D. Hummel Planetarium
Eastern Kentucky University
Richmond, Kentucky 40475
606-622-1547, Seats 164

John James Audubon Museum
Audubon State Park
Henderson, Kentucky 42420
502-826-2247

Museum of History and Science
727 W. Main Street
Louisville, Kentucky 40202
502-561-6111 (*)

Rauch Memorial Planetarium
University of Louisville
Louisville, Kentucky 40292
502-588-6665, Seats 100

Weathertord Planetarium
Berea College
Berea, Kentucky 40404
606-986-9342, ext. 6240, Seats 51

Observatories

Roberts Observatory
Berea College
Berea, Kentucky 40404
606-986-9342 ext. 6240

Louisiana
Museums and Planetariums

Lafayette Natural History Museum
637 Girard Park Drive
Lafayette, Louisiana 70503
318-268-5544 (*), Seats 58

Louisiana Arts and Science Center
P. O. Box 33N
Baton Rouge, Louisiana 70821
504-344-9465 (*), Seats 248

Louisiana Nature and Science Center, Inc.
Joe W. Brown Park
P. O. Box 870610
New Orleans, Louisiana 70187
504-246-5672 (*), Seats 66

Louisiana Tech University Planetarium
P. O. Box 3182
Ruston, Louisiana 71272
318-257-4303, Seats 120

St. Martin Parish Science Center
P. O. Box 42
St. Martinville, Louisiana 70582
318-394-6967 (*), Seats 60

Observatories

Freeport McMoRan Observatory and Planetarium
409 Williams Boulevard
Kehner, Louisiana 70062
504-468-7229

Maine
Museums and Planetariums

Children's Museum of Maine
746 Stevens Avenue
Portland, Maine 04103
207-797-5483

Francis M. Malcolm Science Center
P. O. Box 186
Easton, Maine 04740
207-488-5451 (*), Seats 50

Maine State Museum
State House Complex
Augusta, Maine 04333
207-289-2301

The Natural History Museum
College of the Atlantic
Bar Harbor, Maine 04609
207-288-5015

Nylander Museum
393 Main Street
Caribou, Maine 04736
207-493-4474

Southworth Planetarium
University of Southern Maine
96 Falmouth Street
Portland, Maine 04103
207-780-4249, Seats 62

State of Maine Marine Resources
Laboratory
McKown Point
West Boothbay Harbor, Maine 04575
207-633-5572

University of Maine Planetarium
Physics Department
Wingate Hall
Orono, Maine 04469
207-581-1341, Seats 50

Maryland
Museums and Planetariums

Anne Arundel Natural History Museum
Carrie Weedon Center
Galesville, Maryland 20765
301-224-5000

K. Price Bryan Planetarium
College of Notre Dame of Maryland
4701 N. Charles Street
Baltimore, Maryland 21210
301-532-5702, Seats 60

**Community College of Baltimore
Planetarium**
2901 Liberty Heights Avenue
Baltimore, Maryland 21215
301-396-7994, Seats 50

Cylburn Nature Museum
Cylburn Mansion
4915 Greenspring Avenue
Baltimore, Maryland 21209
301-396-0180

Frostburg State University Planetarium
Department of Astronomy
Frostburg, Maryland 21532
301-689-4270, Seats 38

**Maryland Science Center and
Allan C. Davis Planetarium**
601 Light Street
Baltimore, Maryland 21230
301-685-2370, Seats 144

Montgomery College Planetarium
Takoma Avenue and Fenton Street
Takoma Park, Maryland 20012
301-587-4090, Seats 60

NASA-Goddard Space Flight Center
Visitor Center, Code 130
Greenbelt, Maryland 20771
301-286-8981

Howard B. Owens Science Center
9601 Greenbelt Road
Seabrook, Maryland 20706
301-577-8718 (*), Seats 174

U. S. Naval Academy Planetarium
Annapolis, Maryland 21402
301-267-3586, Seats 115

**Washington County Planetarium and
Space Science Center**
823 Commonwealth Avenue
Hagerstown, Maryland 21740
301-791-4172, Seats 72

Watson-King Planetarium-Observatory
Towson State University
Baltimore, Maryland 21204
301-830-3020, Seats 45

Observatories

University of Maryland Observatory
Astronomy Program
College Park, Maryland 20742
301-405-3001

Massachusetts
Museums and Planetariums

Peter Andrews Planetarium
Deerfield Academy
Deerfield, Massachusetts 01342
413-772-0241, Seats 100

Bassett Planetarium
Department of Astronomy
Amherst College
Amherst, Massachusetts 01002
413-542-2138, Seats 60

**Boston Museum of Science and
Charles Hayden Planetarium**
Science Park
Boston, Massachusetts 02114
617-723-2500, Seats 300

**Cape Cod Museum of Natural History,
Inc.**
Route 6A
Brewster, Massachusetts 02631
617-896-3867

The Children's Museum
Museum Wharf
300 Congress Street
Boston, Massachusetts 02210
617-426-8855

Framingham State College Planetarium
State Street
Framingham, Massachusetts 01701
508-626-4764, Seats 72

Museum of Comparative Zoology
26 Oxford Street
Cambridge, Massachusetts 02138
617-495-2463

New England Science Center
222 Harrington Way
Worcester, Massachusetts 01604
508-791-9211 (*), Seats 103

Peabody Museum of Salem
East India Square
Salem, Massachusetts 01970
508-745-1876 (founded 1799)

The Pratt Museum of Natural History
Amherst College
Amherst, Massachusetts 01002
413-542-2165

Springfield Science Museum
236 State Street
Springfield, Massachusetts 01103
413-733-1194 (*), Seats 100

Observatories

Amherst College Observatory
Amherst College
Department of Astronomy
Amherst, Massachusetts 01002
413-542-2138

Boston University Observatory
Department of Astronomy
725 Commonwealth Avenue
Boston, Massachusetts 02215
617-353-5700 (*), Seats 40

Harvard-Smithsonian Center for Astrophysics (Harvard College Observatory and Smithsonian Astrophysical Observatory)
60 Garden Street
Cambridge, Massachusetts 02138
617-495-7461

Haystack Observatory
Route 40
Westford, Massachusetts 01886
508-692-4764

Hopkins Observatory
Williams College
Williamstown, Massachusetts 01267
413-597-2188 (*)

Maria Mitchell Observatory
3 Vestal Street
Nantucket, Massachusetts 02554
508-228-9273

Wallace Astrophysical Observatory
Department of Earth Sciences
MIT Room 54-426
Cambridge, Massachusetts 02139
617-253-6315

Wheaton College Observatory
Norton, Massachusetts 02766
508-285-7722

Whitin Observatory
Wellesley College
Wellesley, Massachusetts 02181

Woodside Observatory and Planetarium
13 Friend Court
Wenham, Massachusetts 01984
508-468-4815, Seats 20

Michigan
Museums and Planetariums

Abrams Planetarium
Michigan State University
East Lansing, Michigan 48824
517-355-4676, Seats 252

The Ann Arbor Hands-On Museum
219 E. Huron Street
Ann Arbor, Michigan 48104
313-995-5437

Jesse Besser Museum Planetarium
491 Johnson Street
Alpena, Michigan 49707
517-356-2202, Seats 60

Children's Museum
Detroit Public Schools
67 E. Kirby
Detroit, Michigan 48202
313-494-1210 (*), Seats 35

Detroit Science Center
5020 John Road
Detroit, Michigan 48202
313-577-8400 (*), Seats 30

Dinosaur Gardens, Inc.
11160 U.S. 23 South
Ossineke, Michigan 49766
517-471-5477

Exhibit Museum Planetarium
University of Michigan
Ann Arbor, Michigan 48109
313-764-0478, Seats 36

Great Lakes Area Paleontological Museum
381 S. Long Lake Road
Traverse City, Michigan 49684
616-943-8850

Impression 5 Science Museum
200 Museum Drive
Lansing, Michigan 48933
517-485-8116

Kalamazoo Public Museum
315 S. Rose Street
Kalamazoo, Michigan 49007
616-345-7092 (*), Seats 85

Kingman Museum of Natural History
W. Michigan Avenue at 20th Street
Battle Creek, Michigan 49017
616-965-5117 (*), Seats 30

Lansing Community College Planetarium
P. O. Box 40010
Lansing, Michigan 48910
517-483-1092, Seats 135

Robert T. Longway Planetarium
1310 E. Kearsley Street
Flint, Michigan 48503
313-760-1181, Seats 290

McMath Planetarium
Cranbrook Institute of Science
500 Lone Pine Road
Bloomfield Hills, Michigan 48013
313-645-3235, Seats 83

Public Museum of Grand Rapids and Roger B. Chaffee Planetarium
54 Jefferson, SE
Grand Rapids, Michigan 49503
616-456-3200, Seats 88

Sloan Museum
1221 E. Kearsley Street
Flint, Michigan 48503
313-762-1170

The University of Michigan-Exhibit Museum
1109 Geddes Avenue
Ann Arbor, Michigan 48109-1079
313-763-4191

The Wayne State University Museum of Natural History
Wayne State University
637 Science Library
Detroit, Michigan 48202
313-577-2886

Observatories

Brooks Observatory
Physics Department
Central Michigan University
Mt. Pleasant, Michigan 48859
517-774-3321

Michigan State University Observatory
Physics and Astronomy Department
East Lansing, Michigan 48824
517-353-4540

Peach Mountain Observatory
9287 Chestnut Circle
Dexter, Michigan 48130

James C. Veen Observatory
3308 Kissing Rock Road
Lowell, Michigan 49331
616-897-7065

Stargate Observatory
P. O. Box 1505
Warren, Michigan 48090-1505

Minnesota
Museums and Planetariums

Marshall Alworth Planetarium
University of Minnesota-Duluth
Duluth, Minnesota 55812
218-726-7129, Seats 64

Minneapolis Planetarium
300 Nicollet Mall
Minneapolis, Minnesota 55401
612-372-6644, Seats 180

Moorhead State University Planetarium
Moorhead, Minnesota 56560
218-236-3982, Seats 60

Paulucci Space Theatre
Highway 169 and E. 23rd Street
Hibbing, Minnesota 55746
218-262-6720 (*), Seats 61

St. Cloud State University Planetarium
St. Cloud, Minnesota 56301
612-255-2013, Seats 65

Science Museum of Minnesota
30 E. 10th Street
St. Paul, Minnesota 55101
612-221-9488

Southwest State University Planetarium
Marshall, Minnesota 56258
507-537-6196, Seats 60

Observatories

Macalester College Observatory
1600 Grand Avenue
St. Paul, Minnesota 55105
612-696-6383

Mississippi
Museums and Planetariums

Russell C. Davis Planetarium and McNair Space Theater
201 E. Pascagoula Street
Jackson, Mississippi 39201
601-960-1550, Seats 230

Observatories

Kennon Observatory
Department of Physics and Astronomy
University of Mississippi
University, Mississippi 38677
601-232-7046

Rainwater Observatory and Planetarium
French Camp Academy
French Camp, Mississippi 39745
601-547-6113 (*), Seats 40

Speer-Lyell Observatory
4120 Old Canton Road
St. Andrew's School
Jackson, Missisippi 39216
601-856-3033

Missouri
Museums and Planetariums

Kansas City Museum Planetarium
3218 Gladstone Boulevard
Kansas City, Missouri 64123
816-483-7827, Seats 50

St. Louis Science Center and McDonnell Star Theater
5100 Clayton Road
Forest Park
St. Louis, Missouri 63110
314-289-4444 (*), Seats 228

Observatories

Laws Observatory
Department of Physics and Astronomy
University of Missouri
Columbia, Missouri 65211
314-882-3335

Powell Observatory
P. O. Box 400
Blue Springs, Missouri 64013

Montana
Museums and Planetariums

Museum of the Rockies (Taylor Planetarium)
Montana State University
Bozeman, Montana 59717
406-994-2251, Seats 104

Nebraska
Museums and Planetariums

Jenson Planetarium
Physics Department
Nebraska Wesleyan University
Lincoln, Nebraska 68504
402-465-2246, Seats 70

Lueninghoener Planetarium
Midland Lutheran College
900 N. Clarkson
Fremont, Nebraska 68025
402-721-5480, Seats 70

J. M. McDonald Planetarium
1330 N. Burlington
Hastings, Nebraska 68901
402-461-2399, Seats 55

Ralph Mueller Planetarium
University of Nebraska at Lincoln
212 Morrill Hall
Lincoln, Nebraska 68588
402-472-6302, Seats 80

Observatories

Behlen Observatory
Department of Physics and Astronomy
University of Nebraska
Lincoln, Nebraska 68588
402-472-2770

Nevada
Museums and Planetariums

Community College of Southern Nevada Planetarium
3200 E. Cheyenne Avenue
North Las Vegas, Nevada 89030
702-644-5059, Seats 64

Fleischmann Planetarium
University of Nevada-Reno
Reno, Nevada 89557
702-784-4812, Seats 54

New Hampshire
Museums and Planetariums

Libby Museum
Route 109 North
Wolfeboro, New Hampshire 03894
603-569-1035

Christa McAuliffe Planetarium
3 Institute Drive
Concord, New Hampshire 03301
603-271-2842, Seats 92

Science Center of New Hampshire
Route 113
Holderness, New Hampshire 03245
603-968-7194

Observatories

Shattuck Observatory
Department of Astronomy
Wilder Hall
Dartmouth College
Hanover, New Hampshire 03755
603-646-2034

University of New Hampshire Observatory
Physics Department
DeMeritt Hall
Durham, New Hampshire 03824
603-862-1950

New Jersey
Museums and Planetariums

Bergen Museum of Art and Science
Ridgewood Avenue and Fairview Avenue
Paramus, New Jersey 07652
201-265-1248

Liberty Science Center
251 Phillip Street
Jersey City, New Jersey 07305
201-200-1000

The Newark Museum
49 Washington Street
Box 540
Newark, New Jersey 07101
201-596-6615 (*), Seats 58

New Jersey State Museum
205 W. State Street, CN 530
Trenton, New Jersey 08625
609-292-6347 (*), Seats 140

Robert J. Novians Planetarium
Ocean County College, CN 2001
Toms River, New Jersey 08754
908-255-0343, Seats 119

The Planetarium of the County College of Morris
214 Centre Grove Road
Cohen Hall
Randolph, New Jersey 07869
201-328-5070, Seats 82

Princeton University Museum of Natural History
Princeton University, Guyot Hall
Princeton, New Jersey 08544
609-452-4102

Trailside Nature and Science Center
Coles Avenue and New Providence Road
Mountainside, New Jersey 07092
908-789-3670 (*), Seats 42

Observatories

New Jersey Astronomical Association Observatory
Voorhees State Park
P. O. Box 214
High Bridge, New Jersey 08829
908-638-8500

Princeton University Observatory
Peyton Hall
Princeton, New Jersey 08544
609-258-3800

Willlam Miller Sperry Observatory
Union County College
1033 Springfield Avenue
Cranford, New Jersey 07016
908-549-0615

New Mexico
Museums and Planetariums

Robert H. Goddard Planetarium
11th and N. Main
Roswell, New Mexico 88201
505-624-6744, Seats 120

Hefferan Planetarium
Albuquerque Public Schools
Career Enrichment Center
807 Mountain Road NE
Albuquerque, New Mexico 87102
505-247-3658, Seats 66

Meteorite Museum
Institute of Meteoritics
200 Yale NE
Albuquerque, New Mexico 87131
505-277-2747

Space Center
Top of N. M. Highway 2001
Alamogordo, New Mexico 88311
800-545-4021 (*), Seats 113

Observatories

Apache Point Observatory
P. O. Box 59
Sunspot, New Mexico 88349
505-437-6822

National Solar Observatory–Sacramento Peak (division of the National Optical Astronomy Observatories)
P. O. Box 62
Sunspot, New Mexico 88349
505-434-7000

University of New Mexico and Capilla Peak Observatory
Department of Physics and Astronomy
200 Yale NE
Albuquerque, New Mexico 87131
505-277-2616

National Radio Astronomy Observatory
(Very Large Array Radio Telescope and Very Long Baseline Array Radio Telescope)
P. O. Box O
Socorro, New Mexico 87801
505-835-7000

New York
Museums and Planetariums

American Museum of Natural History-Hayden Planetarium
Central Park West at West 79th Street
New York, New York 10024
212-769-5100, Seats 650

Andrus Planetarium
511 Warburton Avenue
Yonkers, New York 10701
914-963-4550, Seats 135

Buffalo Museum of Science
1020 Humboldt Parkway
Buffalo, New York 14211
716-896-5200

The Discovery Center of Science and Technology
321 S. Clinton Street
Syracuse, New York 13202
315-425-9068 (*), Seats 45

The Gregory Museum: Long Island Earth Science Center
Heitz Place
Hicksville, New York 11801
516-822-7505

Gustafson Planetarium
Fresh Air Fund
R. D. #3, Box 276
Van Wyck Lake Road
Fishkill, New York 12524
914-897-4320, Seats 50

Herkimer County Boces Planetarium
Gros Boulevard
Herkimer, New York 13350
315-867-2088, Seats 60

Edwin P. Hubble Planetarium
1600 Avenue L
Brooklyn, New York 11230
718-258-9283, Seats 40

Jones Planetarium Theater
Human Resources School
I. U. Willets and Searingtown Roads
Albertson, New York 11507
516-747-5400, Seats 30

Junior Museum
282 Fifth Avenue
Troy, New York 12182
518-235-2120 (*), Seats 40

Link Planetarium
Roberson Museum and Science Center
30 Front Street
Binghamton, New York 13905
607-772-0660, Seats 70

Longwood School District Planetarium
Middle Island-Yaphank Road
Middle Island, New York 11953
516-345-2741, Seats 64

Museum of Long Island Natural Sciences
Earth and Space Sciences Building
State University of New York at Stony Brook
Stony Brook, New York 11794
516-632-8230

Newburgh Free Academy Planetarium
201 Fullerton Avenue
Newburgh, New York 12550
914-563-7500, Seats 88

New York Hall of Science
47-01 111th Street
Flushing Meadows Corona Park
Corona, New York 11368
718-699-0005

New York State Museum
Cultural Education Center
Empire State Plaza
Albany, New York 12230
518-474-5877

Northeast Bronx Planetarium
750 Baychester Avenue
Bronx, New York 10475
718-379-1616, Seats 175

Pember Museum of Natural History
33 W. Main Street
Granville, New York 12832
518-642-1515

Potsdam College Planetarium
Pierrepont Avenue
Potsdam, New York 13676
315-267-2284, Seats 70

Rochester Museum and Science Center and Strasenburgh Planetarium
657 East Avenue
Rochester, New York 14603
716-271-4320, Seats 229

Schenectady Museum and Planetarium
Nott Terrace Heights
Schenectady, New York 12308
518-382-7890, Seats 70

Science Museum of Long Island
Leeds Pond Preserve
1526 North Plandome Road
Manhasset, New York 11030
516-627-9400

Sci-Tech Center of Northern New York
317 Washington St., N.Y.S. Office Building
Watertown, New York 13601
315-788-1340

Southern Cayuga Atmospherium-Planetarium
Poplar Ridge, New York 13139
315-364-8426, Seats 60

Staten Island Institute of Arts and Sciences
75 Stuyvesant Place
Staten Island, New York 10301
718-727-1135

SUNY at Brockport Planetarium
Brockport, New York 14420
716-395-5578, Seats 50

SUNY at Fredonia Planetarium
Jewett Hall
Fredonia, New York 14063
716-473-3370, Seats 75

SUNY at Oneonta Planetarium
Oneonta, New York 13820
607-431-3197, Seats 75

SUNY Northcountry Planetarium
Box 44
Hudson Hall
Plattsburgh, New York 12901
518-564-3166, Seats 55

**Vanderbilt Museum: Mansion,
Marine Museum, Planetarium**
180 Little Neck Road
Centerport, New York 11721
516-262-7800, Seats 238

Wagner College Planetarium
631 Howard Avenue
Staten Island, New York 10301
718-390-3432, Seats 80

Whitworth Ferguson Planetarium
Buffalo State College
1300 Elmwood Avenue
Buffalo, New York 14222
716-878-4911, Seats 70

Observatories

Alfred University Observatory
Alfred, New York 14802
607-871-2208

Custer Institute Observatory
Main Bayview Road
Southold, New York 11971
516-722-3850

Dudley Observatory
69 Union Avenue
Schenectady, New York 12308
518-382-7583

Fuertes Observatory
Cornell University
Ithaca, New York 14853
607-255-3557

**Kopernik Space Science Center and
Observatory**
c/o Roberson Museum and Science Center
30 Front Street
Binghamton, New York 13905
607-772-0660

Martz Observatory
176 Robin Hill Road
Frewsburg, New York 14738
716-664-4506

North Carolina
Museums and Planetariums

Catawba Science Center
243 Third Avenue NE
Hickory, North Carolina 28603
704-322-8169 (*), Seats 30

Colburn Gem and Mineral Museum, Inc.
Civic Center Complex
Haywood Street
Asheville, North Carolina 28801
704-254-7162

Discovery Place
301 N. Tryon Street
Charlotte, North Carolina 28202
704-372-6262

Kelly Planetarium
Science Museums of Charlotte, Inc.
1658 Sterling Road
Charlotte, North Carolina 28209
704-372-6261, Seats 65

Morehead Planetarium
University of North Carolina
E. Franklin Street, CB# 3480
Chapel Hill, North Carolina 27599
919-549-6863

Natural Science Center of Greensboro
(Edward R. Zane Planetarium)
4301 Lawndale Drive
Greensboro, North Carolina 27408
919-288-3769, Seats 86

Nature Museum
1658 Sterling Road
Charlotte, North Carolina 28209
704-372-6261

Nature Science Center
Museum Drive
Winston-Salem, North Carolina 27105
919-767-6730 (*), Seats 34

**North Carolina Museum of Life and
Science**
433 Murray Avenue
Durham, North Carolina 27704
919-477-0431

North Carolina State Museum of Natural Science
102 N. Salisbury Street
Raleigh, North Carolina 27611
919-733-7450

Robeson County Planetarium and Educational Resource Center
Box 2909
Lumberton, North Carolina 28359
919-739-3302, Seats 90

Schiele Museum of Natural History and Planetarium, Inc.
1500 E. Garrison Boulevard
Gastonia, North Carolina 28053
704-866-6900

Margaret C. Woodson Planetarium
Horizons Unlimited
1636 Parkview Circle
Salisbury, North Carolina 28144
704-639-3462, Seats 76

Observatories

Three College Observatory
Department of Physics and Astronomy
University of North Carolina at Greensboro
Greensboro, North Carolina 27412
919-334-5669

North Dakota

Museums and Planetariums

Center for Aerospace Sciences/ Atmospherium
Box 8216, University Station
Grand Forks, North Dakota 58202
701-777-2791 (*), Seats 200

Valley City State University Planetarium
Valley City, North Dakota 58072
701-845-7452, Seats 50

Observatories

Minot State University Observatory
Earth Science Department
Minot State University
Minot, North Dakota 58701
701-256-3620

Ohio

Museums and Planetariums

Ward Beecher Planetarium
Youngstown State University
410 Wick Avenue
Youngstown, Ohio 44555
216-742-3616, Seats 140

Bowling Green State University Planetarium
Department of Physics and Astronomy
Bowling Green, Ohio 43403
419-372-8666, Seats 118

Cincinnati Museum of Natural History (and Planetarium)
1720 Gilbert Avenue
Cincinnati, Ohio 45203
513-345-8505, Seats 96

Cleveland Museum of Natural History
1 Wade Oval Drive
University Circle
Cleveland, Ohio 44106
216-231-4600, Seats 85

Columbus Center of Science and Industry
280 E. Broad Street
Columbus, Ohio 43215
614-228-2674, Seats 100.

Copernicus Planetarium
Lourdes College
6832 Convent Boulevard
Sylvania, Ohio 43560
419-885-3211, Seats 60

Dayton Museum of Natural History/ Apollo Observatory
2629 Ridge Avenue
Dayton, Ohio 45414
513-275-7431, Seats 80

Lake Erie Nature and Science Center and Schuele Planetarium
28728 Wolf Road
Bay Village, Ohio 44140
216-835-9912, Seats 75

McKinley Museum of History, Science, and Industry
(Hoover-Price Planetarium)
800 McKinley Monument Drive
Canton, Ohio 44701
216-455-7043, Seats 65

NASA-Lewis Research Center
Visitor Center
21000 Brookpark Road, MS 8-1
Cleveland, Ohio 44135
216-433-2001

Ohio State University Planetarium
174 W. 18th Avenue
Columbus, Ohio 43210
614-292-1773, Seats 80

Toledo Museum of Natural Sciences
2700 Broadway
Toledo, Ohio 43609
419-385-5721, Founded 1938

Wilderness Center Planetarium
9877 Alabama Avenue SW
Wilmot, Ohio 44689
216-359-5235, Seats 25

Observatories

Cincinnati Observatory
3489 Observatory Place
Cincinnati, Ohio 45208
513-321-5186

Perkins Observatory
Box 449
Delaware, Ohio 43015
614-363-1257

Warren Rupp Observatory
P. O. Box 1118
Mansfield, Ohio 44901
419-524-7814

S. B. P. Observatory
Box 601
Cedarville College
Cedarville, Ohio 45314
513-766-2211

Warner & Swasey Observatory
Department of Astronomy
Case Western Reserve University
Cleveland, Ohio 44106
216-368-3729

Weitkamp Observatory
Otterbein College
Westerville, Ohio 43081
614-898-1516 (*), Seats 25

Oklahoma
Museums and Planetariums

Omniplex Science Museum and Kirkpatrick Planetarium
2100 NE 52nd Street
Oklahoma City, Oklahoma 73111
405-424-5545, Seats 120

Oregon
Museums and Planetariums

Chemeketa Community College Planetarium
P. O. Box 14007
4000 Lancaster Drive NE
Salem, Oregon 97309
503-399-5161, Seats 65

Mt. Hood Community College Planetarium
26000 SE Stark Street
Gresham, Oregon 97030
503-667-7297, Seats 70

Oregon Museum of Science and Industry
4015 SW Canyon Road
Portland, Oregon 97221
503-222-2828 (*), Seats 132

Observatories

Pine Mountain Observatory
P. M. O. Bend-Burns Star Route
Bend, Oregon 97701
503-382-8331

Vernonia Peak Observatory
55371 McDonald Road
Vernonia, Oregon 97064
503-429-2430

Pennsylvania
Museums and Planetariums

Academy of Natural Sciences of Philadelphia
19th and The Parkway
Philadelphia, Pennsylvania 19103
215-299-1000

Allegheny College Planetarium
Physics Department
Meadville, Pennsylvania 16335
814-332-5364, Seats 60

The Carnegie Museum of Natural History
4400 Forbes Avenue
Pittsburgh, Pennsylvania 15213
412-622-3131

Carnegie Science Center
One Allegheny Avenue
Pittsburgh, Pennsylvania 15212
412-237-3300 (*), Seats 150

Dallastown Area School District Planetarium
R. D. 1
Dallastown, Pennsylvania 17313
717-244-4021, Seats 90

Detwiler Planetarium
Lycoming College
Williamsport, Pennsylvania 17701
717-321-4284, Seats 80

Fred W. Diehl Planetarium
600 Walnut Street
Route 11
Danville, Pennsylvania 17821
717-275-4111, Seats 60

The Frost Entomological Museum
The Pennsylvania State University
Patterson Building, Department of Entomology
University Park, Pennsylvania 16802
814-863-1863

Edinboro University Planetarium
Edinboro, Pennsylvania 16444
814-732-2493, Seats 85

Erie Historical Museum
356 W. Sixth Street
Erie, Pennsylvania 16507
814-453-5811 (*), Seats 40

Everhart Museum
Nay Aug Park
Scranton, Pennsylvania 18510
717-346-8370 (*), Seats 40

The Franklin Institute Science Museum
Ben Franklin Parkway at 20th Street
Philadelphia, Pennsylvania 19103
215-448-1200 (*), Seats 330

Indiana University of Pennsylvania Planetarium
Geoscience Department
114 Walsh Hall
Indiana, Pennsylvania 15705
412-357-2379, Seats 75

McDonald Planetarium
Centennial Schools
666 Reeves Lane
Warminster, Pennsylvania 18974
215-441-6157, Seats 100

Museum of Scientific Discovery (Spectrum)
P. O. Box 934
Strawberry Square
Harrisburg, Pennsylvania 17108
717-233-7969

North Museum
Franklin and Marshall College
Box 3003
Lancaster, Pennsylvania 17604
717-291-3941 (*), Seats 101

Reading School District Planetarium
1211 Parkside Drive S.
Reading, Pennsylvania 19611
215-371-5854, Seats 150

State Museum of Pennsylvania
Box 1026
Third and North Streets
Harrisburg, Pennsylvania 17108
717-783-9914 (*), Seats 100

Strait Planetarium
Mansfield University
Mansfield, Pennsylvania 16933
717-662-4750, Seats 110

Ulmer Planetarium
Lock Haven University
Lock Haven, Pennsylvania 17745
717-893-2075, Seats 60

University Museum of Archeology and Anthropology
University of Pennsylvania
Spruce and 33rd Streets
Philidelphia, Pennsylvania 19104
215-898-4000

Wagner Free Institute of Science
17th Street and Montgomery Avenue
Philadelphia, Pennsylvania 19121
215-763-6529

West Chester University Planetarium
Department of Geology and Astronomy
West Chester, Pennsylvania 19383
215-436-2727, Seats 75

Observatories

Allegheny Observatory
Observatory Station
University of Pittsburgh
Pittsburgh, Pennsylvania 15214
412-321-2400

Bucknell University Observatory
Department of Physics
Lewisburg, Pennsylvania 17837
717-524-1139

Edinboro University of Pennsylvania Observatory
Edinboro, Pennsylvania 16444
814-732-2469

Keystone Junior College Observatory
Public Relations
P. O. Box 50
La Plume, Pennsylvania18440
717-945-5141

Kutztown University Observatory
Kutztown, Pennsylvania 19530
215-683-4438 (*)

Swarthmore College Observatory
Swarthmore, Pennsylvania 19081
215-328-8272

Villanova University Observatory
Department of Astronomy and
Astrophysics
Fourth Floor, Mendel Hall
Villanova, Pennsylvania 19085
215-645-4820 (*), Seats 40

Nicholas E. Wagman Observatory
Deer Lakes Park
Pittsburgh, Pennsylvania 15116

Rhode Island
Museums and Planetariums

Middletown Planetarium
Aquidneck Avenue
Middletown, Rhode Island 02840
401-846-6395, Seats 60

Museum of Natural History and Cormack Planetarium
Roger Williams Park
Providence, Rhode Island 02905
401-785-9450, Seats 61

Observatories

Community College of Rhode Island Observatory
400 East Avenue
Warwick, Rhode Island 02886
401-825-2178

Ladd Observatory
210 Doyle Avenue
Providence, Rhode Island 02912
401-863-2314

South Carolina
Museums and Planetariums

Gibbes Planetarium
1112 Bull Street
Columbia, South Carolina 29201
803-799-2810, Seats 55

Howell Memorial Planetarium
Bob Jones University
Greenville, South Carolina 29614
803-242-5100, Seats 90

Museum of York County and Settlemyre Planetarium
4621 Mount Gallant Road
Rock Hill, South Carolina 29730
803-329-2121, Seats 64

Roper Mountain Science Center
504 Roper Mountain Road
Greenville, South Carolina 29615
803-297-0232 (*), Seats 172

South Carolina State Museum
301 Gervais Street
Columbia, South Carolina 29201
803-737-4921

Spartanburg County Nature-Science Center
385 S. Spring Street
Spartanburg, South Carolina 29301
803-583-2777

Stanback Museum and Planetarium
South Carolina State College
Orangeburg, South Carolina 29117
803-536-7174, Seats 82

Observatories

Charles E. Daniel Observatory
504 Roper Mountain Road
Greenville, South Carolina 29615
803-297-0232

Francis Marion College Observatory
Highway 301 N.
Francis Marion College
Florence, South Carolina 29501
803-661-1250 (*), Seats 73

Melton Memorial Observatory
Department of Physics and Astronomy
University of South Carolina
Columbia, South Carolina 29208
803-777-4180

Tennessee

Museums and Planetariums

M. D. Anderson Planetarium
Lambuth College
Jackson, Tennessee 38301
901-425-3283, Seats 76

Bays Mountain Nature Center
853 Bays Mountain Park Road
Kingsport, Tennessee 37660
615-229-9447 (*), Seats 107

Children's Museum of Oak Ridge, Inc.
461 W. Outer Drive
Oak Ridge, Tennessee 37830
615-482-1074

**Cumberland Science Museum and
Sudekum Planetarium**
800 Ridley Boulevard
Nashville, Tennessee 37203
615-862-5160, Seats 127

**East Tennessee Discovery Center and
Akima Planetarium**
Box 6204
Knoxville, Tennessee 37914
615-637-1121, Seats 57

**East Tennessee State University
Planetarium**
Johnson City, Tennessee 37614
615-929-4112, Seats 50

**Memphis Pink Palace Museum and
Planetarium**
3050 Central Avenue
Memphis, Tennessee 38111
901-454-5609, Seats 165

University of Tennessee Planetarium
Chattanooga, Tennessee 37403
615-755-4133

Observatories

**A. J. Dyer Observatory of Vanderbilt
University**
1000 Oman Drive
Brentwood, Tennessee 37027
615-373-4897

**Cleveland State Community College
Observatory**
P. O. Box 3570
Cleveland, Tennessee 37320
615-472-7141

Jones Observatory
Department of Physics and Astronomy
University of Tennessee at Chattanooga
Chattanooga, Tennessee 37402
615-755-4546 (*)

**Middle Tennessee State University
Observatory**
Murfreesboro, Tennessee 37132
615-898-2956

Texas

Museums and Planetariums

Angelo State University Planetarium
Department of Physics
San Angelo, Texas 76909
915-942-2136, Seats 118

**Stephen F. Austin State University
Planetarium**
Department of Physics and Astronomy
P. O. Box 13044, SFA Station
Nacagdoches, Texas 75962
409-568-3001, Seats 70

Marian Blakemore Planetarium
1705 W. Missouri
Midland, Texas 79701
915-683-2882, Seats 125

Cooke County College Planetarium
1525 W. California
Gainesville, Texas 76240
817-668-7731, Seats 65

El Paso Planetarium
6531 Boeing Drive
El Paso, Texas 79925
915-779-4317, Seats 120

Fort Worth Museum of Science and History
(Noble Planetarium)
1501 Montgomery Street
Fort Worth, Texas 76107
817-732-1631, Seats 70

Don Harrington Discovery Center
1200 Streit Drive
Amarillo, Texas 79106
606-355-9547 (*), Seats 68

Houston Museum of Natural Science and Burke Baker Planetarium
1 Hermann Circle Drive
Houston, Texas 77030
713-526-4273, Seats 232

Sam Houston State University Planetarium
Physics Department
Huntsville, Texas 77340
409-294-1601, Seats 50

Hudnall Planetarium
Tyler Junior College
P. O. Box 9020
Tyler, Texas 75711
903-510-2312, Seats 115

Insights
El Paso Science Center, Inc.
303 N. Oregon Street
El Paso, Texas 79901
915-542-2990

Morgan Jones Planetarium
P. O. Box 981
Abilene, Texas 79604
915-673-2751, Seats 70

Museum of Texas Tech University and Moody Planetarium
Fourth and Indiana
Lubbock, Texas 79409
306-742-2432, Seats 62

NASA-Johnson Space Center
2101 NASA Road 1
Houston, Texas 77058
713-483-4321 (recorded information)

Nature Center and Planetarium of Brazosport, Inc.
P. O. Box 1464
Lake Jackson, Texas 77566
409-265-7731, Seats 72

Richland College Planetarium
12800 Abrams Road
Dallas, Texas 75243
214-238-6013, Seats 100

St. Mark's Planetarium and Observatory
10600 Preston Road
Dallas, Texas 75230
214-363-6491, Seats 90

San Antonio College Planetarium
1300 San Pedro Avenue
San Antonio, Texas 78212
512-733-2910, Seats 95

The Science Place
(Southwest Museum of Science and Technology)
P. O. Box 151469
Dallas, Texas 75315-1469
214-428-7200 (*), Seats 60

University of Texas-Arlington Planetarium
Physics Department
Box 19059
Arlington, Texas 76019
817-273-2266, Seats 64

Wichita Falls Museum and Art Center
2 Eureka Circle
Wichita Falls, Texas 76308
617-692-0923 (*), Seats 60

Observatories

Stephen F. Austin State University Observatory
Department of Physics and Astronomy
Box 13044
Nacogdoches, Texas 75962
409-568-3001

George Observatory
P. O. Box 268
Damon, Texas 77430
409-553-3400

McDonald Observatory
P. O. Box 1337
Fort Davis, Texas 79734
915-426-3640

Utah

Museums and Planetariums

Hansen Planetarium
15 S. State Street
Salt Lake City, Utah 84111
801-538-2104

Ott Planetarium at Weber State University
Bob Tillotson
2336 W. 5650 S
Roy, Utah 84067
801-773-8106

Sarah Summerhays Planetarium
Brigham Young University
297 Eyring Science Center
Provo, Utah 84602
801-378-2805

Observatories

Physics Department Observatory
University of Utah
201 James Fletcher Building
Salt Lake City, Utah 84112
801-581-7140

Vermont

Museums and Planetariums

Discovery Museum
51 Park Street
Essex Junction, Vermont 05452
802-878-8687

Fairbanks Museum and Planetarium
Main and Prospect Streets
St. Johnsbury, Vermont 05819
802-748-2372, Seats 55

Montshire Museum of Science, Inc.
Montshire Road
Norwich, Vermont 05055
802-649-2200

Shelburne Museum, Inc.
U.S. Route 7
Shelburne, Vermont 05482
802-985-3346

Observatories

Green Mountain Observatory
P. O. Box 782
Williston, Vermont 05495
802-878-3459

Virginia

Museums and Planetariums

Arlington Planetarium
1426 N. Quincy Street
Arlington, Virginia 22207
703-358-6070, Seats 70

Chesapeake Planetarium
300 Cedar Road
Chesapeake, Virginia 23320
804-547-0153, Seats 120

Eastern Mennonite College Museum and Planetarium
Harrisonburg, Virginia 22801
703-432-4400, Seats 79

D. Ralph Hostetter Museum of Natural History
Eastern Mennonite College
Harrisonburg, Virginia 22801
703-433-2771

Museum of the Geological Sciences
Virginia Polytechnic Institute and State University
Derring Hall
Blacksburg, Virginia 24061
703-231-6029

NASA-Langley Visitor Center
NASA-Langley Research Center, MS 480
Hampton, Virginia 23665
804-864-6000

NASA-Wallops Flight Facility
Visitor Center
Goddard Space Flight Center
Wallops Island, Virginia 23337
804-824-1344

Norfolk State University Planetarium
2401 Corprew Avenue
Norfolk, Virginia 23504
804-683-8240, Seats 120

Pittsylvania County Planetarium
Educational and Cultural Center
37 Pruden Street
P. O. Box 232
Chatham, Virginia 24531
804-432-2761, Seats 87

Mary D. Pretlow Planetarium
Old Dominion University
Hampton Boulevard
Norfolk, Virginia 23508
804-440-4108, Seats 200

Science Museum of Virginia
2500 W. Broad Street
Richmond, Virginia 23220
804-367-1013 (*), Seats 281

Science Museum of Western Virginia and Hopkins Planetarium
1 Market Square
Roanoke, Virginia 24011
703-342-5710, Seats 140

Virginia Beach City Public Schools Planetarium
3080 S. Lynnhaven Road
Virginia Beach, Virginia 23452
804-431-4067, Seats 120

Virginia Living Museum
524 J. Clyde Morris Boulevard
Newport News, Virginia 23601
804-595-1900 (*), Seats 75

Virginia Marine Science Museum
717 General Booth Boulevard
Virginia Beach, Virginia 23451
804-425-3474

Virginia Museum of Natural History
1001 Douglas Avenue
Martinsville, Virginia 24112
703-666-8600

John C. Wells Planetarium
Physics Department
James Madison University
Harrisonburg, Virginia 22807
703-568-6109, Seats 70

J. Calder Wicker Planetarium
Fork Union Military Academy
Route 15
P. O. Box 278
Fork Union, Virginia 23055
804-842-3212, Seats 70

Observatories

Keeble Observatory
Randolph-Macon College
Ashland, Virginia 23005
804-752-7344

Leander McCormick Observatory
University of Virginia
P. O. Box 3818
Charlottesville, Virginia 22903
804-924-7494

Washington
Museums and Planetariums

Eastern Washington Science Center
Riverfront Park
N. 507 Howard
Spokane, Washington 99201
509-456-5507 (*), Seats 30

Eastern Washington University Science Center
W. 705 First Avenue
Spokane, Washington 99205
509-458-6326 (*), Seats 75

Geer Planetarium
Bellevue Community College
3000 Landerholm Circle SE
Bellevue, Washington 98007
206-641-2321, Seats 65

Pacific Science Center
200 Second Avenue N.
Seattle, Washington 98109
206-443-2001 (*), Seats 40

Washington State University Planetarium
Program in Astronomy
Pullman, Washington 99164
509-335-8518, Seats 60

Observatories

Goldendale Observatory
1602 Observatory Drive
Goldendale, Washington 98620
509-773-3141

West Virginia
Museums and Planetariums

Benedum Natural Science Theater
Oglebay Resort and Conference Center
Wheeling, West Virginia 26003
304-243-4034, Seats 150

Berkeley County Planetarium
Hedgesville High School
Route 1, Box 89
Hedgesville, West Virginia 25427
304-754-3354, Seats 25

Dwight O. Conner Planetarium
2101 Dudley Avenue
Parkersburg, West Virginia 26101
304-420-9595, Seats 75

Geology Museum
Marshall University
3rd Avenue and Hal Greer Boulevard
Huntington, West Virginia 25755
304-696-6720

Sunrise Children's Museum
746 Myrtle Road
Charleston, West Virginia 25314
304-344-8035 (*), Seats 60

Observatories

National Radio Astronomy Observatory
P. O. Box 2
Green Bank, West Virginia 24944
304-456-2011

Brooks Nature Center Observatory
Oglebay Resort and Conference Center
Wheeling, West Virginia 26003
304-243-4000

Wisconsin
Museums and Planetariums

Buckstaff Planetarium
University of Wisconsin
800 Algoma Boulevard
Oshkosh, Wisconsin 54901
414-424-7103, Seats 50

Cable Natural History Museum Inc.
County Highway M and Randysek Road
Cable, Wisconsin 54821
715-798-3890

Milwaukee Public Museum
800 W. Wells Street
Milwaukee, Wisconsin 53233
414-278-2702

The Museum of Natural History
University of Wisconsin
900 Reserve Street
Stevens Point, Wisconsin 54481
715-346-2858

L. E. Phillips Planetarium
Department of Physics and Astronomy
University of Wisconsin
Eau Claire, Wisconsin 54702
715-836-3148, Seats 50

University of Wisconsin-LaCrosse Planetarium
Physics Department
Cowley Hall
LaCrosse, Wisconsin 54601
608-785-8669, Seats 60

University of Wisconsin Planetarium
Department of Physics
River Falls, Wisconsin 54022
715-425-3196, Seats 50

University of Wisconsin Planetarium
Department of Physics and Astronomy
Stevens Point, Wisconsin 54481
715-346-2208, Seats 70

Observatories

Hobbs Observatory
Beaver Creek Reserve
Route 2, Box 94
Fall Creek, Wisconsin 54742
715-877-2787

Modine-Benstead Observatory
Racine Astronomical Society, Inc.
P. O. Box 085694
Racine, Wisconsin 53403

Pine Bluff Observatory
4065 Observatory Road
Cross Plains, Wisconsin 53528
608-262-3071

Washburn Observatory
University of Wisconsin-Madison
475 N. Charter Street
Madison, Wisconsin 53706
608-262-9274

Whitewater Observatory
Old Main Hill
Department of Physics
University of Wisconsin
Whitewater, Wisconsin 53190
414-472-5766

Yerkes Observatory
Public Information
c/o 373 W. Geneva Street
P. O. Box 258
Williams Bay, Wisconsin 53191
414-245-5555

Wyoming
Museums and Planetariums

Casper Planetarium
904 N. Poplar
Casper, Wyoming 82601
307-577-0310, Seats 95

University of Wyoming Planetarium
Department of Physics and Astronomy
Box 3905
Laramie, Wyoming 82071
307-766-6150, Seats 80

Observatories

Wyoming Infrared Observatory
Department of Physics and Astronomy
University of Wyoming
Laramie, Wyoming 82071
307-766-6150 (*), Seats 80

Canada
Museums and Planetariums

Alberta Science Centre/Centennial Planetarium
P. O. Box 2100
Mewata Park, Calgary, Alberta T2P 2M5
403-221-3700, Seats 244

Doran Planetarium
Laurentian University
Sudbury, Ontario P3E 2C6
705-675-1151, Seats 72

Edmonton Space and Science Centre
11211 142nd Street
Edmonton, Alberta T5M 4A1
403-452-9100 (*), Seats 220

Lockhart Planetarium
University of Manitoba
500 Dysart Road
Winnipeg, Manitoba R3T 2M8
204-474-9785, Seats 60

H. R. MacMillan Planetarium
Vanier Park
1100 Chestnut Street
Vancouver, British Columbia V6J 3J9
604-736-4431, Seats 275

National Museum of Science and Technology
P. O. Box 9724
Ottawa Terminal, Ottawa, Ontario
K1G 5A3
613-991-9219

Ontario Science Centre
770 Don Mills Road
Don Mills, Ontario M3C 1T3
416-429-4100 (*), Seats 50

Planetarium Dow of the Ville de Montreal
1000, rue St. Jacques Ouest
Montreal, Quebec H3C 1G7
514-872-4530, Seats 385

Royal Ontario Museum and McLaughlin Planetarium
100 Queens Park
Toronto, Ontario M5S 2C6
416-586-5736, Seats 340

Seneca College Planetarium
1750 Finch Avenue E
North York, Ontario M5S 5T7
416-491-5050, Seats 61

Observatories

Burke-Gaffney Observatory
Saint Mary's University
Halifax, Nova Scotia B3H 3C3
902-420-5633

Climenhaga Observatory
Department of Physics and Astronomy
University of Victoria
Victoria, British Columbia V8W 3P6
604-721-7750

Devon Observatory
Department of Physics
University of Alberta
Edmonton, Alberta T6G 2J1
403-492-5410

Dominion Astrophysical Observatory
5071 W. Saanich Road
Victoria, British Columbia V8X 4M6
604-363-0001

David Dunlap Observatory
Box 360
Richmond Hill, Ontario L4C 4Y6
416-884-2112

Observatoire Astronomique du Mont Megantic
C. P. 24
Notre-Dame-des-Bois, Quebec J0B 2E0
514-343-6718

Rothney Astrophysical Observatory
Physics and Astronomy Department
University of Calgary
Calgary, Alberta T2N 1N4
403-220-5385

Science North Solar Observatory
100 Ramsey Lake Road
Sudbury, Ontario P3E 5S9
705-522-3701

Gordon MacMillian Southam Observatory
1100 Chestnut Street
Vancouver, British Columbia V6J 3J9
604-738-2855

University of British Columbia Observatory
2219 Main Hall
Vancouver, British Columbia V6T 1Z4
604-822-6186

University of Saskatchewan Observatory
Department of Physics
Saskatoon, Saskatchewan S7N 0W0
306-966-6396

University of Western Ontario Observatory
Astronomy Department
London, Ontario N6A 3K7
519-661-3183

ZOOS AND AQUARIUMS

Alabama

Birmingham Zoo
P. O. Box 74022
2630 Cahaba Road
Birmingham, Alabama 35253
205-879-0408

Montgomery Zoo
Box ZEBRA
329 Vandiver Boulevard
Montgomery, Alabama 36110
205-240-4900

Alaska

Alaska Zoo
4731 O'Malley Road
Anchorage, Alaska 99516
907-346-2133

Arizona

Arizona-Sonora Desert Museum
2021 N. Kinney Road
Tucson, Arizona 85473
602-883-1380

The Phoenix Zoo
5810 E. Van Buren
Phoenix, Arizona 85008
602-273-1341

Reid Park Zoo
1100 S. Randolph Way
Tucson, Arizona 85716
602-791-3204

Wildlife World Zoo
Litchfield Park
16501 W. Northern Avenue
Litchfield, Arizona 85340
602-935-9453

Arkansas

Little Rock Zoological Garden
1 Jonesboro Drive
Little Rock, Arkansas 72205
501-666-2406

California

Fresno Zoo
(Chaffee Zoological Gardens of Fresno)
894 W. Belmont
Roeding Park
Fresno, California 93728
209-488-1549

The Living Desert
47-900 Portola Avenue
Palm Desert, California 92260
619-346-5694

Los Angeles Zoo
5333 Zoo Drive
Los Angeles, California 90027
213-666-4650

Marine World Africa USA
2001 Marine World Parkway
Vallejo, California 94589
707-644-4000

Micke Grove Zoo
Micke Grove Regional Park
11793 North Micke Grove Road
Lodi, California 95240
209-331-7270

Oakland Zoo
Knowland Park
9777 Golf Links Road
Oakland, California 94605
415-632-9525

Sacramento Zoo
Willam Land Park
3930 William Land Park Drive
Sacramento, California 95822
916-449-5166

San Diego Wild Animal Park
15500 San Pasqual Valley Road
Escondido, California 92027
619-747-8702

San Diego Zoo
P. O. Box 551
San Diego, California 92112
619-234-3153

San Francisco Zoo
Sloat Boulevard and 45th Avenue
San Francisco, California 94132
415-753-7080

Santa Ana Zoo
1801 E. Chestnut Avenue
Santa Ana, California 92701
714-836-4000

Santa Barbara Zoo
500 Ninos Drive
Santa Barbara, California 93103
805-962-5339
805-962-6310 (for taped information)

Colorado

Cheyenne Mountain Zoological Park
P. O. Box 158
Colorado Springs, Colorado 80901
719-633-0917

Denver Zoological Gardens
City Park
Denver, Colorado 80205
303-331-4118

Pueblo Zoo
Pueblo City Park
Pueblo Boulevard and Goodnight Avenue
Pueblo, Colorado 81003
719-561-9664

Connecticut

Beardsley Zoological Gardens
1875 Noble Avenue
Bridgeport, Connecticut 06610
203-576-8126

Maritime Center
10 North Water Street
Norwalk, Connecticut 06360
203-852-0700

Mystic Marinelife Aquarium
55 Coogan Boulevard
Mystic, Connecticut 06355-1997
203-536-9631

Delaware

Brandywine Zoo
1001 N. Park Drive
Wilmington, Delaware 19802
302-571-7788

District of Columbia

National Zoological Park
3000 Block of Connecticut Avenue NW
Washington, D.C. 20008
202-673-4717

Florida

Busch Gardens Zoological Park
P. O. Box 9158
Tampa, Florida 33674
813-988-5171

Central Florida Zoo
U. S. Highway 17/92 at Interstate 4
Lake Monroe, Florida 32747
407-323-4450

Cypress Gardens
P. O. Box I
Cypress Gardens, Florida 33884
813-324-2111

Discovery Island Zoo
Walt Disney World
P. O. Box 10000
Lake Buena Vista, Florida 32830
407-824-2875

Dreher Park Zoological Park
P. O. Box 6597
1301 Summit Boulevard
West Palm Beach, Florida 33405
407-533-0887

Jacksonville Zoological Park
8605 Zoo Road
Jacksonville, Florida 32218
904-757-4463

Jungle Larry's Zoological Park
1590 Goodlette Road
Naples, Florida 33962
813-262-5409

Lowry Park Zoological Garden
7530 N. Boulevard
Tampa, Florida 33604
813-935-8552

Miami MetroZoo
12400 SW 152nd Street
Miami, Florida 33177
305-251-0400

Miami Seaquarium
4400 Rickenbacker Causeway
Miami, Florida 33152
305-361-5703

Monkey Jungle
14805 SW 216th Street
Miami, Florida 33170
305-235-1611
(damaged by Hurricane Andrew in 1992;
call first)

Parrot Jungle and Gardens
11000 SW 57th Avenue
Miami, Florida 33156
305-666-7834

St. Augustine Alligator Farm
P. O. Drawer E, Route A1A South
St. Augustine, Florida 32085
904-824-3337

Santa Fe Teaching Zoo
3000 NW 83rd Street
P. O. Box 1530
Gainesville, Florida 32602
904-395-5604

The ZOO
5701 Gulf Breeze Parkway
Gulf Breeze, Florida 32561
904-932-2229

Georgia

Aquarium of the University of Georgia
Skidaway Island
McWhorter Road
Savannah, Georgia 31401
912-598-2496

**NYZP St. Catherine's Island Wildlife
Survival Center**
Route 1, Box 207-Z
Midway, Georgia 31320
912-884-5005

Zoo Atlanta
Grant Park
800 Cherokee Avenue
Atlanta, Georgia 30304
404-624-5600

Hawaii

Honolulu Zoo
Kapiolani Park
151 Kapahulu Avenue
Honolulu, Hawaii 96815
808-971-7171

Sea Life Park
Makapuu Point, Oahu
Waimanalo, Hawaii
808-259-7933

Waikiki Aquarium
2777 Kalakausa Avenue
Honolulu, Hawaii 96815
808-923-9741

Idaho

Boise City Zoo
Julia Davis Park
Boise, Idaho 83706
208-384-4260

Illinois

Brookfield Zoo
3300 Golf Road
Brookfield, Illinois 60513
708-485-0263

Glen Oak Zoo
2218 N. Prospect
Peoria, Illinois 61603
309-686-3365

Henson Robinson Zoo
1100 E. Lake Drive
Springfield, Illinois 62707
217-529-2097

Lincoln Park Zoological Gardens
2200 N. Cannon Drive
Chicago, Illinois 60614
312-294-4660

Miller Park Zoo
P. O. Box 3157
1020 S. Morris Avenue
Bloomington, Illinois 61702
309-823-4250

John G. Shedd Aquarium
1200 South Lake Shore Drive
Chicago, Illinois 60605
312-939-2438

Indiana

Columbian Park Zoo
South Street
Lafayette, Indiana 47901
317-447-9353

Fort Wayne Children's Zoo
3411 Sherman Boulevard
Fort Wayne, Indiana 46808
219-482-4610

Indianapolis Zoo
White River State Park
1200 W. Washington Street
Indianapolis, Indiana 46222
317-630-2001

Mesker Park Zoo
Bement Avenue
Evansville, Indiana 47712
812-428-0715

Potawatomi Zoo
Potawatomi Park
500 S. Greenlawn Boulevard
South Bend, Indiana 46615
219-284-9800

Iowa

Blank Park Zoo of Des Moines
7401 SW 9th Street
Des Moines, Iowa 50315
515-285-4722

Greater Iowa Aquarium
501 East 30th Street
Des Moines, Iowa 50318
515-263-0612

Kansas

Emporia Zoo
Soden's Grove Park
P. O. Box 928
Emporia, Kansas 66801
316-342-7306

Lee Richardson Zoo
Finnup Park
P. O. Box 499
Garden City, Kansas 67846
316-276-1250

Sedgwick County Zoo & Botanical Garden
5555 Zoo Boulevard
Wichita, Kansas 67212
316-942-2213

Sunset Zoological Park
11th and Poyntz
Manhattan, Kansas 66502
913-537-0063

Topeka Zoological Park
635 Gage Boulevard
Topeka, Kansas 66606
913-272-5821

Kentucky

Louisville Zoological Garden
P. O. Box 37250
1100 Trevilian Way
Louisville, Kentucky 40233
502-459-2181

Louisiana

Alexandria Zoological Park
City Park Boulevard
P. O. Box 71
Alexandria, Louisiana 71309
318-473-1386

Aquarium of the Americas
111 Iberville Street
New Orleans, Louisiana 70113
504-595-3474

Greater Baton Rouge Zoo
Greenwood Park
3601 Thomas Road
P. O. Box 458
Baton Rouge, Louisiana 70821
504-775-3877

Maine

Mount Desert Oceanarium
Mount Desert Island
Bar Harbor, Maine 04609
207-244-7330

Maryland

Baltimore Zoo
Druid Hill Park
Baltimore, Maryland 21233
301-396-7102

National Aquarium in Baltimore
Pier 3
501 East Pratt Street
Baltimore, Maryland 21233
301-576-3800

Salisbury Zoological Park
City Park
P. O. Box 3163
Salisbury, Maryland 21802
301-548-3188

Massachusetts

Aquarium of the National Marine Fisheries Service
Water Street
Woods Hole, Massachusetts 02543
508-548-7684

Cape Cod Aquarium
281 Route 6A
Brewster, Massachusetts 02631
508-385-9252

Franklin Park Zoo
Dorchester, Massachusetts 02110
617-442-0991

Michigan

Belle Isle Zoo and Aquarium
c/o Detroit Zoo
P. O. Box 39
Royal Oak, Michigan 48068
313-267-7159 (aquarium)
313-267-7160 (zoo)

Binder Park Zoo
7400 Division Road
Battle Creek, Michigan 49017
616-979-1351

Detroit Zoological Park
P. O. Box 39
8450 W. 10 Mile Road
Royal Oak, Michigan 48068
313-398-0903

John Ball Zoological Garden
1300 W. Fulton
Grand Rapids, Michigan 49504
616-776-2590

Potter Park Zoo
1301 S. Pennsylvania Avenue
Lansing, Michigan 48933
517-483-4221

Saginaw Children's Zoo
1461 S. Washington
Saginaw, Michigan 48605
517-759-1657

Minnesota

Lake Superior Zoological Gardens
7210 Fremont Street
Duluth, Minnesota 55807
218-624-1502

Minnesota Zoo
13000 Zoo Boulevard
AppleValley, Minnesota 55124
612-432-9000

St. Paul's Como Zoo
Midway Parkway and Kaufmane Drive
St. Paul, Minnesota 55103
612-488-4041

Mississippi

Jackson Zoological Park
2918 W. Capitol Street
Jackson, Mississippi 39209
601-352-2585

Missouri

Dickerson Park Zoo
3043 N. Fort
Springfield, Missouri 65803
417-833-1570

Kansas City Zoological Gardens
6700 Zoo Drive
Swope Park
Kansas City, Missouri 64132
816-333-7406

St. Louis Zoological Park
Forest Park
St. Louis, Missouri 63110
314-781-0900

Montana

Red Lodge Zoo
Box 820
Red Lodge, Montana 59068
406-446-1133

Nebraska

Folsom Children's Zoo
1300 S. 27th Street
Lincoln, Nebraska 68502
402-475-6742

Omaha's Henry Doorly Zoo
10th Street and Deer Park Boulevard
Omaha, Nebraska 69107
402-733-8011

New Jersey

Cape May County Park Zoo
Route 9 and Pine Lane
Cape May Court House, New Jersey 08210
609-465-5271

New Jersey State Aquarium at Camden
1 Riverside Drive
Camden, New Jersey 08101
609-365-3300

Space Farms Zoological Park and Museum
Beemerville Road
Sussex, New Jersey 07461
201-875-5800

Turtle Back Zoo
560 Northfield Avenue
South Mountain Reservation,
New Jersey 07052
201-731-5800

Van Saun Zoo
216 Forest Avenue
Paramus, New Jersey 07652
201-262-3771

New Mexico

Rio Grande Zoological Park
903 10th Street SW
Albuquerque, New Mexico 87102
505-843-7413

New York

Aquarium at Niagara Falls
701 Whirlpool Street
Niagara Falls, New York 14302
716-285-3575

Bear Mountain Trailside Museum and Zoo
Bear Mountain State Park
Bear Mountain, New York 10911
914-786-2701

Buffalo Zoological Garden
Delaware Park
Buffalo, New York 14214
716-837-3900

Burnet Park Zoo
500 Burnet Park Drive
Syracuse, New York 13201
315-435-8511

Central Park Zoo
830 Fifth Avenue
New York, New York 10021
212-439-6500

Garvies Point Museum and Preserve
Barry Drive
Glen Cove, New York 11542
516-671-0300

New York Zoological Park
(The Bronx Zoo)
Fordham Road and Bronx River Parkway
Bronx, New York
718-367-1010

Queens Zoo
Flushing Meadow Park
53-51 111th Street
Flushing, New York
718-861-6030

Ross Park Zoo
185 Park Avenue
Binghamton, New York 13903
607-724-5461

Seneca Park Zoo
2222 Saint Paul Street
Rochester, New York 14621
716-342-2744

Staten Island Zoological Society
614 Broadway
Staten Island, New York 10310
718-442-3101

Trevor Zoo
Millbrook School
Millbrook, New York 12545
914-677-3704

Utica Zoo
Roscoe Conkling Park
Steele Hill Road
Utica, New York 13501
315-738-0472

North Carolina

North Carolina Aquarium at Fort Fisher
U. S. Highway 421
Fort Fisher, North Carolina
919-458-8257

North Carolina Zoological Park
Zoo Parkway
Route 4, Box 83
Asheboro, North Carolina 27203
919-879-7000

North Dakota

Dakota Zoo
Dakota Zoological Society
Sertoma Park
P. O. Box 711
Bismarck, North Dakota 58501
701-223-7543

Roosevelt Park Zoo
1215 Burdick Expressway East
P. O. Box 538
Minot, North Dakota 58702
701-852-2751

Ohio

Akron Zoological Park
50 Edgewood Avenue
Akron, Ohio 44307
216-434-8645

Cincinnati Zoo and Botanical Gardens
3400 Vine Street
Cincinnati, Ohio 45234
513-281-4701

Cleveland MetroParks Zoological Park
3900 Brookside Park Drive
Cleveland, Ohio 44109
216-661-6500

Columbus Zoological Gardens and Arthur C. Johnson Aquarium
P. O. Box 400
9990 Riverside Drive
Powell, Ohio 43065
614-645-3400

Kings Island Wild Animal Habitat
Kings Island, Ohio 45034
513-241-5600

Toledo Zoological Garden
2700 Broadway
Toledo, Ohio 43609
419-385-572

Oklahoma

Oklahoma City Zoological Park
2101 NE 50th Street
Oklahoma City, Oklahoma 73111
405-424-3344

Tulsa Zoological Park
5701 E. 36th Street N
Tulsa, Oklahoma 74115
918-596-2400

Oregon

Metro Washington Park Zoo
4001 SW Canyon Road
Portland, Oregon 97221
503-226-1561

Wildlife Safari
P. O. Box 1600
Winston, Oregon 97496
503-679-6761

Pennsylvania

Clyde Peeling's Reptiland, Ltd.
Route 15
Allenwood, Pennsylvania
717-538-1869

Erie Zoological Garden
423 West 38th Street
P. O. Box 3268
Erie, Pennsylvania 16508
814-864-4093

Philadelphia Zoological Garden
34th Street and Girard Avenue
Philadelphia, Pennsylvania 19104
215-243-1100

Pittsburgh Aviary
Allegheny Commons West
Pittsburgh, Pennsylvania 15212
412-323-7234

Pittsburgh Zoo
P. O. Box 5250
Pittsburgh, Pennsylvania 15206
412-665-3639

Zooamerica
100 W. Hersheypark Drive
Hershey, Pennsylvania 17033
717-534-3861
800-437-7439

Rhode Island

Roger Williams Park Zoo
Roger Williams Park
Providence, Rhode Island 02905
401-785-9450

South Carolina

Brookgreen Gardens
U. S. Highway 17 S
Murrells Inlet, South Carolina 29576
803-237-4218

Greenville Zoo
150 Cleveland Park Drive
Greenville, South Carolina 29601
803-240-4310

Riverbanks Zoological Park
P. O. Box 1060
Columbia, South Carolina 29202-1060
803-779-8717

South Dakota

Great Plains Zoo
15th and Kiwanis
Sioux Falls, South Dakota 57102
605-339-7059

Tennessee

Grassmere Wildlife Park
3777 Nolensville Road
Nashville, Tennessee 37211
615-833-1534

Knoxville Zoological Park
P. O. Box 6040
915 Beaman Street at Chilhowee Park
Knoxville, Tennessee 37914
615-637-5331

Memphis Zoo and Aquarium
2000 Galloway
Memphis, Tennessee 38112
901-726-4787

Nashville Zoo
1710 Ridge Road Circle
Joelton, Tennessee
615-370-3333

Tennessee Aquarium
101 West Second Street
Chattanooga, Tennessee 37401
615-265-0695

Texas

Abilene Zoo
P. O. Box 60
Abilene, Texas 79604
915-672-9771

Caldwell Zoo
P. O. Box 4280
Tyler, Texas 75701
214-593-0121

Central Texas Zoo
Route 10, Box 173E
Waco, Texas 76708
817-752-0363

Dallas Zoo
Marsalis Park
620 East Clarendon Drive
Dallas, Texas 75260
214-670-6825

El Paso Zoo
4001 E. Paisano
El Paso, Texas 79905
915-544-2402

Fort Worth Zoological Park
2727 Zoological Park Drive
Fort Worth, Texas 76110
817-870-7051

Fossil Rim Wildlife Center
Route 1, Box 210
Glen Rose, Texas 76043
817-897-2960

Houston Zoo
1513 N. MacGregor
Houston, Texas 77030
713-525-3300

Gladys Porter Zoo
500 Ringgold Street
Brownsville, Texas 78520
512-546-7187

The San Antonio Zoo
3903 N. St. Mary's Street
San Antonio, Texas 78212
512-734-7184

Texas State Aquarium
One Shoreline Plaza
Corpus Christi, Texas 78408
800-477-4853

The Texas Zoo
P. O. Box 69
110 Memorial Drive
Victoria, Texas 77902
512-573-7681

Ellen Trout Zoo
P. O. Drawer 190
Lufkin, Texas 75902
409-634-6313

Utah

Utah's Hogle Zoo
2600 E. Sunnyside Avenue
Salt Lake City, Utah 84108
801-582-1632

Virginia

Mill Mountain Zoological Park
Mill Mountain Road
Roanoke, Virginia 24001
703-343-3241

**National Zoological Park Conservation
and Research Center**
Front Royal, Virginia 22630
703-635-4166

Virginia Zoological Park
3500 Granby Street
Norfolk, Virginia 23504
804-441-2374

Washington

Northwest Trek Wildlife Park
11610 Trek Drive E.
Eatonville, Washington 98328
206-832-6116

Point Defiance Zoo and Aquarium
5400 N. Pearl
Tacoma, Washington 98407
206-591-5337

Seattle Aquarium
Pier 59
Waterfront Park
Seattle, Washington 98109
206-386-4320

Woodland Park Zoo
5500 Phinney Avenue N.
Seattle, Washington 98103
206-684-4800

West Virginia

Oglebay's Good Children's Zoo
Oglebay Park
Wheeling, West Virginia 26003
304-242-3000

Wisconsin

Henry Vilas Zoo
702 S. Randall Avenue
Madison,Wisconsin 53715
608-266-4732

Milwaukee County Zoo
1001 W. Bluemound Road
Milwaukee, Wisconsin 53228
414-771-3040

Racine Zoo
2131 N. Main Street
Racine, Wisconsin 53402
414-636-9189

University of Wisconsin Zoological Museum
Lowell Noland Building
Madison, Wisconsin 53706
608-262-3766

Canada

Calgary Zoo, Botanic Gardens, and Prehistoric Park
Box 3036, Station B
Calgary, Alberta T2M 4R8
403-265-9310

Metropolitan Toronto Zoo
Box 280, West Hill
Toronto, Ontario MIE 4R5
416-392-5900

BOTANICAL GARDENS

Alabama

Birmingham Botanical Garden
2612 Lane Park Road
Birmingham, Alabama 35223
205-879-1227

Arizona

Arizona-Sonora Desert Museum
2021 N. Kinney Road
Tucson, Arizona 85743
602-883-1380

Boyce Thompson Southwestern Arboretum
P. O. Box AB
Superior, Arizona 85273
602-689-2811

Desert Botanical Garden
1201 North Galvin Parkway
Phoenix, Arizona 85008
602-941-1225

California

Huntington Library, Art Collections, and Botanical Garden
1151 Oxford Road
San Marino, California 91108
818-405-2100

Los Angeles State and County Arboretum
301 N. Baldwin Avenue
Arcadia, California 91006
818-446-8251

Mendocino Coast Botanical Gardens
18220 Route 1
Fort Bragg, California 95437
707-964-4352

Santa Barbara Botanical Gardens
1212 Mission Canyon Road
Santa Barbara, California 94122
415-661-1316

Colorado

Denver Botanic Gardens
909 York Street
Denver, Colorado 80206
303-331-4000

Delaware

Winterthur Museum and Gardens
Winterthur, Delaware 19735
800-448-3883

District of Columbia

U.S. National Arboretum
3501 New York Avenue
Washington, D.C. 20002
202-475-4815

Florida

Bok Tower Gardens
P. O. Box 3810
Lake Wales, Florida 33859
813-676-1408

Marie Selby Botanical Gardens
811 S. Palm Avenue
Sarasota, Florida 33577
813-366-5730

Georgia

Atlanta Botanical Gardens
P. O. Box 77246
Atlanta, Georgia 30357
404-876-5858

Calaway Gardens
Pine Mountain, Georgia 31822
800-282-8181

Hawaii

National Tropical Botanical Gardens
P. O. Box 340
Lawai, Kauai, Hawaii 96765
808-332-7324

Illinois

Chicago Botanic Garden
Lake Cook Road
P. O. Box 400
Glencoe, Illinois 60022
708-835-5440

Iowa

Des Moines Botanical Center
909 E. River Drive
Des Moines, Iowa 50316
515-283-4148

Massachusetts

Arnold Arboretum
Arbor Way
Jamaica Plain, Massachusetts 02130
617-524-1718

**Botanical Museum, Harvard University
Museums of Cultural and Natural
History**
26 Oxford Street
Cambridge, Massachusetts 02138
617-495-1910

Michigan

**Carl G. Fenner Arboretum and
Environmental Education Center**
2020 E. Mt. Hope Road
Lansing, Michigan 48910
517-483-4224

**Fernwood Nature Center and Botanical
Gardens**
13988 Rangeline Road
Niles, Michigan 49120
616-695-6491

Nebraska

Nebraska Statewide Arboretum
University of Nebraska
Lincoln, Nebraska 68508
402-472-2971

New Jersey

Cora Hartshorn Arboretum
324 Forest Drive S.
Short Hills, New Jersey 07078
201-376-3587

New York

Brooklyn Botanic Garden
1000 Washington Avenue
Brooklyn, New York 11225
718-622-4433

The Cloisters
Fort Tryon Park
New York, New York 10040
212-923-3700

Cornell Plantations
One Plantation Road
Ithaca, New York 14850
607-255-3020

New York Botanical Gardens
Southern Boulevard
Bronx, New York 10458
718-220-8700

North Carolina

Biltmore House and Garden
U. S. 23
Asheville, North Carolina 28802
704-274-1776

Ohio

Garden Center of Greater Cleveland
11030 East Boulevard
Cleveland, Ohio 44106
216-721-1600

Holden Arboretum
9500 Sperry Road
Mentor, Ohio 44060
216-256-1110

Oregon

Japanese Gardens
Kingston Avenue
Portland Oregon 97201
503-223-1321

Pennsylvania

Longwood Gardens
Route 1, P. O. Box 501
Kennett Square, Pennsylvania 19348
215-388-6741

Morris Arboretum of the University of Pennsylvania
9414 Meadowbrook Road
Chestnut Hill
Philadelphia, Pennsylvania 19118
215-247-5777

Tennessee

Cheekwood Botanical Gardens
Forrest Park Drive
Nashville, Tennesse 37205
615-353-2148

Virginia

Monticello
Route 53
Charlottesville, Virginia 22902
804-295-8181

Mount Vernon
Mount Vernon Memorial Highway
Mount Vernon, Virginia 22121
703-780-2000

Wisconsin

University of Wisconsin Arboretum–Madison
1207 Seminole Highway
Madison, Wisconsin 53711
608-263-7888

NATIONAL PARKS LISTING

The following lists selected sites in the National Parks System—or areas intended to preserve and highlight some aspect of the natural environment. For a complete listing of all sites in the National Park System, contact the National Park Service headquarters, 202-208-4747.

Alabama

Russell Cave National Monument
Route 1, Box 175
Bridgeport, Alabama 35740
205-495-2672

Alaska

Alagnak Wild River
P. O. Box 7
King Salmon, Alaska 99613
907-246-3305

Aniakchak National Monument and Preserve
P. O. Box 7
King Salmon, Alaska 99613
907-246-3305

Bering Land Bridge National Preserve
P. O. Box 220
Nome, Alaska 99762
907-443-2522

Denali National Park and Preserve
P. O. Box 9
McKinley Park, Alaska 99755
907-683-2294

Gates of the Arctic National Park and Preserve
P. O. Box 74680
Fairbanks, Alaska 99707
907-456-0281

Glacier Bay National Park and Preserve
Gustavus, Alaska 99826
907-697-2230

Katmai National Park and Preserve
P. O. Box 7
King Salmon, Alaska 99613
907-246-3305

Kenai Fjords National Park
P. O. Box 1727
Seward, Alaska 99664
907-224-3874

Kobuk Valley National Park
P. O. Box 1029
Kotzebue, Alaska 99752
907-442-3890

Lake Clark National Park and Preserve
701C Street, P. O. Box 61
Anchorage, Alaska 99513
907-781-2218

Noatak National Preserve
P. O. Box 1029
Kotzebue, Alaska 99752
907-442-3890

Wrangell-St. Elias National Park and Preserve
P. O. Box 20
Glennalien, Alaska 99588
907-822-5234

Yukon-Charley Rivers National Preserve
P. O. Box 64
Eagle, Alaska 99588
907-547-2233

Arizona

Grand Canyon National Park
P. O. Box 129
Grand Canyon, Arizona 86023
602-638-7888

Organ Pipe Cactus National Monument
Route 1, Box 100
Ajo, Arizona 85321
602-524-6228

Petrified Forest National Park
Arizona 86028
602-524-6228

Saguaro National Monument
3693 S. Old Spanish Trail
Tucson, Arizona 85730-5699
602-296-8576

Sunset Crater National Monument
Route 3
Box 149
Flagstaff, Arizona 86004
602-467-2241

Arkansas

Buffalo National River
P. O. Box 1173
Harrison, Arkansas 72601
501-741-5443

Hot Springs National Park
P. O. Box 1860
Hot Springs, Arkansas 71902
501-623-1433

California

Channel Islands National Park
1901 Spinnaker Drive
Ventura, California 93001
805-644-8157

Devils Postpile National Monument
c/o Sequoia and Kings Canyon National
Parks
Three Rivers, California 93271
209-565-3456

Kings Canyon National Park
Three Rivers, California 93271
209-565-3341

Lassen Volcanic National Park
P. O. Box 100
Mineral, California 96063
916-595-4444

Lava Beds National Monument
P. O. Box 867
Tulelake, California 96134
916-677-2282

Point Reyes National Seashore
Point Reyes, California 94956
415-663-1092

Redwood National Park
111 Second Street
Crescent City, California 95531
707-464-6101

Sequoia National Park
Three Rivers, California 93271
209-565-3341

Yosemite National Park
P. O. Box 577
Yosemite National Park, California 95389
209-372-0200

Colorado

Mesa Verde National Park
Colorado 81330
303-529-4465

Rocky Mountain National Park
Estes Park, Colorado 80517
303-586-2371

District of Columbia

Rock Creek Park
5000 Glover Road, NW
Washington, D.C. 20015
202-426-6832

Florida

Big Cypress National Preserve
Star Route, Box 110
Ochopee, Florida 33943
813-695-2000

Biscayne National Park
P. O. Box 1369
Homestead, Florida 33090
305-247-7275

Canaveral National Seashore
P. O. Box 6447
Titusville, Florida 32782
407-267-1110

Dry Tortugas National Park
P. O. Box 6208
Key West, Florida 33041
305-247-6211

Everglades National Park
P. O. Box 279
Homestead, Florida 33030
305-242-7700

Gulf Islands National Seashore
1801 Gulf Breeze Parkway
Gulf Breeze, Florida 32561
904-934-2600

Timucuan Ecological and Historic Preserve
13165 Mt. Pleasant Road
Jacksonville, Florida 32225
904-221-5568

Georgia

Cumberland Island National Seashore
P. O. Box 806
St. Marys, Georgia 31558
912-882-4336

Hawaii

Haleakala National Park
P. O. Box 369
Makawao, Hawaii 96768
808-572-9306

Hawaii Volcanoes National Park
Hawaii National Park, Hawaii 96718
808-967-7311

Idaho

City of Rocks National Reserve
P. O. Box 169
Almo, Idaho 83312
208-733-8398

Craters of the Moon National Monument
P. O. Box 29
Arco, Idaho 83213
208-527-3257

Hagerman Fossil Beds National Monument
P. O. Box 570
Hagerman, Idaho 83332
208-837-4793

Indiana

Indiana Dunes National Lakeshore
1100 North Mineral Springs Road
Porter, Indiana 46304
219-926-7561

Kentucky

Mammoth Cave National Park
Mammoth Cave, Kentucky 42259
502-758-2328

Maine

Acadia National Park
P. O. Box 177
Bar Harbor, Maine 04609
207-288-3338

Appalachian National Scenic Trail
Appalachian Trail Conference
P. O. Box 236
Harpers Ferry, West Virginia 25425
304-535-6331
(The Appalachian Trail continues for 2,114 miles [3,220 kilometers], from Mount Katahdin, Maine, to Springer Mountain, Georgia.)

Maryland

Assateaque Island National Seashore
Route 2, Box 294
Berlin, Maryland 21811
410-641-1441

Catoctin Mountain Park
6602 Foxville Road
Thurmont, Maryland 21788
301-663-9343

Massachusetts

Cape Cod National Seashore
South Wellfleet, Massachusetts 02633
508-255-3421

Michigan

Isle Royale National Park
87 North Ripley Street
Houghton, Michigan 49931
906-482-0984

Pictured Rocks National Lakeshore
P. O. Box 40
Munising, Michigan 49862
906-387-3700

Sleeping Bear Dunes National Lakeshore
P. O. Box 277
9922 Front Street
Empire, Michigan 49630
616-326-5134

Minnesota

**Mississippi National River
and Recreation Area**
175 East Fifth Street
Suite 418
Box 41
St. Paul, Minnesota 55101
612-290-4160

Voyageurs National Park
P. O. Box 50
International Falls, Minnesota 56649
218-283-9821

Mississippi

Gulf Islands National Seashore
3500 Park Road
Ocean Springs, Mississippi 39564
601-875-9057

Missouri

Ozark National Scenic Riverways
P. O. Box 490
Van Buren, Missouri 63965
314-323-4236

Montana

Glacier National Park
West Glacier, Montana 59936
406-888-5441

Nebraska

Niobrara National Scenic River
P. O. Box 591
O'Neill, Nebraska 68763
402-336-3970

Nevada

Great Basin National Park
Baker, Nevada 89311
702-234-7331

New Mexico

Carlsbad Caverns National Park
3225 National Parks Highway
Carlsbad, New Mexico 88220
505-785-2232

New York

Fire Island National Seashore
120 Laurel Street
Patchogue, New York 11772
516-289-4810

North Carolina

Blue Ridge Parkway
700 Northwestern Plaza
Asheville, North Carolina 28801
704-259-0779

Cape Hatteras National Seashore
Route 1, Box 675
Manteo, North Carolina 27954
919-473-2111

Cape Lookout National Seashore
P. O. Box 690
Beaufort, North Carolina 28516
919-728-2250

North Dakota

Theodore Roosevelt National Park
P. O. Box 7
Medora, North Dakota 58645
701-623-4466

Oregon

Crater Lake National Park
P. O. Box 7
Crater Lake, Oregon 97604
503-594-2211

**John Day Fossil Beds National
Monument**
420 W. Main Street
John Day, Oregon 97845
503-575-0721

Oregon Caves National Monument
19000 Caves Highway
Cave Junction, Oregon 97523
503-592-2100

Pennsylvania

**Upper Delaware Scenic and
Recreational River**
P. O. Box C
Narrowsburg, New York 12764
717-729-7135

South Carolina

Congaree Swamp National Monument
Suite 607, 1835 Assembly Street
Columbia, South Carolina 29201
803-776-4396

South Dakota

Badlands National Park
P. O. Box 6
Interior, South Dakota 57750
605-433-5361

Jewel Cave National Monument
R. R. 1, Box 60AA
Custer, South Dakota 57730
605-673-2288

Wind Cave National Park
Hot Springs, South Dakota 57747
605-745-4600

Tennessee

Big South Fork National River
P. O. Drawer 630
Oneida, Tennessee 37841
615-879-4890

Great Smoky Mountains National Park & Recreational Area
Gatlinburg, Tennessee 37738
615-436-1200

Obed Wild and Scenic River
P. O. Box 429
Wartburg, Tennessee 37887
615-346-6294

Texas

Alibates Flint Quarries National Monument
c/o Lake Meredith Recreation Area
P. O. Box 1438
Fritch, Texas 79036
806-857-3152

Big Bend National Park
Big Bend National Park, Texas 79834
915-477-2251

Big Thicket National Preserve
3785 Milam
Beaumont, Texas 77701
409-839-2689

Guadalupe Mountains National Park
H. C. 60, Box 400
Salt Flat, Texas 79847-9400
915-828-3251

Padre Island National Seashore
9405 S. Padre Island Drive
Corpus Christi, Texas 78418-5597
512-937-2621

Rio Grande Wild and Scenic River
c/o Big Bend National Park
Big Bend National Park, Texas 79834
915-477-2251

Utah

Arches National Park
P. O. Box 907
Moab, Utah 84532
801-259-8161

Bryce Canyon National Park
Bryce Canyon, Utah 84717
801-834-5322

Canyonlands National Park
125 West 200 South
Moab, Utah 84532
801-259-7164

Capitol Reef National Park
Torrey, Utah 84775
801-425-3791

Natural Bridges National Monument
Box 1
Lake Powell, Utah 84533
801-259-5174

Rainbow Bridge National Monument
c/o Glen Canyon National Recreation Area
P. O. Box 1507
Page, Arizona 86040
602-645-8200

Timpanogos Cave National Monument
R. R. 3, Box 200
American Fork, Utah 84003
801-756-5238

Zion National Park
Springdale, Utah 84767-1099
801-772-3256

Virginia

Prince William Forest Park
P. O. Box 209
Triangle, Virginia 22172
703-221-7181

Shenandoah National Park
Route 4, Box 348
Luray, Virginia 22835
703-999-2243

Virgin Islands

Buck Island Reef National Monument
P. O. Box 160
Christiansted, St. Croix,
Virgin Islands 00820
809-773-1460

Salt River Bay NHP and Ecological Preserve
(not open to the public)

Virgin Islands National Park
P. O. Box 7789
Charlotte Amalie, St. Thomas, Virgin Islands 00801
809-775-6238

Washington

Mount Rainier National Park
Tahoma Woods, Star Route
Ashford, Washington 98304
206-569-2211

North Cascades National Park
2105 Highway 20
Sedro Woolley, Washington 98284
206-856-5700

Olympic National Park
600 E. Park Avenue
Port Angeles, Washington 98362
206-452-0330

West Virginia

Bluestone National Scenic River
c/o New River Gorge National River
P. O. Box 1189
Oak Hill, West Virginia 25901
304-466-0417

New River Gorge National River
P. O. Box 1189
Oak Hill, West Virginia 25901
304-465-0508

Wisconsin

Apostle Islands National Lakeshore
Route 1, Box 4
Bayfield, Wisconsin 54814
715-779-3397

Lower Saint Croix National Scenic Riverway
P. O. Box 708
St. Croix Falls, Wisconsin 54024
715-483-3284

Saint Croix National Scenic Riverway
P. O. Box 708
St. Croix Falls, Wisconsin 54024
715-483-3284

Wyoming

Devils Tower National Monument
Devils Tower, Wyoming 82714
307-467-5283

Fossil Butte National Monument
P. O. Box 527
Kemmerer, Wyoming 83101
307-877-4455

Grand Teton National Park
P. O. Drawer 170
Moose, Wyoming 83012
307-733-2880

Yellowstone National Park
P. O. Box 168
Yellowstone National Park,
Wyoming 82190
307-344-7381

NATIONAL WILDLIFE REFUGES

Note: Names in parentheses represent refuges administered from headquarters on another refuge.

Washington Office

Director
National Wildlife Refuges
U.S. Department of the Interior
U.S. Fish and Wildlife Service
1849 C Street NW
MIB 3012
Washington, D.C. 20240
202-208-4717

Alabama

Bon Secour National Wildlife Refuge
P. O. Box 1650
Gulf Shores, Alabama 36542
205-968-8623

Choctaw National Wildlife Refuge
Box 808
Jackson, Alabama 36545
205-246-3583

Eufaula National Wildlife Refuge
Route 2, Box 97-B
Eufaula, Alabama 36027
205-687-4065

Wheeler National Wildlife Refuge
(Blowing Wind Cave, Fern Cave,
Watercress Darter)
Route 4, Box 250
Decatur, Alabama 35603
205-353-7243

Alaska

Alaska Maritime Headquarters
(Alaskan Peninsula Unit, Bering Sea
Unit, Chukchi Sea Unit, Gulf of Alaska
Unit)
202 W. Pioneer Avenue
Homer, Alaska 99603
907-235-6546

Alaska Peninsula National Wildlife Refuge
(Becharof)
P. O. Box 277
King Salmon, Alaska 99613
907-246-3339

Aleutian Islands Unit
Box 5251, Naval Air Station Adak, FBO
Seattle, Washington 98791
907-592-2406

Arctic National Wildlife Refuge
Box 20, 101-12th Avenue
Fairbanks, Alaska 99701
907-456-0250

Innoko National Wildlife Refuge
Box 69
McGrath, Alaska 99627
907-524-3251

Izembek National Wildlife Refuge
Box 127
Cold Bay, Alaska 99571
907-532-2445

Kanuti National Wildlife Refuge
Box 11, 101-12th Avenue
Fairbanks, Alaska 99701
907-456-0329

Kenai National Wildlife Refuge
P. O. Box 2139
Soldotna, Alaska 99669-2139
907-262-7021

Kodiak National Wildlife Refuge
1390 Buskin River Road
Kodiak, Alaska 99615
907-487-2600

Koyukuk National Wildlife Refuge
Box 287
Galena, Alaska 99741
907-656-1231

Nowitna National Wildlife Refuge
Box 287
Galena, Alaska 99741
907-656-1231

Selawik National Wildlife Refuge
Box 270
Kotzebue, Alaska 99572
907-442-3799

Tetlin National Wildlife Refuge
Box 779
Tok, Alaska 99780
907-883-5312

Togiak National Wildlife Refuge
P. O. Box 270
Dillingham, Alaska 99576
907-842-1063

Yukon Delta National Wildlife Refuge
P. O. Box 346
Bethel, Alaska 99559
907-543-3151

Yukon Flats National Wildlife Refuge
Box 14, 101-12th Avenue
Fairbanks, Alaska 99701
907-456-0440

Arizona

Buenos Aires National Wildlife Refuge
P. O. Box 109
Sasabe, Arizona 85633
602-823-4251

Cabeza Prieta National Wildlife Refuge
1611 N. Second Avenue
Ajo, Arizona 85321
602-387-6483

Cibola National Wildlife Refuge
Box AP
Blythe, California 92225
619-857-3253

Havasu National Wildlife Refuge
Box 3009
Needles, California 92363
619-326-3853

Imperial National Wildlife Refuge
Box 72217
Martinez Lake, Arizona 85364
602-783-3371

Kofa National Wildlife Refuge
Box 6290
Yuma, Arizona 85364
602-783-7861

Arkansas

Big Lake National Wildlife Refuge
Box 67
Manila, Arkansas 72442
501-564-2429

Cache River National Wildlife Refuge
P. O. Box 279
Turrell, Arkansas 72384
501-343-2595

Felsenthal National Wildlife Refuge
(Overflow)
P. O. Box 1157
Crossett, Arkansas 71635
501-364-3167

Holla Bend National Wildlife Refuge
(Logan Cave)
Route 1, Box 59
Dardanelle, Arkansas 72834-9074
501-229-4300

Northeast Arkansas Refuges
P. O. Box 279
Turrell, Arkansas 72384
501-343-2595

Wapanocca National Wildlife Refuge
Box 279
Turrell, Arkansas 72384
501-343-2595

White River National Wildlife Refuge
Box 308
321 W. 7th Street
De Witt, Arkansas 72042
501-946-2591

California

Chibola (see Arizona)

Havasu (see Arizona)

Hopper Mountain National Wildlife Refuge
P. O. Box 5839
Ventura, California 93005
805-644-5185

Humboldt Bay National Wildlife Refuge
1020 Ranch Road
Loleta, California 95551
707-733-5406

Imperial (see Arizona)

Kern National Wildlife Refuge
Box 670
Delano, California 93216-0219
805-725-2767

Klamath Basin Refuges
(Bear Valley [OR], Clear Lake [OR], Lower
Klamath [OR/CA], Tule Lake, Upper
Klamath [OR])
Route 1, Box 74
Tulelake, California 96134
916-667-2231

Modoc National Wildlife Refuge
Box 1610
Alturas, California 96101
916-233-3572

Sacramento Valley Refuges
(Butte Sink Wildlife Management Area,
Colusa, Delevan, Sacramento River,
Sutter, Willow Creek-Lurline Wildlife
Management Area)
Route 1, Box 311
Willows, California 95988
916-934-2801

Salton Sea National Wildlife Refuge
(Coachella Valley)
P. O. Box 120
Calipatria, California 92223
619-348-5278

**San Francisco Bay National Wildlife
Refuge**
(Antioch Dunes, Castle Rock, Ellicott
Slough, Farallon, Salinas River, San Pablo
Bay)
Box 524
Newark, California 94560
415-792-0222

San Luis National Wildlife Refuge
(Grasslands Wildlife Management Area,
Kesterson, Merced, San Joaquin River)
Box 2176
Los Banos, California 93635
209-826-3508

Southern California Coastal Complex
(Tijuana Slough, Seal Beach, Sweetwater
Marsh)
P. O. Box 355
Imperial Beach, California 91933
619-575-1290

Colorado

**Alamosa/Monte Vista National Wildlife
Refuge**
9383 El Rancho Lane
Alamosa, Colorado 81101
719-589-4021

Arapaho National Wildlife Refuge
(Bamforth [WY], Hutton Lake [WY],
Pathfinder [WY])
Box 457
Walden, Colorado 80480
303-723-8202

Browns Park National Wildlife Refuge
1318 Highway 318
Maybell, Colorado 81640
303-365-3613

Connecticut

**Stewart B. McKinney National Wildlife
Refuge**
P. O. Box 1030
Westbrook, Connecticut 06498
203-399-2513

Delaware

Bombay Hook National Wildlife Refuge
Route 1, Box 147
Smyrna, Delaware 19977
302-653-9345

Prime Hook National Wildlife Refuge
Route 3, Box 195
Milton, Delaware 19968
302-684-8419

Florida

**Chassahowitzka National Wildlife
Refuge**
1502 S. Kings Bay Drive
Crystal River, Florida 32629
904-563-2088

J. N. "Ding" Darling National Wildlife Refuge
(Caloosahatchee, Island Bay, Matlacha Pass, Pine Island)
One Wildlife Drive
Sanibel, Florida 33957
813-472-1100

Florida Panther National Wildlife Refuge
3860 Tollgate Road
Naples, Florida 33942-5444
813-353-8442

Lake Woodruff National Wildlife Refuge
Box 488
DeLeon Springs, Florida 32028
904-985-4673

Lower Suwannee National Wildlife Refuge
(Cedar Keys)
Route 1, Box 1193C
Chiefland, Florida 32626
904-493-0238

Arthur R. Marshall Loxahatchee
(Hobe Sound)
Route 1, Box 278
Boynton Beach, Florida 33437-9741
407-732-3684

Merritt Island National Wildlife Refuge
(Pelican Island, St. Johns)
Box 6504
Titusville, Florida 32780
407-867-0667

National Key Deer Refuge
(Crocodile Lake, Great White Heron, Key West)
P. O. Box 430510
Big Pine Key, Florida 33043-0510
305-872-2239

St. Marks National Wildlife Refuge
Box 68
St. Marks, Florida 32355
904-925-6121

St. Vincent National Wildlife Refuge
Box 447
Apalachicola, Florida 32320
904-653-8808

Georgia

Okefenokee National Wildlife Refuge
(Banks Lake)
Route 2, Box 338
Folkston, Georgia 31537
912-496-7366

Piedmont National Wildlife Refuge
(Bond Swamp)
Route 1, Box 670
Round Oak, Georgia 31038
912-986-5441

Savannah Coastal Refuges National Wildlife Refuge
(Blackbeard Island, Harris Neck, Pinckney Island [SC], Savannah [SC/GA], Tybee [SC], Wassaw, Wolf Island)
Box 8487
Savannah, Georgia 31412
912-944-4415

Hawaii

Hakalau Forest National Wildlife Refuge Complex
154 Waianuenue Avenue, Room 219
Hilo, Hawaii 96720
808-969-9909

Hawaiian and Pacific Islands National Wildlife Refuge Complex
300 Ala Moana Boulevard, Room 5302
Honolulu, Hawaii 96850
808-541-1201

Johnston Atoll
P. O. Box 396
APO AP 96558
808-621-3044

Kaui National Wildlife Refuge Complex
(Kilauea Point, Huleia, Hanalei)
Box 87
Kilauea, Kauai, Hawaii 96754
808-828-1413

Midway Atoll
P. O. Box 1, Midway Atoll
FPO AP 96516
808-471-1110

Oahu/Molokai/Maui National Wildlife Refuge Complex
(James C. Campbell, Kakahaia, Kealia Pond, Pearl Harbor)
P. O. Box 340
Haleiwa, Hawaii 96712-0340
808-637-6330

Remote Islands National Wildlife Refuge Complex
(Baker Island, Hawaiian Islands, Howland Island, Rose Atoll)
300 Ala Moana Boulevard, Room 5302
Honolulu, Hawaii 96813
808-541-1201

Idaho

Bear Lake (affiliated with Southeast Idaho NWR Complex)
370 Webster, Box 9
Montpelier, Idaho 83254
208-847-1757

Camas (affiliated with Southeast Idaho NWR Complex)
2150 E. 2350 N.
Hamer, Idaho 83245
208-662-5423

Deer Flat National Wildlife Refuge
13751 Upper Embankment Road
Nampa, Idaho 83653
208-467-9278 (or 888-5582)

Grays Lake (affiliated with Southeast Idaho NWR Complex)
74 Grays Lake Road
Wayan, Idaho 83285
208-574-2755

Kootenai National Wildlife Refuge
HCR 60, Box 283
Bonners Ferry, Idaho 83805
208-267-3888

Minidoka (affiliated with Southeast Idaho NWR Complex)
Route 4, P. O. Box 290
Rupert, Idaho 83350
208-436-3589

Southeast Idaho National Wildlife Refuge Complex
1246 Yellowstone Avenue, A-4
Pocatello, Idaho 83201
208-237-6616

Illinois

Brussels District (affiliated with Mark Twain NWR)
HRC, Box 107
Brussels, Illinois 62013
618-883-2524

Chautauqua National Wildlife Refuge (Meredosia)
Rural Route 2
Havana, Illinois 62644
309-535-2290

Crab Orchard National Wildlife Refuge
Box J
Carterville, Illinois 62918
618-997-3344

Cypress Creek
Route 1, Box 53D
Ullin, Illinois 62992
618-634-2231

Mark Twain National Wildlife Refuge
1704 North 24th
Quincy, Illinois 62301
217-224-8580

Savannah District (affiliated with Upper Mississippi River National Wildlife & Fish Refuge)
Post Office Building
Savannah, Illinois 61074
815-273-2732

Upper Mississippi River National Wildlife and Fish Refuge (see Minnesota)

Indiana

Muscatatuck National Wildlife Refuge
Route 7, Box 189 A
Seymour, Indiana 47274
812-522-4352

Patoka River National Wetlands Project
510 1/2 Morton Street, Box 217
Oakland City, Indiana 47660
812-749-3199

Iowa

DeSoto National Wildlife Refuge
Route 1, Box 114
Missouri Valley, Iowa 51555
712-642-4121

Mark Twain (see Illinois)

McGregor District (affiliated with the Upper Mississippi River National Wildlife & Fish Refuge)
P. O. Box 460
McGregor, Iowa 52157
319-873-3423

Union Slough National Wildlife Refuge
1710 360th Street
Titonka, Iowa 50480
515-928-2523

Upper Mississippi River National Wildlife and Fish Refuge (see Minnesota)

Walnut Creek National Wildlife Refuge
P. O. Box 399
Prairie City, Iowa 50228
515-994-2415

Wapello District (affiliated with Mark Twain NWR)
10728 Country Road X-61
Wapello, Iowa 52653
319-523-6982

Kansas

Flint Hills National Wildlife Refuge
Box 128
Hartford, Kansas 66854
316-392-5553

Kirwin National Wildlife Refuge
Route 1, Box 103
Kirwin, Kansas 67644
913-543-6673

Quivira National Wildlife Refuge
Route 3, Box 48A
Stafford, Kansas 67578
316-486-2393

Louisiana

Bayou Cocodrie National Wildlife Refuge
P. O. Box 1772
Ferriday, Louisiana 71334
318-992-5261

Cameron Prairie National Wildlife Refuge
Route 1, Box 643
Bell City, Louisiana 70630
318-598-2216

Catahoula National Wildlife Refuge
P. O. Drawer Z
Rhinehart, Louisiana 71363
318-992-5261

D'Arbonne National Wildlife Refuge (Upper Ouachita)
Box 3065
Monroe, Louisiana 71201
318-325-1735

Lacassine National Wildlife Refuge
HRC 63, Box 186
Lake Arthur, Louisiana 70549
318-774-5923

Lake Ophelia National Wildlife Refuge (Grand Cote)
P. O. Box 256
Marksville, Louisiana 71351
318-253-4238

Sabine National Wildlife Refuge
Highway 27 S., 3000 Main Street
Hackberry, Louisiana 70654
318-762-3816

SE Louisiana Refuges (Bogue Chitto, Bayou Sauvage, Breton, Delta)
1010 Gause Boulevard, Building 936
Slidell, Louisiana 70458
504-646-7555

Tensas River National Wildlife Refuge
Route 2, Box 295
Tallulah, Louisiana 71282
318-574-2664

Maine

Moosehorn National Wildlife Refuge (Cross Island, Franklin Island, Seal Island)
Box 1077
Calais, Maine 04619
207-454-3521

Parker River National Wildlife Refuge (see Massachusetts)

Petit Manan (affiliated with Moosehorn NWR)
P. O. Box 279
Milbridge, Maine 04658
207-546-2124

Rachel Carson National Wildlife Refuge
Route 2, Box 751
Wells, Maine 04090
207-646-9226

Pond Island (see Massachusetts)

Sunkhaze Meadows National Wildlife Refuge
1033 South Main Street
Old Town, Maine 04468
207-827-6138

Maryland

Blackwater National Wildlife Refuge
(Martin, Susquehanna)
2145 Key Wallace Drive
Cambridge, Maryland 21613
410-228-2677

Chincoteague (see Virginia)

Eastern Neck National Wildlife Refuge
1730 Eastern Neck Road
Rock Hall, Maryland 21661
301-639-7056

Patuxent National Wildlife Refuge
Route 197
Laurel, Maryland 20708
301-498-0253

Massachusetts

Conte National Wildlife & Fish Refuge
VA Medical Center, Box 6
Northampton, Massachusetts 01060
413-582-3174

Great Meadows National Wildlife Refuge
(John Hay [NH], Massasoit, Nantucket, Oxbow, Wapack [NH])
Weir Hill Road
Sudbury, Massachusetts 01776
508-443-4661

Monomy (affiliated with Great Meadows NWR)
Wikis Way, Morris Island
Chatam, Massachusetts 02633
508-945-0594

Parker River National Wildlife Refuge
(Pond Island [ME], Thacher Island)
Northern Boulevard, Plum Island
Newburyport, Massachusetts 01950
508-465-5753

Michigan

Seney National Wildlife Refuge
(Harbor Island, Huron)
HCR 2, Box 1
Seney, Michigan 49883
906-586-9851

Shiawassee National Wildlife Refuge
(Michigan Islands, Wyandotte)
6975 Mower Road
Saginaw, Michigan 48601
517-777-5930

Minnesota

Agassiz National Wildlife Refuge
R. R. 1, Box 74
Middle River, Minnesota 56737
218-449-4115

Big Stone National Wildlife Refuge
25 NW 2nd Street
Ortonville, Minnesota 56278
612-839-3700

Crane Meadows National Wildlife Refuge
P. O. Box 306
Little Falls, Minnesota 56345
612-632-1575

Detroit Lakes Wildlife Management District (affiliated with Minnesota Waterfowl and Wetland Management Complex)
Route 3, Box 47D
Detroit Lakes, Minnesota 56537
218-847-4431

Fergus Falls Wildlife Management District (affiliated with Minnesota Waterfowl and Wetland Management Complex)
Route 1, Box 76
Fergus Falls, Minnesota 56537
218-739-2291

Hamden Slough (affiliated with Minnesota Waterfowl and Wetland Management Complex)
Route 1, Box 32
Detroit Lakes, Minnesota 56501
218-439-6319

Litchfield Wildlife Management District
(affiliated with Minnesota Waterfowl and
Wetland Management Complex)
971 E. Frontage Road
Litchfield, Minnesota 55355
612-693-2849

**Minnesota Valley National-Wildlife
Refuge**
3815 E. 80th Street
Bloomington, Minnesota 55420-1600
612-854-5900

**Minnesota Waterfowl and Wetlands
Management Complex**
Route 1, Box 76
Fergus Falls, Minnesota 56537
218-739-2291

Morris Wildlife Management District
(affiliated with Minnesota Waterfowl and
Wetland Management Complex)
Route 1, Box 877
Morris, Minnesota 56267
612-589-1001

Rice Lake National Wildlife Refuge
(Mille Lacs)
Route 2
McGregor, Minnesota 55760
218-768-2402

Sherburne National Wildlife Refuge
17076 293rd Avenue
Zimmerman, Minnesota 55398
612-389-3323

Tamarac National Wildlife Refuge
HC-10, Box 145
Rochert, Minnesota 56578
218-847-2641

**Upper Mississippi River Wildlife & Fish
Refuge** (or Upper Mississippi River
Complex)
(Iowa, Illinois, Minnesota, and Wisconsin)
51 E. 4th Street, Room 101
Winona, Minnesota 55987
507-452-4232

Windom Wildlife Management District
(affiliated with Minnesota Waterfowl and
Wetland Management Complex)
Route 1, Box 273A
Windom, Minnesota 56101
507-831-2220

Mississippi

Mississippi Sandhill Crane Complex
7200 Crane Lane
Gautier, Mississippi 39553
601-497-6322

Mississippi Wildlife Management District
(Dahomey, Tallahatchie)
P. O. Box 1070
Grenada, Mississippi 38901
601-226-8286

Noxubee National Wildlife Refuge
Route 1, Box 142
Brooksville, Mississippi 39739
601-323-5548

Panther Swamp (affiliated with Yazoo
NWR)
Route 5, Box 25
Yazoo City, Mississippi 39194
601-746-5060

**St. Catherine Creek National Wildlife
Refuge**
P. O. Box 18639
Natchez, Mississippi 39122
601-442-6696

Yazoo National Wildlife Refuge
(Hillside, Mathews Brake, Morgan Brake)
Route 1, Box 286
Hollandale, Mississippi 38748
601-839-2638

Missouri

Annada District (affiliated with Mark
Twain NWR)
(Clarence Cannon)
P. O. Box 88
Annada, Missouri 63330
314-847-2333

Mark Twain (see Illinois)

Mingo National Wildlife Refuge
(Pilot Knob)
Route 1, Box 103
Puxico, Missouri 63960
314-222-3589

Squaw Creek National Wildlife Refuge
Box 101
Mound City, Missouri 64470
816-442-3187

Swan Lake National Wildlife Refuge
R. R. 1, Box 29A
Sumner, Missouri 64681
816-856-3323

Montana

Benton Lake National Wildlife Refuge
Box 450
Black Eagle, Montana 59414
406-727-7400

Bowdoin National Wildlife Refuge
(Black Coulee, Creedman Coulee, Hewitt
Lake, Lake Thibadeau)
Box J
Malta, Montana 59538
406-654-2863

**Charles M. Russell National Wildlife
Refuge**
(Hailstone, Halfbreed Lake, Lake Mason,
UL Bend, War Horse)
Box 110
Lewistown, Montana 59457
406-538-8706

Ft. Peck Wildlife Station
(affiliated with Charles M. Russell NWR)
P. O. Box 166
Fort Peck, Montana 59223
406-526-3464

Jordan Wildlife Station (affiliated with
Charles M. Russell NWR)
P. O. Box 63
Jordan, Montana 59337
406-557-6145

Lee Metcalf National Wildlife Refuge
Box 257
Stevensville, Montana 59870
406-777-5552

Medicine Lake National Wildlife Refuge
(Lamesteer)
HC 51, Box 2
Medicine Lake, Montana 59247
406-789-2305

**National Bison Range National Wildlife
Refuge**
(Nine-Pipe, Pablo)
State Highway 212
Moiese, Montana 59824
406-644-2211

**Northwest Montana Wildlife
Management District**
(Swan River)
780 Creston Hatchery Road
Kalispell, Montana 59901
406-755-9311

**Red Rock Lakes National Wildlife
Refuge**
Monida Star Route, Box 15
Lima, Montana 59739
406-276-3347

Sand Creek Wildlife Station (affiliated
with Charles M. Russell NWR)
P. O. Box 89
Roy, Montana 59471
406-464-5181

Nebraska

**Crescent Lake National Wildlife Refuge
Complex**
(North Platte)
P. O. Box 748
Morrill, Nebraska 69358
308-247-3495

DeSoto National Wildlife Refuge
(see Iowa)

**Fort Niobrara/Valentine National
Wildlife Refuge**
Hidden Timber Route, HC 14, Box 67
Valentine, Nebraska 69201
402-376-3789

Karl E. Mundt National Wildlife Refuge
(see South Dakota)

**Rainwater Basin Wetland Management
District**
Box 1686
Kearney, Nebraska 68847
308-236-5015

Nevada

Ash Meadows (affiliated with Desert
Refuge Complex)
P. O. Box 2660
Pahrump, Nevada 89041
702-372-5435

Desert National Wildlife Range
(affiliated with Desert Refuge Complex)
Box 14, HRC 38
Las Vegas, Nevada 89124
702-646-3401

Desert Refuge Complex
(Amargosa Pupfish Station, Moapa Valley)
1500 North Decatur Boulevard
Las Vegas, Nevada 89108
702-646-3401

Pahranagat (affiliated with Desert Refuge
Complex)
Box 510
Alamo, Nevada 89001
702-725-3417

Ruby Lake National Wildlife Refuge
Box 60-860
Ruby Valley, Nevada 89833
702-779-2237

Stillwater National Wildlife Refuge
(Anaho Island, Fallon)
Box 1236
Fallon, Nevada 89408
702-423-5128

New Hampshire

Great Bay National Wildlife Refuge
601 Spaulding Turnpike, Suite 17
Portsmouth, New Hampshire 03801
603-431-7511

John Hay National Wildlife Refuge
(see Massachusetts)

Lake Umbagog National Wildlife Refuge
Box 279
Erroll, New Hampshire 03579
603-482-3415

Wapack National Wildlife Refuge
(see Massachusetts)

New Jersey

Barnegat Division (affiliated with Edwin
B. Forsythe NWR)
70 Collinstown Road, P. O. Box 544
Barnegat, New Jersey 08005
609-698-1378

Cape May National Wildlife Refuge
15 South Main Street, Suite 3
Cape May Court House, New Jersey
08210-4207
609-463-0994

**Edwin B. Forsythe National Wildlife
Refuge**
(Brigantine Division)
15 South Main Street, Suite 3
Cape May Court House, New Jersey
08210-4207
609-652-1665

Great Swamp National Wildlife Refuge
Pleasant Plains Road, RD 1, Box 152
Basking Ridge, New Jersey 07920
201-425-1222

Wallkill River National Wildlife Refuge
P. O. Box 383
Sussex, New Jersey 07461
201-702-7266

New Mexico

Bitter Lake National Wildlife Refuge
Box 7
Roswell, New Mexico 88202
505-622-6755

**Bosque del Apache National Wildlife
Refuge**
Box 1246
Socorro, New Mexico 87801
505-835-1828

Grulla (see Texas)

Las Vegas National Wildlife Refuge
Route 1, Box 399
Las Vegas, New Mexico 87701
505-425-3581

Maxwell National Wildlife Refuge
Box 276
Maxwell, New Mexico 87728
505-375-2331

San Andres National Wildlife Refuge
P. O. Box 756
Las Cruces, New Mexico 88004
505-382-5047

Sevilleta (affiliated with Bosque del
Apache NWR)
P. O. Box 1248
Socorro, New Mexico 87801
505-864-4021

New York

Iroquois National Wildlife Refuge
P. O. Box 517, Casey Road
Alabama, New York 14003
716-948-9154

**Long Island National Wildlife Refuge
Complex**
(Amagansett, Conscience Point,
Elizabeth A. Morton, Lido Beach Wildlife
Management Area)
P. O. Box 21
Shirley, New York 11967
516-286-0485

Montezuma National Wildlife Refuge
3395 Route 5/20 E.
Seneca Falls, New York 13148
315-568-5987

Oyster Bay and Target Rock (affiliated
with Wertheim NWR)
P. O. Box 21
Shirley, New York 11967
516-271-2409

Seatuck (affiliated with Wertheim NWR)
P. O. Box 21
Shirley, New York 11967
516-581-1538

Wertheim National Wildlife Refuge
P. O. Box 21
Shirley, New York 11967
516-286-0485

North Carolina

Alligator River National Wildlife Refuge
P. O. Box 1969
Manteo, North Carolina 27954
919-473-1131

Great Dismal Swamp (see Virginia)

MacKay Island National Wildlife Refuge
(Currituck)
Box 39
Knotts Island, North Carolina 27950
919-429-3100

Mattamuskeet National Wildlife Refuge
(Cedar Island, Pungo, Swanquarter)
Route 1, Box N-2
Swanquarter, North Carolina 27885
919-926-4021

Pea Island National Wildlife Refuge
(affiliated with Alligator River NWR)
Box 1969
Manteo, North Carolina 27954
919-987-2394

Pee Dee National Wildlife Refuge
Box 92
Wadesboro, North Carolina 28170
704-694-4424

Pocosin Lakes National Wildlife Refuge
Route 1, Box 195-B
Creswell, North Carolina 27928
919-797-4431

Roanoke River National Wildlife Refuge
102 Dundee Street, Box 430
Windsor, North Carolina 27983
919-794-5326

North Dakota

**Arrowwood National Wildlife Refuge
Complex**
7745 11th Street SE
Pingree, North Dakota 58476-8308
701-285-3341

Audubon National Wildlife Refuge
R. R. 1
Coleharbor, North Dakota 58531
701-442-5474

Chase Lake Prairie Project (affiliated
with Arrowwood NWR Complex)
R. R. 1, Box 144
Woodworth, North Dakota 58496
701-752-4218

Crosby Wildlife Management District
(affiliated with Des Lacs Complex)
P. O. Box 148
Crosby, North Dakota 58730
701-965-6488

**Des Lacs National Wildlife Refuge
Complex**
(Lake Zahl)
Box 578
Kenmare, North Dakota 58746
701-385-4046

Devils Lake Wetland Management District
(Lake Alice)
Box 908
Devils Lake, North Dakota 58301
701-662-8611

Kulm Wetland Management District
Box E
Kulm, North Dakota 58456
701-647-2866

Lake Ilo (affiliated with Audubon NWR Complex)
Dunn Center, North Dakota 58626
701-548-8110

Long Lake National Wildlife Refuge Complex
R. R. 1, Box 23
Moffit, North Dakota 58560
701-387-4397

Lostwood (affiliated with Des Lacs NWR Complex)
R. R. 2, Box 98
Kenmare, North Dakota 58746
701-848-2466

J. Clark Salyer National Wildlife Refuge
Box 66
Upham, North Dakota 58789
701-768-2548

Tewaukon National Wildlife Refuge
R. R. 1, Box 75
Cayuga, North Dakota 58013
701-724-3598

Upper Souris National Wildlife Refuge
R. R. 1
Foxholm, North Dakota 58738
701-468-5467

Valley City Wildlife Management District
(affiliated with Arrowwood NWR Complex)
11515 River Road
Valley City, North Dakota 58072-9619
701-845-3466

Ohio

Ottawa National Wildlife Refuge
(Cedar Point, West Sister Island)
14000 W. State Route 2
Oak Harbor, Ohio 43449
419-898-0014

Oklahoma

Little River National Wildlife Refuge
(Little Sandy)
P. O. Box 340
Broken Bow, Oklahoma 74728
405-584-6211

Salt Plains National Wildlife Refuge
Route 1, Box 76
Jet, Oklahoma 73749
405-626-4794

Sequoyah National Wildlife Refuge
(Oklahoma Bat Caves)
Route 1, Box 18A
Vian, Oklahoma 74962
918-773-5252

Tishomingo National Wildlife Refuge
Route 1, Box 151
Tishomingo, Oklahoma 73460
405-371-2402

Washita National Wildlife Refuge
(Optima)
Route 1, Box 68
Butler, Oklahoma 73625
405-664-2205

Wichita Mountains Wildlife Refuge
Route 1, Box 448
Indiahoma, Oklahoma 73552
405-429-3221

Oregon

Ankeny (affiliated with the Western Oregon Refuge Complex)
2301 Wintel Road
Jefferson, Oregon 97352
503-588-2701

Baskett Slough (affiliated with the Western Oregon Refuge Complex)
10995 Highway 22
Dallas, Oregon 97338
503-623-2749

Bear Valley (see California)

Deer Flat (see Idaho)

William L. Finley (affiliated with the Western Oregon Refuge Complex)
26208 Finley Refuge Road
Corvallis, Oregon 97333
503-757-7236

Hart Mountain National Antelope Refuge (affiliated with the Sheldon/Hart Mountain NWR Complex)
P. O. Box 21
Plush, Oregon 97637
503-947-3315

Klamath Basin Refuges (see California)

Klamath Forest
HC 63, Box 303
Chiloquin, Oregon 97624
503-783-3380

Lewis and Clark National Wildlife Refuge (see Washington)

Malheur National Wildlife Refuge
HC 72, Box 245
Princeton, Oregon 97721
503-493-2612

McNary (affiliated with Umatilla NWR)
P. O. Box 544
Burbank, Washington 99323
509-547-4942

Oregon Coastal Refuges (affiliated with the Western Oregon Refuge Complex)
2030 Marine Science Drive
Newport, Oregon 97365-5296
503-867-4550

Sheldon/Hart Mountain National Wildlife Refuge Complex
Box 111
U.S. Post Office Building, Room 308
Lakeview, Oregon 97630
503-947-3315

Toppenish (affiliated with the Umatilla NWR)
1671 Pumphouse Road
Toppenish, Washington 98948
509-865-2405

Umatilla National Wildlife Refuge
(Cold Springs, McKay Creek)
P. O. Box 239
Umatilla, Oregon 97882
503-922-3232

Upper Klamath (see California)

Western Oregon Refuges Complex
(Bandon Marsh, Cape Meares, Nestucca Bay, Oregon Islands, Siletz Bay, Three Arch Rocks)
26208 Finley Refuge Road
Corvallis, Oregon 97333
503-757-7236

Pennsylvania

Erie National Wildlife Refuge
RD 1, Wood Duck Lane
Guy Mills, Pennsylvania 16327
814-789-3585

John Heinz National Wildlife Refuge at Tinicum
(Supawna Meadows)
Tinicum National Environmental Center
Scott Plaza 2, Suite 104
Philadelphia, Pennsylvania 19113
215-521-0662

Ohio River Islands (see West Virginia)

Puerto Rico

Caribbean Islands National Wildlife Refuge
(Buck Island [VI], Cabo Rojo, Desecheo, Green Cay [VI], Laguna Cartagena , Sandy Point [VI])
Box 510
Boqueron, Puerto Rico 00622
809-851-7297

Culebra (affiliated with the Caribbean Islands NWR)
P. O. Box 190
Culebra, Puerto Rico 00775
809-742-0115

Rhode Island

Ninigret National Wildlife Refuge
(Block Island, Pettaquamscutt Cove, Sachuest Point, Trustom Pond)
Shoreline Plaza, Route 1A, Box 307
Charlestown, Rhode Island 02813
401-364-9124

South Carolina

Ace Basin National Wildlife Refuge
P. O. Box 848
Hollywood, South Carolina 29449
803-889-3084

Cape Romain National Wildlife Refuge
5801 Highway 17, North
Awendaw, South Carolina 29429
803-928-3368

Carolina Sandhills National Wildlife Refuge
Route 2, Box 330
McBee, South Carolina 29101
803-335-8401

Pinckney Island (see Georgia)

Santee National Wildlife Refuge
Route 2, Box 66
Summerton, South Carolina 29148
803-478-2217

Savannah (see Georgia)

Tybee (see Georgia)

South Dakota

Lacreek National Wildlife Refuge
HWC 3, Box 14
Martin, South Dakota 57551
605-685-6508

Lake Andes National Wildlife Refuge
(Karl E. Mundt)
Route 1, Box 77
Lake Andes, South Dakota 57356
605-487-7603

Lake Andes Wetland Management District
200 4th Street SW, Room 113
Federal Building
Huron, South Dakota 57350-2470
605-352-7014

Madison Wetland Management District
Box 48
Madison, South Dakota 57042
605-256-2974

Sand Lake National Wildlife Refuge
(Pocasse)
R. R. 1, Box 25
Columbia, South Dakota 57433
605-885-6320

Waubay National Wildlife Refuge
R. R. 1, Box 79
Waubay, South Dakota 57273
605-947-4521

Tennessee

Cross Creeks National Wildlife Refuge
643 Wildlife Road
Dover, Tennessee 37058
615-232-7477

Hatchie National Wildlife Refuge
(Chickasaw, Lower Hatchie, Sunk Lake)
Box 187
Brownsville, Tennessee 38012
901-772-0501

Reelfoot National Wildlife Refuge
(Lake Isom)
4343 Highway 157
Union City, Tennessee 38261
901-538-2481

Tennessee National Wildlife Refuge
Box 849
Paris, Tennessee 38242
901-642-2091

Texas

Anahuac National Wildlife Refuge
(Moody)
Box 278
Anahuac, Texas 77514
409-839-2680

Aransas National Wildlife Refuge
(Matagorda)
Box 100
Austwell, Texas 77950
512-286-3559

Attwater Prairie Chicken National Wildlife Refuge
Box 518
Eagle Lake, Texas 77434
409-234-5940

Balcones Canyonlands
300 E. 8th Street, Room 873
Austin, Texas 78701
512-482-5700

Brazoria National Wildlife Refuge
(Big Boggy)
Box 1088
Angleton, Texas 77515-1088
409-849-6062

Buffalo Lake National Wildlife Refuge
P. O. Box 179
Umbarger, Texas 79091
806-499-3382

Hagerman National Wildlife Refuge
Route 3, Box 123
Sherman, Texas 75090
214-786-2826

Laguna Atascosa National Wildlife Refuge
Box 450
Rio Hondo, Texas 78583
512-748-3607

Lower Rio Grande Valley/Santa Ana Complex
320 N. Main Street, Room A-103
McAllen, Texas 78501
210-630-4636

Lower Rio Grande Valley (affiliated with the Lower Rio Grande Valley/Santa Ana Complex)
Route 2, Box 202A
Alamo, Texas 78516
210-787-3079

McFaddin/Texas Point (affiliated with the Anahuac NWR)
P. O. Box 609
Sabine Pass, Texas 77655
409-971-2909

Muleshoe National Wildlife Refuge
(Grulla [NM])
Box 549
Muleshoe, Texas 79347
806-946-3341

San Bernard (affiliated with the Brazoria NWR)
Route 1, Box 1335
Brazoria, Texas 77422
409-964-3639

Santa Ana National Wildlife Refuge
(affiliated with the Lower Rio Grande Valley/Santa Ana Complex)
Route 2, Box 202A
Alamo, Texas 78516
512-787-3079

Utah

Bear River Migratory Bird Refuge
862 S. Main Street
Brigham City, Utah 84302
801-723-5887

Fish Springs National Wildlife Refuge
Box 568
Dugway, Utah 84022
801-522-5353

Ouray National Wildlife Refuge
1680 W. Highway 40, Room 1220
Vernal, Utah 84078
801-789-0351

Vermont

Missisquoi National Wildlife Refuge
Box 163
Swanton, Vermont 05488
802-868-4781

Virginia

Back Bay National Wildlife Refuge
(Plum Tree Island)
4005 Sandpiper Road, Box 6286
Virginia Beach, Virginia 23462
804-721-2412

Chincoteague National Wildlife Refuge
(Wallops Island)
Box 62, Maddox Boulevard Ext.
Chincoteague, Virginia 23336
804-336-6122

Eastern Shore of Virginia National Wildlife Refuge
(Fisherman Island)
RFD 1, Box 122B
Cape Charles, Virginia 23310
804-331-2760

Great Dismal Swamp National Wildlife Refuge
(Nansemond)
3100 Desert Road, P. O. Box 349
Suffolk, Virginia 23434
804-986-3705

MacKay Island (see North Carolina)

Mason Neck National Wildlife Refuge
(Featherstone, Marumsco)
14416 Jefferson Davis Highway, Suite 20A
Woodbridge, Virginia 22191
703-690-1297

Presquile/James River National Wildlife Refuge
Box 189
Prince George, Virginia 23875
804-733-8042

Washington

Columbia National Wildlife Refuge
(Saddle Mountain)
735 E. Main Street, P. O. Drawer F
Othello, Washington 99344
509-488-2668

Conboy Lake (affiliated with the
Ridgefield NWR)
100 Wildlife Refuge Road, Box 5
Glenwood, Washington 98619
509-364-3410

**Julia Butler Hansen Refuge for the
Columbian White-tail Deer**
P. O. Box 566
Cathlamet, Washington 98612
206-795-3915

McNary (see Oregon)

Nisqually National Wildlife Refuge
(San Juan Islands)
100 Brown Farm Road
Olympia, Washington 98506
206-753-9467

Pierce (affiliated with the Ridgefield
NWR)
MP 36-06-R, SR 14
Stevenson, Washington 98648
509-427-5208

Ridgefield National Wildlife Refuge
(Franz Lake, Steigerwald Lake)
301 N. Third Street, P. O. Box 457
Ridgefield, Washington 98642
206-887-4106

Toppenish (see Oregon)

Turnbull National Wildlife Refuge
26010 Smith Road
Cheney, Washington 99004
509-235-4723

Umatilla National Wildlife Refuge (see
Oregon)

Washington Coastal Refuges
(Copalis, Dungeness, Flattery Rocks, Grays
Harbor, Protection Island, Quillayute
Needles, Washington Islands)
1638 Barr Road South
Port Angeles, Washington 98382
206-457-8451

Willapa National Wildlife Refuge
(Lewis and Clark [OR])
HC 01, Box 910
Ilwaco, Washington 98624-9707
206-484-3482

West Virginia

**Ohio River Islands National Wildlife
Refuge**
P. O. Box 1811
Parkersburg, West Virginia 26102
304-422-0752

Wisconsin

Horicon National Wildlife Refuge
(Fox River, Gravel Island, Green Bay)
W 4279 Headquarters Road
Mayville, Wisconsin 53050
414-387-2658

Leopold Wetland Management District
W 4279 Headquarters Road
Mayville, Wisconsin 53050
414-387-2658

Necedah National Wildlife Refuge
W 7996-20th Street W
Necedah, Wisconsin 54646
608-565-2551

Trempealeau National Wildlife Refuge
Route 1, Box 1602
Trempealeau, Wisconsin 54661
608-539-2311

**Upper Mississippi River National
Wildlife and Fish Refuge** (see Minnesota)

Wyoming

Bamforth (see Colorado)

Hutton Lake (see Colorado)

National Elk Refuge
675 E. Broadway
Jackson, Wyoming 83001
307-733-9212

Pathfinder (see Colorado)

Seedskadee National Wildlife Refuge
P. O. Box 700
Green River, Wyoming 82935
307-875-2187

NOTABLE CAVES AND CAVERNS

Deepest Caves Measured

Snezhnaya, Russia	4,397 feet (1,340 meters)
Puertas de Illamina, Spain	4,390 feet (1,330 meters)
Pierre–St. Martin, France and Spain	4,334 feet (1,321 meters)
Huautla, Mexico	4,067 feet (1,240 meters)

Longest Caves Measured

Mammoth–Flint Ridge, Kentucky	235.6 miles (379.2 kilometers)
Holloch, Switzerland	86.9 miles (139.8 kilometers)
Jewel Cave, South Dakota	66.6 miles (107.2 kilometers)
Greenbrier-Organ, West Virginia	44.7 miles (72 kilometers)

Most Visited United States Caves

Blanchard Springs Caverns,
Mountain View, Arkansas

Carlsbad Caverns,
Carlsbad, New Mexico

Cave of the Winds,
Manitou Springs, Colorado

Cumberland Caverns,
McMinnville, Tennessee

Endless Caverns,
New Market, Virginia

Fantastic Caverns,
Springfield, Missouri

Howe Caverns,
Howes Cave, New York

Lake Shasta Caverns,
O'Brien, California

Luray Caverns,
Luray, Virginia

Jewel Cave,
Custer, South Dakota

Mammoth Caves,
Mammoth Cave, Kentucky

Meramec Caverns,
Stanton, Missouri

Natural Bridge Caverns,
Natural Bridge Caverns, Texas

Oregon Caves National Monument,
Cave Junction, Oregon

Polar Caves,
Plymouth, New Hampshire

Russell Cave National Monument,
Bridgeport, Alabama

Sea Lion Caves,
Florence, Oregon

Timpanogos Cave National Monument,
American Fork, Utah

Wind Cave National Park,
Hot Springs, South Dakota

USEFUL SCIENCE INFORMATION

Nobel Prize Awards (1901–1994)

The Nobel Prizes have been awarded since 1901 in the fields of chemistry, physics, physiology or medicine, literature, and peace; a prize in economics was added in 1969. They were established through a bequest of Alfred Nobel, the Swedish chemical engineer and inventor of dynamite; part of the money is also given as a gift from the Bank of Sweden. Chemistry, physics, and economic awards are chosen by the Royal Swedish Academy of Stockholm; physiology or medicine, by the Nobel Assembly at the Karolinska Institute, Stockholm.

The recipients of the awards are informed early in the fall of each year; the formal presentation of the awards is on December 10, the anniversary of Nobel's death. The following lists the Nobel Prizes in science from 1901 to 1994:

Chemistry

1901   **Van't Hoff, Jacobus Henricus (Netherlands)**—discovery of osmotic pressure in solution and the laws of chemical dynamics.

1902   **Fischer, Hermann Emil (Germany)**—work on sugar and the synthesis of purine.

1903   **Arrhenius, Svante August (Sweden)**—work on electrolytic theory of dissociation.

1904   **Ramsay, Sir William (Great Britain)**—work on inert gaseous elements in the air and their place on the periodic table.

1905   **Von Baeyer, Johann F. Adolf (Germany)**—work on organic dyes and hydroaromatic compounds that helped the advancement of organic chemistry and the chemical industry.

1906   **Moissan, Henri (France)**—work on fluorine; development of an electric furnace (named after him).

1907   **Buchner, Eduard (Germany)**—discovery of cell-free fermentation.

1908   **Rutherford, Lord Ernest (Great Britain)**—work on the disintegration of the elements; and chemistry of radioactive elements.

1909   **Ostwald, Wilhelm (Germany)**—work on catalysis and development of principles governing chemical equilibria and rates of reaction.

1910   **Wallach, Otto (Germany)**—work on organic chemistry, especially alicyclic compounds.

1911   **Curie, Marie (France)**—discovery of radioactive elements radium and polonium; and the isolation of radium and the study of its nature and compounds.

1912   **Grignard, Victor (France)**—discovery of the Grignard reagent (used in organic chemistry).

        Sabatier, Paul (France)—discovery of a method of hydrogenating organic compounds in the presence of finely disintegrated metals.

1913   **Werner, Alfred (Switzerland)**—work on atomic linkages in molecules (which opened such fields as inorganic chemistry).

1914   **Richards, Theodore William (U.S.)**—accurately determined the atomic weight of many chemical elements.

1915   **Willstätter, Richard Martin (Germany)**—discovery of plant pigments, especially chlorophyll.

1916–1917   **not awarded**

1918   **Haber, Fritz (Germany)**—synthesized ammonia from its elements.

1919   **not awarded**

1920   Nernst, Walther Hermann (Germany)—work in thermochemistry.

1921   Soddy, Frederick (Great Britain)—work on chemistry of radioactive substances, including the origin and nature of radioactive isotopes.

1922   Aston, Francis William (Great Britain)—discovery of isotopes in many nonradioactive elements; also enunciated the whole-number rule.

1923   Pregl, Fritz (Austria)—invented microanalysis of organic substances.

1924   not awarded

1925   Zsigmondy, Richard Adolf (Germany)—determined the heterogeneous nature of colloid solutions; and for the methods he used, which became fundamental in the study of modern colloid chemistry.

1926   Svedberg, The (Theodor) (Sweden)—work on disperse systems.

1927   Wieland, Heinrich Otto (Germany)—work on bile acids and related substances.

1928   Windaus, Adolf Otto Reinhold (Germany)—work on sterols and their connection with vitamins.

1929   Harden, Sir Arthur (Great Britain) and von Euler-Chelpin, Hans (Sweden)—investigations on the fermentation of sugar; and determined how fermentative enzymes work.

1930   Fischer, Hans (Germany)—determined the constitution of haemin and chlorophyll; synthesized haemin.

1931   Bosch, Carl (Germany) and Bergius, Friedrich (Germany)—invented and developed chemical high-pressure methods.

1932   Langmuir, Irving (U.S.)—work in surface chemistry.

1933   not awarded

1934   Urey, Harold Clayton (U.S.)—discovery of heavy hydrogen.

1935   Joliot, Frédéric (France) and Joliot-Curie, Irene (France)—synthesis of several new radioactive elements.

1936   Debye, Petrus Josephus W. (Netherlands)—investigations on the molecular structure through work on dipole moments and diffraction of X rays and electrons in gases.

1937   Haworth, Sir Walter Norman (Great Britain)—work on carbohydrates and vitamin C.

          Karrer, Paul (Switzerland)—work on carotenoids, flavins, and vitamins A and B_2.

1938   Kuhn, Richard (Germany)—work on carotenoids and vitamins.

1939   Butenandt, Adolf Friedrich Johann (Germany)—work on sex hormones.

          Ruzicka, Leopold (Switzerland)—work on polymethylenes and higher terpenes.

1940–1942   not awarded

1943   De Hevesy, George (Hungary)—work on using isotopes as tracers to study chemical processes.

1944   Hahn, Otto (Germany)—discovered fission of heavy nuclei.

1945   **Virtanen, Artturi Ilmari (Finland)**—work in agricultural and nutritional chemistry, including his fodder preservation method.

1946   **Sumner, James Barcheller (U.S.)**—discovered that enzymes can be crystallized.

Northrop, John Howard (U.S.) and **Stanley, Wendell Meredith (U.S.)**—work on preparing enzymes and virus proteins in pure form.

1947   **Robinson, Sir Robert (Great Britain)**—work on plant products of biological importance, including the alkaloids.

1948   **Tiselius, Arne Wilhelm Kaurin (Sweden)**—work on electrophoresis and absorption analysis, especially studies and discoveries on the complex nature of serum proteins.

1949   **Giauque, William Francis (U.S.)**—work on chemical thermodynamics, including the behavior of certain substance at low temperatures.

1950   **Diels, Otto P.H. (Germany)** and **Alder, Kurt (Germany)**—discovery and development of the diene synthesis.

1951   **McMillan, Edwin Mattison (U.S.)** and **Seaborg, Glenn Theodore (U.S.)**—discoveries in the chemistries of the transuranium elements.

1952   **Martin, Archer John Porter (Great Britain)** and **Synge, Richard Laurence Millington (Great Britain)**—invention of partition chromatography.

1953   **Staudinger, Hermann (Germany)**—discoveries in macromolecular chemistry.

1954   **Pauling, Linus Carl (U.S.)**—discovery of the nature of the chemical bond, including its application to the structures of complex substances.

1955   **Du Vigneaud, Vincent (U.S.)**—work on sulfur compounds that were important to biochemistry, especially for the first synthesis of a polypeptide hormone.

1956   **Hinshel Wood, Sir Cyril Norman (Great Britain)** and **Semenov, Nikolaj Nikolajevic (U.S.S.R.)**—work on the mechanisms behind chemical reactions.

1957   **Todd, Lord Alexander R. (Great Britain)**—work on nucleotide co-enzymes and nucleotides.

1958   **Sanger, Frederick (Great Britain)**—work on the structure of proteins, especially insulin.

1959   **Heyrovsky, Jaroslav (Czechoslovakia)**—invented polargraphic methods of analysis.

1960   **Libby, Willard Frank (U.S.)**—determined that carbon-14 could be used for dating objects; used in archeology, geology, geophysics, and other branches of science.

1961   **Calvin, Melvin (U.S.)**—worked on carbon dioxide assimilation in plants.

1962   **Perutz, Max Ferdinand (Great Britain)** and **Kendrew, Sir John Cowdery (Great Britain)**—work on the structures of globular proteins.

1963   **Ziegler, Karl (Germany)** and **Natta, Giulio (Italy)**—worked on high polymers, which advanced studies in chemistry and technology.

1964   **Hodgkin, Dorothy Crowfoot (Great Britain)**—developed the structures of important biochemical substances using X-ray techniques.

1965   **Woodward, Robert Burns (U.S.)**—worked on the art of organic synthesis.

1966   **Mulliken, Robert S. (U.S.)**—work with chemical bonds and the electronic structures of molecules using the molecular orbital method.

1967   **Eigen, Manfred (West Germany), Norrish, Ronald George Wreyford (Great Britain)**, and **Porter, Sir George (Great Britain)**—for their work on extremely fast chemical reactions, effected by disturbing the equilibrium by means of very short pulses of energy.

1968   **Onsager, Lars (U.S.)**—discovered a relation that is fundamental for the thermodynamics of irreversible processes.

1969   **Barton, Sir Derek H. R. (Great Britain)** and **Hassel, Odd (Norway)**—discovered the idea and application of conformation in chemistry.

1970   **Leloir, Luis F. (Argentina)**—discovered sugar nucleotides, including their role in the biosynthesis of carbohydrates.

1971   **Herzberg, Gerhard (Canada)**—worked on electronic structure and geometry of molecules, especially free radicals.

1972   **Anfinsen, Christian B. (U.S.)**—work on amino acid ribonuclease, including its connection between it and biological activity.

        Moore, Stanford (U.S.) and **Stein, William H. (U.S.)**—work on the connection between chemical structure and catalytic activity in the active center of a ribonuclease molecule.

1973   **Fischer, Ernst Otto (West Germany)** and **Wilkinson, Sir Geoffrey (Great Britain)**—independently worked on the chemistry of organo-metallic compounds (sandwich compounds).

1974   **Flory, Paul J. (U.S.)**—work on the physical chemistry of macromolecules.

1975   **Cornforth, Sir John Warcup (Australia and Great Britain)**—work on stereochemistry of enzyme-catalyzed reactions.

        Prelog, Vladimir (Switzerland)—work on stereochemistry of organic molecules and their reactions.

1976   **Lipscomb, William N. (U.S.)**—work on structure of boranes illuminating problems of chemical bonding.

1977   **Prigogine, Ilya (Belgium)**—work on nonequilibrium thermodynamics, especially the theory of dissipative structures.

1978   **Mitchell, Peter D. (Great Britain)**—worked to understand biological energy transfer through the formulation of the chemiosmotic theory.

1979   **Brown, Herbert C. (U.S.)** and **Wittig, Georg (Germany)**—developed the use of boron- and phosphorus-containing compounds into important reagents in organic synthesis.

1980   **Berg, Paul (U.S.), Gilbert, Walter (U.S.)**, and **Sanger, Frederick (Great Britain)**—determined the base sequences in nucleic acids.

1981   **Fukui, Kenichi (Japan)** and **Hoffmann, Roald (U.S.)**—independently developed theories on the course of certain chemical reactions.

1982   **Klug, Aaron (Great Britain)**—worked on crystallographic electron microscopy, determining the structure of certain biologically significant nucleic acid–protein complexes.

1983   **Taube, Henry (U.S.)**—worked on the mechanisms of electron transfer reactions, particularly in metal complexes.

1984   **Merrifield, Robert Bruce (U.S.)**—determined a way to produce chemical synthesis on a solid matrix.

1985   **Hauptman, Herbert A. (U.S.)** and **Karle, Jerome (U.S.)**—developed direct methods to determine crystal structures.

1986   **Herschbach, Dudley R. (U.S.), Lee, Yuan T. (U.S.), and Polanyi, John C. (Canada)**—determined the dynamics of chemical elementary processes.

1987   **Cram, Donald J. (U.S.), Lehn, Jean-Marie (France), and Pedersen, Charles J. (U.S.)**—work in the development and use of molecules that had structure-specific interactions of high selectivity.

1988   **Deisenhofer, Johann (U.S.), Huber, Robert (West Germany), and Michel, Hartmut (West Germany)**—determined the three-dimensional structure of a photosynthetic reaction center.

1989   **Altman, Sidney (U.S.)** and **Cech, Thomas R. (U.S.)**—independently discovered the catalytic properties of RNA.

1990   **Coret, Elias J. (U.S.)**—developed the theory and methodology of organic synthesis.

1991   **Ernst, Richard R. (Switzerland)**—refined the technology involved in nuclear magnetic resonance imaging (NMRI).

1992   **Marcus, Rudolph A. (U.S., born Canada)**—mathematically determined the cause and effect of electrons jumping from one molecule to another.

1993   **Kary B. Mullis (U.S.)**—discovered the polymerase chain reaction that allows scientists to make trillions of DNA copies from small samples.

1994   **George A. Olah (U.S.)**—discovered the hydrocarbon reactions of superacids that capture fast-disappearing "carbocations" and stabilize them for hours.

Physics

1901   **Röntgen, Wilhelm Conrad (Germany)**—discovery of the rays that are named after him.

1902   **Lorenzt, Hendirk Antoon (Netherlands)** and **Zeeman, Pieter (Netherlands)**—discovered the influence of magnetism on radiation phenomena.

1903   **Becquerel, Antoine Henri (France)**—discovered spontaneous radioactivity.

        Curie, Pierre (France) and **Curie, Marie (France)**—joint research on the radiation phenomena discovered by Becquerel.

1904   **Rayleigh, Lord (John William Strutt) (Great Britain)**—investigations of the densities of the most important gases; discoverer of argon.

1905   **Lenard, Philipp Eduard Anton (Germany)**—work on cathode rays.

1906   **Thomson, Sir Joseph John (Great Britain)**—work on theoretical and experimental investigations on the conduction of electricity by gases.

1907   **Michelson, Albert Abraham (U.S.)**—work on optical precision instruments and the spectroscopic and metrological investigations carried out with their aid.

1908   **Lippmann, Gabriel (France)**—reproduced colors photographically based on the phenomenon of interference.

1909   **Marconi, Guglielmo (Italy)** and **Braun, Karl Ferdinand (Germany)**—contributed to the development of wireless telegraphy.

1910   **van der Waals, Johannes D. (Netherlands)**—work on the equation of state for gases and liquids.

1911   **Wien, Wilhelm (Germany)**—discoveries on the laws governing the radiation of heat.

1912   **Dalén, Nils Gustaf (Sweden)**—invented automatic regulators for use in conjunction with gas accumulators for illumination lighthouses and buoys.

1913   **Kamerlingh-Onnes, Heike (Netherlands)**—investigated the properties of matter at low temperatures which lead, inter alia, to the production of liquid helium.

1914   **von Laue, Max (Germany)**—discovered the diffraction of X rays by crystals.

1915   **Bragg, Sir William Henry (Great Britain)** and **Bragg, Sir William Lawrence (Great Britain)**—(father and son) analyzed crustal structure by means of X rays.

1916   **not awarded**

1917   **Barkla, Charles Glover (Great Britain)**—discovered the characteristic Röntgen radiation of the elements.

1918   **Planck, Max Karl Ernst Ludwig (Germany)**—discovered energy quanta.

1919   **Stark, Johannes (Germany)**—discovered the Doppler effect in canal rays and the splitting of spectral lines in electric fields.

1920   **Guillaume, Charles Edouard (Switzerland)**—discovered anomalies in nickel steel alloys.

1921   **Einstein, Albert (Germany and Switzerland)**—discovered the law of the photoelectric effect.

1922   **Bohr, Niels (Denmark)**—investigated the structure of atoms and of the radiation emanating from them.

1923   **Millikan, Robert Andrews (Great Britain)**—work on the elementary charge of electricity and on the photoelectric effect.

1924   **Siegbahn, Karl Manne Georg (Sweden)**—work in the field of X-ray spectroscopy.

1925   **Franck, James (Germany)** and **Hertz, Gustav (Germany)**—discovered the laws governing the impact of an electron upon an atom.

1926   **Perrin, Jean Baptiste (France)**—work on the discontinuous structure of matter, especially for his discovery of sedimentation equilibrium.

1927   **Compton, Arthur Holly (U.S.)**—discovered the effect named after him.

       Wilson, Charles Thomson Rees (Great Britain)—determined a method of making the paths of electrically charged particles visible by condensation of vapor.

1928   **Richardson, Sir Owen Willans (Great Britain)**—work on the thermionic phenomenon, especially for the discovery of the law named after him.

1929   **De Broglie, Prince Louis-Victor (France)**—discovered the wave nature of electrons.

1930   **Raman, Sir Chandrasekhara Venkata (India)**—work on the scattering of light, and discovered the effect named after him.

1931   **not awarded**

1932   **Heisenberg, Werner (Germany)**—created quantum mechanics, the application which has, inter alia, led to the discovery of the allotropic forms of hydrogen.

1933   **Schrödinger, Erwin (Austria)** and **Dirac, Paul Adrien Maurice (Great Britain)**—discovered new productive forms of atomic theory.

1934   **not awarded**

1935   **Chadwick, Sir James (Great Britain)**—discovered the neutron.

1936   **Hess, Victor Franz (Austria)**—discovered cosmic radiation.

        Anderson, Carl David (U.S.)—discovered the positron.

1937   **Davidsson, Clinton Joseph (U.S.)** and **Thomson, Sir George Paget (Great Britain)**—experimental discovery of the diffraction of electrons by crystals.

1938   **Fermi, Enrico (Italy)**—demonstrated the existence of new radioactive elements produced by neutron irradiation; and his related discovery of nuclear reactions brought about by slow neutrons.

1939   **Lawrence, Ernest Orlando (U.S.)**—invented and developed the cyclotron; and the results of the cyclotron, especially with regard to artificial radioactive elements.

1940–1942   **not awarded**

1943   **Stern, Otto (U.S.)**—developed the molecular ray method and discovered the magnetic moment of the proton.

1944   **Rabi, Isidor Isaac (U.S.)**—developed the resonance method for recording the magnetic properties of atomic nuclei.

1945   **Pauli, Wolfgang (Austria)**—discovered the Pauli principle.

1946   **Bridgman, Percy Williams (U.S.)**—invented an apparatus to produce extremely high pressures; and other discoveries in high pressure physics.

1947   **Appleton, Sir Edward Victor (Great Britain)**—investigated the upper atmosphere and discovered the layer named after him.

1948   **Blackett, Lord Patrick Maynard Stuart (Great Britain)**—developed the Wilson cloud chamber method; discoveries in the fields of nuclear physics and cosmic radiation.

1949   **Yukawa, Hideki (Japan)**—predicted the existence of mesons on the basis of theoretical work on nuclear forces.

1950   **Powell, Cecil Frank (Great Britain)**—developed the photographic method of studying nuclear processes; and discoveries regarding mesons with this method.

1951   **Cockcroft, Sir John Douglas (Great Britain)** and **Walton, Ernest Thomas Sinton (Ireland)**—work on the transmutation of atomic nuclei by artificially accelerated atomic particles.

1952   **Bloch, Felix (U.S.)** and **Purcell, Edward Mills (U.S.)**—developed new methods for nuclear magnetic precision measurements, and discoveries with such measurements.

1953   **Zernike, Frits (Frederik) (Netherlands)**—demonstrated the phase contrast method; invented the phase contrast microscope.

1954   **Born, Max (Great Britain)**—research in quantum mechanics, especially the statistical interpretation of the wave function.

   Bothe, Walther (Germany)—developed the coincidence method and discoveries from the method.

1955   **Lamb, Willis Eugene (U.S.)**—discovered the fine structure of the hydrogen spectrum.

   Kusch, Polykarp (U.S.)—determined the magnetic moment of an electron.

1956   **Shockley, William (U.S.), Bardeen, John (U.S.),** and **Brattain, Walter Houser (U.S.)**—research on semiconductors and discovered the transistor effect.

1957   **Yang, Cheng Ning (China)** and **Lee, Tsung-Dao (China)**—investigated so-called parity laws, which lead to important discoveries with elementary particles.

1958   **Cerenkov, Pavel Aleksejvic (U.S.S.R.), Frank, Il'ja Michajlovic (U.S.S.R.),** and **Tamm, Igor Jevgen'evic (U.S.S.R.)**—discovered and interpreted the Cerenkov effect.

1959   **Segrè, Emilio Gino (U.S.)** and **Chamberlain, Owen (U.S.)**—discovered the antiproton.

1960   **Glaser, Donald A. (U.S.)**—invented the bubble chamber.

1961   **Hofstadter, Robert (U.S.)**—studied electron scattering in atomic nuclei; discoveries concerning the structure of the nucleons.

   Mössbauer, Rudolf Ludvig (Germany)—researched the resonance absorption of gamma radiation and discovered the effect that bears his name.

1962   **Landau, Lev Davidovic (U.S.S.R.)**—determined theories on condensed matter, especially liquid helium.

1963   **Wigner, Eugene P. (U.S.)**—contributed to the theory of the atomic nucleus and the elementary particles, especially through the discovery and application of fundamental symmetry principles.

   Goeppert-Mayer, Maria (U.S.) and **Jensen, J. Hans D. (Germany)**—discovered aspects of nuclear shell structure.

1964   **Townes, Charles Hard (U.S.), Basov, Nicolai Gennadievic (U.S.S.R.),** and **Prochorov, Aleksandre Mikhailovic (U.S.S.R.)**—fundamental work in the field of quantum electronics, which led to the construction of oscillators and amplifiers based on the maser-laser principle.

1965 **Tomonaga, Sin-Itiro (Japan), Schwinger, Julian (U.S.),** and **Feynman, Richard P. (U.S.)**—fundamental work in quantum electrodynamics, with deep-ploughing consequences for the physics of elementary particles.

1966 **Kastler, Alfred (France)**—discovered and developed optical methods for studying Hertzian resonances in atoms.

1967 **Bethe, Hans Albrecht (U.S.)**—contributed to the theory of nuclear reactions, especially discoveries concerning energy production in stars.

1968 **Alvarez, Luis W. (U.S.)**—contributed to elementary particle physics, in particular the discovery of a large number of resonance states, made possible by his development of the technique of using the hydrogen bubble chamber and data analysis.

1969 **Gell-Mann, Murray (U.S.)**—contributions and discoveries concerning the classification of elementary particles and their interactions.

1970 **Alfvén, Hannes (Sweden)**—work and discoveries in magnetohydrodynamics with fruitful application in different parts of plasma physics.

     Néel, Louis (France)—work and discoveries concerning anti-ferromagnetism and ferrimagnetism, which lead to important applications in solid-state physics.

1971 **Gabor, Dennis (Great Britain)**—invented and developed the holographic method.

1972 **Bardeen, John (U.S.), Cooper, Leon N. (U.S.),** and **Schrieffer, J. Robert (U.S.)**—jointly developed the theory of superconductivity (usually called the BCS theory).

1973 **Esaki, Leo (Japan)** and **Giaever, Ivar (U.S.)**—experimental discoveries regarding tunneling phenomena in semiconductors and superconductors, respectively.

     Josephson, Brian D. (Great Britain)—developed theoretical predictions of the properties of a supercurrent through a tunnel barrier, especially the Josephson effects.

1974 **Ryle, Sir Martin (Great Britain)** and **Hewish, Antony (Great Britain)**—pioneering research in radio astrophysics (Ryle for his observations and inventions of the aperture synthesis technique; Hewish for his decisive role in the discovery of pulsars).

1975 **Bohr, Aage (Denmark), Bottelson, Ben (Denmark),** and **Rainwater, James (U.S.)**—discovered the connection between collective motion and particle motion in atomic nuclei and the development of the theory of the structure of the atomic nucleus based on this connection.

1976 **Richter, Burton (U.S.)** and **Ting, Samuel C.C. (U.S.)**—discovered a heavy elementary particle of a new kind.

1977 **Anderson, Philip W. (U.S.), Mott, Sir Nevill F. (Great Britain),** and **van Vleck, John H. (U.S.)**—developed fundamental theoretical investigations of the electronic structure of magnetic and disordered systems.

1978 **Kapitsa, Peter Leonidovitch (U.S.S.R.)**—basic inventions and discoveries in the area of low temperature physics.

     Penzias, Arno A. (U.S.) and **Wilson, Robert W. (U.S.)**—discovered cosmic microwave background radiation.

1979   **Glashow, Sheldon L. (U.S.), Salam, Abdus (Pakistan),** and **Weinberg, Steven (U.S.)**—contributed to the theory of the unified weak and electromagnetic interaction between elementary particles, including inter alia the prediction of the weak neutral current.

1980   **Cronin, James W. (U.S.)** and **Fitch, Val L. (U.S.)**—discovered the violations of fundamental symmetry principles in the decay of neutral K-mesons.

1981   **Bloembergen, Nicolaas (U.S.)** and **Schawlow, Arthur L. (U.S.)**—contributed to the development of laser spectroscopy.

        Siegbahn, Kai M. (Sweden)—contributed to the development of high resolution electron spectroscopy.

1982   **Wilson, Kenneth G. (U.S.)**—developed the theory on critical phenomena in connection with phase transitions.

1983   **Chandrasekhar, Subrahmanyan (U.S.)**—developed theoretical studies of the physical processes of importance to the structure and evolution of the stars.

        Fowler, William A. (U.S.)—theoretical and experimental studies of the nuclear reactions of importance in the formation of the chemicals elements in the universe.

1984   **Rubbia, Carlo (Italy)** and **van der Meer, Simon (Netherlands)**—contributed to the large project that led to the discovery of the field particles W and Z, communicators of weak interaction.

1985   **von Klitzing, Klaus (Germany)**—discovered the quantized Hall effect.

1986   **Ruska, Ernst (Germany)**—fundamental work in electron optics; designed the first electron microscope.

        Binnig, Gerd (Germany) and **Rohrer, Heinrich (Switzerland)**—designed the first scanning tunneling microscope.

1987   **Bednorz, J. Georg (Germany)** and **Muller, K. Alexander (Switzerland)**—made an important breakthrough in the discovery of superconductivity in ceramic materials.

1988   **Lederman, Leon M. (U.S.), Schwartz, Melvin (U.S.),** and **Steinberger, Jack (U.S.)**—discovered the neutrino beam method; demonstrated the doublet structure of the leptons through the discovery of the nuon neutrino.

1989   **Ramsey, Norman F. (U.S.)**—invented the separated oscillatory fields method and its use in the hydrogen maser and other atomic clocks.

        Dehmet, Hans G. (U.S.) and **Paul, Wolfgang (Germany)**—developed the ion trap technique.

1990   **Friedman, Jerome I. (U.S.), Kendall, Henry W. (U.S.),** and **Taylor, Richard E. (Canada)**—pioneering investigations concerning deep inelastic scattering of electrons on protons and bound neutrons, which have been of essential importance for the development of the quark model in particle physics.

1991   **de Gennes, Pierre-Giles (France)**—studied the changes that take place in liquid crystals when the orientation of the molecules changes from a random to an aligned state.

1992   **Charpak, George (France, born Poland)**—devised an electronic detector that recorded the trajectories of subatomic particles in atom smashers.

1993   **Joseph H. Taylor (U.S.) and Russel A. Hulse (U.S.)**—discovered a binary pulsar, and determined its pulse rate.

1994   **Shull, Clifford G. (U.S.) and Brockhouse, Bertram N. (Canada)**—each independently developed neutron-scattering techniques for studying solids and liquids.

Physiology or Medicine

1901   **von Behring, Emil (Germany)**—work on serum therapy, especially its application against diphtheria.

1902   **Ross, Sir Ronald (Great Britain)**—work on malaria, showing how it enters the organism.

1903   **Finsen, Niels Ryberg (Denmark)**—work on the treatment of diseases, especially lupus vulgaris, with concentrated light radiation, whereby he opened a new avenue for medical science.

1904   **Pavlov, Ivan Petrovic (Russia)**—work on the physiology of digestion.

1905   **Koch, Robert (Germany)**—investigations and discoveries in relation to tuberculosis.

1906   **Golgi, Camillo (Italy) and Ramon y Cajal, Santiago (Spain)**—work on the structure of the nervous system.

1907   **Laveran, Charles Louis Alphonse (France)**—work on the role played by protozoa in causing diseases.

1908   **Mecnikov, Ilja Il'jic (Russia) and Ehrlich, Paul (Germany)**—work on immunity.

1909   **Kocher, Emil Theodor (Switzerland)**—work on the physiology, pathology, and surgery of the thyroid gland.

1910   **Kossel, Albrecht (Germany)**—contributed to our knowledge of cell chemistry through his work on proteins, including the nucleic substances.

1911   **Gullstrand, Allvar (Sweden)**—work on the dioptrics of the eye.

1912   **Carrel, Alexis (France)**—work on vascular suture and the transplantation of blood vessels and organs.

1913   **Richet, Charles Robert (France)**—work on anaphylaxis.

1914   **Bárány, Robert (Austria)**—work on the physiology and pathology of the vestibular apparatus.

1915–1918   **not awarded**

1919   **Bordet, Jules (Belgium)**—discoveries relating to immunity.

1920   **Krogh, Schack August Steenberger (Denmark)**—discovered the capillary motor regulating mechanism.

1921   **not awarded**

1922   **Hill, Sir Archibald Vivian (Great Britain)**—discovery relating to the production of heat in the muscle.

           Meyerhof, Otto Fritz (Germany)—discovery of the fixed relationship between the consumption of oxygen and the metabolism of lactic acid in the muscle.

1923   Banting, Sir Frederick Grant (Canada) and Macleod, John James Richard (Canada)—discovered insulin.

1924   Einthoven, Willem (Netherlands)—discovered the mechanism of the electrocardiogram.

1925   **not awarded**

1926   Fibiger, Johannes Andreas Grib (Denmark)—discovered the Spiroptera carcinoma.

1927   Wagner-Jauregg, Julius (Austria)—discovered the therapeutic value of malaria inoculation in the treatment of dementia paralytica.

1928   Nicolle, Charles Jules Henri (France)—work on typhus.

1929   Eijkman, Christiaan (Netherlands)—discovered the anti-neuritic vitamin.

Hopkins, Sir Frederick Gowland (Great Britain)—discovered the growth-stimulating vitamins.

1930   Landsteiner, Karl (Austria)—discovered human blood groups.

1931   Warburg, Otto Heinrich (Germany)—discovered the nature and mode of action of the respiratory enzyme.

1932   Sherrington, Sir Charles Scott (Great Britain) and Adrian, Lord Edgar Douglas (Great Britain)—discovered the functions of neurons.

1933   Morgan, Thomas Hunt (U.S.)—discovered the role played by the chromosome in heredity.

1934   Whipple, George Hoyt (U.S.), Minot, George Richards (U.S.) and Murphy, William Parry (U.S.)—discoveries concerning liver therapy in cases of anemia.

1935   Spemann, Hans (Germany)—discovery of the organizer effect in embryonic development.

1936   Dale, Sir Henry Hallett (Great Britain) and Loewi, Otto (Austria)—discoveries relating to chemical transmission of nerve impulses.

1937   Szent-Györgyi, Albert (Hungary)—discoveries in connection with the biological combustion processes, with a special reference to vitamin C and the catalysis of fumaric acid.

1938   Heymans, Corneille Jean (Belgium)—discovered the role played by the sinus and aortic mechanisms in the regulation of respiration.

1939   Domagk, Gerhard (Germany)—discovered the antibacterial effects of prontosil.

1940–1942   **not awarded**

1943   Dam, Henrik Carl Peter (Denmark)—discovered vitamin K.

Doisy, Edward Adelbert (U.S.)—discovered the chemical nature of vitamin K.

1944   Erlanger, Joseph (U.S.) and Gasser, Herbert Spencer (U.S.)—discoveries relating to the highly differentiated functions of single nerve fibers.

1945   Fleming, Sir Alexander (Great Britain), Chain, Sir Ernst Boris (Great Britain) and Florey, Lord Howard Walter (Great Britain)—discovered penicillin and its curative effect in various infectious diseases.

1946   Muller, Hermann Joseph (U.S.)—discovered the production of mutations by means of X-ray irradiation.

1947   **Cori, Carl Ferdinand (U.S.)** and **Cori, Gerty Theresa (U.S.)**—discovered the course of the catalytic conversion of glycogen.

   Houssay, Bernardo Alberto (Argentina)—discovered the part played by the hormone of the anterior pituitary lobe in the metabolism of sugar.

1948   **Müller, Paul Hermann (Switzerland)**—discovered the high efficiency of DDT as a contact poison against several arthropods.

1949   **Hess, Walter Rudolf (Switzerland)**—discovered the functional organization of the interbrain as a coordinator of the activities of the internal organs.

   Moniz, Antonio de Egas (Portugal)—discovered the therapeutic value of leucotomy in certain psychoses.

1950   **Kendall, Edward Calvin (U.S.), Reichstein, Tadeus (Switzerland),** and **Hench, Philip Showalter (U.S.)**—discoveries relating to the hormones of the adrenal cortex, their structure, and biological effects.

1951   **Theiler, Max (South Africa)**—discoveries concerning yellow fever and how to fight against it.

1952   **Waksman, Selman Abraham (U.S.)**—discovered streptomycin, the first antibiotic effective against tuberculosis.

1953   **Krebs, Sir Hans Adolf (Great Britain)**—discovered the citric acid cycle.

   Lipmann, Fritz Albert (U.S.) - discovered the co-enzyme A and its importance for intermediary metabolism.

1954   **Enders, John Franklin (U.S.), Weller, Thomas Huckle (U.S.),** and **Robbins, Frederick Chapman (U.S.)** - discovered the ability of the poliomyelitis viruses to grow in cultures of various types of tissues.

1955   **Theorell, Axel Hugo Theodor (Sweden)**—discoveries concerning the nature and mode of action of oxidation enzymes.

1956   **Cournand, André Frédéric (U.S.), Forssmann, Werner (Germany),** and **Richards, Dickinson W. (U.S.)**—discoveries of heart catherization and pathological changes in the circulatory system.

1957   **Bovet, Daniel (Italy)**—discoveries relating to the synthetic compounds that inhibit the action of certain body substances, and especially their action on the vascular system and the skeletal muscles.

1958   **Beadle, George Wells (U.S.)** and **Tatum, Edward Lawrie (U.S.)**—discovered that genes act by regulating definite chemical events.

   Lederberg, Joshua (U.S.)—discoveries concerning the genetic recombination and the organization of genetic material of bacteria.

1959   **Ochoa, Severo (U.S.)** and **Kornberg, Arthur (U.S.)**—discovered the mechanisms in the biological synthesis of ribonucleic acid and deoxyribonucleic acid.

1960   **Burnet, Sir Frank Macfarlane (Australia)** and **Medawar, Sir Peter Brian (Great Britain)**—discovered acquired immunological tolerance.

1961   **von Békésy, Georg (U.S.)**—discoveries of the physical mechanism of stimulation within the cochlea.

1962   Crick, Francis Harry Compton (Great Britain), Watson, James Dewey (U.S.), and Wilkins, Maurice Hugh Frederick (Great Britain)—discoveries of the molecular structure of nuclear acids and its significance for information transfer in living material.

1963   Eccles, Sir John Carew (Australia), Hodgkin, Sir Alan Lloyd (Great Britain), and Huxley, Sir Andrew Fielding (Great Britain)—discoveries of the ionic mechanisms involved in excitation and inhibition in the peripheral and central portions of the nerve cell membrane.

1964   Bloch, Konrad (U.S.) and Lynen, Feodor (Germany)—discoveries concerning the mechanism and regulation of the cholesterol and fatty acid metabolism.

1965   Jacob, François (France), Lwoff, André (France), and Monod, Jacques (France)—discoveries in the genetic control of enzyme and virus synthesis.

1966   Rous, Peyton (U.S.)—discovered tumor-inducing viruses.

Huggins, Charles Brenton (U.S.)—discoveries of hormonal treatment of prostatic cancer.

1967   Granit, Ragnar (Sweden), Hartline, Haldan Keffer (U.S.), and Wald, George (U.S.)—discoveries in the primary physiological and chemical visual processes in the eye.

1968   Holley, Robert W. (U.S.), Khorana, Har Gobind (U.S.), and Nirenberg, Marshall W. (U.S.)—interpreted the genetic code and its function in protein synthesis.

1969   Delbrück, Max (U.S.), Hershey, Alfred D. (U.S.), and Luria, Salvador E. (U.S.)—discoveries in the replication mechanism and the genetic structure of viruses.

1970   Katz, Sir Bernard (Great Britain), von Euler, Ulf (Sweden), and Axelrod, Julius (U.S.)—discoveries in the humoral transmitters in the nerve terminals and the mechanism for their storage, release, and inactivation.

1971   Sutherland, Earl W., Jr. (U.S.)—discoveries in the mechanisms of the action of hormones.

1972   Edelman, Gerald M. (U.S.) and Porter, Rodney R. (Great Britain)—discoveries in the chemical structure of antibodies.

1973   von Frisch, Karl (Germany), Lorenz, Konrad (Austria), and Tinbergen, Nikolaas (Great Britain)—discoveries in the organization and elicitation of individual and social behavior patterns.

1974   Claude, Albert (Belgium), de Duve, Christian (Belgium), and Palade, George E. (U.S.)—discoveries of the structural and functional organization of the cell.

1975   Baltimore, David (U.S.), Dulbecco, Renato (U.S.), and Temin, Howard Martin (U.S.)—discoveries of the interaction between tumor viruses and the genetic material of the cell.

1976   Blumberg, Baruch S. (U.S.) and Gajdusek, D. Carleton (U.S.)—discoveries of new mechanisms for the origin and dissemination of infectious diseases.

1977   Guillemin, Roger (U.S.) and Schally, Andrew V. (U.S.)—discoveries in peptide hormone production of the brain.

Yalow, Rosalyn (U.S.)—for the development of radioimmunoassays of peptide hormones.

1978 Arber, Werner (Switzerland), Nathans, Daniel (U.S.), and Smith, Hamilton O. (U.S.)—discovered restriction enzymes and their application to problems of molecular genetics.

1979 Cormack, Allan M. (U.S.) and Hounsfield, Sir Godfrey N. (Great Britain)—developed the computer assisted tomograph (CAT).

1980 Benacerraf, Baruj (U.S.), Dausset, Jean (France), and Snell, George D. (U.S.)—discoveries of genetically determined structures on the cell surface that regulate the immunological reactions.

1981 Sperry, Roger W. (U.S.)—discoveries of the functional specialization of the cerebral hemispheres.

Hubel, David H. (U.S.) and Wiesel, Rorsten N. (Sweden)—discoveries in information processing in the visual system.

1982 Bergström, Sune K. (Sweden), Samuelsson, Bengt I. (Sweden), and Vane, Sir John R. (Great Britain)—discoveries in prostaglandins and related biologically active substances.

1983 McClintock, Barbara (U.S.)—discovered mobile genetic elements.

1984 Jerne, Niels K. (Denmark), Köhler, Georges J.F. (Germany), and Milstein, César (Great Britain and Argentina)—developed theories concerning the specificity in development and control of the immune system and the discovery of the principle for production of monoclonal antibodies.

1985 Brown, Michael S. (U.S.) and Goldstein, Joseph L. (U.S.)—discoveries of the regulation of cholesterol metabolism.

1986 Cohen, Stanley (U.S.) and Levi-Montalcini, Rita (Italy and U.S.)—discoveries of growth factors.

1987 Tonegawa, Susumu (Japan)—discovered the genetic principle for generation of antibody diversity.

1988 Black, Sir James W. (Great Britain), Elion, Gertrude B. (U.S.) and Hitchings, George H. (U.S.)—discoveries of important principles for drug treatment.

1989 Bishop, Michael J. (U.S.) and Varmus, Harold E. (U.S.)—discovered the cellular origin of retroviral oncogenes.

1990 Murray, Joseph E. (U.S.) and Thomas, E. Donnall (U.S.)—discoveries of organ and cell transplantation in the treatment of human disease.

1991 Neher, Erwin (Germany) and Sakmanna, Bert (Germany)—work on uncovering basic cell functions.

1992 Fischer, Edmond H. (U.S.) and Krebs, Edwin G. (U.S.)—discovered (in the 1950s) a cellular regulatory mechanism used to control a variety of metabolic processes.

1993 Richard J. Roberts (Great Britain) and Phyllip A. Sharp (U.S.)—discovered genes are composed of several segments; it would lead to gene splicing and better understanding of hereditary disease and cancer.

1994   **Martin Rodbell (U.S.)** and **Alfred G. Gilman (U.S.)**—identified G proteins, which translate and integrate external signals for the cell's second messengers.

Scientific Organizations

Note: Publications of certain organizations in parentheses.

Biology

American Birding Association, Inc.
P. O. Box 6599
Colorado Springs, Colorado 80934
(*Birding*)

Botanical Society of America, Inc.
1735 Neil Avenue
Columbus, Ohio 43210
(*American Journal of Botany*)

National Association of Biology Teachers
11250 Roger Bacon Drive
Reston, Virginia 22090
(*American Biology Teacher*)

Biomedical Science

Alzheimer's Disease and Related Disorders Association
919 N. Michigan Avenue, Suite 1000
Chicago, Illinois 60611-1676
800-621-0379

American Allergy Association
P. O. Box 7273
Menlo Park, California 94026
415-322-1663

American Diabetes Association
505 Eighth Avenue
New York, New York 10018
800-232-3472

American Heart Association
7320 Greenville Avenue
Dallas, Texas 75231
214-373-6300

American Liver Foundation
998 Pompton Avenue
Cedar Grove, New Jersey 07009
800-223-0179

American Lung Association
1740 Broadway
New York, New York 10019
212-245-8000

American Psychiatric Association
1400 K Street NW
Washington, D.C. 20005
202-682-6000

American Psychological Association
1200 17th Street NW
Washington, D.C. 20036
202-955-7600

American Red Cross
17th and D Street NW
Washington, D.C. 20006
202-737-8300

American Red Cross
AIDS Educational Office
17th and D Street NW
Washington, D.C. 20006
202-737-8300

Asthma and Allergy Foundation of America
1717 Massachuestts Avenue, Suite 305
Washington, D.C. 20036
202-265-0265

Brain Research Foundation
134 South LaSall Street
Chicago, Illinois 60603
312-782-4311

Cystic Fibrosis Foundation
6931 Arlington Road
Bethesda, Maryland 20814

March of Dimes Birth Defects Foundation
1275 Mamaroneck Avenue
White Plains, New York 10605

Muscular Dystrophy Association
810 Seventh Avenue
New York, New York 10019

National AIDS Network
1012 14th Street NW, Suite 601
Washington, D.C. 20005
202-347-0390

National Cancer Institute
Cancer Information Service
NCU Building 31
Bethesda, Maryland 20205
800-422-6237 (800-4CANCER)

National Down's Syndrome Society
141 Fifth Avenue
New York, New York 10010
National Down's Syndrome Congress—
800-232-6372

National Health Information Center
P. O. Box 1133
Washington, D.C. 20013-1133
800-336-4797

National Kidney Foundation
2 Park Avenue
New York, New York 10016
212-889-2210

National Multiple Sclerosis Society
205 East 42nd Street
New York, New York 10017
212-986-3240

Phobia and Anxiety Disorders Clinic
State University of New York at Albany
1535 Western Avenue
Albany, New York 12203
518-456-4127

Chemistry

American Chemical Society
1155 16th Street NW
Washington, D.C. 20036
202-872-4400
(*American Chemical Society Journal*)

Physics and Astronomy

American Astronomical Society
American Institute of Physics
335 E. 45th Street
New York, New York 10017
(*Astronomical Journal; Astrophysical Journal*)

American Institute of Aeronautics and Astronautics
370 L'Enfant Promenade SW
Washington, D.C. 20560
(*AIAA Journal*)

Astronomical Society of the Pacific
390 Ashton Avenue
San Francisco, California 94112
(*Mercury: The Journal of the Astronomical Society of the Pacific*)

Universities Space Research Association
P. O. Box 391
Boulder, Colorado 80306
303-440-9160

Earth Science and Meteorology

American Geological Institute
4220 King Street
Alexandria, Virginia 22302

American Geophysical Union
2000 Florida Avenue NW
Washington, D.C. 20009
(*EOS*)

American Petroleum Institute
1220 L Street NW
Washington, D.C. 20005
202-682-8120

Geological Society of America
3300 Penrose Place
P.O. Box 9140
Boulder, Colorado
(*GSA Bulletin; Geology*)

Mineralogical Society of America
1130 17th Street NW
Suite 330
Washington, D.C. 20036
(*American Mineralogist*)

National Geophysical Data Center
325 Broadway
Boulder, Colorado 80303
303-497-6761

Environmental Science

Center for Environmental Information, Inc.
46 Prince Street
Rochester, New York 14607-1016
716-546-3796

Environmental Defense Fund
Toxics Program
1616 P Street NW
Washington, D.C. 20036
202-387-3500

National Audubon Society
950 Third Avenue
New York, New York 10022

National Wildlife Federation
1412 16th Street NW
Washington, D.C. 20036

Natural Resources Defense Council
40 West 20th Street
New York, New York 10011
212-727-2700

World Resources Institute
1709 New York Avenue NW
Washington, D.C. 20006

Engineering

American Ceramic Society
757 Brooksedge Plaza Drive
Westerville, Ohio 43081

The American Institute of Architecture
1735 New York Avenue NW
Washington, D.C. 20006

American Institute of Chemical Engineers
345 East 47th Street
New York, New York 10017
(numerous journals)

American Nuclear Society
555 N. Kensington Avenue
LaGrange Park, Illinois 60525
(*Nuclear Science and Engineering*)

American Society for Engineering Education
11 Dupont Circle
Suite 200
Washington, D.C. 20036

American Society of Civil Engineers
345 E. 47th Street
New York, New York 10017
(numerous journals)

American Society of Mechanical Engineers
345 E. 47th Street
New York, New York 10017
(numerous journals)

American Society of Safety Engineers
1800 East Oakton
Des Plaines, IL 60018

Institute of Electrical and Electronics Engineers
345 E. 47th Street
New York, New York 10017-2394
(numerous journals)

The Metallurgical Society of the American Institute of Mining, Metallurgical, and Petroleum Engineers
410 Commonwealth Drive
Warrendale, Pennsylvania 15086

National Society of Professional Engineers
1420 King Street
Alexandria, Virginia 22314
(*Engineering Times*)

Society of Women Engineers
United Engineering Center
345 East 47th Street
New York, New York 10017
(*United States Woman Engineer: Magazine of the Society of Women Engineers*)

Government Agencies

Centers for Disease Control and Prevention
1600 Clifton Road NE
Atlanta, Georgia 30333
404-639-3311
As part of the Department of Health and Human Services, the CDC provides information to the public on specific diseases.

Consumer Product Safety Commission
Chemical Hazards Program
5401 Westbard Avenue
Washington, D.C. 20207
800-638-2772
The federal program that regulates consumer products and provides information on chemicals, particularily those often used in the home.

Department of Energy
Forrestal Building PA-3
1000 Independence Avenue SW
Washington, D.C. 20585
Department responsible for energy research and development, regulatory programs, conservation, and data collection and analysis.

Environmental Protection Agency
401 M Street SW
Washington, D.C. 20460
202-260-2080
Provides information about the EPA
regulatory and informational programs,
including health and exposure (to
chemicals) assessment.

Federal Energy Regulatory Commission
825 N. Capitol Street NE
Washington, D.C. 20426
202-208-0680
Agency responsible for regulating all
energy sources other than nuclear.

Food and Drug Administration
Freedom of Information Office
5600 Fishers Lane
Rockville, Maryland 20857
301-443-6310
Responds to written requests for information on the safety of foods; and also some
questions on low-level exposure to toxic
chemicals.

**National Aeronautics and Space
Administration**
NASA Headquarters
Washington, D.C. 20546
202-453-1000
A government agency responsible for the
United States space program.

National Institute of Mental Health
5900 Fishers Lane
Rockville, Maryland 20857
301-443-2403
A government agency responsible for the
promotion of research and support in
mental health.

**National Oceanic and Atmospheric
Administration**
Environmental Research Laboratories
325 Broadway
Boulder, Colorado 80303
303-497-3000
A government agency that is responsible
for, among other duties, weather information dissemination.

National Science Foundation
1800 G Street NW
Washington, D.C. 20550
202-357-9498
Independent federal government agency
responsible to promote basic research in
science and engineering.

**Occupational Safety and Health
Administration**
200 Constitution Avenue NW
Washington, D.C. 20210
202-523-8148
Part of the Department of Labor, OSHA
enforces the federal Occupational Safety
and Health Act.

Office of Nuclear Energy
U.S. Department of Energy
MS NE-12
Washington, D.C. 20585
202-586-4316
Government office that handles the
civilian nuclear research and development
programs for the Department of Energy.

United States Geological Survey
Department of the Interior
12201 Sunrise Valley Drive
Reston, Virginia 22092
703-648-4460
Government office that handles the
dissemination of information concerning
geology and geophysics.

Popular Science Publications
General Science

Omni
324 W. Wendover Avenue
Greensboro, North Carolina 27408
A monthly magazine that covers science
fact, fiction, and fantasy for readers of all
ages, backgrounds, and interests. (The
magazine is mainly offered in cyberspace.)

Popular Science
2 Park Avenue
New York, New York 10016
A monthly publication that stresses
current popular science, new products, and
technology for general audiences.

Science Frontiers
Sourcebook Project
P. O. Box 107
Glen Arm, Maryland 21057
This bimonthly publication is a collection
of scientific anomalies in the current
scientific literature.

Science News
1719 N Street NW
Washington, D.C. 20036
A weekly publication for a general
audience that calls itself "The Weekly
Newmagazine of Science."

Scientific American
415 Madison Avenue
New York, New York 10017
A monthly publication for serious amateur
and professional scientists with detailed
articles on all fields of science.

Biology

American Forests
1516 P Street NW
Washington, D.C. 20005
A bimonthly magazine of trees and forests,
stressing management and intellegent use
of forests, soil, water, and wildlife.

American Horticulturist
American Horticultural Society
7931 E. Boulevard Drive
Alexandria, Virginia 22308-1300
A bimonthly magazine covering gardening.

The Herb Companion
201 E. 4th Street
Loveland, Colorado 80537
A bimonthly magazine that covers the
culture, history, culinary uses, and crafts of
herbs, with some medicinal information.

Living Bird
Cornell Laboratory of Ornithology
159 Sapsucker Woods Road
Ithaca, New York 14850
Published four times each year, covering
conservation of and news about birds, with
an emphasis on amateur birding.

International Wildlife
National Wildlife Federation
8925 Leesburg Pike
Vienna, Virginia 22184-0001
A bimonthly magazine for persons
interested in natural history, outdoor
adventure, and the environment.

National Gardening
National Gardening Association
180 Flynn Avenue
Burlington, Vermont 05401
A bimonthly magazine on all aspects of
food gardening and ornamentals.

National Wildlife
National Wildlife Federation
8925 Leesburg Pike
Vienna, Virginia 22184-0001
A bimonthly magazine that emphasizes
wise use of the nation's natural resources
and the conservation and protection of
wildlife and its habitat.

Natural History
Central Park West at 79th Street
New York, New York 10024
A monthly magazine for the serious
amateur scientist, which stresses all fields
of science except physics and chemistry,
and with an emphasis on biology and
anthropology.

Organic Gardening
33 E. Minor
Emmaus, Pennsylvania 18098
Published nine times each year, the
magazine covers organic gardening for
general audiences.

Wildlife Conservation Magazine
New York Zoological Society
185th Street and Southern Boulevard
Bronx, New York 10460-1068
Bimonthly magazine covering wildlife—
including animals and their conservation.

**Zoo Life: Zoos, Aquariums, and
Wildlife Parks**
11661 San Vicente Boulevard
Los Angeles, California 90049
A quarterly magazine that reports on
conservation, education, research and
captive breeding efforts of zoos, aquariums,
and wildlife parks.

Biomedical Science

American Health Magazine
28 W. 23rd Street
New York, New York 10010
A monthly general interst magazine
that covers health and lifestyle aspects of
medicine, fitness, nutrition, and
psychology.

Health
301 Howard Street
San Francisco, California 94105
Published seven times each year, on
health, fitness, and nutrition for general
audiences.

Longevity
1965 Broadway
New York, New York 10023-5965
A monthly magazine for general audiences
that stresses articles on leading a more
productive and healthy life.

Prevention
Rodale Press
33 East Minor Street
Emmaus, Pennsylvania 18098
A monthly magazine for general audiences
that emphasises preventive health and
nutrition maintenence to lead a healthier
life.

Earth Science, Meteorology, and Environmental Science

Archaeology
Archaeological Institute of America
135 William Street
New York, New York 10038
A bimonthly magazine on archaeology
for the general public.

Audubon
National Audubon Society
700 Broadway
New York, New York 10003-9501
A bimonthly magazine that focuses on
the environment—from energy to forests
and wetlands.

Earth
21027 Crossroads Circle
Waukesha, Wisconsin 53187
A bimonthly magazine for the amateur
earth scientist.

Environment
1319 18th Street NW
Washington, D.C. 20036-1802
Published ten times each year, the
magazine stresses the environmental effects
of technology, and articles on science in
public affairs.

National Parks
1776 Massachusetts Avenue, NW
Washington, D.C. 20036
A bimonthly magazine for persons
interested in preservation of the National
Park System's natural areas and habitats.

Natural Hazards Observer
Natural Hazards Research and
Applications Information Center
Institute of Behavioral Science #6
University of Colorado
Boulder, Colorado 80309-0482
Bimonthly newsletter to strengthen
communication among researchers and
individuals, organizations, and agencies
concerned with mitigating the effects of
natural hazards.

Ocean Realm: Magazine of the Sea
342 West Sunset Road
San Antonio, Texas 78209
Published four times each year, emphasizing ocean flora, fauna, and conservation
of the oceans' natural resources.

Rocks and Minerals: For Everyone Interested in Rocks, Mineral, and Fossils
4000 Albermarle Street NW
Washington, D.C. 20016
A bimonthly magazine for rock and
mineral hobbists, written for general
audiences.

Sea Frontiers
The International Oceanographic
Foundation/University of Miami/Nature
America
UM Knight Center
400 SE 2nd Avenue
4th Floor
Miami, Florida 33131-2116
A bimonthly publication that covers
marine flora, fauna, and ocean
environments.

Sierra
Sierra Club
730 Polk Street
San Francisco, California 94109
A bimonthly magazine that emphasizes
conservation and environmental politics.

**Trilogy: The Magazine for Outdoor
Enthusiasts**
310 Old E. Vine Street
Lexington, Kentucky 40507-1534
A bimonthly magazine that covers
recreation, industry, and the environment.

Physics and Astronomy

Ad Astra
922 Pennsylvania Avenue
Washington, D.C. 20003-2140
A bimonthly magazine for general
audiences that covers the space
exploration(national and international).

Air & Space/Smithsonian
Smithsonian Institution
National Air and Space Museum
900 Jefferson Drive
Washington, D.C. 20560
A bimonthly publication with a broad
spectrum—from aviation history to the
latest advances in space science.

Astronomy
P. O. Box 1612
Waukesha, Wisconsin 53187-1612
A monthly magazine covering astronomy
for the hobbiest.

Aviation Week and Space Technology
1222 Avenue of the Americas
New York, New York 10020
Weekly news and feature magazine on
aeronautics and space flight.

Final Frontier
1017 S. Mountain
Monrovia, California 91016
A bimonthly magazine for general
audiences that covers space science and
exploration.

Sky & Telescope
P. O. Box 9111
Belmont, Massachusetts 02178
A monthly magazine for serious amateur
and professional astronomers.

Computer, Mathematical, and Engineering

Byte Magazine
1 Phoenix Mill Lane
Peterborough, New Hampshire 03458
A monthly magazine covering computers
for professional users.

COMPUTE
1965 Broadway
New York, New York 10023-5965
Published monthly, emphasizing home,
educational, and recreational computing.

Computer Shopper
One Park Avenue
New York, New York 10016
A monthly magazine of about 700 plus
pages, consisting of advertising for
computer hardware, software, and other
products. It also contains reviews and
feature stories.

Incider/A+
80 Elm Street
Peterborough, New Hampshire 03458
A monthly magazine for Apple II and
Macintosh users.

**PC: The Independent Guide to IBM-
Standard Personal Computing**
1 Park Avenue
New York, New York 10016
A biweekly magazine for users and owners
of IBM personal computers and compatible
systems.

PC World
501 2nd Street
San Francisco, California 94107
A monthly magazine that emphasizes
reviews, news, how-to, and feature articles
on software and hardware.

PC/Computing
19th Floor
950 Tower Lane
Foster City, California 94404-2121
A monthly magazine for advanced users
of personal computers.

Technology Review
Building W59
Massachusetts Institute of Technology
Cambridge, Massachusetts 02139
Published eight times each year and
stresses what is new in scientific research
and technology.

Children's Science Publications

Dolphin Log
The Cousteau Society, Inc.
8440 Santa Monica Boulevard
Los Angeles, California 90069
A bimonthly magazine that emphasizes
marine animals and plants, mainly for
children ages 8 to 14.

National Geographic World
National Geographic Society
17th and M Streets NW
Washington, D.C. 20036
A monthly magazine that covers science,
sports, animals, and archaeology.

Odyssey
7 School Street
Peterborough, New Hampshire 03458
603-924-7209
A children's astronomy magazine,
emphasizing space technology and science
and activities for children (ages 8 to 14)
interested in all facets of astronomy.

Owl
Young Naturalist Foundation
56 The Esplanade, Suite 304
Toronto, Ontario M5E 1A7 Canada
Published ten times each year for young
children, emphasizing nature, science, and
the world around them.

P3: the earth-based magazine for kids
P3 Foundation, Inc.
P. O. Box 52
Montgomery, Vermont 05470
An ecology magazine published 10 times
each year to educate children about
protecting the planet.

Ranger Rick
National Wildlife Federation
1400 16th Street NW
Washington, D.C. 20036
A monthly magazine for ages 6 to 12,
emphasizing nature, conservation, and the
environment.

3-2-1 Contact
1 Lincoln Plaza
New York, New York 10023
Published ten times each year, and
emphasizes science and technology for
children 8 to 14 years old.

Your Big Backyard
National Wildlife Federation
8925 Leesburg Pike
Vienna, Virginia 22184-0001
A monthly magazine for ages three to five,
emphasizine the natural world.

Zoobooks
Wildlife Education, Ltd.
3590 Kettner Boulevard
San Diego, California 92101
Published 10 times each year, and features
one animal per issue, describing everything
about the animal, from anatomy to habitat.

ADDITIONAL SOURCES OF INFORMATION: GENERAL SCIENCE BOOKS

Asimov, Isaac, and Janet Asimov. *Frontiers II: More Recent Discoveries About Life, Earth, Space, and the Universe*. Dutton-Truman Talley, 1993.

Bunch, Bryan. *The Henry Holt Handbook of Current Science & Technology*. Henry Holt, 1992.

Carnegie Library of Pittsburgh, Science and Technology Department. *Science and Technical Desk Reference*. Gale Research, 1993.

Feldman, David. *Do Penguins Have Knees?*; *When Do Fish Sleep?*; *Why Do Dogs Have Wet Noses?*; *Who Put the Butter in Butterfly?* The Imponderable Series. HarperPerennial, 1990–1992.

Gibilisco, Stan. *The Concise Illustrated Dictionary of Science and Technology*. TAB Books, 1993.

The Macmillan Visual Dictionary. Macmillan, 1992.

McGrayne, Sharon Bertsch. *365 Surprising Scientific Facts, Breakthroughs, and Discoveries*. John Wiley & Sons, 1994.

Ronan, Colin A., ed. *Science Explained: The World of Science in Everyday Life*. Henry Holt, 1993.

Trefil, James. *1001 Things Everyone Should Know About Science*. Doubleday, 1992.

Index

A

Aardvark, 126
Abacus, 497, 528
Abbe, Cleveland, 451
Abiogenesis, 144
ABO blood group, 153–54
Absolute zero, 283
Absorption, 144, 266
Abstract number, 29
Acceleration, 273, 275
ACE inhibitor, 219
Achiral objects, 35
Acid rain, 476
Acids, 251–53
Acoustical engineers, 525
Acquired immunodeficiency syndrome (AIDS), 187
Acre, 2
ACTH (adrenocorticotropic hormone), 162
Actinoids, 239
Activation energy, chemical, 245
Acupressure, 204
Acupuncture, 204
Adams, John Couch, 354
Ada (programming language), 507
Addition, 28–29
Adenine, 180
Adhesion, 266
Adler, Alfred, 212
Admiralty mile, 2
Adrenaline, 162, 219
Adrenocorticotropic hormone, 162
Adrian, Edgar, 626

Adsorption, 266
Aerolites, 329
Aeronautical engineers, 525
Aeronomy, 420
Aerospace engineers, 525
Africanized honeybees, 121
Agassiz, Jean, 407
Aging, theories on, 161
Agnatha, 123
Agricola, Georgius, 407
Agricultural engineers, 525
AICD. See Automatic implantable cardiac defibrillator
AIDS. See Acquired immunodeficiency syndrome
Aiken, Howard, 513
Air bubbles, 482
Aircraft inspectors, 525
Airframe mechanics, 525
Air mass, 428
Airplane, 46
Airplane mechanic, 525
Air pollution, 470–72
Air temperature, 429, 432
Aitken, Robert Grant, 342
Alchemy, 226
Alcohol, 266
Alder, Kurt, 617
Alfvén, Hannes, 623
Algae, 100, 108
Algology, 88
Alkadienes, 249
Alkanes, 249
Alkenes, 249
Alkynes, 249
Alleles, 178, 179
Allergens, 219

Allergies, 193
    types of, 194
Alloys, 242, 546
Alphabets
    early, 46–47
    Greek, 48–49
Alpha Centauri, 340
Alpha-particle, 255, 295, 296, 298
Alpha-particle-induced reactions, 300
Alternating current, 292
Alternator, 546
Altitude, 19
Altman, Sidney, 619
Altocumulus clouds, 436, 437
Altostratus clouds, 436, 437
Alvarez, Luis, 302, 407, 623
Alveolus, 174
Alvin (submarine), 88
Alzheimer's disease, 194
Amalgam, 242
Amber, 131–32
Amino acids, 156, 180, 183
    definition of, 144, 219
    as self-replicating mechanisms, 90
    symbols for, 56
Ammeter, 546
Amor asteroids, 327
Amp, 292
Ampere, 7, 18
Ampère, André Marie, 302
Amphibia (class), 122
Amphibians, 122, 132
Amplitude, 285, 290
Analgesics, 219
Analogue multimeter, 22

Anaximander, 451
Anderson, Carl David, 621
Anderson, Philip, 623
Anemia, 155, 194
Anesthetics, 219
Aneurysm, 194
Anfinsen, Christian, 618
Angina pectoris, 192
Angioplasty, 201
Angiosperms, 107
Angle of refraction, 289
Angles, ratio of common, 35
Angstrom, 17
Angular momentum, 275
Animals
    daily patterns, 124
    diseases borne by, 200–201
    distinguished from plants,
        101
    endangered, 134–35
    extinct, 132–34
    fastest, 131
    invertebrates, 120–22
    lifespan, 131
    mass extinction, 92
    navigation, 129
    poisonous, 129–30
    records set by, 130
    reproduction, 101, 120
    symbols for, 54
    typical cell, 103
    vertebrates, 122–24
    wildlife refuges, 487–88,
        598–613
Anion, 231
Annelid, 120
Annular eclipse, 334
Anomalistic year, 70
Anorexia nervosa, 194
Antacid, 219
Antarctica, 488
Antelope, 130
Antibiotics, 220
Antibodies, 220
Anticoagulant, 220
Antidepressant, 220
Antifreeze, 229–30
Antigen, 153, 220

Antihistamine, 220
Anti-inflammatories, 220
Antimatter, 309
Antiparticle, 297, 309
Antipsychotic drugs, 220
Antiseptic, 220
Antiuniverse, 316
Anxiety disorders, 211
AOL (America Online), 512
Aphelion, 369
Aplastic anemia, 155
Apollo asteroids, 327
Apollo missions, *332*, 348–49
Appendicitis, 194
Appleton, Sir Edward, 451, 621
Appliances, household, 293
Applications programmers, 526
Applications programs, 505
Aquariums, by state, 580–89
Aqueous solutions, 228
Aral Sea, 473
Aratus, 451
Arber, Werner, 136, 629
Arc, measurement of, 9
Archaebacteria, 96, 100
Archaeopteryx, 123
Archimedes, 35
Architectural engineers, 525
Arctic lupine, 110
Area
    formulas for, 33–34
    measurement of, 6, 8
    U.S.-SI equivalents, 8
Aristotle, 354, 451
Arjuna asteroids, 327
Aromatics, 249
Arrhenius, Svante, 90, 259, 615
Arrhythmia, 195
Arterioles, 220
Arthritis, 192
Arthropods, 121
Arthroscopic surgery, 201–2
Artificial intelligence, 510
Artiodactyla (order), 124
ASCII code, 508–10
Ascorbic acid. *See* Vitamin C
Asexual reproduction
    animal, 120
    plant, 109

Assembly languages, 506
Asteroid belt, 326
Asteroids, 90, 326–27, 353
Asthenosphere, 377, 379
Asthma, 195
Aston, Francis, 616
Astrological signs and symbols,
    47
Astronautics
    Apollo missions to Moon,
        332, 348–49
    Moon probes, 333
    recent and future
        unmanned spacecraft,
        350–51
    space firsts, 347–48
    special spacecraft, 349–50
    unmanned spacecraft to
        planets, 351–54
Astronomical distances, 27–28
Astronomy
    common terms in, 362–65
    definition of, 314
    major scientists, 354–60
    scientific organizations, 631
    scientific publications, 636
    significant discoveries,
        360–62
    symbols in, 58
    theories, 316–17
Atavism, 144
Aten asteroids, 327
Atherosclerosis, 195
Atmosphere, 420
    color of, 422
    composition of dry air at
        sea level, 423
    divisions of, 420–22
    sunlight through, 422
Atomic mass, 231, 266, 296
Atomic number, 231, 266
Atomic time, 77
Atoms
    Dalton's theory, 226, 258
    decay, 255, 296
    models, 233, 295–96
    nomenclature, 231
    nucleus, 299

physics of, 295
radioactivity, 296
size of, 299
splitting, 299–300
structure of, 230–35
See also Isotopes
Atom smashers. *See* Particle accelerators
Atrial fibrillation, 192
Audiologist, 184
Audubon, John James, 136
Aurora australis, 330
Aurora borealis, 330
Australopithecines, 404
Australopithecus afarensis, 404, 405, 407
Autoimmune disease, 220
Automatic implantable cardiac defibrillator (AICD), 202
Automobiles
    antifreeze, 229–30
    electric, 254–55, 487
    gasoline alternatives, 487
    history of, 528
Autoradiography, 202
Autotrophs, 96
Avery, Oswald Theodore, 212
Aves (class), 123
Avicenna, 212
Avogadro, Lorenzo, 259
Avogadro's law, 257
Axelrod, Julius, 628
Azimuth, 19

B

Baade, Wilhelm, 355
Babbage, Charles, 513
Babcock, Harold, 355
Babinet, Jacques, 302
Bacteria, 99
    as disease carrier in blood, 155
Baekeland, Leo, 530
Baer, Karl Ernst von, 136
Baily, Francis, 355
Balance (instrument), 40

Balanced universe model, 315
Balfour, Francis Maitland, 136
Balmer, Johann, 355
Baltimore, David, 212, 628
Banach, Stefan, 35
Banks, Sir Joseph, 136
Banting, Sir Frederick, 626
Bárány, Robert, 625
Barbiturate, 220
Bard, Allan J., 90
Bardeen, John, 622, 623
Barkla, Charles, 620
Barnard, Edward, 355
Barometric air pressure, 434–35
Barringer, Daniel, 355
Barrow, Isaac, 35
Bartholin, Caspar, 212
Bartlett, Neil, 242
Barton, Sir Derek, 618
Baryon, 298
Basal cell cancer, 177
Bases, 180, 251–53
BASIC (programming language), 507
Basov, Nicolai, 622
Bates, Henry Walter, 136
Bateson, William, 136
Bats, 125
Batteries, electrochemistry of, 253–54
Baud rate, 501
Bauhin, Caspar, 136
Bayer, Johann, 355
Beaufort, Sir Francis, 426
Beaufort wind scale, 426–27
Beaumont, William, 212
Becquerel, Antoine, 255, 302, 619
Bednorz, J. Georg, 624
Bee, killer, 121
Bell, Jocelyn, 355
Belon, Pierre, 136
Benacerraf, Baruj, 629
Benign, definition of, 220
Benign prostatic hypertrophy, 195
Bentham, George, 136
Benz, Karl, 528

Benzene, 249–50
Benzodiazepines, 220
Berg, Paul, 618
Bergeron, Tor, 451
Bergius, Friedrich, 616
Bergström, Sune, 629
Berliner, Emile, 530
Bernard, Claude, 212
Bernoulli, Daniel, 35, 259
Bernoulli disks, 499, 502
Bernoulli's principle, 258
Berosus, 71
Berzelius, Jöns Jacob, 260
Bessel, Friedrich Wilhelm, 355
Beta-blocker, 220
Beta-particle, 296, 298
Bethe, Hans, 623
Bibliographic Retrieval Service, 512
Big Bang theory, 314–15
Bilharz, Theodor, 136
Binary compound, 266
Binary computing, 496
Binnig, Gerd, 624
Biochemical engineers, 525
Biofeedback, 204
Biogenesis, 144
Biological clock. *See* Circadian rhythm
Biological oxygen demand, 491
Biology
    common terms in, 144–49
    definition of, 88
    and life, 88–91
    major scientists, 136–41, 212–17
    scientific organizations, 630
    scientific publications, 634
    significant discoveries, 141–44
    symbols, 54
Bioluminescence, 102, 288. *See also* Luminescence
Biomedical engineers, 525
Biomedical science
    common terms, 219–23
    laboratory technology, 201–3

(continued)

Biomedical science (*cont.*)
    major scientists, 212–17
    scientific organizations,
        630–31
    scientific publications, 635
    significant discoveries,
        217–19
    symbols, 55
Biomes, 461, 491
Biopharmaceuticals, 220
Biopsy, 220
Biosphere, 145
Biosynthesis, 145
Biotechnical engineers, 526
Biotin, 158
Bipolar disorder, 210
Birds, 123
    endangered, 134–35
    extinct, 132–33
Bishop, Michael, 629
Biston betularia moth, 93
Bjerknes, Jakob, 451
Bjerknes, Vilhelm, 451
Black, James, 212
Black, Sir James Whyte, 212,
    629
Black dwarf, 338
Blackett, Patrick, 621
Black hole, 278, 317, 338
Blackwell, Elizabeth, 212–13
Black widow spider, 129
Bladder, 164
    interstitial cystitis, 197
Blizzard, 454
Bloch, Felix, 622
Bloch, Konrad, 628
Bloembergen, Nicolaas, 624
Blood, 163
    common disorders, 155
    composition of, 152–53
    definition of, 152
    disease carriers in, 155–56
    donated, 154–55, 156
    types, 153–54
Blood pressure, 165, 197, 198
Blood vessels, 163
Blue-green algae, 100

Blue supergiants, 338
Blumberg, Baruch, 628
B lymphocytes, 153
Bock, Jerome, 136
Bode, Johann, 336, 355
Body. *See* Human body
Bohr, Aage Niels, 623
Bohr, Niels H.D., 233, 258, 295,
    302, 620
Bohr model, 233, 258, 295–96
Boiling point, 235–36
Bok, Bart Jan, 355
Bolide, 329
Boltwood, Bertram, 407
Boltzmann, Ludwig, 302
Bonding, chemical, 246–47
Bone marrow, 220
Bones, 174, 175
    Flat (compact), 174
    See also Osteoporosis
Boole, George, 513
Bora winds, 425
Bordet, Jules, 625
Borlaug, Norman Ernest, 136
Born, Max, 302, 622
Bosch, Carl, 616
Bose, Satyendra Nath, 303
Bose, Sir Jagadis Chandra, 136
Bosons, 297
Botanical gardens, by state,
    589–91
Botany, 88, 104
Bothe, Walther, 622
Bottelson, Ben, 623
Bovet, Daniel, 627
Bowman, Sir William, 213
Bow shock, 371
Boyle, Robert, 260
Boyle's law, 258
Bradycardia, 192
Bragg, Sir William Henry, 620
Bragg, Sir William Lawrence,
    620
Bragg equation, 258
Brahe, Tycho, 324, 342, 358
Brahmagupta, 35, 355
Brain, 167, 168

Brainstem, 167
Brattain, Walter, 622
Braun, Karl, 620
Breezes, land and sea, 424–25
Brewster, Sir David, 303
Bridgman, Percy, 621
Briggsian logarithms, 23
Broca, Pierre Paul, 213
Bronchioles, 174
Bronchitis, 195
Brongniart, Alexandre, 329
Brown, Herbert C., 618
Brown, Michael Stuart, 213, 629
Brown, Robert, 136
Brown, Robert Hanbury, 355
Brown algae, 108
Brown spider, 129
BRS (Bibliographic Retrieval
    Service), 512
Brückner, Edouard, 451
Brunfels, Otto, 136–37
Bryophytes, 107
Bubble chamber, 309
Bubbles, 90, 482
Buchner, Eduard, 615
Buckminsterfullerenes, 251, 384
Buckyballs, 251, 384
Buildings, tallest, 524
Bulimia, 195
Bullock, William, 530
Bunsen, Robert, 260
Buran wind, 425
Burbank, Luther, 137
Burbridge, Margaret, 355
Burnet, Sir Frank, 627
Burnham, Sherburne Wesley,
    342
Bursitis, 195
Butenandt, Adolf, 616
Buys Ballot, Christoph, 452

C

C (programming language), 507
C++ (programming language),
    507

CABG. *See* Coronary artery bypass graft
CAD/CAM (computer-aided design/computer-aided manufacturing), 511
Caesar, Julius, 79
Calciferol. *See* Vitamin D
Calcitonin, 162
Calcium channel blocker, 220
Calculator, 497
Calendar, 78–81
Calvin, Melvin, 90, 617
Camerarius, Rudolph Jacob, 137
Cancer, 177, 192
Candela, 7
Candolle, Augustin Pyrame de, 137
Cannizzaro, Stanislao, 260
Cannon, Annie Jump, 355
Cantor, Georg, 35
Capacity, measurement of, 9
Carbohydrates, 89, 156–57
Carbon, 90, 382, 384
Carbon cycle, 458, 459
Carbon dating, 257
Carbon dioxide, 481, 492
Carbon monoxide, 470
Carcinogen, 220, 492
Carcinoma, 192, 220
Cardiac problems. *See* Heart
Cardiac muscle, 167
Cardiologist, 184
Cardiovascular system, 163
Carnivore, 96, 125, 492
Carpal tunnel syndrome, 195
Carrel, Alexis, 625
Carrier, disease, 191
Carson, Rachel, 489
Cartilage, 174
Caselli, Abbe, 529
Cassini, Giovanni, 356
Castner, Hamilton Young, 260
Catalyst, 248
Cataract, 195
Catheter, 220
Cathode ray tube (CRT), 498, 517, 546

Cation, 231
CAT scan. *See* Computerized axial tomography
Cauchy, Augustin Louis, 36
Cavendish, Henry, 260
Caves and caverns, 488, 614
CD-ROM, 500
Cech, Thomas, 619
Cell
    animal, 101, 103
    comparisons, 102, 104, 160–62
    definition of, 102
    plant, 101, 103
    See also Cytology
Cellular telephone, 528
Celsius, Anders, 282, 303
Celsius scale, 282
Cenozoic era, 388
Centauri star system, 340
Central nervous system, 167
Central processing unit (CPU), 498, 499, 506
Centrifugal force, 274
Centripetal force, 274
Ceramic engineers, 526
Ceramic matrix composites, 546
Cerebellum, 167
Cerebral hemispheres, 167
Cerebral hemorrhage, 199
Cerebral infarction, 199
Cerebrovascular accident. *See* Stroke
Cerenkov, Pavel, 622
Cesium clocks, 77
Cetacea (order), 125
CETI. *See* Communication with extraterrestrial intelligence (CETI) programs
CFCs. *See* Chlorofluorocarbons
Chadwick, Sir James, 303, 621
Chain, Ernst Boris, 213
Chain reactions, 299
Challenger space shuttle, 350
Chamberlain-Moulton theory. *See* Tidal theory
Chamberlin, Thomas, 407

Chandler, Seth, 356
Chandrasekhar, Subrahmanyan, 356, 624
Chaos, 506–7
Charge, electric, 4, 291
Charge-cloud model, 233, 296
Charge-coupled devices, 344
Charles, Jacques, 260
Charles II (king of England), 226
Charles's law of pressures, 258
Charpak, George, 624
Chemical charges, symbols for, 57
Chemical energy, 277
Chemical engineer, 526
Chemical equilibrium, 245
Chemistry
    acids and bases, 251–53
    bonding, 246–47
    branches of, 227
    classifying matter, 227–30
    common substances, 249
    common terms, 248, 266–70
    definition of, 226
    early studies, 226–27
    formulas and equations, 244–45
    laws and rules, 257–59
    major chemists, 259–63
    Nobel Prize awards, 615–19
    organic, 249–51
    radiochemistry, 255–57
    reactions, 244–45
        types of, 247–48
    scientific organization, 631
    significant discoveries, 263–66
    symbols in, 56–58
Chemotherapy, 202, 220
Chicken pox, 187
Chicxulub Crater, 402
Children's scientific publications, 637
Chinook winds, 425
Chirality, 35

Chiron (comet), 64

Chiropractor, 184

Chiroptera (order), 125

Chittenden, Russell Henry, 213

Chlamydia, 189

Chlorine monoxide (ClO), 483

Chlorofluorocarbons (CFCs), 481, 483

Chlorophyll, 145

Cholesterol, 159–60

Chondrichthyes, 123

Chorionic gonadotropin, 162

Chromium, 157

Chromosomes, 145, 179–80

Chromosphere, 319

Chronic rheumatic heart disease, 195

Chu Shih-Chieh, 36

Cinder volcanoes, 393

ClO. *See* Chlorine monoxide

Circadian rhythm, 68–69

Circle
    definition of, 32
    formula for finding area of, 34
    formula for finding perimeter of, 34
    measurement of, 9, 33

Circuit, 546

Circulatory system, 163–64

Cirrocumulus clouds, 436, 437

Cirrostratus clouds, 436, 437

Cirrus clouds, 436, 437

Civil engineer, 526

Clark, Alvan, 356

Classical physics, 272

Claude, Albert, 137, 628

Clausius, Rudolf, 283, 303

Clavius, Christopher, 79

Clay, 90–91

Cleavage, of minerals, 382, 413

Climate
    definition of, 454
    Earth's ancient, 482
    and El Niño, 484
    global warming, 480–81
    zones, 461
    See also Weather

Clinical depression. *See* Major depression

Clocks and watches
    cesium, 77
    early, 73

Closed universe model, 315

Cloudburst, 441

Clouds
    definition of, 455
    high, 436, 437
    high-altitude, 435
    low, 436, 437
    middle, 436, 437
    symbols for, 62
    types of, 435–37
    vertically developing, 436, 437

Clusters, star, 342

Cobalamin, 158

COBE. *See* Cosmic Background Explorer

COBOL (programming language), 507

Cobra, 129

Cockcroft, Sir John, 622

Coconut, 110

Codon, 180

Coelenterate, 121

Cohen, Stanley H., 137, 629

Cohn, Ferdinand Julius, 137

Cold front, 429, 430

Colds, 187

Colitis, 195

Colliding plate boundaries, 379

Colligative properties, 229

Collision theory (birth of solar system), 317

Colloidal dispersions (suspensions), 230

Colloidal micelles, 230

Colloidal particles, 472

Colonoscopy, 202

Color
    of atmosphere, 422
    dispersion of, 288
    of minerals, 382

Colugos, 125

Combination, chemical, 247

Comet Grigg-Skjellerup, 353

Comet Halley, 90, 353

Comets, 324–26, 327, 328

Commensalism, 145

Commerson's dolphin, 130

Commoner, Barry, 489

Common logarithms, 23

Communication programs, 504

Communication with extraterrestrial intelligence (CETI) programs, 354

Communities, ecological, 461

Complex numbers, 29

Composite volcanoes, 393

Compound, chemical, 227–28, 267

Compressed natural gas, 487

Compton, Arthur Holly, 620

CompuServe, 512

Computer hardware specialists, 496

Computerized axial tomography (CT/CAT scan), 202

Computer programmers, 496, 526

Computers, 528–29
    adding on to, 501
    definition of, 496
    high-performance, 505–6
    minicomputers, 504
    necessities, 499–500
    personal, 498–505
    up-to-date, 502
    viruses, 497–98
    workings of, 512–13

Computer science
    binary computing, 496
    common terms in, 516–22
    definition of, 496
    early computing, 497
    information and retrieval services, 511–12
    languages, 506–8
    major scientists, 513–14
    scientific publications, 636–37
    significant discoveries, 514–16

terminology, 501
uses in science and
technology, 510–11
Concentrated solution, 229, 267
Condensation point, 236
Conductors, 292
Condylomata acuminata. See
Human papillomavirus
Cone, formula for finding
volume of, 34
Congestive heart failure, 192
Conic sections, 34
Coniferous forests, 464, 465
Conjunctivitis, 195
Conon of Samos, 36
Constant acceleration due to
gravity, 273
Constellations, 336
Constipation, 195
Continents, 375, 380
Contraceptives, 221
Convective zone, 319
Conybeare, William, 407
Cooper, Leon, 623
Coordinated Universal Time, 82
Cope, Edward, 408
Copernicus, Nicolaus, 356
Copper, 157
Coral reefs, 413, 469
Core, of Earth, 377
Coret, Elias, 619
Cori, Carl, 627
Coriolis, Gustave-Gaspard, 303,
452, 455
Coriolis effect, 424, 445
Cormack, Allan, 629
Cornforth, Sir John, 618
Corona, 319
Coronary arteries, 221
Coronary artery bypass graft
(CABG), 202
Correns, Karl Franz Joseph
Erich, 137
Corrosion, 248
Corti, Alfonso, 213
Cortical sex hormones, 162
Cosmic Background Explorer
(COBE), 315, 350

Cosmic rays, 330
Cosmology, 315
Coulomb, Charles, 291
Coulomb (unit), 18, 291
Counting devices, 497
Cournand, André, 627
Cousteau, Jacques-Yves, 408
Covalent bonds, 246
CPU. *See* Central processing
unit
Cram, Donald, 619
Craters, 327, 328, 414
Crick, Francis, 213, 628
Crohn's disease, 195
Cronin, James, 624
Crookes, Sir William, 260
CRT. *See* Cathode ray tube
Crust, of Earth, 377, 378–79
Crustal plates. *See* Plate
tectonics
Cryosurgery, 202
Crystals, 382–84
definition of, 414
ice, 443
shape, 382
CT scan. *See* Computerized axial
tomography
Cube
definition of, 32
formula for finding area of,
34
formula for finding volume
of, 34
Cubic measurement. *See*
Volume
Cugnot, Nicolas Joseph, 528
Cumulonimbus clouds, 436,
437
Cumulus clouds, 436, 437
Curie, Marie, 255, 260, 615,
619
Curie, Pierre, 255, 260, 619
Current, electric. *See* Electric
current
Currents, ocean, 398
Cushing, Harvey William, 213
Cuvier, Georges, 137, 213, 408
Cyclones, 445

Cylinder
definition of, 32
formula for finding volume
of, 34
Cystic fibrosis, 190–91
Cystitis, 195–96
Cystoscopy, 202
Cytology, 88, 102
Cytoplasm, 145, 221
Cytosine, 180

D

Daguerre, Louis, 529
Daimler, Gottlieb, 528
Daisy-wheel printers, 503
Dale, Sir Henry, 626
Dalén, Nils, 620
Dalton, John, 226, 233, 258,
259, 260
Dam, Henrik, 626
Dampier, William, 452
Dana, James, 408
Dark matter, 316
Dark nebulas, 342
Darlington, Cyril Dean, 213
Darwin, Charles, 91, 137
Darwin, Erasmus, 213
Darwin, George, 331
Dassies, 125
Database programs, 504
Database services, 511–12
Data bits, 501
Dausset, Jean, 213, 629
Davaine, Casimir, 213
Davenport, Charles Benedict,
137
Davidsson, Clinton, 621
Davis, William Morris, 408
Davy, Sir Humphry, 260
Dawes, William Rutter, 356
Day, 71–72
Daylight Savings Time, 85
DDT, 492
Death rate, by selected causes,
206–8

de Broglie, Louis Victor, 260, 303, 621
de Broglie waves, 302
Debye, Peter, 303, 616
Decibels, 17–18, 290
Deciduous forests, 464, 465
Decimals
     binary equivalents, 496
     equivalents of common fractions, 30
Decomposers, 96
Decomposition, 247, 492
de Duve, Christian, 628
De Forest, Lee, 529
Deforestation, 481–82
de Gennes, Pierre-Giles, 624
De Hevesy, George, 616
Dehmet, Hans, 624
Deisenhofer, Johann, 619
Delbrück, Max, 628
Delirium, 221
Delusional disorder, 210
Delusions, 209
Democritus, 226
Dendrochronology, 78
Density
     of common substances at 68 degrees F, 236–37
     measurement of, 18–19
     of Sun, 319
Dental technology, 209
Dentist, 184
Deoxyribonucleic acid (DNA), 181
     and amino acids, 90, 180
     definition of, 180
     genetic code in, 182
     genetic fingerprinting, 182
     symbols for, 55
Depression (mental), 210
Dermatitis, 196
Dermatologist, 184
Dermoptera (order), 125
Descartes, René, 452
Desert, 375, 467–68
de Sitter, Willem, 356
Desktop publishing, 511
Desmarest, Nicholas, 408

Deuteron-induced reactions, 300
de Vries, Hugo Marie, 137
Dew, 455
Diabetes, 183, 193
Dialog (database service), 512
Diamond, 289, 382, 384
Diaphragm, 174
Diarrhea, 196
Diastolic blood pressure, 165
Diatomic elements, 247
Diatomic molecules, 247
Diels, Otto, 617
Diesel, Rudolf, 528
Digestive hormones, 162
Digestive system, 165–66
Digital multimeter, 22
Dinosaur, 401, 402, 404, 414
Diode, 546
Diophantus of Alexandria, 36
Diphtheria, 187
Diplopia, 196
Dirac, Paul, 621
Direct current, 292
Disease. *See* Medicine and health; *specific diseases*
Disk drive, 500
Disks, computer, 499–500, 502
Dispersion, 288, 289
Dissociative disorders, 211
Dissolved matter, 472
Distance
     astronomical, 27–28
     U.S.-SI equivalents, 8
Distillation, 226
Diuretic, 221
Diverticulitis, 196
DNA. *See* Deoxyribonucleic acid
Dobereiner, Johann, 238
Doisy, Edward, 626
Dokuchaiev, Vasilii, 408
Domagk, Gerhard, 626
Dominant characteristics, 94
Dominant genes, 178
Doppler, Christian, 291, 303 451
Doppler effect, 291, 363, 451
Dot-matrix printers, 503
Double helix, 180

Double replacement, chemical, 248
Douglass, Andrew Ellicott, 78
Down's syndrome, 179, 191
Drake, Edwin, 408
Draper, Henry, 356
Dreyer, Johann, 342, 356
Dry cell battery, 253–54
Duggar, Benjamin Minge, 137
Dugongs, 126
Dujardin, Félix, 137
Dulbecco, Renato, 628
Dumps. *See* Landfills
Dutton, Clarence, 408
Du Vigneaud, Vincent, 617
Dynamo, 546
Dyspepsia, 196

E

Ear, 168, 170
Earth
     changes through time, 381
     circumference of, 2–3, 6
     distance to Sun, 369, 372
     early, 368
     effect on Moon, 76
     impacts on, 327–28, 402
     layers of, 377–78
     magnetic field, 371, 380, 382
     movement through galaxy, 371
     as planet, 320–23
     precession, 370–71
     revolution of, 369
     rotation of, 368–69, 370
     statistics on, 372–73
     See also Atmosphere
Earthquakes, 389
     famous, 391
     major zones, 392
     Mercalli scale, 390
     Richter scale, 390–91
Earth science
     common terms in, 412–17
     major scientists, 407–11

scientific organizations, 631

scientific publications, 635–36

significant discoveries in, 411–12

symbols in, 59–61

Eastman, George, 530

EBCDIC code, 508

Eccles, Sir John, 628

ECG. *See* Electrocardiograph

Echinoderm, 121

Echocardiogram, 203

Eckert, John Presper, 513

Eclipse, 334–35

Eclipse year, 70

Ecological succession, 492

Ecology, 461

definition of, 458

freshwater, 469

marine, 469

terrestrial, 463–68

Ecotone, 492

Eddington, Sir Arthur, 356

Edelman, Gerald, 628

Edentata (order), 125

Edison, Thomas, 529, 530

Edward I (king of England), 2

EEG. *See* Electroencephalograph

EEPROM (electrically erasable programmable read-only memory), 503

Efficiency

measurement of, 6

U.S.-SI equivalents, 9

Egg-laying mammals, 126

Ehrlich, Paul, 213, 489, 625

Eichler, August Wilhelm, 137

Eigen, Manfred, 618

Eijkman, Christiaan, 626

Einstein, Albert, 68, 279–81, 296, 300–301, 303, 620

Einstein Observatory, 347

Einthoven, Willem, 626

EKG. *See* Electrocardiograph

Ekman, Vagn Walfrid, 408

Elasticity, 546

Electrical energy, 277

Electrical engineering, symbols in, 65

Electrical engineers, 526

Electrical multimeters, 22

Electrical units, 18

Electric cars, 254–55, 487

Electric charge, 4, 291

Electric current, 291–92, 294

Electricity, 291–93

Electric light, 529

Electrocardiograph (ECG/EKG), 203

Electroencephalograph (EEG), 203

Electrolytes, 229

Electromagnet, 546

Electromagnetic fields (EMFs), 480

Electromagnetic waves, 286–87

Electromagnetism, 281, 283, 294–95

Electromotive force, 546

Electron, 230, 231, 233–34, 291, 292, 295, 298, 301

Electronics, 529

Electronics engineers, 526

Electrostatics, 291

Electroweak theory, 281

Elementary particles. *See* Subatomic particles

Elements

chemical, 226, 227–28

activity of, 241

electron configurations, 234

naming of, 243

symbols for, 57

human, 101

See also Periodic Table of the Elements

Elephants, 126, 130

Elion, Gertrude, 629

Ellipse, formula for finding area of, 34

Elliptical orbit, 278

El Niño, 369, 394, 484

Elton, Charles, 489

Embolism, 199

EMFs. *See* Electromagnetic fields

Emission nebulas, 342

Emphysema, 196

Empirical formula, 244

Encephalitis, 200

Encke, Johann, 356

Endangered animals, 134–35

Endemic, definition of, 221

Enders, John, 213, 627

Endocarditis, 192

Endocrine glands, 161, 162

Endocrinologist, 184

Endometriosis, 196

Endorphins, 221

Endoscopy, 202

Energy

equivalent of mass, 280

in physics, 276–77, 310

sources, 486–87

Engelmann, George, 138

Engine, 546

Engineering

common terms in, 546–48

definition of, 524

scientific organizations, 632

scientific publications, 636–37

types of, 524–28

Engineer's scale, 21

Engler, Adolf, 138

Enterprise space shuttle, 350

Entropy, 284

Environment

current concerns, 476–80

definition of, 458

preservation of nature, 487–88

See also Pollution

Environmental science

common terms in, 491–94

definition of, 458

Earth's environments, 461–69

major environmentalists, 489

natural cycles on Earth, 458–60

(continued)

Environmental science (*cont.*)
scientific organizations,
631–32
scientific publications,
635–36
significant discoveries in,
490–91
symbols in, 64
Enzyme, 221
Ephemeris time, 77
Epidemic, 201
Epidemiologist, 184
Epilepsy, 196
Epinephrine, 162
EPROM (erasable programmable
read-only memory), 503
Epstein-Barr virus. *See*
Mononucleosis
Equations
chemical, 244
definition of, 41
Maxwell's, 294–94
Equinox, 75, 370–71
Erasistratus of Chios, 213–14
Eratosthenes, 2–3, 356
Erlanger, Joseph, 626
Erlenmeyer, Richard, 260
Ernst, Richard, 619
Erosion, 480
Erythroblastosis fetalis, 154
Erythrocytes. *See* Red blood
cells
Erythropoietin, 162
Esaki, Leo, 623
Escape velocity, 278
Esophagus, 165
Espy, James, 452
Essential amino acids, 156
Ethanol, 487
Euclid, 30, 36
Euclidean geometry, 506
Euler, Leonhard, 36
Europa (moon of Jupiter), 400
European earth salamander, 129
Eutrophication, 492
Evolution
current, 93
definition of, 91

early, 92
of living organisms, 93
stages of human, 404–6
Ewing, William, 408
Exclusion principle. *See* Pauli
exclusion principle
Exocrine glands, 161, 162
Exosphere, 420, 421
Expansion joint, 546
Experimental physics, 272
Expert systems, 510
Exponent, 31–32
Extinction
animal, 132–34, 401
caused by space objects, 402
definition of, 146
mass, 92
Extraterrestrial life, 354
Eye, 168, 170

F

Fabrici, Girolamo. *See* Fabricius
ab Aquapendente,
Hieronymus
Fabricius ab Aquapendente,
Hieronymus, 214
Fabry, Charles, 483
Facsimile machine, 529
Faculae, 319
Fahrenheit, Daniel Gabriel, 283,
303
Fahrenheit scale, 283
Fallopius, Gabriel, 214
Faraday, Michael, 303
Faraday's laws, 258
Fats, 89, 159
Fatty acids, 159
Fax. *See* Facsimile machine
Female reproductive system,
171–72
Fermat, Pierre de, 36
Fermi, Enrico, 303, 621
Fermions, 297
Ferrel, William, 423, 452
Ferrel cells, 423

Feynman, Richard, 303, 623
Fiber, 221
Fiber optics, 290, 529
Fibiger, Johannes, 626
Fibonacci, Leonardo, 36
Fibroblasts, 186
Fibroid tumors, 196
Fielding, Sir Andrew, 628
Filament, 547
Finsen, Niels, 625
Fireball, 329
Fischer, Edmond, 629
Fischer, Ernst, 618
Fischer, Hans, 616
Fischer, Hermann, 625
Fish, 123
endangered, 135
extinct, 133
Fisher, R.A., 94
Fission, 299
Fitch, Val, 624
Fitzroy, Robert, 452
Flagella, 146
Flamsteed, John, 342, 356
Flatworms, 122
Fleming, Sir Alexander, 214,
626
Fleming, Sir John Ambrose, 303,
529
Flood, 414
Floppy disk drive, 500
Florey, Sir Howard Walter, 214
Flory, Paul John, 260, 618
Flourens, Jean Pierre Marie, 214
Flowering plants, 105–6, 107–8
Flowers, germination tables for,
119
Flu. *See* Influenza
Fluid volume, 5, 7
Fluorescence, 268, 288
Fluorine, 157
Flying lemurs, 125
Folic acid (folacin), 158
Food chain, 92, 462
Food irradiation, 257
Food pyramid, 462–63
Food web, 462
Fool's gold. *See* Pyrite

Foot (measurement), 2
Forbes, Edward, 138
Force, 274
Forests, 464, 465–66
     See also Deforestation
Forssmann, Werner, 627
FORTRAN (programming
     language), 507
Fossil fuels, 486, 492
Fossils, 60, 401–4, 407
Foucault, Jean, 303–4
Fourier, Jean Baptiste Joseph,
     Baron, 36
Fourth-generation languages,
     506
Fowler, William, 624
Fox, Sydney, 90
Fractals, 506
Fractions
     definition of, 42
     percent and decimal
          equivalents, 30
Fracture, of minerals, 382, 414
Franck, James, 620
Frank, Il'ja, 622
Franklin, Benjamin, 304
Franklin, Rosalind, 214
Fraunhofer, Josef von, 304
Free radicals, 161
Freezing
     for organ transplantation,
          203
     red blood cells, 156
     as weather condition,
          440–41
Freezing point, 229–30, 235,
     236
Frege, Friedrich Ludwig Gottlob,
     36
Frequency (sound), 285
Freshwater ecology, 460
Fresnel, Augustin, 304
Freud, Sigmund, 214
Friction, 275
Friedman, Jerome, 624
Frisch, Karl von, 138
Frost, 440
Fruit, 105, 146

FSH (follicle-stimulating
     hormone), 162
Fuchs, Leonhard, 138
Fujita, T. Theodore, 449
Fujita and Pearson wind damage
     scale, 449
Fukui, Kenichi, 618
Fuller, R. Buckminster, 251, 384
Fullerenes, 251, 384
Functional groups (chemistry),
     250
Fungi, 96, 100
Fuse, 547
Fusion, 300, 319, 486
Fuzzy logic, 510

G

Gabor, Dennis, 529, 623
Gaertner, Karl Friedrich von,
     138
Gaia hypothesis, 492
Gajdusek, D. Carleton, 628
Galapagos Rift, 88–89
Galaxy, 315
     definition of, 340
     shapes of, 341
     See also Milky Way
Galen, 214
Galileo Galilei, 73, 273, 356,
     530
Galle, Johann, 356
Gall stones, 196
Galton, Francis, 452
Galvani, Luigi, 260–61
Galvanometer, 547
Game port, 500
Games, computer, 504, 511
Gamma globulin, 221
Gamma-ray, 296
Gamma-ray-induced reactions,
     300
Gamma-Ray Observatory, 347,
     351
Gamow, George, 356
Ganglion, 196

Garbage, 477, 478, 485
Gases, 235–36
     Boyle's law, 258
     and chemical kinetics, 245
     Dalton's law, 258
     density of, 237
     noble, 242
Gasket, 547
Gasohol, 487
Gasoline, 487
Gas pressure, 235
Gastritis, 196
Gastroenteritis, 197
Gastrointestinal system. *See*
     Digestive system
Gates, computer, 512–13
Gates, William, 513
Gause's principle, 492
Gauss, Karl Friedrich, 36
Gay-Lussac, Joseph-Louis, 261
Gay-Lussac's law. *See* Charles's
     law of pressures
Geiger, Hans, 304
Gell-Mann, Murray, 623
Gemini missions, 349
Gene, 94, 146, 178
Generator, 547
Genetic disease, 190–91
Genetic engineering, 183
Genetic engineers, 526
Genetics, 93–94, 178–83
     classical, 178–79
     modern, 179–80
     See also Deoxyribonucleic
          acid
GEnie (General Electric
     Network for Information
     Exchange), 512
Genital warts, 189
Geodesy, 3
Geoffroy Saint-Hilaire, Étienne,
     138
Geological engineers, 526
Geologic time, 78, 387–88
Geology
     branches of, 376
     definition of, 376
     symbols for maps, 59

Geometric shapes, 32–33
    formulas for, 33–34
Geometry, 506
Geostationary satellites, 450
Geothermal energy, 486
Gerard, John, 138
German measles. *See* Rubella
Gesner, Conrad, 138
Geysers, 415
Giaever, Ivar, 623
Giauque, William, 617
Gibbs, Josiah, 261
Gilbert, Grove Karl, 408
Gilbert, Walter, 618
Gilbert, William, 408
Gill, Sir David, 357
Gill, Theodore Nicholas, 138
Gilman, Alfred, 630
Girder, 547
Glacier, 415
Glaser, Donald, 304, 622
Glashow, Sheldon, 281, 624
Glass, 236
Glauber, Johann, 261
Glaucoma, 197
Glaze, 440
Global warming, 480–81
Globular clusters, 342
Glomeruli, 164
Glucagon, 162
Glucocorticoids, 162
Glucose, 147
Glycerol, 159
Glycolysis, 147
Gnawing mammals, 126
Goddard, Robert, 357
Gödel, Kurt, 36
Gödel's proof, 42
Goeppert-Mayer, Maria, 622
Gold, Thomas, 357
Goldmark, Peter, 530
Goldstein, Joseph, 214, 629
Golgi, Camillo, 214, 625
Gonadotropic hormones, 162
Gondwanaland, 380
Gonorrhea, 189
Gould, Benjamin, 357
Gould, Gordon, 529

Gout, 197
Government agencies, 632–33
Gradual evolution, 91
Graham, Thomas, 261
Graham's law, 258
Gram, 6
Grand mal seizures, 196
Grand unified theory (GUT),
    281–82
Granit, Ragnar, 628
Graph, 42
Graphics programs, 504
Graphics tablet, 499, 504
Graphic symbol, 46
Grassi, Giovanni Battista, 138
Grasslands, 466, 467
Grassmann, Hermann Günther,
    36
Gravitational collapse, 310
Gravitational lensing, 316
Gravity and gravitation, 281,
    282
    constant acceleration due
        to, 273
    definition of, 272
    general theory of relativity,
        280–81
    Newton's universal law of,
        277
    waves, 278
Greek alphabet, 48–49
Green, George, 36
Green algae, 108
Greenhouse effect, 480–81
Greenstein, Jesse, 357
Greenwich Mean Time, 82
Gregorian calendar, 78–80
Gregory, James, 357
Gregory XIII (pope), 79
Grew, Nehemiah, 138
Grignard, Victor, 615
Grimaldi, Francesco, 304
Groundwater, 415
Growth hormone, 162
Guanine, 180
Guillaume, Charles, 620
Guillemin, Roger, 628
Gullstrand, Allvar, 625

GUT. *See* Grand unified theory
Gutenberg, Beno, 408
Gutenberg, Johannes, 530
Gutenberg discontinuity, 377
Gymnosperm, 107, 147
Gynecologist, 184
Gyroscope, 310

H

Haber, Fritz, 261, 615
Habitat, 492
Haboob, 425
Hadley, George, 423, 452
Hadley cells, 423
Hadron, 298
Haeckel, Ernst, 458
Hahn, Otto, 261, 616
Hahnemann, Samuel, 204
Hail, 440, 455
Halberg, Frans, 68
Hale, George Ellery, 357
Hales, Stephen, 138
Half-life, 255, 256, 296
Hall, Asaph, 357
Hall, James (1761–1832), 409
Hall, James (1811–1898), 408
Halley, Edmund, 357
Hallucination, 209
Halo, 442
Hamilton, Sir William Rowan,
    37
Han-ch'ing. *See* Chu
    Shih-Chieh
Hansen, Armauer, 214
Hansen's disease. *See* Leprosy
Hard disk drive, 500
Harden, Sir Arthur, 616
Hard water, 232–33
Hardy, Godfrey Harold, 37
Hares, 125
Hariot (Harriot), Thomas, 37
Hartline, Haldan, 628
Harvey, William, 214
Hashimoto, Hakaru, 214
Hassel, Odd, 618

Hauptman, Herbert, 619
Hawking, Stephen, 278, 357
Haworth, Sir Walter, 616
HDL. *See* High-density lipo-
protein
Health. *See* Medicine and health
Hearing, 168
Heart, 163, 164
cardiac problems, 192–93
Heart attack. *See* Myocardial
infarction
Heartburn, 197
Heart rate, 163
Heat
definition of, 282
entropy, 284
See also Thermodynamics
Heat index chart, 433
Heavy lepton, 298
Hebrew calendar, 78–79
Hecataeus, 529
Heidenhain, Rudolf, 214
Heisenberg, Werner, 302, 304,
621
Heisenberg's uncertainty
principle, 233, 258, 296,
301–2
Helmholtz, Hermann, 304
Hemoglobin, 152
Hemophilia, 155, 191
Hemorrhoids, 197
Hench, Philip, 627
Henry, Joseph, 304
Henry I (king of England), 2
Hepatitis, 187
Herb, 117–18
Herbivore, 96
Heredity. *See* Genetics
Hernia, 197
Hero of Alexandria, 37
Herophilus of Chalcedon, 214
Herpes simplex, 187–88
Herpes zoster. *See* Chicken pox
Herschbach, Dudley, 619
Herschel, Caroline, 357
Herschel, Sir John, 342, 357
Herschel, Sir William, 342, 357
Hershey, Alfred, 628

Hertz, Gustav, 620
Hertz, Heinrich, 304
Hertzsprung, Ejnar, 357
Hertzsprung-Russell diagram,
337
Herzberg, Gerhard, 618
Hess, Germain Henri, 261
Hess, Harry Hammond, 409
Hess, Victor, 621
Hess, Walter, 627
Hess's law, 259
Heterogeneous mixtures, 228
Heterosphere, 420, 421
Heterotroph, 96
Hevelius, Johannes, 357
Hewish, Antony, 357, 623
Hexagon, 34
Heymans, Corneille, 626
Heyrovsky, Jaroslav, 617
Higgins, William, 261
Higgs particle, 298
High blood pressure, 197
High-density lipoprotein (HDL),
159
High-level languages, 506,
507–8
High-performance computers,
505–6
Hill, Sir Archibald, 625
Hinshel Wood, Sir Cyril, 617
Hipparchus, 357
Hippocrates of Cos, 215
Hitchings, George, 629
HIV. *See* Human immuno-
deficiency virus
Hoarfrost, 441
Hodgkin, Dorothy Crowfoot,
261, 617
Hodgkin, Sir Alan, 628
Hoffmann, Roald, 618
Hofstadter, Robert, 304, 622
Hollerith, Herman, 497, 513
Holley, Robert, 628
Holmes, Arthur, 409
Holography, 529
Homeopathy, 204
Homeostasis, 221
Hominoids, 404, 407, 415

Homo erectus, 405, 406
Homogeneous mixtures, 228
Homo habilis, 404–6
Homo neanderthalensis. See
Neanderthals
Homo sapiens, 405, 406
Hooke, Robert, 304, 358
Hooker, Sir Joseph Dalton, 138
Hooker, Sir William Jackson,
138
Hopkins, Sir Frederick, 626
Hopper, Grace Murray, 513
Hormonal system, 161–63
Hormones
definition of, 161, 221
major, 162–63
Horrocks, Jeremiah, 358
Horton, Robert, 409
Hot subdwarfs, 338
Hot vents, 396
Hounsfield, Sir Godfrey, 629
Hour, 73–74
Houssay, Bernardo, 627
Howard, Luke, 435, 452
Hoyle, Sir Fred, 358
Hubble, Edwin, 315, 358
Hubble constant, 315–16
Hubble Space Telescope, 351
Hubel, David, 629
Huber, Robert, 619
Huggins, Charles, 628
Hull, Albert, 529
Hulse, Russel, 625
Human body
nonblood components and
needs of, 156–60
systems, 161–77
See also Blood; Organ
Human immunodeficiency virus
(HIV), 187
Human papillomavirus, 189
Humboldt, Alexander, 409
Humidity, 433–34, 455
Humus, 147
Huntington's disease, 191
Hurricanes, 445
major, 446–47
names for, 447

(continued)

Hurricanes *(cont.)*
  Saffir-Simpson damage
    potential scale, 448
Hussey, Joseph, 342
Hutton, James, 409
Huxley, Sir Andrew Fielding,
  215
Huygens, Christiaan, 358
Hydrocarbons, 249–50, 492
Hydrogen
  bonding, 247
  as gasoline alternative, 487
Hydrometeors, 438
Hydrophobia. *See* Rabies
Hydropower, 486
Hydrothermal vents, 89
Hylonomus, 123
Hypatia, 37
Hypertension, 197
Hyperthyroidism, 197
Hypotension, 198
Hypothalamic-releasing/
  inhibiting hormones, 162
Hypothyroidism, 197
Hyracoidae (order), 125
Hyraxes, 125

I

Ice, 389, 440–41
  air bubbles in, 482
  crystals, 443
Ice age, 415
Icon, 46
Ideogram, 46
IgE. *See* Immunoglobulin E
IgG. *See* Immunoglobulin G
IgM. *See* Immunoglobulin M
Igneous rocks, 385–86
Imaginary numbers, 29
Immune system, 174, 221
Immunization, 221
Immunoglobulin E (IgE), 194
Immunoglobulin G (IgG), 194
Immunoglobulin M (IgM), 194
Incandescence, 288
Inch, decimal equivalents of
  fractions for, 30–31

Incineration, 486
Incomplete dominance, 179
Incontinence, 197
Index of refraction, 289
Indicators, chemical, 253
Industrial engineers, 526–27
Inertia, 272, 274, 275
Infantile paralysis. *See* Polio
Infarction. *See* Myocardial
  infarction
Infectious mononucleosis. *See*
  Mononucleosis
Inflationary universe model, 315
Influenza, 188
Infrared Astronomical Satellite,
  347
Infrasonic pitch, 17
Ink jet printers, 503
Inoculation, 221
Insect-eaters, 125
Insectivora (order), 125
Insects, diseases borne by,
  200–201
Instinct, 147
Insulators, 292, 547
Insulin, 162, 183
Intensity, sound, 290
Interference
  measurement of, 23
  wave, 287
Interferometer, 23, 310, 346
Interferon, 221
Internal reflection, 289–90
International Date Line, 82
International nautical mile, 2
International System of Units.
  See SI system
Internet, 512
Interplanetary dust, 330
Interstitial cystitis, 197
Inventions, table of significant,
  531–45
Invertebrate, 120–22
In vitro, 221
In vivo, 221
Involuntary muscle, 166
Iodine, 157
Ion, 231–32
Ionic bond, 246

Ionosphere, 421, 422
Iron (body mineral), 157
Irrational number, 29
Irreversible cell battery. *See* Dry
  cell battery
Isotope, 202, 255, 296

J

Jacob, François, 628
Jacquard, Joseph-Marie, 497,
  513, 528
Jansky, Karl, 346, 358
Janssen, Hans, 529
Janssen, Pierre, 358
Janssen, Zacharias, 529
Jastrow, Robert, 358
Jeans, Sir James, 358
Jeffreys, Sir Harold, 358
Jenner, Edward, 215
Jensen, J. Hans, 622
Jerne, Niels, 629
Jet lag, 69
Jet streams, 429
Jobs, Steven, 513
Johanson, Don, 407
Joliot, Frederic, 255, 304, 616
Joliot-Curie, Irene, 255, 304,
  616
Josephson, Brian, 623
Joule, James, 283, 304
Joystick, 519
Julian calendar, 79
Jung, Carl Gustav, 215
Jupiter (planet), 17, 320–23, 352
Jussieu, Antoine Laurent de, 138
Juvenile rheumatoid arthritis,
  192

K

Kamerlingh-Onnes, Heike, 620
Kapitsa, Peter, 623
Karle, Jerome, 619
Karrer, Paul, 616
Kastler, Alfred, 623
Katz, Sir Bernard, 628

Kellner, Karl, 260
Kelvin (temperature), 7
Kelvin, Baron. *See* Thomson,
    William
Kelvin scale, 283
Kemeny, John, 507
Kendall, Edward, 627
Kendall, Henry, 624
Kendrew, Sir John, 617
Kepler, Johannes, 277, 324, 342,
    358
Kernighan, Brian, 507
Kerr, Roy Patrick, 305
Keyboard, computer, 498, 499
Khorana, Har Gobind, 628
Kidney, 164
        stones, 197
Killer bee, 121
Kilogram, 6, 7
Kilowatt, 293
Kinetic energy, 276, 303
Kinetics, chemical, 245
Kingdom (organism classifica-
    tion), 94–100
Kingdom Animalia, 96
Kingdom Archaebacteria, 96,
    100
Kingdom Fungi, 96, 100
Kingdom Monera, 96, 98–99
Kingdom Plantae, 96
Kingdom Prokaryotae, 96
Kingdom Protista, 96, 100
Kirchhoff, Gustav Robert, 305
Kirkwood, Daniel, 358
Kitasato, Baron Shibasaburo,
    215
Klug, Aaron, 619
Knight, Andrew, 138
Koch, Robert, 625
Kocher, Emil, 625
Köhler, Georges, 629
Kolbe, Adolph, 261
Köppen, Wladimir, 452
Kornberg, Arthur, 627
Kossel, Albrecht, 625
Krebs, Edwin, 629
Krebs, Sir Hans, 627
Krogh, Schack, 625
Kuhn, Richard, 616

Kuiper, Gerard, 358
Kuiper Belt, 359
Kurtz, Thomas, 507
Kusch, Polykarp, 622

L

Lacunar infarction, 199
Lagomorpha (order), 125
Lagrange, Joseph Louis, 358
Lakes, largest, 373
Lamarck, Jean Baptiste, 139
Lamb, Sir Horace, 37
Lamb, Willis, 622
Lambert, Johann Heinrich, 37
Lamp, 529
LAN. *See* Local access network
Land, Edwin, 305
Landau, Lev, 622
Land breeze, 424–25
Landfills, 477, 478
Landsteiner, Karl, 626
Langley, Samuel Pierpont,
    528
Langmuir, Irving, 261, 616
Language interpretation,
    computer, 510
Lanthanoid, 239
Laparoscopy, 202
Laplace, Pierre Simon de, 358
Laptop computer, 504
Large intestine, 166
Larmor, Sir Joseph, 305
Lartet, Édouard, 409
Larva, 147
Larynx, 174
Lasers, 529
        optical disks, 500
        printers, 503
        surgery, 202
        workings of, 301
Latitude, 81
Laurasia, 380
Lava dome, 393
Laveran, Charles, 625
Lavoisier, Antoine, 226, 261
Law of Conservation of Energy,
    259

Law of Conservation of Mass,
    259
Law of Conservation of
    Momentum, 275–76
Law of Constant Acceleration,
    275
Law of Constant Proportions,
    259
Law of Inertia, 275
Law of Multiple Proportions,
    259
Law of Octaves, 259
Lawrence, Ernest, 305, 621
Laxative, 221
LCD. *See* Liquid crystal display
LDL. *See* Low-density lipo-
    protein
Lead, 470, 475, 479
Lead storage battery, 254, 254
Leaf, 105
        cross-section, 107
Leakey, Louis, 409
Leakey, Mary, 409
Leakey, Richard, 409
Leap second, 80
Leap year, 81
Leavitt, Henrietta, 359
Le Chatelier, Henri Louis, 261
Le Chatelier's principle, 259
Lederberg, Joshua, 627
Lederman, Leon, 305, 624
Lee, Tsung-Dao, 622
Lee, Yuan, 619
Leeuwenhoek, Anton van, 139,
    529
Legendre, Adrien-Marie, 37
Lehn, Jean-Marie, 619
Leibniz, Gottfried Wilhelm von,
    37, 497, 514
Leith, Emmet, 529
Leloir, Luis, 618
Lenard, Philipp, 619
Length
        definition of, 4, 6
        U.S.-SI equivalents, 8
Leonardo of Pisa. *See* Fibonacci,
    Leonardo
Leopold, Aldo, 489
Leprosy, 188

Lepton, 298
Letters, Greek and Roman used in science, 48–50
Leuckart, Karl Georg, 139
Leukemia, 155
Leukocytes. *See* White blood cells
Leverrier, Urbain, 359
Levi-Montalcini, Rita, 629
Lewis, Gilbert, 261
Lexis/Nexis, 512
Libavius, 226
Libby, Willard, 617
Life
    building blocks of, 89
    definition of, 88
    "new" under sea, 88–89
    and space connection, 90
    theories of origin of, 89–90
Life span
    of animals, 131
    expectancy tables by race, sex, and age, 205–6
    human, 161
Ligament, 174
Light
    definition of, 287–88
    electric, 529
    pollution, 475
    reflection and refraction, 288–90
    speed of, 279–80
    waves, 287–90
Lightning, 444–45
Lindemann, Carl Louis Ferdinand von, 37
Linear measurement, 5, 7–8
Line printers, 503
Lines of force, 293, 294, 371
Link, Edwin, 529
Linnaeus, Carolus, 95, 139
Liouville, Joseph, 37
Lipids, 89, 159, 221
Lipmann, Fritz, 627
Lipoprotein, 159–60
Lipoprotein-a (Lp-a), 160

Lippershey, Hans, 530
Lippmann, Gabriel, 620
Lipscomb, William, 618
Liquid crystal display (LCD), 498, 519
Liquid crystal shutter printer, 503
Liquids, 235
    density of, 237
LISP (programming language), 507, 510
Literal numbers, 29
Lithosphere, 377, 379
Lithotripsy, 203
Liver, 187
Local access network (LAN), 508
Local Group (galaxies), 341
Loewi, Otto, 626
Logarithm, 23
Long (cortical) bones, 174
Longitude, 81
Longitudinal waves, 286
Lorenz, Konrad, 139, 628
Lorentz, Hendirk, 619
Loudness, 17–18, 290
Lovell, Sir Bernard, 359
Low blood pressure, 198
Low-density lipoprotein (LDL), 159
Lowell, Percival, 359
Lp-a. *See* Lipoprotein-a
Lubricant, 547
"Lucy" (fossil skeleton), 407
Lumen, 221
Luminescence, 102, 288. *See also* Bioluminescence
Lunar eclipse, 334–35
Lunar halo, 442
Lungs, 173–74
Lupus, 192, 193
Luria, Salvador, 628
L-waves, 389
Lwoff, André, 628
Lyell, Sir Charles, 376, 409
Lyme disease, 200
Lymphatic system, 174, 176

Lymphocytes, 153, 174
Lynen, Feodor, 628

M

MacArthur, Robert, 489
Mach, Ernst, 305
Machine language, 506
Machines
    basic, 528
    definition of, 547
MACHOs. *See* Massive compact halo objects
Macleod, John James, 626
Magma, 415
Magnetic disk, 499
Magnetic field, 293–94, 371, 380
Magnetic force lines. *See* Lines of force
Magnetic moment of the particle, 297
Magnetic resonance imaging (MRI), 203
Magnetic tape, 499
Magnetism, 293–94, 382
    See also Electromagnetism
Magnetopause, 371
Magnetosphere, 371
Magnetron, 529
Magnitude, 42, 415
Maiman, Theodore, 529
Mainframe computer, 505
Major depression, 210
Malaria, 200
Male reproductive system, 171
Malnutrition, 198
Malocclusion, 221
Malpighi, Marcello, 139, 215
Malthus, Thomas, 489
Mammalia (class), 123
Mammals
    endangered, 134
    extinct, 133
    gestation periods, 127–28
    orders of, 124–26

records set by, 130
subclasses of, 126
Mammography, 203
Manatees, 126
Manganese, 157
Manic depression. *See* Bipolar
    disorder
Manic syndrome, 210
Mantell, Gideon, 409
Mantissa, 3
Mantle, of Earth, 377
Maps, 529
    geological symbols, 59
    topographical symbols, 61
Marbut, Curtis, 409
Marconi, Guglielmo, 530, 620
Marcus, Rudolph, 619
Marine ecology, 460
Marine life
    and hot vents, 396
    invertebrates, 121
    See also Fish
Marine science. *See* Oceans
Mars (planet), 320–23, 330, 352
Marsh, George, 489
Marsh, Othniel, 409
Marsupials, 126
Martin, Archer, 617
Mass
    definition of, 4, 272
    distribution in solar system,
        318
    energy equivalent of, 280
    measurement of, 18–19
    in SI system, 7
    U.S.-SI equivalents, 9
Massage, 204
Mass extinction, 92
Massive compact halo objects
    (MACHOs), 316
Massive parallel processing, 506
Mass number, 231
Materials engineers, 527
Mathematics
    common terms in, 40–43
    major mathematicians,
        35–38

and measurement, 28–32
scientific publications,
    636–37
significant discoveries,
    39–40
signs and symbols, 51–53
See also Numbers
Matter, 228, 230, 235
    physical properties of,
        236–37
Mauchly, J.W., 513
Maury, Matthew, 410
Maxwell, James Clerk, 281, 294,
    305
Maya calendar, 78
Mayr, Ernst Walter, 139
McCarthy, John, 507, 510
McClintock, Barbara, 629
McMillan, Edwin, 617
Mean sidereal day, 71–72
Mean solar day, 71
Measles, 188
Measurement, 1–44
    of astronomical distances,
        27–28
    common terms in, 40–43
    definition of, 42
    early, 2–3
    electrical, 293
    importance to science, 2
    of logarithms, 23
    and mathematics, 28–32
    of molecules, 235
    scientific scales, 20–22
    significant discoveries in,
        39–40
    SI system, 6–8
    of speed, 20
    of temperature, 23–27
    U.S. conventional system,
        5–6
    U.S.-SI conversion tables,
        10–15
    U.S.-SI equivalents, 8–9
Mechanical energy, 277
Mechanical engineer, 527
Meckel, Johan Friedrich
    (1724–1774), 215

Meckel, Johann Friedrich
    (1781–1833), 215
Mecnikov, Ilja, 625
Medawar, Sir Peter, 627
Medicine and health
    and air pollution, 470–71
    chronic diseases, 192–93
    common terms, 219–23
    communicable diseases,
        187–90
    disease carriers in blood,
        155–56
    hereditary/genetic diseases,
        190–91
    invasive laboratory
        techniques, 201–2
    major scientists, 212–17
    methods for maintaining
        health, 204
    miscellaneous problems,
        193–200
    Nobel Prize awards, 625–30
    noninvasive laboratory
        techniques, 202–3
    significant discoveries,
        217–19
    types of providers, 184–86
    and water pollution, 474–75
    *See also specific diseases and
        conditions*
Meditation, 204
Megachannel Extraterrestrial
    Assay (META), 354
Megaloblastic anemia, 155
Meiosis, 147, 180
Meitner, Lise, 243
Melanoma, 177
Melatonin, 162
Melting point, 235
Memory, computer, 500, 503
Menaquinone. *See* Vitamin K
Mendel, Gregor, 93–94, 139,
    178
Mendeléev, Dmitri, 238, 262
Meningitis, 188
Menopause, 172
Menstruation, 172

Mercalli, Giuseppe, 390, 410
Mercalli scale, 390, 410
Mercury (metal), 242
Mercury (planet), 281, 320–22, 351
Mercury missions, 349
Mergenthaler, Ottmar, 530
Meridian, 81
Merrifield, Robert, 619
Mersenne, Marin, 30
Mersenne primes, 30
Meson, 298
Mesosphere, 420, 421
Mesozoic era, 388
Messenger RNA, 183
Messier, Charles, 342, 359
META. *See* Megachannel Extraterrestrial Assay
Metabolism, 222
Metallic bonding, 247
Metallurgical engineer, 527
Metallurgy, 527
Metals
    alloys, 242, 546
    noble, 242
    in Periodic Table, 240–41
    properties of, 241
    trace, 494
Metamorphic rock, 385–86
Metastasis, 222
Meteor, 328–29
Meteorite, 329–30
Meteoroid, 328
Meteorology
    common terms in, 454–56
    definition of, 420
    major meteorologists, 451–54
    scientific organizations, 631
    scientific publications, 635–36
    significant discoveries, 453–54
    symbols for, 62–63
    See also Weather; *specific weather conditions*
Meter, 6, 7
Methane, 100, 481

Metric scale, 21
Metric system, 6–8
Meyer, Lothar, 238
Meyerhof, Otto, 625
Michel, Harmut, 619
Michelson, Albert, 305, 620
Microbiology, 88
Microburst, 426, 444
Microcomputers. *See* Personal computers
Microgravity, 279
Microlensing, 316
Micrometer, 22
Microorganism, 147
Microphone, 547
Microscope, 529
Migraines, 193
Mile, 2
Milky Way, 340, 341, 371
Miller, Stanley, 90, 139
Miller, William Hallowes, 410
Millikan, Robert, 620
Milne, John, 410
Milstein, César, 629
Mineralocorticoids, 162
Minerals
    crystals, 382–84
    hardness, 382, 384, 415
    for health, 157
    properties of, 382
Mines, deepest, 378
Minicomputers, 504
Mining engineer, 528
Minkowski, Hermann, 37
Minot, George, 626
Minute, 74
Mir space station, 349
Mistral, 425
Mitchell, Peter, 618
Mitosis, 147, 180
Mixed number, 29
Mixture, 228
Möbius, August Ferdinand, 37
Modem, 501
Modern physics, 272
Mohammed, 79
Mohl, Hugo von, 139
Mohorovičić, Andrija, 410

Mohorovičić discontinuity, 377
Mohs, Friedrich, 384, 410
Mohs hardness scale, 384
Moissan, Henri, 615
Molar mass, 235
Mole (measurement), 7, 235
Molecule, 235
Mollusks, 121–22
Momentum, 274, 275
Monera, 96, 98–99
Monitor, computer, 498
Moniz, Antonio de Egas, 627
Monod, Jacques, 628
Monomer, 251
Mononucleosis, 188
Monosaccharide, 89
Monotremata (subclass), 126
Monsoon, 425
Month, 70–71
Montlivault, Sales-Guyon de, 90
Mood disorders, 209–10
Moon
    Apollo missions to, 332, 348–49
    and calendar, 78, 79
    eclipse, 334–35
    effect on Earth, 76
    faces of, 332
    orbit around Earth, 331
    origin of, 331
    phases of, 333
    probes to, 333
    statistics on, 330–31
    and tides, 76, 400
Moore, Stanford, 618
Morgan, Thomas Hunt, 626
Morley, Edward, 305
Morse, Samuel Finley Breese, 530
Moseley, Henry, 238
Mössbauer, Rudolf, 622
Motion, 273–76
    Kepler's laws of planetary, 324
    Newton's laws, 275–76
Motor, 547
Mott, Sir Nevill, 623

Mountain, 468
    definition of, 415
    peaks, 375
    See also Volcanoes
Mount Pinatubo, 394, 483
Mouse, computer, 498–99
MRI. *See* Magnetic resonance
    imaging
Muir, John, 489
Muller, Hermann Joseph, 626
Müller, Johann, 37
Müller, Johannes Peter, 215
Muller, K. Alexander, 624
Müller, Paul Hermann, 489, 627
Mulliken, Robert, 618
Mullis, Kary, 619
Multimedia, 511
Multimeter, 22
Multiple bonding, chemical, 247
Multiple personality disorder,
    211
Mumps, 188
Mu-neutrino, 298
Muon, 298
Murchison, Sir Roderick, 410
Murphy, William Parry, 626
Murray, Joseph, 629
Muscle system, 166–67
Muscular dystrophy, 191
Museums, by state, 550–80
Muslim calendar, 78–79
Mycology, 88
Myocardial infarction, 193
Myopia, 198

N

Nanotechnology, 531
Napier, John, 38, 497
Napier's bones, 497
Narcotics, 222
Nathans, Daniel, 629
National parks, by state, 592–97
Natural logarithms, 23
Natural numbers, 29
Natural wonders, 376
Nature, preservation of, 487–88

Naturopathologist, 184
Naturopathy, 204
Naudin, Charles, 139
Nausea, 222
Nautical distance, 9
Nautical mile, 2
Navel orange, 110
Neanderthals, 405, 406
Neap tide, 400–401
Nebular (centrifugal-force)
    hypothesis, 317
Nebulas, 342
Needham, John, 139
Néel, Louis, 623
Negative number, 29
Neher, Erwin, 629
Neptune (planet), 320–22, 324,
    353
Nernst, Walther, 262, 616
Nerve, 222
Nervous system, 167–71
Net electric charge, 231
Neural network, 510
Neuron, 222
Neuroses, 210–11
Neurotransmitter, 222
Neutralization, chemical, 253
Neutrino, 298–99
Neutron, 230, 295, 298
Neutron-induced reactions, 299
Neutron star, 338
Newlands, John, 262
Newlands's law, 259
NewsNet, 512
Newton, Sir Isaac, 275, 277, 305
Niacin, 158
Nicolle, Charles, 626
Niepce, Joseph, 529
Nimbostratus clouds, 436, 437
Nitrates, 475
Nitrogen cycle, 458, 460
Nitrogen oxides, 470, 481
Nitroglycerin, 222
NMR. *See* Magnetic resonance
    imaging
Nobel, Alfred, 262, 614
Nobel Prize, 614
    in chemistry, 615–19
    in physics, 619–25

    in physiology or medicine,
        625–30
Noble gases, 242
Noctilucent clouds, 435
Noise pollution, 475
Nondisjunction, 191
Noniconic sign, 46
Nonmetals, 241
Nonruminators, 124
Nonsteroidal anti-inflammatory
    drugs (NSAIDs), 222
Noradrenaline, 162
Nor'easter, 425
Norepinephrine, 162
Norrish, Ronald, 618
North celestial pole, 370
Northern Hemisphere
    constellations, 336
    sun and seasons, 75, 370
    telescopes in, 344
Northrop, John, 617
Notebook computer, 504
"Not in my backyard" syndrome,
    478
Nova, 338
NSAIDs. *See* Nonsteroidal
    anti-inflammatory drugs
Nuclear fusion. *See* Fusion
Nuclear physics, 299–300
Nuclear power, 486
Nuclear reactions, 299–300
Nuclear waste, 478–79
Nucleic acids, 89
Nucleotides, 90, 180
Numbers
    evolution of, 28
    naming, 29
    scientific notation, 3–4
    symbols for prefixes, 51
Nutation, 416
Nutrient cycle, 493

O

Obesity, 198
Obliquity of the ecliptic, 370
Observatories, by state, 550–80

Obsessive-compulsive disorder, 211
Occluded front, 429, 430
Occupational safety and health specialists, 528
Oceans, 395
    composition of sea water, 396–97
    features, 399
    hot vents, 396
    hydrothermal vents, 89
    life in, 396
    need for, 395
    "new" life under, 88–89
    planetary, 400
    shoreline, 397
    statistics on, 395–96
    surface currents, 398
    zones, 399
Ochoa, Severo, 627
Octagon, 34
Ohm (unit), 18, 292
Ohm, Georg, 305
Ohm's law, 293
Olah, George, 619
Olds, Ransom Eli, 528
Olfactory system, 168, 170
Oliphant, Sir Mark, 305
Omar Khayyám, 38
Omnivore, 96
On-line data services, 511–12
Onsager, Lars, 618
Oort, Jan Hendrik, 359
Oort Cloud, 359
Open cluster, 342
Open universe model, 315
Operating system, computer, 500
Oppenheimer, Julius, 305
Optical disk, 500
Optical fiber links. See Fiber optics
Optical scanner, 501
Oranges, 110
Orbital model, 233
Orbits, 278–79
Oresme, Nicolas, 38

Organ
    definition of, 160
    transplants, 203
Organic chemistry, 249–51
Organisms
    classification of, 94–95
    composition of, 101
    and ecology, 461
    evolutionary relationships, 95
    evolution of, 93
    five-kingdom classification, 97–98
    groups of, 96
    luminescence, 102, 288
    See also Extinction
Oscillating universe model, 315
Osmosis, 148
Osteichthyes, 123
Osteoarthritis, 192
Osteopathy, 204
Osteoporosis, 198
Ostwald, Friedrich Wilhelm, 262, 615
Oughtred, William, 38
Overpopulation, 484
Ovulation, 172
Owen, Sir Richard, 410
Oxidation-reduction reactions, 248
Oxygen atom, 231
Oxygen cycle, 458, 460
Oxytocin, 163
Ozone, 471, 481, 482–84
Ozonosphere, 420, 421, 483

P

Pacioli, Luca, 38
Pad computer. See Graphics tablet
Pain, 222
Pain oncology nursing, 204
Palade, George, 628
Paleontology, 401
    symbols, 60

Paleozoic era, 388
Palmtop computer, 504
Panagea, 380
Pandemic, 222
Pangolin, 126
Panspermia, 90
Pantothenic acid, 158
Papanicolaou, George, 215
Pappus of Alexandria, 38
Paracelsus, 226
Parallel port, 500
Parallels, 42, 81
Parasites, 96
Parathormone, 163
Parhelia, 442
Parkes, Alexander, 530
Parkinson, James, 215
Parkinson's disease, 198
Parks, national, by state, 592–97
Partial eclipse, 334
Particle accelerator, 297
Particles, 295–99
    in space, 328, 330
    subatomic, 230, 297–98
    water pollutants, 472
Particulate matter, 471
Pascal (programming language), 507
Pascal, Blaise, 38, 497, 507, 513
Paschen, Louis, 306
Pasteur, Louis, 215
Pathogen, 222
Paul, Wolfgang, 624
Pauli, Wolfgang, 302, 306, 621
Pauli exclusion principle, 302
Pauling, Linus, 262, 617
Pavlov, Ivan, 215, 625
Payne-Gaposchkin, Cecilia, 359
PCs. See Personal computers
Pearson, Allen, 449
Pedersen, Charles, 619
Peltier effect, 547
Pelvic inflammatory disease (PID), 189
Penck, Albrecht, 410
Penck, Walther, 410
Penicillin, 222

Penrose, Roger, 38
Pentagon, 34
Penumbral eclipse, 334
Penzias, Arno, 314, 623
Peptide, 222
Percent
    definition of, 43
    equivalents of common
        fractions, 30
    measuring in solution, 4
Perfect (ideal) gas law, 259
Perfect number, 29
Perihelion, 369
Perimeter, formulas for finding,
    34
Period (sound wave), 285
Period (table of elements), 238,
    239–40
Periodic law, 238
Periodic Table of the Elements,
    226
    definition of, 238
    divisions of, 239
    groups of, 238, 240–42
    history of, 238
    Mendeléev's version, 238,
        239
    periods of, 238, 239–40
Peripheral nervous system, 167
Perissodactyla (order), 126
Peristalsis, 222
Perkin, Sir William Henry, 262
Perrin, Jean Baptiste, 620
Personal computers, 498–505
Pertussis. *See* Whooping cough
Perutz, Max, 617
Petit mal seizure, 196
Petroleum engineer, 528
PET (or PETT) scan, 202
Phagocyte, 153, 174
Phagocytosis, 186
Phenomena, measurement of, 2
Pheresis, 154
Philipp, Ferdinand Ludwig. *See*
    Cantor, Georg
Phlebitis, 198
Phobias, 211–12

Pholidata (order), 126
Phonograph records, 530
Phosphorescence, 288
Photoelectric effect, 300
Photography, 529–30
Photolithography, 531
Photon, 298, 301
Photosphere, 319
Photosynthesis, 110, 148, 493
pH scale, 252–53
Phylum Annelida, 120
Phylum Arthropoda, 121
Phylum Coelenterata, 121
Phylum Echinodermata, 121
Phylum Mollusca, 121–22
Phylum Nematoda, 122
Phylum Platyhelminthes, 122
Phylum Porifera, 122
Physical anthropology, 404
Physical laws, 2, 310
Physics
    of atom, 295
    basic forces in nature,
        281–82
    branches of, 272
    common terms, 309–12
    definition of, 272
    Einstein's relativity theories,
        279–81
    grand unified theories,
        281–82
    major physicists, 302–7
    Nobel Prize awards, 619–25
    nuclear, 299–300
    quantum, 300–302
    scientific organizations, 631
    scientific publications, 636
    significant discoveries,
        307–9
    symbols in, 59
    work and energy, 276–77
    See also Gravity and
        gravitation; Motion
Phytoplankton, 108
Piazzi, Giuseppe, 359
Piccard, Auguste, 452
Pickering, Edward, 359

Pickering, William, 359
PID. *See* Pelvic inflammatory
    disease
Piezoelectric effect, 310
Pikas, 125
Pinchot, Gifford, 489
Pinnipeda (order), 126
Pion, 298
Pitch, 17, 290, 291
Pitcher plant, 109
Plages, 319
Planck, Max, 300, 306, 620
Planck's constant, 302
Planetariums, by state, 550–80
Planetary nebulas, 342
Planetary winds, 423–24
Planets, 320
    distances from Sun, 321
    Kepler's laws of motion, 324
    oceans on, 400
    particles between, 330
    in relation to Earth, 322
    satellites of, 323–24
    size comparisons, 322
    statistics on, 321
    unmanned spacecraft to,
        351–53
    See also specific planets
Plants
    botanical names of, 110–14
    categories of, 108
    definition of, 104
    distinguished from animals,
        101
    flowering, 106, 107–8
    germination tables, 119
    growth of, 105
    land, 107–8
    life cycle, 108
    meat-eating, 109
    parts of, 105–6
    photosynthesis, 110, 148,
        493
    poisonous, 115–17
    and pollution, 114–15
    reproduction, 101, 109
    symbols for, 54

(continued)

Plants (*cont.*)
    time period of existence,
      104–5
    typical cell, 103
    water, 108
    See also Botany
Plaque, 159–60, 222
Plasma, 152, 236
Platelets, 153, 154, 186
Plate tectonics, 379–80
Playfair, John, 410
Pliny the Elder, 452
Pliny the Younger, 410
Pluto (planet), 320–22, 324
Pneumonia, 188
Poison
    animals, 129–30
    definition of toxic
      substance, 493
    plants, 115–17
    toxic air pollutants, 471
Poisson, Siméon, 306
Polanyi, John, 619
Polar cells, 423
Polar coordinates, 15
Polarization, 310
Polio, 188
Pollutant, 470, 493
Pollution, 469
    air, 470–72
    definition of, 493
    and plants, 114–15
    water, 472
Polycythemia, 155
Polygon
    definition of, 32
    names for, 33
Polymer, 251, 530, 547
Polyp, 222
Polypeptide, 222
Polysaccharide, 89
Pons, Jean Louis, 359
Porpoise, 125
Porter, Rodney, 628
Porter, Sir George, 618
Ports, computer, 500
Positive number, 29
Positron, 298

Positron emission transaxial
    tomography (PET or PETT),
    202
Potential energy, 276, 277
Pouched mammal, 126
Powell, Cecil, 621
Powell, John Wesley, 410, 489
Power
    mathematical, 31–312
    measurement of, 6
    in physics, 276
    U.S.-SI equivalents, 9
Power plant mechanics, 525
Prandtl, Ludwig, 306
Precambrian era, 388
Precession of the equinoxes,
    370–71
Precipitation
    definition of, 438, 456
    high and low records, 439
    highest normal in U.S., 440
    liquid, 438–39
    in selected U.S. cities,
      431–33
    symbols for, 62
Precision decisions, 510
Pregl, Fritz, 616
Prelog, Vladimir, 618
Presbyopia, 222
Pressure-point massage. *See*
    Acupressure
Prevailing wind, 424
Priestley, Joseph, 226, 262
Prigogine, Ilya, 618
Primate, 126
Prime Meridian, 81, 82
Prime number, 29, 30
Primordial soup, 90
Pringsheim, Nathanael, 139
Printer, computer, 501, 502–3
Printing, 530
Proboscidea (order), 126
Prochorov, Aleksandre, 622
Prodigy, 512
Products, chemical, 244
Progesterone, 163
Programmed senescence theory,
    161

Programmer-analysts, 526
Programmers, 496, 526
Programming codes, 508
Programming languages, 506,
    507
Programs, computer. *See*
    Software
Prolactin, 163
PROM (programmable read-
    only memory), 503
Prominences (filaments), 319
Prostatitis, 198
Prosthesis, 222
Prosthodontist, 186
Protein, 89, 156, 223
Proteinoid sphere, 91
Protist, 100
Protoavis texensis, 123
Proton, 230, 231, 291, 295
Proton-induced reactions, 300
Protoplanet hypothesis, 317, 368
Protozoa, 100
Proust, Joseph, 259, 262
Proxima Centauri, 340
Psoriasis, 198
Psychiatrist, 186
Psychoses, 209–10
Ptolemy, 359
Puberty, 223
Publications, scientific, 633–37
Puffer fish, 129
Pulley, 547
Pulsar, 338
Punctuated evolution, 91
Purcell, Edward, 622
P-wave, 389
Pyramid, formula for finding
    volume of, 34
Pyridoxine, 158
Pyrite, 91
Pythagoras, 38
Pytheas, 410

Q

Q fever, 200
Quanta, 300

Quantum jump, 301
Quantum-mechanical model, 233
Quantum mechanics, 300–301
Quantum physics, 300–302
Quark, 297, 298
Quasar, 364

R

Rabbit, 125
Rabies, 200
Rabi, Isidor, 621
Radar
    definition of, 547
    for weather watching, 450–51
Radian, 7
Radio
    definition of, 547
    development of, 530
    frequencies, 287
Radioactive dating, 257
Radioactive isotopes, 202, 255
Radioactivity, 255–57, 296
Radiochemistry, 255–57
Radiologist, 186
Radio telescope, 346–47
Radiotherapist, 186
Radon, 479
Rain. *See* Precipitation; Rainstorm
Rainbow, 441–42
Rainforest, 464, 465–66
Rainstorm, 441
Rainwater, James, 623
RAM (random-access memory), 501, 503
Raman, Sir Chandrasekhara, 621
Ramanujan, Srinivasa Aaiyangar, 38
Ramon y Cajal, Santiago, 625
Ramsay, Sir William, 615
Ramsey, Norman, 624
Rare earth series, 239
Rational number, 29

Ray, John, 139
Rayleigh, John, 306, 619
Raynaud, Maurice, 215
Raynaud's disease, 198
Reactant, 244
Reaction, chemical, 244–45
Reaction, in physics, 311
Real number, 29
Réamur, René, 139
Reber, Grote, 346
Recessive characteristics, 94
Recessive genes, 178
Rectangle
    definition of, 32
    formula for finding area of, 33
    formula for finding perimeter of, 34
Rectangular coordinates, 15
Rectangular prism, 32
Rectangular solid, formula for finding volume of, 34
Rectum, 166
Recycling, 477, 484–85
    signs, 64–65
Red algae, 108
Red blood cells, 152
    freezing, 156
Redfield, William, 452
Red giant, 338
Redox reactions. *See* Oxidation-reduction reactions
Red supergiant, 338
Reflection, 288–90, 442
Reflective nebulas, 342
Refraction, 288–89, 441, 442
Refuse, 477
Regional winds, 425–26
Regolith, 386
Reiche, Harald, 90
Reichstein, Tadeus, 627
Relative humidity, 433–34
Relativity theory. *See* Theory of general relativity; Theory of special relativity
Removable cartridges, 499
Renin, 163
Replacement, chemical, 247–48

Reproduction
    animal, 101, 120
    plant, 101, 109
Reproductive system, 171–72
Reptiles, 123–24
    endangered, 135
    extinct, 134
Resonance, 290
Respiratory system, 173–74
Resultant, 274
Retinol. *See* Vitamin A
Reye, Ralph, 215
Rh blood type, 154
Rheostat, 547
Rheumatoid arthritis, 192
Rhinitis, 198
Riboflavin, 158
Ribonucleic acid (RNA),
    and amino acids, 90, 183
    definition of, 182–83
    symbols for, 56
Richards, Dickinson, 627
Richards, Theodore, 615
Richardson, Sir Owen, 306, 621
Richet, Charles, 625
Richter, Burton, 623
Richter, Charles, 390, 410
Richter scale, 390–91
Rickettsal diseases, 200–201
Riemann, Georg Friedrich Bernhard, 38
Rime, 441, 456
Ring of Fire, 393
Ritchie, Dennis, 507
Rivers, 374, 472
RNA. *See* Ribonucleic acid
Robbins, Frederick, 627
Robdell, Martin, 630
Roberts, Richard, 629
Robinson, Sir Robert, 617
Robotics, 510–11, 521
Roche, Édouard, 359
Rocks
    symbols for, 60
    types of, 385–86
Rocky Mountain spotted fever, 201
Rodentia (order), 126

Roentgen, Wilhelm, 255, 306, 619

Rohrer, Heinrich, 624

ROM (read-only memory), 501, 503

Rømer, Ole, 359

Röntgen, Wilhelm. See Roentgen, Wilhelm

Root, plant, 105

Ross, Sir Ronald, 625

Rossby, Carl-Gustaf, 452

Roundworm, 122

Rous, Peyton, 628

Royal Society of London, 226

Rubbia, Carlo, 624

Rubbish, 477

Rubella, 188–89

Ruler (measuring device), 20–21

Rumford, Benjamin, 306

Ruminator, 124

Ruska, Ernst, 306, 624

Russell, Bertrand, 38

Russell, Henry Norris, 359

Rutherford, Daniel, 262

Rutherford, Ernest, 233, 295, 306, 615

Ruzicka, Leopold, 616

Rydberg, Johannes, 306

Ryle, Sir Martin, 623

S

Sabatier, Paul, 615

Sabin, Albert, 215

Sachs, Julius von, 139

Safety engineer, 528

Saffir-Simpson damage potential scale, 44

Sagan, Carl, 359

Sakmanna, Bert, 629

Salam, Abdus, 281, 624

Salamander, 129

Salk, Jonas, 215

Salmon, Daniel Elmer, 216

Salyut space stations, 350

Samuelsson, Bengt, 629

Sanger, Frederick, 617, 618

Santa Ana wind, 425

Sarcoidosis, 198

Sarcoma, 192

Satellites, artificial, 450, 530

Saturated solution, 229

Saturn (planet), 320–23, 352

Savanna, 466–67

Scavenger, 96

Schally, Andrew, 628

Schawlow, Arthur, 624

Scheele, Karl, 226, 262

Schiaparelli, Giovanni, 359

Schizophrenia, 210

Schleiden, Matthias Jakob, 139

Schmidt, Bernhard, 360

Schmidt, Maarten, 360

Schrieffer, J. Robert, 623

Schrödinger, Erwin, 295, 306, 621

Schrödinger's model, 296

Schultze, Max Johann, 139

Schwabe, Heinrich, 319

Schwann, Theodor, 140

Schwartz, Melvin, 624

Schwinger, Julian, 623

Scientific measurement. See Measurement

Scientific method, 2

Scientific notation, 3–4

Scientific scales, 20–22

SCSI. See Small computer system interface

Seaborg, Glenn, 617

Sea breeze, 424–25

Sea-floor spreading, 379, 380

Seal (animal), 126

Search for extraterrestrial intelligence (SETI) program, 354

Seas. See Oceans

Seasons, 74–75, 370

Sea water. See Oceans

Second
definition of, 74
leap second, 80
in SI system, 7

Secondary wind, 424–25

Sedgwick, Adam, 410

Sedimentary rock, 385–86

Seebeck effect, 311

Seed plant, 107

Seeds, 105, 109, 110

Segrè, Emilio, 622

Seismic wave, 389

Seizure, 196

Semenov, Nikolaj, 617

Semiconductor, 242, 292

Semimetal. See Semiconductor

Senses, 167–68

Serial port, 500

SETI. See Search for extra-terrestrial intelligence (SETI) program

Set theory symbols, 53

Sexual disorders, 211

Sexually transmitted diseases (STDs), 189–90

Sexual reproduction
animal, 120
plant, 109

Seyfert, Carl, 360

Shapley, Harlow, 360

Sharp, Phyllip, 629

Shells, electron, 231

Shergotty-Nakhla-Chassigny meteorites, 330

Sherrington, Sir Charles, 626

Shield volcano, 393

Shingles, 190

Shockley, William, 622

Shoemaker, Carolyn, 360

Shoemaker, Eugene, 360

Sholes, Christopher, 530

Short-tailed shrew, 129

Shull, Clifford, 625

Sickle-cell anemia, 155, 191

Sidereal day, 71–72

Sidereal month, 70

Sidereal year, 70

Siderite, 329

Siderolite, 329

SIDS. See Sudden infant death syndrome

Siebold, Karl, 140

Siegbahn, Kai M., 624

Siegbahn, Karl Manne, 620

Sight, 168
Sigmoid colon, 166
Signed number, 29
Signs and symbols
    animal, 54
    astrological, 47
    astronomical, 58
    biomedical, 55
    chemical, 56–58
    definition of, 46
    early, 46–47
    in earth science, 59–61
    electric, 293
    in electrical engineering, 65
    in environmental science,
        64
    mathematical, 51–53
    in meteorology, 62
    number prefixes, 51
    in physics, 58
    plant, 54
Silicon, 242
Silicon chip, 513
Silviculture, 493
Simulators, flight, 529
Sine wave, 284
Sinusitis, 198
Siple, Paul A., 427
Sirenia (order), 126
Sirocco, 425
SI system, 6–8
Skeletal muscle. *See* Voluntary
    muscle
Skeletal system, 174, 175
Skin, 174, 177
    cancer, 177
Skull, 406
Sky, 422
Skylab, 350
Sleeping sickness. *See* Encepha-
    litis
Sleet, 441
Small computer system interface
    (SCSI), 500
Small intestine, 166
Smallpox, 190
Smell, 168
Smith, Hamilton, 629

Smith, William, 410
Smog, 493
Smooth muscle. *See* Involuntary
    muscle
Snakes, poisonous, 129, 130
Snell, George, 629
Snow
    greatest annual falls in U.S.,
        444
    in selected U.S. cities,
        431–33
    storms, 442
Soddy, Frederick, 262, 616
Software, 504–5, 521
Soil, 386–87
    erosion, 480
    pollution, 475
Solar day, 71, 72, 74
Solar eclipse, 334–35
Solar flare, 319, 330
Solar halo, 442
Solar power, 486
Solar system
    birth of, 317–18, 368
    definition of, 317
    distribution of mass in, 318
    most distant bodies in, 325
    See also Planets; Sun;
        Universe
Solar wind, 330
Solids, 235
    density of, 236
    formula for finding volume
        of rectangular, 34
Solid waste, 477
Solstice, 75, 370
Solubility curve, 228–29
Solution
    common solutes, 229
    definition of, 228
    kinds of, 228
    measuring parts and
        percent, 4
Solvent, 228
Somnolence, 223
Sonic boom, 18
Sørensen, Søren, 253, 263
Sosigenes, 79

Sound
    Doppler effect, 291
    speed of, 18, 290–91
    units, 17
    waves, 284–85, 290–91
Southern Hemisphere
    constellations, 336
    solstice, 370
    telescopes, 344–45
Soyuz spacecraft, 350
Space
    cataloging celestial objects,
        342
    life connection, 90
    major scientists, 354–60
    orbits in, 278–79
    search for extraterrestrial
        life, 354
    telescopes, 347
    time travel, 68
    See also Astronautics
Space shuttle, 350
Space-time curvature, 280–81
Spasm, 223
Species
    endangered, 134–35
    numbers of, 95
Specific gravity, 382
Spectrum, 311
Speed
    definition of, 273, 311
    of light, 279–80
    measurement of, 20
    of sound, 18, 290–91
Spemann, Hans, 216, 626
Sperm, 171
Sperry, Roger, 216, 629
Sphere
    definition of, 32
    formula for finding area of,
        34
    formula for finding volume
        of, 34
Spherical coordinates, 16
Sphygmomanometer, 165
Spicule, 319
Spider, 129
Spleen, 163

Sponge, 122
Spore plant, 107
Spreadsheet program, 504
Spring tide, 400–401
Squamous cell cancer, 177
Square
    definition of, 32
    formula for finding area of,
        33
    formula for finding perim-
        eter of, 34
Square measurement. *See* Area
Square wave, 284
Standard time, 82, 85
Standard units, 4
Stanley, Wendell, 617
Stark, Johannes, 620
Stars, 337
    brightest, 339
    catalogs, 342
    classification of, 337
    closest, 339–40
    lives of, 337
    types of, 338–39
Static electricity, 291
Stationary front, 429, 430
Staudinger, Hermann, 617
STDs. *See* Sexually transmitted
    diseases
Steady state model, 315
Stein, William, 618
Steinberger, Jack, 624
Steller, Georg, 140
Stem, plant, 105
Steno, Nicolaus, 411
Steradian, 7
Stern, Otto, 621
Stirling, James, 38
Stoichiometry, 244
Stokes, Sir George, 306
Stokes, William, 216
Stomach, 165–66
Storms, 441, 442, 444–49, 450
Strasburger, Eduard, 140
Stratocumulus clouds, 436, 437
Stratosphere, 420, 421
Stratus clouds, 436, 437
Streak, of minerals, 382

Streams (particle collections),
    328
Strep throat, 198
Striations, 382
String theories, 282
Stroke, 198–99
Strong nuclear force, 281, 282
Sturgeon, William, 306
Sty, 199
Subatomic particles, 230,
    297–98
Subduction, 379
Sudden infant death syndrome
    (SIDS), 199
Sugar-phosphate combination,
    180
Sukhovey, 426
Sulfur oxide, 471
Sumner, James, 617
Sun
    density of, 319
    eclipse, 334–35
    equinox, 75
    layers of, 319–20
    and seasons, 74, 75
    solstice, 75
    statistics on, 318–19
    through atmosphere, 422
Sundial, 71
Sun pillar, 442
Sunspot, 319
Supercomputer, 505
Superconductivity, 270, 284
Supernova, 338
Supersaturated solution, 229,
    270
Supersonic boom, 18
Superstring theories, 282
Surgery
    arthroscopic, 201
    laser, 202
Suspended particles, 472
Sutherland, Earl, Jr., 628
Svedberg, Theodor, 616
Swan, Joseph Wilson, 529
S-waves, 389
Sydenham, Thomas, 216
Symbiosis, 149

Symbols. *See* Signs and symbols
Synapse, 223
Synge, Richard, 617
Synodic month, 70
Synthetic polymer, 530
Syphilis, 189–90
System analyst, 526
Systematics. *See* Taxonomy
Systemic lupus erythematosus.
    See Lupus
Systems programmer, 526
Systems programs, 505
System unit, computer, 498
Systolic blood pressure, 165
Szent-Györgyi, Albert, 626

T

Tachyon, 279, 298
Taiga, 464, 465
Takamine, Jokichi, 263
Talbot, William Henry, 530
Tamm, Igor, 622
Tansley, Sir Arthur, 140
Tape drive, 500
Tar pit, 131
Tartaglia (Niccoló Fontana), 38
Taste, 168, 171
Taube, Henry, 619
Taxonomy, 95
Taylor, Brook, 38
Taylor, Joseph H., 625
Taylor, Richard, 624
Tay-Sachs disease, 191
Technical science
    common terms in, 546–48
    definition of, 524
    highlights of, 528–31
    nanotechnology, 531
    significant discoveries and
        inventions, 531–45
Teeth, 209
    dentist, 184
Teisserenc De Bort, Léon, 453
Tektite, 330
Telegraph, 530

Telephone, 530
  cellular, 528
Telescope, 530
  charge-coupled devices, 344
  common, 342–43
  largest, 344–46
  radio, 346–47
  reflecting and refracting, 343
  in space, 347
Television, 530, 548
Temin, Howard, 216, 628
Temperate forest, 464, 465
Temperature, 23–27
  absolute zero, 283
  air, 429, 431
  common scales, 282–83
  conversions, 23, 25–27
  definition of, 282, 456
  entropy, 284
  and humidity, 433–34
  and ice crystals, 443
  ranges in universe, 24
  in selected U.S. cities, 431–33
  of Sun, 320
  world's high and low, 433
Temperature inversion, 493
Temporomandibular disorder (TMD), 199
Tendonitis, 199
Terrestrial ecology, 463–68
Testes, 171
Testosterone, 163
Thalassemia, 191
Theiler, Max, 216, 627
Theophrastus, 140
Theorell, Axel, 627
Theoretical physics, 272
Theory, 2, 272
Theory of everything. *See* Grand unified theory
Theory of general relativity, 280–81
Theory of special relativity, 68, 279–80
Thermal energy, 277
Thermal printer, 503

Thermocline, 395
Thermocouple, 548
Thermodynamics, 283, 311
Thermoelectricity, 548
Thermonuclear reactions, 300, 319
Thermosphere, 420, 421
Thiamin, 180
Thiamine, 158
Thomas, E. Donnall, 629
Thomson, Sir Charles Wyville, 140
Thomson, Sir George, 621
Thomson, Sir Joseph John, 306, 619
Thomson, William (Baron Kelvin), 90, 258, 283, 304
Thorium, 257, 296
Thornwaite, Charles, 453
Thrombocytes. *See* Platelets
Thrombosis, 155, 199
Thunberg, Carl P., 140
Thunder, 444–45
Thunderstorm, 444
Thymosin, 163
Thyroxine, 163
Tidal theory, 317
Tidal wave, 389
Tidal zone, 469
Tides, 17, 400, 416
  average high and low, 76
  as energy source, 487
  and Moon, 76, 400
  neap and spring, 400–401
Time
  accuracy around the world, 77
  atomic, 77
  common divisions of, 69
  Coordinated Universal, 82
  Daylight Savings, 85
  ephemeris, 77
  future, 76
  geologic, 78
  importance to science, 68
  international zones, 84
  measured, 4, 68
  seasonal, 74–75

  Standard, 82, 85
  tidal, 76
  travel, 68
  Universal, 82
  U.S. zones, 83
  worldwide variations, 85
  years, months, and days, 69–74
  See also Calendar; Clocks and watches
Tinbergen, Nikolaas, 140, 628
Tincture, 228
Ting, Samuel, 623
Tiselius, Arne, 617
Tissue, 160, 223
Tissue plasminogen activator (tPA), 223
Titan (moon of Saturn), 90, 400
Titius, Johann, 360
T lymphocytes, 153
TMD. *See* Temporomandibular disorder
TMJ. *See* Temporomandibular disorder
Tocopherol. *See* Vitamin E
Todd, Alexander, 617
Tombaugh, Clyde, 360
Tomonaga, Sin-Itiro, 623
Tonegawa, Susumu, 629
Tonsillitis, 199
Toothless mammals, 125
Topographical symbols, for maps, 61
Tornadoes, 448–49
Torque, 274
Torricelli, Evangelista, 307, 453
Total eclipse, 334
Townes, Charles, 622
Toxic substances. *See* Poison
tPA. *See* Tissue plasminogen activator
Trabecular bones, 174
Trace metals, 494
Trachea, 173
Trackball, 499
Tradescant, John (1570–1633), 140

Tradescant, John (1608–1662), 140
Transcendental number, 29
Transcription, RNA, 183
Transfer RNA, 183
Transform boundary plate, 379
Transformer, 548
Transistor, 531
Transition element, 239
Translation, RNA, 183
Transplant, organ, 203
Transuranic element, 243–44
Transuranic waste, 478
Transverse wave, 286
Trash, 477
Trauma, 223
Traumatologist, 186
Tree ring, 78
Trees. *See* Deforestation; Forests
Trembley, Abraham, 140
Triangle
    definition of, 32
    formula for finding area of, 33
    formula for finding perimeter of, 34
Trichomoniasis, 190
Trigeminal neuralgia, 199
Triglycerides, 159
Tritium, 257
Tropical depression, 445
Tropical forest, 464, 465–66
Tropical storm, 445, 446
Tropical year, 69
Troposphere, 420, 421
Tschermak von Seysenegg, Erich, 140
TSH (thyroid-stimulating hormone), 163
Tsiolkovsky, Konstantin, 360
Tsunami, 389–90, 416
Tube (valve), 548
Tuberculosis, 190
Tubulidentata (order), 126
Tull, Jethro, 140
Tumor, 199
Tundra, 464–65
Turing, Allan, 514

Typhoid fever, 199
Typhoon, 445
Typhus, 201

U

Ulcer, 199
Ultrasonic pitch, 17
Ultrasound, 203
Ultraviolet telescope, 347
Uncertainty principle, 233, 258, 296, 301–2
Ungulate, 124
Universal donor, 154
Universal Time, 82
Universe
    age of, 315–16
    cosmology, 315
    first moments of, 314–15
    particles of, 295–99
    scale of, 16
    temperature ranges in, 24
Unsaturated solution, 229
Upatnieks, Juris, 529
Uranium
    fission, 299
    nuclear reactions, 300
    radioactive dating of, 256, 257
Uranus (planet), 320–24, 352
Urbanization, 484
Urethra, 164
Urethritis, 199
Urey, Harold, 90, 140, 360, 616
Uric acid, 223
Urinary tract, 164, 165
Urologist, 186
Uterine prolapse, 199

V

Vaccination, 156, 223
Vacuum, 311

Vacuum tube, 529
Valence, 231
Valence electron, 231
Valence number, 231
Vallisneri, Antonio, 216
Van Allen, James, 371, 411
Van Allen radiation belt, 371
van de Graaff, Robert, 307
van der Meer, Simon, 624
van de Waals, Johannes, 307, 619
van de Waals force, 247
Vane, Sir John, 629
van't Hoff, Jacobus Henricus, 263, 615
van Vleck, John H., 623
Variable resistor, 548
Variable star, 338
Varicose vein, 199
Variola. *See* Smallpox
Varmus, Harold, 629
Vascular plants, 107
Vascular system, 223
Vasopressin, 163
Vaucanson, Jacques de, 497
Vector, 273, 311
Vector sum, 274
Vegetables, germination tables for, 119
Velocity, 273, 311
Venereal warts. *See* Human papillomavirus
Venus (planet), 320–22, 351
Venus-flytrap, 109
Vernier, Pierre, 38
Vertebrate, 122–24
Vertigo, 223
Very low density lipoprotein (VLDL), 159
Vesalius, Andreas, 216
Video graphics adapter (VGA), 522
Viper, 130
Virologist, 186
Virtanen, Artturi, 617
Virtual reality, 511
Viruses, as disease carriers in blood, 155

Visceral muscle. *See* Involuntary muscle
Viscosity, 312
Vitamin A, 158
Vitamin B₁. *See* Thiamine
Vitamin B₂. *See* Riboflavin
Vitamin B₃. *See* Niacin
Vitamin B₆. *See* Pyridoxine
Vitamin B₁₂. *See* Cobalamin
Vitamin C, 158
Vitamin D, 158
Vitamin E, 159
Vitamin K, 159
Vitamins, 157–59
VLDL. *See* Very low density lipoprotein
Voicebox. *See* Larynx
Volcanoes, 393
    deep-sea, 396
    major zones, 392
    Mount Pinatubo, 394, 483
    recent active, 393–94
Volt, 18, 292
Volta, Alessandro, 307
Voltage, 291
Voltmeter, 548
Volume
    formulas for finding, 34
    measurement of, 5, 7, 8, 18–19
    U.S.-SI equivalents, 8
Voluntary muscle, 166
von Baeyer, Johann, 615
von Behring, Emil, 625
von Békésy, Georg, 627
von Euler, Ulf, 628
von Euler-Chelpin, Hans, 616
von Frisch, Karl, 628
von Klitzing, Klaus, 624
von Laue, Max, 620
von Lieben, R., 529
von Neumann, John, 514
von Willebrand's disease, 191
Voskhod spacecraft, 350
Vostok spacecraft, 350
Voyager missions, 353–54
VRAM (video random-access memory), 503

W

Waddington, Conrad, 216
Wagner-Jauregg, Julius, 626
Waksman, Selman, 627
Wallace, Alfred Russel, 140
Wallach, Otto, 615
Walrus, 126
Walton, Ernest, 622
Warburg, Otto, 216, 626
Warm front, 429, 430
Warming cycle, 480–81
Warts
    definition of, 199
    genital, 189
Wassermann, August von, 216
Waste, human, 475
Waste disposal, 477–79
Water
    on Earth, 473
    pollution, 472, 474–75
    softening, 232–33
    unusual properties of, 237
    use in U.S., 473–74
    vapor pressure of, 245
Water cycle, 458, 459
Waterfall, 374
Waterspout, 448
Water table, 417
Watson, James Dewey, 216, 628
Watt, 292
Wave
    diagram of, 285
    Doppler effect, 291
    electromagnetic, 286
    gravity, 278
    interference, 287
    light, 287–90
    parts, 284–85
    properties, 286
    relationships, 286
    seismic, 389
    sound, 284–85, 290–91
    and uncertainty principle, 301–2
Wave crest, 285

Wavelength, 285
Wave trough, 285
W boson, 298
Weak interaction, 281, 282
Weather
    air masses, 428
    barometric air pressure, 434–35
    definition of, 456
    forecasting, 435, 450–51
        old ways of, 428–29
        satellites, 450, 530
    fronts, 429, 430, 455
    humidity, 433–34
    jet streams, 429
    major meteorologists, 451–53
    See also Clouds; *specific weather conditions*
Weather station data symbols, 62
Wegener, Alfred, 411
Weight
    definition of, 272
    measurement of, 5, 7
    U.S.-SI equivalents, 9
Weinberg, Steven, 281, 624
Weiss, Pierre, 307
Weller, Thomas, 627
Went, Friedrich August, 140
Werner, Abraham, 411
Werner, Alfred, 615
Wetlands, 476
Whales, 125
Wharton, Thomas, 216
Wheatstone, Sir Charles, 307
Whipple, Fred, 360
Whipple, George, 626
White, Gilbert, 140, 489
White blood cells, 152–53, 174, 186
White dwarf, 338
White hole, 316, 339
Whittaker, Sir Edmund Taylor, 38
Whole number, 29
Whooping cough, 190
Wieland, Heinrich, 616

Wien, Wilhel, 620
Wiesel, Rorsten, 629
Wigner, Eugene, 307, 622
Wildlife refuges, 487–88
    by state, 598–613
Wilkes, Maurice, 514
Wilkins, Maurice, 217, 628
Wilkinson, Sir Geoffrey, 618
Willis, Thomas, 217
Williwaws, 426
Willstätter, Richard, 615
Willughby, Francis, 141
Willy-willys, 445
Wilson, Alexander, 141
Wilson, Charles Thomson Rees, 307, 620
Wilson, Edmund Beecher, 141, 217
Wilson, Edward Osborne, 489
Wilson, Kenneth G., 307, 624
Wilson, Robert, 314
Wind
    Beaufort scale, 426–27
    chill, 427–28
    definition of, 456
    Earth's general circulation, 424
    as energy source, 487

major circulation cells, 423
planetary, 423–24
prevailing, 424
regional, 425–26
secondary, 424–25
shear, 426
Windaus, Adolf, 616
Winkler, Clemens, 263
Winslow, Jakob, 217
Wirth, Niklaus, 507, 508
Wittig, Georg, 263, 618
Wöhler, Friedrich, 263
Woodward, Robert, 618
Word-processing programs, 505
Work, in physics, 276
World calendar, 80
Worm, 120, 130
Wormhole (astronomy), 316
Wound, healing of, 186
Wozniak, Stephen, 514
Wragge, Clement L., 447
Wright brothers, 528
Write-protected disk, 522

X

Xenophanes, 411

Y

Yalow, Rosalyn, 629
Yang, Cheng Ning, 622
Yard, 2
Year, 69–70
    See also Leap year, Tropical year
Young, Robert, 307
Young, Thomas, 217
Yukawa, Hideki, 621

Z

Zeeman, Pieter, 619
Zernike, Frits, 622
Zero law, 283
Ziegler, Karl, 263, 617
Zinc, 157
Zinder, Norton, 217
Zodiacal light, 330
Zoology, 88, 120
Zoos, 135
    by state, 580–89
Zsigmondy, Richard, 616
Zwicky, Fritz, 360
Zworykin, Vladimir, 530